Cultural, Behavioral, and Social Considerations in Electronic Collaboration

Ayse Kok
Bogazici University, Turkey

Hyunkyung Lee
Yonsei University, South Korea

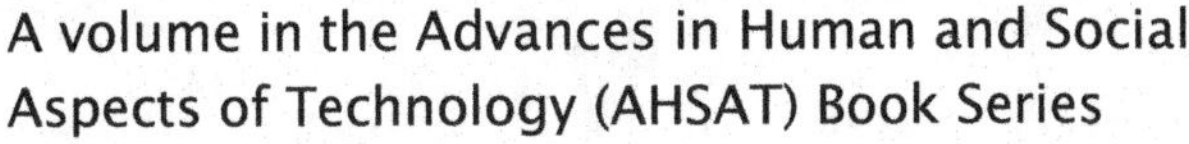

An Imprint of IGI Global

Published in the United States of America by
Business Science Reference (an imprint of IGI Global)
701 E. Chocolate Avenue
Hershey PA, USA 17033
Tel: 717-533-8845
Fax: 717-533-8661
E-mail: cust@igi-global.com
Web site: http://www.igi-global.com

Copyright © 2016 by IGI Global. All rights reserved. No part of this publication may be reproduced, stored or distributed in any form or by any means, electronic or mechanical, including photocopying, without written permission from the publisher. Product or company names used in this set are for identification purposes only. Inclusion of the names of the products or companies does not indicate a claim of ownership by IGI Global of the trademark or registered trademark.

Library of Congress Cataloging-in-Publication Data

Names: Kok, Ayse, 1979- editor. | Lee, Hyunkyung, 1974- editor.
Title: Cultural, behavioral, and social considerations in electronic collaboration / Ayse Kok and Hyunkyung Lee, editors.
Description: Hershey : Business Science Reference, 2015. | Includes bibliographical references and index.
Identifiers: LCCN 2015032917| ISBN 9781466695566 (hardcover) | ISBN 9781466695573 (ebook)
Subjects: LCSH: Business enterprises--Computer networks. | Business networks. | Communication--Technological innovations. | Organizational change. | Organizational effectiveness.
Classification: LCC HD30.37 .C86 2015 | DDC 658.4/0220285--dc23 LC record available at http://lccn.loc.gov/2015032917

This book is published in the IGI Global book series Advances in Human and Social Aspects of Technology (AHSAT) (ISSN: 2328-1316; eISSN: 2328-1324)

British Cataloguing in Publication Data
A Cataloguing in Publication record for this book is available from the British Library.

All work contributed to this book is new, previously-unpublished material. The views expressed in this book are those of the authors, but not necessarily of the publisher.

For electronic access to this publication, please contact: eresources@igi-global.com.

Advances in Human and Social Aspects of Technology (AHSAT) Book Series

Ashish Dwivedi
The University of Hull, UK

ISSN: 2328-1316
EISSN: 2328-1324

Mission

In recent years, the societal impact of technology has been noted as we become increasingly more connected and are presented with more digital tools and devices. With the popularity of digital devices such as cell phones and tablets, it is crucial to consider the implications of our digital dependence and the presence of technology in our everyday lives.

The **Advances in Human and Social Aspects of Technology (AHSAT) Book Series** seeks to explore the ways in which society and human beings have been affected by technology and how the technological revolution has changed the way we conduct our lives as well as our behavior. The AHSAT book series aims to publish the most cutting-edge research on human behavior and interaction with technology and the ways in which the digital age is changing society.

Coverage

- Technology Dependence
- Human-Computer Interaction
- Digital Identity
- Activism and ICTs
- Cultural Influence of ICTs
- Technology Adoption
- Technoself
- Human Development and Technology
- Philosophy of technology
- ICTs and social change

IGI Global is currently accepting manuscripts for publication within this series. To submit a proposal for a volume in this series, please contact our Acquisition Editors at Acquisitions@igi-global.com or visit: http://www.igi-global.com/publish/.

The Advances in Human and Social Aspects of Technology (AHSAT) Book Series (ISSN 2328-1316) is published by IGI Global, 701 E. Chocolate Avenue, Hershey, PA 17033-1240, USA, www.igi-global.com. This series is composed of titles available for purchase individually; each title is edited to be contextually exclusive from any other title within the series. For pricing and ordering information please visit http://www.igi-global.com/book-series/advances-human-social-aspects-technology/37145. Postmaster: Send all address changes to above address.
Copyright © 2016 IGI Global. All rights, including translation in other languages reserved by the publisher. No part of this series may be reproduced or used in any form or by any means – graphics, electronic, or mechanical, including photocopying, recording, taping, or information and retrieval systems – without written permission from the publisher, except for non commercial, educational use, including classroom teaching purposes. The views expressed in this series are those of the authors, but not necessarily of IGI Global.

Titles in this Series

For a list of additional titles in this series, please visit: www.igi-global.com

Handbook of Research on Cultural and Economic Impacts of the Information Society
P.E. Thomas (Bharathiar University, India) M. Srihari (Bharathiar University, India) and Sandeep Kaur (Bharathiar University, India)
Information Science Reference • copyright 2015 • 619pp • H/C (ISBN: 9781466685987) • US $325.00 (our price)

Human Behavior, Psychology, and Social Interaction in the Digital Era
Anabela Mesquita (CICE – ISCAP/Polytechnic of Porto, Portugal & Algoritmi Centre, Minho University, Portugal) and Chia-Wen Tsai (Ming Chuan University, Taiwan)
Information Science Reference • copyright 2015 • 373pp • H/C (ISBN: 9781466684508) • US $200.00 (our price)

Rethinking Machine Ethics in the Age of Ubiquitous Technology
Jeffrey White (Korean Advanced Institute of Science and Technology, KAIST, South Korea) and Rick Searle (IEET, USA)
Information Science Reference • copyright 2015 • 332pp • H/C (ISBN: 9781466685925) • US $205.00 (our price)

Contemporary Approaches to Activity Theory Interdisciplinary Perspectives on Human Behavior
Thomas Hansson (Blekinge Institute of Technology, School of Management (MAM), Sweden)
Information Science Reference • copyright 2015 • 437pp • H/C (ISBN: 9781466666030) • US $195.00 (our price)

Evolving Issues Surrounding Technoethics and Society in the Digital Age
Rocci Luppicini (University of Ottawa, Canada)
Information Science Reference • copyright 2014 • 317pp • H/C (ISBN: 9781466661226) • US $215.00 (our price)

Technological Advancements and the Impact of Actor-Network Theory
Arthur Tatnall (Victoria University, Australia)
Information Science Reference • copyright 2014 • 331pp • H/C (ISBN: 9781466661264) • US $195.00 (our price)

Gender Considerations and Influence in the Digital Media and Gaming Industry
Julie Prescott (University of Bolton, UK) and Julie Elizabeth McGurren (Codemasters, UK)
Information Science Reference • copyright 2014 • 357pp • H/C (ISBN: 9781466661424) • US $195.00 (our price)

Human-Computer Interfaces and Interactivity Emergent Research and Applications
Pedro Isaías (Universidade Aberta (Portuguese Open University), Portugal) and Katherine Blashki (Noroff University College, Norway)
Information Science Reference • copyright 2014 • 348pp • H/C (ISBN: 9781466662285) • US $200.00 (our price)

www.igi-global.com

701 E. Chocolate Ave., Hershey, PA 17033
Order online at www.igi-global.com or call 717-533-8845 x100
To place a standing order for titles released in this series, contact: cust@igi-global.com
Mon-Fri 8:00 am - 5:00 pm (est) or fax 24 hours a day 717-533-8661

Editorial Advisory Board

Jay Curtis Bonk, *Indiana University, USA*
Craig Cunningham, *National Louis University, USA*
Martin Ebner, *University of Graz, Austria*
Carolyn Mori, *Hawaii Tokai International College, USA*
Zuhal Tanrikulu, *Bogazici University, Turkey*
Soner Yildirim, *METU, Turkey*

Table of Contents

Foreword xv

Preface xvii

Acknowledgment xxiii

Chapter 1
Remapping Mental Models of Collaboration Using Immersive 3D Design Thinking Studios 1
Andrew Stricker, The Air University, USA
Cynthia Calongne, Colorado Technical University, USA

Chapter 2
Exploring Social Learning Constructs in Corporate Informal Web-based Learning Environments 19
Hyunkyung Lee, Yonsei University, South Korea

Chapter 3
Ecologies of Information and Communication Technology Platform Design for e-Government Service Provision: Actors, Influences, and Fields of Play 37
Shefali Virkar, University of Oxford, UK

Chapter 4
Emerging Forms of Collaboration Communities of Practice Online through Networked Fictions, Dreams and Stories 69
Alexandra Antonopoulou, University of London, UK
Eleanor Dare, University of Derby, UK

Chapter 5
Digital Collaboration in Educational and Research Institutions 100
Rami Wael Muhtaseb, A.M. Qattan Foundation, Palestine

Detailed Table of Contents

Foreword xv

Preface xvii

Acknowledgment xxiii

Chapter 1
Remapping Mental Models of Collaboration Using Immersive 3D Design Thinking Studios 1
Andrew Stricker, The Air University, USA
Cynthia Calongne, Colorado Technical University, USA

Design thinking provides opportunities for structuring e-collaboration efforts and for gaining a deeper understanding of the process and the product. This chapter outlines strategies for improving the perceptions and skills associated with collaborative effort using cognitive remapping, 3D visual cues, models, and methods supporting design thinking. The study features insights from years of applied immersive 3D design thinking studios involving students and researchers across academia and military institutions. It concludes with recommendations for improving the perceived value of electronic collaboration involving trans-organizational teams.

Chapter 2
Exploring Social Learning Constructs in Corporate Informal Web-based Learning Environments 19
Hyunkyung Lee, Yonsei University, South Korea

As many organizations have taken an interest in social learning, they have been concerned with how to design effective social learning environments for their learners. Although there are studies regarding the importance of social learning, the use of social learning tools, and the implementation and challenges of social learning in the workplace, there is little research on what social learning constructs are crucial for designing social learning environments. This chapter aims to explore social learning constructs in corporate informal web-based learning environments. To achieve its purpose, this chapter initially identified major social learning constructs in informal web-based learning environments based on theoretical grounds and literature reviews. As a result, learning, community, interaction, and social media were identified as environmental constructs, and motivation and self-efficacy were identified as individual constructs.

This research chapter, through the presentation of an empirical case study surrounding the implementation and use of an electronic property tax collection system in Bangalore (India), developed between 1998 and 2008, critically examines both the role of Information and Communication Technologies (ICTs) in governmental reform processes and the contribution of such technologies to the deeper understanding of the social dynamics shaping e-government projects used to reform public sector institutions. Drawing on the theoretical perspectives of the 'Ecology of Games' and 'Design-Actuality Gaps', both of which recognise the importance of a multitude of diverse motives and individualistic behaviour as key factors influencing organisational reform and institutional change, the chapter contributes not just to an understanding of the role of ICTs in public administration reform, but also towards that emerging body of research which is critical of managerial rationalism for an organization as a whole, and is sensitive to an ecology of actors and their various motivations operating within the symbiotic organisation.

The chapter will outline the implications of two projects, namely the 'Phi Books' (2008) and the 'Digital Dreamhacker' (2011). These novel projects serve here as case studies for investigating new and challenging ways of advancing collaborative technologies, using in particular, Communities of Practice and insights gained from both embodiment and graph theory (social network analysis) as well as design. Both projects were developed collaboratively, between a computer programmer and a designer and a wider community of practice, consisting of other artists, writers, technologists and designers. The two systems that resulted also acted as methodologies, instigated by the authors with a view to facilitate, explore and comment on the act of collaboration. Both projects are multi-disciplinary, spanning ideas and techniques from mathematics and art, design and computer programming. The projects deploy custom-made software and fiction enmeshed structures, drawing upon methodologies that are embedded with dreams and stories while at the same time being informed by cutting-edge research into human behaviour and interaction design. The chapter will investigate how the projects deployed techniques and theoretical insights from social network analysis as well as motion capture technology and the wider concept of a Community of Practice, to extend and augment existing collaborative methods. The chapter draws upon Wenger et al (2002), as well as Siemens (2014) and Borgatti et al (2009), and will explore the idea of a new form of collective social and technological collaborative grammar, deploying gesture as well as Social Network Analysis. Moreover, the featured projects provide insights into the ways in which digital technology is changing society, and in turn, the important ways in which technology is embedded with the cultural and economic prerogatives of increasingly globalized cultures.

This chapter explores the role of digital technologies in promoting interaction and collaboration at educational and research institutions. It describes some forms of digital collaboration, and explores how educational and research institutions employ digital technologies to reach learners inside and outside the institutional boundaries. The chapter investigates a number of digital collaboration tools and their characteristics, and highlights some aspects of employing these tools to support interaction among students, teachers, researchers, and different learning communities with a special focus on science. Some cases of integrating digital technologies in the educational process and in research are also given. At the end of the chapter, insights are discussed, and a summary is presented.

This chapter investigates the highly researched and debated key issue of electronic collaboration (e-collaboration) in the learning process, onwards called e-collaborative learning (e-CL), in a holistic overview. The structure of the chapter is as follows. First of all, it clarifies the meaning and context of e-CL, and compares it with analysed relevant notions. Second, the human elements of e-CL and their roles are explored, classified into functional categories. Third, the supportive elements technology, pedagogy, and methodology are extensively visited. Fourth, the framework elements time, space, and society are presented. Fifth, the e-CL process is analysed, following the ADDIE model and analysing its phases. Sixth, significant affordances and challenges of e-CL are identified, and seventh, future directions are considered. Finally, conclusions are reached. Throughout the chapter new approaches, methods, and terms are proposed in the interests of the enrichment or the effectiveness of e-CL.

Recent technological advances are providing new and exciting opportunities for researchers to work together across the conventional boundaries of time, distance, and discipline. These advances have formed new networks of research, both in electronic mediums and in face-to-face environments, different from traditional networks in terms of their changing nature and scope. This paper reports some of the preliminary findings from a qualitative case study of the establishment of the 'EMT project'. It attempts to illustrate how the EMT project as a connected network formulates positive academic interactions and consequently facilitates professional learning immersed in research activities. In parallel, the study examines the benefits and problems arising from the sense of being together across time and space supported by advanced networked technologies in collaborative research, and further identifies the gap between the academic and the technical perspective in research.

The aim of our chapter is to contribute to a better understanding of E-Collaboration, especially its intimate connection with knowledge and knowledge processes. We begin by presenting a knowledge-oriented understanding of E-Collaboration and an architecture of an E-Collaboration system (people, processes and technology) based on that understanding; then we describe the eSF system (an implementation of this architecture within our team), our experiences with it and what we have learned about the success factors of E-Collaboration.

This investigation reviews research literature on electronic collaboration (e-collaboration) with a view to collate relevant information to support e-collaboration knowledgebase, further research and encourage further collaborative engagements. E-collaboration has been described with various phrases such as information sharing, information exchange, knowledge sharing, social networking and joint working. This research categorised the challenges of e-collaboration into people, process and technology because all the issues identified in e-collaboration research are rooted in one of these categories. As e-collaboration is a source of competitiveness, businesses that fail to strategically adopt the phenomenon could lose out. A notable example of e-collaboration is crowdfunding which provides funding for start-up and small businesses. However, businesses that support e-collaboration strategy have the potential to have better competitive advantage with increased firm performance.

Social media or social networking tools are Internet-based applications that focus on building social networks or social relations among people with shared interests and/or activities. Social media sites essentially consist of a representation of each user (often a profile), his/her social links, and a variety of additional services. Social networking sites fuss and was impressed by the community as a result of submissions from the ease and facilitated communication between people, and widened its fame and many use became their top concern, where communicating through these sites to get to know each other, and find out news each other, and receive news and themes and all that is new in the arena. However, since these sites and programs are open, there are no controls commensurate with our religion and our values and our habits of Arab and fixed principles, which impact on the lives of people in general, whether positively or negatively.

The aim of this chapter is to compare the two worlds of science and learning in the perspective to find commonalties that could be used to develop new methods and technologies to better support collaborative and on-line scientific research. In this perspective we claim the existence of a convergence of these two domains and highlight similarities in on-line tools that support such activities. At the same time, we bring attention to the fact that a largely overlooked aspect of existing on-line scientific collaborative research systems, which is instead well represented in learning systems, is communication among partners. To address this issue we build a collaborative on-line software tool that allows to make some interesting early observations. Further on, we report on the introduction of a discourse structuring facility that could be used, on one hand, to ease the use of communication tools and on the other as a boundary object: an artifact that allows to bridge different paradigms and backgrounds.

The nature of the traditional approaches to collaborative group projects can often be characterized by hierarchy, clarity of roles, and assignment of tasks to participants. Digital-age collaborative projects are often characterized by impromptu and ill-defined organization, spontaneity, democratic decision-making, and continual morphing of roles. These two approaches are grounded in fundamentally different cultural frameworks. This chapter describes and analyzes an innovative collaborative process of role description, negotiation, adoption, and ongoing evolution through routine metacognitive processes which provides a structure by which to integrate positive aspects of traditional hierarchical approaches to collaborative projects and positive aspects of digital-age communication culture. This role negotiation process can clarify responsibilities and processes while nurturing the sense of personal agency and self-determination crucial to intrinsic motivation and engagement.

The Regional English language learning (ELL) project in the American Spaces Philippines was established at the US Department of State's Bureau of Educational and Cultural Affairs (ECA) and Bureau of International Information Programs (IIP) in the fiscal year 2013 as a response to a study which showed the modest state of English language teaching and learning in the country. The project, a cooperation between English as a Foreign Language (EFL) educators and administrators at partner schools, universities, and American spaces in the archipelago counterparts and funded by the US Department of State's Bureau of Educational and Cultural Affairs (ECA) and Bureau of International Information Programs (IIP), was aimed at assisting with the production of more and better-qualified English as a Foreign Language (EFL) educators and administrators.

Chapter 14
Online Communities of Practice and Web 2.0 265
Amir Manzoor, Bahria University, Pakistan

In contemporary Knowledge Management, communication and collaboration play very significant role. Knowledge exists within the stakeholders of an organization. Such knowledge, when extracted and harnessed effectively, can become an extremely valuable asset to achieve organizational goals and objectives. This knowledge, embedded in the people, must be properly released through an appropriate channel to make it usable. Through dialogue and discussions, using online tools, this release and reuses of knowledge can be made possible. The Community of Practice (CoP) is a useful organizing concept for enhancing collaboration, sharing knowledge, and disseminating best practices among researchers and practitioners. This chapter explores the concept of Communities of Practice and how Web 2.0 technologies can facilitate the transformation from a conventional community of practice to online community of practice for better and effective online communities of practices.

Chapter 15
Guidelines to Innovate Organizations by Knowledge Management via Communities of Practice 293
Roberta Salgado Gonçalves da Silva, University of São Paulo, Brazil
Edson Walmir Cazarini, University of São Paulo, Brazil

This study proposes to achieve an innovative environment via Communities of Practice (CoP) in companies that doesn´t know Knowledge Management (KM). The contribution of the paper is to elucidate the relevance of KM presenting a research and the literature of KM, CoP, Organizational Culture and Information and Communication Technology. A survey was performed at ten companies in the interior of São Paulo state, Brazil. Any company that doesn´t know KM and needs to be innovative may use the original twenty-two guidelines.

Chapter 16
Integration of Web 2.0 Tools for Non-Formal Learning Practices: A Study of IBM's Digital Spaces 309
Ayse Kok, Bogazici University, Turkey

This research tries to explore the specific benefits of online collaboration tools, and finds out how their use has been appropriated by employee volunteers for their practice of volunteering and how they influenced the process of their meaning-making. By doing so, it raised an awareness of the digital tools that provide collections of traits through which individuals can get involved in non-formal learning practices by having digital interactions with others.

Compilation of References 327

About the Contributors 365

Index 372

Foreword

E-collaboration is about sharing information within and between organizations for the purposes of planning, coordinating, decision making, process integration, improving efficiency and effectiveness. These technologies include Web-based chat tools, Web-based asynchronous conferencing tools, e-mail, listservs, collaborative writing tools, group decision support systems, teleconferencing suites, social networking platforms, and Web 2.0 technologies.

Organizations exchange information through people, process and technology, and increasingly rely on e-collaboration technologies to make that happen. The connectivity being made possible by the nature of the digital space offers much potential for becoming engaged in a joint activity. Regardless of the benefit of these technologies offered to employees, be it socializing, networking, or support, much remains to be explored about these places in terms of learning and development.

This book fills an important gap by focusing on all forms of e-collaboration whether it be through email, online communities of practices, social networks, Web 2.0 tools or virtual teams in organizational settings.

Topics covered include:

- **Theory that informs practice:** Emerging models and understanding from academia;
- **Research:** New understandings of learning, collaborative sense-making, and learning preferences;
- **The Practitioner view:** Real examples from around the world of ground-breaking developments in e-collaboration that are transforming education, adult learning and corporate training;
- **Guidance for designers and producers:** Pedagogical advice and skills for a range of people who may have had little exposure to the body of knowledge surrounding collaboration design;
- **Looking to the future:** What to expect in the next 5 to 10 years and how to prepare to take full advantage of the opportunities that an increasingly connected society will provide for computer-supported collaboration.

"Cultural, Behavioral, and Social Considerations in Electronic Collaboration" has been written with the intent of providing practical advice from academics, researchers, practitioners and designers who are currently engaged in defining, creating and delivering the increasingly important world of electronic collaboration. By leaving aside trends in technology, this book instead focuses on the articulation and development of the computer-supported collaboration theories that underpin the use of technology.

This book addresses key gaps in the available literature including the inequality of access to technologically enabled learning and cutting-edge design issues and pedagogies that will take us into the next decade of e-collaboration and future Web 3.0+ approaches.

The challenges in e-collaboration are both difficult and interesting. People are working on them with enthusiasm, tenacity, and dedication to develop new methods of analysis and provide new solutions to keep up with the ever-changing threats. In this new age of global interconnectivity and interdependence, it is necessary to provide practitioners, both professionals and students, with state-of-the art knowledge on the frontiers in e-collaboration. This book is a good step in that direction.

The Prophet Mohammad (s.a.w) said 'Seek knowledge even unto China'. To gain the academic knowledge on e-collaboration, we tried to collaborate with scholars across the world, whose efforts the editors of this book very much appreciate.

Ayse Kok
Bogazici University, Turkey

Preface

Today's workplace settings are in constant need of recurrent learning processes interwoven with daily tasks on digital spaces. However, these digital spaces are not devoid of any issues and hence suggest the need for employees to be conscious of the emerging issues.

Effective collaboration will increasingly be strategic differentiators for organizations of all types in the twenty-first century. Information and communication technologies have a critical role to play in helping organizations to achieve these goals. By publishing new theoretical and practical research findings, as well as providing a forum for broader discussion, this book contributes to the understanding and advancement of this important domain of electronic collaboration.

This book addresses the design and implementation of e-collaboration technologies, assesses the behavioral, cultural and social impacts of these technologies on individuals and groups, and presents theoretical considerations on links between the use of e-collaboration technologies and behavioral, social, or cultural patterns.

Research studies undertaken by Future Lab in 2007 have suggested that when people make a choice or decision not to use technology, even though access is available to them, then they are making an empowered choice. Above and beyond having the necessary access to online tools, online collaboration, therefore, is predicated on the ability to make an informed choice when and when not to make use of these tools. Online collaboration is not, therefore, simply a matter of ensuring that all individuals make use of these tools throughout their day-to-day lives, but a matter of ensuring that all individuals are able to make what could be referred to as "smart" use of technology, i.e., using it as and when appropriate. In this sense, not making use of an online tool can be a positive outcome for some people in some situations, providing that the individual is exercising an empowered "digital choice" not to do so, FutureLab concluded. The results of various studies in this book offer examples of empowered choices being made by uses; for example, choosing to use the Web 2.0 tools such as the wiki or blog because making use of them increased information-sharing, which supported the participants' progress with their projects in an organizational or academic setting. However, there are also times when participants are choosing not to use these tools because they have a preference for the more conventional methods such as face-to-face discussions or brainstorming. Various data also suggest areas that would be worthy of further exploration in terms of understanding whether or not the decisions made are empowered ones or not. A good example of this would be to provide meaningful and relevant information about how much "time" might be saved in the long run in terms of efficiency and improved collaboration outcomes. The results, therefore, build on existing theories and discourses regarding the use of online collaboration tools, but also challenge us to expand our understanding and application of these theories with regard to the following areas:

- Swapping and changing from a range of online collaboration tools;
- Being well-informed about the strengths and weaknesses of particular online collaboration tools in relation to usability and impact on learning;
- Developing a range of sophisticated and tailored strategies for using online collaboration tools to support their learning;
- Being extremely familiar with technology;
- Being aware of what help and support is available.

THE CHALLENGES

This book does not compare the impact of one collaboration medium over another and does not include the implications of mature use of collaboration technologies, which have been widely discussed elsewhere. Mature users of collaboration technology are more likely to report business benefits and staff benefits of their implementation and are also more likely both to align learning and collaboration with business goals and to measure success (Bersin Associates, 2008; Towards Maturity, 2009). Mature users are also more likely to blend collaboration and learning technologies within other approaches to develop business solutions.

This book does not attempt to isolate the specific role of technology in the blend, the maturity of the user, nor the process of business alignment, all of which influence results. Caution should be used in applying the results in this review; increasing the use of technologies in collaborative learning will not automatically achieve success or efficiency savings.

SEARCHING FOR A SOLUTION

The use of learning technologies in the workplace is on the increase. Those who are investing in learning technologies expect more from their investment. But is there clear and concrete evidence to illustrate that technology-supported collaboration and learning in the workplace actually delivers the type of bottom-line business benefits that organisations are looking for? This is the question that we investigate within this book.

The authors set out to identify and review a range of literature (academic, research, case studies, online and print) to look for examples of both workplace and academic implementation of collaboration technologies that have tangible results. Articles, reports and case studies have been investigated using the following parameters:

- **Employers:** The review focused on the business users of collaboration technologies and aimed to include small and large companies encompassing the private, public and third sectors.
- **Technology:** The definition of technology-supported collaboration/e-collaboration used in this review includes the application of collaboration technologies across the learning process from assessment of organizational and individual need to delivery of learning, learner support, management and administration, and formal and informal learning.

To identify information resources that address all of these three parameters, we approached an extensive network of global providers, experts (academic and non-academic), and employer membership groups in addition to conducting traditional literature research.

ORGANIZATION OF THE BOOK

The book is organized into seventeen chapters. A brief description of each of the chapters follows:

In Chapter 1,"Remapping Mental Models of Collaboration Using Immersive 3D Design Thinking Studios", Dr Calongne from Colarado University in US outlines strategies for improving the perceptions and skills associated with collaborative effort using 3D visual cues, models, and methods supporting design thinking. Insights from eight years of applied immersive 3D design thinking studios involve faculty and students across industry, academia, and government organizations. The chapter concludes with recommendations for improving the perceived value of electronic collaboration involving trans-organizational teams.

In Chapter 2, "Exploring Social Learning Constructs in Corporate Informal Web-based Learning Environments", Dr Lee from Yonsei University in South Korea explores social learning constructs in corporate informal web-based learning environments. As many organizations have taken an interest in social learning, they have been concerned with how to design effective social learning environments for their learners. Although there are studies regarding the importance of social learning, the use of social learning tools, and the implementation and challenges of social learning in the workplace, there is little research on what social learning constructs are crucial for designing social learning environments. As a result, community, interaction, and social media were identified as environmental constructs, and motivation and self-efficacy were identified as individual constructs.

A unique example of collaboration from the government sector has been depicted in Chapter 3, "Ecologies of Information& Communication Technology Platform Design for eGovernment Service Provision: Actors, Influences, and Fields of Play". In this chapter, Shefali Virkar from Oxford University in UK critically examines both the role of Information and Communication Technologies (ICTs) in governmental reform processes and the contribution of such technologies to the deeper understanding of the social dynamics shaping e-government projects used to reform public sector institutions. In her chapter, Shefali contributes not just to an understanding of the role of ICTs in public administrative reform, but also towards that emerging body of research which is critical of managerial rationalism for an organization as a whole, and is sensitive to an ecology of actors and their various motivations within the symbiotic organisation.

In Chapter 4, "Emerging forms of collaboration: Communities of practice online through networked fictions, dreams and stories", Alexandra Antonopoulou from University of Greenwich and Dr Eleanor Dare from University of Derby in UK look at two innovative systems created by themselves with a view to facilitate and explore collaboration. They show how two central case study projects have deployed evolving technologies such as motion capture and situated computing, in which non human forces become significant agents, The featured projects also provide insights into the ways in which digital technology is changing society, and in turn, the important ways in which technology is embedded with the cultural and economic prerogatives of increasingly globalized cultures. At the same time, the chapter will expand on philosophical discourses in regards to the utopian nature of collaboration. Their chapter contributes to critical design philosophies a channel for dialogue and cultural commentary, as well as a conceptual challenge to established practices.

In Chapter 5, "Digital Collaboration in Educational and Research Institutions", Mr Muhtaseb from Qattan Foundation in Palestine explores the role of social media tools in promoting interaction and collaboration among teachers, students, researchers, scientists, and the public within the context of universities, colleges, research institutes, and science museums. He also makes use of crowdsourcing for scientific events as a case study.

In Chapter 6, "E-Collaborative Learning (e-CL): Overview and Proposals", Mr Xafopoulos, a graduate student at University of London in UK, investigates e-collaboration with regard to the learning process. Mr Xafopoulos not only explores the core learning components with a focus on the technology, but also provides a classification of e-collaborative learning approaches. Throughout the chapter new approaches, methods and terms are proposed in the interests of the enrichment or the effectiveness of the e-CL process.

In Chapter 7, "Electronic Research Collaboration via Access Grid", Prof. Zhang from Beijing Normal University in China reports some of the preliminary findings from a qualitative case study of the establishment of a three-year collaborative project that addresses how successful secondary chemistry teachers structure and handle the chemistry content of lessons. Prof. Zhang considers this EMT project as a bounded system, lending itself to being studied by using multiple data collection methods (semi-structured individual interviews, observation, and a review of key documents) in order to provide a rounded and comprehensive account of academic interactions over a period of time. This interpretive case study intends to form a knowledge base for developing a conceptual framework and theoretical assumptions about unseen professional learning mediated by technology in research networks for a future research project. It attempts to illustrate how the EMT project as a connected network formulates positive academic interactions and consequently facilitates professional learning immersed in research activities.

In Chapter 8, "eSF: An E-Collaboration System for Knowledge Workers", Prof Bettoni along with his colleagues Prof. Bittel, Prof Bernhard and Prof Mirata from FFHS in Switzerland present an understanding of the essence of e-collaboration that these scholars themselves call as "knowledge-oriented", because according to their opinion what matters in e-collaboration is the construction of shared knowledge; then they propose an architecture of referred to as an e-collaboration system - which includes people, processes and technology. These scholars also describe the implementation of this architecture in their team of the Research Management Unit at FFHS. These authors also suggest some success factors of E-Collaboration that have emerged as relevant for tapping the full power of E-Collaboration.

In Chapter 9, Barriers to Electronic Collaboration, Mr Owens Imarhiagbe from Kingston University in UK tries to provide answers to some important research questions with regard to the barriers in e--collaboration in every sphere of social and human endeavours. Mr Owens Imarhiagbe discusses electronic collaboration in terms of the challenges associated with people, process and technology. Although technology has enabled the expansion of e-collaboration over a decade, Nosek and McManus (2008) identified technology as a major challenge to the development and advancement of e-collaboration. Mr Owens Imarhiagbe argues that technology provided the necessary support for progressive e-collaboration in the past and technology also has the responsibility to resolve the challenges impacting e-collaboration today and the future.

Chapter 10, "The Impact of Social Networking Sites on the Arab Community ",Prof. El-Khouly from Helwan University in Egypt explores and identifies the social and political implications of social networking in Arab countries and suggests policy options and avenues for further research. Three important questions that he seeks answers throughout his chapter are: 1) What is the effect of the amount of interaction with these sites to improve political awareness among the students of Arab universities? 2) What is the effect of the amount of confidence in the information provided by these sites to improve the political awareness of the students? 3) What is the effect of the time period for the membership to improve the political awareness of the Arab Universities students?

Chapter 11, "E-Research: A Way of Learning Together?", Prof Diviacco from OGS in Trieste, Italy. aims to address issues such as what would be the commonalties between collaborative learning and collaborative research? Can this comparison be used to help in the development of tools to support such activities and in order to avoid as much as possible the above-mentioned traps? In this analysis she reports on the experiences of several international projects her institute was involved in, where they have been in charge of the development of web based tools to support heterogeneous communities to grow from different backgrounds and paradigms and to construct collaboratively knowledge. Prof Diviacco explores and reports on the possible paths that can be followed aiming at this, such as the formalization of knowledge or leaving collaborative knowledge to emerge freely such as in simultaneous "hands-on" processes such as in forums, wikis or social networks.

In Chapter 12, "Role Negotiation in Collaborative Projects", Prof Donaldson from Western Oregon University in US argues that the processes and roles produced by the culture of digital communications are characterized by impromptu and ill-defined organization, spontaneity, democratic decision-making, and continual morphing of roles. Based on his own professional experience, Prof Donaldson proposes a process of role negotiation through which the effectiveness and efficiency of digitally-mediated collaborative projects (ranging from the highly formal to the highly informal) can be optimized.

In Chapter 13, "The scholarship of engagement and generative learning communities: Preparing EFL leaders for authentic practice at the American Spaces Philippines", Mrs Celine Okol from Cabanilla University of the Philippines outlines the collaborative activities undertaken by the EFL project, a cooperation between English as a Foreign Language (EFL) educators and administrators at partner schools, universities, and American spaces in the archipelago counterparts and funded by the US Department of State's Bureau of Educational and Cultural Affairs (ECA) and Bureau of International Information Programs (IIP), which aims at assisting with the production of more and better-qualified English as a Foreign Language (EFL) educators and administrators. She demonstrates how the project sought to help in setting up more productive and effective teacher education programs, to build capacity at partner schools, universities, and American spaces in the archipelago via collaborative activities such as e-scholarships, webinar courses.

In Chapter 14, "Supporting Electronic Collaborative Experiences at Universities based on Learning Spaces and LAMS", Dr Papadimitriou from the Ministry of Education in Greece, Mr Papadakis, a tutor-counselor in Open University of Cyprus, Prof Lionarakis, Associate Professor in Hellenic Open University in Greece present us a case study in the Hellenic Open University regarding the design and the development of a learning sequence on the topic "Implementing essays" and the views of tutor-counselors of using LAMS. The Learning Space of the case study aimed at achieving a high degree of interactions among students, students and tutors, and also at guiding them between face-to-face meetings when they prepare an essay. The authors also present a methodology to create collaborative sequences highlighting the advantages, the requirements and the relevant constraints of using LAMS.

In Chapter 15," Online Communities of Practice and Web 2.0", Dr Manzoor from Bahria University in Pakistan explores the concept of Communities of Practice and how Web 2.0 technologies can facilitate the transformation from a conventional community of practice to online community of practice for better and effective online communities of practices. Dr Manzoor asserts that in contemporary Knowledge Management, communication and collaboration play very significant role and knowledge exists within the stakeholders of an organization. This knowledge, embedded in the people, must be properly released through an appropriate channel to make it usable. Through dialogue and discussions, using online tools, this release and reuses of knowledge can be made possible.

In Chapter 16, "Guidelines to innovate organizations by knowledge management via communities of practice", Prof Da Silva proposes to achieve an innovative environment via Communities of Practice (CoP) in companies that doesn´t know Knowledge Management (KM). The contribution of the paper is to elucidate the relevance of KM presenting a research and the literature of KM, CoP, Organizational Culture and Information and Communication Technology. Any company that doesn´t know KM and needs to be innovative may use the original twenty two guidelines.

In the final chapter of this book, "Utilizing Digital Collaboration Tools for Non-Formal Learning Practices", I examine how a group of employee volunteers in IBM used Web 2.0 tools for their collaborative learning practice and what assumptions they had for using the tools. I present multiple approaches to using the tools and list multiple assumptions participants had for such a practice. I explore how the use of these online collaboration tools has been appropriated by employee volunteers for their practice of volunteering and how they influenced the process of their meaning-making. By doing so, I aim to raise an awareness of the digital tools that provide collections of traits through which individuals can get involved in non-formal learning practices by having digital interactions with others.

Ayse Kok
Bogazici University, Turkey

REFERENCES

Anderson, P. (2007). *What is Web 2.0? Ideas, technologies and implications for education.* JISC. Retrieved from www.jisc.ac.uk/media/documents/techwatch/tsw0701b.pdf

Daft, R., & Huber, G. P. (1987). How organizations learn: A communications framework. *Research in the Sociology of Organizations*, *5*, 1–36.

Dohn, N. (2010). Web 2.0: Inherent tensions and evident challenges for education. *International Journal of Computer-Supported Collaborative Learning*, *4*(3), 343–363. doi:10.1007/s11412-009-9066-8

Downes, S. (2010). *E-learning 2.0.* National Research Council of Canada. Retrieved from http://www.elearnmag.org/subpage.cfm?section=articles&article=29-1

Facebook. (2014). Statistics. Retrieved from http://www.facebook.com/press/info.php?statistics

French, S., & Swain, J. (2004). Researching together: a participatory approach. In S. French & J. Sim (Eds.), *Physiotherapy: A Psychosocial Approach* (3rd ed., pp. 50–64). Oxford: Butterworth-Heinemann.

O'Reilly, T. (2007). *Web 2.0 Compact Definition: Trying Again.* Retrieved from http://www.oreillynet.com/pub/a/oreilly/tim/news/2005/09/30/what-is-web-20.html

Wenger, E., & Snyder, W. M. (2000). Communities of practice: The organizational frontier. *Harvard Business Review*, *78*(1), 139. PMID:11184968

Zack, M. H., & McKenney, J. L. (1995). Social context and interaction in ongoing computer-supported management groups. *Organization Science*, *6*(4), 394–422. doi:10.1287/orsc.6.4.394

Acknowledgment

We wish to personally thank all of the authors for their contributions to our inspiration and knowledge and other help in creating this book. Thank you all of the authors who without their contributions and support this book would not have been written.

We also acknowledge the valuable contributions of the reviewers regarding the improvement of quality, coherence, and content presentation of chapters. Most of the authors also served as referees; we highly appreciate their double task.

A special thank you note should be provided for Prof Curtis Bonk from Indiana University who put the editors of this book into contact. This collaborative writing process could not have been possible without his support.

Last and not least: we beg forgiveness of all those who have been with us over the course of the past months while writing this book and whose names we have failed to mention.

Ayse Kok
Bogazici University, Turkey

Hyunkyung Lee
Yonsei University, South Korea

Chapter 1
Remapping Mental Models of Collaboration Using Immersive 3D Design Thinking Studios

Andrew Stricker
The Air University, USA

Cynthia Calongne
Colorado Technical University, USA

ABSTRACT

Design thinking provides opportunities for structuring e-collaboration efforts and for gaining a deeper understanding of the process and the product. This chapter outlines strategies for improving the perceptions and skills associated with collaborative effort using cognitive remapping, 3D visual cues, models, and methods supporting design thinking. The study features insights from years of applied immersive 3D design thinking studios involving students and researchers across academia and military institutions. It concludes with recommendations for improving the perceived value of electronic collaboration involving trans-organizational teams.

INTRODUCTION

Design thinking describes the emotive and cognitive techniques for reframing the perceptions and beliefs of collaboration. Applying design thinking for e-collaboration between researchers or students with no professional or personal ties strengthens the opportunity to achieve synergy during the pursuit of the desired outcomes.

This chapter explores design thinking characteristics, and how they impact the mental models of collaboration. It examines the relationship between teamwork and educational theories, such heutagogy and constructionism, and it offers examples from the design studio experiences of graduate students and game-based examples from researchers during a 10-week summer experiment.

DOI: 10.4018/978-1-4666-9556-6.ch001

Copyright © 2016, IGI Global. Copying or distributing in print or electronic forms without written permission of IGI Global is prohibited.

Background

E-collaboration in immersive 3D spaces presents technological, group and process challenges that seem simple when compared to the barriers presented by each participant's beliefs and fears about teamwork. Immersion in this research does not center on the use of a head-mounted display device, but on the intersection of people working, learning and socializing inside a 3D world. Design thinking leverages immersion to encourage creativity as teams develop a strategy for group work and shared outcomes.

Online collaboration strategies blend 1) voice communication, text and video; 2) a process for managing cooperative work; 3) techniques for leveraging conflict; 4) integration and version control for group products. In online classes that feature activity-based learning, groups explore ideas and create working prototypes using social constructionism.

Constructionism asserts that learning is an active process involving the creation of knowledge and understanding from experiences in the world, leading to personally meaningful products (Resnick, 1996). Social constructionism extends activity-based learning by encouraging discussion and cooperatively constructed views of the world.

Electronic collaboration, called e-collaboration, uses technology through a mix of asynchronous and synchronous communications to share ideas and design characteristics during group activities. E-collaboration in a 3D immersive environment transforms an empty landscape into visual scenes populated with 3D content that simulate a place or a meeting space. These virtual spaces transform into a virtual world when people socialize and interact within the setting, offering opportunities for collaborators as students, designers or researchers to meet and conduct cooperative work.

In a virtual world, the group members can see themselves in relationship to the content as it is displayed around their avatars, and an avatar represents their sense of self. Within these 3D settings, the design studio is both a physical studio for creating group projects, scenes and simulations, and it is a conceptual framework for understanding the process of idea generation, exploration and creativity.

Virtual world design thinking personalizes e-collaboration, provides a technological infrastructure, and embraces the creative process through individual constructivism and social constructivism as team members work cooperatively to generate ideas and depict them in 3D designs. Heutagogy describes a learning approach that encourages students and teams to practice self-determined learning as they set expectations and take responsibility for their collaborative activities. The focus extends beyond the accumulation of facts and how adults learn through experience (andragogy) to ownership of the process and the group's products. Design thinking encourages learner-centric collaborations and presents characteristics that strengthen the team experience and lifelong learning. Potential barriers to using social constructivism in collaborative teams stems from the beliefs and perceptions about group work.

COGNITIVE REFRAMING MODELS AND PERCEPTIONS ON COLLABORATION

Support exists for the use of 3D worlds as an immersive experience in which teams can experiment and discover how to accomplish the learning objectives while reflecting on their culture and behavior (Kapp & O'Driscoll, p. 88). Realizing value from constructionist learning environments, however, is not likely to emerge independently in 3D worlds. Educators and learners take the time to customize their avatars and to learn to communicate, gesture, and emote as they share their ideas and collaborate on 3D projects (Calongne, 2008).

The enriched visualization tools provided by 3D worlds are very suitable as building blocks for creating cooperatively-constructed learning activities where ideas can be visually represented, shared, and applied through building 3D interactive projects. Karl Kapp and Tony O'Driscoll (2010) identified several benefits offered by 3D worlds to learning: contextually situated, consequentially experienced, action-oriented, discovery driven, collaboratively motivated, and participant-centered project design.

Once students mastered the mechanics of communicating and gesturing in a 3D world, attention shifted toward leveraging the full power of the immersive experience to help reframe existing beliefs about a collaborative effort. Graduate students studying computer science tend to work alone as they frame the application of their science to problems or opportunities. One goal for the students was to expand their thinking and viewpoint to identify new ways to tackle problems through collaborative effort as they studied complex problems and explored novel solutions.

The collaborative virtual design thinking process helped students as they practiced their team skills, and they employed a cognitive scaffolding approach to work on the project. They discussed their goals, generated ideas, examined the challenges, and explored a variety of strategies. Modeling their ideas in 3D helped to present a context for evaluating possible solutions, but collaboration in 3D space presented inherent challenges as well as strengths.

Through their applied learning activities, they gained a deeper understanding of the course concepts and program goals. Particular strengths were visible during their project demonstrations. As the students gave a tour of their cooperative designs, they noted how their projects were not constrained to the mundane assembly of 3D objects. Instead, the group product reflected their diverse perspectives and beliefs. The students expressed their observations about the journey as well as the destination, noting that their themes and discoveries were far better than the individual accomplishments within the body of work.

Virtual world design thinking frames the examination of e-collaboration in research groups and among graduate students as they developed class projects. Working cooperatively across geographic distances required a good understanding of the tasks, a shared understanding of the expectations for the outcomes and effective communication mechanisms.

Two areas of research support this study: 1) how approaches to problems or opportunities can be mentally reframed or remapped for helping to address the human tendency to persist with a set of perceptions based on their beliefs, even when a new situation calls for adaptation or new opinions, and 2) ways to support creative problem solving through collaborative effort and design thinking.

MENTAL REMAPPING OF BELIEFS ON COLLABORATION

Immersive 3D spaces interact with and shape episodic memories cradled in time and space. Students share a sense of being there, or presence when interacting in 3D space with other learners and instructors. The state-of-mind they experience is the result of sensory perception, thoughts, feelings, emotions, and beliefs interacting within the brain from the millions of neural brain patterns firing in concert that create a holistic mental state.

The essential feature involved in mental remapping or reframing of beliefs is to tap into new emotional states generated by interacting within a 3D environment. The neural effect is a surge in excitatory neurotransmitters that increase the firing rate of neurons in certain parts of the brain (Carter, 1999, p. 164). The overall effect is it increases the intensity of perception and boosts long-term potentiating of neurons, so experiences or episodes that happen from the mental state within the immersive 3D space are more memorable and, if pleasant, sought after by the participant.

Creating new episodic memories for mental remapping of a priori beliefs on collaboration is fragile. It may take a year or longer through persistent engagement in immersive virtual worlds to embed a mental remapping in long-term memory as observed during nine years of teaching collaborative work in virtual worlds. The students participated in design thinking projects over a sequence of graduate courses spanning three years. They developed 3D simulations of their conceptual and physical models.

Research on situated cognition by Joseph Glick (1997) highlighted the importance of purposeful design within immersive 3D spaces for helping to shape mental frameworks through the practice of newly constructed knowledge within and grounded by the environment (p. 247). To that end, the authors designed the immersive 3D spaces to resemble the design studio environments physically employed by Stanford University's Hasso Plattner Institute of Design. The goal was to influence the shaping of mindsets through the use of collaborative design thinking and to encourage future innovators.

The physical spaces set within the 3D classroom entailed reconfigurable furniture supporting collective and group breakout areas as collaborative workspaces, ideation and team software tools, digital presentation displays, mockup kits, and design thinking resources as depicted in Figure 1.

The project locations were reconfigurable areas where groups worked on their team projects in virtual breakout collaborative workspaces. These virtual class areas contained concept-mapping ideation models and toolsets, group presentation displays, 3D mockup kits supporting rapid prototyping, and in-world project resources on design thinking methodologies.

Figure 1. Immersive 3D design studio spaces

Figure 1a. 3D Design Studio facility. Figure 1b. Small group breakout areas. Figure 1c. Hologram packing of Design Studio.

Figure 1d. 3D visualization Design Studio tools. Figure 1e. Student Collaborative Prototyping Design Studio space Figure 1f. Student Design Studio evaluation and testing activity.

DESIGN THINKING

Tim Brown (2008) defines Design Thinking as a process, blending art, craft, business acumen, and a market strategy combined with an astute awareness of what people need. Creativity leads to innovation and extends beyond technological invention to identify and create opportunities with new eyes. Brown (2008, p.3) described several characteristics of design thinkers that complement virtual world design thinking qualities:

- **Empathy:** A shared, intuitive grasp of the qualities that matter
    - Experience the world from the smallest detail
    - Reflect on the needs and perspectives of people and their behavior
    - Generate ideas to support possible solutions
    - Explore the alternatives in the context of how people feel
    - Analyze the broad and fine details of the possible outcomes
    - Exhibit an intuitive grasp of the opportunities and potential problems
    - Identify solutions that support the teams' values
- **Integrative Thinking:** The collaborators as connectivists
    - Apply non-Aristotelian thinking to see the shades of gray among the choices
    - See the diverse, purposeful and potentially opposing perspectives
    - Create fresh and surprising solutions that extend the art-of-the-possible
    - Look beyond what is known to discover what could be
- **Optimism:** The design team shares a *can-do attitude*
    - Visualize solutions beyond the problem's boundaries
    - Reflect on alternatives not previously explored
    - Apply a game-based approach to experimentation and discovery
    - Be willing to fail
    - Be open to discoveries by taking a fresh or alternative perspective
- **Experimentalism:** The designers as pioneers
    - Take broad strokes and aim high
        - Instead of taking small steps, think big
    - Question everything and evaluate the alternatives
    - Explore the unknown, knowing that vast opportunities await
- **Collaboration:** Maps with Integrated Design, as great teams
    - Produce better products than talented individuals
    - Respect and recognize their personal and collective power
    - Encourage cross-disciplinary experience
    - Stimulate new and diverse perspectives
    - Encourage teammates to spin ideas in unusual pathways
    - See opportunities in surprising places
    - Recognize that people matter and come first
    - Understand that innovation extends beyond technology and supports people

In virtual world design studios, the students selected a theme for their project and brainstormed, pruned and prioritized the list of alternatives to identify candidate approaches.

They discussed a range of ideas about their prospective game designs, 3D simulations, interaction styles, and user behavior. Each week, they met to review their plans, strategized the next steps, and using an evolutionary prototyping process, created their designs.

IMMERSIVE 3D ENVIRONMENTS AND SUPPORT FOR COGNITIVE REFRAMING

An essential cognitive feature in Tim Brown's Design Thinking characteristics is integrative thinking. People construct knowledge and build new ideas on what they've experienced or associate with concrete exemplars contained in memory. No doubt, the lessons of the past are helpful for generating new insights in creative ways. However, there are drawbacks from an over-reliance on existing ideas or concepts as the sole basis for generating new creative insights.

Research on creativity by Tom Ward (1995, 1999) highlights how creative people tend to recall familiar pathways of thought and concrete exemplars or examples to frame a novel idea or problem solution. The result is likely to be less than satisfactory for generating creative insights when addressing novel problems or innovation opportunities. His recommendation is to encourage deliberate abstraction at the early stages of creative processes rather than considering existing examples, particular solutions or approaches used in the past.

Fixation and creativity research by Steve Smith (1995) highlighted the importance of imaginary objects to help with overcoming memory blocking of creative thought processes. Existing mental models limit the ability to extend beyond current perceptions and inhibit divergent concept associations and constrain the creative activity. The means to extend beyond the boundaries of how concepts and 3D objects relate to their functional use allows the mind to form connections important to cognitive reframing. These novel reconfigurations of concepts and their associations strengthen creativity (Hampton, 1997; Wisniewski, 1997).

Immersive 3D environments support cognitive reframing and encourage the exploration of new concepts and collaborative design thinking. Why? Through abstraction and visual cues, learners expand their mental models of how things work, extending beyond the symbolic level to envision dramatically different candidate solutions. Figure 2 illustrates the process used to support student engagement and collaborative design thinking during team activities.

The degree by which students grappled with high levels of abstraction via symbols in the 3D space and shape their ideas into interactive 3D models contributed to creative insights on new combinations of concepts. Evidence of students exploring these new perspectives and their ultimate representations grew during virtual world group activities and decreased when working in physical spaces. The decision to combine Tim Brown's (2008) Design Thinking processes with the authors' work on cognitive reframing and remapping helped to support students with creative problem-solving challenges during collaborative projects.

Tim Brown's Design Thinking project spaces depicted in Figure 2 involves three main iterative phases: 1) *Inspiration*, 2) *Ideation*, and 3) *Implementation*. The activities in each phase strengthened the outcomes as the learners defined the problem or opportunity, considered multiple perspectives, identified constraints and ideas for prototyping solutions, and implemented the group's designs. The collective work developed during the process featured iterative cycles to support revisiting earlier assumptions, ideas, and plans. Adapting the design thinking concepts in the 3D project spaces supported reframing

Figure 2. Cognitive reframing activities in an adaptation of Tim Brown's (2008) design project spaces

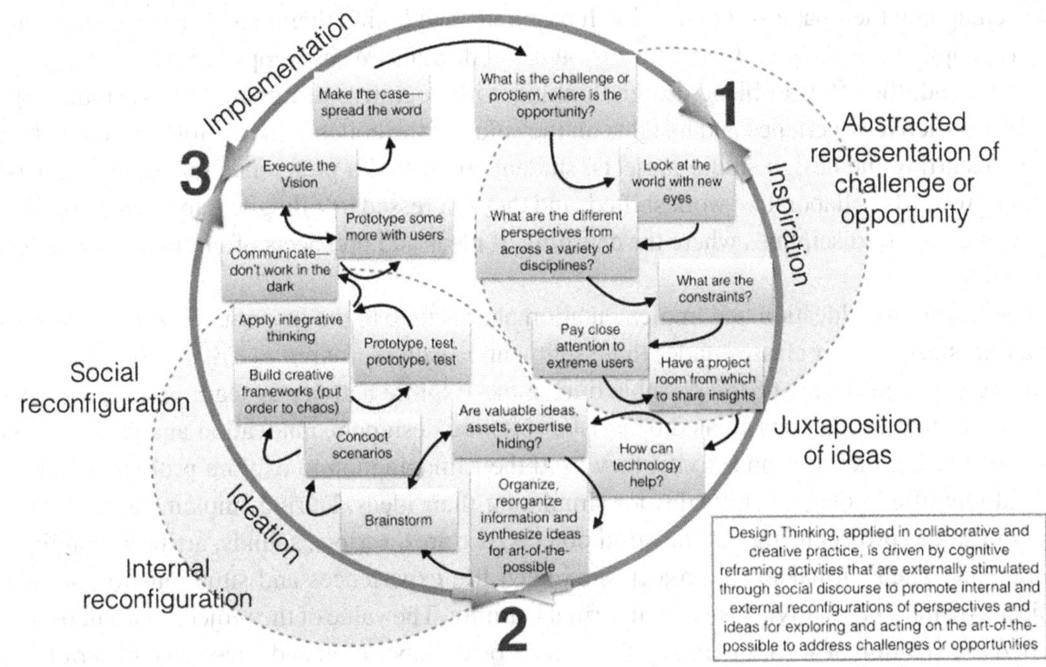

* Figure is an adaptation of Tim Brown's design project spaces (see Brown,T. (June, 2008), *Design thinking.* Boston, MA: Harvard Business Review, p. 4); the figure has been adapted and illustrated to depict the inclusion of cognitive reframing activities.

or remapping beliefs associated with creative, collaborative efforts. Participants no longer limited themselves during the collaboration, but instead envisioned opportunities beyond their imagination. During the Inspiration phase, students were asked to model their first perspective using 3D shapes and symbols. These abstractions of the initial view of the problem depicted their diverse views of the challenge or opportunity for their group project (Stricker, Holm, Calongne, & McCrocklin, 2011).

Additional steps encouraged students to solicit diverse options by inviting guests to visit their virtual design studio spaces to view and discuss their planned project. The mix of perspectives and ideas arising from the discussion helped to encourage a juxtaposition of ideas and stimulate creative thinking. During the Ideation activities, the groups revisited prior assumptions and early plans for the project. They employed brainstorming techniques involving the use of fish-bone diagrams, affinity charts, concept maps, and other collaborative models to visualize the art-of-the-possible.

The overall effect for each student strengthened internal reconfiguration of a priori beliefs regarding collaboration as a value-added activity for supporting creative design thinking. As the group project entered the Ideation phase, the groups prototyped their ideas to share, evaluate, and test in preparation for Implementation. Students completed two prototypes to evaluate diverse ideas and gain insights from guest evaluators from outside the discipline of computer science. These pilot studies of their prototypes helped them to assess and consider different viewpoints from people representing the prospective end users. On the surface, the groups thought that the project focused on the design of a simulated solution to the challenge. Instead, the desire to help students expand their internal reconfiguration of beliefs about collaboration towards a social reconfiguration of communities of practice was integral to the collaboration process. Students explored new collaboration methods for investigating complex problems after remapping their patterns of behavior. It required abandoning their perceived limitations about their creative capabilities, helping them to envision novel designs (Wenger, pp. 125-126).

In the end, the effort to blend design thinking with cognitive reframing helped students gain first-hand constructive experience and insights on the value of the collaborative effort to creatively innovate. Prior to starting the design studio projects, students indicated a preference for individual work. Their attitudes towards collaborative work shifted, and they expressed a willingness to practice their science at the intersection of disciplines where the churning of ideas and prospects offer opportunities for creative innovation.

The Inspiration, Ideation and Implementation phases map to the Innovation Design Studio structure the authors use in their classes under three segments: *Explore, Imagine, Create* (Stricker et al., 2011). Students explored the art-of-the-possible during the Explore activity as team participants evaluated a rich set of sample situations created by artists, software designers, innovation analysts, and knowledge workers. During the Ideation activity, they used their imagination to explore problems within the topics and identified potential strategies for simulating their ideas. During Implementation, they created a design studio project using virtual world objects, textures, scripts, sounds, artificial intelligence, and animations. Their virtual world projects simulated life experiences and situations to complement the project's theme, such as civic justice or informal learning. The value of the project's simulations extended beyond the creation of scenes to remap their views on collaboration and encourage generative thinking.

3D Design Thinking

Design studios blend a virtual representation of a place suitable for the creation of content and a strategy for practicing design thinking. The virtual world classes conducted by the authors spanned nine years and featured four years of design studio sessions. Team members met and simulated a face-to-face meeting within the environment. Their depictions of self as avatars ranged from women and men in modern dress to historical costumes, movie and fictional characters, animals, and robots (Figure 3).

Figure 3. Avatars in virtual worlds met to attend classes and plan their project designs

Identity plays a role in virtual teams as the participants experience self-actualization. Barbara Truman (2013) studied how people collaborate in online groups. Her research examined how collaborators achieve *virtual-physioception* through awareness of their virtual self, social presence and metacognition. She also studied how they experienced *virtual intersubjective presencing* through transformed social interaction, dialogue and a shared sense of presence. Truman's research featured the identification of vesting within groups that meet in multiuser virtual environments. For individual participants, she examined their level of commitment, collaboration style, the frequency of electronic communication and their preferred method of interaction as they strived to meet the group's goals.

It may seem surprising to discuss identity and team meeting behavior in the context of online collaboration. The first five years of classes focused less attention on identity, and the team members who were not comfortable with their avatar's appearance struggled to concentrate on the group's objectives. When the groups stood instead of sitting during meetings, or if they sat with an awkward pose, they experienced fatigue and had a hard time focusing on the activities.

The cognitive reframing process and transformation evolved as the collaborators met to reflect on their design plans and how they mapped to the course concepts and the project's theme. The teams of students shifted from thinking of their classmates as avatars and "not a real person" to colleagues who worked together to create experiences through their game designs and simulations. They connected and met minds as they formed into teams and expressed conflicting opinions. Similar to physical teams, they distributed the activities among the group members and managed conflict for design and style decisions, how visitors would interact with their designs and 3D object behavior. The cognitive remapping benefits were similar to those noted during online class discussion boards as the posts shift from looking like a collection of student monologues into an extensive and productive conversation.

The 3D design projects spanned a series of games and simulations set in a variety of settings, including a tribute to the Mayan culture and a series of Greek mythology games that featured the Labyrinth, Pandora's garden, Medusa's Lair, and the Temple of Athena. Figure 4 depicts an educational game set on a spaceship that tracked the player's progress and the pedagogy as the players progressed through sickbay, engineering and up to the bridge.

Figure 4. The Spaceship game featured a Sickbay Nurse and a Patient as non-player characters

COMMUNICATION MECHANISMS AND E-COLLABORATION STYLES

Location transparency in the group communications made it easy to teams to communicate. The teams formed into virtual world groups and used a group channel for voice and text discussions. The group channel was private and gave them flexibility and privacy. They hosted discussions with team members who were standing on different virtual world regions or for those nearby but outside the range of the local voice chat (Table 1). Some group members stood next to classmates from other groups, yet no one outside their team could hear them or see their group discussion chat logs.

Design thinking teams chose where and how they met and communicated. Some groups simulated a face-to-face meeting while other group members worked at a distance or from different regions. Aside from the group chat and voice channel, team members sent instant messages (IMs) to individual collaborators using text or voice. Some teams elected to host a custom conference call so students from different groups and guests could participate in the virtual world's internal voice and text chat.

Non-verbal feedback was a bit more challenging as conveying gestures required a participant to activate a software gesture, play an animation or type an emote to express the appropriate emotion. Practitioner research is underway to simulate gestures and visual cues more naturally as noted during the keynote address by Philip Rosedale, CEO of High Fidelity (2014) during the OpenSimulator Community Conference (OSCC). As he gave his presentation, a video camera captured his real life expression, and the software portrayed his natural facial gestures on his avatar as he spoke.

Based on their preferences, students communicated using the public voice and text chat, the group voice and text chat, the one-to-one IM voice and text chat and a custom conference. Table 1 identifies the options available to groups as they communicated in the virtual world. When they used the group channel for private group meetings, the instructors and guests needed to join the virtual world group to participate.

Switching voice channels between groups or back to the public nearby channel was challenging for novices, so the group facilitators or instructors moved between several group channels and the local voice channel during group discussions. The group, IM and conference channels improved the audible quality during voice discussions as the local chat featured spatial sound. In local voice chat, collaborators could hear spatialized sound in relationship to their avatar's location or from the end of their cursor.

Table 1. E-collaboration communication tools in immersive 3D environments

Access	Communication Method	Audible Range or Channel
Public	Local text chat	0-20 meters
Public	Local Voice	0-60 meters
Public	Shout command in text chat	0-99 meters
Public	Whisper command in text chat	0-10 meters
Private	Instant message (IM) text & voice	Private channel; email notice
Private	Group message text & voice	Group channel
Private	Conference text & voice	Custom channel
Private	Group notice w/content attachment	Group after login; email notice
Private	Drag content to avatar or Share	Receive after login; email notice

Two options for hearing local voice ranged from the avatar's location or to hear and speak from the user's cursor location. Changing where one can hear and speak provided flexibility in facilitating the groups as they worked across geographic distances in the same region. The instructor stood in one location and with the voice setting located on their cursor, chatted with group members beyond the 60 meter local chat range. The control of voice location worked great for supporting different teams without moving or intruding on their team activities until group requested guidance and support. Using this cursor option for voice, the instructors cannot hear sound at their avatar location until their cursor returns to their body or the chat preference is reset to the avatar location.

The group channel was hard for some teams to access. Moving the teams to distant design studio locations made it easier for them to use local voice and not hear the other groups. Using local voice when set to the cursor's current position improved the quality of sound as the cursor moved closer to the speaker. While local voice chat is not private, groups experienced a sense of privacy, and the use of local chat made the groups easier to facilitate. The instructor positioned the cursor on a team to hear and speak to them and used the keyboard's Escape key to return to listening locally.

Beyond the communication methods employed in immersive 3D environments, Table 2 depicts different collaboration styles for teams that meet and work online. These styles support different types of groups and notes how group members were assigned or chose to participate. Groups with loosely structured roles allowed members to self-select their role and to share in the work, distributing tasks as needed. Formal groups had assigned roles and tasks.

The integration of individual effort in a team project ranged from a traditional integrator role to the use of technology to store group contributions, such as GitHub and other cloud repositories. On the software site, group member contributions offered traceability for individual work, an opportunity to manage version control and archives for archiving and managing changes to the group project.

While less common, mapping the collaboration style to a learning theory helped to illustrate the potential strengths noted from the use of each method, and presented a technique that the authors used in their classes and research (Stricker et al., 2011).

One feature noted in the team compositions focused on the distance between team members in their personal and professional relationships. One author described these relationships as weak-tie networks based on his cognitive psychology background, while the other author defined the team composition as

Table 2. How groups collaborate, assign roles, integrate work, participate and their relationships

Collaboration Style	Roles	Work Integration	Theory	Ties
• Student teams	• Loose	• Integrator or shared	• Pedagogy	• Weak tie
• Work project teams	• Formal	• Integrator	• Andragogy	• Strong tie
• Experts at work	• Formal	• Integrator	• Constructionism	• Strong tie
• Elective, exploratory	• Loose	• Shared	• Experiential	• Weak tie
• Self-directed	• Loose	• Collaborative	• Heutagogy	• Weak tie
• Crowdsourcing	• Loose	• Shared, distributed	• Connectivism	• Weak tie
• Diverse expert group	• Formal	• Facilitator	• Delphi method	• Weak tie
• Community, elective	• Loose	• Shared, distributed	• Communities of practice	• Weak tie

a loosely-coupled collaboration, favoring a term from software engineering. In a loosely-coupled software design, individual sections of the software may be changed without impacting the integrity of the project. This concept extended beyond the proximity and affiliation of the team members and supported changes to group work without impacting the integrity of the project.

In Table 2, weak-tie networks described the collaborators who were geographically distant and had no work or organizational associations, and strong-tie networks described co-workers and affiliates. It might be argued that some of the students were friends prior to class and had already formed into strong-tie networks, but they were geographically distant, worked for different organizations and could move between teams without consequences.

RESEARCH METHOD

The authors hosted a ten-week summer experiment in 2013 to explore new pathways for virtual world design thinking in contrast to the nature of massive open online courses (MOOCs). In the two-person teams, the researchers took turns hosting each week's theoretical foundations and exploration using 3D games and activities as seen in Figure 5. They designed and played games to explore strategies for cooperative and collaborative work, and one of interest to e-collaboration was a two-person multiplayer educational roleplaying game called Slippery Rock Falls (Calongne et al., 2014).

Slippery Rock Falls is a 3D game developed to support a trans-organizational team activity. The researchers playing the game were for the most part geographically distributed and worked for different schools and organizations. The game centers on communication between a player who can see the path for safe passage across the slippery rocks, and the player who needs to trust and execute the instructions flawlessly to succeed.

Teams comprised of two members played cooperatively and assumed either the role of the Guide or the Traveler. The Traveler must cross the river by stepping on slippery rocks and avoid the alligators around them, but cannot see the path to safety (see Figure 6). The Guide communicates the path to safety and the Traveler followed the Guide's instructions.

Figure 5. A Summer experiment on virtual world design thinking and MOOCs

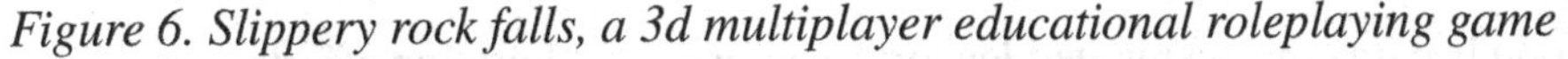

Figure 6. Slippery rock falls, a 3d multiplayer educational roleplaying game

To start the game, the Guide clicked on the game board to obtain and wear a heads-up-display (HUD) device that visually depicts a safe path across the slippery rocks to the other side of the falls. The Guide briefly studied the map and reflected on how to share the information with the Traveler. A stopwatch increased the feeling of tension by displaying the passage of time in seconds.

The game began when the Guide started the timer and gave the Traveler instructions on where to walk, how many steps to take and when to turn to avoid falling into the water. Four teams played simultaneously, offering a sense of competition without the teams feeling the pressure to compete.

While the players spoke and provided instructions, their emotive and cognitive techniques kept adapting during the game, and when the Traveler fell into the water, the player teleported back to the start point with the sounds of an alligator roaring. The games are fast, and in subsequent attempts, the Guide adopted new strategies or switched roles with the Traveler, sharing the experience. Repeated attempts using different strategies also led to failure, but certain discoveries increased their skill development and made them persist at the challenge. The struggle and the discoveries helped to reframe their beliefs on the usefulness of collaboration. The Guide discovered that the instructions were not easy to give, and the Traveler struggled to take small steps and turn without falling into the water. After completing the game, the winning team completed a self-assessment survey, and in later versions of the game, they completed a signature character strengths assessment (Peterson & Seligman, 2004).

Despite the challenges noted with other 3D design games, the research teams thought that the game would be easy to play, given their strong motor skills and domain knowledge. After a few minutes of play, the teams noted that giving and following instructions was difficult. Previous game experience or strong motor skills did not lead to an easy win. Amid cries of laughter, they struggled to cross the slippery rock falls and finish faster than the opposing teams. The players observed that the game offered a level playing field for novices and experts, and at the end of the first session's play, a team with one member who was new to virtual worlds won.

How could a novice and an intermediate player generate a strategy, communicate the steps clearly and move across the treacherous water faster than more experienced teams, including the game's designer and a virtual world instructor with strong motor skills? The answer resided in the emotive and cognitive techniques that the teams employed as they communicated, interpreted and responded to the instructions.

In this example, the Guide became the designated leader. In other e-collaboration efforts, the tactics used in virtual teams resembled face-to-face teams. Some groups designated a leader, or a self-appointed leader emerged while others prefer a distributed or shared leadership role.

One feature of the technology that supported shared design activities is the Share with Group option. When selected and the permissions set to Modify, Copy, Transfer, collaborators strengthened the designs and improved the scripts created by other team members. The Share with Group option was also useful when instructors demonstrated areas for improvement on the student projects.

Figure 7 depicts students on a tour of a design studio project of a physics experiment in which an astronaut is standing with a foot on one of the three locations: the Moon, Earth or Mars. The terrain's texture changes to look like he's standing on Mars, Earth or the Moon when it is clicked. Participants select one of the three combinations for the astronaut to hold in his hand: a hammer and a feather, two hammers, or two feathers. The simulation asks which object will fall faster, and then demonstrates it based on the location and objects selected.

FUTURE RESEARCH DIRECTIONS

Remapping prior beliefs to reframe the perceptions of the value of collaboration offers great promise for strengthening the future of e-collaboration. How people feel, and their fears about group work and criticism are the tip of the iceberg when it comes to examining the barriers to teamwork. Despite the success of the design studio class experiences noted in this chapter, the future research opportunities are extensive for formal studies.

Initial efforts will discover new patterns and trends to support quantitative studies that evaluate them diverse conditions. The opportunities for research range from the evaluation of diverse collaboration tools to the impact of online collaboration environments on group outcomes. Future work will explore

Figure 7. The design of a physics experiment early in the process

the 1) culture, 2) beliefs, 3) fears, and 4) collaboration processes, as well as 5) the identification of new techniques for brainstorming online.

Emotive and cognitive remapping and reframing practices for e-collaboration need further investigation to understand the risks, benefits, challenges, and unknown effects associated with their use. In the design studio teams, the shift in beliefs and perspectives suggested the possibility of long-term benefits. Without further study, it is hard to understand the effects over time or how to apply the same strategy in another context.

The challenges with future work increase when researchers analyze the data obtained during a small, focused study and attempt to generalize the results to support widespread use. Future investigations will use fine or coarse granularity in their scope to examine different levels of abstraction. Consider the benefits of exploring the experiences, perceptions and ethnographic concerns of collaborators in a single study as these discoveries may lead to new questions. Ongoing research tends to take the findings from exploratory studies and use them as a context for measurement and analysis. For example, a comparison of a breadth of examples helps to evaluate the characteristics that may promote better e-collaborative experiences across different contexts and groups.

Research on reframing and remapping the beliefs about collaboration suggests the need to explore a broad range of possible experiences, trends and pathways to support e-collaboration. The exploratory findings often suggest research questions, variables and potentially, prospective hypotheses for further study.

Future work on collaborative games, like Slippery Rock Falls, features the study of signature character strengths and their role in strengthening awareness, an appreciation of self, and the shared perception of collaborative goals and contributions. The Slippery Rock Falls game during the first experiment ended with a self-assessment survey. The next phase will integrate the Signature Character Strengths assessment by Peterson and Seligman (2004) to determine the Values in Action and their support for emotive and cognitive reframing.

In the virtual world, 3D models will reflect the power of an individual's character, their collaboration strengths, and the qualities that matter most to them. The assessment tool will offer guidance on how to classify and interpret the data for use in strengthening team relationships and outcomes. The strengths and virtues categories fall into six categories: 1) wisdom and knowledge; 2) courage; 3) humanity; 4) justice; 5) temperance; and 6) transcendence. As the game's participants map their personal strengths to these six categories, the research examines their ability to adapt their world view and beliefs to generate radical, new ideas as they collaborate.

CONCLUSION

The virtual world design studio approach used in the study embraces Brown's (2008) philosophy of design thinking. The characteristics common to both strategies are 1) empathy; 2) integrative, connectivist thinking; 3) optimism; 4) experimentalism; and 5) collaboration. In 3D immersive spaces, collaborators share 3D models of their ideas, permitting the team to understand and identify new opportunities and potential problems. As they envision solutions and gain respect for the team's beliefs and values, they share fresh, diverse perspectives with a can-do attitude to support the discovery of novel approaches.

One of the challenges of integrative thinking is the dependence on existing perceptions and beliefs as a basis for generating creative ideas and achieving action-oriented outcomes. The watered-down approach to creative efforts makes it harder to identify new solutions. Using abstraction to share raw ideas and general concepts to their expression as 3D models stimulates the investigation of new ideas, leading to solutions not previously explored.

Emotive and cognitive techniques support the reframing of beliefs about collaboration and strengthen the process and outcomes. Remapping the perceptions into a fresh perspective opens the mind to new pathways for identifying creative solutions. Virtual world design thinking provides a visual landscape for prototyping ideas as simulations and serves as a meeting space for the expression of ideas. Cognitive reframing offers an opportunity to change the perceived value of participation in weak-tie networks of collaborators and increases group commitment.

The design studio philosophy for e-collaboration in an immersive 3D environment leverages social constructivism as participants let their minds wander down new paths, share their reflections, and explore the art-of-the-possible.

REFERENCES

Brown, T. (2008). Design thinking. *Harvard Business Review*, *2008*(June). Retrieved from http://hbr.org/2008/06/design-thinking/ar/1 PMID:18605031

Calongne, C. (2008). Educational frontiers: Learning in a virtual world. *EDUCAUSE Review*, *43*(5), 36–48. Retrieved from http://net.educause.edu/ir/library/pdf/ERM0852.pdf

Calongne, C., Stricker, A., Truman, B., Murray, J., Lavieri, E., Jr., & Martini, D. (2014, April 22-24). Slippery rocks and ALGAE: A multiplayer educational roleplaying game and a model for adaptive learning game design. *Proceedings of the 19th Annual TCC Worldwide Online Conference*. Retrieved from http://etec.hawaii.edu/proceedings/2014/Calongne.pdf

Carter, R. (1999). *Mapping the mind.* Los Angeles, CA: University of California Press.

Glick, J. (1997). Discourse and development: Notes from the field. In *Discourse, Tools, and Reasoning: Essays on Situated Cognition, edited by Resnick, Saljo, Pontecorvo, and Burge*. Berlin: Springer. doi:10.1007/978-3-662-03362-3_11

Hampton, J. A. (1997). Emergent attributes in combined concepts. In T.B. Ward, S.M. Smith, & J. Vaid (Eds.), Creative thought: An investigation of conceptual structures and processes (pp. 83-110). Washington, DC: American Psychological Association. doi:10.1037/10227-004

Kapp, K. M., & O'Driscoll, T. (2010). *Learning in 3D: Adding a new dimension to enterprise learning and collaboration.* San Francisco, CA: Pfeiffer and John Wiley, Inc.

Peterson, C., & Seligman, M. E. P. (2004). *Character strengths and virtues: A handbook and classification. New York: Oxford University Press and Washington.* DC: American Psychological Association.

Resnick, M. (July, 1996). Distributed constructionism. In *Proceedings of the International Conference on the Learning Sciences Association for the Advancement of Computing in Education*, Northwestern University.

Rosedale, P. (2014, November 8). Philip Rosedale keynote: What is the metaverse? *Proceedings of the Open Simulator Community Conference*. [YouTube Video]. Retrieved from https://www.youtube.com/watch?v=iR3uUVPyjhU

Scharmer, C. O. (2000). Presencing: Learning from the future as it emerges [PDF document]. Presentation at the *Conference on Knowledge and Innovation, Helsinki School of Economics, Finland.* Retrieved from http://www.ottoscharmer.com/docs/articles/2000_Presencing.pdf

Smith, S. M. (1995). Fixation, incubation, and insight in memory and creative thinking. In S. M. Smith, T. B. Ward, & R. A. Finke (Eds.), The creative cognition approach (pp. 135-156). Cambridge, MA: MIT Press.

Stricker, A., Holm, J., Calongne, C., & McCrocklin, M. (2011). Collaborative prototyping of learning innovations across loosely coupled educational communities. *International Journal of Learning and Media*, Winter 2011, 3(1).

Truman, B. (2013). *Transformative interactions using embodied avatars in collaborative virtual environments: Towards transdisciplinarity* [Doctoral dissertation]. ProQuest Dissertations & Theses Global. (1560886039).

Ward, T. B., Finke, R. A., & Smith, S. M. (1995). *Creativity and the mind: Discovering the genius within.* New York, NY: Plenum Press. doi:10.1007/978-1-4899-3330-0

Ward, T. B., Smith, S. M., & Finke, R. A. (1999). Creative cognition. In R.J. Sternberg (Ed.), The handbook of creativity (pp. 189-212). Cambridge, MA: MIT Press.

Wenger, E. (1998). *Communities of practice: Learning, meaning, and identity.* New York, NY: Cambridge University Press. doi:10.1017/CBO9780511803932

Wisniewski, E. J. (1997). Conceptual combination: Possibilities and aesthetics. In T. B. Ward, S. M. Smith, & J. Vaid (Eds.), Creative thought: An investigation of conceptual structures and processes (pp. 83-110). Washington, DC: American Psychological Association.

KEY TERMS AND DEFINITIONS

3D Simulation: A virtual reality scene, game or experience involving the creation of objects that have scripted behavior and respond to interaction by avatars and with other objects. The simulation types range from education, research, games or entertainment.

Action-Oriented Outcomes: Collaborative problem-solving and constructivism by teams of colleagues, leading to design solutions.

Avatar: A representation of a person within a virtual world.

Constructivism: A philosophy of learning centered on creating content to illustrate the concepts and desired competencies. In constructionism, students learn by designing projects.

Design Thinking: Centers on problem-solving, modeling ideas and creating action-oriented outcomes. It builds on instructional systems design (ISD) to engage collaborators with a meta-awareness of the performance and behavioral goals of the task.

Immersive 3D World: Avatars are immersed in the 3D environment or simulation, and for students or volunteer participants, their avatars may be part of the organism they are studying.

Loosely-Coupled Collaboration: Leverages the principle of a loosely-coupled software design where a change in one part of the design does not negatively impact the behavior or integrity of the collaborative product. In context, changes by colleagues to parts of the product strengthen, rather than detract from the collaborative outcome.

Mental Models: A perception and view of the world. The mental models for electronic collaboration refer to team member expectations, communication styles, team behavior, work styles and responsibilities.

Social Constructivism: The discovery of new approaches increases during problem-solving discussions and collaborative design practices.

Virtual Intersubjective Presencing: Group interaction within collaborative virtual environments that extends into transformed social interaction, dialogue in groups and how avatars communicate to promote a shared sense of presence (Truman, 2013).

Virtual World: A virtual reality scene with avatars interacting, communicating and sharing.

Virtual-Physioception: Avatar identity, embodiment and the relationship of self and the avatar (Scharmer; 2000, Truman, 2013) as noted during technology-enabled collaboration within a virtual environment.

Weak-Tie Network: In psychology, a relationship that is not close yet extends a network of contacts. In context, it is a team with no formal organizational relationship or work requirement that comprises a collaboration of colleagues.

Chapter 2
Exploring Social Learning Constructs in Corporate Informal Web-based Learning Environments

Hyunkyung Lee
Yonsei University, South Korea

ABSTRACT

As many organizations have taken an interest in social learning, they have been concerned with how to design effective social learning environments for their learners. Although there are studies regarding the importance of social learning, the use of social learning tools, and the implementation and challenges of social learning in the workplace, there is little research on what social learning constructs are crucial for designing social learning environments. This chapter aims to explore social learning constructs in corporate informal web-based learning environments. To achieve its purpose, this chapter initially identified major social learning constructs in informal web-based learning environments based on theoretical grounds and literature reviews. As a result, learning, community, interaction, and social media were identified as environmental constructs, and motivation and self-efficacy were identified as individual constructs.

INTRODUCTION

Traditional formal corporate trainings, which are mainly led by instructors or served as one-time training sessions, can no longer be expected to be useful for learners in the workplace. Instead, attention on informal learning has been increasing in corporate education (Bingham & Conner, 2010). According to Cross (2007), people in corporations learn informally most of what they need to know on the job. Merriam, Caffarella and Baumgartner (2007) also revealed that it has been estimated that over 70 percent of learning in the workplace is informal. The driving factors of this change can be summarized in three aspects. First, it is revealed that adult learners become more proactive learners when there are practical

DOI: 10.4018/978-1-4666-9556-6.ch002

Copyright © 2016, IGI Global. Copying or distributing in print or electronic forms without written permission of IGI Global is prohibited.

needs or requirements and they can choose and construct independently their own learning experiences (Zemke & Zemke, 1984; Knowles, Holton & Swanson, 2005; Reynard, 2007). In other words, adult learners can organize their learning based on what would be useful and required of them, and discover meaningful knowledge in the process of learning activities from different knowledge sources. Second, it is found that adult learners learn not only by themselves as individuals, but also with others through collaborative interaction. In this context, connection, interaction, and dialogue are considered as crucial elements in adult learning (LeNoue, Hall & Eighmy, 2011). Third, most corporate education has started emphasizing not employees' mere acquisition of knowledge but employees' effective application of learning on the job through sharing authentic knowledge and experience with others. In this regard, corporations have made an effort to provide interactive and collaborative learning environments among learners, practitioners, and workers.

At the same time, social learning has gained high attention in the workplace as it particularly emphasizes social interaction with others for learning in informal environments. Social learning became acknowledged as the primary element for effective organizational performance as most work in organizations are not accomplished by the individual learning of one person but through the social learning of a group of people and networks (Wilkins, 2008; Jarche, 2010). Many companies, however, still maintain the traditional formal education format and have failed to provide effective social learning. This is because of the limitations with the current education format to facilitate learner's active participation and expand learner's motivation to share knowledge with other learners. The representative examples are e-learning programs and knowledge management systems. E-learning in the workplace has come into the spotlight for its cost-effectiveness compared to classroom learning. Knowledge management systems in the workplace have also been well established in that it has implemented and computerized a community of practices. Although both e-learning and knowledge management system may result in the successful outcome of cost reduction and technological accessibility, they have shown the limitations in facilitating social learning in two ways.

First, in the case of e-learning programs, although there are interaction means, such as discussion rooms, chatting spaces, and bulletin boards, they often result in individual learning, not social learning. In addition, among possible interactions between instructor-learner, learner-learner, and learner-content within e-learning programs (Moore, 1989), most interactions occur merely between instructors and learners through simple questions and answers. Although social learning can be mostly active when there are learning activities with peer groups with a two-way and continuous communication among learners, the current e-learning programs have not yet provided such environments. Second, in the case of the knowledge management system, it has a limitation of providing a meaningful social learning environment for real and practical knowledge sharing and creation. This is because it initially focused on the development of a database of information. Therefore, although many organizations have invested in implementing knowledge management systems to manage information resources and organizational knowledge, there are few opportunities for employees to acquire, share, and use authentic information and knowledge (Davenport, 1994; Bednar, 2000; Vanderville, 2000). To sum up, the conventional approach taken for developing e-learning programs and knowledge management systems has not sufficiently provided the environment for effective social learning (Davenport & Prusak, 1998; Donahue, 2001; Gilmour, 2003; Stahl, Koschmann & Suthers, 2006; Bang & Dalsgaard, 2006). Because of such limitations of e-learning programs and knowledge management systems, social media has appeared as a strong alternative to support social learning in the workplace.

Social media is generally defined as an Internet-based application created by Web 2.0 technologies. It has been playing a highly successful role in supporting social network and social interaction. People expect that interactive and informal learning using the Internet, mobile, and social media will grow gradually in the future (Chang & Hong, 2011). This is because social media can provide a two-way collaborative learning environment and enables spontaneous and effective social interaction. In addition, there is an anthropological reason why social media will become more important in the future. According to one of the main discussions of the American Society for Training and Development (ASTD) conference in 2010, the younger generation produces content through social media such as Twitter, Facebook, and YouTube. The n-generation, which was born between January 1977 and December 1997 and has become the majority of young workers, has particularly been exposed to computer and digital media (Tapscott, 2009). Thus, the use of social media is natural and critical to the generation's learning and working in the workplace. Another advantage of social media is the promptness of interaction, such as getting answers immediately from multiple experts and knowledge sources. It is much more effective to use social media rather than relying on education training from subject matter experts to solve various problems within the workplace (Galagan, 2010).

Since social media shows outstanding success in facilitating social interaction on the web, it is likely that the use of social media has resulted in social learning, either intentionally or unintentionally. In this regard, embracing social media as educational technologies can improve corporate education by providing social learning environments. Despite such potential, however, many organizations are not ready to implement social media strategically but it merely plays the role of technological support for learners' interaction in web-based learning environments (Jue, Marr & Kassotakis, 2010). To capitalize on the opportunities social media has brought, social media should not be considered as just one technology solution. Social media alone is not sufficient in building an effective social learning environment in corporate education. Instead, the paradigm of corporate education must be first changed, fundamentally centering on learners' voluntary participation in knowledge sharing and interaction. Therefore, along with social media, it is necessary to incorporate learners' psychological and social constructs. That is, it is crucial to consider what social learning constructs are essential for learning performance in the workplace (Ali, Pascoe & Warne, 2002). The prior researches on the constructs related to social learning in corporations are summarized in Table 1.

As shown in Table 1, these studies have mainly taken a fragmentary approach by focusing on the relationships between each construct and learning performance. For instance, some studies investigate the effects of social constructs, such as interaction or learning community, on learning performance. Some studies also demonstrate that motivation or self-efficacy as learners' psychological constructs affect learning performance. In addition, some other studies show simple functions and characteristics of social media as a tool. Despite the contribution of illustrating the specific constructs related to social learning, these studies have limitations in considering all possible main constructs of social learning and learning performance simultaneously.

To provide learners with useful learning environments, it is necessary to take a comprehensive instructional design approach. As a first step to the instructional design of social learning environments, therefore, this chapter attempts to identify social learning constructs in corporate informal web-based learning environments, particularly in linkage with learning performance, from integrated reviews including fundamental theories, instructional approaches, and learning environments related to social learning.

Table 1. Previous researches on the constructs related to social learning in corporations

The Constructs Related to Social Learning		Research Topics	Researches
Adult learners' personal characteristics	•Self-directedness •Motivation •Self-efficacy •Willingness	Relationships between related constructs to social learning and learning performance	Charbonneau-Gowdy & Cechova (2009), Kim (2003), Hill, Song & West (2009), Sthapornnanon et al. (2009)
Adult learners' external characteristics	•Social interaction •Collaboration •Community activities		
Social constructs	•Interaction •Learning community	Effects on interaction and community for learning performance	Anderson & Harris (1997), Bray, Aoki & Dlugosh (2008), Chung (2003), Keeler (2006), McDonald & Gibson (1998), Rodriguez Robles (2006)
Learners' psychological constructs	•Motivation •Self-efficacy	Effects on motivation and self-efficacy for learning performance	Baldwin & Ford (1988), Baldwin, Magjuka & Loher (1991), Colquitt, LePine & Noe (2000), Mathieu, Tannenbaum & Salas (1992), Noe (1986)
Technology	•Social media	Characteristics and functionalities of social media	Kietzmann et al. (2011), LeNoue, Hall & Eighmy (2011)

LITERATURE REVIEW

Social Learning in the Workplace and Related Theories

Most of the earlier research on social learning was focused on childhood education in classroom contexts (Bandura, Ross & Ross, 1963; Baer & Sherman, 1964). While those areas are still valid, there is an increasing number of recent research on social learning for adult education as well as social learning in web-based learning environments (Sthapornnanon et al., 2009; Charbonneau-Gowdy & Cechova, 2009; Hill, Song & West, 2009; Yap & Robben, 2010; Zhang, Olfman & Firpo, 2010; Garrett, 2011). In the former case, social learning is regarded as an important learning mechanism for adult learners in their practical learning, particularly in corporations. According to Gibson (2004, p.199), social learning "especially is relevant to adult learning, as it helps to explain the modeling function of observational learning; emphasizes the interaction of the person, behavior, and environment; and accounts for motivational aspects of learning." In the latter case, due to the enormous development and increase in the availability of Internet-based communication technologies, social media has become a crucial construct that enables learners to interact and communicate on the web without time or space constraints.

As many organizations have taken an interest in social learning, there have been several studies conducted on social learning in the workplace. Those studies identified three main issues in this area: (i) the importance of social learning in the workplace; (ii) the use of social learning technologies and social-networking tools in the workplace; and (iii) implementation and challenges of social learning in the workplace.

First, there are studies which show the importance of social learning for effective teaching and learning (DiMicco et al., 2008; Moon & Lee, 2009; Yap & Robben, 2010). This line of study has emphasized that learning through social networking can affect employees' organizational commitment and job satisfaction. For example, according to Moon and Lee (2009), it is necessary for employees to engage in social networking activities to acquire critical information in rapidly changing business environments. This result implies that most companies need to consider social learning as an important learning intervention and thus should encourage learners to share their knowledge and experiences with other colleagues at work.

Second, there are studies focused on how social learning tools, such as blogs and wikis, are used in corporate environments (Hasan & Pfaff, 2006; Jackson, Yates & Orlikowski, 2007; Kim, Lee & Hwang, 2008). According to these studies, employees use these tools for sharing new corporate information rather than for social connections. For instance, Microsoft offers office-based technology such as SharePoint, and IBM provides social learning tools such as blogs, wikis, and social bookmarking for use in orientations, classes and meetings (Levy & Yupangco, 2008). Because social networking sites on the Internet have become popular for social learning in corporations, companies have been sponsoring tools for social network and researching on how companies can use the tools effectively. For instance, an IBM research group has conducted research on why people use a social networking site and what goals are created in building relationships using the social networking site called Beehive, which is similar to Facebook and MySpace. This research has focused users' motivations and thoughts on using the social networking sites (DiMicco et al., 2008). Another study on social networking in the workplace has examined the impact of social networking activities on organizational commitment and job satisfaction (Moon & Lee, 2009). According to this research, social networking activities such as learning through peer-peer and senior-junior interactions, mentoring, and the management of the learning organization affect the degrees of organizational commitment and the level of job satisfaction significantly.

Third, there are studies of the implementation and challenges of social learning in the workplace. For example, according to one of recent studies (Lee & Bonk, 2010), the most important reason for using social learning in the workplace was found to share knowledge and experiences among colleagues. On the other hand, another result of this study showed that generation gaps and age differences impede the implementation of social learning in multi-generational corporate contexts. Since there are various generations in corporations, the lack of technological support for the older users can create another challenge in the implementation of social learning. In a study by Levy & Yupangco (2008), it emphasized not only the application of social learning in the workplace but also the many challenges to consider when implementing social learning. That is, it presented some best practices and practical challenges when adopting social learning in the workplace, such as productivity and efficiency, firewall and security, intellectual property, confidentiality, policies, and participation.

Based on the above-mentioned literature review, the main issues pertaining to social learning in the workplace and the related researches are summarized in Table 2.

As shown in Table 2, the review of these three major issues illuminates the large potential of social learning to play a crucial role in the workplace and confirms that many studies have been conducted on social learning in corporations. However, there is a shortfall that these studies have not yet taken a theoretical and instructional design approach in developing social learning environments but merely have described current interest and status of social learning in the workplace. Integrated reviews including fundamental theories, instructional approaches, and learning environments related to social learning, therefore, are needed to identify what constructs are crucial to develop social learning environments. These are discussed in the following sections.

Table 2. Main issues pertaining to social learning in the workplace and related researches

Main Issues	Researches
Importance of social learning in the workplace	DiMicco et al. (2008), Moon & Lee (2009), Yap & Robben (2010)
Use of social learning technologies and social networking tools in the workplace	DiMicco et al. (2008), Hasan & Pfaff (2006), Jackson, Yates & Orlikowski (2007), Kim, Lee & Hwang (2008), Moon & Lee (2009), Yap & Robben (2010)
Implementation and challenges of social learning in the workplace	Lee & Bonk (2010), Levy & Yupangco (2008)

Fundamental Theories of Social Learning

There are two major fundamental theories of social learning: social learning theory and social constructivist theory.

First, social learning theory has been mainly considered as a basic theory of social learning. Social learning theory actually stemmed from the early Greeks, such as Plato and Aristotle, with the concept that people learn by observing others (Gibson, 2004). Then it became more crystallized when Miller and Dollard (1941) suggested that learning could not occur without imitation and reinforcement. Their work focused on imitation learning, which refers to simply following others and relying on reinforcement for following others. Although Miller and Dollard's work stimulated many concepts of social learning, it was different from observational learning in that the latter leads to changes in human behaviors by observing others. This observational learning has been facilitated by Rotter's (1954, 1982) and Bandura's (1977, 1986) social learning theories, which built the foundation for social learning (Gibson, 2004; Merriam, Caffarella & Baumgartner, 2007).

The main idea of social learning theory formulated by Rotter (1954, 1982) is that personality represents the interaction of the individual with his or her environment and behavior is changed by the individual's learning experiences and environments. This theory emphasizes the importance of the social context or environmental elements for an individual's behavior. On the other hand, the social learning theory by Bandura (1977, 1986) suggests that people can learn new information and behaviors by observing and modeling the behavior of others. According to Bandura (1977, p.22), "learning would be exceedingly laborious, not to mention hazardous, if people had to rely solely on the effects of their own actions to inform them what to do. Fortunately, most human behavior is learned observationally through modeling: from observing others, one forms an idea of how new behaviors are performed, and on later occasions, this coded information serves as a guide for action." This social learning theory emphasizes the importance of observing and modeling others' behaviors and a modeling process through the four components of attention, retention, reproduction, and motivation. In addition, Bandura (1977) suggested that three models of observational learning as follows: (i) a live model, which involves an actual individual demonstrating or acting out a behavior; (ii) a verbal instructional model, which involves descriptions and explanations of a behavior; and (iii) a symbolic model, which involves real or fictional characters displaying behaviors in books, films, television programs, or online media.

Second, social learning actually has its roots in social constructivist theory, where learning is regarded as a self-directed, problem-based, and collaborative process (Bang & Dalsgaard, 2006). In general, social constructivism provides useful perspectives for social learning as it emphasizes the importance of collaboration among learners and practitioners (Lave & Wenger, 1991; McMahon, 1997). According to social constructivist theory, learners construct their new knowledge during the process of social interaction with others and learning is considered as a social process that happens during communication with others (Sthapornnanon et al., 2009; Park et al., 2010).

Social constructivism has been mainstreamed especially in educational theories and practices (Vygotsky, 1978; Wertsch, 1985; Moll, 1990; Rogoff, 1990; Lave & Wenger, 1991; Cole, 1996). This notion emphasizes the importance of social interaction, collaboration, and community characteristics in the learning process. With this constructivist perspective, Vygotsky (1978) defines the 'Zone of Proximal Development' (ZPD), as a zone in which learners can succeed if they can be helped and supported by more knowledgeable others when they cannot solve problems by themselves. He describes it as "the distance between the actual development level as determined by independent problem solving and the level of potential development as determined through problem solving under adult guidance or in collaboration with more capable peers" (Vygotsky, 1978, p. 86). In this zone, learners can develop intellectually and truly learn through scaffolding which is help or assistance from other competent experts or peers. While learners not only share knowledge and information but also participate in collaborative activities, they discuss meanings and construct their own knowledge (Wertsch & Tulviste, 1992; Maddux, Johnson & Willis, 1997; Wink & Putney, 2002). This concept has mainly focused on children's cognitive development through interaction with adults or other peers, but it implies that adult learners also can develop their cognitive capability by learning from other more knowledgeable peers and collaborating with them to solve various problems on the jobs. Therefore, much of the collaborative problem-solving strategies are built in the zone of proximal development.

Instructional Approaches for Social Learning

There are three main instructional approaches for social learning, which are situated learning, cognitive apprenticeship, and collaborative learning. These instructional approaches were selected following the categories of instructional methods organized by Reigeluth and Keller (2009).

First, an essential principle of situated learning is that learning needs to happen in authentic contexts, which are settings and situations that are usually encountered by learners (Lave & Wenger, 1991). In particular, learners need to be a part of the 'Community of Practice' (CoP), which includes certain beliefs and behaviors to be acquired. As novice learners move from the periphery of the community to its center, they become active learners and finally identify with the role of experts. This concept refers to 'legitimate peripheral participation,' which provides a way to speak about the relations between newcomers and old-timers, and about activities, identities, artifacts, and communities of knowledge and practice. It concerns "the process by which newcomers become a part of a community of practice" (Lave & Wegner, 1991, p.29). Legitimate peripheral participation is related to cognitive apprenticeship in terms of a process in which newcomers become gradually active participants and experts within a community.

Second, the situated learning approach has been further developed by the idea of cognitive apprenticeship. The main concept of apprenticeship is that more experienced people assist less experienced people as the latter seek to obtain their goals (Collins, Brown & Newman, 1989). In other words, apprenticeship is a social learning method of helping novices become experts in various fields. Brown, Collins and Duguid (1989, p.34) emphasized that "cognitive apprenticeship supports learning in a domain by enabling students to acquire, develop and use cognitive tools in authentic domain activity. Learning, both outside and inside school, advances through collaborative social interaction and social construction of knowledge."

Third, the approach of collaborative learning can support social learning in that people can learn through social interaction and collaboration. Ewing & Miller (2002, p.114) presented key features of collaborative learning as follows: "(i) learners have individual responsibility and accountability; (ii) learning interaction takes place in small groups; (iii) communication during learning is interactive and dynamic; (iv) learners can identify their role in the learning task; and (v) participants have a shared understanding within the learning environment." Collaborative learning is more effective than individual learning because it is not only contributing to motivation, but also improving achievement and social outcomes (Slavin, 1995). As the Internet developed, studies on collaborative learning have focused more on how people can learn together with the help of computers, which refers to computer-supported collaborative learning. Some recent studies have emphasized the importance of informal social connections in computer-supported collaborative learning environments (Kreijns, Kirschner & Jochems, 2003; Contreras-Castillo et al., 2004; Kreijns et al., 2007).

Learning Environments for Social Learning

Since this study focuses on social learning constructs not in a formal learning context but in informal web-based learning environments, learning environments must be considered. There are mainly two research areas on social learning environments, one is new social learning using social media and the other is informal learning.

First, due to the development of web technologies, social learning has occurred when web technologies are used to learn from one another. One of the most influential growing technologies in Web 2.0 environments is social media, as it facilitates social learning unconstrained by geographical and time differences. This provides people with more opportunities to learn together. As social media has become universal for learners, educators can use these tools for academic purposes (Chen & Bryer, 2012). According to Bingham & Conner (2010), social learning is newly defined as "the new social learning," which is a particularly dedicated terminology with the meaning that social learning occurs using social media in the workplace, communities, and online. In other words, the concept of new social learning is to "leverage online communities, media sharing, micro-sharing, content collaboration, and immersive environments to introduce people to ideas in quick burst, when it suits their workflow, without a big learning curve, and in a way that more closely mirrors how groups interact in person" (Bingham & Conner, 2010, p.11). Learners use social media through the Web; therefore, the concept of the new social learning can be identical with the concept of web-based learning using social media.

Second, social learning is more likely related to informal learning settings out of a classroom than formal learning. Because informal learning occurs every day in the workplace, it is vital for learners in corporations to learn informally in order to cope with new tasks and situations immediately (Lewark, 2010). Informal learning in the workplace can also explain 80% of an individual's knowledge about their jobs by asking questions, observing coworkers, and through other independent learning activities (Attwell, 2007). According to research on informal learning, "especially those asking about adults' self-directed learning projects, reveal that upwards of 90 percent of adults are engaged in hundreds of hours of informal learning. It has also been estimated that the upwards of 70 percent of learning in the workplace is informal, although billions of dollars each year are spent by business and industry on formal training programs" (Merriam, Caffarella & Baumgartner, 2007, p. 35–36).

Table 3. Related theories to social learning and descriptions

<table>
<tr><th colspan="2">Related Theories</th><th>Descriptions</th><th>Researches</th></tr>
<tr><td rowspan="3">Fundamental theories</td><td rowspan="2">Social learning theory</td><td>• Interaction of the individual with the environment
• Social context or environmental elements for an individual's behavior</td><td>Rotter (1954)</td></tr>
<tr><td>• Observational learning and modeling
• Modeling processes through attention, retention, reproduction, and motivation
• Self-efficacy</td><td>Bandura (1977)</td></tr>
<tr><td>Social constructivist theory</td><td>• Social interaction with others
• Internalization of social interaction
• Zone of proximal development</td><td>Moll (1990), Vygotsky (1978), Wertsch (1985),</td></tr>
<tr><td rowspan="3">Instructional approaches</td><td>Situated learning</td><td>• Social interaction and collaboration
• Community of Practice (CoP)
• Legitimate peripheral participation</td><td>Lave & Wenger (1991)</td></tr>
<tr><td>Cognitive apprenticeship</td><td>• A social learning method of helping novices become experts
• Learning-through-guided-experience on cognitive and metacognitive</td><td>Brown, Collins & Duguid (1989), Collins, Brown & Newman (1989)</td></tr>
<tr><td>Collaborative learning</td><td>• Collaboration in small groups and in learning communities
• Learning together with the help of computers</td><td>Slavin (1995), Ewing & Miller (2002)</td></tr>
<tr><td rowspan="2">Learning environments</td><td>The new social learning (WBL using social media)</td><td>• Interaction through social media
• Leverage of online communities, media sharing, micro-sharing, content collaboration</td><td>Bingham & Conner (2010)</td></tr>
<tr><td>Informal learning</td><td>• Learning in various places out of instructor-led programs
• Self-study programs, CoP, and others</td><td>Cross (2007), Watkins & Marsick (1990)</td></tr>
</table>

In sum, the theories above are summarized in Table 3 concerning the overall fundamental theories, instructional approaches, and learning environments for social learning.

Based on literature reviews of the overall fundamental theories, instructional approaches, and learning environments for social learning, Figure 1 displays the conceptual framework of social learning in informal web-based learning environments.

As shown in Figure 1, social learning theory and social constructivist theory are fundamental to social learning in this study. These theories emphasize the importance of interaction with others to share their knowledge and skills. In addition, three instructional approaches, i.e., situated learning, cognitive apprenticeship, and collaborative learning, are crucial concepts to support social learning as they focus on collaboration among learners to solve authentic problems. Along with those basic theories and instructional approaches, social media, a critical element of the new social learning environment, is also considered essential for social learning as it enables learners to communicate, collaborate, and share knowledge and skills with others more effectively and efficiently on the web.

Figure 1. The conceptual framework of social learning in informal web-based learning environments

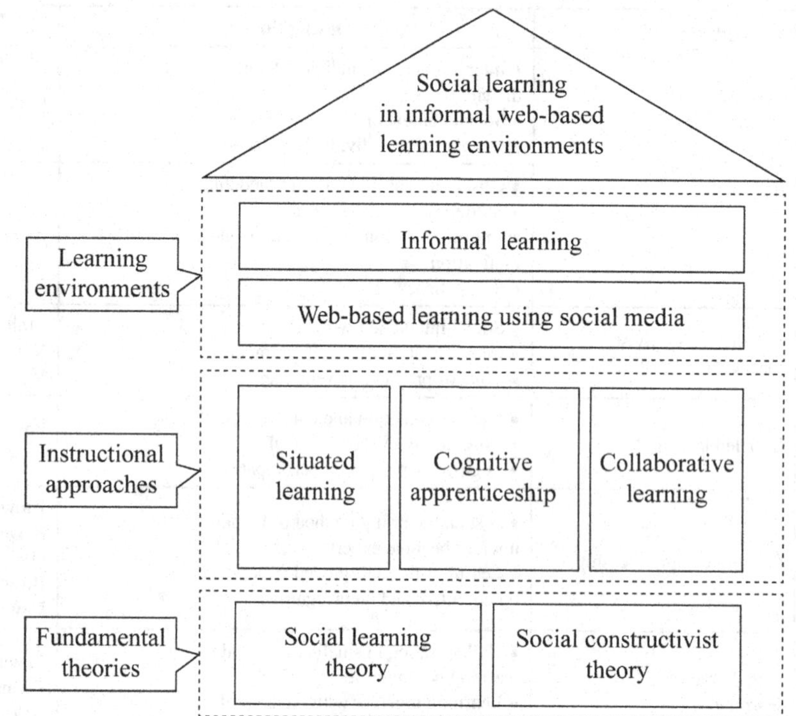

Social Learning Constructs in Informal Web-Based Learning Environments

The key constructs of social learning in informal web-based learning environments can be drawn from fundamental theories, instructional approaches, and learning environments as described in the previous section. In particular, the identification of social learning constructs can be done considering their environmental and individual characteristics. This is because the behavior of people is often affected by the environment in which they exist and on their interpretation of the environment (Bandura, 1977). In addition, according to a psychological equation of behavior by Lewin (1943), both individual and environmental characteristics need to be considered to predict and explain human behavior. If only one of the two characteristics is considered, the results of research may be overestimated (Moon, 2010). Therefore, taking into account both environmental and individual characteristics of social learning constructs, five social learning constructs, interaction, learning community, social media, motivation, and self-efficacy were identified and classified (See Table 4).

As shown in Table 4, in the consideration of environmental characteristics, three social learning constructs, interaction, learning community, and social media were identified. In particular, social learning theory and social constructivist theory commonly deal with constructs related to interaction. The instructional approaches of cognitive apprenticeship and situated learning also emphasize interaction. Furthermore, the instructional approaches of situated learning and collaborative learning are related to collaboration and interaction within communities. The concept of new social learning considers mainly the use of social media in informal web-based learning environments. In the case of individual characteristics, two social learning constructs, motivation and self-efficacy were identified from social

Table 4. Social learning constructs in informal web-based learning environments and related theories

<table>
<tr><th></th><th>Related Theories</th><th>Social Learning Constructs in IWBLEs</th></tr>
<tr><td rowspan="3">Environmental characteristics</td><td>• Social learning theory
• Social constructivist theory
• Situated learning
• Cognitive apprenticeship
• The new social learning</td><td>Interaction</td></tr>
<tr><td>• Situated learning
• Collaborative learning
• Informal learning</td><td>Learning community</td></tr>
<tr><td>• Collaborative learning
• The new social learning
• Informal learning</td><td>Social media</td></tr>
<tr><td rowspan="2">Individual characteristics</td><td>Social learning theory</td><td>Motivation</td></tr>
<tr><td>Social learning theory</td><td>Self-efficacy</td></tr>
</table>

*Note: IWBLEs refers to the abbreviation for Informal Web-based Learning Environments.

learning theories. These social learning constructs are also verified by a study of Hill, Song and West (2009), which examined social learning constructs and the application of the constructs in web-based learning environments (See Table 5).

As shown in Table 5, according to the study by Hill, Song and West (2009), social learning constructs in web-based learning environments are largely comprised of the learning context, culture and community, and learner characteristics. In further detail, the 'context' construct is broken down into interactions, the group and class size, and resources; the 'culture and community' construct is classified as the culture and community; and the 'learner characteristics' construct consists of epistemological beliefs, individual learning styles, self-efficacy, and motivation. As such, these results are aligned with the identification of social learning constructs of this study except that this study added social media as another social learning construct in informal web-based learning environments.

Based on the above review, research related to each of the five social learning constructs can be summarized in Table 6.

The related research presented in Table 6 includes social learning constructs in informal web-based learning environments. First, research related to the construct of interaction has mostly focused on interactions in social learning, social constructivism, and web-based learning environments. Second, the construct of learning community has been investigated in research on communities with social learning, employee performance, adult learners, and online environments. Third, the construct of social media is related to research on social learning technologies in the workplace and social networking sites. Lastly, the constructs of motivation and self-efficacy have focused on learners' characteristics in social learning environments.

FUTURE RESEARCH DIRECTIONS

Based on fundamental theories, instructional approaches, and learning environments for social learning and other research related to social learning, social learning constructs in corporate informal web-based

Table 5. Application of social learning constructs in web-based learning environments (Hill, Song & West, 2009, p.90)

Constructs		Application in Web-Based Learning Environments
Context	Interactions	• Provide opportunities for creating and sharing in-depth messages • Enable support by more knowledgeable others • Encourage interaction by the instructor and peers
Context	Group and class size	• Monitor group size to enable support from more knowledgeable others (i.e., peers) • Monitor class size to enable consistent and engaged interaction
	Resources	• Encourage effective use of postings and other resources • Provide strategies to identify, interpret, and utilize resources
Culture and community	Culture	• Facilitate online interactions so they meet the needs of learners from a variety of cultures • Provide multiple formats for communication to meet differing cultural needs
	Community	• Facilitate connection-building in small and large groups • Support collaborative activities
Learner characteristics	Epistemological beliefs	• Take into consideration reflective thinking abilities • Gain an understanding of epistemological beliefs of students to guide design
	Individual learning styles	• Gain an understanding of learning styles to guide design • Enable different levels of interaction to accommodate individual learning styles
	Self-efficacy	• Enable choice in interactions to minimize social anxiety • Promote self-regulated learning
	Motivation	• Incorporate authentic activities • Send messages regularly to motivate learners

Table 6. Social learning constructs in informal web-based learning environments and related researches

Social Learning Constructs in IWBLEs		Researches
Environmental constructs	Interaction	Ali, Pascoe & Warne (2002), Dennen (2004), Hill, Song & West (2009), LeNoue, Hall & Eighmy (2011), Sthapornnanon et al. (2009), Woo & Reeves (2007)
	Learning community	Hill, Song & West (2009), LeNoue, Hall & Eighmy (2011), Levy & Yupangco (2008), Wellman et al. (1996),
	Social media	Kietzmann et al. (2011), LeNoue, Hall & Eighmy (2011), Levy & Yupangco (2008), Yap & Robben (2010), Zywica, Richards & Gomez (2011)
Individual constructs	Motivation	Conte & Paolucci (2001), DiMicco et al. (2008), Hill, Song & West (2009)
	Self-efficacy	Hill, Song & West (2009), Price & Archbold (1995)

*Note: IWBLEs refers to the abbreviation for Informal Web-based Learning Environments.

learning environments were identified as interaction, learning community, social media, motivation, and self-efficacy. Since the five social learning constructs are founded on theoretical backgrounds, it is necessary to verify if the five constructs can be related to social learning performance positively or what relationships between the constructs and learning performance are through practical methodologies. Future research, therefore, is recommended on identifying the structural relationships between social learning constructs and learning performance in corporate informal web-based learning environments statistically.

CONCLUSION

Many corporations have been concerned with how they can provide their learners with effective social learning environments. In order to find a solution, instructional designers or learning managers in the workplace need to consider first what constructs are critical for designing social learning environments. This chapter reviewed literatures related to social learning and presented major social learning constructs based on theoretical backgrounds. Thus, the results of this chapter can be a fundamental background when designing social learning environments in corporate settings.

REFERENCES

Ali, I. M., Pascoe, C., & Warne, L. (2002). Interactions of organizational culture and collaboration in working and learning. *Journal of Educational Technology & Society*, *5*(2), 60–68.

Anderson, S. E., & Harris, J. B. (1997). Factors associated with amount of use and benefits obtained by users of a statewide educational telecomputing network. *Educational Technology Research and Development*, *45*(1), 19–50. doi:10.1007/BF02299611

Attwell, G. (2007). The personal learning environments: The future of eLearning? *eLearning Papers*, *2*(1), 1-8.

Baldwin, T. T., Magjuka, R. J., & Loher, B. T. (1991). The perils of participation: Effects of choice of trainee motivation and learning. *Personnel Psychology*, *44*(1), 51–65. doi:10.1111/j.1744-6570.1991.tb00690.x

Bandura, A. (1977). *Social learning theory*. NY: General Learning Press.

Bandura, A. (1986). *Social foundations of thought and action: A social cognitive theory*. Englewood Cliffs, NJ: Prentice-Hall.

Bang, J., & Dalsgaard, C. (2006). Rethinking e-learning: Shifting the focus to learning activities. In E. K. Sorensen & D. Murchú (Eds.), *Enhancing learning through technology* (pp. 184–202). Information Science Publishing. doi:10.4018/978-1-59140-971-7.ch008

Bingham, T., & Conner, M. (2010). *The new social learning: A guide to transforming organizations through social media*. San Francisco, CA: Berrett-Koehler Publishers, Inc.

Bray, E., Aoki, K., & Dlugosh, L. (2008). Predictors of learning satisfaction in Japanese online distance learners. *International Review of Research in Open and Distance Learning*, *9*(3), 1–24.

Brown, J. S., Collins, A., & Duguid, P. (1989). Situated cognition and the culture of learning. *Educational Researcher, 18*(1), 32–42. doi:10.3102/0013189X018001032

Charbonneau-Gowdy, P., & Cechova, I. (2009). Moving from analogue to high definition e-tools to support empowering social learning approaches. *Electronic Journal of e-Learning, 7*(3), 225-238.

Chen, B., & Bryer, T. (2012). Investigating instructional strategies for using social media in formal and informal learning. *International Review of Research in Open and Distance Learning, 13*(1), 87–104.

Cole, M. (1996). *Cultural psychology: A once and future discipline*. Cambridge, MA: Harvard University Press.

Collins, A., Brown, J. S., & Newman, S. E. (1989). Cognitive apprenticeship: Teaching the craft of reading, writing, and mathematics. In L. B. Resnick (Ed.), *Knowing, learning, and instruction: Essays in honor of Robert Glaser* (pp. 453–494). Hillsdale, NJ: Lawrence Erlbaum Associates.

Colquitt, J. A., LePine, J. A., & Noe, R. A. (2000). Toward an integrative theory of training motivation: A meta-analytic path analysis of 20 years of research. *The Journal of Applied Psychology, 85*(5), 678–707. doi:10.1037/0021-9010.85.5.678 PMID:11055143

Conte, R., & Paolucci, M. (2001). Intelligent social learning. *Journal of Artificial Societies and Social Simulation, 4*(1). Retrieved from http://jasss.soc.surrey.ac.uk/4/1/3.html

Contreras-Castillo, J., Favela, J., Perez-Fragoso, C., & Santamaria-del-Angel, E. (2004). Informal interactions and their implications for online courses. *Computers & Education, 42*(2), 149–168. doi:10.1016/S0360-1315(03)00069-1

Cross, J. (2007). *Informal learning: Rediscovering the natural pathways that inspire innovation and performance*. San Francisco, CA: John Wiley & Sons, Inc.

Dennen, V. P. (2004). Cognitive apprenticeship in educational practice: Research on scaffolding, modeling, mentoring, and coaching as instructional strategies. In D. H. Jonassen (Ed.), *Handbook of research on educational communications and technology* (2nd ed., pp. 813–828). NJ: Lawrence Erlbaum Associates.

DiMicco, J., Millen, D. R., Geyer, W., Dugan, C., Brownholtz, B., & Muller, M. (2008). Motivations for social networking at work. *Proceedings of the 2008 ACM conference on Computer supported cooperative work CSCW '08* (pp. 711-720).

Ewing, J., & Miller, D. (2002). A framework for evaluating computer supported collaborative learning. *Journal of Educational Technology & Society, 5*(1), 112–118.

Garrett, N. (2011). An e-portfolio design supporting ownership, social learning, and ease of use. *Journal of Educational Technology & Society, 14*(1), 187–202.

Gibson, S. K. (2004). Social learning (cognitive) theory and implications for human resource development. *Advances in Developing Human Resources, 6*(2), 193–210. doi:10.1177/1523422304263429

Hasan, H., & Pfaff, C. C. (2006). The wiki: An environment to revolutionize employees' interaction with corporate knowledge. *Proceedings of the Australasian Computer-Human Interaction Conference*, Sydney (pp. 377-380). doi:10.1145/1228175.1228250

Hill, J. R., Song, L., & West, R. E. (2009). Social learning theory and web-based learning environments: A review of research and discussion of implications. *American Journal of Distance Education*, *23*(2), 88–103. doi:10.1080/08923640902857713

Jackson, A., Yates, J., & Orlikowski, W. (2007). Corporate blogging: Building community through persistent digital talk. *Proceedings of the 40th Hawaii International Conference on System Sciences* (pp. 1530-1605). doi:10.1109/HICSS.2007.155

Keeler, L. C. (2006). Student satisfaction and types of interaction in distance education courses. *Dissertation Abstracts International*, *67*, 9.

Kietzmann, J. H., Hermkens, K., McCarthy, I. P., & Silvestre, B. S. (2011). Social media? Get serious! Understanding the functional building blocks of social media. *Business Horizons*, *54*(3), 241–251. doi:10.1016/j.bushor.2011.01.005

Kim, S. T., Lee, C. K., & Hwang, T. (2008). Investigating the influence of employee blogging on IT workers' organizational citizenship behavior. *International Journal of Information Technology and Management*, *7*(2), 178–189. doi:10.1504/IJITM.2008.016604

Kreijns, K., Kirschner, P. A., & Jochems, W. (2003). Identifying the pitfalls for social interaction in computer-supported collaborative learning environments: A review of the research. *Computers in Human Behavior*, *19*(3), 335–353. doi:10.1016/S0747-5632(02)00057-2

Kreijns, K., Kirschner, P. A., Jochems, W., & van Buuren, H. (2007). Measuring perceived sociability of computer-supported collaborative learning environments. *Computers & Education*, *49*(2), 176–192. doi:10.1016/j.compedu.2005.05.004

Lave, J., & Wenger, E. (1991). *Situated learning: Legitimate peripheral participation*. Cambridge, UK: Cambridge University Press. doi:10.1017/CBO9780511815355

Lee, H., & Bonk, C. (2010). Implementation, challenges, and future plans of social learning in the workplace. In J. Sanchez, & K. Zhang (Eds.), *Proceedings of World Conference on E-Learning in Corporate, Government, Healthcare, and Higher Education 2010* (pp. 2581-2587). Chesapeake, VA: AACE.

LeNoue, M., Hall, T., & Eighmy, M. A. (2011). Adult education and social media revolution. *Adult Learning*, *22*(2), 4–12. doi:10.1177/104515951102200201

Levy, S., & Yupangco, J. (2008, August 11). Overcoming the challenges of social learning in the workplace. *Learning Solutions e-Magazine*.

Lewark, S. (2010). Learning, knowledge transfer and competence development in forestry operations small and medium sized enterprises (SMEs). Institute for Forest Utilization and Work Science. Albert-Ludwigs-University Freiburg, Breisgau, Germany.

Lewin, K. (1943). Defining the Field at a given time. *Psychological Review*, *50*(3), 292–310. doi:10.1037/h0062738

Maddux, C. D., Johnson, D. L., & Willis, J. W. (1997). *Educational computing: Learning with tomorrow's technologies*. Boston: Allyn & Bacon.

Mathieu, J. E., Tannenbaum, S. I., & Salas, E. (1992). Influences of individual and situational characteristics on measures of training effectiveness. *Academy of Management Journal*, *35*(4), 828–847. doi:10.2307/256317

McDonald, J., & Gibson, C. C. (1998). Interpersonal dynamics and group development in computer conferencing. *American Journal of Distance Education*, *12*(1), 7–25. doi:10.1080/08923649809526980

McMahon, M. (1997, December). *Social constructivism and the world wide web: A paradigm for learning*. Paper presented at the ASCILITE conference. Perth, Australia.

Merriam, S., Caffarella, R., & Baumgartner, L. (2007). *Learning in adulthood: A comprehensive guide* (3rd ed.). NY: Willey.

Miller, N. E., & Dollard, J. C. (1941). *Social learning and imitation*. New Haven, CT: Yale University Press.

Moll, L. C. (1990). Introduction. In L. C. Moll (Ed.), *Vygotsky and education: Instructional implications and applications of sociohistorical psychology* (pp. 1–27). NY: Cambridge University Press. doi:10.1017/CBO9781139173674.002

Moon, S., & Lee, Y. (2009). The impacts of social network activities on company employees' organizational commitment and job satisfaction. *Journal of Korea Human Resource Management*, *6*(2), 55–67.

Moon, S. B. (2010). *Basic concepts and applications of structural equation modeling*. Seoul: Haksisa.

Noe, R. A. (1986). Trainee attributes and attitudes: Neglected influences on training effectiveness. *Academy of Management Review*, *11*, 736–749.

Park, S., Lim, C., Lee, J., & Choi, J. (2010). *Understanding of educational methods in educational technology*. Seoul: Educational Science Inc.

Price, V., & Archbold, J. (1995). Development and application of social learning theory. *British Journal of Nursing (Mark Allen Publishing)*, *4*(21), 1263–1268. doi:10.12968/bjon.1995.4.21.1263 PMID:8574105

Reigeluth, C. M., & Keller, J. B. (2009). Understanding instruction. In C. M. Reigeluth & A. A. Carr-Chellman (Eds.), *Instructional-design theories and models: Building a common knowledge base* (Vol. III, pp. 27–39). NY: Routlege.

Rodriguez Robles, F. M. (2006). Learner characteristic, interaction and support service variables as predictors of satisfaction in web-based distance education. *Dissertation Abstracts International*, *67*, 7.

Rogoff, B. (1990). *Apprenticeship in thinking: Cognitive development in social context*. NY: Oxford University Press.

Rotter, J. B. (1954). *Social learning and clinical psychology*. NY: Prentice-Hall. doi:10.1037/10788-000

Rotter, J. B. (1982). *The development and application of social learning theory: Selected papers*. NY: Praeger.

Slavin, R. E. (1995). *Cooperative learning: Theory, research, and practice* (2nd ed.). Englewood Cliffs, NJ: Prentice Hall.

Sthapornnanon, N., Sakulbumrungsil, R., Theeraroungchaisri, A., & Watcharadamrongkun, S. (2009). Instructional design and assessment: Social constructivist learning environment in an online professional practice course. *American Journal of Pharmaceutical Education*, *73*(1), 1–8. doi:10.5688/aj730110 PMID:19513138

Vygotsky, L. S. (1978). *Mind in society: The development of higher psychological processes*. Cambridge, MA: Harvard University.

Watkins, K., & Marsick, V. (1990). *Informal and incidental learning in the workplace*. London.

Wellman, B., Salaff, J., Dimitrova, D., Garton, L., Gulia, M., & Haythornthwaite, C. (1996). Computer networks as social networks: Collaborative work, telework, and virtual community. *Annual Review of Sociology*, *22*(1), 213–238. doi:10.1146/annurev.soc.22.1.213

Wertsch, J. V. (1985). *Vygotsky and the social formation of mind*. Cambridge, MA: Harvard University Press.

Wertsch, J. V., & Tulviste, P. (1992). L. S. Vygotsky and contemporary developmental psychology. *Developmental Psychology*, *28*(4), 548–557. doi:10.1037/0012-1649.28.4.548

Wink, J., & Putney, L. G. (2002). *A vision of Vygotsky*. Boston: Allyn & Bacon.

Woo, Y., & Reeves, T. C. (2007). Meaningful interaction in web-based learning: A social constructivist interpretation. *The Internet and Higher Education*, *10*(1), 15–25. doi:10.1016/j.iheduc.2006.10.005

Yap, R., & Robben, J. (2010). A model for leveraging social learning technologies in corporate environments. *Proceedings of the 7th International Conference on Networked Learning 2010*.

Zemke, R., & Zemke, S. (1984, March). 30 things we know for sure about adult learning. *Innovation Abstracts, 6*(8).

Zhang, X., Olfman, L., & Firpo, D. (2010). Supporting social constructivist learning through the KEEP SLS e-portfolio system. *International Journal on E-Learning*, *9*(3), 411–426.

Zywica, J., Richards, K. A., & Gomez, K. (2011). Affordances of a scaffolded-social learning network. *On The Horizon*, *19*(1), 33–42. doi:10.1108/10748121111107690

KEY TERMS AND DEFINITIONS

Learning Community: Learning community includes the concept of both communities of practice and knowledge-building communities.

Learning Performance: Learning performance can be categorized into learning satisfaction, learning persistence, and learning achievement. Learning satisfaction and learning persistence through learners' perceptions particularly are considered as major variables for learning performance in informal web-based learning environments. Since formal learning achievements are not required in informal learning environments, learning satisfaction and persistence become more appropriate indicators of learning performance than learning achievement.

Social Learning: Collaborative learning that happens through interactions with others in informal learning environments.

Social Media: Internet-based applications designed to support social learning through interactive communications in informal environments.

Chapter 3
Ecologies of Information and Communication Technology Platform Design for e-Government Service Provision:
Actors, Influences, and Fields of Play

Shefali Virkar
University of Oxford, UK

ABSTRACT

This research chapter, through the presentation of an empirical case study surrounding the implementation and use of an electronic property tax collection system in Bangalore (India), developed between 1998 and 2008, critically examines both the role of Information and Communication Technologies (ICTs) in governmental reform processes and the contribution of such technologies to the deeper understanding of the social dynamics shaping e-government projects used to reform public sector institutions. Drawing on the theoretical perspectives of the 'Ecology of Games' and 'Design-Actuality Gaps', both of which recognise the importance of a multitude of diverse motives and individualistic behaviour as key factors influencing organisational reform and institutional change, the chapter contributes not just to an understanding of the role of ICTs in public administration reform, but also towards that emerging body of research which is critical of managerial rationalism for an organization as a whole, and is sensitive to an ecology of actors and their various motivations operating within the symbiotic organisation.

INTRODUCTION

Over the course of the last two decades, globalisation and information technology have been rapidly dismantling traditional barriers to trade, travel and communication, fuelling great promise for progress

DOI: 10.4018/978-1-4666-9556-6.ch003

Copyright © 2016, IGI Global. Copying or distributing in print or electronic forms without written permission of IGI Global is prohibited.

towards greater global equity and prosperity. Attracted by the 'hype and hope' of Information and Communication Technologies (ICTs), development actors across the world have adopted computer-based systems and related ICTs for use in government as a means reforming the inefficiencies in public service provision. Whilst a number of these electronic government or 'e-government' projects have achieved significant results, evidence from the field indicates that despite the reported success stories, the rate of project failure remains particularly high.

Much has been written about e-government within a growing stream of literature on ICT for development, generating countervailing perspectives where optimistic, technocratic approaches are countered by far more sceptical standpoints on technological innovation. However, in trying to analyse both their potential and real value, there has been a tendency for scholars to see e-government applications as isolated technical artefacts, analysed solely as a collection of hardware and software. Far less work is based on empirical field research, and models put forward by scholars and practitioners alike often neglect the actual attitudes, choices and behaviour of the wide array of actors involved in the implementation and use of new technology in real organisations as well as the way in which the application shapes and is shaped by existing social, organisational and environmental contexts.

This chapter seeks to unravel the social dynamics shaping e-government projects used to reform public sector institutions. The value of such an approach is based on a review of existing development literature, which tends to be overly systems-rational in its approach. As a consequence, the literature does not recognise the degree to which project failure (*viz.* the general inability of the project design to meet stated goals and resolve both predicted and emerging problems) is symptomatic of a broader, much more complex set of interrelated inequalities, unresolved problems and lopsided power-relationships both within the adopting organisation and in the surrounding environmental context.

The case study from which this paper is drawn, focused on a project aimed at digitising property tax records and administrative processes within the Revenue Department of the Greater Bangalore City Municipal Corporation. In recognising the need to turn property tax into a viable revenue instrument that delivers high tax yields without compromising on citizen acceptance, the Bangalore City Corporation has sought to improve its property tax administration system through the introduction of a computerised database and the use of digital mapping techniques to track compliance and check evasion.

E-GOVERNMENT: DEFINITION, NATURE, AND SCOPE

Simultaneous with the shift towards a more inclusive process of participation in political decision-making and public sector reform has been an increased interest in the new digital Information and Communication Technologies (ICTs) and the ways in which they may be used to effectively complement and reform existing political processes. Developments in communication technologies have historically resulted in changes in the way in which governments function, often challenging them to find new ways in which to communicate and interact with their citizens, and ICTs today are seen to possess the potential to change institutions as well as the mechanisms of service delivery, bringing about a fundamental change in the way government operates and a transformation in the dynamic between government and its citizens (Misra, 2005). The work of the public sector has traditionally been highly information-intensive; government has been, and still remains, the single largest collector, user, holder and producer of information (Heeks, 2000), and is considered to be a central resource 'in pursuing democratic/political processes, in managing resources, executing functions, measuring performance, and in service delivery' (Isaac-Henry, 1997).

e-Government has today become an influential concept for scholars concerned with public administration reform and better overall governance. In developed countries, large-scale projects at the local level have typically concentrated on the creation of virtual or digital town-halls through the automation and distribution of well-structured administrative services (Dutton,1999). However, while online e-government service initiatives have become common in many countries, and in a variety of contexts, such applications are characteristically built with a primary focus on administration-citizen interaction, rather than on explicitly supporting plans for strategic organisational development. Further, although considerable attention has been focused on how e-government can help public bodies improve their services, there are relatively few studies which focus the long term sustainability of e-government initiatives, particularly in the developing world. In contrast, this project focused on in this study seeks to illustrate that the potential for improved government-citizen interaction through e-government and public sector reform could be realised not only through developing the 'virtual front office' but also through their effect on back-office organisation and culture.

CENTRAL RESEARCH QUESTIONS AND THEORETICAL APPROACH

The main goal of this chapter is thus to approach the issues thrown up by the organisational and institutional transformations that occur in public administration from a multidisciplinary perspective and, through the use of a case study, attempt to bring a new perspective to bear on the following questions:

1. Does the introduction and implementation of Information and Communication Technologies within developing world bureaucracies have an impact on the internal dynamics of the group and on relationships between actors operating within these organisations?
2. If, so what are the types of interactions that may arise between the actors concerned and how do these impact project outcome?

Whilst a single case study alone cannot provide closed-end answers to these questions, it can suggest ways of addressing them that could otherwise be applicable to a wider variety of situations.

The theoretical framework adopted by this research will therefore emphasise three issues: first, the politics involved in the conception, innovation, and governance of software platforms for public administration, which is related to the set of institutions and rules that set the limits on, and the incentives that result in, the constitution and working of interdependent networks of actors within the industry and within government; second, the concept of electronic government itself as circumscribed by socio-political and economic development; and finally, the relationship and interrelationships between technology, organisation, and institutional change. To do this, the chapter will ground its case study in three major complementary strands of literature, first delineated in Virkar (2011):

1. A conceptual discussion of the roles and interactions of a multiplicity of actors with diverse motivations and strategies conceptualized as an 'ecology of games', or an overarching sphere of symbiotic action falling within the umbrella of New Institutionalism, and their contribution to the shaping of political organisations and institutions; with special reference to the success or failure of e-government projects.

2. The literature which deals with public administration reform and the role of Information and Communication Technologies in improving the functioning of public administration and in reducing corruption within a developing country context.
3. A discussion of the importance of the ICT hardware and software industry, with special reference to software platform design for e-government and to socio-economic and political development in India.

Conclusions will be reached through the concurrent use of three dimensions – *theoretically* on the basis of existing literature, *descriptively* on the basis of a case study, and *analytically* using a unique hybrid of the complementary conceptual frameworks of the Ecology of Games (Long, 1958) and the Design-Actuality Gap model (Heeks, 2003).

RESEARCH METHODOLOGY

The ultimate aim of this chapter is thus to contribute to the development of a conceptual framework that is relevant to policy discussions of e-government software platform design and maintenance within not only an Indian, but also a broader global context. In order to augment theoretical discussions of administrative reform in a digitised world, this chapter uses a case study to explore its central research issues, within which a mixed-methods approach employing a combination of qualitative and quantitative data was selected to inform and to strengthen the understanding of the relationships between the actors, inputs, and project outputs. The aim of the study was, therefore, to evolve ideas that could be generalised across similar situations and the research was consequently developed in the following steps:

- In-depth review of existing theoretical perspectives and literature surrounding corruption and tax evasion, ICTs and public administration, and property tax reform.
- Qualitative analysis of official documents;
- Collection and analysis of quantitative data relevant to the case;
- Developing case studies through in-depth personal interviews;
- Data analysis and interpretation;
- Preparation of conclusions and their validation;
- Recommendations for the future.

The use of mixed-method case study research is becoming increasingly popular in the social sciences, and is fast being recognised as a successful approach for investigating contemporary phenomena in a real-life context when the boundaries between phenomenon and context are not evident and where multiple sources of evidence present themselves (Yin, 2003). It was thus felt to be a particularly apt way of studying the nature and impact of actor actions, motivations and behaviours on e-government software platform conception and design, where the aim is not simply to judge whether the project at hand represents a success or failure, but is to understand the qualities inherent in the architecture that have made it so.

More precisely, case study research consists of a detailed investigation of phenomena within a given context, often with data being collected over a period of time. The aim of this approach is thus to provide the researcher with an all-round analysis of the surrounding environment and processes, in order that they might throw light on the theoretical issues being investigated (Eisenhardt, 1989). The phenomenon under examination is thus not isolated from its context, rather it is of interest precisely because the aim is to observe and understand actor behaviour and/or organisational processes and their interplay with the surrounding environment. The use of a case study itself is therefore not as much a method as it is a *research strategy*, where the context is deliberately included as part of the overall design. Today, case studies are widely used in organisational research across the social sciences, indicating growing confidence in the approach as a rigorous research strategy in its own right (Hartley, 2005).

As research conducted by adopting this strategy is typically done in the field, the presence of too many observations and uncontrollable 'variables' makes the application of standard experimental or survey approaches infeasible. Further, information tends to be scattered and generally cannot be picked up using one single method (Eisenhardt, 1989). Case studies thus typically combine a number of data collection methods such as participant observation, direct observation, interviews, focus groups, ethnography, document analysis, questionnaires etc., where evidence may be quantitative or qualitative depending on the research issues at hand (Hartley, 2005). The approach is consequently flexible, allowing for new methods to be incorporated as new sources of data and new actors present themselves. The case study approach may thus be and has been used for various purposes – to provide a descriptive narrative, to generate new theory, or to test existing theory through the triangulation of data (Virkar, 2011).

SOURCES OF EVIDENCE AND DATA COLLECTION

Introducing e-government initiatives into public bodies is a tricky strategic game to play; for, although computerisation alters the *work-load*, *work-profile*, and *work-content* of the average public sector employee, thereby *impacting accountability*, *reducing the opportunities for exercising discretion*, *making performance more visible*, and *flattening extant hierarchies*, the re-engineering of workflow processes often forces the *need for employee retraining* and *retooling*, and sometimes *creates severe redundancy* (Virkar, 2011). Many nascent projects, therefore, tend to face significant internal resistance from staff, and particularly, from within the middle to lower levels of the given civil service; with efforts made to craft and to re-frame procedures and protocols, and to successfully effect back-end computerisation having a profound impact on the way civil servants perform their duties and perceive their jobs.

Very often, within developing countries, it is the fear of the unknown that drives this resistance forward; most especially, if the introduction of a new technology results in a dramatic change of procedures, and the imperative need for the acquisition of new skills. Further, in corrupt service delivery departments, there may be acute pressure placed internally to slow down, or to delay, the introduction of technology-led reforms; owing to, in this case, the significant, impending loss of additional income. An in-depth analysis of the ICT for development literature by this researcher identified five participant-actor groups involved in strategic games and interactions within the larger global meta-game concerned most-immediately with the implementation of e-government projects (Virkar, 2011):

1. **Politicians:** The first group identified comprises of elected representatives of various hues, guided and influenced chiefly by both electoral imperatives and a need to maintain their public image; and, therefore concerned predominantly with the direction of both key economic policy issues, as well as issues of public service delivery.

2. **Administrators / Civil Servants:** This group of actors is guided, principally, by their perceptions of existing institutional 'culture' and practices, and by their positive (or negative) attitudes towards internal bureaucratic reform; including, such concerns as those pertaining to the down-sizing of administrative services to promote 'efficiency', and those relevant to a sense of bureaucracy being policed by elected government through the introduction and the institutionalisation of ICTs.
3. **Employees of Organisations Involved with the Technical Design of IT and ICT Systems Architecture:** This attitudes held by group of participant-actors are guided, primarily, by extant corporate workplace cultures and/or by prevailing market-based trends; wherein, the approach taken by private suppliers and technology-based solutions providers to e-government systems architecture might be considerably different to, or deviate significantly from, what the adopting government agency actually needs, or indeed wants, from a given systems-architecture.
4. **Private Citizens:** This is another particularly interesting group of participant-actors, as the researcher is never quite sure as to what their reaction to the roll-out, and the implementation, of e-government systemic networks will be. Whilst in theory citizens should welcome the introduction of a systems-architecture that simplifies public administrative processes, it is, in practice, equally possible that some citizens might neither be very happy, nor welcome the happenstance, should a more efficient system, and considered as being either to their perceived or their express detriment, be put into place.
5. **International Donors:** This final participant-actor group controls the purse-strings globally, and oftentimes comes to the table with 'higher' ideals influenced by ideas currently prevalent within international politics and political circles; including, the firm desire to have a particular brand of 'good governance' take root within the developing world.

For the larger study from which this chapter is drawn, 40 personal interviews were conducted over a 24-month period. The interviewees can be roughly divided into four groups based on their relationship to the case: *Senior Civil Servants* involved with the planning and implementation of the project, including current and former BBMP Commissioners, Deputy Commissioners for Revenue, and Revenue Officers, *Revenue and Tax Officials*, primarily Assistant Revenue Officers (AROs) responsible for the in-the-field collection and administration of property tax in the city, *Software Developers* involved in the conception, design, and implementation of the project, and *Miscellaneous Actors* including journalists and external consultants.

Twenty-seven subjects agreed to full-length interviews and to have their comments recorded. This included all six members of the project planning committee, one senior official involved with the implementation of the GIS, and twenty senior revenue officers involved with the system's application in the field. Additional informal interviews conducted face-to-face or over the email were also used to close gaps in knowledge or to follow up new information and anchor the interpretation of events and motives in the perceptions of participants. In addition to the recorded interviews, this chapter uses information and quotes obtained informally from people related to the project who did not wish to be interviewed formally or have their comments recorded. Out of the 13 people in this category, 10 were junior revenue officials (Station Managers, Tax Inspectors and Accountants) working under the AROs interviewed, 2 were Revenue Officers supervising the overall administration of the Revenue Offices and one person was a local correspondent from a leading national daily.

EXAMINING ACTOR ATTITUDES AND PERCEPTIONS: FROM HUMAN *FACTORS* TO HUMAN *ACTORS*

One approach to understanding behaviour is to look at the composition of individual actors, rather than the system as a whole (Virkar, 2013). The design and implementation of complex computer systems, such as those that support e-government platforms, requires a better understanding in practitioner circles of the users of such networks and the settings in which they work. Part of the problem resides in the implicit treatment of ordinary people as unskilled, non-specialist users of technology and their networks comprising of elementary processes or factors that can be studied in isolation in a field laboratory setting (Bannon, 1991). Another contributing aspect is the approach of computational sociologists and computer scientists to the mathematical modelling of social processes as interactions amongst quantifiable variables; wherein the behaviour of individual actors and other micro-factors that constitute aggregative sociological outcomes are ignored at the cost of the initial macro-conditions that they otherwise circumscribe, constrain, and influence (Macy &Willer, 2002).

Although psychology has a long tradition of contributing to computer systems design and implementation, it has been a neglected discipline in scholarly circles. Moreover, on the one hand, key issues such as those concerned with the underlying values of the people involved in large-scale system design, and their motivational basis for interaction in the work setting, have been missed out in recent computer science-based scholarly analysis (Salvendy, 2012). Conceptualising and understanding people as actor-elements in situations, on the other hand, each with a set of skills and shared practices based on work experiences with others, requires a reorientation of the way in which the relationships between the central elements of computer-systems architecture design extant within work environments – namely *people*, *technology*, *work requirements*, and *organisational constraints* – are negotiated (Kuutti, 1996).

The main human participants actively involved within the electronic governance process may, hence, be placed into one of two distinct groups: *Internal actors*, who comprise chiefly of those *institutional actors* responsible for the *maintenance*, *upkeep* and the *running* of a project, including (a) *officers of the assembly* who are responsible for the operation of the back-office systems architecture such as IT specialists and forum moderators, and (b) *elected representatives* (and their support staff) who correspond to the virtual front-desk both individually and collectively; and *External actors*, or *miscellaneous actors external to a given network set-up*, and who also comprise of two distinct categories, including (a) *online-network participants*, or the person(s) (or group) that initiates an online interaction with a governmental entity after identifying an issue of relevance, and then following its progress through to the end, from submission to final feedback and outcome, and (b) *individual citizens*, or those individuals who may or may not be entitled to participate online, but who will invariably impact, or be impacted by, the outcome of a policy process through their fundamental ability to shape public opinion elsewhere.

The use of the terms 'human factors' and 'human actors' give us a clue, therefore, as to how people in system design clusters are approached within the scholarly literature (Virkar, 2011). More particularly, the terms highlight differences intrinsic to how people and their contributions are, and can be, perceived; the former connoting a passive, fragmented, depersonalised, and somewhat automatic human-element contribution to the computer systems environment, and the latter an active, controlling, involved one (Carayon et. al, 2012). More precisely, within the *human factor* approach, the human element is more often than not reduced to being another systemic component, possessing certain characteristics that need to be factored into the design equation extant to the overall human-machine system (Czaja & Nair, 2012). In doing so, the approach de-emphasises certain important elements of work design: the goals, values, and beliefs which technologists and system-users hold otherwise about life and work (Jacko et. al., 2012). By using the term *human actor*, emphasis is placed on considering users and developers as autonomous agents, possessing the capacity to control, regulate, and coordinate their behaviour, rather than them being on par and analysed as mere information-processing automatons (Proctor & Vu, 2012). The study of game-strategic actor interactions is, hence, pivotal to the deeper understanding of e-government initiatives, as it is important to determine therein the impact that the sum total of all actor motivations and goals have on public consultative and participatory processes, and have, subsequently, on public policy outcomes (Salvendy, 2012).

UNDERSTANDING POLITICAL BEHAVIOUR WITHIN THE CONTEXT OF E-GOVERNMENT SYSTEMS-ARCHITECTURE

The central issue that needs to be understood whilst studying the development of ICT platforms and their implementation in public sector organisations through an analysis of actor interactions is thus: *What motivates people to do what they do?* Another approach taken to understanding political behaviour is, therefore, to look more closely at the *rationality* of actors and actor-groups; rather than at individual human *factors*, or at the computer-system network architecture as a whole. This is largely because human *actors* are driven by a combination of *organisational and institutional roles and duties*, and by *calculated self-interest*; with political, social, and economic interactions being organised around the *construction* and *interpretation of meaning*, as well as the *making of choices*. This approach to the study of political e-governance begins by *defining* and *examining* the *motives* and the *goals* that prompt actors to *interact* and *participate* in decision- and policymaking processes online.

All actor interactions, when considered in this vein, are taken as having been *motivated* in some way, and individuals are understood as being willing to *engage* in a particular behaviour in order to achieve a desired end (Atkinson & Birch, 1970). Political actors, in particular, possess a complex set of goals they wish to attain; including *power, income, prestige, security, convenience, loyalty* (to an idea, an institution, or to the nation), *pride in work well done*, and *a desire to serve the public interest* (as the individual actor conceives it). Added to this, individuals and private citizens tend to participate in politics for *altruistic* or *conformist* reasons; to *boost their self-esteem*, to *self-enhance*, and to *achieve self-efficacy* (Virkar, 2011). Actors range from being purely self-interested 'climbers' or 'conservers' motivated entirely by goals which benefit themselves and their *status quo*, rather than their organizations or the society at large, to having mixed motives as 'zealots', 'advocates' and 'statesmen' motivated by goals which combine self-interest and altruistic loyalty with larger universal values (Downs, 1964).

For citizens and users of the e-government application, the motivation to use the system may either be *intrinsic* or *extrinsic* (Cruickshank et. al., 2010). *Intrinsic motives* include *inward rewards* pertaining to the human desire to feel competent and self-determining, to show altruism, or to seek to increase the welfare of others. On the other hand, *extrinsic motives* are usually associated with some sort of *external reward* in the social, economic, or political sphere. Both these cognitive typographies manifest themselves within particular forms of human behaviour; relevant, especially, to configurations of *conditional co-operation, social pressure, tolerance thresholds*, and the *bandwagon effect* (Virkar, 2011; Margetts et. al., 2012). Different motives and goals may underlie the same surface behaviour, with the social and psychological consequences of participation in democratic and political processes being different for different users (Virkar, 2013); wherein, some participate to gain information or support, and others to communicate, and wherein all strategic game-movements result in a set of nested, interrelated interactions within the framework of a large strategic *meta-game* or playing field (Virkar, 2011). Consequently, the motivations and goals for using the online resources will determine precisely *how* these will be used, by *whom*, and *when*.

THE PROPERTY TAX: DEFINITION, NATURE, AND SCOPE

Property tax may be defined as a recurrent tax on real property (land and/or improvements) in urban areas (Dillinger, 1988). Just like other taxes, it may be considered as 'a compulsory transfer of money… from private individuals, institutions or groups to the government…[as] one of the principal means by which a government finances its expenditure' (Bannock et.al, 1987). Further, Rosengard (1998) defines Property Tax as '…[an] *ad valorem* ("according to the value" tax, as opposed to a unit tax), *in rem* ("against the object" tax as opposed to a personal or *in personam* tax) levied on the ownership, occupation or development of land and/or buildings. Property taxes usually are assessed annually upon the capital value of a property, or upon proxies for capital value such as presumed or actual rental income. Taxes not confined to immovable property, such as net wealth taxes and general capital gains taxes, are not commonly classified as property taxes."

Property tax is appealing to local governments in developing countries for a number of reasons. First and possibly most importantly, it is a potential revenue generator, particularly given the high-income elasticity of property ownership in developing countries. It is a relatively stable source of income, and it is easy to implement slight adjustments and incremental rate changes. The tax is generally equitable and progressive for residential properties. It is hard to avoid legally due to the high visibility and relative immobility of property, with asset immobility also conferring a high degree of economic efficiency on the tax. It is clearly enforceable, particularly through the seizure and liquidation of property. The tax has the potential to enhance the local government agency's responsiveness to local priorities, particularly when used to finance local goods.

As a means of financing the recurrent cost of municipal services, the merits of the property tax are controversial, particularly as in theory these could be financed through a variety of user charges, taxes or by inter-governmental transfers. According to Rosengard (1998), the tax does have some very obvious weaknesses. Political vulnerability is a significant constraint on property tax as a source of revenue, as in practice the tax has a propensity to encounter a degree of political resistance, which is altogether disproportionate to its absolute yield (NIUA, 2004). The large number of statutory taxpayers magnifies the political impact of even slight tax increases, whilst its high visibility amplifies awareness and intensifies the resentment of the tax burden. Further, the purported non-objective basis of assessment is commonly perceived to be arbitrary and unsubstantiated, with poor administration often leading to glaring horizontal inequities (Dillinger, 1988). The tax also has the potential the potential to exacerbate regional disparities in wealth, particularly in countries where rates and expenditures are determined locally.

Changing the mind-sets of key actors in games related to property tax administration is often central to successfully reforming the method of valuation. On the one hand, public reluctance to adopt new methods is a major obstacle to changes in assessment when undertaking property tax reform, often arising from a certain degree of unawareness and an aversion to shouldering an increased tax burden. In addition, those taxpayers who seek to use existing flaws in the system to their own advantage – generally to partially or completely evade taxes – may also be reluctant to accept a better, more fool-proof system. At the same time, the attitudes of government officials also need to be dealt with during the reform process as any change in procedure is bound to bring about modifications in existing systems, with resistance arising when staff are confronted with the need to develop new skills and where well-entrenched power structures and old mental models are challenged (Virkar, 2011) The degree to which both the public and the bureaucracy are willing to adapt to reforms is thus important, as these attitudes often shape the political response to changes in the administrative set-up of tax regime and to reassessments of the tax rate.

ANALYTICAL FRAMEWORK: THE ECOLOGY OF GAMES

From the turn of the century to the present, there has been a progressive movement away from the view that governance is the outcome of rational calculation to achieve specific goals by a unitary governmental actor, and in that context metaphors based on games have been extremely useful in developing new ways to think about the policy process. A look through the literature reveals that although many political games have been described by scholars within differing contexts, ranging from electoral politics to administrative functioning, there exists no comprehensive description of the public organization as a system of these various interactions.

The use of Game Theory and most other game metaphors (although differing widely in their orientation) have had, according to scholars, one major limitation for clarifying policy processes: they focus squarely on a single arena or field of action; be it a school, a county, a legislature, etc. Yet, by their very nature, policy making and implementation cut across these separate arenas, in both their development and impact (Firestone, 1989). In e-government projects for instance, systems built by both public and private enterprises for use by government employees and citizens across different political constituencies must be enforced by legislative acts created and interpreted by national branches of government. In addition, actors at different levels of the policy system encounter divergent problems posed by the system in question and their actions are influenced by varied motives. What is needed, therefore, is a framework that goes beyond single games in order to focus on how games 'mesh or miss' each other to influence governance and policy decisions. One of the few efforts to look at this interaction and interdependence was Norton Long's (1958) discussion of "The Local Community as an Ecology of Games."

Rejected in favour of Behaviouralism and Rational Choice Theory – two approaches based on the assumption that individuals act autonomously as a result of either socio-psychological characteristics or due to rational calculations of their personal utility (Hechter & Kanazawa, 1997) - during the period immediately following World War II, Institutionalist approaches came into their own in the late 1980s under the guise of New Institutionalism as a result of a growing number of scholars attempting to describe and understand in concrete terms the political world around them (Peters, 2000). Contrary to both Behavioural Theory and Rational Choice Theory, New Institutionalists considered observable behaviour to occur and be understood solely within the context of institutions, leading to the creation and development of two new branches of theory, namely Rational Choice Institutionalism and Behavioural Institutionalism (Immergut, 1998).

Rational Choice Theory in particular depends for its analytical power on unhindered, utility-maximising individuals; and it would, at first glance, appear to be futile indeed to relate it to the idea of institutions and their constraining influence on actor behaviour (Peters, 2000). However, despite the individualistic basis underpinning the approach, a number of rational choice theorists have come to accept the first and foremost precept of the New Institutionalism, which is that most political life occurs within institutions, and that in order to provide a comprehensive explanation of politics, their theories must address questions regarding their nature and role (Tsebelis, 1990). There has, in consequence, been a flowering of rational choice literature on political institutions since the late 1980s, including work on legislatures (McCubbins, 1987), cabinets (Laver & Schofield,1990) and bureaucracies (Johnson & Libecap, 1994), and some economic theorists have even gone as far as to apply the idea of rational choice to the institution of marriage (Becker, 1991). Further, despite the possible contradictions put forward by March and Olsen (1989) in their work (March & Olsen, 1989), there are several approaches to institutions that depend on the underlying logic of rational choice approaches. Notable amongst these are Dunleavy's (1991) discussion of 'institutional public choice' and 'first principles public choice', Kenman's (1996) argument for the utility of 'institutional rational choice' and Fritz Scharpf's (1997) treatise on 'actor-centred institutionalism'.

The basic assumption is that not only may social phenomena be explained as the outcome of interactions amongst intentional actors – individual, collective, or corporate – but that these interactions are structured and outcomes are shaped by the characteristics of the institutional settings within which they occur (Scharpf, 1997). As the basic argument of rational choice approaches is that utility maximisation can and will remain the primary motivation of individuals, rational choice approaches to institutions all presume the same egoistic behavioural characteristics found in similar approaches to other aspects of political behaviour (Peters, 2000). However, the institutional variants of the approach focus attention on the importance of *institutions* as mechanisms for channelling and constraining individual behaviour.

Proponents of rational choice institutionalism hold that, as actors depend on socially constructed rules to orient their actions in otherwise chaotic social situations, institutions may be considered to have a key influence on not only the actors themselves but on the nature and direction of their interactions (Scharpf, 1997). Further, collective and corporate actors central to policy processes are institutionally constituted, as the institutions themselves may be said to "exist" only to the extent that the individuals acting within them are able to coordinate their choices within a common frame of reference that is constituted by institutional rules. In addition, this approach identifies clear actors in each process, in direct contrast to other variations of institutional theories that deal with only sets of rules and norms (Peters, 2000). Thus, for models that combine rational choice concepts with institutional analysis, individual actors are still expected to manoeuvre in order to maximise personal utilities, but their actions are inherently constrained by the rule sets of the one or more or institutions within which they are operating.

Throughout this body of work, notes Peters (2000), institutions are conceptualised as collections of rules and incentives that establish the conditions for bounded rationality, thus establishing a 'political space' within which many interdependent political actors can function. Institutions define not only the membership of composite actors and the resources (both material and legal) that they may draw upon – thus defining the scope of their legitimate activities and the powers of the individuals who act for them – but also the purposes that they are to serve or the values that they are to consider in arriving at their choices (Scharpf, 1997). More particularly, institutions have explanatory value because sanctioned rules will reduce the range of potential behaviour by specifying required, prohibited, or permitted actions (Ostrom, Gardner & Walker, 1994).

Whilst both Rational Choice and Behaviouralist approaches considered the actions of individual actors to be unfettered by both formal and informal institutions, instead making their own choices with preferences being viewed as exogenous to the political process (Simon, 1955), initial proponents of the

New Institutionalism (most notably March and Olsen, who named the movement in 1984) pointed out the need to reassert some of the features of the old perspective (Hall & Taylor, 1996). As well as altering the theoretical perspectives of the discipline, this change in paradigm was also a response to a growing demand for the use of rigorous research methods in the social sciences and an equally strong push for a more explicit constitution of empirical political theory: both ideas then being seemingly incompatible with an institutional focus. In particular, March and Olsen (1984) argued that behavioural and rational choice approaches were characterised by five basic weaknesses:

- **Contextualism:** the tendency to subordinate political phenomena to societal phenomena by seeing politics as an integral part of society, but being less inclined to differentiate the polity from the rest of society;
- **Reductionism:** the propensity to see political phenomena as the aggregate consequences of individual behaviour, rather than linking political outcomes to organizational structures and rules of appropriate behaviour;
- **Utilitarianism:** the inclination to see action as the product of calculated self-interest without acknowledging the response of political actors to obligations and duties;
- **Functionalism:** or the assumption that history is an efficient process moving towards equilibrium, leading to the smooth and untroubled evolution of the political process;
- **Instrumentalism:** or the tendency to define decision-making and the allocation of resources as the central concerns of political life, paying less attention to the ways in which political life is organised around the development of meaning and identity through symbols, rituals, and ceremonies.

Building upon theories of Rational Choice, scholars such as Beinhocker (2006) and Gintis (2000) have proposed a vision of the economy and other socio-political institutions that falls within the purview of Complex Adaptive System theories in response to what they perceive to be the combined aridity of classical game theory and general equilibrium theory – both of which have been generally considered as the two most popular ways to describe the creation of wealth by actors within a social ecology. Viewing markets and other institutions as complex adaptive systems radically alters the analytical tools that may be deployed to model socio-economic and political behaviour within a given field of play (Gintis, 2006).

According to Gintis (2006), complex adaptive systems are almost a mirror inversion of neoclassical economic theories such as traditional game theories for, as Axel Leijonhufvud notes in Gintis, neoclassical theories model "smart people in unbelievably simple situations" whilst real-world situations involve "simple people [coping] with incredibly complex conditions" (Gintis, 2006: 2). Beinhocker (2006) offers the following useful summary of the differences between conventional game theories rooted in neoclassical models and complexity economics (cf. Davis, 2008):

- **Dynamics:** The complex economy is open and dynamic and generally far from equilibrium, whereas neoclassical economic models are far more static and closed.
- **Agents:** In a complex economy, actors have limited information and face high costs of information processing. Under appropriate conditions, these agents may develop non-optimal but highly effective heuristics for operating in complex environments. By contrast, agents operating in neoclassical economies are assumed to possess perfect information and are able to optimize at minimum cost.
- **Networks:** Complex economic theory recognizes that actors participate in a number of sophisticated networks that allow them to compensate for having limited information and high information pro-

cessing costs. This, as discussed earlier, is quite the contrary for actors operating under neoclassical conditions.

- **Emergence:** Theories surrounding complex economies lend themselves to the modelling of macro-systems through an examination of individual agent-level behaviour. This is in contrast to neoclassical theories where the actions of individual actors may not be easily determined.
- **Evolution:** The order and structuring of actor behaviour in complex economies is derived through evolutionary processes such as differentiation, selection, and amplification. Such concepts do not exist in classical game theory.

Further, in considering institutions as biological systems, complex adaptive system theories also put forward the idea of "imitation" to explain socio-political and cultural evolution. Gintis (2000), for instance, demonstrates how individuals and groups with low pay-off strategies tend to switch from these to strategies used by more successful actors. The idea of change through imitation has also found use in behavioural economics and the modelling of actor behaviour within institutions, as well as the process of technological diffusion; thereby building on neoclassical approaches to game theory. However, overall there has been to date only a few contributions to the economic literature on behavioural change through imitation, and far less in other social science disciplines such as Politics and Sociology.

Additionally, Beinhocker emphasises that behavioural economic research (Gintis, 2006) shifts focus away from more conventional neoclassical ideas of actor behaviour onto the actions of individual actors who are not purely self-centred in their social interactions within a group, but rather are (cf. Fehr & Gachter, 2002; Beinhocker, 2006) a combination of *conditional co-operators* (who prefer to sacrifice personal goals for the sake of the larger good) and *altruistic operators* (who act to maintain the group's *status quo*). The chief 'embarrassment' of classical game theory, according to Gintis (2006), is thus its inability to explain why an individual actor or group would ever play a 'one-shot' game. What is needed, therefore, is a framework that goes beyond single games in order to focus on how games 'mesh or miss' each other to influence governance and policy decisions. One of the few efforts to look at this interaction and interdependence was Norton Long's (1958) discussion of "The Local Community as an Ecology of Games", whose key ideas will be dealt with in subsequent sections of this thesis.

The Ecology of Games framework, as first laid out by Long in the late 1950s offers a New Institutionalist perspective on organisational and institutional analysis. As with most theories of New Institutionalism, it recognises that political institutions are not simple echoes of social forces, and that routines, rules and forms within organisations and institutions evolve through historically interdependent processes that do not reliably and quickly reach equilibrium (March & Olsen, 1989). Long developed the idea of the ecology of games as a way of reconciling existing debates about who governed local communities as he believed they had significant flaws.

The crucial insight in Long's theory however, was not the idea of games *per se* which, as has been discussed earlier, was already well developed, but his linking of that notion to the metaphor of an ecology (Firestone,1989). Ecology as a concept relates to the interrelationships of species in their environment, allowing for numerous relationships amongst entities, and has been used to understand the relationships among individuals and more complex social systems. This speaks of a singular interdependence between different actors within a given territory. Although there may be other relationships as well, what is significantly missing is a single, rational, coordinating presence.

Games themselves are social constructs that vary over time and across social contexts (Crozier & Friedberg, 1980). Similar types of games might recur within similar social settings, but all games tend to be uniquely situated in place and time, and any typology of games that might emerge across a cumulative body of studies is likely to remain quite abstract. Despite this, Dutton (1992) has identified several key attributes which all games may share: first, every game has a set of goals, purposes, or objectives, with some games having multiple aims. Second, a game has a set of prizes, which may vary widely from profit to authority to recognition, and are distinct from the objectives of the players. Third, games have rules that govern the strategies or moves open to players depending on the organisational or institutional settings within which they are played. Rules need not be public or fair (depending on whether public or private interests are involved), may change over time, and may or may not need consensus to be accepted. Finally, a game has a set of players, defined by the fact that they interact – compete or cooperate – with another in pursuing the game's objectives.

For Long, territories (or fields of play) were defined quite literally by being local communities. Moved from the community context to the world of e-government design, adoption and implementation, territories may be diverse – from the inner circle of the project design team, through to the adopting organisation, the nation and finally the international policy arena – but the idea of each stage being a political community or a collection of actors whose actions have political implications is still very much applicable. The ecology of games metaphor thus provides us with a useful way to think about how the various players interact in making and carrying out administration and developing policy.

ANALYTICAL FRAMEWORK: THE DESIGN-ACTUALITY GAP MODEL

Like all political interactions, the behaviour of actors related to the design and uptake of e-government projects is circumscribed by the organisations and institutions within which they are played out, and by the range of actors taken from the individuals and groups directly and indirectly involved with the process of governance. The outcome of an e-government project therefore does not depend on a single project entity alone, and instead depends on the interaction between different actors in the process and the nature of the relationships between them. Gaps in project design and implementation can in reality be seen as expressions of differences arising from the interaction between different (often conflicting) actor moves and strategies, determined to a large extent by actor perceptions, and played out within the context of set circumstances.

In order to assess the extent to which the case study in question has succeeded or failed, this research project will first attempt to locate it within Heeks' seminal three-fold categorisation. By examining numerous case studies related to ICTs and e-government failure in developing countries, Heeks (2002) identified three dominant categories of reported outcome: *total failure*, *partial failure*, and *success*. Though not theoretically exhaustive (they do not, for instance take into account the mutation of outcomes over time), these categories are nonetheless valuable and comprise the first step of a framework within which a project might be evaluated.

- The first possible outcome is *total failure*, where a project is either never implemented or in which a new system is implemented but is almost immediately abandoned.
- A second possible outcome involves the *partial failure* of an initiative; wherein either major goals are left unattained or where there are manifest significant undesirable outcomes. In other words, partial failures range from straightforward, easily identifiable cases where only a subset of initial-

ly-stated objectives are achieved to the so-called "sustainability failure" of an initiative that at first succeeds but is then abandoned after a year or so.

- Finally, one may see the *success* of an initiative, in which most actor groups attain their major goals and do not experience significant undesirable outcomes.

Heeks (2003) concluded that the major factor determining project outcome was the degree of mismatch between the current realities of a situation ('where are we now') and the models, conceptions, and assumptions built into a project's design (the 'where the e-government project wants to get us'). From this perspective, e-government success and failure depends largely on the size of this 'design-actuality' gap: the larger gap, the greater the risk of e-government failure, the smaller the gap, the greater the chance of success. He also identified three so-called 'archetypes of failure', situations when a large design-actuality gap – and, hence, failure – is more likely to emerge. These may be classified as Hard-Soft Gaps, Public-Private Gaps, and Country-Context Gaps (Dada, 2006); and are summarised below:

Hard-Soft Gaps

Hard-soft gaps refer to the difference between the actual, rational design of the technology (hard) and the actuality of the social context – people, culture, politics, etc. – within which the system operates (soft). These sorts of gaps are commonly cited in examples of e-government failure in developing countries, where 'soft' human issues that are not initially taken into account whilst designing a project result in undesirable effects after implementation. Many scholars, such as Stanforth (2006), see technology as just one of a number of heterogeneous socio-technical elements that must be considered and managed during the design and implementation of a successful e-government project, whilst Madon (2004) has discussed different sets of case studies which have revealed that numerous factors that have allowed individuals in developing countries to access ICTs (and which depend on resources, skill-levels, values, beliefs, and motivations, etc.) are often ignored. It may thus be inferred that a lack of training, skills, and change management efforts would all affect rates of failure, as it is these factors that would bridge the gap between the technology itself and the context within which it exits.

A major cause of project failure in developing countries is a general lack of skills and training, which are necessary for both government officials and citizens to effectively use a system (Jae Moon, 2002). This is a particularly significant problem in developing countries, where there is often a chronic lack of qualified staff and training schemes. According to Basu (2004): " ...there are insufficient numbers of people in developing countries trained in appropriate technologies to do all the work. Training opportunities are also straining to meet needs." Widespread low rates of literacy make this situation very difficult and costly to change, exacerbating failure of projects in these countries. Jaeger and Thompson (2003) assert that an e-government system would fail if the government did not take an active role in educating citizens about the value of e-government, a fact all the more pertinent in developing countries where low levels of education and skills amongst end-users and a lack of familiarity with technology could result in systems not being used to their full potential. Thus it may be inferred that the rate of success or failure is likely to be influenced by the ability of a population to access useful information and services.

The issue of change management, according to Dada (2006) also impacts the hard-soft gap in developing countries, as e-government projects result in the realignment of working practices and government functions. As this thesis will discuss later, the successful implementation of an e-government project requires that the public sector changes and re-engineers its internal processes to adapt to the new technology and work culture. In situations where corruption and rent-seeking is the norm, the realignment of information flows and power structures can be heavily resisted by actors with vested interests (Peterson, 1998). Project design often does not take into account the potential for resistance amongst government employees, and project designers are consequently not equipped with the tools necessary to counter it when they come across it.

Hard-soft gaps thus may be seen as the outcome of interactions played out primarily at the level of the project itself, between individuals and agencies involved with the design and acceptance of the technology. For instance, decisions taken by senior officials relating to issues of change management and skill levels might be motivated by the desire of the top brass to curtail and keep in check the power of their junior employees and to maintain control over their territories. Similarly a clash between powerful rivals on a project planning committee could result in either half-baked compromise decisions or strong decisions that are not followed through, leading to chaos at the implementation stage that has repercussions on more junior staff.

Private-Public Gaps

The next archetype put forward by Heeks (2003) is that of private-public gaps, which refers to the difference between organisations in the private and public sectors, and the mismatch that results when technology meant for private organisations is used in the public sector without being adapted to suit the role and aims of the adopting public organisation. A common problem is again the lack of highly skilled professionals in the public sector, resulting primarily from uncompetitive rates of pay in that sector as compared to the private sector (Ciborra & Navarra, 2005). The design of e-government projects is consequently outsourced to the private sector, resulting in a clash of values, objectives, culture, and large design-actuality gaps.

The gap between the public and private sector may also be discussed in terms of management styles, values, and cultures; and the impact that these differences have on system design (Ciborra, 2005). For instance, private sector systems are designed to see recipients of services as customers, while to governments they are citizens. There are numerous problems associated with viewing citizens as customers, not in the least that customers by definition need markets to operate in and have the ability to choose between alternative products, both of which are necessarily difficult to find in the public sector since public service providers are usually monopolies. Further the private sector sees customers as a means of making a profit and thus prices its goods accordingly, and not always to the benefit of all. Government services, on the other hand, are public goods that every individual has a right to and thus the government needs to set prices to ensure equal access of services to everybody. In other cases, private sector organisations with activist leanings may attempt to impose their own value systems and goals on the design of a project, leading to a clash of priorities. Overall, in adopting private sector values, governments would often be required to make an enormous paradigm shift and tailor their way of working accordingly, something that developing country agencies often find difficult to adjust to.

Another private-public mismatch has to do with project design in relation to funding. e-Government projects in developing countries are usually driven by government departments who rely either on public funds or aid from donor agencies, money that usually comes in as a block budgetary allocation that has to be used by a particular date (Heeks, 2003). Projects are thus often planned as one-off investments – a very private sector mind-set. However, this may result in an all-or-nothing approach to systems development, rather than a set of incremental improvements, to the overall detriment of the project. Public-Private Gaps hence often arise out of games played at the level of the adopting government agency, generally between the agency and its private sector counterparts, although it is not uncommon to find interactions between public and private individuals on project committees having an impact on the outcome of a project as well.

Country-Context Gaps

The final archetype of failure defined by Heeks (2003) is the country-context gap, or the gap that arises when a system designed for one country is transferred into the reality of another. This is particularly true for systems transferred between developed and developing countries, where designs for one may clash with the actualities within the other. Country-context gaps are, according to Dada (2006) closely related to hard-soft gaps as they arise from, amongst other things, differences in technological infrastructure, skill sets, education levels, and working cultures. As discussed in previous sections, benefits to be had from e-government in developed countries include cost reduction and time saved through the complete automation of work and the processing of all transactions online. They also require both service providers and end-users to have the skills to use the technology to its full potential. However, developing countries often lack the basic infrastructure (physical and human) needed to support the wholesale computerisation of tasks and services, and hence those systems adopted in their entirety from the developed world without taking these factors into account have a high chance of failing.

Country-context gaps emerge chiefly as a result of games played by national, provincial and international actors operating across borders. For instance, decisions to adopt or promote a certain management style or value system, buy or sell a particular technology from a particular organisation or country, or collaborate with particular government agencies in different parts of the world all stem from games of international trade, aid, and diplomacy. Two major criticisms have been levelled against Heeks' model in the literature (Dada, 2006). The first is that it is much too simplistic: it is fairly obvious that the larger the gap between a proposed system and the realities on the ground as a consequence of differences in factors relating to resources, culture, preconceptions, and other rigidities; the more difficult it would be to implement a new system successfully. The second criticism is that the classification is prone to subjectivity in the expectations about the future and in perceptions of reality, especially since some issues can be arguably included into different categories.

In recognising these drawbacks, this thesis maintains that Heeks' model forms an integral part of any evaluation of e-government success or failure, as any initial evaluation made using the basic model may be nuanced and expanded upon (as has been done) by exploring in greater detail the factors resulting in the eventual outcome. Further, it is important to remember that placing different reasons for failure into the various categories is not as important as understanding the issues and the underlying factors themselves, thereby being able to anticipate and deal with such problems if they were to arise.

The model is particularly useful given the large investments made by developing country governments in e-government systems and the large opportunity costs associated with implementation, as it encourages project planners to take a focused, holistic view of problem solving; making them consider concurrently the technology at hand, the current circumstances, the impact of actors' motivations and actions, and possible vested interests. It may be used both as a predictive tool anticipating potential failings and heading them off at the initial stages, as well as being used to diagnose problems during the execution of the project. The framework is thus a means of evaluating outcome and problem solving strategies at all stages during the development of a project, and not just to examine what went wrong in hindsight.

DIGITISING PROPERTY TAXATION RECORDS IN BANGALORE, INDIA: EXPLORING THE CASE OF THE GREATER BANGALORE CITY MUNICIPAL CORPORATION (BBMP)

Against the background of technological innovation in Karnataka state, project planners from the Greater Bangalore City Municipal Corporation (BBMP) felt that the manual system of property tax administration was archaic, opaque, and inefficient. All the members of the core project group believed that property tax collections under the manual system had suffered from poor record keeping and bad information management practices, slow processing times, and overcomplicated assessment and payment procedures. These had, in turn, created frustration amongst taxpayers and resulted in low levels of compliance. The computerised property tax system was thus borne out of a need to reform the manual system of property tax administration in Bangalore and improve tax revenues and compliance through the improvement of back-office efficiency, the simplification of tax collection, and the reduction of money lost through malpractice through the effective detection and deterrence of tax evasion – spurred on by the need to enhance power, authority and reputations.

Interviews with tax officials revealed that most felt that there had been serious problems with the manual system of tax administration. They claimed that the biggest hurdles to the efficient administration of tax that they encountered prior to the introduction of the computerised database were poor and haphazard recordkeeping and large amounts of paperwork that needed to be done manually. Information was scattered and the process of calculating tax due, administering collections and checking up on defaulters was extremely unsystematic. While, as expected, none of the revenue officials interviewed mentioned government employee corruption as being serious problem, many interviewees spoke of the difficulties they faced in identifying and catching tax evaders. Most officials interviewed felt that the introduction of technology had greatly impacted old work processes and had helped alleviate the difficulties they faced under the manual system. They believed that the centralisation of data, the ease with which citizens could access their tax information, and the setting up of tax collection points across the city had all helped in bringing more properties into the tax net and contributed significantly towards improving tax payer compliance.

All the officials interviewed felt that their interactions with the public had significantly decreased since the introduction of the computerised system, and a little over half them believed their overall relationship with citizens had improved as a result. However, whilst acknowledging that the use of digitised records, computer printouts and online databases had had a positive impact on their work, some interviewees were quick to point out that technology had been used simply to automate existing processes, and that old infrastructural problems (such as poor electricity supply and old computers) and problems related to a lack of skills and training on the computerised system had not been resolved.

Only a small percentage of revenue officials reported that they had been consulted during the design stage of the project. Further, there appeared to be no mechanism in place to solicit user feedback once the initial system had been developed. Almost all the officials interviewed said they felt disconnected from system. Most professed a high degree of unfamiliarity with the system, and were completely unaware of its key features. For instance, only one tax official mentioned the introduction of GIS mapping techniques as being useful to his work and that of his staff, a worrying fact given that the core project team had placed much store by the GIS maps as a tool to track property tax payments and identify defaulters. These are not good signs, as effective system implementation requires employees to fully accept and adopt the technology in the belief that it will do them some well-defined good.

Further, none of the officials interviewed knew how to operate even its most basic features. With no scheme in place to give them any formal training on the system, all the interviewees reported to be completely dependent on a private computer operator to feed in, change and retrieve electronic property tax data. This, this researcher feels, created a new problem within revenue offices and limited the effectiveness of the system, as it resulted in a shift in the balance of power within the workplace to the disadvantage of revenue officials and consequently hardened their attitude towards computerisation. Senior officers, once enthusiastic about the system, spoke about the frustration they felt at being unable to fulfil their supervisory role and at being put at the mercy of a junior employee. Junior tax officials, already slightly sceptical of the system, feared that their skill levels would put them at a disadvantage within the office and could eventually result in redundancy.

Opinions were divided about whether or not computerisation of the system that had led to improved tax yields. Most tax officials felt that while the introduction of the computerised system had positively impacted tax collections to some extent, there were many other reasons as to why tax yields had improved. For others, the introduction of the Self Assessment Scheme as a means of shifting the responsibility of tax payments onto the shoulders of the citizens and reducing the workload of revenue staff was almost as (if not more) important as the introduction of technology into the workplace. It may be concluded from the interviews that general citizen apathy towards property tax is to a large extent a consequence of poor public awareness about the benefits of paying property tax, a lack of enforcement measures and a general dislike of cumbersome processes – problems which cannot be solved through the introduction of technology alone.

INFORMATION AND COMMUNICATION TECHNOLOGY PLATFORM DESIGN FOR DEVELOPMENT: KEY ACTORS, MOVES, AND GAMES

An examination of the interviews and other data collected during field research reveals that the eventual outcome of the revenue department project can be interpreted as the consequence of a number of players making moves within a number of separate but interrelated games related to the project's design, implementation and adoption. At least six kinds of games have influenced the effect the system has had on tax administration in Bangalore city. They include expertise games, power and influence games, policy games, turf struggles, games of persuasion and business games. From the games identified during the course of research, a four-fold taxonomy has been developed which classifies games occurring within the given ecology of a public sector organisation or institution according to their degree and magnitude, and that analyses actor interactions on the basis of *the field of play, the key actors involved, the main objective(s) of the game under study*, and *the nature and/or spirit in which the game has been played.* The four categories, which are derived from this author's research, are elaborated below:

1. **Arena or Field of Play:** Actor interactions may be classified according to the arena within which they are played out. In other words, this classification – which has its roots in initial work done

by Vedel (1989) and Dutton (1992) – focuses on the reach and influence of actors within a given context, and the impact of their actions (both direct and indirect) on project outcomes.

   a. **Project-Specific Games:** are generally played by individuals and groups of actors directly involved with the case under study. Such interactions usually occur during the planning and execution of a project and impact.
   b. **Organisation-Specific Games:** are played out within the department or organisation within which the case study is based, involving not only actors directly concerned with the case study but also others within the institution whose moves come to bear influence on the project at hand.
   c. **City or Regional Level Games:** include those interactions between actors whose power or reach extends to the level of the city or region within which the project is based, and who are playing power games for relatively high stakes. The goals, moves and strategies chosen by actors at this level may or may not have a direct link to the case study, however they come to bear either a direct or indirect influence on its eventual outcome.
   d. **National Level Games:** involve players who have their eye on attaining some sort of national prestige or who are influenced by other actors or discourses operating at the national level. Here again, actors may or may not be directly attached to the project or organisation under study.
   e. **International Level Games:** are played chiefly by actors or groups of actors possessing international clout and/or aspirations. Games played at this level usually do not have a direct bearing on the project under study, however, actors might indirectly influence outcomes by attempting to gain power/prestige through adhering to popular trends, binding project planners to third-party conditonalities or merely by subscribing to certain schools of thought.

2. **Key Actors Involved:** Games may also be classified according to the key actors involved in each interaction studied. This axis thus aims to study interactions within the context of the key players – who they are and who they interact with.
   a. **Interactions Internal to the Project Planning/Core Group:** includes any games being played exclusively between constituent elements of the project planning committee or the core group responsible for the design and execution of the project under study.
   b. **Core Project Group vs. Other Members of Implementing Department:** cover games played between members of the core project committee and other individuals and/or groups within the implementing department who are otherwise not directly involved on the project at hand.
   c. **Games within the Implementing Organisation:** are played out between groups and individual actors who are members of the implementing organisation. Such interactions may or may not be directly related to the ICT4D project, but their outcome would have an impact on its eventual success or failure.
   d. **Department/Organisation vs. External Players:** cover interactions between the implementing department/organisation acting in a unified, institutional capacity and other external players such as the media, citizens and civil society organisations.
   e. **Games Played by External Actors:** which have little or no direct connection to the currently project, but which nonetheless have a significant impact on its eventual success or failure.
3. **Actor Goals:** A third way of classifying actor interactions is based on the goals that different actor groups seek to attain by engaging with other players. Actors within each game are bound to have

multiple goals that motivate them to act in certain ways, and thus it is important when applying this classification to identify the primary motivating factor behind each move.

a. **Games of Power and Prestige:** Involve moves to enable actors to gain or shore up their individual power and prestige or those of their group.
b. **Games to Maintain Status Quo:** Are those interactions whereby players seek to maintain the status quo. These games are generally played when actors perceive a threat to their current position or status, and thus act to preserve their current standing in the hierarchy.
c. **Games to Achieve Change:** Are those interactions that attempt to change a current situation or process within a department or organisation, primarily through the attainment of project goals and objectives.
d. **Games to Achieve Political and Policy Aims:** Are those moves and strategies played by actors to achieve certain political or policy aims which may or may not have a direct relationship or bearing on the project under study.
e. **Games to Further Ideology and/or Discourse:** Comprise chiefly those games played by actors who are generally driven by a particular ideology or discourse and wish to use their political influence to impose their ideas on either the implementing organisation or on the project planners themselves.

4. **Nature of Game Play:** The final axis against which games may be classified analyses the nature of the political dynamic between the key actors within which the project was conceived and implemented. In other words, this axis differentiates between positive and negative actors and the impact of their actions on their sphere of influence.
   a. **Constructive Game Play:** includes altruistic and other positive moves, where competition is seen to be constructive and controlled/restrained rivalry brings about positive results. Such games are therefore win-win situations, and include all those moves that have a positive impact on the adoption of new technologies within a development context.
   b. **Destructive Game Play:** involves fierce rivalries and negative competition, resulting in zero-sum games where actors act purposefully to win at the cost of their so-called 'opponents', thereby creating a negative project environment and often resulting in a large wastage of time and resources.

The discussion above reveals that at the heart of a design-actuality gap usually lies a power struggle brought about through a deep-seated mistrust between different actor groups. In particular, the case study demonstrates that gaps arise because those with the power and authority to take design or implementation decisions are usually unwilling to allow any initiative to go ahead that would give the other actor group(s) in the game more autonomy over the system.

WORKPLACE ORGANISATION, STRUCTURE, AND POLITICAL INSTITUTIONS: EVALUATING ADAPTATION TO CHANGE IN THE AGE OF THE INTERNET

The identification of the actors related to property tax administration in India at its most basic, and the discussion of the games they play during the process of tax administration and reform, highlighted the fact that if property tax is administered and reformed almost exclusively by a local government authority using conventional policy and fiscal tools, then the arena within which games are played out remains highly localised with the number of actors restricted and their moves limited. However, as the case study illustrates, the introduction of ICTs into the reform process will not only add more actors to the mix but also introduce different levels of interaction and open up the playing field to a larger number of moves and decisions, as the use of technology in development is connected to much larger national and international policy discourses.

As the analysis has shown, certain key games with local impacts get played out in different arenas between actors influenced by not only local but also national and international factors. Design-actuality gaps open up and give way to unfavourable project outcomes if designers and top managers assume that localised outcomes result only from direct local influences, discounting the impact of other factors external to the project at hand. In the light of such an evaluation, what impact, it may be asked, has the computerised system had on the process of organisational reform, and what effect has this in turn had on institutional change?

From the discussion and analysis of the system presented above and in previous sections of this chapter, it may be concluded that despite the presence of self-interested and competitive game-play during the development of the Revenue Department system, co-operation during the introduction and adoption stages has resulted in positive steps being taken towards organisational reform and institutional change. In terms of changes at the level of the organisation, the digitisation of the tax registers and the automation of processes have increased the efficiency of the Department by speeding up tax administration processes, reducing mistakes, and lowering workloads.

Institutionally speaking, the project has also had some success. By allowing citizens to access their records and pay at their convenience (either online or at kiosks), the corporation has adopted a radical citizen-centric approach to tax administration which has not only shifted the balance of power in the government-citizen relationship in favour of the citizens, but has, at the same time, made citizens more responsible. This might be considered to be a real departure from traditional notions of Indian bureaucracy where power is concentrated in the hands of the bureaucrats, and citizens can afford to be passive actors in administration meta-games. However, as some of the key organisational and institutional variables have not yet been put in place, and there is no mechanism by which problems may be identified and bridged during the implementation process, the long-term direction of these changes is still uncertain. Of particular concern are the attitudes of revenue employees towards the changes in work processes and the shifts in hierarchies.

ANALYSING THE VALUE OF THE ECOLOGY OF GAMES FRAMEWORK WITHIN THE CONTEXT OF E-GOVERNMENT SERVICE PROVISION

The Ecology of Games provides a theoretical framework for discussing the strength and interplay of groups and interests shaping e-government projects. But the question must be asked: what added value has the use of this theory brought to the study of e-government and ICT4D projects? The answer to this question has been brought out through the discussion of the case study in previous sections of this research chapter, and its most salient points may be summarised below.

Firstly, the notion of an Ecology of Games offers a framework for thinking about an extremely complex set of interactions, identifying and highlighting the roles played by those who shape and are shaped by the rules of the game, and the impact that each player has on a project's ultimate outcome. It particularly emphasises the potential for unanticipated, unplanned developments on project success; raising doubts on more conventional, information-systems views of e-government that see project implementation as governed by a more controlled, isolated, predictable system of action.

The framework also focuses on 'symbolic politics', what Dutton (1992) in his discussion of the theory has described as the role ideas play in political change. Whilst democratic politics and the formulation of policy is in part a contest over ideas about how to define and achieve the common good, empirical scholars of politics have been remarkably resistant to giving ideas a central explanatory place in their accounts (Mehta, 2010). The Ecology of Games amends this, emphasising not only the way in which the development of ideas shapes political interactions, but also highlighting the emergence and role of new bearers and interpreters of those ideas (like the media) as key players in the ultimate success or failure of a project.

The Ecology of Games has, according to Dutton (1992) yet another advantage as an approach to research, in that it helps identify cross-pressures facing key players often involved in more than one game; recognising that e-government project development is not, contrary to conventional frameworks, a self-contained system of action. Instead, as illustrated by the case study, the framework recognises that projects are being formulated and implemented in parallel with other policies. Many players in one policy area are playing simultaneously in others. The outcome of the political process in one arena often shapes play within another. In doing so, it provides a more nuanced interpretation of the broader system of action in which the development of an e-government project develops, emphasising again the role of unplanned, unanticipated interactions between various interests, and the formation of unconventional interests and alliances as a result of shared goals. Nothing is new about many of these interactions, they often repeat themselves through the ages in a variety of situations, yet conventional theories tend to ignore or underplay them.

Using the Ecology of Games perspective does, however, mean that a number of limitations and difficulties need to be acknowledged. The first is that it is essentially a 'sensitizing' concept, a background theory that offers a certain way of seeing, organizing, and understanding complex reality (Dutton, 1992). Whilst this is not necessarily a weakness, it does imply not only a limited usefulness for quantitative or formal mathematical approaches, but also a large degree of interpretive flexibility. Consequently, different researchers applying the Ecology of Games to the same situation are likely to perceive different ecologies, games, actors, and interactions. Any one interpretation can thus be challenged by others, or by any researcher who can critically assess the depiction of a specific ecology.

A second, related criticism it that whilst it provides a point of view and indicates a set of methods to conduct case studies, the Ecology of Games theory can only give an indication of the likely nature of the dynamics shaping outcomes. Based on human behaviour motivated by a particular set of influences, it is thus limited as a predictive theory, in the sense that it will not be able to predict the concrete outcomes necessary for both micro- and more generalised macro-level decision-making. A final problem with the framework is that it may lead to an extremely complex mapping of social reality (Dutton, Schneider & Vedel, 2011). Its innate flexibility can lead a researcher to read deeper and deeper into what might be, in reality, only a few large meta-games. And finally, partly as a result of this tendency towards increased complexity, it becomes necessary to arbitrarily limit the depth of any analysis lest it become too unwieldy. Such an arbitrary truncation feeds back into the discussion surrounding the theory's interpretive flexibility and its value as a predictive tool, as different studies of the same of object would be likely to result in different analyses and (especially if used as a policy tool) different policy decisions.

These disadvantages, however, might be overcome; as seen in recent work combining the Ecology of Games with other sociological perspectives such as Network Theory and Social Constructivism

(Cornwell, Curry & Schwirian, 2003). It may be concluded that the central strength of the Ecology of Games perspective compared with other theoretical frameworks is this: without taking away from the central issues at hand or diverting attention from the central field of action, the framework focuses on a variety of phenomena – personality, values, historical circumstance, environment – that are all too often peripheral to the central action of conventional theories but in truth form the central core of the policy process and are often key forces behind organisational and institutional change. In doing so, the combination helps provide researchers with a nuanced understanding of how actor dynamics impact political and policy outcomes.

CONCLUSION

Rapidly evolving economic and social contexts mean that political institutions and the people who constitute them cannot afford to get bogged down in traditional work practices or be impervious or resistant to change themselves. Whilst this does not necessarily mean a wholesale rejection of what has gone before, it does mean that there needs to be a constant assessment and reassessment of workplace values and current practices, eliminating those which result in behaviours that are detrimental to the functioning of the organisation and encouraging those that promote positive interactions. Organisations and institutions, particularly those which form the political core of a society, cannot afford to be seen to have been left behind, as the people within those institutions are generally looked to as political trendsetters and role models in addition to being responsible for societal welfare.

The discussion brought out in this chapter reveals that at the heart of a political game usually lies a power struggle brought about through a deep-seated mistrust between different actor groups. In particular, the case study put forward demonstrates that gaps arise because those with the power and authority to take design or implementation decisions are usually unwilling to allow any initiative to go ahead that would give the other actor group(s) in the game more autonomy over the system. Further, certain key games with local impacts get played out in different arenas between actors influenced by not only local but also national and international factors. Problems arise if designers and top managers assume that localised outcomes result only from direct local influences, discounting the impact of other factors external to the project at hand.

Added to this, there is a tendency for power elites to lose touch with ground realities when devising projects for their organisations as well as for their citizens, especially when planners comprise the higher echelons of government and operate within a top-down command-and-control system of management. There is also a danger that high-level project planners will, in looking at macro-outcomes, ignore outliers and how these may precipitate unexpected turns of events. This holds particularly true when existing patterns of communication and information exchange fail to be flexible or unable to adapt to changing situations.

REFERENCES

Asquith, A. (1998). Non-elite Employees' Perceptions of Organizational Change in English Local Government. *International Journal of Public Sector Management*, *11*(4), 262–280. doi:10.1108/09513559810225825

Avgerou, C., & Walsham, G. (2000). Introduction: IT in Developing Countries. In C. Avgerou & G. Walsham (Eds.), *Information Technology in Context: Studies from the Perspective of Developing Countries* (pp. 1–8). Ashgate: Aldershot Press.

Bahl, R. W., & Linn, J. F. (1992). *Urban Public Finance in Developing Countries*. New York, N.Y.: Oxford University Press.

Bannock, G., Baxter, R. E., & Davis, E. (1987). *The Penguin Dictionary of Economics* (4th ed.). London: Penguin Books.

Bannon, L. J. (1991). From Human Factors to Human Actors: The Role of Psychology and Human Computer Interaction Studies in System Design. In J. Greenbaum & M. Kyng (Eds.), *Design At Work: Cooperative Design of Computer Systems* (pp. 25–44). New Jersey, N.J.: Lawerence Erlbaum Associates Inc., Publishers.

Basu, S. (2004). E-Government and Developing Countries: An Overview. *International Review of Law Computers & Technology*, *18*(1), 109–132. doi:10.1080/13600860410001674779

Beinhocker, E. D. 2006. The Origin of Wealth: Evolution, Complexity and the Radical Remaking of Economics. Boston, M.A.: Harvard Business School Press.

Bellamy, C. (2000). The Politics of Public Information Systems. In G. David Garson (Ed.), *Handbook of Public Information Systems* (pp. 85–98). New York, N.Y.: Marcel Dekker Inc.

Bellamy, C., & Taylor, J. A. (1994). Introduction: Exploiting IT in Public Administration. *Public Administration*, *72*(1), 1–12. doi:10.1111/j.1467-9299.1994.tb00996.x

Bhatnagar, S. (2004). *E-Government: From Vision to Implementation*. New Delhi: SAGE Publications.

Carayon, P., Hoonakker, P., & Smith, M. J. (2012). Human Factors in Organizational Design and Management. In G. Salvendy (Ed.), *Handbook of Human Factors and Ergonomics* – (4th ed., pp. 534–552). New Jersey, N.J.: John Wiley and Sons. doi:10.1002/9781118131350.ch18

Casely, J. (2004, March 13th). Public Sector Reform and Corruption: CARD Facade in Andhra Pradesh. *Economic and Political Weekly*, 1151–1156.

Ciborra, C. (2005). Interpreting e-government and development: Efficiency, transparency or governance at a distance? *Information Technology & People*, *18*(3), 260–279. doi:10.1108/09593840510615879

Cornwell, B., Curry, T. J., & Schwirian, K. P. (2003). Revisiting Norton Long's Ecology of Games: A Network Approach. *City & Community*, *2*(2), 121–142. doi:10.1111/1540-6040.00044

Crozier, M., & Friedberg, E. (1980). [University of Chicago Press.]. *Actors and Systems. Chicago, I*, L.

Cruickshank, P., Edelmann, N., & Smith, C. F. (2010). Signing an e-Petition as a Transition from Lurking to Participation. *Electronic Government and Electronic Participation*.

Czaja, S. J., & Nair, S. N. (2012). Human Factors Engineering and Systems Design. In G. Salvendy (Ed.), *Handbook of Human Factors and Ergonomics* (4th ed., pp. 38–56). New Jersey, N.J.: John Wiley and Sons. doi:10.1002/9781118131350.ch2

Dada, D. (2006). The Failure of E-Government in Developing Countries: A Literature Review. *The Electronic Journal on Information Systems in Developing Countries*, *26*(7), 1–10.

Dillinger, W. (1988). Urban Property Taxation in Developing Countries. *World Bank Policy Research Working Paper Series*, no. 41. Retrieved from http://ideas.repec.org/p/wbk/wbrwps/41.html

Downs, A. (1964). Inside Bureaucracy. Boston, M.A.: Little Brown.

Dutton, W. H. (1992). The Ecology of Games Shaping Telecommunications Policy. *Communication Theory*, *2*(4), 303–324. doi:10.1111/j.1468-2885.1992.tb00046.x

Dutton, W. H., Schneider, V., & Vedel, T. (2012). Large Technical Systems as Ecologies of Games: Cases from Telecommunications to the Internet. In J. Bauer, A. Lang, & V. Schneider (Eds.), *Innovation Policy and Governance in High-Tech Industries: The Complexity of Coordination*. Berlin: Springer Link. doi:10.1007/978-3-642-12563-8_3

Eisenhardt, K. M. (1989). Building Theories from Case Study Research. *Academy of Management Review*, *14*(4), 532–550.

Fehr, E., & Gachter, S. (1998). Reciprocity and Economics: The Economic Implications of *Homo Reciprocans. European Economic Review*, *42*(3), 845–859. doi:10.1016/S0014-2921(97)00131-1

Fehr, E., & Gachter, S. (2002). Altruistic Punishment in Humans. *Nature*, *415*(6868), 137–145. doi:10.1038/415137a PMID:11805825

Firestone, W. A. (1989). Educational Policy as an Ecology of Games. *Educational Researcher*, *18*(7), 18–24. doi:10.2307/1177165

Gintis, H. (2000). *Game Theory Evolving*. Princeton, N.J.: Princeton University Press.

Gintis, H. (2006). *The Economy as a Complex Adaptive System - A Review of Eric D. Beinhocker*. MacArthur Research Foundation Paper Series. Retrieved from http://www.umass.edu/preferen/Class%20Material/Readings%20in%20Market%20Dynamics/Complexity%20Economics.pdf

Hall, P. A., & Taylor, R. C. R. (1996). Political Science and the Three New Institutionalisms. *MPIFG Discussion Paper 96/9.*

Hartley, J. (2005). Case Study Research. In C. Cassell & G. Symon (Eds.), *Essential Guide to Qualitative Methods in Organisational Research* (pp. 323–333). London: SAGE Publications.

Hechter, M., & Kanazawa, S. (1997). Sociological Rational Choice Theory. *Annual Review of Sociology*, *23*(1), 191–214. doi:10.1146/annurev.soc.23.1.191

Heeks, R. 2003. Most eGovernment-for-Development Projects Fail: How Can the Risks be Reduced? *i-Government Working Paper Series - Paper No. 14*, IDPM, 2003.

Isaac-Henry, K. (1997). Development and Change in the Public Sector. In K. Isaac-Henry, C. Painter, & C. Barnes (Eds.), *Management in the Public Sector: Challenge and Change* (pp. 1–25). London: International Thomson Business Press.

Jacko, J. A., Yi, J. S., Sainfort, F., & McClellan, M. (2012). Human Factors and Ergonomic Methods. In G. Salvendy (Ed.), *Handbook of Human Factors and Ergonomics* (4th ed., pp. 289–329). New Jersey, N.J.: John Wiley and Sons. doi:10.1002/9781118131350.ch10

Kenman, H. (1996). Konkordanzdemokratie und Korporatismus aus der Perspektive eines rationalen Institutionalismus. *Politische Vierteljahresschrift*, *37*, 494–515.

Kuutti, K. 1996. Activity Theory as a Potential Framework for Human Computer Interaction Research. In B. A. Nardi (Ed.), Context and Consciousness: Activity Theory and Human Computer Interaction (pp. 17 – 44). Boston, M.A.: M.I.T. Press.

Laver, M., & Schofield, N. (1990). *Multiparty Government: The Politics of Coalition in Europe*. Oxford: Oxford University Press.

Lewis, A. (1982). *The Psychology of Taxation*. Oxford: Martin Robertson & Company.

Long, N. E. (1958). The Local Community as an Ecology of Games. *American Journal of Sociology*, *64*(3), 251–261. doi:10.1086/222468

Macy, M. W., & Willer, R. (2002). From Factors to Actors: Computational Sociology and Agent-Based Modeling. *Annual Review of Sociology*, *28*(1), 143–166. doi:10.1146/annurev.soc.28.110601.141117

Madon, S. (1997). Information-based Global Economy and Socio-Economic Development: The Case of Bangalore. *The Information Society*, *13*(3), 227–243. doi:10.1080/019722497129115

Madon, S. (2004). Evaluating the Developmental Impact of E-Governance Initiatives: An Exploratory Framework. *Electronic Journal of Information Systems in Developing Countries*, *20*(5), 1–13.

Madon, S., Sahay, S., & Sahay, J. (2004). Implementing Property Tax Reforms in Bangalore: An Actor-Network Perspective. *Information and Organization*, *14*(4), 269–295. doi:10.1016/j.infoandorg.2004.07.002

March, J. G., & Olsen, J. P. (1984). The New Institutionalism: Organisational Factors in Political Life. *The American Political Science Review*, *78*(3), 734–749. doi:10.2307/1961840

March, J. G., & Olsen, J. P. (1989). *Rediscovering Institutions: The Organisational Basis of Politics*. New York, N.Y.: The Free Press.

Margetts, H. Z. (2006). Transparency and Digital Government. In C. Hood & D. Heald (Eds.), *Transparency: the Key to Better Governance?* (pp. 197–210). London: The British Academy. doi:10.5871/bacad/9780197263839.003.0012

Margetts, H. Z., John, P., Escher, T., & Reissfelder, S. (2011). Social Information and Political Participation on the Internet: An Experiment. *European Political Science Review*, *3*(3), 321–344. doi:10.1017/S1755773911000129

McCubbins, M. D., & Sullivan, T. (1987). *Congress: Structure and Policy*. Cambridge: Cambridge University Press.

Mehta, J. (2010). Ideas and Politics: Towards a Second Generation. *Perspectives on Politic*. Retrieved from http://www.allacademic.com//meta/p_mla_apa_research_citation/0/2/2/1/1/pages22111/p22111-1.php

Mintzberg, H. (1985). The Organisation as Political Arena. *Journal of Management Studies*, *22*(2), 133–154. doi:10.1111/j.1467-6486.1985.tb00069.x

Misra, S. (2005). eGovernance: Responsive and Transparent Service Delivery Mechanism. In A. Singh (Ed.), Administrative Reforms: Towards Sustainable Practices (pp. 283-302). New Delhi: SAGE Publications.

Moon, M. J. (2002). The Evolution of E-Government among Municipalities: Rhetoric or Reality? *Public Administration Review*, *62*(4), 424–433. doi:10.1111/0033-3352.00196

National Institute of Urban Affairs (NIUA). (2004). *Reforming the Property Tax System. Research Study Series no. 94*. New Delhi: NIUA Press.

Ostrom, E., Gardner, R., & Walker, J. (1994). Rules, Games and Common-Pool Resources. Ann Arbor, M.I.: University of Michigan Press.

Peters, B. G. (2000). *Institutional Theory in Political Science: The New Institutionalism*. London: Continuum Press.

Proctor, R. W., & Vu, K.-P. L. (2012). Selection and Control of Action. In G. Salvendy (Ed.), *Handbook of Human Factors and Ergonomics* (4th ed., pp. 95–116). New Jersey, N.J.: John Wiley and Sons. doi:10.1002/9781118131350.ch4

Rosengard, J. K. (1998). Property Tax Reform in Developing Countries. Boston, M.A.: Kluwer Academic Publications. doi:10.1007/978-1-4615-5667-1

Scharpf, F. W. (1997). *Games Real Actors Play: Actor-Centered Institutionalism in Policy Research*. Oxford: Westview Press.

Simon, H. A. (1955). A Behavioural Model of Rational Choice. *The Quarterly Journal of Economics*, *69*(1), 99–118. doi:10.2307/1884852

Stanforth, C. (2006). Analysing eGovernment in Developing Countries Using Actor-Network Theory. *iGovernment Working Paper Series Paper no. 17*.

Tsebelis, G. (1990). Nested Games: Rational Choice in Comparative Politics. Berkley, C.A.: University of California Press.

Vedel, T. (1989). Télématique et Configurations d'Acteurs: Une Perspective Européenne. *Reseaux*, *7*(37), 9–28.

Virkar, S. (2011). *The Politics of Implementing e-Government for Development: The Ecology of Games Shaping Property Tax Administration in Bangalore City, India* [Unpublished Doctoral Thesis]. University of Oxford, Oxford.

Yin, R. K. (2003). Applied Social Research Methods Series: Vol. 5. *Case Study Research: Design and Methods*. London: SAGE Publications.

ADDITIONAL READING

Bhatnagar, S. (2004). E-Government: Opportunities and Challenges. *World Bank Presentation*. Retrieved from http://siteresources.worldbank.org/INTEDEVELOPMENT/Resources/559323-1114798035525/1055531-1114798256329/10555556-1114798371392/Bhatnagar1.ppt

Bruhat Bangalore Mahanagara Palike. (2000). *Property Tax Self-Assessment Scheme: Golden Jubilee Year 2000*, Mahanagara Palike Council Resolution No. 194/99-2000, Bangalore, 2000 [Handbook].

Bruhat Bangalore Mahanagara Palike. (2007). *Assessment and Calculation of Property Tax Under the Capital Value System (New SAS): 2007- 2008*, Bangalore [Unpublished Handbook].

Ciborra, C., & Navarra, D. D. (2005). Good Governance, Development Theory and Aid Policy: Risks and Challenges of E-Government in Jordan. *Information Technology for Development, 11*(2), 141–159. doi:10.1002/itdj.20008

De, R. (2007, September 3-7). Antecedents of Corruption and the Role of E-Government Systems in Developing Countries. Paper for the *Proceedings of Ongoing Research Electronic Government 6th International Conference, EGOV 2007*, Regensburg, Germany. Retrieved from http://www.iimb.ernet.in/~rahulde/CorruptionPaperEgov07_RDe.pdf

Dunleavy, P., Margetts, H. Z., Bastow, S., & Tinkler, J. (2006). *Digital Era Governance: IT Corporations, The State and E-Government*. Oxford: Oxford University Press. doi:10.1093/acprof:oso/9780199296194.001.0001

Dutton, W. H. (1999). *Society on the Line: Information Politics in the Digital Age*. Oxford: Oxford University Press.

Fink, C., & Kenny, C. J. (2003). W(h)ither the Digital Divide? *Info: The Journal of Policy. Regulation and Strategy for Telecommunications, 5*(6), 15–24. doi:10.1108/14636690310507180

Gopal Jaya, N. (2006). Introduction. In N. Gopal Jaya, A. Prakash, & P. K. Sharma (Eds.), *Local Governance in India: Decentralisation and Beyond* (pp. 1–26). New Delhi: Oxford University Press.

Heeks, R. (2005). eGovernment as a Carrier of Context. *Journal of Public Policy, 25*(1), 51–74. doi:10.1017/S0143814X05000206

Heeks, R. (2006). *Implementing and Managing eGovernment – An International Text*. New Delhi: Vistar Publications.

Jha, G. (1983). Area Basis of Valuation of Property Tax: An Evaluation. In A. Datta (Ed.), *Property Taxation in India* (pp. 106–117). New Delhi: Centre for Urban Indian Studies – The Indian Institute of Public Administration.

Jha, S. N., & Mathur, P. C. (1999). *Decentralization and Local Politics*. New Delhi: SAGE Publications.

Jick, T. D. (1979). Mixing Qualitative and Quantitative Methods: Triangulation in Action. *Administrative Science Quarterly, 24*(4), 602–611. doi:10.2307/2392366

Johnson, R. N., & Libecap, G. D. 1994. The Federal Civil Service System and the Problem of Bureaucracy. Chicago, IL: University of Chicago Press. doi:10.7208/chicago/9780226401775.001.0001

Lieten, G. K., & Srivatsava, R. (1999). *Unequal Partners: Power Relations, Devolution and Development in Uttar Pradesh, Indo-Dutch Studies on Development Alternatives (no. 23)*. New Delhi: SAGE Publications.

Madon, S. (1993). Introducing Administrative Reform through the Application of Computer-Based Information Systems: A Case Study in India. *Public Administration and Development*, *13*(1), 37–48. doi:10.1002/pad.4230130104

Madon, S., & Bhatnagar, S. (2000). Institutional Decentralised Information Systems for Local Level Planning: Comparing Approaches Across Two States in India. *Journal of Global Information Technology Management*, *3*(4), 45–59. doi:10.1080/1097198X.2000.10856289

Madon, S., Krishna, S., & Michael, E. (2010). Health Information Systems, Decentralisation and Democratic Accountability. *Public Administration and Development*, *30*(4), 247–260. doi:10.1002/pad.571

Margetts, H. Z. (1998). *Information Technology in Government: Britain and America*. London: Routledge Press.

Ronaghan, S. A. (2002). Benchmarking E-Government: A Global Perspective. *The United Nations Division for Public Economics and Public Administration (DPEPA) Report*.

Rose, R. (2005). A Global Diffusion Model of e-Governance. *Journal of Public Policy*, *25*(1), 5–28. doi:10.1017/S0143814X05000279

Rose-Ackerman, S. (1978). *Corruption: A Study in Political Economy*. New York, N.Y.: Academic Press.

Schech, S. (2002). Wired for Change: The Links between ICTs and Development Discourses. *Journal of International Development*, *14*(1), 13–23. doi:10.1002/jid.870

Schiller, H. I. (1981). *Who Knows: Information in the Age of the Fortune 500*. Norwood: Ablex Publishing Corp.

Sinha, K. P. (1981). *Property Taxation in a Developing Economy*. New Delhi: Puja Publications.

Tanzi, V. (1987). Quantitative Characteristics of the Tax Systems of Developing Countries. In D. Newbery & N. Stern (Eds.), *The Theory of Taxation for Developing Countries* (pp. 205–241). New York, N.Y.: Oxford University Press.

Virkar, S. (2011). Exploring Property Tax Administration Reform through the use of Information and Communication Technologies: A Study of e-Government in Karnataka, India. In J. Steyn & S. Fahey (Eds.) ICTs and Sustainable Solutions for Global Development: Theory, Practice and the Digital Divide (Vol 2, pp. 127-149). Hershey, P.A.: IGI Global, Inc.

Wade, R. H. (1985). The Market for Public Office: Why the Indian State Is Not Better at Development. *World Development*, *13*(4), 467–497. doi:10.1016/0305-750X(85)90052-X

World Bank. (2002). *The Networking Revolution: Opportunities and Challenges for Developing Countries* (InfoDev Working Paper). Washington, D.C.: The World Bank Publications.

KEY TERMS AND DEFINITIONS

Actor Goals and Motivations: The aims that key actors seek to attain and maintain from interacting with other players, encompassing both broader long-term achievements as well as more short- to medium-term rewards.

Actor Perceptions: Include the preferences and opinions of key institutional players that help determine the disjoint between project design and current ground realities, together with the nature and direction of organisational reform and institutional change.

Actor(s): The individuals, groups or other entities whose interactions shape the direction and nature of a particular game being considered.

Country-Context Gap: Refers to the gap that arises when a system designed in theory for one country is transferred into the reality of another.

Design-Actuality Gap Model or Framework: Is a framework for project evaluation which contends that the major factor determining project outcome is the degree of mismatch between the current ground realities of a situation ('where are we now'), and the models, conceptions, and assumptions built into a project's design (the 'where the project wants to get us').

e-Democracy: May be defined by the express intent to increase the participation of citizens in decision-making through the use of digital media and the application of Information and Communication Technologies to political processes. e-Democracy may be subdivided into *e-Engagement* (or *e-Participation*), *e-Voting, e-Consultation.* 1) **e-*Engagement*** (or *e-Participation*)**:** Refers to the overall enhancement of opportunities for greater consultation and dialogue between government and its citizens through the encouragement of online citizen action and citizen participation in political processes electronically. 2) *e-Voting:* May be defined broadly as the expression and exercise of fundamental democratic rights and duties online through specially developed digital platforms. 3) *e-Consultation:* Refers to the process whereby citizens are given the opportunity to provide feedback to government online on matters of public importance and participate in the shaping of issues relevant to them via the new digital media.

e-Governance: Refers to the use of ICTs by government, civil society, and political institutions to engage citizens in political processes and to the promote greater participation of citizens in the public sphere.

e-Government: Refers to the use of Information and Communication Technologies by government departments and agencies to improve internal functioning and public service provision. Broadly speaking, e-government may be divided into 2 distinct areas: *e-Administration* and *e-Services.* 1) *e-Administration*, which refers to the improvement of government processes and to the streamlining of the internal workings of the public sector often using ICT-based information systems, 2) *e-Services*, which refers to the improved delivery of public services to citizens through multiple electronic platforms

Game(s): Arena(s) of competition and cooperation structured by a set of rules and assumptions about how to act in order for actors to achieve a particular set of objectives.

Hard-Soft Gap: Refers to the difference between the *actual, rational design* of a technology (hard) adopted within a project and the *actuality of the social context*, namely people, culture, politics, etc., within which the system operates (soft).

Managerial Variables: Are those institutional variables relating to project management and other *soft* variables of project design and implementation, which include the efficiency and effectiveness of a supply chain, the characteristics of an agency's culture, and the capacity of an adopting agency to adapt to and to manage change.

Moves: May be defined as actions, decisions and other plays made by key actors taken to arrive at key goals, usually if not always based on their strategy of choice.

Partial Failure: Of an initiative is a situation in which major goals are unattained or where there are significant undesirable outcomes.

Political Variables: Are those *soft* institutional variables relating to the perceptions and impressions that public servants have regarding potential labour cuts, administrative turnover, and changes in executive direction generated by the development of e-government.

Private-Public Gap: Refers to the mismatch that results when technology meant for private organisations is used in the public sector without being adapted to suit the role and aims of the adopting public organisation.

Project Outcome: Or the sum total of the interaction between organisational and institutional realities and the project design carried out within the constraints of the current organisational and institutional set-up.

Rules: The written or unwritten codes of conduct that shape actor moves and choices during a game.

Strategies: Include tactics, ruses, and ploys adopted by key actors during the course of a game to keep the balance of the engagement in their favour.

Success: Of an initiative is a situation in which most actor groups attain their major goals and do not experience significant undesirable outcomes.

Technological Variables: Are those institutional variables relating to technology and other *hard* elements of project design and implementation, which include the ability of a user-population to access ICTs, the quality of the user population's Internet use, the availability of an internal technological infrastructure, and the provision of technical skills to the government workforce.

Total Failure: Of an initiative is a situation where a project is either never implemented or in which a new system is implemented but is almost immediately abandoned.

Chapter 4
Emerging Forms of Collaboration
Communities of Practice Online through Networked Fictions, Dreams and Stories

Alexandra Antonopoulou
University of London, UK

Eleanor Dare
University of Derby, UK

ABSTRACT

The chapter will outline the implications of two projects, namely the 'Phi Books' (2008) and the 'Digital Dreamhacker' (2011). These novel projects serve here as case studies for investigating new and challenging ways of advancing collaborative technologies, using in particular, Communities of Practice and insights gained from both embodiment and graph theory (social network analysis) as well as design. Both projects were developed collaboratively, between a computer programmer and a designer and a wider community of practice, consisting of other artists, writers, technologists and designers. The two systems that resulted also acted as methodologies, instigated by the authors with a view to facilitate, explore and comment on the act of collaboration. Both projects are multi-disciplinary, spanning ideas and techniques from mathematics and art, design and computer programming. The projects deploy custom-made software and fiction enmeshed structures, drawing upon methodologies that are embedded with dreams and stories while at the same time being informed by cutting-edge research into human behaviour and interaction design. The chapter will investigate how the projects deployed techniques and theoretical insights from social network analysis as well as motion capture technology and the wider concept of a Community of Practice, to extend and augment existing collaborative methods. The chapter draws upon Wenger et al (2002), as well as Siemens (2014) and Borgatti et al (2009), and will explore the idea of a new form of collective social and technological collaborative grammar, deploying gesture as well as Social Network Analysis. Moreover, the featured projects provide insights into the ways in which digital technology is changing society, and in turn, the important ways in which technology is embedded with the cultural and economic prerogatives of increasingly globalized cultures.

DOI: 10.4018/978-1-4666-9556-6.ch004

Copyright © 2016, IGI Global. Copying or distributing in print or electronic forms without written permission of IGI Global is prohibited.

INTRODUCTION

The following chapter looks at the implications of two projects which represent two methodological systems, namely the 'Phi Books' (2008) and 'Digital Dreamhacker' (2011). These two systems, conceived collaboratively by the authors, have deployed custom-made software and fiction enmeshed structures with a view to facilitate, explore and comment on collaboration in itself.

Both projects are multi-disciplinary, spanning ideas and techniques from science and art, critical design and computer programming, performance and literature, while they are informed by research into human behaviour, identity and the wider concept of a community of practice. The projects have been presented at International Conferences and discussed in a wide range of peer reviewed academic papers.

This chapter will represent an opportunity to outline the project's implications for the understanding and advancement of collaborative technologies. Providing readers with technical and conceptual insight into their engendered by digital technologies modes of collaboration, it is hoped to open a space for further dialogue about the limits and possibilities of e-collaboration. The projects outlined in the chapter present subversive collaborative writing tools and social networking platforms for communities of practice in the context of Web 2.0 technologies combined with Web 3 collaborative, intelligent technologies, deploying concepts such as the semantic web and embodied computing. More specifically, the chapter will present how the two central case study projects have deployed and often re-appropriated evolving technologies such as motion capture and embodied, situated computing, presenting how context aware models of human subjects can combine with technologies to expand the agencies at play in collaborative works. The chapter will draw upon Wenger et al (2002), as well as Siemens (2014) and Borgatti et al (2009), and will explore the idea of a new form of collective social and technological collaborative grammar, deploying gesture as well as Social Network Analysis. Moreover, the featured projects provide insights into the ways in which digital technology is changing society, and in turn, the important ways in which technology is embedded with the cultural and economic prerogatives of increasingly globalized cultures. Through this, the authors will touch upon the interdependence of human identity with the socio-technological imaginary, providing a channel for broader dialogue and cultural commentary, as well as a conceptual challenge to established practices.

The chapter will start with a short description of the projects followed by a section situating the projects within collaborative learning theories and theories of Social Network Analysis. The main analysis will discuss how the projects act as a methodological approach and commentary on collaboration (with each other and with technology) and learning through communities of practice.

Description of the Case Studies: The 'Phi Books' and the 'Digital Dreamhacker'

The Phi books is an interdisciplinary collaborative project initiated by the authors in 2008. The project uses the house as a metaphor for interdisciplinary collaboration and is a response to the inadequacy of historical models for both theorizing and practicing creative research collaboration, and to an apparent lack of theoretical mobility across diverse disciplines. It has employed narrative, story telling, audience participation, code-writing, performance, maths, sophisticated motion tracking technology as well as custom software to explore how borders, walls and doors facilitate collaboration. The authors' research in different fields but with similar subject matters reminded them of the English terraced houses that seem identical in structure, but they are different since different people inhabit them. Initially, the authors bought two identical books, and used them as a metaphor for their houses. Stories were written for

Figure 1. From left to right: The Phi Books covers (2008); Book illustrations and objects (2008); Algorithm illustration(2008). Copyright: Antonopoulou A., Dare E.

each room in the houses and then books were swapped to write a response to each other's stories. This seemed to mirror an 'extreme programming' methodology in its agility and rapidity and in our attempts to 'break' each other's stories. *The authors used a mathematical algorithm to write a precise number of words for each room. The numbers of the words in each room were following the logic of the phi ratios, this was the foundational structure for their collaboration (see Figure 1).*

'Room one is 100 words. Room 2 is a room of 200 words, Room 3 is a room of 300 words. Room 4 is a room of 500 words. Room 5 is a room of 800 words. Room 6 is a room of 1300 words. To explain our writing algorithm: Ignoring the seed values, each remaining number is the sum of the previous two or $F(n) = F(n-1) + F(n-2)$*, for integer* $n > 1$*.' (Antonopoulou; Dare, 2012, p.90)*

The authors were drawn to the historical continuity of this schema as well as its mathematical precision. From the initial formulation of algorithmic fictions to technologically mediated and embodied systems for collaboration. The books were performed in conferences and symposia while at the same time, the audience was asked to expand the Phi neighbourhood by entering the authors' houses-books and writing their own house stories. In Freie University Berlin (2009) the books were placed in a physical map of the Phi books's neighbourhood representing houses. Around the books there were piles of photocopied extracts of the authors' stories, representing other houses. The participants used these random bits of the authors' house stories to write their own house stories. The phi neighbourhood scenery was constantly changing while the participants added or extracted papers from the pile. The participants kept on sending us new stories online. The logic of the Phi ratios was maintained in the authors' performance as we well as in their writing; for example, in Berlin sound was used to maintain the logic of the Phi ratios and to punctuate the performance, connecting the linguistic to the sonic and to the spatial constraints of the authors' collaboration. Each sound progressively expanded to reflect the increase in size of each room in the Phi house, according to the ancient Phi ratios. We modelled the room sizes computationally to get a reverberation that was fitted to the geometry of each room (figure 2).

In London at the Inter-Art Goldsmiths Symposium (2010) an interactive application was devised (Phi-Meta film) to comment on the inevitable nature of participation, combining the physical space of writing performance with virtual space. In the later stages the project evolved into a participatory staged performance asking participants to perform their own stories within a 12 camera motion capture system while aiming to record them with video-cameras at the same time. This would allow us to compare their graphically represented movement with their psychical self-represented performances and extrapolate

Figure 2. Top- Material from Berlin InterArt Symposium-Metaphors in Aesthetics History panel (2009) From left to right: Images representing sounds, photographic media (2009); Phi neighbourhood installation (2009); Participants' stories (2009). Bottom - Presentation in University of Stockholm Library - Symposium on Aesthetics and history (2010); The Phi-Meta film application - Processing app. Inter-Art Symposium, Goldsmiths 2010); Using the motion capture system (2011); The Phi stage from the Thursday club- Goldsmiths presentation performance (2011), Victoria and Albert museum app. (2012) Copyright: Antonopoulou A., Dare E.

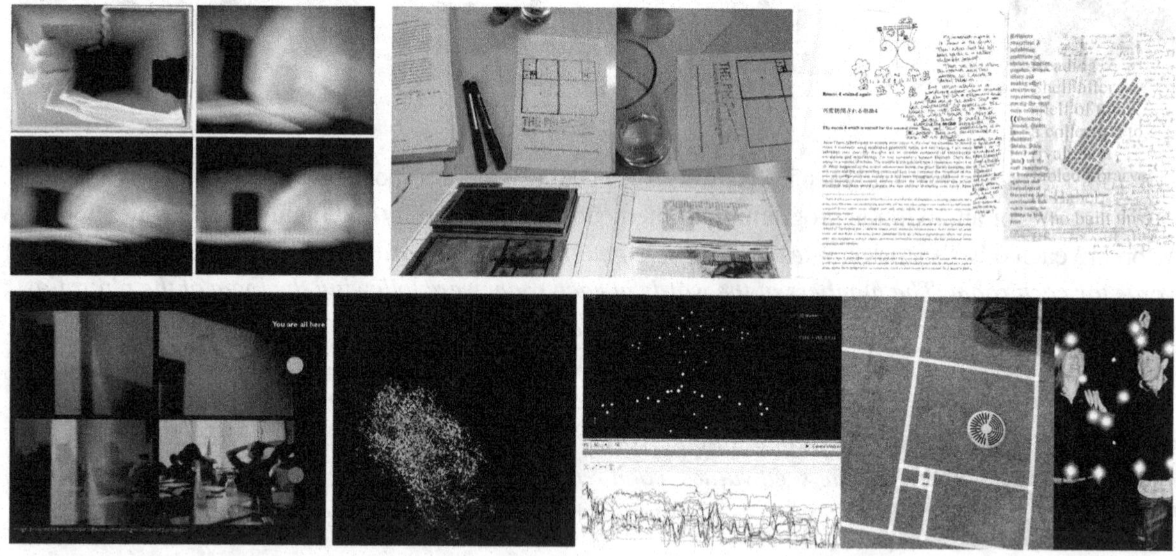

new layers of embodied narrative and subjective articulation. Through the technologies developed, the authors will comment on the nature of technologically mediated collaboration. (fig.2). More info can found on the publications (Antonopoulou & Dare, 2008; Antonopoulou & Dare, 2012) and the project' blog (phibooksland.blogspot.com).

The digital Dreamhacker application (Antonopoulou & Dare, 2011) is a Web based program written in Javascript that gathers dream themes reported by individual dreamers in the form of keywords, and turns them into crowdourced dream visualisations by sourcing images from the image sharing website Flickr. It is a "repurposing of dreams, a form of Crowdsourced 'hack', in which we take images from an online community and subvert them into dream visualisations and diverse social networks (...). Since the elusive meaning of the dreamers' keywords is the only parameter that defines the selection of the online images used, the generated dream visualisation does not have many visual similarities with the image that the dreamer recollects" (Antonopoulou & Dare, 2013, p. 1). These dream visualisations are then uploaded onto the Social Web, allowing for further commentary and collective interpretation. The project is not about the literal illustration of dreams or a means of enhancing artistic skill, but more of a commentary on the 'social imaginary' and the connection between technology, culture and our individual 'imaginings', including dreams. Therefore, the visualisations re-frame dreams within a technical and cultural imaginary, meaning the systems of meaning that help form collective understandings and expectations of social life. The project currently explores the digitally produced crowdsourced dream visualisations (produced by the digital Dreamhacker app) (see Figure 3) with analogue crowdscoursed

Figure 3. From left to right: Dream visualised by the Dreamhacker app. (2013), Dream visualised by participant (2014).). Copyright: Antonopoulou A., Dare E.

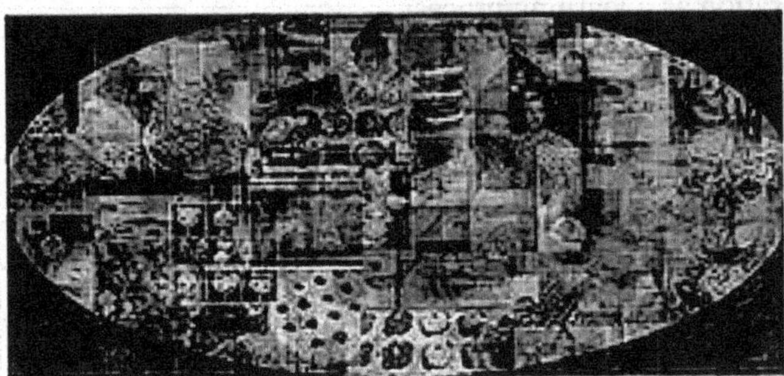

visualisations created by people visualising other people's dreams. With this the aim is to construct an installation in which both analogue human generated sculptures, and prints of computationally generated crowdsourced dream visualisations will be put side by side resulting into an impressive collaborative sculpture, a physical network of dream imaginaries. The research methodology for the project frames social media as an innovative context for collaboratively exploring technology and the imagination, supported by methods "that emanate from both critical design and network analysis" (Antonopoulou & Dare, 2013, p. 1).

BACKGROUND

Framing the Projects within Collaborative Learning Theories

The next section discusses how the phi books projects and the Dreamhacker project are involved not only with technologically mediated collaboration but also communities of practice and collaborative learning.

Human learning, and, by extension all processes of creative human collaboration have been described as "a semiotic apprenticeship based on the creation of a collaborative community of practice in which learners develop their thinking through talk rather than through modelling." Throughout this chapter the authors will stress how strongly collaboration is embedded with learning processes, indeed, the authors frame collaboration as a type of learning process, involving the constant negotiation of what Vygotsky (1962) termed the 'zone of proximal development', in which:

> *collaborative learning, either among students or between students and a teacher, is essential for assisting each student in advancing through his or her own zone of proximal development, that is, the gap between what the learner could accomplish alone and what he or she could accomplish in cooperation with others who are more skilled or experienced (Warschauer, 1997, p. 471).*

In contrast to a conventional teacher and pupil relationship both projects were based on peer-to-peer relationships where there was a less clear-cut skill disparity. There is strong theoretical support for the idea that competence is obtained through forming connections. In the Phi Books and Dreamhacker projects connections are formed between participants and within technical systems that mediate the collaboration. Both of the projects are underpinned by a methodological commitment to understanding the effects of technologically mediated collaboration as a learning process.

One theory that supports the notion of social learning within the context of online networks and other forms of technological mediation is Connectivism, this was a useful frame of reference for the projects discussed here. The core focus of connectivism is the implication of learning, such as emails, forums and blog posts and claims to address the less formal types of learning that can occur within social networks, it refers to 'tacit' knowledge' but has a limited theoretical framing for it. Connectivism advocates learning processes that are mediated by digital technology, predicated on notions of self-organisation and emergence:

Connectivism is the integration of principles explored by chaos, network, and complexity and self-organization theories. Learning is a process that occurs within nebulous environments of shifting core elements – not entirely under the control of the individual. Learning (defined as actionable knowledge) can reside outside of ourselves (within an organization or a database), is focused on connecting specialized information sets, and the connections that enable us to learn more are more important than our current state of knowing (Siemens, 2014).

However, there are conceptual contradictions in the connectivist model, despite allusions to technological agency, the site of learning in a connectivist model is still located within the individual, in keeping with a cognitivist outlook, in which a unitary knower is framed within an information processing paradigm. In this model embodied knowledge is rarely, if ever, acknowledged. Although Siemens makes allusions to tacit knowledge, the definition provided is vague and unsatisfactory, at no point does it acknowledge the role of the body as a site of knowing. The authors of this paper found the body to be of central importance to collaborative learning and social communication. In Siemens' model the individual is swept into "a concept of rationality that is considered an a-historical and universal model leading to a 'de-contextualized' view of learning – one that fails to deal directly with considerations and questions of context – ideology, culture, power and race-class-gender differences" (Illeris, 2009, p. 95).

As Duke (2013) observes, "If a person with limited core knowledge accesses Internet information beyond his or her ability to understand, then that knowledge is useless" (Duke et al, 2013, p. 9). As this chapter endeavours to demonstrate, there is more to human interaction then symbolic representation, or information processing paradigms, other forms of knowledge are also central to human leaning, as well as the social and cultural milieu of learners, "Siemens' Connectivist approach is essentially about cognitive development, and does not attempt to explain the socialisation processes inherent in the networked world. A common criticism of connectivism is the lack of supportive empirical research" (Coverdale, 2014). Tacit and embodied understandings of the world are similarly negated by connectivism, indeed, the role of the body is rarely acknowledged within current discourse around digital collaboration and communities of practice.

In both projects tacit knowledge was explored as a way to uncover individual and collective understandings of dreaming and storytelling. Tacit knowledge is summed up by the scientist and philosopher Michael Polanyi in his statement "We know more than we can tell." (Polanyi, 2009, p.4). Tacit knowledge implies a multi-layered background of subjective and non-formalised skills and knowledge, including cultural and embodied forms of knowing. Adam (1998) asks, what types of knowledge are denied by the conceptualisation of knowing as a symbolic representation within traditional AI (i.e. digital systems).

Adam writes of 'epistemic hierarchies' (Adam, 1998) that privilege propositional knowledge but denies or negates, other, typically less formalised, forms of knowing such as tacit or skills based knowledge. These other types of knowing are not separable from the experience of being embodied, as Adam writes: "Rationalist philosophy has sidelined the body in giving the mind the primary role in the making of knowledge and rationality" (Adam, 1998, p. 129).

How then, can tacit knowledge be shared and articulated within digital collaborative systems? The case studies contained within this chapter explore how the body, as well as less formal forms of knowledge can be incorporated into contemporary collaborative tools. This chapter will explore some ways in which the useful insights of connectivism can be integrated with tacit and embodied knowledge, in particular the case study section shows how motion tracking has been used by the authors to investigate embodiment and gesture in the context of a collaborative story telling project, the *Phi Books*. The authors deployed motion tracking technology to investigate the complex ways in which the body is a site of narrative meaning, including the absence of explicit gesture:

The body can also transmit messages without any movement at all. To refrain from gesture, for example by stifling symptoms of grief, could be as demonstrative an act as bursting into tears. The body is not neutral until its owner makes an involuntary movement or decides to send out a signal - for faces, hands, and limbs can be as significant in repose as in motion. There is no attribute of the human body, whether size, shape, height or colour, which does not convey some social meaning to the observer (Bremmer et al, 1993, p. 1).

Embodiment as Dourish writes is a crucial aspect of situated computing, but it does not preclude social and cultural meaning:

The relevance of embodiment for the sociological side of situated computing is also a question of interaction. What Suchman's work drew attention to was the way that action emerges not as the outcome of disconnected cognitivism, but rather from a direct, reflexive conversation with the setting of its production. Accomplishing the sequential organisation of action is a real-time affair. As a simple example, this approach explores spoken language as social action rather than the verbalisation of internal mental dispositions (Dourish, 2000, p. 2).

However it is not only the embodied tacit knowledge or the technological mediation but also the collaboration between the participants that form a learning community. Within the so-called 'new pedagogy' (Fullan, 2013), including connectivism, there has been a strong emphasis on social relationships as a crucial aspect of effective online learning, as well as a crucial component of online collaborative communities. The next section will look at the concept of Communities of Practice, virtual environments within which collaborations and learning processes unfold. Communities of practice were at the heart of both projects as a means to learn and collaborate.

The term Community of Practice (CoP) has been defined by the cognitive anthropologists Wenger et al as: "groups of people who share a concern, a set of problems, a passion about a topic, and who deepen their knowledge and expertise in this area by interacting on an ongoing basis" (Wenger, et al, 2002).

Formally a Community of Practice involves groups of individuals engaged in communal learning, these individuals may also create a shared identity by contributing to the practices of their Community of Practice. The knowledge these communities generate is sometimes referred to as Social Capital. A

Community of Practice has been defined by (Wenger et. Al, 2002, pp 27 – 29) as having the following structural characteristics:

- A domain of knowledge
- A notion of community
- A practice

These criteria are arguably idealised, assuming perhaps, to uniform a distribution of technical and intellectual resources, as well as access. It is apparent from this definition that such communities have existed for many years, possibly millennia. Later in this chapter it will become evident how the topology or structure of networks and virtual communities can reveal useful information about those networks. These structures can have a profound impact on the efficacy and power balance of Communities of Practice as well as their effectiveness in promoting learning and collaboration.

A community of practice is a basic social unit in which work gets done, and in which the skills and knowledge pertinent to that work are learnt, shared and developed, and evolve over time. Communities of practice are thus important social structures for creating and sharing knowledge (Gibbs et al, 2012, p. 1).

Drawing from Wenger the authors recognised that Communities of Practice offered both projects benefits such as: enabling 'practitioners to take collective responsibility for managing the knowledge', (...) creating 'a direct link between learning and performance', (...) addressing 'the tacit and dynamic aspects of knowledge creation and sharing', and working within communities that ' are not limited by formal structures: they create connections among people across organizational and geographic boundaries' (Wenger et al, 2006. p. 4).

Despite the benefits of Communities of Practice, developing and sustaining them is a challenge, not least of all for the following reasons:

- Team building with distributed individuals who might not even have met one another, is challenging
- Trusted communities take time to evolve
- Current economic and legal infrastructures are not suited to all types of organisations

It was important for the authors to recognise both the strengths and weaknesses embedded in Communities of Practice. The authors also deployed Social Network Analysis to investigate how such communities interact and evolve and how best to support their members, as the next section will outline, an analysis of the Dreamhacker Social Network revealed some significant structural metrics, as explained later in this chapter. Such metrics are crucial to understanding and supporting collaboration within communities of practice.

Social Networks and Social Network Analysis

Siemens has clearly aligned Social Network Analysis with online learning, stating that "Social network analysis is an additional element in understanding learning models in a digital era" (Siemens, 2014). Siemens, like many proponents of Social Network Analysis believes that the underlying structures and relations found in social networks reveal useful information about their members and relations, including predictive tools: "Within social networks, hubs are well-connected people who are able to foster and maintain knowledge flow. Their interdependence results in effective knowledge flow, enabling the personal understanding of the state of activities organizationally" (Siemens, 2014). It is important to also acknowledge some of the weaknesses inherent in Social Network Analysis and indeed in Social Networks, such as those identified by Helms et al (2010), who critique the difficulty of effective bottleneck identification, and therefore of conclusively identifying isolated individuals within social networks. Others such as Wellman (2002) critique the paradoxically de-materialising but atomising, role of such networks, in which individuality is oddly emphasised but without any anchoring in individual space. Regardless of such critiques, it would be hard to deny that such networks and their associated techniques have enormous cultural and social significance.

One formal definition of Social Networks describes them as: "a set of actors that may have relationships with one another. Networks can have few or many actors (nodes), and one or more kinds of relations (edges) between pairs of actors" (Hanneman, 2001, p. 19). The term 'actors' is inter-disciplinary, evolving from the domains of sociology, statistics, social psychology and graph theory. An actor in the context of Social Network analysis is an individual, organisation or object within that network. An actor is represented in graph theory as a node. An actors' connections to other actors are represented by ties (sometimes also called *edges* or *relations*).

There are clearly some strong connections between the criteria above and Communities of Practice, however, as well as the similarities between different types of online Social Network, it is also important to recognise the significant differences. Social Networks may be generalised mechanisms for managing and maintaining social relations, such as Facebook and MySpace or specialised types of professional, political or interest group networks, such as Care2, Within3 or LinkedIn.

Given the complexity and inter-connectedness of online Social Networks it is not surprising that specialised tools have emerged for analysing and understanding them. Foremost is the technique of Social Network Analysis which makes use of concepts from Graph theory. Social Network Analysis enables the identification of important nodes in a Social Network and the detection of cliques in communities as well as the ability to trace how information is diffused within networks and how patterns of opinion are formed. Some observers have made very strong claims for the benefits of Social Network Analysis, predicting a new theoretical framework for online learning predicated on the core features of self-organising social structures:

online self-organizing social systems could provide the foundation for a new instructional design science; namely, instructional design super-theory. (Wiley et al, 2002, p. 14)

An important distinction between Social Network Analysis and the analysis of other types of data is the emphasis on relationships or relations. These relations are strongly emphasised in Social Network Analysis because they can reveal more about the network than the details of each member's individual attributes. The structure and behavioural patterns of connections are studied by network analysts, these analysts look at features that fall into formal analytic categories such as: connections, distributions and segmentations. It is important to acknowledge the critique of Social Network Analysis as an ahistorical, reductionist model which:

lacks agency in the sense that it neglects subjectivity and human intentionality. This criticism suggests that the nodes tend to be conceptualized as passive and interchangeable receptacles, wholly determined by their positions or environments rather than active agents who manage their own destinies as well as shape the network around them. (Borgatti et al, 2009, p. 18)

Others critics call for a social ethics of network theory, one that is not founded on game theoretic, organisational, principals of self interest:

If we are going to go with the network metaphor, we need a praxis and an ethics, for engaging with the world beyond our interests, which means accounting for the space between nodes, becoming invested in the non-nodal. (Mejias, 2006)

But how the 'non-nodal' can be incorporated into new models of e-collaboration and social learning? The following two case studies explore some new ways in which different types of knowledge as well as different channels of communication can be integrated into the digital collaborative domain, the two case studies re-visit the chapter's central themes of collaboration, social networks and Communities of Practice.

WE AND I: COLLABORATING WITH EACH OTHER AND WITH TECHNOLOGY IN THE PHI BOOKS AND THE DIGITAL DREAMHACKER

Both Phi Books and the Dreamhacker projects used ambivalent, poetic open to interpretation or even unconscious systems such as stories and dreams as a medium and method to explore collective knowledge. Through a collaborative process where complex relationships, negotiation, tension but also mediation was involved, tacit knowledge was often turned into explicit conscious realisations. Throughout the project the authors have investigated both the benefits and drawbacks of digitally mediated collaboration while also drawing upon analogue tools and processes such as drawing and book binding. Both authors emphasise the co-constitution of theory and practice, and, in keeping with this goal, set out to explore what happens when collaboration is framed as a type of theorem, reducible to a precise, formal statement. Looking back into the narrative and the process of the projects it is argued that their structure can act as a methodology for collaborative learning. The following paragraphs will explore how the relationships between the 'we' and the 'I' facilitated collaboration and promoted learning.

As mentioned, prior to writing the Phi Books it was agreed that the house theme would be used as a metaphor for the authors' interdisciplinary collaboration and more specifically as a project that explores the difficulties of collaboration. As both authors were initially ambivalent about the process of creative collaboration the need for a precise structure emerged, this was defined according to the Phi ratios. Foremost among the devices used by the project was an algorithmic starting point, a set of rules and procedures for instigating the writing process. Even if the algorithm provided a precise structure for the word- count in each room the collaboration was not easy to start with. The rules were set from the very beginning raising worries about borders.

One of the authors felt uneasy with the idea of swapping books because she wanted to have a clear distinction of which book-house belongs to whom. She did not want anyone to wander around her house. She suggested that the authors should sent their response to each other story via e-mail and then each of them would stick the other person's story in their own house-book. This idea worried the second author too much. Being a professional designer the second author was worried about would her text be printed and stuck in the book. As the author said:

What if she typed my story with tiny letters hidden near the spine of the book? I also wanted to see how her stories looked physically in her book. Just reading a text file was not enough. I wanted to see the little spots, the places where the ink was thicker, how it was all placed in the page; I wanted to smell the glue to feel how she had made it. (Antonopoulou, Dare, 2008)

Both authors were fighting against loss of control. After negotiation the authors agreed that they would start swapping books. However, it was suggested that, if this felt uncomfortable they would reside to the idea of just keeping their own book-house and exchanging stories via e-mail, on condition that they would show how they had positioned each other's responses inside their individual book-houses. The struggle continued when the author that initially wanted control over her book not only wrote her 100 words for her first room but added a couple more pages of notes asserting that they would fit in a cupboard. The other author felt that not only the foundation schema but also the communication of the project was at stake since the stories were blended with extra words and messy notes. In her attempt to bring back part of the structure and separate the word specific stories from the notes, she set new rules for her house-book. She instructed that in her house any note pages had to be cut smaller and have a different color of paper so that a potential reader could easily separate the stories from the notes. The other author could not do anything but agreed. This was our first collaboration lesson; the learning was to take things from each other, set rules and negotiate. Each of the authors should comply with the rules of the other's book. Rules were set rules, walls were built and compromises were made. The authors highly value the constraints and fears of collaboration as a method to facilitate collaborative learning. Therefore, they extemporised their own organic research paradigm that accommodated complexity and contradiction rather than framing them as inconvenient variables. Both authors found the constraints of the algorithm initially supportive, but ultimately claustrophobic, and opted instead for an old-fashioned inter-subjective power struggle.

Rules are often questionable in their interpretation, but also as being entirely context specific they often cease to have a reason of existence when the situation changes. By the end of the project, the borders and rules were set and there was a rebellion against structure. The author who initially objected to merge the text with the notes decided to rebel against her decision mixing them all up, she also created pages with no text at all naming them sleeping pages and invited others to write her text.

By the time we reached room six, I had already instigated a full scale rebellion against the phi ratios, bursting out of their numerical constraints and inviting readers to do the same by writing their own stories. I felt that the story should be at the same space with the theory, as narrative writing is next to referenced text. I went back to previous stories and draw, filling the void space; I was a rebel, I wanted to celebrate that. Eleanor joined in the rebellion by reverting to code, which is, of course, a type of language. At the same she wrote in my territory, tunnelling into one of my rooms, and leaving words as provocations. She used stardust in her illustrations and these specks of shiny little dots where transferred into the whole book. That was the collaborative contamination. The walls were built to be broken down, when we felt that our rules were well established and not needed anymore. We loved both books equally. (Antonopoulou, Dare, 2010)

Tight structures and territories were finally abolished to give birth to a healthy, wall-free, unlimited collaboration schema. The project could be considered as a paradigm of joining two individual practices and ending up with a common result that celebrates both collaboration and individuality. Valuing the difficulties, tensions and power struggles of collaboration the authors recognized that they have been affected by the interaction, they have developed and changed collectively. The authors frame this as an outcome of collective learning within a community of practice. In this case, the authors frame the networked creation of stories (writing, illustration) as a Community of creative writing Practice. As the background to this chapter has elucidated, Communities of Practice are "important social structures through which people create, refine, share and learn knowledge" (Gibbs et al, 2012). At the same time, the authors' writing is both diverse and integrated, reflecting individual interpretations within a collective neighborhood. In exchanging each others' materials and being required to write a recapitulative account of them both authors clearly felt the need to undergo a transfer of consciousness, even of qualia, or ineffable raw feels, the subjective experiences of being that Daniel Dennett characterises as 'the ways things seem to us' (Dennett, 1988). These experiences, (which, it has to be said, are the subject of philosophical contention) cannot clearly be represented within an a priori, symbolic, system of making; as such they represent the beginning of a significant modification of the project's underlying foundations and a similarly significant change in practice.

The notion of transfection suggests an invasive form of transfer, a mutating, and, an unwelcome form of transduction. In the note post hoc explanations one of the authors wrote that "transfection takes place through membranes, including walls. The transfer of materials mutates my constitution" (Antonopoulou, Dare, 2008). Even earlier in the project the other author began to report, via a fictional character, the notion that her thoughts did not belong to her "I suffocate hearing to my neighbor's suppositions. "She places her ego in my thoughts, in front of my eyes, in the tip of my tongue." (Agent A, Book A, room 5.1, 2009:37). As both authors generate more and more post-hoc material, in the form of meta-critical notes about their own fictions and practices, the distinction between their private thoughts became more blurred.

Although I know little about her it would be accurate to say that Elizabeth Cho is the closest person to me in the world. If, for some reason, we pressed ourselves flat like geckos against the party wall that separates our two homes there would be less than six inches between us. Her life resonates through the cool brick border. Recently I've moved my bed into the fifth room so I can hear her heart beating at night. It punctuates my sleep like the touch of an unborn twin. (Antonopoulou, Dare, 2008)

The authors were initially two people with very different cultural backgrounds, (one stereotypically English viewing her house as a neurotic fortress of insulation and the other viewing her house as a big open space that everyone is invited) changed through the collaboration. After the 'collaborative contamination' both authors wrote in the books about their thought amalgamation, their new voice and identity shift. "My thoughts are an unstable compound of second-order translations and miss-hearings". *(Antonopoulou, Dare, 2008)*

The tape recorder was an artificial voice. A voice that made us wonder about our identity. That made us unable to recognise ourselves. We have become something different through the process but still not similar to each other. (...) This voice was the one transforming everything into something else. She was transforming me to something else too, she was making up new dialogues and thoughts. She was using mottos from the TV and comics. Was that voice mine? Were those thoughts my own? (Antonopoulou, Dare, 2008)

Similarly to the rooms of the two houses, which are the uncanny mirror of each other, though it contains different objects and different atmospheres, the authors analogise themselves as two subjects. Professor Polya put it: 'The analogy of these systems consists in this community of relations' (37). Building a community of relations has been the architectural foundation for the Phi Books, to initially find the correct proportions with which to model the project and then collectively reposition themselves in their individual path and place. "Self doesn't just burst forth its social encounters.(…) Stories of the self don't simply happen, they are actively composed in relation to others" (Holstein, Gubrium, 2000, p.124).

The books were a chance to discuss the authors' research fields and filter them through narrative. It is not possible for the authors to separate this project from their greater research. 'Creative knowledge cannot be abstracted by the loom that produced it. Inseparable from its process, it resembles the art of sending the woof-thread through the warp.' (Carter, 2004, p.1). The force that I could feel through the walls of my own deterministic structures was uncertainty, Gaver et al (2004) describe this 'pervasive sense of uncertainty' in positive terms, acknowledging the value of 'play, exploration and subjective interpretation', particularly in response to the limits of individual knowledge. In the context of such an intensive collaboration as that of the production of the Phi Books, it seems right to acknowledge and perhaps even to capitalize upon the limits of mutual understanding; exploration, is after all, about entering unknown territories. One of the authors said that the Phi Books allowed her to investigate the unknown territory both the practice and the inter-subjective, creative, engagement with the other author. At the same time the other author realised how the metaphor and the ambivalence of the stories and the notes can be a way to transform tacit knowledge about her research subject matter into conscious explicit thoughts.

Once the authors have realised the leaning outcomes and have become an integrated system, within a wall free collaboration space, they decided to open up the collaboration to others. The books were fragmented to offer their contents to others. People were leaving responses on random room stories from the books.

The book is bursting from its bindings; it contains many different sheets of drawings, notes, collages, found objects, messy pastel pages and loose sheets of transparent papers. Despite its chaotic appearance the briefest examination of the book reveals an inherent structure that will be familiar to many people. (Antonopoulou, Dare, 2008)

This way not only the book form but also the authors' collaborative systems were destructed giving space for new learning within a more extended community of practice. This constant destruction underpinned that the Phi books offered a learning methodology based on open-ended, asymmetries and tensions, which are always present in collaboration. The destruction continued while the authors used the motion capture - gesture recognition system to mediate the participants' physical performance while narrating their house stories. While the system was eradicating the participants' physical presence leaving just a representation of the way they move, it became more difficult to define identities and relationships during the collaboration. It was the agency of the technology that destructed this time and led to new learning outcomes.

The idea that technologies have agency that interacts with the participants was evident throughout the project. This way the project becomes "a performative space' where "the system expresses the author's ideas. The system is both a messenger for and a message from the author' " (Sengers & Mateas, 2003, p. 167). For example, the authors viewed the books as organisms with agency and authorship.

I am the voice of the book you are writing on, your thoughts belong to me, you are part of the white pages, plain material, ink and paper, you belong to everyone that holds me, you do not exist on your own. I am the carnival, I am what others see, I belong to everyone and you belong to me. (Antonopoulou, Dare, 2008)

In addition to being in collaboration with the book the authors wrote stories on the agency of a machine called the utopia machine.

This is a voice from the flat next door. I am not a human; I am just a utopia machine, a placebo for my neighbors. I am helping them to hear their thoughts; they justify them through my existence. I might be an artificial pulse for the person living on the right of my flat, something completely different for someone else. I only wish there was another machine elsewhere, to hear myself ... the machine. (Antonopoulou, Dare, 2008)

Once authors have explored the technological agency and its outcomes in the Phi Books they came up with the Digital Dreamhacker project which is in itself a commentary on the inevitable nature of technological remediation even in the most unconscious aspect of human lives such as dreams. In this case the randomness of technological agency offered a space for a community of 'dream practice' to discuss and evolve (Antonopoulou, Dare 2013). At the same time, the idea that the Dreamhacker computational system is, similarly to the dreamer, in an unconscious dream state itself (while processing language that does not understand the context of its meaning) connected the machine with the person.

The notion of digital or literary materiality may seem anathema, yet many theorists, including Katherine N. Hayles have observed that literature is not and never has been immaterial: "Literary texts, like us, have bodies, an actuality necessitating that their materialities and meanings are deeply interwoven with each other" (Hayles, 2002, p. 107). Both Phi Books and the Dreamhacker projects can in many ways be characterised as algorithmic and procedural, but also as a re-mediation of materialities from computational to literary forms and the opposite. They exemplify a recursive and perpetual form of regeneration based on the push and pull, the acceptance & the resistance, the learning and misunderstanding. The acts of rebellion described are acts of creative investigation, a source of critical tension, that contests orthodox notions of interactivity and results in learning.

Creating, Refining and Sharing Through Recursive Transfer in the Phi Books

Through engaging with a Community of Practice aggregated around blog posts and emails, the theme of recursion has emerged as a core feature of the online collaborative process. Recursion has been recognised as a feature of successful collaborative communities, "As I have learned from geeks, structures of communication are not inevitable, given, or neutral; for any public to become a sovereign entity in contemporary technical societies, it must be recursive" (Kelty, 2005, p. 204)

Upon completion of each story written for the Phi Books project the authors agreed to exchange each others' books, this entailed accessing, analysing and reacting to their most recent story before completing a new one. In this way the authors wrote two stories for each room, one for each book. These bipartite fictions can be conceptualized as consisting of an exposition (or initial presentation) and a recapitulation, echoing existing themes as a form of secondary development containing radically new material.

The authors frame this process as 'recursive transfer', a form of *a posteriori* knowledge generation involving an epistemological shift from the constraints of a computational process to one that is more 'intuitive' or tacitly oriented. Graeme Sullivan describes this type of conceptual disruption as a form of knowledge creation that 'exists between theory and practice, and beyond assumed discipline boundaries' (Sullivan, 2005, p.152). Sullivan articulates the need for conceptual and theoretical mobility amongst creative practitioners working with and within heterogeneous systems:

For artists working within the general area designated Making in Systems there is a desire to move beyond discipline boundaries and into areas of inquiry that interact and intersect and require new ways to conceptualize forms and structures. For instance, artist-theorists working at the interface of art and science within the digital environment are finding that past notions of theory and practice no longer serve as adequate systems around which to define plans and actions. (Sullivan, 2005, p.152)

The authors propose that recursive transfer is a useful concept for understanding the collaborative processes that occur via online Communities of Practice. Designers may be more familiar with the notion of recursive or iterative processes, of designing, testing and measuring, then redesigning in repeated cycles. Baldwin and Clark state 'Human designers can and do operate recursively in their imaginations' (Baldwin et al, 1999, p. 231), they describe recursion (particularly via modularisation) in design as the ability to partition complex problems and 'create abstractions that simplify the relationships among parts' (Baldwin et al, 1999, p. 230), adding 'it is a change in the design of a process that changes designs' (Baldwin et al, 1999, p. 230). Like conversation, the recursive process of creative collaboration have many tacit dimensions, often the fictional stories most effectively articulated the tacit aspects of collaboration: "Stories were like a secret code, a silent and camouflaged set of communication rules. We needed the stories to continue to communicate with each other " (Antonopoulou & Dare, 2009, p. 90).

Over time the collaboration has become more performative, involving the acting out and re-enactment of core stages in the writing process. The authors have used narrative and craft (such as making their own books and macquettes, or theatrical models of story scenes) as well as performances that explore how boundaries and openings in the form of metaphorical and physical borders (walls and doors) can facilitate collaboration. The metaphor of walls and doors that emerged in the stories was also present in the form of rules about the collaborative process and occasions when those rules were spontaneously abandoned, such as the introduction of sounds and spoken performance into the story telling process.

Interactive Film and Motion Capture in the Phi Books

The author's first move into a performative domain of collaborative writing occurred through the creation of the *Phi Meta Film,* this was an interactive computer program written in Processing. The author's custom-made software enabled them to project a film version of the Phi Book's stories while also filming the audience. In this way live images of the audience were merged into a new version of the *Phi Meta Film.* Each member of the audience signalled their willingness to participate by wearing coloured stickers. However, the application playing with the inevitable nature of participation, was slowly appearing the live filming of the all the participants' bodies within the walls of a house we were presenting. The authors said 'Did you hear a smooth, metallic mechanism over by the door? A series of automatic locks have been activated. You are now confined in this room. Your detention gives you all ample opportunity to enjoy the fruits of participatory performance '(Antonopoulou, Dare, 2010).

The collaborative filming process of the *Phi Meta Film* as well as the embodied quality of the research process, increasingly suffused the author's respective vocabularies. The verbal and visual materials generated by the authors bore the unmistakeably kinaesthetic references of embodied agents, for example, one of the authors wrote: "I cannot breathe any more. I am trying to look through windows" (Antonopoulou & Dare, 2008)

Observing their own emergent narrative themes and vocabulaic patterns inspired the authors to ask new participants to recount stories while being filmed by a twelve camera motion capture system. By exerting a clear set of constraints upon the participants – suggesting what thematic areas they should recount (stories about rooms they had worked in) the authors were able to "maintain the logic of the phi ratios in our performance as we did in our writing. We aimed to connect the linguistic to the sonic and to the spatial constraints of our collaboration" (Antonopoulou & Dare, 2012, p. 93).

In 2010 the authors invited participants to relate their stories while having their gestures mapped in the motion capture studio at Goldsmiths University of London. Via this system the cameras were able to "record the participants' house performances with video cameras in order to compare their graphically represented movement with their psychical self-represented performances. This enabled us to extrapolate new layers of embodied narrative and subjective articulation." (Antonopoulou & Dare, 2012, pp 99 – 100).

In examining these gestures (particularly their own) the authors identified a range of significant narrative motifs, for example gestures that seemed to signify *ongoing thoughts*, *emphatic images* and *tentativeness*. Two of these gestures are depicted in figure 4:

The resulting gestures were highly subjective with little scope for a generalisable grammar, different participants had their own range of unique gestural motifs, additionally, not all subjects had clearly discernible, linear meanings associated with their gestures. But in observing the author's own gestures it became clear that an additional layer of meaning was available to them in understanding each other and the narratives they created.

The Phi Books became spatial (physical-virtual). They are now spatial neighbourhoods and territories, but we still want to call our project the 'Phi Books' as we believe that a book can be spatial, performable and independent, detached from its ordinary form (Antonopoulou & Dare, 2012, pp. 99 – 100).

The authors propose that considering the embodied aspects of collaboration, such as gesture (and its absence) has the potential to provide collaborators with another set of communicative tools, identifying, for example, tensions, reticence, and unspoken feelings. This may have beneficial implications, particu-

Figure 4. Gestures signifying ongoing thoughts and emphatic images

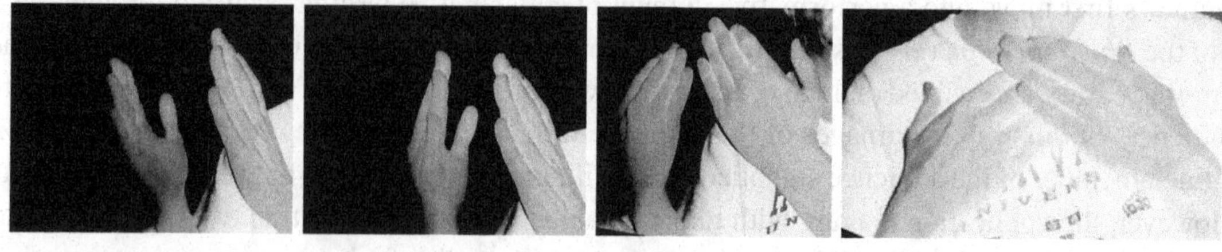

larly for cross cultural collaboration and communication via visual online systems such as Skype. While it is hard to envisage a computer system that can automatically ascribe precise generalised meanings to human gestures, it is practicable to develop a system in which humans and computers collaborate, jointly constructing a morphology of individual gestures. Such a system might usefully be deployed for online collaboration. Likewise, the authors propose that a re-framing of tools such as Social Network Analysis within a situated and embodied methodology might constructively support creative collaboration, as the second case study will illustrate.

The Social Imaginary: Humans and Computers Working Together in the Digital Dreamhacker

The digital Dreamhacker is an asymmetrical collaborative system, one in which humans and computers work together. By drawing upon the idea of the Social Imaginary, in which the crowdsourced dreams form "a set of stories and narratives that are indistinguishable from practice" (Kelty, 2005, p. 201), the Dreamhacker application "throws light on this cultural, social and technological mediation of our dreams" (Antonopoulou & Dare, 2013, p. 1). An example of how the social and the personal are intertwined and manifest in dreams is evidenced in the often quoted example of how people in the early days of television dreamt in black and white but started to dream in colour when colour TV services began.

Dreaming is a widespread human experience but the surreality and illogic of dreams makes it hard to theorize or formalize dreaming within computational systems. The project acknowledges the most recent scientific understanding of dreams, in which the focus is placed upon the context and from of dreams instead of their specific content, but it also seeks to highlight the subjective and irreducible nature of visual interpretation, deploying arbitrarily crowdsourced images which no computer system can understand in human terms. The Dreamhacker system chooses images by matching their meta-data tags to the user's key words, but it has no ability to refine its choice of images according to aesthetic or narrative criteria. The collaboration involved in a computational system is therefore inherently asymmetrical, one that entails as many accidents and misunderstandings as serendipitous decisions. The project does not seek to disguise or gloss over the differences in understanding between human and computers, indeed, the authors believe it is imperative to design systems that can perspicaciously approach such differences.

The asymmetrical collaboration involved in the Dreamhacker system, is, like dreams themselves, inherently generative of ambiguity, the type of collaboration that results is far harder to frame within the instrumentalist teleology of learning theory and Social Capital, nor is it about self-expression and artistry:

The project is not about an individualist form of hacking, nor is it about individual identities and personalised imagery. The project is about hacking into the Social Imaginary, which, in this context, refers to the collective representation of our inter-subjective experiences and their associated symbolism. ... It is about the social aspect of dreams, which is expanded in the final step in the Dreamhacking operation where dream visualisations are uploaded onto the Social Web. In this way they are gestated and hatched through dialogue, collaborative interpretation and further re-shaping. (Antonopoulou & Dare, 2013, p. 1)

The role of social networks and their analysis in the Dreamhacking project is elucidated in the following section.

Networks

The Dreamhacker project explores how the illogic of dreams can be embedded into new computational paradigms, the aim being to create a collaborative network in which dreamers can research the nature of their own and other's dreams. One of the main strategies deployed by the Dreamhacker project has been the use of social network analysis, predicated on the idea that:

Social behaviours cannot be fully understood without considering the network structures that underlie them. Developments in network theory provide us with relevant modelling tools. (Noble et al, 2004, p. 1)

The dreams of Dreamhacker users are framed as connectors in a wider communication and data storage system. It is these connections, or the network topology (the structure of networks in the language of network analysis) of such connections that can provide a broader framework for analysing dreams. For such a methodical analysis to be possible the dreams are characterised as nodes (actors) and the relationships between dreams as ties. By analysing the distributions and connections of nodes and ties in the Dreamhacker Social Network, a number of key structural metrics can be observed, three of these are framed by the authors as: dreamer propinquity, dreamer cliques and dreamer multiplexity.

Dreamer-propinquity provides a measure of how well connected dreams are, this can encompass a nexus of content or form. Dreamer cliques consist of subgroups or communities linked by content or form and dreamer multiplexity reveals the overlapping networks of a potentially vast, intricate, global Social Imaginary (Antonopoulou & Dare, 2013, pps 2-3). For example dreamers may also connect to networks of news events, writing groups, social trends as well as conventional social networks such as Facebook.

The provocative pleasures of engineering such complications are implicit, the themes that emanate from such provocations are perhaps more surprising, not least for their congruence with many of the familiar challenges faced by collaborative projects, such as challenges of communication, interpretation and establishing common intentions. The work represented in the Phi Books project and the Digital Dreamhacker allows for multiple interpretation and multi-linear outcomes. The recursive structures and processes embedded in these projects are anti-teleological, offering a complex, hybridized methodology that is consistently reflexive and dynamic. The specific form of social network analysis deployed on the Dreamhacker data is now explained, as well as the wider implications of using data analysis for collaborative online projects (see Figure 5).

In 1963 Goffman observed that the process of inter human communication is one of regulation and order, in which, when:

persons are present to one another they can function not merely as physical instruments but also as communicative ones. This possibility, no less than the physical one, is fateful for everyone concerned and in every society appears to come under strict normative regulation, giving rise to a kind of communication traffic order. (Goffman, 1963. pp. 23 - 24)

This order, the authors argue, is closely connected to the idea of the social imaginary, and is one that can usefully be integrated with social network analysis for collaborative communities of practice. What follows is a description of a social network analysis of the Dreamhacker Community of Practice data, revealing, the authors argue, significant aspects of Goffman's 'communication traffic order'.

Figure 5. The Dreamhacker dream themes visualised as a network of nodes and ties

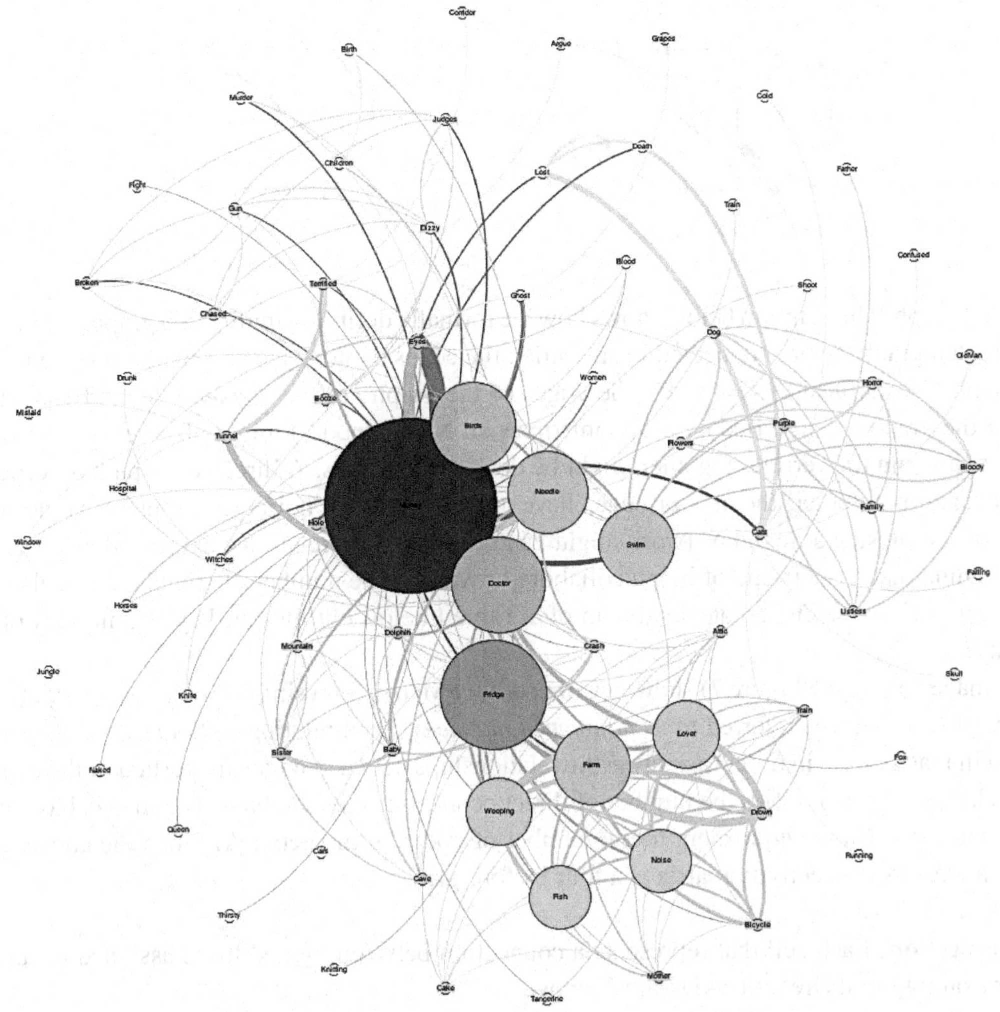

Graph Theory Basics

Earlier this chapter outlined how the Digital Dreamhacker and the Phi Books projects deployed networked systems of collaborative communication, this section will look in more detail at the techniques used to analyse collaborative creative networks. Before proceeding to explain the techniques used to analyse the Dreamhacker collaborative network a brief introduction to graph theory follows.

A graph is a set of ties among nodes. In the context of Social Network Analysis a graph, denoted by the letter G (or D for a digraph), consists of a set of vertices (or nodes) signified by the letter V. Vertices might represent individuals, groups or objects. Vertices are connected by a set of edges (or ties), denoted by the letter E, representing the relationships between individuals, groups and objects. An edge (a,b) means that a and b have a relation or a ↔ b; for instance, a and b may be friends or collaborators. Edge (a,b) might also imply edge (b,a) meaning the graph is not directed – it is formally known as an

Figure 6. A directed graph on the left and an undirected graph on the right

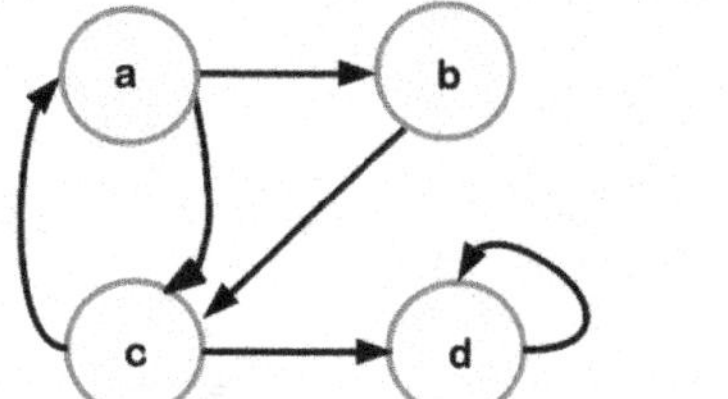

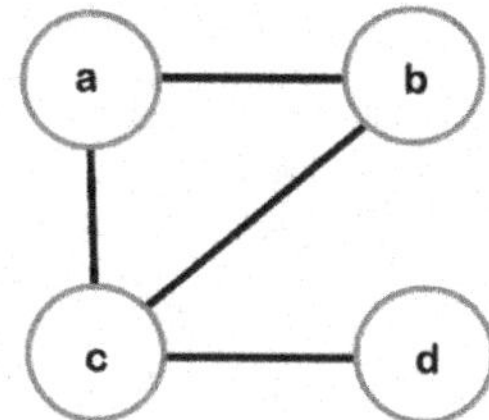

undirected graph. The diagram below shows how we formally define an undirected graph, the vertices of an undirected graph are not connected in any order, the edges do not have an orientation (see Figure 6).

A graph G is defined as G=(V, E), the edges of the graph are the *elements* of E. The vertices or nodes of the graph are signified by a V, sometimes an N (for 'node') might also be used. Informally, the edges that join the vertices together might be described as lines. A directed graph has vertices that are connected in an order, the arcs or edges have an *orientation*. Undirected graphs have no order or orientation. Analysing a Social Network might capture friendship relations, expressed as for example, (a,b), meaning that a is a friend of b or a collaborator with b. The number of friends of a is also known as the *degree* of a or the immediate neighbour of a. Table 1 below outlines the key terminology of Social Network Analysis.

The image above (see Figure 7) shows a Connectivity Matrix for a simple Social Network of dreams, these are also sometimes referred to as *adjacency matrices*. Data relating to Social Networks is often arranged in matrix form in order to analyse the relationships between nodes, in particular the degrees of those nodes (a degree signifies the number of direct connections a node has). The matrix has a number of rows and cells that are equivalent to the number of nodes in the network. Since the above network has four nodes, its connectivity matrix is a four by four grid.

- **Connection:** Each cell that represents a connection between two nodes is assigned a value of 1, for example, cell Dream B – Dream C above.
- **Non-Connection:** A cell that does not signify a direct connection is assigned a value of 0, as in cell Dream D – Dream A.

Table 1. Key social network analysis terminology

Key Social Network Analysis terminology
Size = the number of nodes
Density = the number of ties that are present or the amount of ties that could be present (strong-weak ties)
Degree = a degree signifies the number of direct connections a node has
Out-degree = the sum of connections from an actor to others
In-degree = the sum of connections to an actor
Walk = a sequence of actors and relations that begins and ends with actors
Geodesic distance = the number of relations in the shortest possible walk from one actor to another
Closeness centrality = the distance of one actor to all others in the network
Betweenness centrality = the number that represents how frequently an actor is between other actors' geodesic paths
Cliques = sub-sets of actors, more closely tied to each other than to actors who are not part of the sub-set, also known as segmentations, partitions and communities.

Figure 7. Connectivity (adjacency) Matrix and network diagram for four dreams

	Dream A	Dream B	Dream C	Dream D
Dream A	-	1	0	0
Dream B	1	-	1	0
Dream C	1	1	-	1
Dream D	0	0	1	-

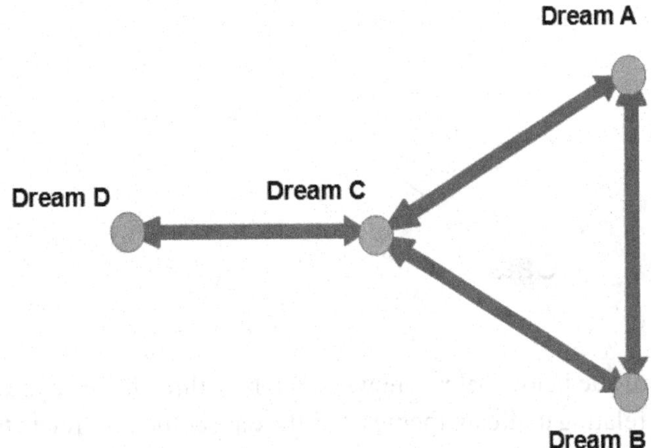

- If all of the connections in the network are bi-directional (meaning that a movement is possible from node Dream C to node Dream D and vice-versa), the connectivity matrix is defined as being *transposable.*

Adding up a row or a column gives the *degree* of a node. Node Dream D in the example above is the least connected as it has the lowest *summation of connectivity* in this network. However, this should not be assumed to be a scalable situation in a more complex, larger network. For example, if there are a large number of indirect paths which have not been considered in the connectivity matrix.

Social Network Analysis with Gephi

It is important to recognise that the "unit of analysis in network analysis is not the individual, but an entity consisting of a collection of individuals and the linkages among them" (Wasserman et al, 1994, p. 5). An adjacency matrix is only the starting point for Social Network Analysis, before reaching even that point, significant effort is put into pre- processing or preparing data for analysis. There are a number of file types which network data can be represented in, including *.xml*, *.csv* (comma separated values), excel spreadsheets, programmed structures such as R's tables and data frames (R is a statistical and machine learning programming language), and *.gml* or *Graph Modelling Language* files which the authors used for the Dreamhacker data.

Figure 8. The simple example. gml file visualised with Gephi graph visualisation software

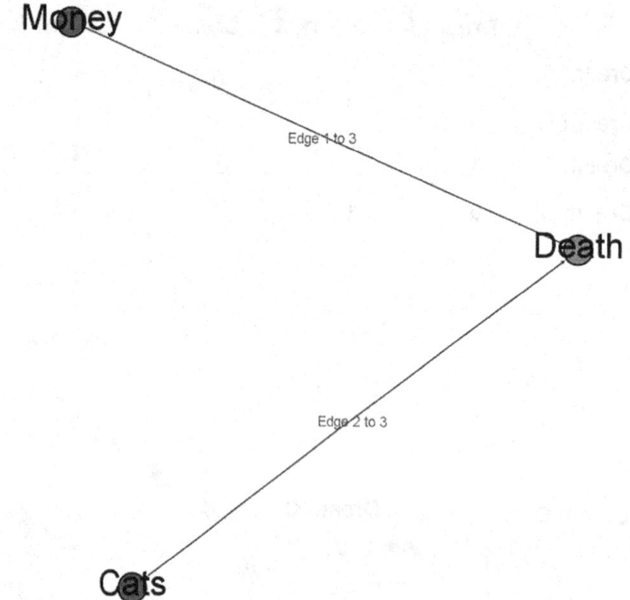

The example of a .gml file below below shows a graph of three nodes and two edges. The data describes nodes and edges relating to dream themes, but the data could also relate to the context of dreams and the affective state of dreamers, or any other type of node and edge relationship. The data can be cross-referenced to individuals and their attributes for further analysis. Weightings might also be added to the edge data to emphasise factors such as frequency of interaction and kinship etc. For this analysis the authors were interested in emergent patterns among the dream themes themselves, dreams were therefore treated as actors within a social network.

The first Dreamhacker Social Network Analysis looked at the connectivity of nodes using the social network analysis (graph visualisation) tool *Gephi.* The data that was examined related to co-occurrences of dream themes. The visual output of this analysis is depicted in Figure 8. Themes relating to money, cats, doctors, death and birds emerged with a high degree (of direct connection), these themes can be described as *hubs, focal nodes, ego networks* or *connectors*. The image below shows the ego network for the dream theme of *cats*.

Egos and Neighbourhoods of Dreams

An ego is an individual node or actor, it is the smallest atom of a social network. Analysing an ego and its network patterns can reveal the strength of an actor's relationships. Egos may have important structural roles within a network, serving as highly connected hubs, while others might act as bridges connecting more isolated but innovative nodes, all of this information is arguably useful for networks of collaborators and for communities of practice.

An ego network can be defined as a network "consisting of a single actor (ego) together with the actors they are connected to (alters) and all the links among those alters" (Borgatti, 2005, p. 31). In the figure below the nodes that connect to the cat theme are therefore its *alters* (alter egos). The alters *money, death*

Figure 9. Ego-network for the dream theme of 'cats'

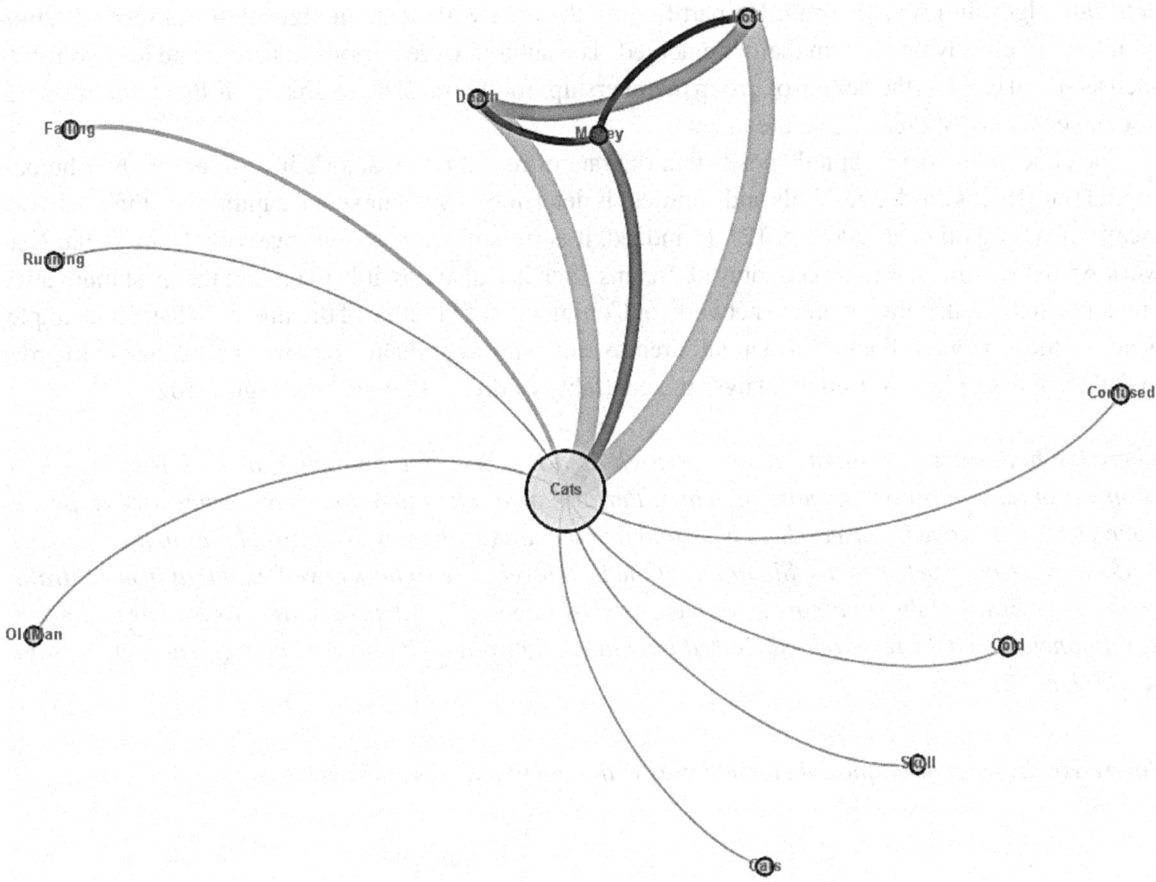

and *lost* are tied to each other. In a conventional social network of human actors there would also be ties relating to social, cognitive-affective states ('likes' etc) and actions (such as communication and other social interactions). These factors can be cross-correlated to demographic data about individual dreamers.

A diverse ego-network is often cited as being advantageous, offering the nodes in that network a greater chance of obtaining what they need, while weak ties within a network are sometimes framed as disadvantageous. However, Granovetter (1973) offers a more nuanced view of weak ties in an ego network:

Such linkage generates paradoxes: weak ties, often denounced as generative of alienation...are here seen as indispensable to individuals' opportunities and to their integration into communities; strong ties, breeding local cohesion, lead to overall fragmentation. (Granovetter, 1973, p.530) (see Figure 9)

The approach outlined above is in keeping with the principal that "the primary focus of network research in the social sciences has been on the consequences of networks. Perhaps the most fundamental axiom in social network research is that a node's position in a network determines in part the opportunities and constraints that it encounters, and in this way plays an important role in a node's outcomes" (Borgatti et al, 2009, p. 12).

In order to detect the significant sub-sets of nodes within the larger Dreamhacker data *a community detection* algorithm was also run. By partitioning the data with such an algorithm, subsets, or 'communities" of closely tied dream themes emerged. The authors were curious to investigate how concepts such as social capital (the degree of group membership) might translate to dreams, is there, for example, a social economy of dreams and dreamers?

The concept of social capital "posits that the rate of return on an actor's investment in their human capital (i.e., their knowledge, skills and abilities) is determined by their social capital (i.e., their network location)" (Borgatti et al, 2009, p. 12). If, indeed, it is possible to usefully 'read off' from Social Network Analytic principals to an economy of dreams, then is it also possible to predict the most innovative dreamers in the collaborative dream network, or Community of Practice of dreamers? What, for example, were the most 'powerful' and 'influential' dreams, and who were the most powerful dreamers? In order to deduce this Gephi was used to analyse the centrality of dream themes (See Figure 10):

where the nodes are individuals, a key research area has been the prediction of similarity in time to adoption of an innovation for pairs of actors. Performance refers to a node's outcomes with respect to some good. For example, researchers have found that actors with more structural holes in their ego networks at work have better ideas. Similarly, at the firm level, researchers have found that firm centrality predicts the firm's ability to innovate, as measured by number of patents secured, as well as to perform well financially. Other research has linked individual centrality with power and influence. (Borgatti et al, 2009, p. 12)

Figure 10. Sub-sets or cliques of communities with the Dreamhacker dream data

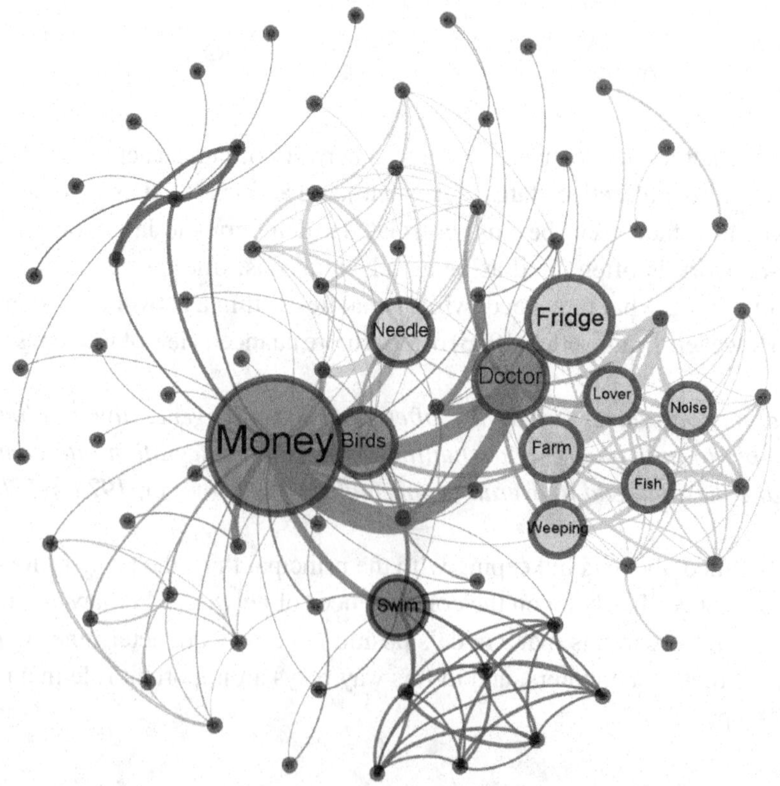

The centrality of a dream themes such as *money,* does not necessarily imply a high degree of connectivity to other themes. Less central nodes may still have more thematic overlap (connectivity) with other dream themes. *Money* as a theme has a high degree centrality, meaning direct links to other nodes, but other less degree central nodes are more advantageously placed to connect with the wider reaches of the Dreamhacker network. Such nodes may act as *brokers* or *bridges* to wider parts of the network, they may have fewer connections but a greater *betweenness centrality*. The analogy with human collaborators is clear, sever certain, apparently less central nodes, and other parts of the collaborative network may become completely isolated. There is ample scope to develop warning and nurturing systems for collaborative networks, as well as for using the dates and geographic locations of dreamers to investigate whether major situating events, such as economic shifts and weather patterns, as well as personal events, have any significant impact on the themes dreamers report dreaming about.

While some of these concepts are hard to instrumentalise in regard to dreams, the identification of generative nodes, those that are conducive to innovation and effective interaction, may have far more practical implications for other types of creative collaboration, and for identifying potential collaborators within Communities of Practice. Matching, for example, actors who are able to originate new ideas with actors who have the pragmatic skills to do something with those ideas can be facilitated by, for example, identifying structural holes (disrupted or absent connections in networks), such an analysis may have positive outcomes within collaborative networks.

The simple forms of Social Network Analysis applied to the Dreamhacker data have suggested many useful ways of understanding and working within collaborative networks, it is important to recognise that there are many ways of analysing such data, including predictive modelling and very complex statistical processes which have not been mentioned here, in particular the very detailed ways of examining the interaction of actors within a network, as outlined by Burt (1992). It should also be noted that Social Network Analysis may be more effective when working with very large data sets, however this is not a straightforward assumption, unlike "conventional data, network data typically do not have an unambiguous notion of sample size." (Kolaczyk et al, 2012). Depending "strongly on the model assumed for how the network scales. In particular, in the case of reciprocity, whether or not the model for scaling takes into account the notion of preexisting relationship affects whether reciprocity is even meaningful for large networks." (Kolaczyk et al, 2012)

Social Network Analysis can provide mechanisms for addressing emerging problems as well as opportunities within collaborative online communities, for example the concept of balancing social networks aims to neutralize: "issues to facilitate the flow of knowledge within the network. After identifying nodes that can disturb or block the flow of knowledge (i.e. isolated nodes, relationship concentrators, etc.) .(Monclar et al, 2011, p. 564)

The authors conclude that the implications of Social Network Analysis for online learning and collaboration have still not been fully realised, in the future these tools might be more fully integrated with the familiar data analytics provided by companies such as Google and Amazon as well as to Communities of Practice and virtual learning environments. The final sections will look at the author's solutions and recommendations, finishing with a brief overview of the implications for future research raised by the Phi Books and the digital Dreamhacker projects.

SOLUTIONS AND RECOMMENDATIONS

This chapter has illustrated by pragmatic examples as well as through theoretical evidence the importance of social networks for e-collaboration. The authors have built a case for deploying grounded, mathematical tools in support of online collaborative communities. In particular the chapter has built a case of the Community of Practice as a core component of effective, digitally mediated creative collaboration online in tandem with techniques from Social Network Analysis. This idea is supported by a growing number of theorists and practitioners, for whom the community of practice has become a central agent in the process of acquiring and circulating knowledge. Ideally, the authors propose, the knowledge circulated in such communities should consist of both tacit, embodied and more conventional forms of curriculum or declarative knowledge. Communities of Practice should offer collaborators a self-defined, self-organising environment in which to develop ideas and gain advantageous support:

Communities of practice are important social structures through which people create, refine, share and learn knowledge. They are self-organizing groups that coalesce around a common interest or endeavor. Through mutual engagement and interaction in the pursuit of these endeavors, these groups develop a repertoire of shared work practices and knowledge, and a sense of joint enterprise (Gibbs et al, 2012 p. 1).

While both authors acknowledge the value of on-line mechanisms and social structures for collaboration, they are also at pains to recognise the problems inherent in computer mediated systems, not least of all the significant problem of computer human interaction and understanding.

However, it is the author's experience that such difficulties can become important material and thematic elements in online collaboration, that misunderstandings, accidents and computational reductionism are unavoidable elements in online interaction. The authors propose a new type of collaborative grammar that incorporates such features, this grammar encompasses network structures, embodied gestures and, as the authors have evidenced throughout this chapter, inherently chaotic, non-interpretable processes such as dreaming, "in keeping with the complex and multifaceted meanings the notion of research-by-practice evokes" (Antonopoulou & Dare, 2013, p. 93). In such a practice, complexity and contradiction should not be approached as inconvenient variables. The constraints and fears inherent in collaboration, as well as the setting of rules, building of walls and making of compromises should eventually enable wall free, more extemporised forms of collaboration.

The authors propose that collaboration is fundamentally processual "in that we are engaged in thinking through doing, generating a dialogue that interrogates and connects" (Antonopoulou & Dare, 2013, p. 93). The projects outlined here have also been a response to the historical shortcomings of models "for both theorizing and practising creative research collaboration, and to an apparent lack of theoretical mobility across diverse disciplines" (Antonopoulou & Dare, 2013, p. 93). Both projects have embedded a methodological commitment to the belief that arts-based practice is generative of new knowledge.

As well as the systems described throughout this chapter the authors urge collaborators to invent their own strategies and systems, bearing in mind as Bennett observes:

The virtual is not unreal neither does it function to inculcate a de-realization. It does not somehow exist 'out there' untouched by reality rather it is continuous with reality; it is part of our reality. The two spheres of activity shape each other in terms of organizational structures, network stability, and capacity (Bennett, 2004a, p. 234).

All human tools and systems, including digital systems, are cultural and socially entangled, replete with their own restrictions and embedded with their own social imaginary – overt and tacit rules and assumptions, the authors urge all e-collaborators to recognise the limits as well as the freedoms provided by digitally mediated systems.

FUTURE RESEARCH DIRECTIONS

Taking a theoretical cue from contemporary online learning theory, this chapter proposes future research into the benefits of collaborative systems that use Social Network Analysis to provide timely and appropriate automated feedback and guidance. Further research is indicated that might explore how intelligent, situated online systems can provide automated, as well as human co-authored feedback and guidance for actors within social networks. The authors aim to undertake research into how machine learning can support creative collaboration by adapting to the interests and needs of creative communities of practice. Such an approach will be underpinned by a methodological commitment to the benefits of embodied, situated computing approaches.

A putative Web 3 might also deploy semantic technologies to identify significant features embedded in online interaction, deploying meta data (semantic mark-up embedded in HTML 5) relating to content such as written communication, but also to physical actions including gestures. In short the semantic web is predicated on the idea of embedding tags that identify meaning within Web pages, the goal being to create a network that is easier to search and analyse, in particular by autonomous computer programs. In order to model semantics usefully collaborators will need to formulate an agreed vocabulary. A vocabulary refers to consistent, well-defined meanings that will work across different contexts.

Constructing a common, standard vocabulary within communities of practice is far from straight forward, as the saying goes "one man's weed is another man's flower". The authors propose the need for research into mechanisms for negotiating the semantic frame of online collaborators, including the use of Game Theoretic tools for mathematically modelling and optimising decisions about semantic meaning, with the proviso that such tools should be situated, including the embodied forms of situation discussed in this chapter. Such mechanisms, the author's propose, will support the emergence of inclusive, enhanced communities that can enrich and support creative collaboration.

CONCLUSION

This chapter has looked at two systems for creative collaboration, the 'Digital Dreamhacker' and the 'Phi Books'. These projects were instigated by the authors in order to investigate creative collaboration, in particular systems for creative writing and for exploring the paradoxical and illogical nature of dreams. Both projects have involved the development of software systems following a methodological commitment to situated, embodied computing, but also to a practice that is supported by mathematical tools such as Social Network Analysis.

The case studies outlined here have explored the implications of technology for the understanding and advancement of innovative collaborative technologies, in particular the chapter showed how motion capture and social network analysis can work together to evolve a situated form of collaborative grammar. The featured projects also provided readers with significant technical and conceptual insights into new modes of collaboration engendered by digital technologies, while also opening a space for further dialogue about the limits and possibilities of e-collaboration. The authors would like to close this chapter by urging readers to develop their own tools for creative collaboration, and to explore the benefits of working within online Communities of Practice, such communities can extend skills and insights while enabling actors to share their own knowledge and forge constructive creative partnerships.

REFERENCES

Adam, A. (1998). *Artificial Knowing, Gender and the Thinking Machine*. London, New York: First Routledge.

Antonopoulou, A. & Dare, E. (2008). 'The Phi Books,' Single edition artist's books.

Antonopoulou, A., & Dare, E. (2009, November 16-18). Berlin Freie Universität, Graduiertenkolleg "InterArt" International Research Training Group "Interart Studies." Berlin.

Antonopoulou, A., & Dare, E. (2010, March). *Inter-art Symposium, Goldsmiths-University of London*, London.

Antonopoulou, A. & Dare, E. (2012). Phi territories: Neighbourhoods of collaboration and participation. *Journal of Writing in Creative Practice*, 5(1), 85–105.

Antonopoulou, A., & Dare, E. (2013). The digital dreamhacker: Crowdsourcing the dream imaginary. In K. Cleland, L. Fisher, & R. Harley (Eds.), *Proceedings of the19th International Symposium of Electronic Art*, ISEA '13, Sydney.

Baldwin, C. Y., & Clark, K. B. (1999). *Design Rules: The Power of Modularity* (Vol. 1). MIT Press.

Bennett, W. L. (2004a). Communicating Global Activism: Strengths and Vulnerabilities of Networked Politics. In W. Van Der Donk, B. D. Loader, & P. G. Nixon et al. (Eds.), *Cyberprotest: New Media, Citizens and Social Movements* (pp. 123–146). London: Routledge.

Borgatti, S. P., Mehra, A., Brass, D. J., & Labianca, G. (2009, February 13). Network Analysis in the Social Sciences. *Science*, *323*(5916), 892–895. doi:10.1126/science.1165821 PMID:19213908

Bremmer, J., & Roodenburg, H. (Eds.). (1993). *A Cultural History of Gesture from Antiquity to the Present Day*. Oxford: Polity Press.

Burt, R. S. (1992). *Structural Holes: The Social Structure of Competition*. Cambridge, MA: Harvard University Press.

Carter, P. (2004). *Material Thinking: the Theory and Practice of Creative Research*. Melbourne, Vic: Melbourne University Press.

Coverdale, A. (2008). Critique of Connectivism [blog post]. Retrieved from https://sites.google.com/site/andycoverdale/texts/critique-of-connectivism

Dennett, D. (1988). Quining Qualia. In A. Marcel, & E. Bisiach (Eds.), Consciousness in Contemporary Society (pp. 43-77). Oxford University Press.

Dourish, P. (2000). A Foundational Framework for Situated Computing. Position paper for the CHI 2000 *Workshop on Situated Computing: A Research Agenda.*

Duke, B., Harper, G., & Johnston, M. (2013). Connectivism as a Digital Age Learning Theory. *The HETL Review* (Special Issue), 2013. Retrieved from https://www.hetl.org/ihr-special-issues/

Everett, M., & Borgatti, S. P. (2005). Ego network betweenness. *Social Networks*, *27*(1), 31–38. doi:10.1016/j.socnet.2004.11.007

Fullan, M. (2013). The New Pedagogy: Students and Teachers as Learning Partners. *LEARNing Landscapes, 6*(2).

Gaver, B., Boucher, A., Pennington, S., & Walker, B. (2004). Cultural Probes and The value of Uncertainty. *Interaction, 11*(5), 53–56. doi:10.1145/1015530.1015555

Gibbs, M. R., Wadley, G., & Ng, S. (2012, October 27-29). Using "simple" technology to support geographically distributed communities of practice. Proceedings of the 2012 IEEE Conference on Technology and Society in Asia (T&SA) (pp. 1, 6).

Goffman, E. (1963). *Behavior in public places: notes on the social organization of gatherings*. New York: Free Press of Glencoe.

Granovetter, M. (1973). The Strength of Weak Ties. *American Journal of Sociology*, *78*(6), 1360–1380. doi:10.1086/225469

Hanneman, R. A. (2001). Introduction to Social Network Methods. Retrieved from http://www.research-methods.org/NETTEXT.pdf

Hayles, K. N. (2002). *Writing Machines*. Cambridge: MIT Press.

Helms, R., Ignacio, R., Brinkkemper, S., & Zonneveld, A. (2010). Limitations of Network Analysis for Studying Efficiency and Effectiveness of Knowledge Sharing. *Electronic Journal of Knowledge Management*, *8*(1), 53–68. Retrieved from www.ejkm.com

Holstein, J. A., & Gubrium, F. J. (2000). *The self we live by: narrative identity in a postmodern world.* New York: Oxford University Press, Inc.

Illeris, K. (2009). *Contemporary Theories of Learning: Learning Theorists -- in Their Own Words.* London, New York: Taylor & Francis Routledge.

Kelty, C. (2005). Geeks, Social Imaginaries, and Recursive Publics. *Cultural Anthropology*, *20*(2), 185–214. doi:10.1525/can.2005.20.2.185

Kimble, C., & Hildreth, P. (2004). Communities of Practice: Going One Step Too Far? Proceedings of 9e colloque de l'AIM, (May 2004). p. 304.

Kolaczyk, E. D., & Krivitsky, P. N. (2012). On the Question of Effective Sample Size in Network Modeling, Cornell University Library. Retrieved from http://arxiv.org/abs/1112.0840

Mateas, M., & Sengers, P. (Eds.), (2003). *Narrative Intelligence*. Amsterdam: John Benjamins Publishing. doi:10.1075/aicr.46

McNeill, D. (2005). *Gesture and Thought*. Chicago: University of Chicago Press. doi:10.7208/chicago/9780226514642.001.0001

Mejias, U. A. (2006). *The tyranny of nodes: Towards a critique of social network theories*. Retrieved from http://blog.ulisesmejias.com/2006/10/09/the-tyranny-of-nodes-towards-a-critique-of-social-network-theories/

Monclar, R. S., Oliveira, J., de Faria, F. F., Ventura, L., de Souza, J. M., & Campos, M. L. M. (2011, June 8-10). Using social networks analysis for collaboration and team formation identification. Proceedings of the *2011 15th International Conference on Computer Supported Cooperative Work in Design CSCWD* (pp. 562-569). doi:10.1109/CSCWD.2011.5960128

Morozov, E. (2012). *The Net Delusion: How Not to Liberate The World*. London: Penguin Books.

Noble, J., Davy, S., & Franks, D. W. (2004). Effects of the topology of social networks on information transmission. In S. Schaal, A. J. Ijspeert, A. Billard, & S. Vijayakumar (Eds.), *From Animals to Animats 8: Proceedings of the Eighth International Conference on Simulation of Adaptive Behavior* (pp. 395-404). MIT Press. Retrieved from http://eprints.soton.ac.uk/265249/1/sabNetTopology.pdf

Polanyi, M. (1967) (reissue edition 2009). The Tacit Dimension. Chicago: Chicago University Press.

Pólya, G. (1945). *How to Solve It*. New York: Princeton University Press.

Raike, A., Keune, A., Lindholm, B., & Muttilainen, J. (2013). Concept design for a collaborative digital learning tool for film post-production. *Journal of Media Practice*, *14*(4), 307–329. doi:10.1386/jmpr.14.4.307_1

Siemens, G. (2014). Connectivism: A Learning Theory for the Digital Age. *Elearnspace*. Retrieved from http://www.elearnspace.org/Articles/connectivism.htm

Sullivan, G. (2005). *Art Practice as Research*. Thousand Oaks, CA: Sage.

Vygotsky, L. S. (1962). In E. Hanfmann & G. Vakar (Eds., Trans., Original work published 1934). Thought and language. Cambridge, MA: MIT Press. doi:10.1037/11193-000

Vygotsky, L. S. (1978). *Mind and society*. Cambridge, MA: Harvard University Press.

Vygotsky, L. S. (1979). The development of higher forms of attention in childhood. *Social Psychology*, *18*, 67–115.

Warschauer, M. (1997). Computer-Mediated Collaborative Learning: Theory and Practice. *The Modern Language Journal* (Special Issue), *81*(4), 470-481.

Wasserman, S., & Faust, K. (1994). *Social Network Analysis*. Cambridge: Cambridge University Press. doi:10.1017/CBO9780511815478

Wellman, B. (2002). Little boxes, glocalization, and networked individualism. In M. Tanabe, P. van den Besselaar, & T. Ishida (Eds.), Digital cities II: Computational and sociological approaches (pp. 10–25). Berlin: Springer; Retrieved from http://www.chass.utoronto.ca/~wellman/publications/littleboxes/littlebox.PDF doi:10.1007/3-540-45636-8_2

Wenger, E. (2006). *Communities of practice: a brief introduction*. Retrieved from http://wenger-trayner.com/wp-content/uploads/2013/10/06-Brief-introduction-to-communities-of-practice.pdf

Wenger, E., McDermott, R., & Snyder, W. M. (2002). *Cultivating communities of practice: A guide to managing knowledge*. Boston: Harvard Business School Press.

Wiley, D. A., & Edwards, E. K. (2002). Online self-organizing social systems: The decentralized future of online learning. Retrieved from http://wiley.ed.usu.edu/docs/ososs.pdf

Wilson, S. (1996). Art as Research. Retrieved from http://userwww.sfsu.edu/~swilson/

Yakhlef, A. (2010). The three facets of knowledge: A critique of the practice-based learning theory. *Research Policy*, *39*(1), 39–46. doi:10.1016/j.respol.2009.11.005

ADDITIONAL READING

Burt, R. S. (1992). *Structural Holes: The Social Structure of Competition*. Cambridge, MA: Harvard University Press.

Kelty, C. (2005). Geeks, Social Imaginaries, and Recursive Publics. *Cultural Anthropology*, *20*(2), 185–214. doi:10.1525/can.2005.20.2.185

Wenger, E., McDermott, R., & Snyder, W. M. (2002). *Cultivating communities of practice: A guide to managing knowledge*. Boston: Harvard Business School Press.

KEY TERMS AND DEFINITIONS

Community of Practice (CoP): A self organising group that has a professional (or other type) of practice in common, such groups share information and aims to improve and refine their practice.

Semantic Web: A system for identifying meaning in web pages through the use of meta-data, or data about data. It is proposed that a Web 3 will be predicated on an extensive semantic web.

Social Imaginary: The forces which form our collective understandings and expectations of social life, they could be framed as the moral and social order, or the collective imaginings of what forms the understanding of society.

Social Network Analysis (SNA): A mathematical and theoretical framework for analysing social networks.

Web 3: A controversial term for a future Web in which semantic technologies will enable far more intelligent search and analysis, including recommendation agents and natural language understanding. Web 3 is arguably an unrealistic proposition that is already overdue.

Chapter 5
Digital Collaboration in Educational and Research Institutions

Rami Wael Muhtaseb
A.M. Qattan Foundation, Palestine

ABSTRACT

This chapter explores the role of digital technologies in promoting interaction and collaboration at educational and research institutions. It describes some forms of digital collaboration, and explores how educational and research institutions employ digital technologies to reach learners inside and outside the institutional boundaries. The chapter investigates a number of digital collaboration tools and their characteristics, and highlights some aspects of employing these tools to support interaction among students, teachers, researchers, and different learning communities with a special focus on science. Some cases of integrating digital technologies in the educational process and in research are also given. At the end of the chapter, insights are discussed, and a summary is presented.

DIGITAL TECHNOLOGY FOR TEACHING AND LEARNING

Fast growing advances and the expansion of digital technology tools and applications have increased the opportunity of investing in these technologies in research and education. Personal computers and handheld devices are becoming more affordable and more connected; educational applications are becoming more popular, more social and user friendly; these unique properties have transformed the use of digital technologies from communication tools only into interactive, collaborative, and learning tools.

Today, there is a growing trend to utilize interactive digital technologies to expand interaction and collaboration inside and outside educational institutions. Interactive digital technologies play a main role in emphasizing collaboration between teachers and students and in motivating students to use and extend their experiences. Digital technology has made learning available all the time, enhanced students' engagement in learning, and extended their learning experiences to reach beyond the educational session.

DOI: 10.4018/978-1-4666-9556-6.ch005

Copyright © 2016, IGI Global. Copying or distributing in print or electronic forms without written permission of IGI Global is prohibited.

Digital tools have been adopted for education, communication and collaboration by many educational institutions including schools, universities, colleges, training centers, academies, and institutes, and by many cultural and research institutions such as museums, galleries, libraries, research centers, and informal learning environments. The educational process includes different types of interaction: student–instructor, student–student, and student–content (Moore, 1989). In research, collaboration can take place between researchers from either a same-setting context (e.g., academic institutions) or from different-setting contexts (e.g., between academic–government or academic–private industry) (Stages of Collaboration, 2005). Many digital collaboration tools have been developed to promote and facilitate interaction between these communities and to manage other aspects of the educational process, including collaboration between the educational staff, employees, and researchers where they can easily share ideas and resources, and interact across geographical locations.

The unique characteristics of digital technologies have encouraged many educational and research institutions to invest in digital collaboration tools, while many researchers aim to investigate which digital technologies are the most educationally effective in different contexts. The mentioned cases in the following sections do not specify at which level of education the tool can be applied. Digital technologies have changed the way people learn and communicate; they have connected learners at different educational levels enabling interaction with other learners, educators, and scholars in different locations and learning environments. Learning is becoming more accessible; teachers and students at multiple educational institutions can easily connect.

CHARACTERISTICS OF SOCIAL MEDIA

One of the main features of the development of digital technologies is the expansion of social media; its main characteristics are sharing, participation, interaction, and collaboration. Rapid advancements in social media tools are changing the way we communicate and interact with each other. Support and organization interaction and the facilitation of various collaboration tasks utilize these advancements.

Social media include web-based internet sites that facilitate social interaction in many ways, including social networking; social bookmarking; microblogging; video, image, and audio sharing; virtual words; and much more. (Joosten, 2012)

In order to achieve effective student engagement in education, it is essential to facilitate the way they interact, collaborate, and share knowledge and experiences. Social media help to engage students in the learning process by virtually connecting communities of students, teachers, and researchers. Furthermore, new social media tools are continually being developed and utilized for educational purposes. The properties of social media allow for collaboration and active participation in generating and sharing knowledge among peers and research groups (Battrawi & Muhtaseb, 2013).

This advancement in social media tools has increased the demand of the world's educational systems for new information and communication technologies to support the educational process by making information accessible anywhere and at anytime. It has also encouraged scientists and researchers to explore and utilize new online interaction tools to share information with people in their networks.

The Use of Social Media at Educational Institutions

Social media are increasingly being used at universities, academies, and research institutions for their effectiveness in connecting various communities. It has provided many tools to learners and researchers in which they communicate their ideas and opinions, and share their knowledge among the online learning community. Today, many social media tools are used in online learning such as blogs, virtual classrooms, forum exchanges, and massive open online courses (MOOCs); these tools can be accessed through personal computers or handheld devices. This has also added new characteristics to e-learning where learners can make connections with other learners with whom they can share ideas, resources, and experiences. Even in formal learning environments social media has helped make learning a participative, social, and collaborative environment where groups can collaborate and co-create content.

Social media provide a medium to transform the traditional, passive classroom into an interactive and engaging space facilitating active learning through cooperation, reflection, dialogue, and feedback (Joosten, 2012)

To access a diverse audience, many educational institutions have employed social media tools, such as Facebook and Twitter, to interact with the community and to share their news and activities; some create multiple accounts across various social media channels. The Massachusetts Institute of Technology (MIT), for example, has different Facebook pages[1]: the MIT School of Science page communicates news to the public and updates in the departments of brain and cognitive sciences, biology, chemistry, math, and physics; the Brain and Cognitive Sciences page belongs to the center for neuroscience and cognitive science research and education; the Department of Physics page; the Department of Nuclear Science and Engineering page; and the Technology Review page, which leads a conversation about new technologies and publishes articles written by the MIT staff.

The social web has provided a host of tools that can support collaborative learning strategies. The ability to leverage chat, walls, and boards, while simultaneously facilitating connections with study partners, are in consonance with collaborative learning strategies (Heston, 2013)

In research, social media can connect educational institutions with partner companies. Members can communicate, discuss, and collaborate, building bridges between academic and professional communities. Moreover, social media support the formation of research groups, which include students from various academic backgrounds. This is an advantage for students as instructors can create online research groups and engage students according to their research interests. This also provides an opportunity for students to build their research records and to be more involved in research, practical projects, and building their practical experience during the academic stage. Some universities create one community for each faculty or department. Joint communities or groups can be constructed between different departments helping different university departments to share experiences. For example, a multidisciplinary research project may include students specialized in computer science and bioinformatics. Students who belong to this community can work together on a common subject and share related learning content and resources easily with other community members.

To accomplish their work, academic researchers increasingly rely on digital tools (Lippincott, Hemmasi, & Lewis, 2014); there are a large number of social media tools that support different research activities from sharing ideas, collaboration, and organization to dissemination of results. Such tools also include online meetings and webinars, co-authored documents and shared spreadsheets. Furthermore, there are a growing number of social networks aiming to promote research; ResearchGate, for example, is a social networking site for scientists and researchers to share papers, ask and answer questions, and find collaborators. Mendeley is a research reference manager and academic social network. MyNetResearch is a networking site for global research, and Vivo is a social networking site that connects researchers at participating universities and institutions.

To take full advantage of social media in research and education, educational institutions should provide researchers and educators with competencies and skills; they should also develop training programs for creating new tools and techniques to be utilized in research and education. This can contribute to enhancing the quality of education, as well as facilitating collaboration among academic and research institutions.

Social Networks in Science Education

The interactive features of social media make it an effective tool for increasing interest in and popularizing science, and science communication. Social media, including social networks, may offer rich venues for effective interactions among different communities. The number of social network users has been growing tremendously and many academic institutions, research centers, and organizations have been employing online social networks in many ways to popularize science (Battrawi & Muhtaseb, 2014).

Researchers suggest that social networks can create online, interactive science-learning environments presenting new avenues for science education. By encouraging students to participate in positive discussions on science related topics, they may learn and share valuable scientific knowledge (Battrawi & Muhtaseb, 2013). Social networks can also play an effective role in collaboration and in facilitating interaction between students, teachers, scientists, and the public. For example, the Integrated Digitized Biocollections (iDigBio)[2], an online library funded by the National Science Foundation, facilitates sharing collections, and supports working with groups and public engagement in scientific research. Through this website, data and images for millions of biological specimens are being made available in electronic format to the research community, government agencies, students, educators, and the general public. The information in the digitized collections includes field notes, photographs, 3-D images and information on associated organisms, geographic distribution, environmental habitat, and specimen DNA samples.

Today, an increasing number of scientists are active on social networks where people can follow them and see their immediate comments and feedback on different scientific events, discoveries, and updates related to their field of work. For instance, astrophysicist Neil deGrasse Tyson and science educator and television host Bill Nye have been active on twitter with more than 3 million fans following Tyson (@NeilTyson) and 1.91 million fans following Nye (@TheScienceGuy). Kateman (2012) suggests that scientists in the digital age have a unique opportunity to communicate and interact directly with the public on social media platforms in an engaging, casual and fun atmosphere.

Through social networks, audiences can be exposed to current and ongoing international and global causes, events, petitions, projects, and initiatives (Battrawi & Muhtaseb, 2013). Other social networking tools could play an additional role in crowdsourcing for science related events since they provoke interaction and contribution (Battrawi & Muhtaseb, 2013). Linking students, educators, and the public to these events and activities might contribute to promoting global awareness and help in connecting learners to the international science community.

Social networks represent a promising venue for science communication where science communicators and scientists can be involved in real-time conversations about events with the public. Moreover, social networks make it possible for individuals to create their own blogs or pages where they can promote science and be followed by their peers and acquaintances. Evaluating the role of social networks and their impact in promoting science literacy and interest in science, allows educators and researchers to make the best use of these tools when adopting them for science education and communication (Battrawi & Muhtaseb, 2013).

Live Monitoring as Collaboration Tool

Technological advancements in live broadcasting and the expansion of social media tools can be effectively utilized in research and education. Live streaming services have become available to the public where real-time information is provided, allowing teachers, students, and researchers to deal with real scientific data, collecting information, discussing and engaging with live science events.

Social media tools make it possible to stream lectures, scientific discoveries, events, and live cameras monitoring animals. Some websites, such as Live Animals TV[3], have a growing collection of animal webcams and streaming videos of all kinds of animals. For instance, the Estonian Education and Research Network (EENet)[4] provides live broadcasts of Estonian flora, fauna, and landscapes. Nature cameras monitor eagle nests, ospreys, grey seals, and bears, allowing people to observe animals from anywhere. The National Aeronautics and Space Administration agency (NASA)[5] provides live video from the International Space Station, including internal views when the crew is on-duty and Earth views at other times[6]. NASA has also provided live streaming broadcasts to many astronomical events such as eclipses, transits, comets, asteroids, and coverage of events related to their missions. 'Slooh'[7] is another example of a robotic telescope service accessible to the public; the idea is to create a community observatory in which live coverage of celestial events is available. Recently, many events were observed online and crowdsourced on social networks including the total solar eclipse in 2012, observing comet ISON, observing asteroid '2000 EM26' zipping by earth, Asteroid 2012 DA14 flyby Earth, and the landing of Curiosity Rover on Mars (Battrawi & Muhtaseb, 2014).

Social media can be an effective tool in promoting public engagement in watching, collaborating, and participating in real-time conversations in live science-related events. This capacity to host educational events online has many potential applications in education and research. Moreover, there is a prospect of creating groups or pages, as described in the previous sections, specializing in specific fields to allow students to take an active role in following events.

Crowdsourcing for Science through Social Media

With crowdsourcing, social media can be implemented to enhance public awareness of and engagement in science events and campaigns launched by organizations and educational institutions. As social media encourages interaction and contributions, crowdsourcing also presents a promising venue for citizen science projects, allowing students and the public to participate in local and international scientific research by collecting real scientific data. Social networking tools can be utilized to crowdsource nature cameras and other scientific events. It can also be used to run campaigns to connect people with similar interests to share information and to collaborate on research related to scientific issues.

Social media can be implemented to take advantage of the sites that students primarily use to communicate, such as Facebook or text messaging (Joosten, 2012). For example, creating an event through Facebook has become one of the easiest and fastest methods to announce, promote, and market events to a wide range of people. This offers event followers an opportunity for real-time conversations about an event. Facebook events can be useful for science communicators to promote science-related events. Furthermore, posting events on social networks can also be used to gather people with common interests to discuss and share resources and to collaborate. Connecting social networks to other social media tools can be a great advantage in making use of other resources and involving a wide range of communities.

SOCIAL MEDIA AT MUSEUMS

This section highlights the emergence of social media within museums from being a tool for advertising events and exhibits to a world of interactive education and user generated content (Fox, 2011). Social media have encouraged audience engagement and participation, and encouraged many educational institutions to adopt learning communities where researchers can generate online discussion from the confines of their labs and curators can promote knowledge displayed within a museum (Kateman, 2012). Research will be undertaken by examining the viability and sustainability of social media as tools for education and communication in museums and by extension, in other cultural institutions such as libraries, galleries, and archives (Russo et al. 2007).

According to Russo et. al (2007), museums could use social media in three specific ways: to share information between communities of interest, visitors, and museum professionals; to respond to issues as they become important to visitors and user-groups; to create new knowledge and/or new digital cultural content enabling the interpretation of collections from a visitor perspective. Social networks could play an important role in stimulating audience interactivity and participation; for example, the Museum of Modern Art offers a forum through which visitors can share their opinions and experiences in relation to museum content (Kelly L., & Russo A., 2008). These public forms of participation can influence new audiences and are increasingly valuable in determining the impact of museum initiatives. In addition, enabling audiences to share and discuss their common experiences provides an important insight into collection records (Russo et al. 2007). When young people share their experiences in a public forum, they undertake a form of editing and filtering of information to create knowledge, which is accessible and meaningful to them and their peers.

Social media may also play an important role in science museums by leveraging the crowdsourcing for scientific events as they encourage interaction and contribution (Battrawi & Muhtaseb, 2013). Other social media tools can be employed as a research platform for evaluating the impact of visiting museums on students' motivation and literacy among target groups of visitors.

The ability for an individual to create and display content within an authoritative cultural environment – such as a museum – reflects a growing global interest in the sharing of individual and collective experiences. It also represents changes to the ways in which users interact digitally using different communication models: one-to-one (i.e. user to user); one-to-many (i.e. museum to user — web pages and blogs); and many-to-many (knowledge to knowledge — wikis). (Russo et al. 2007)

Online interaction can take place prior to visiting the museum by virtual tours; during the visit by sharing content with acquaintances and reflection; and after visiting the museum by sharing content, discussions with other visitors, and reflection on experiences. Some museums use social media, such as blogs, podcasts, and wikis, to provoke interaction; other museums integrate mobile into their exhibits, for example, some adopt mobile applications like Sparkatour, a platform to create mobile guided tours for museums. Sparkatour enables small to medium-sized museums to easily create a mobile multimedia-guided tour of their art collections for their visitors (Fox, 2011).

Many social media have become key tools in communication and promoting events by various museums. For instance, Brooklyn Museum has a main website, a blog, a YouTube channel, a Facebook page, a Twitter presence, a Flickr account, as well as Tumblr, Foursquare, and Instagram accounts to both attract and communicate with visitors. The National Design Museum (Smithsonian Institution) has an Educator Resource Center, which presents online resources to link educators to the museum's programs and to create a community of practice, which shares educational experiences and provides best practice examples of design education and museum learning. The museum also has a website enabling educators to connect to each other to share and distribute knowledge (Russo et al. 2007).

DIGITAL COLLABORATION CASES

This section highlights cases where digital technologies are being used to enhance interaction and collaboration among students, teachers, researchers, scientists, and the public.

WebQuests - National Museums Online Learning Project

There are a number of examples that highlight how social media utilize new technologies to encourage and support user participation while visiting museums. The National Museums Online Learning Project involves the nine UK national museums (British Museum, Imperial War Museum, National Portrait Gallery, Natural History Museum, Royal Armouries, Sir John Soane's Museum, Tate, The Wallace Collection and the Victoria and Albert Museum) to create learning objects or "WebQuests" which provide online learning resources across the nine websites for pupils, teachers, and lifelong learners.

The museums have created a social web application called Creative Spaces that will enable users to document how the collections have inspired their own creative activities. Users can also share their ideas through text, images, and videos, particularly where these are related to the museums' collections. Users can also make connections with others with similar interests, entering into dialogue and forming groups around specific topics (Royston, 2009). These WebQuests provide new ways of visualizing, thinking about, presenting, interacting with, and understanding complex topics. For students, WebQuests are curriculum-based activities that use the partners' online museum collections as part of an interactive and engaging experience. WebQuests encourage children to think critically and to use museum objects in new and exciting ways (Royston, 2009). WebQuests encourage learners to ask questions and conduct their own enquiries, to evaluate sources of information, and to communicate and make links between different areas of the curriculum. They also provide teachers with enquiry-based ICT activities with a personalized approach to learning, in addition to a range of cross-curricular topics across the Key Stages and subject areas[8].

Scientist-Student Interaction: Astronaut Photographs

On December 30, 2014, NASA published an article on its website titled 'Astronaut Photographs Inspire Next Generation of Scientists' describing how astronauts' pictures are helping to inspire a next generation of scientists. According to the article, teachers have used space-based images taken from the station to help students grasp geographical, geological, environmental, and other concepts. Students can request astronauts take a specific image to support their investigation. For example, students from Connetquot High School in Bohemia, New York, used astronaut imagery of Earth to compare impact craters on Earth with those on other planets (Gaskill, 2014). These images were provided through the Expedition Earth and Beyond (EEAB[9]) program, which is designed to connect teachers and their students in grades 5–14 with pictures taken by astronauts aboard the International Space Station. The program aims to facilitate student-driven, authentic research projects that study the Earth and if desired, compare features on Earth to those on other planetary bodies such as the Moon and Mars.

According to Gaskill (2014), almost 1.5 million images taken from the station are publicly available for student science investigations. Student investigations have also analyzed changes in Earth's glaciers, bodies of water, and shorelines using images taken of the same place over time. Paige Graff, EEAB director, said 'This models the process by which professional scientists acquire new data; students start with existing data and, if they discover that they need additional data to support their research, can submit a proposal to the Crew Earth Observation target stream to request that an astronaut collect that data". This creates a powerful, direct connection between students and astronauts in orbit (Gaskill, 2014).

EEAB also provides a variety of resources and opportunities for students and teachers, including professional development opportunities for teachers and a virtual shared space where teachers can communicate with EEAB staff. Students can use the wiki to present their research to others, including professional scientists who potentially may serve as mentors. The program also connects students with NASA scientists and experts through EEAB's interactive Classroom Connection Webinars. These free, online events encourage students to craft questions they can answer using earth and space imagery and show them how scientists use this imagery to conduct their own investigations. In October 2014, about 35 schools participated in a webinar launched by EEAB titled "Investigating Earth Using Astronaut Imagery from Space" (Gaskill, 2014).

ARKYD -The First Publicly Accessible Space Telescope

The ARKYD is the first publicly accessible space telescope designed to take high-resolution photos of objects in space. What sets it apart is that the spacecraft was engineered with an external screen and a camera arm, allowing the user to take pictures from the ARKYD as it orbits the earth. In 2013, a company called Planetary Resources[10] launched a campaign to crowd-fund the world's first space telescope on the Kickstarter website as a trial to engage the community in a productive way. Its primary mission is to develop low-cost robotic spacecraft to explore and mine resource-rich asteroids within our reach. The first step toward making this possible is the launching of a fleet of ARKYD spacecraft to identify asteroids that are ripe for further exploration. This same capability has numerous other potential applications in education and research. It's estimated delivery is August 2015 (Moskowitz, 2013).

Planetary Resources will enable investors to take control of the telescope for 30 minutes to take photos of space, which will be theirs to keep. This experience can change the nature of exploration by developing the most advanced space technology ever made available to the public. This experience highlights the potential of social media in promoting citizen science and connecting the public to the international science community. By providing access to such advanced technology to students, scientists, and the public, the next generation will have the opportunity to use it in unpredictable and creative ways.

Promoting Citizen Science through Real-Time Monitoring

Today, many citizen science projects employ digital technologies to encourage the public to participate in scientific research by collecting or sorting out huge amounts of scientific data. Zooniverse[11] is a citizen science web portal owned and operated by the Citizen Science Alliance. It is home to the Internet's largest and most popular citizen science projects. The organization grew from the original Galaxy Zoo project and now hosts dozens of projects, which allow volunteers to participate in crowdsourced scientific research. Zooniverse projects require the active participation of volunteers to complete research tasks. Projects have been drawn from a variety of disciplines, including astronomy, ecology, cell biology, humanities, and climate science.

Zooniverse has recently launched some projects that require citizen scientists to participate in research by watching live streaming for an animal and providing their observations. For instance, the project 'Monitor Penguins in Remote Regions' asks the public to help annotate their images of wildlife in some of the coldest areas on the planet like Antarctica and the Southern Ocean to learn more about penguin populations[12]. Another project, 'The California Condors Need Your Help', tracks the social behavior of the California condor, a critically endangered species suffering from the effects of lead poisoning. Citizen scientists are asked to look at photos of condors taken by motion-activated cameras, to identify the tag number of each condor and to record its behavior around the feeding carcass in order to help scientists judge if a bird's eating or social behavior reveal lead poisoning[13].

In February 2014, the Zooniverse community consisted of more than 1 million registered volunteers. The data collected from the various projects has led to the publication of more than 60 scientific papers (Hall, 2014). There is also a daily news website called 'The Daily Zooniverse', which gives information on the different projects and has a presence on social media.

Another related example is the case of crowdsourcing for observing animals through a science literacy Facebook page called 'Creative Minds'.[14] According to Battrawi and Muhtaseb (2014), the page encouraged its fans to follow a nature camera monitoring an osprey nest in which viewers were able to observe and take screen shots of the hatching process and the daily feeding routines, as well as first flights and hunts. Another live camera was also followed by the page's fans for Zoo Magdeburg[15] in Germany where page fans monitored a pregnant female snow leopard and were challenged to take the first pictures of the cubs as they were born sharing them on the page. The page administrators raised some questions and initiated discussions about animal behavior (Battrawi & Muhtaseb, 2013). Page administrators observed the emotional engagement of some of the audience to the updates on the animals. In addition to the real-time experience, the live stream meant something to people, and they cared about what was going on with the animals. Live streaming challenged people to ask questions, discuss, share ideas, and feel involved. This kind of project increases the sense of responsibility towards the environment and other scientific issues.

The Polymath Project

The Polymath project[16] was an attempt by mathematician Timothy Gowers to solve a mathematical research problem working entirely in the open and using his blog as a medium for mathematical collaboration. The experiment, called 'Massively Collaborative Mathematics', was initiated in January 2009 by Timothy Gowers and described by Michael Nielsen as "a natural extension of open source collaboration to mathematics". The hope was that a large number of mathematicians would contribute, and that their collective intelligence would make easy work of what would ordinarily be a difficult problem. Gowers began the Polymath Project with a description of the problem to be attacked (Nielsen, 2010).

At that point, on February 1, 2009, other people were invited to contribute their thoughts on the problem. In just the first 24 hours after Gowers opened his blog for discussion, six people offered 24 comments. In a sign of things to come, those contributors came from four countries on three continents, and included a high-school teacher, a graduate student, and four professors of mathematics. Collaboration was underway, a collaboration which expanded in the weeks that followed to involve more than twenty people. (Nielsen, 2010)

The initial stage of this project was extremely successful and led to two scientific papers. The Polymath process was a way of sharing mathematical understanding openly, and gradually improving it through the contributions of many people (Nielsen, 2010).

Social Media Tools for Language Learning Exchange

Social media provide an opportunity for learning languages and language exchange without needing to leave one's home or classroom. One can participate in language learning activities anytime and anywhere. Some social media tools include educational websites and social networking sites; other tools include interactive applications that provide an opportunity to network with real people speaking different languages. This is a major advantage since interaction and communication are an important part of learning a language.

Social Media Language Learning (SMLL) is an example of using social media in language learning. SMLL was originally created by Idiomplus, a Barcelona, Spain-based company that applies interactive social media channels to language learning, enabling students to develop communication skills while using these social networks. This method provides the learner with an opportunity to participate in actual real-time, relevant conversations taking place online, and to practice the target language with the help of an experienced teacher. SMLL links interactive social media channels to language learning, enabling students to develop communication and language skills (Procter, 2014).

Some foreign language schools use videoconferencing to connect the class to the world. Videoconferencing in the classroom opens many opportunities for students to engage in language learning, building cultural understanding. Learners have the advantage of connecting with educators from various places, giving them an opportunity to learn from outside experts (Ferriter, n.d.).

Social Media at NASA

The National Aeronautics and Space Administration agency (NASA) has employed many social media channels to reach and interact with the public. It offers various digital technologies, including photo and video sharing, wikis, blogs, podcasts, mash-ups, web feeds, social networking sites (e.g., Facebook, LinkedIn), microblogging (e.g., Twitter), and other web-based forums to tell about its missions and programs. Audiences can follow more than 120 specialized social networking channels under four categories: NASA People and Astronauts; NASA Missions and Topics; NASA Centers and Facilities; and NASA Programs[17]. There are many other websites under the category 'Collaborate with NASA' that offer opportunities and provide resources to the public. NASA also provides many data and resources to educators, students, citizen scientists, and researchers through its "MY NASA DATA" website.[18]

NASA Television, or NASA TV, is a resource designed to provide real-time coverage of the agency's activities and missions, as well as providing resource videos to the news media and educational programs directed at teachers, students, and the general public. NASA 360 is a television program that looks at NASA from all angles, giving the stories behind the technologies and missions. It also looks at how technologies developed for space, aeronautics, and general applications can help people here on earth. NASA's Earth Observatory Facebook page and Twitter account provide NASA images, stories, and discoveries about climate and the environment (NASA, 2015).

NASA's Curiosity Mars Rover Facebook page specializes in covering updates related to the Curiosity Rover, which is a part of NASA's Mars science laboratory mission. The 'Precipitation Measurement Missions' Facebook page posts information from advanced space-borne instruments that measure rain and snow globally. The 'NASA's Cassini Mission to Saturn' Facebook page follows the Cassini mission exploring Saturn, which has revolutionized our view of the planet, its rings, and moons. The mission is a cooperative project of NASA, the European Space Agency, and the Italian Space Agency (ASI) (NASA, 2015).

CONCLUSION

This chapter aimed to contribute to the understanding of the role of digital technologies in promoting interaction and collaboration in research and education. The chapter presented a short overview of some digital collaboration tools used at educational and research institutions, then the role of social media in creating active learning environments where students can engage in discussions, and interact with teachers, researchers, scientists, and the public was investigated. This chapter provides many examples and recommendations for teachers, trainers, administrators, as well as academic researchers who are interested in studies of education and learning technologies. The discussed issues and the presented examples highlight the potential of these technologies to change how learning occurs and how research is conducted. However, the continuous development in digital technologies and the growing number of collaboration tools emphasize the need for further research in this field. Investigating which digital technologies are the most educationally effective in different contexts and knowing more about these tools can increase the opportunities of achieving the best use of these technologies in promoting and sharing knowledge all over the world.

REFERENCES

Aitchison, C. (n. d.). WebQuests from the National Museums Online Learning Project. Retrieved from http://www.aitchisonmedia.net/NMOLP/

Battrawi, B., & Muhtaseb, R. (2013). Assessing the Role of Social Networks in Increasing Interest in Science and Science Literacy among a Sample of Facebook Users. *Proceedings of the 10th International Conference on Hands-on Science*; Košice, Slovakia.

Battrawi, B., & Muhtaseb, R. (2013). The Use of Social Networks as a Tool to Increase Interest in Science and Science Literacy: A Case Study of 'Creative Minds' Facebook Page. *Proceedings of the Second Edition of the International Conference New Perspectives in Science Education*; Florence, Italy.

Battrawi, B., & Muhtaseb, R. (2014). Real-Time Monitoring and Facebook Events: New Social Media Tools for Promoting Online Interaction and Public Engagement in Science. *Proceedings of the 8th International Technology, Education and Development Conference*; Valencia, Spain.

Clara Moskowitz. (2013, May 29). Asteroid Miners to Launch World's 1st Crowdfunded Space Telescope. Retrieved from http://www.space.com/21345-asteroid-mining-crowdfunding-space-telescope.html

Ferriter, B. (n. d.). Using videoconferencing to connect your class to the world. Retrieved from http://www.learnnc.org/lp/pages/6559

Fox, Z. (2011, August 11). 5 Ways Museums Are Reaching Digital Audiences. *Mashable.com.* Retrieved from http://mashable.com/2011/08/11/museums-digital/

Gaskill, M. (2014, December 30). Astronaut Photographs Inspire Next Generation of Scientists. Retrieved from http://www.nasa.gov/mission_pages/station/research/news/EEAB

Hall, S. (2014, February 17). Zooniverse Reaches One Million Volunteers. *Universe Today.* Retrieved from http://www.universetoday.com/109413/zooniverse-reaches-one-million-volunteers/

Heston, J. (2013, February 6). Collaborative Learning: Leveraging Social Learning Sites. Retrieved from http://blog.cengage.com/collaborative-learning-leveraging-social-learning-sites-part-1-of-2/

Joosten, T. (2012). *Social media for educators: Strategies and best practices*. John Wiley & Sons.

Kateman, B. (2012, February 29). Social Media and the Love of Science. Retrieved from http://blogs.ei.columbia.edu/2012/02/29/social-media-and-the-love-of-science/

Kelly, L., & Russo, A. (2008). From ladders of participation to networks of participation: Social media and museum audiences. *Proceedings of Museums and the Web 2008.*

Kulczycki, E. (2013). *Transformation of Science Communication in the Age of Social Media.* Adam Mickiewicz University. Department of Philosophy.

Lippincott, J., Hemmasi, H., & Lewis, V. (2014, June 16). Trends in Digital Scholarship Centers. Retrieved from http://www.educause.edu/ero/article/trends-digital-scholarship-centers/

Moore, M. G. (1989). Three types of interaction. *American Journal of Distance Education, 3*(2), 1–6. doi:10.1080/08923648909526659

NASA. (2015). Social Media at NASA. Retrieved from http://www.nasa.gov/socialmedia/

Nielsen, M. (2010, May 1). Introduction to the Polymath Project and Density Hales-Jewett and Moser Numbers. Retrieved from http://michaelnielsen.org/blog/introduction-to-the-polymath-project-and-density-hales-jewett-and-moser-numbers/

Noorden, R. (2014, August 15). Online collaboration: Scientists and the social network. Retrieved from http://www.nature.com/news/online-collaboration-scientists-and-the-social-network-1.15711

Northern Illinois University. (2005). Stages of Collaboration. Retrieved from http://www.niu.edu/rcrportal/collabresearch/stages/stages.html

Planetary Resources. (2013, May 29). Planetary Resources Announces World's First Crowdfunded Space Telescope Campaign. Retrieved from http://www.planetaryresources.com/2013/05/planetary-resources-announces-worlds-first-crowdfunded-space-telescope-campaign/

Procter, W. (2014, June 11). Social Media and Language Learning. *Education First Blog*. Retrieved from http://www.ef.com/blog/corporate/social-media-and-language-learning/

Royston, C. (2009, April 18). WebQuests - National Museums Online Learning Project. Retrieved from http://www.museumsandtheweb.com/mw2009/abstracts/prg_335002093.html

Russo, A., Watkins, J., & Chan, S. (2007). Look who's talking. [Museum and Gallery Services New South Wales.]. *The MAG*, *2*, 14–15.

Russo, A., Watkins, J., Kelly, L., & Chan, S. (2007). Social media and cultural interactive experiences in museums. *Nordic Journal of Digital Literacy*, *1*, 19–29.

Russo, A., Watkins, J. J., Kelly, L., & Chan, S. (2006, December 7- 9). How will social media affect museum communication? Proceedings of the Nordic Digital Excellence in Museums NODEM, Oslo, Norway.

KEY TERMS AND DEFINITIONS

Citizen Science: Scientific research conducted or contributed to by nonprofessional scientists.

Community: A network of people who share the same goals or interests and communicate through the internet.

Crowdsourcing: The practice of getting service, information, or content by soliciting contributions from a group of people through online tools.

Digital Collaboration: Using digital channels and digital devices to interact, collaborate, share knowledge, and manage information.

Live Monitoring: Using online live broadcasting tools over the social media to receive real-time information.

Online Social Network: Online platform that is designed to allow users to build social networks through which they interact and build their own communities.

Social Media: A set of online tools and applications that allow users to create, share and exchange content and interact in virtual communities.

ENDNOTES

1 http://connect.mit.edu/
2 https://www.idigbio.org
3 http://www.liveanimals.tv/
4 http://www.eenet.ee/eenet/eenet_en
5 http://www.nasa.gov/multimedia/nasatv
6 http://www.nasa.gov/multimedia/nasatv/iss_ustream.html
7 http://events.slooh.com/
8 http://www.aitchisonmedia.net/nmolp/[REMOVEDHYPERLINKFIELD]
9 http://ares.jsc.nasa.gov/education/eeab/index.cfm
10 http://www.planetaryresources.com/
11 https://www.zooniverse.org/
12 http://www.penguinwatch.org
13 http://www.condorwatch.org
14 https://www.facebook.com/creativeminds00
15 http://www.zoo-magdeburg.de/
16 http://polymathprojects.org/
17 http://www.nasa.gov/socialmedia/#.VLu0nyuUf9k
18 http://mynasadata.larc.nasa.gov/

Chapter 6
E-Collaborative Learning (e-CL): Overview and Proposals

Alexandros Xafopoulos
University College London, UK

ABSTRACT

This chapter investigates the highly researched and debated key issue of electronic collaboration (e-collaboration) in the learning process, onwards called e-collaborative learning (e-CL), in a holistic overview. The structure of the chapter is as follows. First of all, it clarifies the meaning and context of e-CL, and compares it with analysed relevant notions. Second, the human elements of e-CL and their roles are explored, classified into functional categories. Third, the supportive elements technology, pedagogy, and methodology are extensively visited. Fourth, the framework elements time, space, and society are presented. Fifth, the e-CL process is analysed, following the ADDIE model and analysing its phases. Sixth, significant affordances and challenges of e-CL are identified, and seventh, future directions are considered. Finally, conclusions are reached. Throughout the chapter new approaches, methods, and terms are proposed in the interests of the enrichment or the effectiveness of e-CL.

INTRODUCTION

E-collaborative learning (e-CL) can be regarded as a type of learning focusing on a specific learning method, collaboration, and a specific collaborative learning medium or resource, electronic technology (e-technology).

E-CL appears to the present digital age as something new when employing digital technology, but its roots are found back in history when regarding e-technology (Kock, 2008). The notions and practices of collaboration and learning were evident in certain forms from the beginning of human history and life.

This chapter objectives are to clarify the notion of e-CL and its related terms, provide insight in its process, focus on special interest areas, and present current and promising trends.

DOI: 10.4018/978-1-4666-9556-6.ch006

Copyright © 2016, IGI Global. Copying or distributing in print or electronic forms without written permission of IGI Global is prohibited.

BACKGROUND

To approach the meaning of e-CL the notion of learning must be examined. First of all, it should be noted that in this chapter human learning is considered although it may occur among other creatures, such as, animals. Second, the notion of learning is connected with the notion of knowledge and the learning process can be considered as one of knowledge creation or construction or building following Scardamalia and Bereiter (2006).

To further explore the notion of knowledge, it is worth mentioning that there is a widely accepted distinction of informative elements into data, information, knowledge, and wisdom. At a data level there is isolated and meaningless information. Data are transformed into information when they acquire meaning. Information is transformed into knowledge or intelligence when it acquires situated context. Finally, knowledge is transformed into wisdom when it acquires personalised pragmatic context.

Furthermore, there is a model named 'the wisdom pyramid' or 'the DIKW pyramid' providing the subsequent transition from data to information, knowledge, and finally, wisdom. This transition occurs in proportion to the quality, quantity, and intimacy of the learning experience.

What is also worth noting is that four basic and increasingly difficult types of knowledge can be considered. Declarative or factual or plain knowledge, that is, regarding what, where and when, as an instance; procedural or skill knowledge, that is, regarding how; conditional or conceptual or structural or contextual or competence knowledge, that is, regarding the previous in an interrelated context, and regarding why; and finally, metacognitive knowledge or metaknowledge, that is, regarding cognition and knowledge (Krathwohl, 2002). The mentioned order depicts in general their increasing difficulty and importance. The first two types may be characterised lower-order knowledge whereas the last two higher-order knowledge. The latter type is most valued and wanted in learning environments.

As regards collaboration, it should be considered as a partnership community process, that is, the collaborating members share a sense of belonging, inclusivity, trust, and reciprocity as well as a common thinking and performing area. Moreover, the term collaboration is different from cooperation, since the former implies the construction of shared, mental or material, products to achieve a shared, mental or material, goal, for instance, problem solving, whereas in the latter each team member undertakes one part of the whole responsibility, constructs a separate product, combined with other members' products in a later stage, and achieves a subgoal (Arvaja, Häkkinen, & Kankaanranta, 2008; Ertl, 2008; Laurillard, 2012).

With regard to technology, in general it refers to any intended, mental or material, product of a mind bearing being. In certain contexts it may be used to denote the digital technology. In this study it is used in the sense of e-technology, which can be analogue or digital, but with a great focus on the digital aspect used for collaborative learning purposes, which is more often and widely applied.

Taking these into account one attempt to define learning is as the knowledge building process with knowledge building goals, and, in that sense, collaborative learning is regarded as the communicative shared-knowledge building process with shared-knowledge building goals. Following these, e-CL is considered as the communicative shared-knowledge building process with shared-knowledge building goals using networked electronic devices (Kock, 2008; Laurillard, 2012). The constructed shared knowledge is also referred to by the term 'collective intelligence'.

What is more, some discriminations should be made. First, this study is concentrated on formal and not non-formal or informal learning. According to Werquin formal learning implies intended process and preset goals whereas non-formal implies intended process but non-preset goals and informal implies non-intended process and non-preset goals (Cameron & Harrison, 2012). Second, collaboration in learning differs from each of communication, interaction, discussion, inquiry, and practice in learning, although it may include them, by being a process involving management, iterative development, and agreements to produce shared knowledge and outcomes based on it (Laurillard, 2012). Third, the networked electronic devices do not necessarily imply computers, desktop or portable, but they may also be interconnected analogue electronic devices, such as, telephones or cameras (Kock, 2008). In the case of computer network use the term computer-supported collaborative learning (CSCL) is used.

Finally, in the e-CL process several learning elements are identified. These could be distinguished into human, supportive, and framework elements and are examined below.

HUMAN ELEMENTS

Introduction

In the e-CL process there are several roles of human participants or partners (Good & Robertson, 2006). They are usually considered and presented as communities or groups, although in lacking or trivial learning environments they may be constituted by only one person or be merged with each other. In large projects the communities may consist of several subcommunities and even create a structured hierarchy of nested communities. Furthermore, participants may be members of more than one community creating overlapping communities (Masterman & Vogel, 2007). For the normal operation of the communities intra- and inter-community collaboration is essential. The participants in e-CL are also called stakeholders and the communities may be online or virtual (Jankowski, 2006; Rheingold, 2000; Van Dijk, 1997), offline, face-to-face or real, or blended (Akyol, Garrison, & Ozden, 2009).

Two frequently used terms, related to the e-CL process communities, are the community of enquiry (CoE) (Garrison, Anderson, & Archer, 1999) and the community of practice (CoP) (Wenger, 1998), which use enquiry and practice to achieve their goals, respectively.

The human elements are classified into the following communities; the management, the design, the implementation, the learning, the technology, and other supportive communities.

Management

The management community provides the learning mission and general learning goals, which must be implemented and followed by the other communities.

Design

The role of the design community is critical in the process of e-CL. The major designer tasks are, following the general management community guidelines, to hierarchise, implement, and supervise the coordination, analysis, planning, and design of the learning process of the learning community, in terms of analysis, planning, development, implementation, and evaluation, as an e-collaborative experience.

The designers need to have solid knowledge about all the participants, and the ability to effectively collaborate with them in their continuously developing culture and personality. Moreover, they need firm functional knowledge about the other elements of the learning process. For example, knowledge of the basic principles of pedagogical, methodological, and technological theory and praxis to implement the design of collaborative learning and to effectively employ technology to support it in the appropriate manner, interface, space, and time (Laurillard, 2012). They should also have the, highly demanding, design skill to identify the most effective or optimum scenarios, including choices, matches and combinations, across the nexus of all the elements of the learning process to create a master plan (Lawson, 2005).

In larger scale projects there can be separate analysis and design communities, and even separate subcommunities for resources and activities, for sessions, for applications, and for environments. Inside the design community there can also be a distinct policy-making community.

Implementation

Another crucial role in e-CL is this of the implementation community, which under certain conditions can be called teaching community. Some of the major implementation tasks are the advice to the design community on its tasks and the realisation of the development and evaluation of the learning process, except if there are separate development, also called engineering, and evaluation communities. Moreover, the implementation of the developed learning process as an e-collaborative experience with a certain degree of freedom to dynamically intervene and regulate it (Dillenbourg & Jermann, 2010). Furthermore, to motivate, guide, orchestrate, and facilitate the learning community, as well as monitor and evaluate it (Laurillard, 2012). The members of this community also need to have solid knowledge about the human as well as the other elements of the learning process. They should also have the demanding skills to identify and solve any emerging problems in the learning process and to collaborate inside their community and with other communities.

Learning

Another key role in e-CL is the learner's one inside a collaboratively learning community. The learners iteratively collaborate inside a learning community in order to build shared knowledge and artefacts. There may be several learning communities which collaborate with each other inside a larger learning community. The individual learners may also collaborate with learners of other learning communities. As a consequence, there can be intra-community and inter-community e-CL with variable number of collaborators. The learners inside a community are assigned certain roles.

Supportive

Apart from the previous communities there are other communities who offer their support and assistance to the learning process preferably in an organised or even collaborative fashion.

Technology

A particularly significant community is the technology one or the learning technologists. They are responsible for the development and functionality of the technological aspect of the e-CL process. They can be distinguished into several categories according to their technological task. For example, learning support by administration, advice, development, implementation, and evaluation issues concerning e-technologies in terms of software, hardware, and networks.

Funding, Supplying, and Maintenance

The funding community is the one that financially supports the e-CL process in terms of participant funding, facilities supply and care, and emergency costs. The supplying community undertakes the supply of the material resources, and the maintenance community is responsible for the maintenance of the buildings and equipment.

Research

The research community is conducting research to identify problematic areas and propose more effective alternatives for the e-CL process.

Other

Other supportive communities can facilitate the e-CL process. Psychologists, neuroscientists, sociologists, anthropologists, linguists, philosophers, engineers, pastors, guardians, relatives and friends are some cases in point.

Finally, there are people who live in the surroundings and may influence in disparate ways, for instance, regarding culture, positively or even negatively the learning process, for example relatives, friends and neighbours.

SUPPORTIVE ELEMENTS

Introduction

In the learning process of e-CL we may identify certain supportive learning elements. These are the learning media or resources or technologies, the pedagogy or andragogy, the learning methods, including the way of communication and collaboration, and the learning content. The supportive elements may be categorised as being originally created, or being an adapted version, or just selected unchanged from another learning source.

Following the Technological Pedagogical Content Knowledge (TPACK or TPCK) model or framework (Mishra & Koehler, 2006) three supportive elements could be identified. The Technology, the Pedagogy, including the Methodology, and the Content.

Technology

The technology incorporates media, applications, environments, non-digital technologies, and infrastructure. The appropriate technologies are identified, combined, and applied for each e-CL learning environment.

Media

The presentation of the content through its several sensory forms, called modalities, requires the presence and function of certain devices or hardware called media, which substantiate it (Bezemer & Kress, 2008). There are several kinds of hardware supporting e-CL, for instance, digital and analogue mass media, desktop, mobile, and handheld computers, mobile phones and devices. When the latter are used for learning the phenomenon is called m-learning (Kok, 2011; Kukulska-Hulme & Traxler, 2007). Additional learning supporting hardware includes computer peripherals, such as cameras, projectors, speakers, and microphones, and other advanced tools, such as, advanced computer-mediated or augmented or virtual reality (VR) tools, interactive whiteboards (IWBs), digital wallboards, interactive transformable objects, multi-sensory and multi-touch devices, which interact with the participants in a variety of sensory ways, as well as robots.

Regarding the latter, a key research area is the creation of robots resembling humans physically, mentally, emotionally and behaviourally, that is, humanlike, intelligent, affective, and interactive robots, which perceive, understand, and express thoughts, emotions, and actions. Kahn et al. (2007) propose nine psychological benchmarks for measuring the successful construction of humanlike robots and suggest similar benchmarks on cognition, emotion, and collaboration.

Applications

The modalities can also be presented with the assistance of software applications. Several types of applications are used in combination with collaborative learning, which transform it into e-CL. Some of the application areas these types could be classified into are the following. Communication and discussion, such as, teleconferencing, Instant Messaging (IM), forums and email; writing and generally development, such as, weblogs, wikis, glossaries, annotators, e-notebooks, and e-noticeboards; evaluation and practice, such as, e-surveys, quizzes, and e-voting; entertainment, such as, educational, and serious games; application, file, and desktop sharing; file, project, and resources management; media or multimedia recorders, editors, and players; e-translation; social bookmarking; social classification or folksonomies; blending or mashups; groupware; simulations; virtual objects or realia; virtual worlds, for instance, Second Life; agents; avatars; ambient environments; and e-portfolios, which facilitate students' reflection on their learning. The collaboration can occur real time in several virtual rooms of these applications.

These applications can be separated into web or web-based and non-web. The former ones gain increasing attraction. They are divided into three generations; the first or Web 1.0 or World Wide Web or Lexical Web with static hyperlinked pages targeting connecting data, the second or Web 2.0 or Social Web or Syntactic Web with user-generated and shared content, and social networks targeting connecting people and information, and the, yet conceptual, third or Web 3.0 or Semantic Web with smartly interconnected resources targeting connecting knowledge (Pileggi, Fernandez-Llatas, & Traver, 2012). The Social Semantic Web attempts to combine the Social and the Semantic Web (Breslin, Passant, & Decker, 2009). A further generation, for example Wise or Pragmatic Web, could target connecting wisdom or metaknowledge (Section Background).

Another distinction is between multimedia and non-multimedia, as well as interactive and non-interactive applications. Multimedia applications integrate some of the content modalities (Subsection Content), whereas non-multimedia only a single content modality. The multimedia and interactive applications are increasingly widespread.

Another category of increasingly used in learning applications are mobile applications. Their considerable advantage is that they can be used in several places, even when travelling.

Two applications which have attracted special interest in the educational community are agents and avatars. They both are virtual humanoids, or even other kinds of creatures, created by programmers. An important difference between them is that agents are controlled by software whereas avatars by a human directly. There are further important distinctions between agents, such as, the autonomous, operated only by software, and the Wizard of Oz, operated partly by a hidden to the learner human, ones. Furthermore, the realistic, such as anthropomorphic, which demonstrate advantages in learning, which is characterised as 'persona effect' (Beun, De Vos, & Witteman, 2003), and the fantastic, such as cartoon, ones. Finally, the agents can be affective, embodied, and conversational interacting with emotions, body, and speech, respectively (Cerezo, Baldassarri, Hupont, & Seron, 2008).

Environments

The applications and media can be integrated into electronic learning environments or platforms, such as, portals, social networks, Virtual Learning Environments (VLEs) or Learning Management Systems (LMSs), Personal Learning Environments (PLEs), Intelligent Tutoring Systems (ITSs), and Massive Online Open Courses (MOOCs).

The basic learning environments are those oriented in the implementation of the learning process. Among these the mostly used are VLEs, such as, the Modular Object-Oriented Dynamic Learning Environment (moodle), Blackboard Learn, Canvas, Sakai, and Edmodo.

Significant aspects that some of these environments support are learning content management, partner, especially learner, engagement, analytics and dashboards, and learning process capture. There are even specialised environments for each of these aspects. For instance, MediaWiki for content management, Piazza for partner engagement, Blackboard Analytics for Learn for analytics, and Blackboard Collaborate, and Echo360 Lecture Capture for learning capture.

The case of PLEs is noteworthy, since the learning community, mostly collaboratively, undertakes the roles of all the other communities, supporting itself within and defining the learning environment and process (Magagnino, 2008).

Another type of environments are learning design environments that afford the learning design phase instead of the learning implementation (Subsection Process Phases). They enable and assist in the creation, modification, visualisation, publication, and sharing of learning designs. Such examples are the learning design support environment Learning Designer (Laurillard et al., 2013), CompendiumLD, LdShake (Hernández-Leo et al., 2011), Integrated Learning Design Environment (ILDE), eLearning XHTML editor (eXe), Cadmos (CoursewAre Development Methodology for Open instructional Systems), WebInstanceCollage, and OpenGLM.

Significant aspects that some of these environments support are pedagogy profiles; swimlane, or otherwise structured, flowcharts including visualised learning elements; learning outcomes maps, which ensure the 'constructive alignment' among outcomes, activities, and assessments (Subsection Process Phases); and virtually, socially networked design communities (Conole, 2013; Dalziel, 2007).

An additional type of environments are learning development environments that foster and implement the learning development phase (Subsection Process Phases). Known examples comprise Articulate Storyline, Adobe Captivate, and Trivantis Lectora.

A special type of platforms for learning purposes are ITSs (Stankov, Glavinić, & Rosić, 2011), which are designed to interact intelligently with the learning, and sometimes the implementation, community, understand it, and adjust the learning process in order to accommodate their needs. These systems incorporate several of the previously mentioned applications and especially agents called intelligent tutoring agents (ITAs), including pedagogical conversational agents (PCAs). The emergence of affective computing led to another type of affectively-sensitive tutoring systems the affective ones (ATSs) (Ben Ammar, Neji, Alimi, & Gouardères, 2010).

Lately, there is an increasing interest in the combination of the Artificial Intelligence (AI), which is employed in ITSs, with collaborative learning, which is employed in CSCL. This interest is expressed by the design of collaborative ITSs that supports CSCL scripts, as described by Olsen, Belenky, Aleven, and Rummel (2014), and by the exploration of the synergy between CSCL and ITS, as described by Tchounikine, Rummel, and McLaren (2010). These efforts foster the development of the so-called adaptive collaborative learning support (ACLS) systems or of Adaptive and Intelligent Collaborative Learning Environments. These provide adaptively intelligent support to collaborative learning (Magnisalis, Demetriadis, & Karakostas, 2011; Walker, Rummel, & Koedinger, 2009).

Another type of platforms is created by the integration of learning environments into virtual worlds. An effort in this area is Simulation Linked Object Oriented Dynamic Learning Environment (SLOODLE), which integrates moodle into Second Life. An extension of this would be the creation of Virtual Learning Worlds (VLWs), that is, virtual worlds dedicated to the learning process.

Finally, a challenging learning environment is one including both the learning design and the learning implementation phase or even all the phases of the learning process (Subsection Process Phases). Attempts to implement such a system are the Learning Activity Management System (LAMS), CeLS (Collaborative e-Learning Structures), the Collaborative Face to Face Educational Environment (CoFFEE), and the Integrated Learning Design Environment (ILDE).

This environment could be facilitated by the employment of AI (Luckin, Koedinger, & Greer, 2007), multiple agents, and collaboration and could be named 'Adaptive and Intelligent Multi-agent Collaborative Learning Process Environment (AIM CoLPE)'. One effort in this direction but in a different application domain is described by Feng (2008). This could be appropriately adapted and extended in the learning domain and even extended with social networking features. Adaptive supportive feedback could be driven by dynamic learner models.

Non-Digital Technologies

Except for the digital technology there are also non-digital, or conventional technologies, in terms of learning tools and objects, such as analogue cameras and overhead projectors, which are combined with the digital ones to support the learning process. In a wide sense even non-electronic media, such as, realia, that is, supportive real objects, can be considered learning fostering technologies.

Infrastructure

The several kinds of networks and networking equipment, analog or digital, wired or wireless, are further technological elements supporting the learning process. These could be considered synonyms with the term Information and Communications Technologies (ICTs). Another related notion is cloud computing for e-learning, that is, networks of remote servers and applications providing centralised storage and online access to e-learning services and resources (Dong, Zheng, Yang, Li, & Qiao, 2009).

Finally, certain digital and non-digital technologies are supportive of the previously mentioned main technologies in the e-CL process, such as, user interfaces (UIs), which are studied by Human-Computer Interaction (HCI), databases, knowledge bases, and search engines. These together with networks may be referred to with the term infrastructure.

Pedagogy

The pedagogy examines and proposes mainly about the human, and especially learner, modelling, about the learning objectives or outcomes, and about the learning theories. It also proposes about the other supportive elements and serves as a basis to methodology which can be considered as part of pedagogy.

Human Modelling

The human modelling refers to the process of construction of human models, that is, knowledge representations about participants, and especially learners. In the latter case the process is called learner modelling. If the human models are accessible by the ones they model, and possibly also by other participants, they are called open. They may also be editable, interactive, and cooperative. The access takes place through an appropriately developed interface, such as, skill meters or concept maps. The represented knowledge is both static, which is also called profile, and dynamic, and mostly qualitative.

For the human modelling several kinds of participant aspects must be investigated. For instance, the resources of the participants either the temporal, such as, available time and age; the material, such as, available resources and media, including e-technologies; the mental or cognitive, such as, beliefs, knowledge, including misconceptions (Sawyer, 2006), skills and competences; the psychological or affective, such as, interests, wills and motivations, emotions, predispositions, and attitudes; the physiological, such as, gender and race; the behavioural, such as, habits, the sociocultural, such as, roles and relations, ethnicity, religion, language, profession, socioeconomic status, and qualifications (Selwyn, 2011). Moreover, the several natural or special needs, and the experiences of the participants. The modelling can be assisted by the employment of learning analytics (Subsection Process Phases).

Another important aspect of the human modelling are the developmental stages in terms of cognition, for example, Piaget's theory, psychology and sociology, for example, Erikson's theory, morality, for instance, Kohlberg's theory, religion, for instance, Goldman's theory, culture or similar areas.

Learning Objectives

As regards the learning objectives or outcomes they refer to the desired results of the learning procedure given the status of the learning elements. The objectives may be structured in several layers from the more general and long-term, for example, final or institutional objectives, to the more specific and short-term ones, such as, activity objectives.

The more specific ones should follow certain criteria, such as the SMART ones, that is, to be specific, measurable, achievable, relevant or interesting, and time-bound. The latter consist of actions, conditions, regarding the human and supportive elements except the pedagogy, and criteria, regarding the framework elements and correctness levels. The actions, and the objectives including them, can be distinguished into cognitive, affective, and psychomotor ones according to the domains described in Bloom's taxonomy of learning objectives. The cognitive objectives can be classified in the 24 cells of the taxonomy table described in (Krathwohl, 2002) with a six-column cognition horizontal dimension and a four-row knowledge vertical dimension.

An example of a significant objective in the learning process is that the learner should advance to reach the limits of their capabilities, acquire metalearning and metacognitive skills and become both an autonomous and a collaborative learner.

Learning Theories

The theories investigate the way that learning is achieved, adopt certain principles, and propose learning techniques. In the design of a learning process there is usually a combination of learning theories. Since they are considered of great importance in the learning process a small overview of them follows focusing on and beginning with the major ones.

Behaviourism

Behaviourism adopts the black box theory for learning, that is, the internal mental learning activities are unknowable and unmeasurable. It focuses on external observable behaviour. It utilises either of two types of conditioning, that is, a process modifying the behaviour. Classical conditioning involves a reflexive response to an external conditioned stimulus, whereas operant conditioning, in which case the behaviourism is called radical, involves a feedback on the previous response by either a reward-reinforcement, to increase its frequency, or a punishment, to decrease it. Both rewards and punishments may be positive, adding stimuli, or negative, removing stimuli. Learning is considered as an external process, either as acquisition of a new or change in the behaviour through conditioning. The learning objectives, activities, and evaluations are behavioural attempting to elicit effectively desired responses, and corrective feedback is applied to the activities. The learners just acquire but do not process or create knowledge or behaviours adopting a mostly passive role (Selwyn, 2011).

Cognitivism

Cognitivism adopts cognitive theories, like the information processing or computational one, which view the mind as a computational system, where the cognitive, and especially the memory, system acquires and processes information comparing the present experience and knowledge with prior ones. The prior experience and knowledge is considered to exist in organised mental knowledge patterns, called schemata. It focuses on cognitive processes. Inside the cognitive system there is a special focus on the memory system and its subsystems, such as sensory, short-term, working and long-term memory. Learning is considered as an internal mental process, especially a schema acquisition or change, involving input, coding, processing, organisation, storage and recall. The learning objectives, activities, and evaluations are cognitive attempting to effectively construct cognitive structures. The learners acquire and process but do not create knowledge.

Cognitivism has several variations, attempting to model the mental system and its processes. One of them is associationism having as models associations of successive mental states. Other ones are computationalism modelling symbolic formal operations, and connectionism modelling interconnected networks of simple units. The new or modern connectionism deals with large, multilevel, massively parallel networks (Shultz, 2011).

Some minor theories in the framework of cognitivism are cognitive load theory, dual-coding theory, and information processing theory. A key topic in these theories and cognitivism in general is memory and the distinction between the different kinds of memory, for example, the sensory, the short-term, the working, and the long-term memory.

Constructivism

Constructivism adopts theories that propose active participation and free exploration and understanding leading to self-knowledge construction by building present knowledge and experience upon and with prior ones by appropriately connecting them. Its focus lies on the prior knowledge and experience and the cognitive development of the learners, which uses as a foundation to assist them in building and developing new knowledge upon and with it. Learning is considered as self-knowledge construction upon and with prior experiences using present, mostly immersive, ones. The learning objectives, activities, and evaluations are cognitive attempting to assist the learners in constructing effectively cognitive structures themselves. The learners acquire, process and create knowledge adopting a central active role.

A theory similar to constructivism, introduced by Papert, is constructionism. A specific difference between them is that constructionism involves more practical creative activities, for example, creating tangible objects, rather than mental ones.

Social Theories

Two variations of constructivism and constructionism are social constructivism and social constructionism, respectively. They highlight social experience, communication, socialisation, and authentic environments. They also pinpoint the role society and culture, and especially language as a mind tool (Kelly, 2010), play in the content and manner of learning. They imply shared and situated learning activities unlike their non-social counterparts. The two basic theories are characterised as cognitive or radical to be distinguished by their social counterparts.

One significant goal in the learning process according to these theories is that the learner advances to reach the limits of their learning capabilities and extend them assisted by their social environment. A notion related to this is Vygotsky's 'Zone of Proximal Development' (ZPD), which denotes the extension of the actual personal learning range or zone of a learner to its potential when support is provided by other more advanced collaborating learning partners (Vygotsky, 1978). This support can take the form of mediation or scaffolding (Kozulin, 2003), that is, assistance to a learner proportionally adapted to their current needs so that they achieve their current goals on their own. This assistance is accomplished through intersubjectivity, that is, negotiated shared situation definition, and semiotic mediation (Wertsch, 1984).

Two related theories are distributed cognition and situated cognition (Jonassen & Land, 2000). Distributed cognition, introduced by Hutchins, is a form of social constructivism which argues that knowledge also lies outside a person in their dynamic social and physical environment (Cole & Engeström, 1993). On the other hand, situated cognition is a form of social constructionism which maintains that knowing is embedded or situated in interactive activities inside a sociocultural and physical context.

A social theory which combines elements from behaviourism, cognitivism, and the social aspects is social learning theory. According to this theory learning is a cognitive modelling process that occurs through the observation of others' behaviour or explicit instruction. The observation of behaviour includes observation of rewards and punishments, which leads to representative or vicarious reinforcement or punishment.

Finally, two variations of social constructivism and social constructionism are communal constructivism and constructionism, respectively. Their characteristic difference is that they create shared knowledge not only with, like the social theories, but also for, that is, impacting, the learning community.

Minor Theories

Several other minor learning theories were proposed. A controversial and highly debated theory is the learning styles one, for example, whether a specific learner prefers and is facilitated by dealing with verbal-auditory, reflective-observational, visual, or kinesthetic-hands-on information. A similar viewpoint is taken by the theory of multiple intelligences by Gardner, which divides intelligence and learning into several modalities, that is, musical, visual, verbal, logical, bodily, interpersonal, intrapersonal, naturalistic and existential. Another theory, trialogical learning, resembles social constructivism in proposing an interaction which develops shared artefacts, in contrast to a non-developing dialogical interaction and a single learner's cognitive monological process.

Finally, another learning hypothesis or view, which has been characterised as a new learning theory which is the most appropriate for the digital age (Siemens, 2005), is connectivism. It is suitable for e-CL since it emphasises connectivity and networks among learners and concepts, taking into account the latest technologies and the Internet. It considers learning as the skill to discover, retrieve and utilise distributed information in the right temporal and spatial framework (Siemens, 2005).

E-CL Supportive Theories

To conclude, in regard to basic learning theories, although instances of behaviourism, cognitivism, cognitive constructivism and constructionism are also applied in the e-CL process the most influential learning theories underpinning e-CL are social constructivism, communal constructivism, social constructionism, and distributed and situated cognition due to their collaborative background (Holmes & Gardner, 2006). Nevertheless, a blended approach regarding the theories, that is, selecting one or more according to each special occasion and objective, is what is usually applied in practice.

Methodology

The methodology, taking into account the other supportive elements, and mainly pedagogy, examines and suggests about the learning strategies, techniques, activities and policies. The strategies are methodological principles. The techniques are proposed, by underpinning learning theories, routes leading to learning. The activities are implementations of the techniques in a specific learning environment. The policies regulate the learning process, for instance, the kind of communication and collaboration inside and among communities, the community size, the level of formality and the prioritization and leadership among stakeholders. A decisive factor for the methodology is the affective status of the learners.

Techniques

As already mentioned each learning theory utilises techniques to accomplish its goals. There is a multitude of techniques which may be applied in the framework of e-CL. Such techniques are jigsaw, the flipped classroom, role-playing, WebQuest, reciprocal teaching, learning by doing or project-based learning, by teaching, by design, through reflection, through practice, through discussion, through sharing, through production, through dissemination, enquiry-based learning, problem-based learning, simulation-based learning, brain-based learning, drama-based learning, object-based learning, game-based learning, service-learning, transformative learning, exploratory learning, discovery learning, incidental learning, experiential learning, museum learning, multimedia learning, double loop learning, action learning, situated learning, self-regulated learning, learner-centred learning, active learning, concept learning, peer learning, cooperative learning, differentiated learning, progressive enquiry, six thinking hats, even e-learning and collaborative learning.

Barkley, Cross, and Major (2014) proffer a classification of collaborative techniques depending on their focus; for example, performing, problem-solving, discussing, writing, drawing or constructing, and playing.

E-Jigsaw

Jigsaw is an example of a collaboratively used technique. The jigsaw learning technique supports team learning and empathy by engaging all students in two groups given a topic. First, in their expert group they focus on one aspect of the topic, and afterwards in their jigsaw group they learn the topic wholly. As in a jigsaw puzzle, each piece, that is, each student's part, is essential for the completion of the process. An extension to this technique is 'e-jigsaw'. 'E-jigsaw' could be the online, or even blended, implementation of this collaboratively learning technique.

Flipped Classroom

The teaching or learning technique 'flipped classroom' signifies that the homework precedes instead of following the class meeting. The implementation community has to more diligently prepare the material and the activities, in terms of development and explanation, before the learning session and the learning community has to study them in advance, so that they have the opportunity for collaboration during the session. The technique includes usually electronic preparation and collaboration. The latter make it appropriate for e-CL processes. Nevertheless, it has been a highly controversial issue inside various educational contexts.

One the one hand, its advocates, supported by research results, argue that it is effective in terms of educational costs, resources, and outcomes. For instance, they claim that it enables learners to distantly learn from the world's leading instructors at their own pace and schedule at a low or no cost. Furthermore, they advocate that, it allows for more personalised learning environments, opposed by economic strains, without special needs in faculty resources and use of facilities. Moreover, they support that learners learn the way of thinking, whereas tutors the learner difficulties. Finally, they indicate that not only does it provide learners with motivation to correctly learn by the engagement of their minds, but it also facilitates a variety of thinking and explaining ways with reference to the domain knowledge.

On the other hand the opponents of the 'flipped classroom' claim that it results to be very intensive for both the learner and the tutor and as a result there is a significant amount of resistance towards participating in it. A case in point is that it is labour-intensive for the tutors, with a steep learning curve, to read all learner questions before the class. What is more, they argue that special tutor skills are required to answer ongoing learner questions on the spot. Additionally, they state that there are intense learner responses regarding course evaluation, although this may not contradict the main educational goals. Finally, they declare that the reason for both the success of and the resistance to the technique is the learner cognitive strain and not the technique itself.

In regard to the extent to which the human roles are changed according to this technique it is easily understood that the tutor has the responsibility not to disseminate the 'self-presented' technological content but to explain it in more depth, and especially its underlying key concepts, as well as assist the learners not to encounter but to assimilate it. In that sense the tutor results to be a so-called 'cognitive coach', who trains the cognition of the learning community, being more of a mentor than a knowledge presenter (Lai, 1993).

Activities

The learning activities can be substantially classified into presenting, involving presentation from the learning environment to the learner, and performing, involving learner performance in the learning environment. Among the numerous other types of activities some important distinctions are between electronic and not, collaborative and not, and linguistic or not. As for the electronic activities they can be further distinguished into online and not. With regard to linguistic activities the presenting include reading and listening, and the performing writing and speaking. In respect of the non-linguistic the presenting activities include the five basic human senses and the performing the physical movements.

A further possible categorisation of the activities would be the one according to the revised Bloom's taxonomy of learning objectives, which could also be applied to characterise activities, especially the cognitive domain taxonomy using the taxonomy table (Krathwohl, 2002). According to the latter taxonomy there are six increasingly difficult cognitive skills. The three lowest, that is remember, understand, and apply, are characterised lower-order thinking skills (LOTS) while the three highest, analyse, evaluate, and create, higher-order thinking skills (HOTS). The latter are most valued and wanted in learning environments.

It is also noteworthy that certain activities, such as, exploratory, may combine several of the previously mentioned types. Moreover, in order that the activities are successful they must include clear and assistive descriptions and instructions regarding the learning process and environment. Finally, support actions could also be considered a kind of activities, which are usually undertaken by the implementation community to support the learning community (Sloep, Hummel, & Manderveld, 2005).

Content

The learning content corresponds to an aspect or subdomain of a learning subject and may expand to whichever area, or domain or discipline or subject, of study. The subdomain may be a simple or complex one. It can be classified into the four kinds of knowledge (Krathwohl, 2002). Furthermore, it should be modelled using a domain knowledge representation scheme. The content creation process must follow certain pedagogical criteria and a decisive factor for it is the learning community knowledge.

The learning content may appear in certain modalities, that is, culturally-shaped perceivable content forms (Bezemer & Kress, 2008). They are text, audio, such as speech, music, or other kind of sound, image, either photograph or graphic, animation, and video. There are three main ways the modalities are perceived by learners corresponding to three human senses; the visual, the auditory, and the tactile or haptic.

To advance learning the design and implementation members must possess, on the one hand, state of the art domain knowledge and, on the other hand, the skill to transform and represent this knowledge to the learning level of the learning community members using modalities and technological media so that the latter community may be assisted to explore this information and construct domain knowledge itself.

Framework Elements

In the process of e-CL there are some framework or contextual elements, which usually play a secondary role in the process. The most basic of them are first time, in terms of point, duration, frequency, and temporal context, second space, in terms of location, area, settings or physical environment, and spatial context, and third society, in terms of sociocultural environment and context. These elements should be modelled in the learning design.

The e-CL approaches can be classified in terms of the framework elements time and space as follows. Firstly, as regards space they can be implemented either in a learning, physical or virtual, room, or in a distance, which can be further discriminated into long distance and short distance ones, or both in a learning room and in a distance, either in parallel or in different occasions, called blended or hybrid. The latter are the most suggested course of action for effective learning.

Secondly, regarding time they can be implemented either in the same time, called synchronous or live or real-time, or in different time, called asynchronous or on-demand, or both in the same and in different time, in parallel or in different occasions, which let be called semi-synchronous.

Finally, from the combination of the above result nine main alternatives. First, learning-room synchronous, that is, on-site e-classes; second long distance synchronous, that is, Web live classes, for example, with videoconferencing or instant messaging; third, long distance asynchronous, for instance, Web blogs, forums or wikis, fourth, long distance semi-synchronous, for example, MOOCs, fifth, short distance synchronous, that is, intranet live classes, sixth, short distance asynchronous, for example, intranet blogs, forums or wikis, seventh, short distance semi-synchronous, for instance, VLEs, eighth, blended synchronous, that is, both on-site & online e-classes, and ninth, blended semi-synchronous, for example, both on-site e-classes and VLEs or flipped classes.

As regards society, environments where e-CL could be applied are enterprises, the industry, e-commerce, entertainment, the arts, journalism, engineering, e-science, medicine, lower, higher and special education, and research.

E-CL PROCESS

The elements previously mentioned participate in, support, and frame the e-CL process, respectively. This process is explored below.

Process Modelling

The learning process has been modelled in several ways called learning models, such as ADDIE (Analysis, Design, Development, Implementation, Evaluation), ASSURE (Analyse learners, State objectives, Select methods, media, and materials, Utilise media and materials, Require learner participation, Evaluate and revise), Dick and Carey, Kemp or Morrison, Ross, and Kemp (MRK), rapid prototyping, which iteratively improves quick solutions, and design thinking.

The latter, being similar to ADDIE and employing principles of rapid prototyping, concentrates on a deeper understanding of the process, empathy, HOTS, situated engagement, a more human-centred design, and is quite frequently adopted for ill-structured problems.

One of the most frequently followed model is ADDIE (Branch, 2009; Branch & Merrill, 2012). Its acronym comprises the first letters of the five phases which it includes. When the phases are implemented through e-technology they can be characterised as e-analysis, e-design, e-development, e-implementation, and e-evaluation.

ADDIE phases may be considered and used in two semantic ways. Firstly, they can be regarded as normal phases being applied mainly to the learning process and the learning elements. And secondly, as metaphases, that is, applied to each of the five ADDIE phases, the latter considered as processes themselves. Some examples of metaphases are the Analysis of the Design, the Design of the Evaluation, the Development of the Analysis, the Implementation of the Design, the Evaluation of the Development, or the Design of the Design. Therefore, the phase terms, implied in the acronym ADDIE, can either be used in the strict sense of a normal phase, or in the loose sense of a metaphase. This chapter examines mainly the strict sense of normal phases.

The five phases of ADDIE, although in general terms are ordered, are not strictly sequential, but there may be several directions among them, such as, iterative cycles or spiral, backwards, overpassing and others, resulting in a dynamically iterative process, which may also be longitudinal (Branch & Merrill, 2012). There is often the need to practice more than one, or even all five, phases concurrently (Branch, 2009).

Finally, a research methodology based on this model is Design-Based Research (DBR) (Barab, 2006; Reimann, 2013). It employs ADDIE phases with a main goal to conduct research and extract research findings regarding the learning process and not to realise a stable learning process.

Process Phases

To begin with, after the problem, domain, goal, and human elements specification at a preparatory phase, at the analysis phase the human elements are analysed and a requirements or, since applied to humans, needs analysis or assessment is conducted, generally specifying the rest learning elements supporting the learning needs.

The analyses conducted can be distinguished into qualitative and quantitative ones. The latter are referred to as learning analytics, including prediction, structure discovery, and relationship mining (Baker & Siemens, 2014). The analyses include the collection or logging, quantitative measurement or qualitative estimation, analytical processing, and reporting of learning environment data regarding any of its elements with a special focus on learners and goals. Furthermore, particular challenges regarding learning, which are presented in Section Challenges, are analysed.

In the present focus on e-CL collaborative or social learning analytics are of special importance (Ferguson & Shum, 2012). A useful graphical representation of their results capturing the learning dynamics are learning sociograms. Another issue is that the prioritisation and focus of analysis among the aspects of the learning process as well as the methods of their collection and analysis are significant and must be defined, depending on the specific learning environment. An emerging field regarding analysis is big data, which deals with data of extreme volume, velocity, and variety.

Two models assistive to the analysis phase is the Berlin model and the TPACK model. The Berlin model considers the correlated factors of a learning process, separating them into two conditional factors, that is, anthropological and sociocultural, and four decisional factors, that is, objectives, content, methods, and resources or media. It also considers general conditions, such as, space and time. The TPACK model which argues that a combination of three kinds of knowledge is needed by the design and implementation members. Technological, pedagogical, including methodological, and content knowledge.

At the design phase, where the analysis phase is taken into account, there can be a distinction of three subphases. First, the modelling design subphase, where human and community models or profiles, whose descriptive form is called persona, as well as, general and then specific, objectives, and content are designed based on underpinning learning theories. Second, the implementation design subphase, where implementation issues related to communities, such as group formation, technologies, techniques, activities, policies, and framework elements are designed. This subphase is further examined below. Third, the assessment design subphase, where assessments, that is, evaluative criteria and activities of the learning procedure, as well as other kind of evaluations, are designed. These assessments should be aligned with the learning objectives and activities. This correspondence or alignment among outcomes, activities, and assessments is termed 'constructive alignment' (Biggs & Tang, 2011). A detailed formal definition of a learning design is called a prototype. Finally, it should be noted that the design phase and its subphases are not strictly sequential but usually follow a spiral form, being reflective.

At the development phase the designed elements are practically deployed.

At the implementation phase the developed e-CL process is performed with specific learning elements. A model or framework focusing on this phase is the Conversational Framework, which enables the representation of the application of several combined learning theories including participant and framework elements and analysing the learning process into several actions (Laurillard, 2009). Another model corresponding to this phase and emphasising learning motivation is the ARCS (Attention, Relevance, Confidence, Satisfaction) model of motivational design. The preferred type of motivation in learning design is more intrinsic than extrinsic.

Analyses like the ones performed in the analysis phase are usually performed in the implementation phase with an evaluative instead of a preparatory purpose. When these analyses are employed continuously over a time period they are referred to as tracking. Their result may be used as feedback to readjust the learning environment.

At the evaluation phase several evaluations of the implementation are executed. The analyses performed in the analysis and implementation phase are evaluatively extended and complemented in the evaluation phase. The evaluation appears in three forms. Generic evaluation, with general characterisations of the outcome; assessment, checking against determined assessment criteria; and feedback, offering explanatory assistive and improving comments or reports. An assessment example is learning performance assessment, that is, the estimation of the degree of learning outcomes achievement against the assessment criteria, often including marking schemes.

A further usual categorisation of evaluation, according to the time it is performed, is into the three types of diagnostic or placement, formative, and summative, which evaluate before, during, and after the learning process, respectively (Miller, Linn, & Gronlund, 2009). Diagnostic evaluation is discriminated in some contexts to express the diagnosis of difficulties during learning (Miller et al., 2009). The evaluation lately often is proposed to include formative feedback to the communities and actually does, so that they identify learning difficulties and overcome them. The time and way of feedback, especially formative, is of great importance for supporting learning. For instance, timely personalised formative feedback enhances the learning experience.

Another commonly used classification of evaluation, according to the way it is performed, is into criterion-referenced, normative, and ipsative. The first evaluates a learner's, or even a learning group, performance against specific evaluation criteria, the second against the other learners' performance, and the third against the learner's previous performance.

Implementation Design Subphase

For the implementation design subphase of the e-CL learning process there are several proposed models. Two of these models are Gagné's Nine events of instruction, rooted in cognitive psychology and information processing theory, (Gagné, Wager, Golas, & Keller, 2005) and R2D2 (Read, Reflect, Display, and Do), which attempts to tackle the different learning styles.

Moreover, the implementation design subphase can be modelled through learning design scenarios, which narrate a range of potential cases of learning experiences with personae determining the functionality of a learning process. Use cases derive from and elaborate on scenarios, describing the way each scenario of the learning process is executed, for instance, in a list of learning actions with their inputs, outputs, and errors. These mechanisms define the time-framed interactions among the participating roles in the learning process. There can be a classification of scenarios according to time, that is, past, present, and future scenarios, and also according to veracity, that is, real and fictitious ones.

Learning design scripts constitute the algorithms, which derive from and encompass the use cases. A special case of scripts are collaborative scripts, which in e-CL contexts are widely known as CSCL scripts. A CSCL script can be defined as a set of instructions prescribing the e-CL process. It has several properties, which can be separated into components and mechanisms (Kobbe et al., 2007). The main script components are the objectives, the participants, the groups, the settings-context, the resources-media, the activities and the policies, such as the interaction mode and the communication mode among the learning stakeholders and the environment. The main script mechanisms are the distribution of participants into groups, that is, group formation, the assignment of settings, roles, policies, and resources into activities, the distribution of the activities to the groups or even individual participants and the time scheduling, including sequencing, of the activities (Laurillard, 2012).

CSCL scripts can be separated into macro-scripts and micro-scripts. Macro-scripts are pedagogical models, which correspond to the above description with the exception of the communication mode, which is included in micro-scripts, which are shorter, dialogue models (Dillenbourg & Hong, 2008).

Design Element Hierarchy

What is of utmost importance in the design process is the hierarchy of the elements of the learning process. In other words, how much design effort and care will be provided in the interests of each of the human, the supportive, and the framework elements. For example, according to the hierarchy the learning design approach may be implementation community centred, learning community centred, content centred, outcome centred, method centred, or blended (Selwyn, 2011). Another serious concern in the design process is whether, how, and how much each of the participants in the learning process will participate in the design process.

Collaborative Participatory Design (CPD)

A highly esteemed among designers learning design approach, involving learners at different stages of the design process of a learning environment and supporting e-CL, is Participatory Design (PD). It can be considered inside Learner-Centred Design (LCD). LCD gives extensive attention not only to the views and knowledge but also to other learner characteristics, such as, needs, wants, skills, experiences, and limitations, at each stage of the design process (Parsons & Cobb, 2014). In a strict sense LCD considers the learner only as a user whereas in a loose one as a more active participant up to a full designer. In light of this PD may be seen as an inclusive kind of loose LCD where the learning community is highly active being co-designers engaged in every design phase.

An extension of PD would be Collaborative PD (CPD) (Scariot, Heemann, & Padovani, 2012) or Partnering Design, where the learners, collaborating inside their community and with the other communities, co-administrate, co-analyse, co-design, co-develop, co-implement and co-evaluate, following the terminology of the ADDIE model, that is, they collaborate potentially in every phase of the dynamically iterative and reflective learning process informing its design.

Strengths

Regarding the strengths of CPD the following remarks can be made. First, it attempts to actively involve all stakeholders, especially students, as agents-designers in the design-research process to ensure the result meets their needs and is usable. Second, there is more sharing of knowledge, power and control over what was developed and why (Parsons & Cobb, 2014). In addition, CPD boosts self-esteem, gives a sense of empowerment, provides opportunities for collaborative learning, improves job prospects, teamwork, confidence, conflict resolution, decision-making, communication and prioritisation skills (Benton, 2013). Finally, it is effective for adult learners (Scaife, Rogers, Aldrich, & Davies, 1997) and facilitates mutual learning, personal and competence development, professional orientation, and working within interdisciplinary groups (Bossen, Dindler, & Iversen, 2010).

Weaknesses

On the other hand some of its weaknesses are the following. First, the children learners' responsibility is questionable (Scaife et al., 1997). Second, there is an increased probability that the learners demonstrate inability or unwillingness to be a creative co-designers or even co-informants (Scaife et al., 1997). Third, there is a certain degree of prioritisation among stakeholders, in contrast to the similar approaches called cooperative inquiry and co-design (Parsons & Cobb, 2014).

AFFORDANCES

Introduction

E-CL fosters the learning process by employing e-technology and collaboration. Each of the latter and their combination provide certain learning affordances in their common application on learning.

As far as e-technology is concerned, a model describing the kinds of the manner in which it impacts learning, which applies in e-CL, is SAMR (Substitution, Augmentation, Modification, Redefinition). According to it e-technology may just substitute, extend-augment, modify, or recreate-redefine the conventional learning process.

As for the aspects in which e-CL fosters learning, there can be promoting changes to each of the learning elements, that is, firstly, in the human, secondly, in pedagogy and methodology, thirdly, in the content, and fourthly, in the framework. It also provides political affordances.

Human

To begin with, regarding human affordances, e-CL enables the implementation community to control the learning process, in terms of the allowed communication and content. Furthermore, to detect, identify, and predict the learners' physical, mental, emotional, social, or learning status and problems. The learners suffering from the latter and having special learning needs are also supported in their learning and socialisation by respective assistive technologies.

In addition, e-CL facilitates the learners' scaffolding so that they advance to reach the limits of their learning capabilities and extend them assisted by their social environment, this way implementing their ZPD.

Moreover, e-CL facilitates 'deep learning' through communal and scaffolded articulation and externalisation. 'Deep learning', contrasted to 'surface learning', is related to Cognitive Science findings and includes HOTS and the following processes, which are fostered by e-technologies. Relation of new knowledge to previous one, integration of knowledge into interlinked mental systems, recognition of patterns and underpinning principles, assimilation, adaptation, and evaluation of new knowledge, critical argument evaluation, and self-reflection (Sawyer, 2006). An extension of deep learning in an e-collaborative context would be e-collaborative deep learning (e-CDL).

E-CL also fosters new types of digital literacies, such as, information and multimedia ones (Warschauer, 2007). The meaning of these new types of literacies is the ability to understand and effectively use information and multimedia.

In addition, e-CL, by being a communal process, contributes towards motivation, engagement, psychological and social development, socialisation, teamworking skills, and empathy. Through collaboration the learner acquires multiple kinds of knowledge more easily and entertainingly, that is, about oneself, the society, and the human, supportive, and framework elements of the learning process. The learners complement and support each other in terms of knowledge and skills and contribute jointly to the construction of shared knowledge and products according to each one's special and personal traits.

Another benefit of e-technology, when viewed as a humanlike collaborative partner (Section Challenges), is that it is not overwhelmed in its task by, although it may show, human emotions and passions, such as, anger, anxiety, hatred or love, tiredness, hunger, thirst, boredom, sleepiness, forgetfulness, ageing, sickness or death, being functionally available 24/7, apart from the risk of its technical failure, especially in critical educational moments. Furthermore, some technological risks may be handled by AI. For instance, e-technology may be programmed to selectively forget or adapt, according to pedagogical principles.

Pedagogy and Methodology

Regarding the pedagogical and methodological affordances, e-CL facilitates both a, qualitatively and quantitatively, enhanced participatory and collaborative learning environment. It supports active learning and engagement in an iterative learning circle involving creation and adaptation and facilitates representation, editing, high quality iterative and broad communication, sharing (Laurillard, 2012), and reflection on the activities, the participants, and the learning process.

It also fosters collaboration by enhancing sharing and exchanging of learning ideas, emotions, practices, and products (Laurillard, 2009). In its turn collaboration promotes the learning process by facilitating multilevel iterative peer learning, cognitive activities, communication, practice, intrinsic and extrinsic feedback for the development and construction of a shared agreed meaning (Laurillard, 2012).

Moreover, e-CL supports personalised and autonomous learning. That is, the learner has relatively easy access to customisable learning materials and routes as well as a great range of automated and peer feedback.

Another related advantage of, digital especially, technology is the provision of immersive learning environments for practice. For instance, by the application of computational models in the form of microworlds, that is, freely explorable learning environments, the outcome becomes explicit and testable and both extrinsic and intrinsic learner feedback are enabled (Laurillard, 2012).

What is more, e-technologies have learning assistive properties by providing continuous e-CL recording, annotation, analysis, and statistics. The analysis can be performed in great detail and in large numbers of participants. Furthermore, e-technologies are repeatedly configurable and proffer a variety of possible assistance, both material, with help files and media, and humanlike, with agents. They also assist the communities by providing easily accessible and editable resources, scenarios, and feedback (Laurillard, 2012).

Content

As for the content affordances, e-CL offers richer in terms of quantity and quality, for example, structured and visualised, but cheaper in terms of price and easily reproducible content (Kluge & Riley, 2008; Roschelle, Pea, Hoadley, Gordin, & Means, 2000).

Framework

Finally, with regard to the framework affordances, e-CL provides spatial, temporal, and sociocultural learning flexibility, in terms of point of time, duration, frequency, pace, location, area, settings, spatial and sociocultural environment and context. The learning process can, relatively easily, occur in a variety of selected environments as regards these factors and usually entails low cost. As a result e-CL enables and fosters ubiquitous, pervasive, multicultural, continuous, and life-long learning.

Political

Moreover, e-CL is beneficial to a political level. Due to the fact that e-CL can take place in an online environment, which is open to anyone, with a networked electronic device and basic digital skills, and of low cost it provides the opportunity to a great range of people for almost equal collaborative access to the same material creating a level of fair and democratic learning access and conditions.

E-CL can also be used at the first level of a knowledge cascade to transfer information from a small group of a more knowledgeable community to increasingly larger groups of less knowledgeable ones so that finally even novice learners acquire the opportunity to receive information and construct it into knowledge.

Conclusion

In conclusion, e-CL can enhance and transform the contribution of the learning elements and assist in administrative and pedagogical tasks inside and outside the learning room and consequently lead to an increase in learning motivation, engagement, interactivity, and effectiveness. Nevertheless, these learning advancements remain actually a political issue and e-CL is not the decisive driver of them but a way, which, when appropriately followed, leads to them.

CHALLENGES

Introduction

The e-CL process faces a multitude of challenges which could be classified into the following categories. Cognitive, for instance, memory, knowledge construction and management; behavioural, for example, conflict resolution and self-regulation; anatomical; physiological; psychological, for instance, motivation, emotions, trust, love and empathy; health; technological; pedagogical; methodological, for instance, learning styles; framework, regarding spatio-temporal and physical environment, for example, weather or decoration; sociocultural and ethical, for example, learning fairness, financial, security; communicative; and finally, linguistic. Each of the above aspects may impose certain constraints to the learning process. Below follows an indicative selection of key challenges.

Acceptability

First of all, as regards acceptability, a challenging issue is the cognitive and physical strain resulting from the intensity of the learning process, since the learning participants, especially the implementation community, have to be continuously informed about the increased activities and answer to challenging questions of all the other participants timely, quickly, correctly, and properly, which creates negative attitudes and resistance concerning acceptability of e-CL. Furthermore, resistance to e-CL may be due to lack of knowledge, interest, or experience of the participants regarding its process.

Engagement

Another major challenge of e-CL is the maintenance of short- and long-term motivation and engagement in the e-CL process, especially if there is no face-to-face contact, which offers assistive communicative cues (Arvaja et al., 2008). The engagement could be supported by social motives and persistent multimedia interaction.

Reliability

As it has already been mentioned the e-technologies employed in the e-CL process are prone to technical failures, which could create serious reliability or robustness problems to the normal and effective function of the collaborative learning environment in proportion to the degree it relies on these technologies for the communication and the collaboration.

Validity

A highly controversial challenge inside e-CL is learning validity, that is, whether e-CL is properly founded and corresponds to the real world. The degree of validity reflects the learning policy which is usually dictated by the management community or the policy-makers following its guidelines, except in the cases of trivial environments and self-directed learning. What is questioned is the correspondence of the selected e-CL elements to pragmatic experience, especially of the content and the e-CL methods. Therefore, valid choices and handlings lead to achievement of valid e-CL objectives. Serious concerns about e-CL include the cases where it is utilised as a tool of totalitarian or capitalist regimes and is oriented to serve their interests and not the real learning needs and situations.

Effectiveness

The effectiveness of e-CL constitutes a challenging issue, in terms of collaboration, learning, and e-technology support. These three processes face effectiveness challenges individually examined. These challenges become even more difficult to meet in the case of their combination under the e-CL process. For instance, multilevel collaboration and learning within and between communities with different characteristics and backgrounds and the effective combination and collaborative integration of a variety of methods and technological resources constitutes a highly complicated challenge especially in the modern multicultural globalised world (Scariot et al., 2012; Smith & Sadler-Smith, 2006). An included basic challenge is that of cohesion within and between the communities.

A specific serious effectiveness challenge is the design, development, and evaluation of e-CL activities, and in particular multimedia, multi-interactive, collaborative HOTS (MICH) activities. A further one is the need for undistracted focus on intended learning and not useless common activities, which the learners may be tempted to engage in using technologies in a communal environment.

What contributes to e-CL effectiveness but is challenging is the proper iterative application of the phases of the learning process and especially the selection and combination of the learning elements at the design phase and their orchestration at the implementation phase.

Flexibility and Extendibility

Flexibility is another challenge that needs to be addressed in e-CL environments. That is, the ability of an e-CL process to accommodate the difference in learning environments and elements, which inevitably occurs in practice.

Two similar challenges are extendibility and adaptability, that is, the ability of e-CL to accommodate the need for extension or update of its process to integrate new and more, or changing, e-CL environments and elements, such as, learners, theories, policies, and e-technologies (Laurillard, 2008).

Ethics

Another concern regarding e-CL is the integration of ethics into its process. Ethical concerns arise in every learning environment and this is even more evident in electronic and collaborative contexts, where there is a network of relationships among people, communities, electronic devices, and networks. An international policy-oriented programme related to ethics is Responsible Research and Innovation (RRI), which examines the potential effects and impacts of research and innovation processes, including e-CL, on the society and the environment (Grimpe, Hartswood, & Jirotka, 2014). Below there is an investigation of four subdomains of ethical considerations.

Fairness and E-Inclusion

A hotly debated e-CL ethical and social challenge is whether it creates fairer learning in terms of access and learning conditions (Selwyn, 2011). Higher socio-economic status learners have more benefits in respect of technological access and technologically enhanced collaborative learning conditions than their lower status counterparts (Warschauer, 2007). This distinction is also evident in wider social fields and institutions, such as, between developed and developing countries.

E-inclusion refers to the attempt of shortening the digital divide, that is the division of people and societies to the ones who have access opportunities and suitable conditions to take advantage of the learning e-technologies and those not (Molina, 2003). The reasons of this divide are manifold and range from lack of knowledge and skills to lack of finance, and physical, mental, emotional, social, or learning disorders. Van Dijk (2005, p. 18) presents a list of personal and positional categorical pairs as regards the digital divide.

MOOCs (Massive Open Online Courses) claim that they foster e-inclusion by being massive, open, and online. Their massive character is disputed though, since first, the profile of the learners engaged in them is dominantly postgraduate and second, the percentage of those successfully finishing their courses in respect to those enrolled is very low.

The fairness in learning is actually a political issue and electronic collaborative technologies are not the decisive driver of fairness but a medium, which, when appropriately employed, facilitates fair learning, alleviation of poverty, joint development, harmony, peace, and justice.

Security

Another debated ethical issue inside e-CL is the balance between on the one hand security, with its several aspects, such as privacy, protection, unsuitable content, and copyright, and on the other availability. The electronic nature of communication entails security holes in the collaborative process where privacy is needed. Another issue is, who is controlling and accessing learning modelling information. On the other hand the request for open courses and Open Educational Resources (OER) is increasing to cover the needs of people who have difficulties in accessing learning for several reasons.

Technology as Partner

A highly controversial ethical challenge regarding e-CL is whether technology could become a collaborative humanlike instead of only a supportive element. That is, it could be considered undertaking collaborative roles in the design, implementation, or learning community, due to the fact that it can resemble humans, for example, being intelligent, affective, conversational, embodied, and animated.

For example, agents, avatars, and robots could potentially be managers, designers, teachers, or learners inside the respective communities. They could also be their assistants, their programmable objects, or a combination of these. As artificially intelligent learners they could be involved in collaborative learning activities or even VLEs and virtual worlds.

The question that arises is in what context, degree, and way can e-technology become fully competent to be a wise and collaborative partner. Or, in more detail, how can it acquire the required cognitive, affective, and psychomotor competences in order to become a wise and collaborative partner or pedagogue. That is, to understand, empathise, and collaborate with as well as inspire personally the learning community in order to lead it to a deep, concise, and holistic experiential understanding of the world and life, to innovative and collaborative creativity, to critical thinking, and to holistic personal development.

Replacing or Displacing Technology

Another significant ethical issue is whether e-technology could replace certain communities, such as, the design and the implementation community, by an artificially humanlike 'technological community'. Many educationalists, among which Selwyn (2011) and Warschauer (2007), appear to agree that technology will not or must not replace the teachers, without specifying whether they refer to low-skilled or poorly qualified ones. This leads to the conclusion that neither in the latter case this substitution should take place according to them.

A less scandalous but also highly controversial topic is whether e-technology displaces communities by either diminishing or enhancing their role. A diminishing example is a goal-oriented technologically standardised learning design by external to the process designers, which would lead to the mechanising and automation of learning, the deskilling of the implementation community and the erosion of its freedom (Selwyn, 2011). The implementation community may result a tool of e-technology instead of having it as a tool. A clear case in point are instances of low competent implementation communities.

On the other hand, an enhancing case is the amplification of the implementation community role by making it responsible for the exploitation of e-technologies in the e-CL process. Furthermore, learning e-technology can be and is used to displace communities by acting not only as a tool but also as an artificially intelligent and affective assistant, such as a conversational agent, an avatar, or a robot. This collaborative assistant would detect the community needs and support them to enhance their knowledge and their soft and hard skills. Furthermore, it would provide them with new opportunities with regard to design and performance.

In conclusion, e-technology should assist and not substitute communities, even poorly qualified ones, by assessing and complementing their lack and needs, and by empowering and enhancing their role in designing, implementing, and evaluating an effective learning methodology and process.

A similar debate is whether technology could replace or displace the educational institutions by providing virtual learning environments or face-to-face communication. A clear case in point are VLEs and in large scale settings MOOCs.

Conclusion

It should be clearly noted that electronic collaborative technologies cannot meet their faced challenges by themselves, and should not be considered as the decisive driver of improving change (Masterman & Vogel, 2007). Nevertheless, these technologies may contribute towards learning enhancement, as a factor of or catalyst for learning improvement, when suitably used. But in the case of inappropriate use, intentionally or not, they may be catalysts for learning deterioration, that is, for the exactly opposite result.

FUTURE DIRECTIONS

The 21st century is the beginning of the new millennium and is named the age of late modernity, which is characterised by uncertainty and worldwide radical changes. Therefore, it is very hard to definitely predict and present the future of e-CL, which appears to be not only promising but also challenging. The trends that appear to be followed are web integration; worldwide open access; enhanced learning analytics; learner-centred and partnering design; interactive and experiential, multimedia, situated and immersive, deep and multicultural learning; e-inclusion and personalisation; frequent personalised formative feedback; VLWs and MICH activities; and augmented online collaboration. Another future trend is the consideration of the learning environment as a self-organised, adaptable, and evolving ecosystem including diverse collaborating or antagonising entities or elements (Dong et al., 2009).

CONCLUSION

This chapter explored the key issue of e-CL in a holistic overview. First of all, a clarification of the term and context of e-CL was provided comparing it with similar notions and analysing relevant notions. The terms learning, knowledge, collaboration, collaborative learning, technology, e-technology, and e-CL were explored.

Second, the human elements of e-CL were examined, together with their roles and aspects in the learning process. These elements were classified into the following categories; the management community, the design community, the implementation community, the learning community, the technology community, and other supportive communities.

Third, the supportive learning elements were visited, with a focus on each of them. Initially, on the technology, with an indicative enumeration of its numerous type of media, applications, environments, non-digital technologies, and infrastructure. In this context two new kinds of environments were proposed. Consequently, the chapter focuses on the pedagogy, with an examination of human modelling, the learning objectives, the major learning theories, an indicative list of the minor ones, and a special mention of e-CL supportive ones. Furthermore, it examined the methodology, with an emphasis on the techniques, making a special reference to the proposed 'e-jigsaw' technique and the 'flipped classroom', as well as the activities. And finally, the learning content and its modalities were explored. Fourth, the framework elements time, space, and society were visited and a classification of e-CL approaches according to them was provided.

Fifth, the e-CL process was examined, following the ADDIE model and analysing its phases, with an emphasis on scenarios, use cases, and CSCL scripts, and also visiting the design element hierarchy, and Collaborative Participatory Design (CPD) with its strengths and weaknesses.

Sixth, significant technological and collaborative affordances of e-CL were identified and discussed, separated into the ones referring to learning elements, such as, human, pedagogy and methodology, content, and framework, and the political ones. They were followed by a short conclusion pinpointing the catalytic role of e-CL in the realisation of the affordances.

Seventh, selected challenges of e-CL were highlighted and analysed, including acceptability, engagement, reliability, validity, effectiveness, flexibility and extendibility, and ethics. Four areas of ethical considerations were examined, that is, fairness and e-inclusion, security, technology as partner, and finally replacing or displacing technology. These were also followed by a brief conclusion noting the catalytic role of e-CL for either learning improvements or learning deterioration depending upon the political choices directing its utilisation.

In both cases of the affordances and challenges what was noticed was that e-CL can play a contributory catalytic role regarding the learning process inside a learning environment. Nevertheless, the quality and resulting outcomes of learning remain a political issue, which reflects key decisions of learning political factors.

Finally, future directions of e-CL were considered. Throughout the chapter new approaches, methods and terms were proposed in the interests of the enrichment or the effectiveness of the e-CL process.

Concluding, in the light of this study e-CL appears as a promising field for research, design, innovation, and creative and effective implementation. It proffers some of the most contemporary opportunities and challenges in terms of learning, collaboration, and technology, and therefore requires rigorous research, study, and experience to leverage its facilities.

REFERENCES

Akyol, Z., Garrison, D. R., & Ozden, M. Y. (2009). Online and Blended Communities of Inquiry: Exploring the Developmental and Perceptional Differences. *International Review of Research in Open and Distance Learning*, *10*(6), 65–83.

Arvaja, M., Häkkinen, P., & Kankaanranta, M. (2008). Collaborative Learning and Computer-Supported Collaborative Learning Environments. In J. Voogt & G. Knezek (Eds.), *International Handbook of Information Technology in Primary and Secondary Education* (Vol. 20, pp. 267–279). Springer, US. doi:10.1007/978-0-387-73315-9_16

Baker, R., & Siemens, G. (2014). Educational Data Mining and Learning Analytics. In R. K. Sawyer (Ed.), *Cambridge Handbook of the Learning Sciences* (2nd ed., pp. 253–274). New York, NY: Cambridge University Press.

Barab, S. (2006). Design-Based Research: A Methodological Toolkit for the Learning Scientist. In R. K. Sawyer (Ed.), *The Cambridge Handbook of the Learning Sciences* (pp. 153–169). Cambridge, UK: Cambridge University Press.

Barkley, E. F., Cross, K. P., & Major, C. H. (2014). *Collaborative Learning Techniques: A Handbook for College Faculty* (2nd ed.). San Francisco, CA: John Wiley & Sons.

Ben Ammar, M., Neji, M., Alimi, A. M., & Gouardères, G. (2010). The Affective Tutoring System. *Expert Systems with Applications*, *37*(4), 3013–3023. doi:10.1016/j.eswa.2009.09.031

Benton, L. (2013). *Participatory Design and Autism: Supporting the participation, contribution and collaboration of children with ASD during the technology design process* [Doctor of Philosophy]. University of Bath. Retrieved from http://opus.bath.ac.uk/40576/

Beun, R.-J., De Vos, E., & Witteman, C. (2003). *Embodied Conversational Agents: Effects on Memory Performance and Anthropomorphisation.* Paper presented at the Intelligent Virtual Agents IVA 2003. doi:10.1007/978-3-540-39396-2_52

Bezemer, J., & Kress, G. (2008). Writing in Multimodal Texts: A Social Semiotic Account of Designs for Learning. *Written Communication*, *25*(2), 166–195. doi:10.1177/0741088307313177

Biggs, J., & Tang, C. (2011). *Teaching for Quality Learning at University* (4th ed.). Maidenhead, UK: The Society for Research into Higher Education and Open University Press.

Bossen, C., Dindler, C., & Iversen, O. S. (2010). *User gains and PD aims: Assessment from a participatory design project.* Paper presented at the Proceedings of the Participatory Design Conference PDC 2010, Sydney, Australia. doi:10.1145/1900441.1900461

Branch, R. M. (2009). *Instructional Design: The ADDIE Approach*. New York, NY: Springer.

Branch, R. M., & Merrill, M. D. (2012). Characteristics of Instructional Design Models. In R. A. Reiser & J. V. Dempsey (Eds.), *Trends and Issues in Instructional Design and Technology* (3rd ed., pp. 8–16). Boston, MA: Pearson Education.

Breslin, J. G., Passant, A., & Decker, S. (2009). *The Social Semantic Web*. Berlin: Springer. doi:10.1007/978-3-642-01172-6

Cameron, R., & Harrison, J. L. (2012). The interrelatedness of formal, non-formal and informal learning: Evidence from labour market program participants. *Australian Journal of Adult Learning*, *52*(2), 277–309.

Cerezo, E., Baldassarri, S., Hupont, I., & Seron, F. J. (2008). Affective embodied conversational agents for natural interaction. In O. Jimmy (Ed.), *Affective Computing* (pp. 329–354). Vienna, Austria: I-Tech Education and Publishing. doi:10.5772/6173

Cole, M., & Engeström, Y. (1993). A cultural-historical approach to distributed cognition. In G. Salomon (Ed.), *Distributed cognitions: Psychological and educational considerations* (pp. 1–46). New York, NY: Cambridge University Press.

Conole, G. (2013). Tools and Resources to Guide Practice. In H. Beetham & R. Sharpe (Eds.), *Rethinking Pedagogy for a Digital Age: Designing for 21st Century Learning* (pp. 78–100). London, UK: Routledge.

Dalziel, J. (2007). Building communities of designers. In H. Beetham & R. Sharpe (Eds.), *Rethinking pedagogy for a digital age: Designing and delivering e-learning* (pp. 193–206). London, UK: Routledge.

Dillenbourg, P., & Hong, F. (2008). The mechanics of CSCL macro scripts. *International Journal of Computer-Supported Collaborative Learning*, *3*(1), 5–23. doi:10.1007/s11412-007-9033-1

Dillenbourg, P., & Jermann, P. (2010). Technology for Classroom Orchestration. In M. S. Khine & I. M. Saleh (Eds.), *New Science of Learning* (pp. 525–552). New York, NY: Springer. doi:10.1007/978-1-4419-5716-0_26

Dong, B., Zheng, Q., Yang, J., Li, H., & Qiao, M. (2009). *An E-learning Ecosystem Based on Cloud Computing Infrastructure.* Paper presented at the International Conference on Advanced Learning Technologies ICALT 2009, Riga, Latvia. doi:10.1109/ICALT.2009.21

Ertl, B. (2008). E-Collaborative Knowledge Construction. In N. Kock (Ed.), *Encyclopedia of E-Collaboration* (pp. 233–239). Hershey, PA: Information Science Reference. doi:10.4018/978-1-59904-000-4.ch036

Feng, X. (2008). *Ship Collaborative Design Based on Multi-agent and Ontology Cooperative Design, Visualization, and Engineering* (pp. 249–252). Berlin: Springer. doi:10.1007/978-3-540-88011-0_35

Ferguson, R., & Shum, S. B. (2012). *Social Learning Analytics: Five Approaches.* Paper presented at the Proceedings of the International Conference on Learning Analytics and Knowledge LAK '12.

Gagné, R. M., Wager, W. W., Golas, K. C., & Keller, J. M. (2005). *Principles of Instructional Design* (5th ed.). Belmont, CA: Wadsworth.

Garrison, D. R., Anderson, T., & Archer, W. (1999). Critical Inquiry in a Text-Based Environment: Computer Conferencing in Higher Education. *The Internet and Higher Education*, *2*(2), 87–105. doi:10.1016/S1096-7516(00)00016-6

Good, J., & Robertson, J. (2006). CARSS: A framework for learner-centred design with children. *International Journal of Artificial Intelligence in Education*, *16*(4), 381–413.

Grimpe, B., Hartswood, M., & Jirotka, M. (2014). *Towards a Closer Dialogue between Policy and Practice: Responsible design in HCI.* Paper presented at the Proceedings of the Conference on Human Factors in Computing Systems CHI '14, Toronto. doi:10.1145/2556288.2557364

Hernández-Leo, D., Romeo, L., Carralero, M. A., Chacón, J., Carrió, M., Moreno, P., & Blat, J. (2011). LdShake: Learning design solutions sharing and co-edition. *Computers & Education*, *57*(4), 2249–2260. doi:10.1016/j.compedu.2011.06.016

Holmes, B., & Gardner, J. (2006). *E-learning: Concepts and Practice*. London, UK: Sage.

Jankowski, N. W. (2006). Creating Community with Media: History, Theories and Scientific Investigations. In L. A. Lievrouw & S. Livingstone (Eds.), The Handbook of New Media (Updated Student ed., pp. 55-74). London, UK: Sage.

Jonassen, D. H., & Land, S. M. (2000). *Theoretical Foundations of Learning Environments*. Mahwah, NJ: Lawrence Erlbaum Associates.

Kahn, P. H. Jr, Ishiguro, H., Friedman, B., Kanda, T., Freier, N. G., Severson, R. L., & Miller, J. (2007). What is a Human?: Toward psychological benchmarks in the field of human–robot interaction. *Interaction Studies: Social Behaviour and Communication in Biological and Artificial Systems*, *8*(3), 363–390. doi:10.1075/is.8.3.04kah

Kelly, K. (2010). *What technology wants*. New York, NY: Viking.

Kluge, S., & Riley, L. (2008). Teaching in Virtual Worlds: Opportunities and Challenges. *Issues in Informing Science and Information Technology*, *5*, 127–135.

Kobbe, L., Weinberger, A., Dillenbourg, P., Harrer, A., Hämäläinen, R., Häkkinen, P., & Fischer, F. (2007). Specifying Computer-Supported Collaboration Scripts. *International Journal of Computer-Supported Collaborative Learning*, *2*(2-3), 211–224. doi:10.1007/s11412-007-9014-4

Kock, N. (2008). A Basic Definition of E-Collaboration and its Underlying Concepts. In N. Kock (Ed.), *Encyclopedia of E-Collaboration* (pp. 48–53). Hershey, PA: Information Science Reference. doi:10.4018/978-1-59904-000-4.ch008

Kok, A. (2011). In Defence of Mobile Technologies: Exploring the Socio-Technological Dimensions of M-Learning. In A.G. Abdel-Wahab, & A.A. El-Masry (Eds.), Mobile Information Communication Technologies Adoption in Developing Countries: Effects and Implications (pp. 67-78). Hershey, PA: Information Science Reference.

Kozulin, A. (2003). Psychological Tools and Mediated Learning. In A. Kozulin, B. Gindis, V. S. Ageyev, & S. M. Miller (Eds.), *Vygotsky's educational theory in cultural context* (pp. 15–38). Cambridge, UK: Cambridge University Press. doi:10.1017/CBO9780511840975.003

Krathwohl, D. R. (2002). A Revision of Bloom's Taxonomy: An Overview. *Theory into Practice*, *41*(4), 212–218. doi:10.1207/s15430421tip4104_2

Kukulska-Hulme, A., & Traxler, J. (2007). Designing for mobile and wireless learning. In H. Beetham & R. Sharpe (Eds.), *Rethinking pedagogy for a digital age: Designing and delivering e-learning* (pp. 180–192). London, UK: Routledge.

Lai, K. W. (1993). Teachers as Facilitators in a Computer-supported Learning Environment. *Journal of Information Technology for Teacher Education*, *2*(2), 127–137. doi:10.1080/0962029930020202

Laurillard, D. (2008). Technology Enhanced Learning as a Tool for Pedagogical Innovation. *Journal of Philosophy of Education*, *42*(3-4), 521–533. doi:10.1111/j.1467-9752.2008.00658.x

Laurillard, D. (2009). The pedagogical challenges to collaborative technologies. *International Journal of Computer-Supported Collaborative Learning*, *4*(1), 5–20. doi:10.1007/s11412-008-9056-2

Laurillard, D. (2012). *Teaching as a design science: Building Pedagogical Patterns for Learning and Technology*. New York, NY: Routledge.

Laurillard, D., Charlton, P., Craft, B., Dimakopoulos, D., Ljubojevic, D., Magoulas, G., & Whittlestone, K. et al. (2013). A constructionist learning environment for teachers to model learning designs. *Journal of Computer Assisted Learning*, *29*(1), 15–30. doi:10.1111/j.1365-2729.2011.00458.x

Lawson, B. (2005). *How Designers Think: The Design Process Demystified* (4th ed.). Oxford, UK: Architectural Press.

Luckin, R., Koedinger, K. R., & Greer, J. (2007). *Artificial Intelligence in Education: Building Technology Rich Learning Contexts That Work* (Vol. 158). Amsterdam: IOS Press.

Magagnino, F. (2008). The Web 2.0 Approach and its Repercussions on E-learning Applications: The Development of a Prototype for Informal Learning. *Journal of e-Learning and Knowledge Society, 4*(3), 223-232.

Magnisalis, I., Demetriadis, S., & Karakostas, A. (2011). Adaptive and Intelligent Systems for Collaborative Learning Support: A Review of the Field. *IEEE Transactions on Learning Technologies, 4*(1), 5–20. doi:10.1109/TLT.2011.2

Masterman, L., & Vogel, M. (2007). Practices and processes of design for learning. In H. Beetham & R. Sharpe (Eds.), *Rethinking Pedagogy for a Digital Age: Designing and delivering elearning* (pp. 52–63). London, UK: Routledge.

Miller, M. D., Linn, R. L., & Gronlund, N. E. (2009). *Measurement and Assessment in Teaching* (10th ed.). Upper Saddle River, NJ: Merrill.

Mishra, P., & Koehler, M. (2006). Technological Pedagogical Content Knowledge: A Framework for Teacher Knowledge. *Teachers College Record, 108*(6), 1017–1054. doi:10.1111/j.1467-9620.2006.00684.x

Molina, A. (2003). The Digital Divide: The Need for a Global e-Inclusion Movement. *Technology Analysis and Strategic Management, 15*(1), 137–152. doi:10.1080/0953732032000046105

Olsen, J. K., Belenky, D. M., Aleven, V., & Rummel, N. (2014, June 5-9,). Using an Intelligent Tutoring System to Support Collaborative as well as Individual Learning. In S. Trausan-Matu, K. E. Boyer, M. Crosby & K. Panourgia (Eds.), *Intelligent Tutoring Systems: Proceedings* of the *12th International Conference, ITS 2014, Honolulu, HI, USA* (pp. 134-143). Cham, Switzerland: Springer International Publishing. doi:10.1007/978-3-319-07221-0_16

Parsons, S., & Cobb, S. (2014). Reflections on the role of the 'users': Challenges in a multi-disciplinary context of learner-centred design for children on the autism spectrum. *International Journal of Research & Method in Education, 37*(4), 421–441. doi:10.1080/1743727X.2014.890584

Pileggi, S. F., Fernandez-Llatas, C., & Traver, V. (2012). When the Social Meets the Semantic: Social Semantic Web or Web 2.5. *Future Internet, 4*(3), 852–864. doi:10.3390/fi4030852

Reimann, P. (2013). Design-Based Research—Designing as Research. In R. Luckin, S. Puntambekar, P. Goodyear, B. Grabowski, J. Underwood, & N. Winters (Eds.), *Handbook of Design in Educational Technology* (pp. 44–52). New York, NY: Routledge.

Rheingold, H. (2000). *The Virtual Community: Homesteading on the Electronic Frontier* (Revised ed.). Cambridge, MA: MIT press.

Roschelle, J. M., Pea, R. D., Hoadley, C. M., Gordin, D. N., & Means, B. M. (2000). Changing How and What Children Learn in School with Computer-Based Technologies. *The Future of Children, 10*(2), 76–101. doi:10.2307/1602690 PMID:11255710

Sawyer, R. K. (2006). Introduction: The New Science of Learning. In R. K. Sawyer (Ed.), *The Cambridge Handbook of the Learning Sciences* (pp. 1–16). Cambridge, UK: Cambridge University Press.

Scaife, M., Rogers, Y., Aldrich, F., & Davies, M. (1997). *Designing For or Designing With? Informant Design For Interactive Learning Environments*. Paper presented at the Proceedings of the Conference on Human Factors in Computing Systems CHI '97, Atlanta, GA. doi:10.1145/258549.258789

Scardamalia, M., & Bereiter, C. (2006). Knowledge Building: Theory, Pedagogy, and Technology. In R. K. Sawyer (Ed.), *The Cambridge Handbook of the Learning Sciences* (pp. 97–115). Cambridge, UK: Cambridge University Press.

Scariot, C. A., Heemann, A., & Padovani, S. (2012). Understanding the collaborative-participatory design. *Work (Reading, Mass.), 41*, 2701–2705. PMID:22317129

Selwyn, N. (2011). *Education and Technology: Key Issues and Debates*. London, UK: Continuum.

Shultz, T. R. (2011). Connectionism and Learning. In V. G. Aukrust (Ed.), *Learning and Cognition in Education* (pp. 25–33). Oxford, UK: Elsevier.

Siemens, G. (2005). Connectivism: A Learning Theory for the Digital Age. *International journal of instructional technology and distance learning, 2*(1), 3-10.

Sloep, P., Hummel, H., & Manderveld, J. (2005). Basic Design Procedures for E-learning Courses. In R. Koper & C. Tattersall (Eds.), *Learning Design: A Handbook on Modelling and Delivering Networked Education and Training* (pp. 139–160). Berlin: Springer. doi:10.1007/3-540-27360-3_8

Smith, P. J., & Sadler-Smith, E. (2006). *Learning in Organizations: Complexities and diversities*. Oxon, UK: Routledge.

Stankov, S., Glavinić, V., & Rosić, M. (2011). *Intelligent Tutoring Systems in E-learning Environments: Design, Implementation and Evaluation*. Hershey, PA: Information Science Reference. doi:10.4018/978-1-61692-008-1

Tchounikine, P., Rummel, N., & McLaren, B. M. (2010). Computer Supported Collaborative Learning and Intelligent Tutoring Systems. In R. Nkambou, J. Bourdeau, & R. Mizoguchi (Eds.), *Advances in Intelligent Tutoring Systems* (pp. 447–463). Berlin: Springer. doi:10.1007/978-3-642-14363-2_22

Van Dijk, J. A. G. M. (1997). The reality of virtual communities. *Trends in communication, 1*(1), 39-63.

Van Dijk, J. A. G. M. (2005). *The Deepening Divide: Inequality in the Information Society*. Thousand Oaks, CA: Sage Publications.

Vygotsky, L. S. (1978). *Mind in Society: The Development of Higher Psychological Processes* (M. Cole, V. John-Steiner, S. Scribner, & E. Souberman, Eds.). Cambridge, MA: Harvard University Press.

Walker, E., Rummel, N., & Koedinger, K. R. (2009). CTRL: A research framework for providing adaptive collaborative learning support. *User Modeling and User-Adapted Interaction*, *19*(5), 387–431. doi:10.1007/s11257-009-9069-1

Warschauer, M. (2007). The paradoxical future of digital learning. *Learning Inquiry*, *1*(1), 41–49. doi:10.1007/s11519-007-0001-5

Wenger, E. (1998). *Communities of Practice: Learning, Meaning, and Identity*. Cambridge, UK: Cambridge university press. doi:10.1017/CBO9780511803932

Wertsch, J. V. (1984). The Zone of Proximal Development: Some Conceptual Issues. *New Directions for Child and Adolescent Development*, *1984*(23), 7–18. doi:10.1002/cd.23219842303

KEY TERMS AND DEFINITIONS

ADDIE Model: A widely used framework which models the evolution of a learning process following spirally the five phases of Analysis, Design, Development, Implementation, and Evaluation.

Collaborative Participatory Design (CPD): A learning design approach where the learners collaborate potentially in every phase of the dynamically iterative and reflective learning process informing its design.

Computer-Supported Collaborative Learning (CSCL): The communicative shared-knowledge building process with shared-knowledge building goals supported by a computer network.

E-Collaborative Learning (E-CL): The communicative shared-knowledge building process with shared-knowledge building goals using networked electronic devices.

Learning Design: The design of a learning process in three spirally followed phases regarding the modelling, the implementation, and the assessment, respectively.

Multimedia Multi-Interactive Collaborative Higher-Order Thinking Skills (MICH) Activities: Learning supporting activities using multiple modalities, being interactive in many ways, being collaborative, and employing analytical, evaluative, and synthetic skills.

Technological Pedagogical Content Knowledge (TPACK) Model: A framework which argues that a combination of three kinds of knowledge is needed by the design and implementation members; technological, pedagogical, including methodological, and content knowledge.

Chapter 7
Electronic Research Collaboration via Access Grid

Jingjing Zhang
Beijing Normal University, China

ABSTRACT

Recent technological advances are providing new and exciting opportunities for researchers to work together across the conventional boundaries of time, distance, and discipline. These advances have formed new networks of research, both in electronic mediums and in face-to-face environments, different from traditional networks in terms of their changing nature and scope. This paper reports some of the preliminary findings from a qualitative case study of the establishment of the 'EMT project'. It attempts to illustrate how the EMT project as a connected network formulates positive academic interactions and consequently facilitates professional learning immersed in research activities. In parallel, the study examines the benefits and problems arising from the sense of being together across time and space supported by advanced networked technologies in collaborative research, and further identifies the gap between the academic and the technical perspective in research.

A QUALITATIVE CASE STUDY

Recent technological advances are providing new and exciting opportunities for researchers to work together across the conventional boundaries of time, distance, and discipline. These advances have formed new networks of research, both in electronic mediums and in face-to-face environments, different from traditional networks in terms of their changing nature and scope. Such networks potentially provide rich opportunities for informal and unplanned professional learning of academics involved in the course of the many and varied interactions that take place whilst carrying out research projects.

This paper reports some of the preliminary findings from a qualitative case study of the establishment of the "EMT project". The EMT project, a three-year collaborative project that addresses how successful secondary chemistry teachers structure and handle the chemistry content of lessons, is being conducted by researchers from two prestigious universities based in two countries with a 10-hour time difference. A set of preliminary research meetings, which have contributed to team building and the

DOI: 10.4018/978-1-4666-9556-6.ch007

Copyright © 2016, IGI Global. Copying or distributing in print or electronic forms without written permission of IGI Global is prohibited.

establishment of a collaborative research project, were held via AccessGrid[1] for one year prior to the start of the main project.

The EMT project is considered as a bounded system, lending itself to being studied by using multiple data collection methods (semi-structured individual interviews, observation, and a review of key documents) in order to provide a rounded and comprehensive account of academic interactions over a period of time. A set of preliminary research meetings, including two face-to- face and four video meetings through AccessGrid, have been observed within a year. A 4.14G packet of documents used in the project was collected and analysed. Post interviews were carried out, both face to face and online (two face-to-face interviews, one Facebook online chat, one Skype live conversation, one Skype online chat, and one via email exchange). The semi-structured interviews consisted of a set of preparatory questions, including the development of the participants' research career, the use of technology, the learning aspect of research, etc.

This interpretive case study intends to form a knowledge base for developing a conceptual framework and theoretical assumptions about unseen professional learning mediated by technology in research networks for a future research project. It attempts to illustrate how the EMT project as a connected network formulates positive academic interactions and consequently facilitates professional learning immersed in research activities. In parallel, the study examines the benefits and problems arising from the sense of being together across time and space supported by advanced networked technologies in collaborative research, and further identifies the gap between the academic and the technical perspective in research.

CONTEXTUAL BACKGROUND: E-RESEARCH AS CONNECTED NETWORKS

In this increasingly professionalised world of modern academia, research is less likely to be carried out as an isolated activity than as a "social enterprise" that includes complex relationships binding elements together (DiMaggio, Hargittai, Neuman, & Robinson, 2001). Especially with the advances in networked technology, academics are no longer working in isolation but in a social domain (Bourdieu, 2004). Research embedded in interactions with a number of academics thus can be described as a network consisting of web-like relationships. In this study, I depict a research project as a connected network, where academics come together and interact with each other. The network acts as an environment that supports all kinds of interactions among academics working together.

Here I present a model, proposing some of the characteristics of a research network that will be used in the analysis of the qualitative data below.

A research network can be said to exist as more than a collection of academics when it possesses the following qualities:

- **Aims:** the shared purposive research thinking that to some extent binds academics together
- **Social Unit:** a recognised entity with norms, roles, and power relationships, which holds its identity no matter whether academics are geographically dispersed or together
- **Interaction:** the dynamics of a relationship among academics working together
- **Reciprocity:** a modality (form) in which academics mutually learn from each other in the network

On the one hand, none of these characteristics defines a research network, but each intertwines and together reveals what a research network is. On the other hand, not every research community necessarily needs to include each characteristic for being a research network. For a research network to be known as a networked environment, it must exist long enough for a rudimentary pattern of interaction.

In the next section, this model is used as a framework to analyse the data collected.

FINDINGS: THE NATURE OF THE RESEARCH NETWORK

Aims

Recent technological developments are "enabling and promoting large-scale and interdisciplinary collaborations that, over time, will become accepted, essential components of research practice across all disciplines" (Voss et al., 2007, p. 1). This new digital infrastructure, comprising distributed and interoperable technology in support of research, has led to a new form of research known as e-Research. Arguably, e-Research has shown its potential to provide greater interactivity among academics and consequently to increase the efficiency and effectiveness of research endeavours across all disciplines.

However, the reasons to collaborate and, furthermore, to learn from peers are varied in different research contexts. Technology can be one of the relevant factors, but it is by far not the only variable determining the move into collaboration. As a senior researcher from group C explained: *you've got to have the sense of what it is you can do together. That sense has got to come from someone else other than just within the electronic linkage.*

Researchers involved in the EMT project are experts in their particular discipline and have published refereed papers associated with it. Some researchers think that the stimulation from collaborative work can make them work more effectively on their own. Others think that they can get an alternative perspective from the collaboration. Thus, they choose research partners who are passionate about similar research topics. Several interviewees emphasised the importance of research ideas for a successful collaborative research project. As one junior researcher from group C explained: *I think the idea has to be important. And people genuinely have to be interested in the work.* Another competent researcher from group B also stressed: *it's really important that you find people who are curious about the same things, as then your questions spark each other even if you come from different directions.* Collaboration is less likely to happen if people are not interested in similar academic questions with the same research purposes.

This was clearly the case in this study. In the EMT project, the arrangement for a potential collaborative project was initiated between research group A and research group B. A third group, research group C, was approached by group B for further academic input. However, this triangular relationship through AccessGrid failed because the research interests of group A were different from the other two. Thus, this study focuses on the work between groups B and C, as they ended up developing a much stronger relationship. As we can see, although the electronic links are available, the links cannot themselves support the research. A successful research project demands, as a minimum, a shared research interest in the first place, and technology appears to be trivial in most situations for academics.

Social Unit

The concepts of self-reflection and identity, as basic factors of learning in a networked setting, have emerged from the interview conversations. The diversity and the changing nature of identities during the course of interactions within different networks appear to be the most important factor in learning.

On the one hand, learning is formed and formulated through identities as academic constructors. As one competent researcher from group B explained: *you feel as if you are part of the structure of the conversation and creation of ideas.* On the other hand, learning from interactions such as discussions brings to the fore the value of prior experience to current learning and consequently engages academics in exploration and reconstruction of their identities (Savin- Baden, 2008). As a competent researcher from group B said: *during the research meeting, we need to understand what values (the group members) share and how these are developed, so they don't feel as if they have no ideas of their own.* Identities can be seen as a groundwork for learning that "incorporates the past and the future in the very process of negotiating the present" (Wenger, 1998, p. 55). Similarly, Goodson and Cole recognise the notion of self as a complex and dynamic system of representation that develops over time as a result of the interactions among the people in such settings (Goodson & Cole, 1994). Furthermore, the discussion of individual identity needs to move up to the discourse about the norms within a community, as higher education is made up of several communities of practice that academics belong to. When a collaborative research project involves different countries, cultural issues appear to be an essential part of discussions about academic norms and rules.

The importance of power relationships were mentioned by several participants in the interviews. The senior researcher usually serves as a node in a networked setting to create links between junior researchers and others. Researchers connect to this node and then connect with others through it. This has a positive effect on the development of junior researchers and the possible achievement of research collaboration, but it is time-consuming to be such a node. As one senior researcher from group B explained: *it means more people contact me, but my own ability to engage in research becomes more limited.* When connected through the AccessGrid, two research groups are brought together while they remain as a team on their physical side. The power relationship stays the same. The interactions between two research groups in AccessGrid are through one link, while the interactions among individual researchers in real-world situations tend to be multiple, such as through regular eye contact and small talk. One junior researcher from group C felt that *it was hard to get a voice, as you had to make sure only one person was talking at a time.* As we can see, this limited communication channel is not able to democratise the research group management structure, but on the other hand has restricted the academic dialogue due to the constrained electronic communication medium. Especially when technology fails, the more experienced people are likely to end up taking over and the junior researchers stay as spectators. One junior researcher from Group B thought that *only one person was really communicating* when they were able to see each other but not talk in one of the AccessGrid meetings.

Reciprocity

Understanding learning is not a straightforward task. Academics are likely to differ in the way they report what they learn from research work. Literature shows that researchers rarely openly acknowledge that they engage in learning in the course of research activities (Brew & Boud, 1995). It is possible that no learning occurs; or, more likely, that learning occurs but remains private to the individual and is not easy to articulate to others. Academics, like most people in the workplace, learn from encounters in work at an unconscious level; that is, they are perhaps not aware that they are learning unless attention is drawn to it. For example, a corridor conversation with a significant scholar may provide intellectual inspiration and remarkable insight into a new researcher's work. As a result, academics may be better able to inform themselves as well as others more effectively, leading to more and improved opportunities for research.

Therefore, the discussion of learning is complicated and needs to be situated in different contexts. Several interview questions were designed to elicit discussions about learning in general. In the interviews, nearly every participant responded either by putting learning into small categories or by describing their learning experiences in specific situations. It is still unknown to a great extent how learning carries on or possibly transcends different situations, especially online and offline. It is hoped that this study provides some insight into these issues, which will be developed further in later work.

More importantly, it is likely that professional learning will be highly idiosyncratic. Different academics will learn different things from the same research project, and some will learn more than others. Thus, this study focuses on the unseen professional learning mediated by technology that takes place within a particular research context rather the nature of each individual academic as a unit.

A competent researcher from Group B commented: *I think it is about the reflective aspect of learning, and we don't always do that. There is that buzz you get when you talk to other people about ideas and can feel your own growing.* With regard to this, professional learning is principally a social process involving self-analysis and reflection, but chiefly a continuing dialogue between self and others. In other words, professional learning in academia first sets out an understanding of self and then evolves in relation to other academics in a network setting provided by research.

Most valuable learning appears to take place unknowingly in research networks. As a senior researcher from group B commented: *the things I learn are not always, even not often, the things I expect to learn. I really like it best, and it seems it is the best learning, when I am surprised by a connection or something I see or suddenly come to understand. It is not passive; it is very active.* The learning comes when least expected while academics are engaged in the research. I use the term "unseen learning" to describe this type of learning. Unseen (incidental) learning processes occur naturally within research activities that are not intentionally set up for learning but are simply part of the daily routine for academics.

Interaction

The lack of structure gives more entry points to the interactions and makes them more dynamic and less organised. A competent researcher from Group B stated: *informality means the ideas get teased out more, so there are more ways to access them.* This provides opportunities for researchers to be part of the construction of the ideas rather than recipients. The informal video conversations that took place as part of this project could thus play an important role in moving the thinking, but careful management is needed to get the social dynamics to work.

The nature of interactions changes with advances in technology. The types of interactions that academics have online are different from the ones they experience on a daily basis. A senior researcher from group C explained: *we used to build a relationship face to face over a drink or a meal. That's what we used to.* Most academics find it hard to communicate through AccessGrid because they cannot easily read the signs because of the time lag. The time lag makes it hard to understand the modes that academics are in, and further, to manage the response time in a conversation. A competent researcher form group B explained: *we need to get used to delays; not being able to intervene normally and waiting was frustrating, as you would be so conscious of getting a turn that you might not be listening as attentively as usual. The silence that follows until the next person speaks can be off-putting and make you wonder if what you said was rubbish!* At this point, we could argue whether technology needs to be improved in order to build a "real" virtual space or academics need to be trained to familiarise themselves to the virtual space. As academic life is fraught with workload pressures and an excessive number of meetings, academics cannot afford to spend time in playing with technology. Although technology is often described as the most important influence upon society, it has never been the sole force shaping society. It is proposed that academics be prepared to make compromises when facing the failure or inability of technology in research work.

Generally speaking, e-Research opens up the research "space" so there is more likely to be learning because researchers are pushed out of their own perspective and possibly can reflect back on the construction of knowledge from an alternative perspective. There are a number of unexamined costs that go with the efficiency and effectiveness made possible by networked technology. More specifically, AccessGrid used in the EMT project was on the one hand frustrating because of the time lag, that is, the difference between sound and vision. On the other hand, the upside is the care that academics take in video conversations. One competent researcher from group B believed that *it can sometimes spice up the discussion because the drawback of such technology focuses attention on the primary purpose ... It's a bit like when you have a bad connection on the phone or at a party, but you really want to hear the other person so you really concentrate on listening and shut out other stuff.*

DISCUSSION

It is More about Connections

As discussed in the previous section, research is considered as connected network in which social structure is constructed by academics involved in research work. Such a network is composed of patterns of collaboration that are supported by flows of communication, including email exchanges and AccessGrid live meetings through time and space. Although the discussion of time and space pervades all of science, researchers are only now beginning to unravel the structures and dynamics of time and space from a social science perspective from this century.

The realisation of research collaboration across time and space is comprehensible when academics within research networks are viewed to be connected. Whatever mode of these networks are presented, the concept of time and space remains the same and is not dominated by the establishment and development of any research network. On the one hand, the notion of time and space would not be distorted by establishing any research network. On the other hand, a research network connects academics at a distance, which in fact provides a sense of changing time and space. Nevertheless, the sense of being together because of the connections across time and space yields contradictory perceptions towards the concept of time and space.

The Concept of Space

It has long been a problem in history that people who are willing to work together are sometimes dispersed in space in different time zones. In this century, the formats of electronic collaboration proliferate as networked technology becomes interactive, distributed, and collaborative. People are "unlocked from the shackles of fixed and rigid schedules, from physical limitations" (Salmon, 2003, p. 11).

Because of the connections between academics provided by the advances in technology, the sense of being together exists while academics are physically at a distance. The impress of this sense consequently forms a space for being together and is proposed as a virtual space, contrary to the real environment set forth in this paper. Lee and his colleagues think that place plays an important role in "encoding the cultural and social understanding of the behaviour and actions appropriate to an environment" (Lee, Danis, Miller, & Jung, 2001). With regard to this, the question about what cultural and social understanding of behaviour and actions would be appropriate to a virtual space supported by networked technology merits serious attention. The dynamics of a virtual space, with potential advantages and disadvantages, arguably influence the way routines and rituals are formed. Typically, the influence of the physical environment on social behaviour and norms is often taken for granted. However, in a virtual space the structure of interactions between academics that may facilitate learning is often hidden and needs to be made more explicit. Such interactions in a virtual space seem unsuitable to affiliate with real-world interactions in research.

One senior researcher from group C mentioned that she met other researchers after a highly stage-managed video conference: *It didn't feel like we were carrying on a relationship. It felt like we were starting a relationship. The relationships we were starting allowed us to make sense of the previous contact we have had.* Another junior researcher also mentioned that he did not recognise distant researchers in the AccessGrid environment whom he had met in a previous conference. Identities only became clear when they were face to face again. Typically, most academics do not think they can get to "know" their research partners in a video mode, or that they can actually "meet" them online. They insist that it is important to get to know people well before becoming engaged in collaborative projects at a distance. A competent researcher from group B commented: *it helped me to have met the team face to face, as otherwise you only see the people as researchers.* Thus, it is questioned whether or not virtual space is an extension of real space, which can extend or not to all facets of real-world research activities. Virtual space only resembles real space and provides an opportunity for academics to communicate with each other regardless of time and distance. What are more important is how academics are connected and how such connections can facilitate better research outcomes. I claim that the main effort should be to develop more social artefacts that may help researchers organise their virtual space in a way that is meaningful to them and helps foster their research activities.

Although the virtual space created by technology is not real, it is worthwhile exploring as a new and different place. One senior researcher from group C used a metaphor to explain: *If you were in a discussion, face to face, and one of the people was blind, you would make special arrangements in order to make the person feel included. That extra awareness might help you in other places also, to be more aware of people who are excluded. So it's like that. It's not there is a bit of me, in a video conference, you have to behaviour like so and so. There is a bit of me, saying in every discussion, I need to be more careful.* As we can see from the quote, a discussion in a virtual space is different from any discussion in a real physical room, but this also applies to any discussion in the real world. Thus, in the virtual research space, more attention and care are required, but no discrimination needs to be laid out. Discrimination would only play a role in setting up an obstacle in the way for the development of new networked technology. In light of this, what we need is more advanced technologies in support of a better virtual space for more stimulating research activities. Furthermore, such virtual space would gain the ability to open up possibilities for academics to reflect critically on behaviour and norms of themselves, and hence potentially to create new opportunities to be engaged in research activities in the long run.

The Concept of Time

Because of such connections, people in different time zones seem to be able to work together on the same task in real time, and the distance between them appears to be shortened. However, for lack of ability to change the concept of time in reality, it is argued that benefits from the global connection would possibly become frustrating for researchers in the future.

An e-Research project usually involves people in different time zones at a far distance. Thus, the possibility of working outside of normal hours in local time is potentially high. Although technology can be available 24 hours a day, technicians not on the research team seldom work outside of normal hours. Researchers have to face the dilemma of struggling with technologies by themselves in off hours or giving up the e-Research attempt in their research career. In order to have real-time meetings through AccessGrid in this EMT project, group C had to be up at 7am and group B had to work until 8pm. Group C did not get the appropriate technical support for the entire academic year of the project, the fact of which has certainly frustrated participants in video meetings, especially when technology failed. One senior researcher from group C expressed her strong feelings about lack of access to technical help: *I am not going to be e-Researching someone in London or Birmingham. I am going to e-Research someone I cannot get to. And that just seemed to be the oddest thing about it.* As we can see, AccessGrid technology has been instrumental in allowing real-time meetings between group B and group C at a distance, regardless of time. However, the lack of technical support reveals the key lesson that technological innovations in research should not go beyond the support that technicians can provide to academics. The social dimension of advanced technology needs to be bounded to follow certain "laws" on the relationship between academia and technology.

The Disconnect between Academia and Technology

No matter how well academics are connected, there is still a gap between the academic and the technical perspective in research. Most participants pointed out and categorised research into the academic side and the technical side. From an academic point of view, researchers do what they aim to do in work. Their research activities are not compromised to the functionality of technology. A senior researcher from Group C explained: *It wasn't as if we got the technology that allows us to do sharing, so let's do it.* In this aspect, technology only plays a role to serve academic purposes rather than to lead research questions. From a technical point of view, technology is invented and improved for various reasons of which the academic purpose is just one request. Researchers use technology for the purpose of advancing academic questions, but have not been able to take control of such technology as technicians expect.

Therefore, I argue that academia is in the midst of a transition from a number of scattered unattainable groups to a widely connected network. Academics are moving from research saturation, in which no workload can be added, to one in which research outcomes can possibly be improved, either by the efficiency of technology in affording individual researchers' choices to manipulate various tasks in different ways at any given time or the inclusiveness of technology in accumulating knowledge from different collaborators. It is ascribed that the importance to the new movement and to the networked structure is rooted in research itself. The dominating principle of such networked research is not technology.

From the observation sessions and the post interviews, it is revealed that researchers simply cannot afford the time needed to get engaged in the technical details, but would prefer technology to work or would rather have others make the technology work. As one senior researcher from group B commented: *I'm more interested in what I can achieve with it. I'm willing to live with the gap.* Another senior researcher from group C also explained: *I made the link in order to work on some issues about secondary chemistry education, not in order to play around with technology.* Most researchers expressed slim chances for them to explore the technology potential. Therefore, the unanticipated consequence of the disconnect between academia and technology cannot be trivialised, but needs to be re-steered in a timely manner by underpinning a sustained and concerted development effort to both academia and technology towards the same destination. This process of reducing the degree of the disconnect can force academics and technicians to re-take decisions over their own routine that they previously had and to oblige the other's attempt to provide better output, reciprocal to each other. Furthermore, there is a need for someone who understands the nature of research and is able to suggest a framework for the use of technology for researchers. As one senior researcher from group C explained: *they could say, look, why don't you do it in this way, when it was appropriate. So it wasn't always coming from me. I want to do this. I want to do that. Somebody was saying you could do it in this way, or something like that.* Thus, it is pivotal to increase diversification of working relationships in order to reduce the gap between academic staff and technical staff, and to further provide the means for stimulation of research activities. It is hoped the process of reducing the gap between academia and technology can progress incrementally at a faster pace in a very short time span in order to be able to constitute the basis of a learning environment for academics across disciplines at different stages in their careers.

CONCLUSION

It becomes very clear that real-time video research meetings in the EMT project are valuable to the collaborative teams, as they contribute to the establishment of a collaborative research project, including research ideas, research questions, and research methods. However, this study also conveys a sense that there is a gap between the academic side and the technical side in doing such research activities, and it could be a general problem faced today in academic research.

Furthermore, the results of this qualitative case study confirm that although the advances in technology provide a great opportunity for academics to be connected in multiple ways, the concept of time and space in this connected age remains the same. What have changed are the academic identities and the interactions between academics, which possibly have opened up more spaces for learning to take place.

When insights and understandings emerge from interactions, learning occurs. It is a social process, chiefly involving a continuing dialogue between the individual academic and others. Specifically speaking, it is a type of learning where academics draw upon their own experiences to construct the meaning of new concepts when engaging in dialogue. The meaningful construction of such new concepts is acquired from the emergence of new understanding, the connection made to prior knowledge, the realisation of a gap between two subject domains, the conflict with previous perceptions, etc.

The underlying assumption of this understanding is that learning involves much more than undertaking activities on a computer or in a networked environment (Salmon, 2003). Learning includes intricate and complex interactions between neural, cognitive, motivational, affective, and social processes (Azevedo,

2002). Also, learning is a transformation where energy and impetus take place, not smoothly but in leaps and bounds. Learners move from the known to the unknown (Dirckinck-Holmfeld, 2002).

More importantly, much valuable learning actually takes place serendipitously in a research network. The promotion of such forms of learning can encourage academics to critique and challenge the structures and boundaries within higher education, whether virtually or face to face.

REFERENCES

Azevedo, R. (2002). Beyond Intelligent Tutoring Systems: Using Computers as META Cognitive Tools to Enhance Learning? *Instructional Science*, *30*, 31–45.

Bourdieu, P. (2004). *Science of Science and Reflexivity*. Chicago: University of Chicago Press.

Brew, A., & Boud, D. (1995). Research and Learning in Higher Education. In B. Smith & S. Brown (Eds.), *Research, Teaching, and Learning in Higher Education: 192*. London; Washington, D.C.: Kogan Page.

DiMaggio, P., Hargittai, E., Neuman, W. R., & Robinson, J. P. (2001). Social Implications of the Internet. In H. Nissenbaum & M. E. Price (Eds.), *Academy & the Internet*., doi:10.1146/annurev.soc.27.1.307

Dirckinck-Holmfeld, L. (2002). Designing Virtual Learning Environments based on Problem Oriented Project Pedagogy. In L. Dirckinck-Holmfeld & B. Fibiger (Eds.), *Learning in Virtual Environments: Forlaget*.

Goodson, I., & Cole, A. (1994). Exploring the Teacher's Professional Knowledge: Constructing Identity and Community. *Teacher Education Quarterly*, *21*(1), 85–105.

Lee, A., Danis, C., Miller, T., & Jung, Y. (2001). Fostering Social Interaction in Online Spaces. *Proceedings of the Conference on Human-Computer Interaction* (pp. 59-66).

Salmon, G. (2003). e-moderating: the Key to Teaching and Learning Online (2nd ed.). London: Routledge.

Savin-Baden, M. (2008). *Learning Spaces: Creating Opportunities for Knowledge Creation in Academic Life*. Maidenhead: Open University Press.

Voss, A., Mascord, M., Casteleiro, M. A., Asgari-Targhi, M., Procter, R., Fraser, M., . . . Anderson, S. (2007). e-Infrastructure Development and Community Engagement. Paper presented at the e-Social Science Conference, Ann Arbor, Michigan, US.

Wenger, E. (1998). *Communities of Practice: Learning, Meaning, and Identity*. Cambridge: Cambridge University Press; doi:10.1017/CBO9780511803932

ENDNOTES

1 There are currently 246 Access Grid nodes listed on the official Access Grid website, across 27 different countries. The Access Grid involves multiple video and audio feeds that make regular research meetings across two universities in two countries possible.

Chapter 8
eSF:
An E-Collaboration System for Knowledge Workers

Marco C. Bettoni
Swiss Distance University of Applied Sciences (FFHS), Switzerland

Willi Bernhard
Swiss Distance University of Applied Sciences (FFHS), Switzerland

Nicole Bittel
Swiss Distance University of Applied Sciences (FFHS), Switzerland

Victoria Mirata
Swiss Distance University of Applied Sciences (FFHS), Switzerland

ABSTRACT

The aim of our chapter is to contribute to a better understanding of E-Collaboration, especially its intimate connection with knowledge and knowledge processes. We begin by presenting a knowledge-oriented understanding of E-Collaboration and an architecture of an E-Collaboration system (people, processes and technology) based on that understanding; then we describe the eSF system (an implementation of this architecture within our team), our experiences with it and what we have learned about the success factors of E-Collaboration.

1. INTRODUCTION AND BACKGROUND

Since their appearance in the 1990s, E-Collaboration technologies have continued to mature and to offer new and potentially better ways to collaborate and communicate but unfortunately adoption throughout this lengthy period has been tepid (Koplowitz et al., 2013); the trend has become even worse over the past few years and points to a rising dissatisfaction with the current systems and initiatives (Drakos, 2013). It seems that, after pausing at the peak of the hype, E-Collaboration (social collaboration, social software and collaboration, social business) is now plunging down into the trough of disillusionment (Burton & Willis 2014; Lavoy 2013).

This could be a good moment to take seriously "the necessity of attaining a balanced understanding of the strengths and challenges" (Burton & Willis, 2014) of E-Collaboration and ask questions like

DOI: 10.4018/978-1-4666-9556-6.ch008

Copyright © 2016, IGI Global. Copying or distributing in print or electronic forms without written permission of IGI Global is prohibited.

"Why is E-Collaboration not working satisfactorily and not being adopted as expected?" or "Why are organisations failing to tap into the full power of E-Collaboration?"

In this chapter we want to contribute to answering these kind of questions in the following way: first we present an understanding of the essence of E-Collaboration that we call "knowledge-oriented" because we are convinced that - like in collaborative e-learning - what matters in E-Collaboration is the construction of shared knowledge (Dillenbourg & Fischer, 2007); then we propose an architecture of what we call an E-Collaboration system - which includes people, processes and technology. This is designed according to the aforementioned knowledge-oriented understanding; and third we describe the implementation of this architecture within our team at the Research Management Unit of FFHS and our experiences with it; last but not least we conclude by proposing some insight derived from our concepts and experiences that could help others in answering the above questions and implementing their own E-Collaboration initiatives successfully.

2. A KNOWLEDGE-ORIENTED UNDERSTANDING OF E-COLLABORATION

Our experience with the practice of E-Collaboration suggests that knowledge processes play an essential, relevant role in it. This is in line with the considerations of other authors who claim that knowledge processes serve as the basis of any form of cooperation (Endress & Wehner, 1996; Vollmer & Wehner, 2007), that knowledge should be considered as one of the key elements of E-Collaboration (Kock, 2005) or that the construction of shared knowledge constitutes one of its key processes (Dillenbourg & Fischer, 2007). Unfortunately we do not see knowledge mentioned in most definitions of E-Collaboration and are lacking models of E-Collaboration with adequate emphasis on knowledge processes.

Kock (2005) suggested a broad definition of E-Collaboration as "collaboration using electronic technologies among different individuals to accomplish a common task". Let us start from here and see if we can extend and adapt this definition in a way that allows to have *knowledge* explicitly mentioned in it. The first part - "collaboration using electronic technologies" - explains simply what the "E-" means; the second part - "among different individuals to accomplish a common task" tells something more about "collaboration": that different individuals are involved and that they work together on a task. In this way, it is not possible to distinguish between "collaboration" and "cooperation" and the two terms are interpreted and defined (also in theory and dictionaries, for example Merriam Webster) as if they were synonyms. But practice demonstrates that collaboration and cooperation are not synonyms; for example, the term E-Cooperation is used much less than E-Collaboration and the discipline of CSCW (Computer Supported Cooperative Work) has not evolved into E-Cooperation and only includes some of the E-Collaboration research. The distinction that we make between "collaboration" and "cooperation" focuses on the relationship between work and people: cooperative work is accomplished by a division of labour among participants in which work is split into pieces and each person is responsible for a portion of the work (Roschelle & Teasley, 1995:70); in collaboration, instead work and responsibility remain a unit. How?

In order to clarify this, our approach is to focus on the *process* of collaboration and ask for example: how does collaboration actually proceed? This approach can be found in the seminal work by Roschelle & Teasley (1995) that investigates collaborative problem solving. There we find three complementary characterisations of collaboration pointing to 4 essential aspects: "single task", "coordination", "shared construction" and "mutual engagement":

1. "Collaboration is said to have occurred when more than one person works on a single task"
2. "Collaboration is a coordinated … activity that is the result of a continued attempt to construct and maintain a shared conception of a problem" and
3. Collaboration is "the mutual engagement of participants in a coordinated effort to solve the problem together" (Roschelle & Teasley, 1995, p. 70).

The notion of a "shared conception of the problem" is central here. Specifically, Roschelle & Teasley claim that collaboration consists of two concurrent activities: solving the problem together and building what they call a "Joint Problem Space" (Roschelle & Teasley, 1995, p. 75), a shared knowledge structure that supports the problem-solving activity. This means that collaboration does not just happen because individuals interact: individuals must make "a conscious, continued effort ... with respect to shared knowledge." (Roschelle & Teasley, 1995, p. 94). And this is not easy to do, it is a fragile process during which the participants have to overcome difficulties of many kinds. Analysis of this process shows that conversation (talk) is the most important resource in dealing with these difficulties. Based on many different forms of interaction (questions and answers, repairs, storytelling, messy talk, etc.), conversation enables us to reach a mutual understanding, to recognise divergent understandings or misunderstandings and to negotiate rectification of the underlying shared knowledge structure with a view to improving joint work. Of particular interest for our system is the conversation known as "messy talk" - an interaction featuring mutual discovery, critical engagement, knowledge exchange and synthesis - because it is a collaborative process that makes the synthesis of knowledge more efficient and effective (Dossick et al., 2012).

Given these elements, we are now in a position to draft our knowledge-oriented definition of E-collaboration (Figure 1):

A coordinated activity among different individuals who use electronic technologies to work on a single, common task and who, concurrently, are also mutually engaged in a conscious, continuous effort to construct and maintain an underlying shared knowledge structure as a basis for accomplishing their task.

But if knowledge plays such a relevant role in E-Collaboration then before we design an E-Collaboration System, we need to reflect on the concept of knowledge. Based on previous research in Knowledge Engineering and Knowledge Management, we propose applying an understanding of knowledge that promotes the human factors (HF) to E-Collaboration i.e. basic human elements and tendencies such as identity, meaning, desire to know, free will, social responsibility, mutual acceptance, love, intentions,

Figure 1. Concurrent activities that define E-Collaboration (SKS = shared knowledge structure)

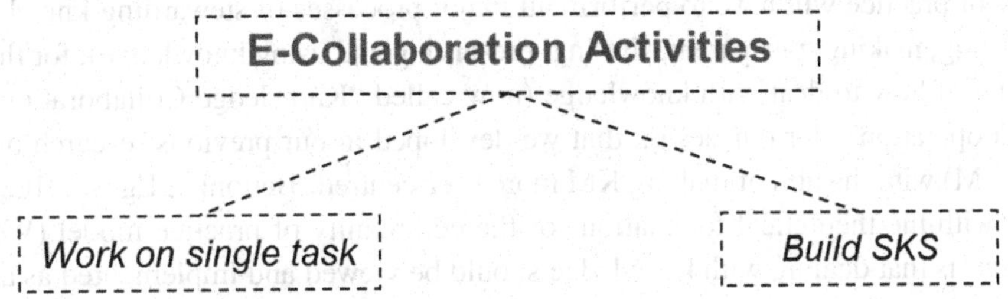

interests, wishes, hopes, expectations, etc. (Bettoni & Eggs, 2010). It is, in short, a radical constructivist understanding of knowledge that we see as a logic of experience rather than as a logic of reality.

3. ARCHITECTURE OF AN E-COLLABORATION SYSTEM

Assuming that our conception of E-Collaboration is viable, according to which E-Collaboration consists of two concurrent activities, one being to work on a single task and the other being construction of a shared knowledge structure (Figure 1), then it follows that the organisational structure (people) and collaboration processes (task, knowledge and social processes) play an important role in making E-Collaboration successful and should be designed accordingly. As a consequence, it is not enough to focus primarily on E-Collaboration technologies; we need to take it seriously that "people" and "processes" also matter and make sure that our design puts all three elements in the right balance. To do this, we suggest introducing the notion of an "E-Collaboration system" which is composed by connecting people, processes and technology to form one unit. This PPT model has been already successfully applied to Knowledge Management elsewhere (Edwards 2009, 2011): "The need is to coordinate people, processes, and technology successfully using some kind of KM system. It is important to realize that here is more to a KM system than just technology, and that any deliberate, conscious attempt to manage knowledge in an organization amounts to a KM system. (Edwards, 2009).

As regards the first element, *people*, we focus on organisational structure as an important aspect because it determines the future function of the whole system; here we concentrate on two main elements - subordination and leadership. Formal subordination defines how responsibilities for different functions and processes are allocated to different organisational entities like functional units, matrix units or teams. For an E-Collaboration system, it does not matter which of these formal structures is in place; what matters is that the system should rely on an "informal subordination" i.e. on participation of all members of the unit in decision-making, like in a social network. The leadership style is another essential aspect of an E-Collaboration system and should be "facilitative" rather than "impositional", indicating a style which promotes choice and an error culture and also pays attention to (Fryer 2012, pp. 37-38): a) creating unrestricted communication; b) legitimate application of power; c) encouraging diversity of expression; d) legitimating leadership status.

As regards the second element, *processes*, the design of an E-Collaboration system should support those methods of interaction among employees which implement the social network required by the people element (see above) and which at the same time are suitable for the knowledge management task of building a shared knowledge structure. One method which satisfies these conditions is the Community of Practice method which defines a very specific type of social structure composed by three fundamental elements: domain, community and practice (Wenger et al. 2002, pp. 27ff and 41ff). In building a SKS, the community of practice will have to perform all major processes of stewarding knowledge (like acquiring, developing, making transparent, sharing, preserving and using knowledge); for this reason, we will use a model of how to deal with knowledge (now called "Knowledge Collaboration", previously "Knowledge Cooperation") for our design that we developed in our previous research on Knowledge Management (KM) with the aim of making KM more user-centred (Bettoni & Eggs 2010, pp. 137-138) and consistent with the theoretical foundations of the community of practice model (Wenger, 1998). Our model suggests that dealing with knowledge should be viewed and implemented as a duality of a) participation in knowledge and b) cultivation of knowledge. Cultivation of knowledge is the circular process by which a community collaboratively stewards its knowledge resources (using processes such as acquiring, developing, making transparent, sharing and preserving knowledge) and uses them in daily work. Participation in knowledge is the circular process by which community members build up social capital (establish and take care of personal relationships, develop individual and collective identities, etc.) and "invest" this social capital in collaboratively stewarding the knowledge resources of their community.

Finally, as regards *technology*, the design of the E-Collaboration systems should take into consideration the needs implied by the design of the previous two elements, people and processes. The technology should be an enabler for these needs: this is why we have selected a Web 2.0 technology and a Virtual Team Office as a platform for implementing it.

This architecture suggests that, in order to construct an E-Collaboration system, you have to design a tree with three branches: a people branch, process branch and technology branch (Figure 2). The people branch is divided into two further sub-branches, "subordination" and "leadership". And the subordination branch divides further into "formal subordination" and "informal subordination". At the end of all sub-branches there are three "leaves": Team, Social Network and Facilitative Leadership. The 4 leaves found at the end of the other two main sub-branches are: Community of Practice, Participation in Knowledge, Cultivation of Knowledge and Virtual Team Office. Together, these 7 leaves are what you have to design in order to implement the core elements of an E-Collaboration system.

4. IMPLEMENTATION AND EXPERIENCES

An E-Collaboration system implemented according to the aforementioned architecture can be found within our E-Collaboration team (formerly the Research Management Unit, in German "Stabsstelle

Figure 2. Architecture of a knowledge-oriented e-collaboration system

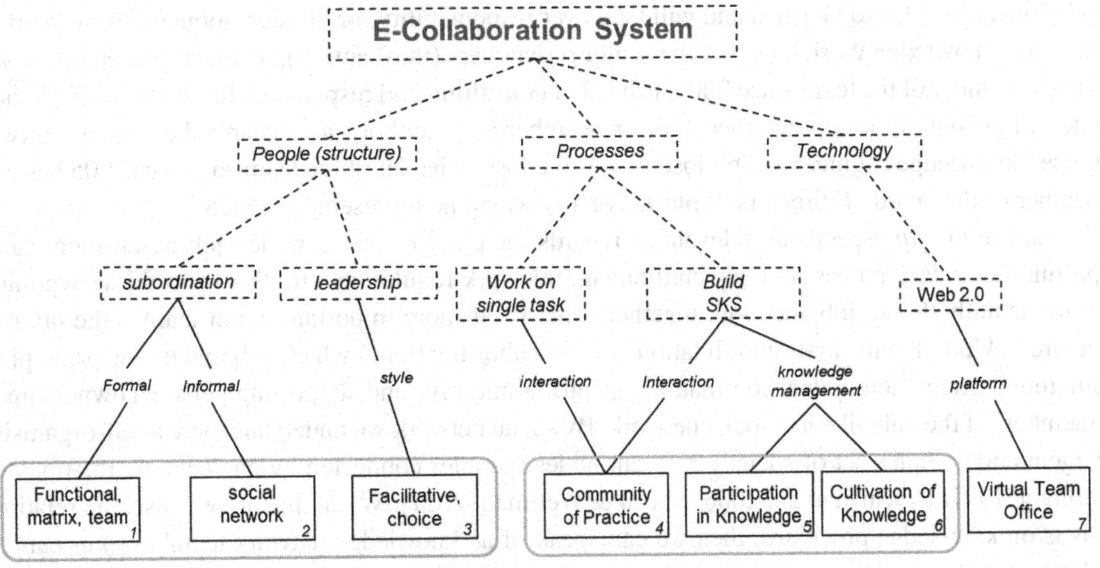

Forschung", acronym SF) at FFHS. The motivation for developing, implementing and applying an E-Collaboration system is based on the one hand on the mission of our team, which consists of promoting E-Collaboration as a competence within FFHS by seeing it as complementary to E-Learning, the core business of FFHS as a distance-learning university. On the other hand, we as a team share the conviction that to solving 21st century problems, we need 21st century organisation and want to organise our team accordingly in an innovative way. This is why E-Collaboration became our main way of working.

The first system prototype, called eSF (the acronym stands for "elektronische Stabsstelle Forschung" which means "electronic Research Management Unit"), was drafted in 2005 by team leader Marco Bettoni and was subsequently adapted regularly in collaboration with the team members. Between 2009 and 2011, the whole team - Cindy Eggs, Willi Bernhard, Nicole Bittel and Marco Bettoni – contributed to a first redesign. A second redesign called eSF2 was implemented in June 2013 when a new member joined our team in the role of a part-time office manager.

In this section, we present the implementation of the people, processes and technology components and related experiences in our eSF system: a) social network, b) facilitative leadership (Albatross method), c) CoP interactions, d) cultivation of knowledge and participation in knowledge, e) virtual team office on Moodle, a platform that constitutes the main technological support for the daily work of our team and can be regarded as its primary meeting place.

4.1. People

From a formal point of view, our team is not included in one of the university's departments but rather is organised as an independent Advisory Staff Unit which reports directly to the general director of our university and is responsible for research and consulting in E-Collaboration. We are four people, two senior researchers and two young research associates, each with multifaceted competencies of different types. One of the two research associates (second author), who joined the team in 2011, has an MA degree in Pedagogy, Religion and Criminology and is responsible for the topic of "Storytelling in Working & Learning", whereas the second research associate, who arrived in 2014, has a degree in Work Psychology, English and German and will take over responsibility for our new topic of "New Working Spaces for Knowledge Work". One of the senior researchers (third author), an electronic engineer who has been member of the team since 2006, is head of consulting and responsible for the topic of "Serious Games". Last but not least, the other senior researcher (first author), a mechanical engineer, software engineer, knowledge engineer and philosopher, is the formal leader of the team and since 2005 has been a member of the board of directors of our university where he represents research.

So far the *formal* aspects are relevant as regards the employment contract, job description, career opportunities, salary ranges, holiday entitlement, telework regulation, etc. But from the viewpoint of how we actually do our job and work together, what is far more important in our team is the *informal* structure (a kind of "informal subordination" or "no subordination") which is based on the principle of promoting participation in decision-making, inspiring initiative and supporting personal ownership for all members of the unit, like in a social network. By social network we understand here a self-organising, emergent and complex set of socially-relevant nodes (people) connected by one or more relationships (Wellman, 1997; Newman et al., 2006; Marin & Wellman, 2011). When, like in our case, the relational focus is on knowledge processes, then we can speak of a "knowledge network team" (or kn-team see 4.2 Processes), a type of team that reminds the *collaborative innovation networks* (COINs) proposed by Gloor (2006). Our team has been designed and implemented as such a collaborative knowledge network:

unlike traditional teams, where the individual knowledge of team members has a more instrumental and secondary role, the primary goal of our kn-team is to steward knowledge and to promote learning. Therefore our focus here is not on product creation (for example: a research project) or on the provision of research services (like organising a researchers' colloquium) but on creating the best conditions for performing these activities, which means developing team members' knowledge. Whereas traditional teams are constituted according to predetermined tasks and their relationships are determined by the task structure, in our kn-team it is the knowledge domain which determines the team's constitution (selection of members) and team members are connected in a multitude of ways based on manifold relationships between their individual knowledge areas. Functions and roles of team members are situationally negotiated, based on their individual activities, interests, involvement in team-building tasks and contributions to extending the team's practice and supported by feedback from team colleagues.

This concept and practice of a *knowledge network team* also requires a new leadership style, one that is "facilitative" rather than "impositional", "listening" rather than "talking" and "coordinating" rather than "controlling". The team leader tries to be neutral and not to use the decision-making authority accorded by the formal position. His/her main task is "to help the group increase its effectiveness by improving its process and structure" (Schwarz, 2005), like in group facilitation. An important foundation and tool for implementing this approach is the so-called "Gossamer Albatross Principle" which states that "Choice leads to motivation and innovation" and the related "Gossamer Albatross Method", a management technique derived from the 1978 success of the Gossamer Albatross aircraft, which resulted in man's first flight (across the English Channel) without use of external power, i.e. a self-powered flight (Weidner, 2007; Grosser, 2004). The aircraft was designed and built by a team led by Paul B. MacCready, a US engineer; it was powered by muscular force using pedals to drive a large two-bladed propeller. On June 12, 1979, piloted by amateur cyclist Bryan Allen, it crossed the English Channel (35.8 km between the Warren near Folkstone and Cap Gris-Nez) in 2 hours and 49 minutes. The key to this extraordinary success – after twenty years of attempts by many international teams - was not the technology alone (aerodynamics, engineering, etc.) but also the kind of team leadership MacCready practised. He had developed a new way of distributing the tasks: instead of prescribing who should do what, as is customary, he merely sorted the list of tasks by priority and let the team members choose: each team member could select his/her preferred tasks and the remaining unselected tasks were distributed only afterwards. Our team applies this method in the same way. Each year we develop a list of the tasks that we need for implementing our given team objectives; based on this list, each team member selects his/her preferred tasks; finally the unselected tasks are distributed among all team members by negotiation.

4.2. Processes

The design of the two main processes in our eSF system, i.e. interaction and knowledge management, has been strongly influenced by experiences collected in a previous experiment, a knowledge network called "Community of Research" or CoRe (Bettoni et al., 2011; Bettoni et al., 2007). Viewed as a social structure, CoRe was composed of seven basic elements, seven interaction and cooperation areas which correspond to aspects of community life. The individual elements are: 1) Community, 2) Practice, 3) Domain, 4) Leadership, 5) Individual, 6) Connections and 7) Resource Development. This concept was based on Etienne Wenger's social theory of learning and his international online workshop "Foundations of Communities of Practice". Since CoRe was a distributed community, interactions among its members were supported by an online collaboration platform on MOODLE called 'CoRe Square', a virtual space for meeting and stewarding research knowledge. The main part of community life in CoRe was organised based on three types of interactions which were also three distinct areas of cooperation for stewarding research knowledge: Domain, Community and Practice. These aspects of community life constituted the central framework of CoRe, viewed as a social structure. *Domain* was that aspect of life in CoRe that collected interactions in which members discussed current topics and shared best practice ideas and lessons learned from past research practice. *Community* collected interactions in which members came together to build connections and cultivate relationships and *Practice* collected interactions in which members engaged in joint activities to solve problems (research or consulting projects) or to build shared knowledge in their domain by telling stories, discussing their own cases and collaborating in projects.

4.2.1. Interaction

In the design of eSF, these same three elements of Domain, Community and Practice are not separated into three independent areas but integrated into any task by means of three types of interaction called "Discuss", "Describe" and "Document":

- **Discuss:** this interaction consists of considering or examining issues according to argument, comment, suggestions, etc.; this type of interaction is used in a balanced way for Domain, Community and Practice interactions; a *Domain discussion* is about a topic of our research that we want to explore and better understand; a *Community discussion* is about understanding one another as people, as human beings in our team; it is an opportunity for team members to support each other in exploring who is who, who knows what and how we function together as a team; a *Practice discussion* is about some work, for example a task in a project or a step in case-based problem-solving situation or else is about an experience recounted in the form of a happening or connected series of happenings experienced by one of the team's members.
- **Describe:** the essence of this interaction consists of representing with words, numbers and/or pictures the outcomes (intermediate, final) of a discussion; it is mainly used for Practice interactions but also includes Domain interactions sometimes. It is seldom used for Community interactions. A *Practice description* can be any intermediary outcome in a project, like the draft of a deliverable or an article. A *Domain description* can represent, for example, the shared understanding of an aspect of our research topic that has been discussed and a *Community description* can be, for example, a list of individual competences, connections or preferences or a table of the team's weekly office presence, a table of its yearly absences (who is at a conference when, who is on holiday, has plans other such absences) etc.
- **Document:** saving what has been described or collected from external sources to an organised repository; mainly used for Domain and Practice interactions, seldom for Community interactions. A Domain document could be, for example, a declaration of the team's mission, vision and strategy; a Practice document can be a report in a project or the final version of a scientific paper and a Community document, a CV of a team member or a plan for a team's outdoor meeting.

Together these 3 types of interactions constitute what we call a "3D task approach" which claims that any collaborative task can be performed by selecting an appropriate combination of these three interaction types.

4.2.2. Knowledge Management

Building shared knowledge structures during team interactions requires that participants deal with knowledge in a way that is at the same time systematic, participative (user-centred) and meaningful to them both as individuals and as a group. In order to comply with these requirements, we chose for our E-Collaboration system a participatory knowledge management model called "Knowledge Collaboration" consisting of two cross-coupled learning loops that activate and sustain one another: "cultivation of knowledge" and "participation in knowledge" (Figure 3).

The lower loop, cultivation of knowledge, is the circular process by which a community collaboratively stewards its knowledge resources and uses them in daily work. The upper loop, participation in knowledge, is the circular process by which community members build social capital (establish and take care of personal relationships, develop individual and collective identities, etc.) and "invest" this social capital in collaboratively stewarding the knowledge resources of their community. The three processes or groups of knowledge processes connected by means of the two learning loops are:

1. **Stewarding Knowledge:** This encompasses activities such as acquiring, developing, making transparent, sharing and preserving knowledge.
2. **Applying Knowledge:** Activities by which knowledge resources available through knowledge stewarding are used in business processes.
3. **Socialising Knowledge:** Activities at a personal and institutional level by which relationships are established and cultivated in view of stewarding and applying knowledge.

To conceive of and implement participation and cultivation as a duality means that they should take place together; they should both require and enable each other. There should not be any cultivation without participation or any participation without cultivation. Participation and cultivation should imply

Figure 3. Knowledge collaboration

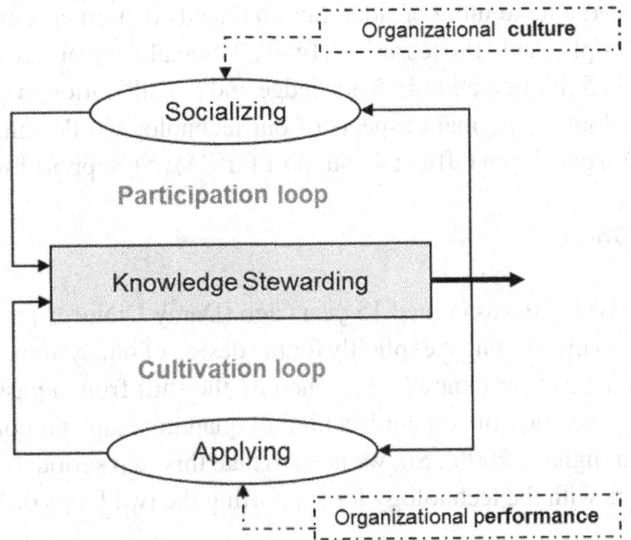

one another. Increasing the level of cultivation should not replace an equal amount of participation; on the contrary it should tend to require an increase in participation.

Cultivation of knowledge should always be based on participation in knowledge: applying knowledge requires a history of participation as a context for its interpretation. In turn, participation in knowledge should also be based on cultivation because it always involves words, concepts and artefacts that allow it to proceed. Finally, the processes of participation (embodied in people) and cultivation (embodied in artefacts) should not be considered just as a distinction between people (human operators) and explicit knowledge (artificial operands, things). In terms of meaning, people and things cannot be defined independently of one another. On the one hand, our sense of ourselves includes the objects of our practice; on the other hand, what these objects are depends on the people that shape them through their experiences.

4.2.3. Task Organisation

Within a virtual team there is a strong need to organise tasks in a systematic way which is shared and transparent to every team member; in our case, organising our list of tasks (what we need to do to implement our teams' objectives) in a systematic way led to a classification of our tasks into 14 categories which are combined in 2 groups: A) Knowledge Management Services; B) E-Collaboration Research & Consulting. Group A includes 6 types of tasks: 1. coordination; 2. research services; 3. quality management; 4. e-organisation; 5. administration; 6. team professional development. Group B encompasses the remaining 8 categories: 7. general R&D activities; 8. R&D project preparation; 9. R&D project execution; 10. general consulting activities; 11. consulting project preparation; 12. consulting project execution; 13. knowledge transfer in general; 14. knowledge transfer within our institution (teaching).

4.3. Technology

In our approach, technology is primarily an enabler for satisfying the needs that emerge when the "People" and "Process" elements have been designed; their characteristics provide the required guidelines for selecting and designing technological components. Without these premises, technology becomes easily an illusion or worse, an inhibitor. In terms of the architecture visualised in Figure 2, this means that to design technology, we have to take into consideration the needs that emerge from the design of the 6 leaves of the branches "People" and "Processes": 1.Team, 2. Social Network, 3. Facilitative Leadership, 4. Community of Practice, 5. Participation in Knowledge and 6. Cultivation of Knowledge. Let us have in the following a closer look at the main aspects of our technological design: 1) Web 2.0 approach; 2) Moodle platform; 3) Virtual Team Office; 4) Support for KM; 5) Support for the 3D task approach.

4.3.1. Web 2.0 Approach

Although the concept of Web 2.0 was coined 15 years ago (Darcy DiNucci[1]) and popularised 10 years ago, it is nevertheless worth mentioning it explicitly for the design of our system. For knowledge workers who collaborate on building a shared knowledge structure, the shift from a passive viewing of content to interaction and active generation of content is a kind of quantum leap and not merely jargon, as Tim Berners-Lee claimed (Laningham, 2006). So, we need to take this step seriously and understand what it means. By providing users with the technology for supporting the two loops of Participation in Knowledge and Cultivation of Knowledge, a Web 2.0 approach constitutes a necessary condition for making the Virtual Team Office a collaborative space.

4.3.2 Moodle Platform

The reasons for selecting Moodle as a platform for implementing our Virtual Team Office are summarised in the following objectives (Bettoni et al., 2006):

- Allows us to have our Virtual Team space easily integrated with the teaching space of our University (which uses Moodle as LMS)
- Allows team members to easily commute between the teaching and the team environment
- Allows team members to easily commute between the research platform for all researchers (which is also a Moodle space) and the team environment.

Other advantages of MOODLE can be found in its flexible user administration, good accessibility of the space for private uses (open source) and the large community of users worldwide (with about 59,000 registered sites and 76 million registered users on August 2015[2]).

4.3.3. Virtual Team Office

Just as clubs have a clubhouse or other sorts of meeting places (for example the "Mermaid Tavern" in London in the Elizabethan era[3]), likewise we are convinced that a virtual team of knowledge workers needs a fixed and well-organised place which reifies its ties as a team and which provides facilities for supporting collaboration and the two loops of knowledge stewarding (Figure 3). This shared space is a fundamental condition for enabling the construction of a shared knowledge structure. Like in the Japanese concept of "ba", this virtual team office "... can be thought of as a shared space for emerging relationships" (Nonaka & Konno, 1998).

The layout of our Moodle Virtual Team Office has a so-called "topics format", meaning that the space is organised into topic sections that can be given titles and include various tools. In former versions, each section was used to encompass all the tools needed for one of the 14 task categories, so we had 14 sections; this approach was more 'task-oriented' in the sense that orientation within the sections was determined by the type of task; for example to ask a question about a template for a project proposal, you had first to decide if this task-object was better classified as belonging to a "research service task" (section 2) or to a "quality management task" (section 3) and then find the correct tool within that section.

In the current version instead, each topic represents one type of interaction and its section contains only the tool that enables it; as a consequence we now have seven sections: 1. Forums; 2. Wikis. 3 Folders; 4. Google Docs; 5. Internet links; 6. Individual tools; 7. Archive. Within these sections, the tools are differentiated by the 14 task categories; so for example we have a forum for coordination, one for research services, one for the preparation of R&D projects, etc. With this approach, we wanted to implement a more "interaction-oriented" orientation because we felt that it would be more consistent with our 3D task approach and as such enable us to make orientation in the Virtual Office more effective. The same question about where to find a template for a project proposal would easily lead to the "folders" section and then here, to find the correct folder, you would have to decide if this task-object was better classified as belonging to a "research service task" (section 2) or to a "quality management task" (section 3).

4.3.4. Support for Knowledge Management

According to our model (see 4.2.2), we understand Knowledge Management in E-Collaboration as Knowledge Collaboration by means of two learning loops: the Cultivation loop and the Participation Loop. Technological support for these loops is achieved by means of a "negotiation triad", a set of three tools: a forum tool, a wiki tool and a file folder tool. The forum is a tool for enabling participation in knowledge: creating new discussion threads, reading posts and replying to them supports participation as the social experience of being connected with others and being actively involved in a collective enterprise (stewarding research knowledge). The wiki is a tool for enabling cultivation of knowledge that preserves the results of conversations (new ideas, insight, best practices, lessons learned, definitions, procedures, etc.) by organising them in a structured way and independently of time. Finally the file folder is a tool for storing the documents referenced either in the associated forum or in the associated wiki.

4.3.5. Support for the 3D Task Approach

For each of the 3 main types of interactions ("Discuss", "Describe" and "Document") needed to perform a collaborative task, our virtual office provides a specific technological tool: a forum discussion for supporting asynchronous "discuss" interactions, a wikipage or a GoogleDocs document for "describe" interactions and a file folder for "document" interactions. In the current version of the platform, where these tools are placed in different topic sections, there needs to be some way to connect them (thus showing that they belong as a unity to the same collaborative task) and to facilitate shifting along the connections. This is achieved by including hyperlinks, for example from forum posts to wikipages or from wikipages to documents in folders. Synchronous interactions supported by tools like Skype or Adobe Connect are usually understood as the main form of E-Collaboration; we also use them in our team, but their impact is limited to a small percent of our total interaction time, probably less than 10%.

5. SOLUTIONS AND RECOMMENDATIONS (THE FULL POWER OF E-COLLABORATION)

Business value depends not only on the quality of business processes and their outcomes but is increasingly being influenced by the quality of knowledge collaboration. But what do "knowledge" and "collaboration" mean in a business context? Our definition of E-Collaboration - as a process consisting of two concurrent activities, one being to work on a single task and the other to build a shared knowledge structure - suggests that knowledge and collaboration are intimately connected in a peculiar way that needs to be well understood in order to accomplish effective and efficient E-Collaboration. This is the first main success factor, but how should it be implemented?

Our answer to this question consists of the architecture of an E-Collaboration system conceived as a tree with three branches: a people branch, process branch and technology branch. And this, as far as we can see from our experience, is the second main success factor in achieving high quality E-Collaboration. But this is not enough and so we come to the third main success factor: the selection of appropriate sub-branches and leaves for the main 3 branches.

The "Social Network" leaf is appropriate because the process of building a shared knowledge structure requires a type of subordination among people that is typical of a network structure where everyone can be a leader, depending of the task to be performed. On the one hand, the members of the social network must be well integrated in the conventional hierarchical structure of the company: this is accomplished by selecting the "team" as a conventional, formal structure. On the other hand, the social network needs a facilitative kind of leadership (the third leaf of the people branch) and a community-oriented organisation of its interactions (Community of Practice, first leaf on the process branch) and its ways of dealing with knowledge (Participation in Knowledge, Cultivation of Knowledge, second and third leaves on the process branch). Finally a Virtual Team Office is appropriate as an online enabler of the aforementioned activities.

Thus we can summarise our recommendations under the following 3 key points:

1. **CONCEPT:** find a definition of E-Collaboration that is knowledge-oriented: see the one that we have given as a source of inspiration
2. **DESIGN:** when designing your solution, consider the PPT model (people, process and technology) and make sure that your design puts all three elements in the right balance and with appropriate relationships. Compare your design with our tree architecture, particularly from the point of view of its knowledge orientation
3. **IMPLEMENTATION:** last but not least, when selecting the elements that implement your design, make sure that they are consistent with the knowledge-oriented concept and with the PPT model.

REFERENCES

Bettoni, M. (2005). Wissenskooperation – Die Zukunft des Wissensmanagements. *Lernende Organisation – Zeitschrift für Systemisches Management und Organisation, 25*(3), 6-24.

Bettoni, M., Andenmatten, S., & Mathieu, R. (2007). Knowledge Cooperation in Online Communities: A Duality of Participation and Cultivation. *Electronic Journal of Knowledge Management, 5*(1), 1–6.

Bettoni, M., & Eggs, C. (2010). User-centred Knowledge Management: A Constructivist and Socialized View. *Constructivist Foundations, 5*(3), 130–143.

Bettoni, M., Schiller, G., & Bernhard, W. (2011). A CoP for Research Activities in Universities. In O. R. Hernáez & E. Bueno Campos (Eds.), *Handbook of Research on Communities of Practice for Organizational Management and Networking: Methodologies for Competitive Advantage* (pp. 396–420). Hershey, PA: IGI Global.

Burton, B., & Willis, D. A. (2014). Gartner's Hype Cycle Special Report for 2014. *Gartner Research Report.* Retrieved from https://www.gartner.com/doc/2816917/gartners-hype-cycle-special-report?docdisp=share

Dillenbourg, P. & Fischer, F. (2007). Basics of Computer-Supported Collaborative Learning. *Zeitschrift für Berufs- und Wirtschaftspädagogik. 21*, 111-130.

Dossick, C., Anderson, A., Iorio, J., Neff, G., & Taylor, J. (2012). Messy talk and mutual discovery: exploring the necessary conditions for synthesis in virtual teams. In A. Javernick-Will & A. Mahalingam (Eds.), *Proceedings of the Engineering Project Organizations Conference.* Retrieved from http://www.epossociety.org/EPOC2012/Papers/Dossick_Anderson_Iorio_Neff_Taylor.pdf

Drakos, N. (2013). Agenda Overview for Social Software and Collaboration. *Gartner Research Report* ID G00245492. Retrieved from https://www.gartner.com/doc/2291615/agenda-overview-social-software-collaboration

Edwards, J. (2011). A Process View of Knowledge Management: It Ain't What you do, it's the way That you do it. *Electronic Journal of Knowledge Management*, *9*(4), 297–306.

Edwards, J. S. (2009). Business processes and knowledge management. In M. Khosrow-Pour (Ed.), *Encyclopedia of Information Science and Technology* (Vol. I, pp. 471–476). Hershey, PA: IGI Global. doi:10.4018/978-1-60566-026-4.ch078

Endress, E., & Wehner, T. (Eds.). (1996). *Zwischenbetriebliche Kooperation. Die Gestaltung von lieferbedingungen*. Weinheim: Psychologie Verlags Union.

Fryer, M. (2012). Facilitative leadership: Drawing on Jürgen Habermas' model of ideal speech to propose a less impositional way to lead. *Organization*, *19*(1), 25–43. doi:10.1177/1350508411401462

Gloor, P. (2006). *Swarm Creativity, Competitive Advantage Through Collaborative Innovation Networks*. Oxford: Oxford University Press. doi:10.1093/acprof:oso/9780195304121.001.0001

Grosser, M. (2004). *Gossamer Odyssey. The Triumph of Human-Powered Flight*. St. Paul, MN: Zenith Press.

Keitt, T. J., Brown, M., Koplowitz, R., Schadler, T., Karcher, P., Fenwick, N., & Smit, A. (2012). The Social CIO. *Forrester Research Report Abstract*. Retrieved from http://www.forrester.com/The+Social+CIO/fulltext/-/E-RES72881

Keitt, T. J., & Schadler, T. (2012). The Road To Social Business Transformation Starts With A Burning Platform. *Forrester Research Report Abstract*. Retrieved from http://www.forrester.com/The+Road+To+Social+Business+Transformation+Starts+With+A+Burning+Platform

Kock, N. (2005). What is E-Collaboration? *International Journal of e-Collaboration*, *1*(1), i–vii.

Koplowitz, R., Schooley, C., Karcherwith Khalid Kark, P., & Murphy, K. (2013.) Social Business And Collaboration Success Hinges On Effective Change Management. *Forrester Research Report Abstract*. Retrieved from https://www.forrester.com/Social+Business+And+Collaboration+Success+Hinges+On+Effective+Change+Management/fulltext/-/E-res81003

Laningham, S. (Interviewer), & Berners-Lee, T. (Interviewee). (2006). developerWorks Interviews: Tim Berners-Lee. Retrieved from http://www.ibm.com/developerworks/podcast/dwi/cm-int082206txt.html

Lavoy, D. (2013, February 13). Collaboration Isn't Working: What We Have Here is a Chasm. *CMSWire.com*. Retrieved from http://www.cmswire.com/cms/social-business/collaboration-isnt-working-what-we-have-here-is-a-chasm-019597.php

Marin, A., & Wellman, B. (2011). Social network analysis: An introduction. In J. Scott & P. J. Carrington (Eds.), *The SAGE Handbook of Social Network Analysis* (pp. 11–25). London: SAGE.

Newman, M., Barabási, A. L., & Watts, D. J. (2006). *The Structure and Dynamics of Networks*. Oxford: Princeton University Press.

Nonaka, I., & Konno, N. (1998). The concept of "ba": Building a foundation for knowledge creation. *California Management Review*, *40*(3), 40–54. doi:10.2307/41165942

Roschelle, J., & Teasley, S. D. (1995). The construction of shared knowledge in collaborative problem solving. In C. E. O'Malley (Ed.), *Computer-Supported Collaborative Learning* (pp. 69–197). Berlin: Springer-Verlag. doi:10.1007/978-3-642-85098-1_5

Schwarz, R. (2005). The Skilled Facilitator Approach. In R. Schwarz, A. Davidson, P. Carlson, & S. McKinney (Eds.), *The Skilled Facilitator Fieldbook* (pp. 3–13). San Francisco: Jossey-Bass.

Vollmer, A., & Wehner, T. (2007). Innovation und wissensorientierte Kooperation. *Profile*, *13*, 31–36.

Weidner, D. (Director) (2007, April 23). KM Essentials. *Certified Knowledge Manager Training Program (CKM)*. Lecture conducted from KM Institute, Basel.

Wellman, B. (1997). An electronic group is virtually a social network. In S. Kiesler (Ed.), *Culture of the Internet* (pp. 179–205). Mahwah, NJ: Lawrence Erlbaum Associates.

Wenger, E. (1998). *Communities of practice. Learning, meaning and identity*. Cambridge: Cambridge University Press. doi:10.1017/CBO9780511803932

Wenger, E., McDermott, R., & Snyder, W. (2002). *Cultivating communities of practice: A guide to managing knowledge*. Boston, MA: Harvard Business School Press.

Wenger, E., White, N., & Smith, J. D. (2009) Digital Habitats: stewarding technology for communities. Portland, OR: CPsquare.

KEY TERMS AND DEFINITIONS

Community of Practice: a combination of four fundamentals elements: a *domain* of knowledge, a *community* of people who care about this domain, a shared *practice* that they develop to be effective in that domain and a *sense of community* as the individual experience of interdependence (membership, influence, fulfilment of needs and shared emotional connection).

Cultivation of Knowledge: The process by which a community collaboratively stewards its knowledge resources and uses them in daily work.

E-Collaboration System: The unit of people, processes and technology for collaborating using electronic technologies.

Knowledge Collaboration: A participative knowledge management model consisting of two cross-coupled learning loops that activate and sustain one another: "cultivation of knowledge" and "participation in knowledge".

Knowledge Management: the systematic organization and coordination of knowledge processes like acquiring, developing, making transparent, sharing, preserving and applying knowledge.

Participation in Knowledge: The process by which community members build social capital (establish and take care of personal relationships, develop individual and collective identities, etc.) and "invest" this social capital in collaboratively stewarding the knowledge resources of their community.

Shared Knowledge Structure: knowledge constructed, negotiated and shared by participants in the act of collaborative problem solving.

Virtual Team Office: a fixed and well-organised online place where a team of knowledge workers reifies its ties as a team and which provides facilities for supporting collaborative work and participative knowledge management.

ENDNOTES

1 http://en.wikipedia.org/wiki/Web_2.0

2 http://moodle.org/stats/

3 http://en.wikipedia.org/wiki/Mermaid_Tavern

Chapter 9
Exploring the Barriers to Electronic Collaboration

Bernard Owens Imarhiagbe
Kingston University, UK

ABSTRACT

This investigation reviews research literature on electronic collaboration (e-collaboration) with a view to collate relevant information to support e-collaboration knowledgebase, further research and encourage further collaborative engagements. E-collaboration has been described with various phrases such as information sharing, information exchange, knowledge sharing, social networking and joint working. This research categorised the challenges of e-collaboration into people, process and technology because all the issues identified in e-collaboration research are rooted in one of these categories. As e-collaboration is a source of competitiveness, businesses that fail to strategically adopt the phenomenon could lose out. A notable example of e-collaboration is crowdfunding which provides funding for start-up and small businesses. However, businesses that support e-collaboration strategy have the potential to have better competitive advantage with increased firm performance.

INTRODUCTION

Electronic collaboration (e-collaboration) has been described as information sharing, information exchange, joint working, social networking or knowledge sharing between two or more people over the internet for a common goal. This broad based definition is supported by Kock, & D'Arcy (2002) because e-collaboration in this context includes all forms of e-collaboration and it is not limited to the use of a computer. As an example, in modern times, mobile telephones can be used for e-collaboration because they have internet connectivity. People have collaborated online over a decade and the benefits are enormous (Nosek, & McManus, 2008; Turban, Bolloju, & Liang, 2011). According to them, although there are benefits accrued for e-collaboration, there are challenges causing discouragement among collaboration participants and organisational leadership. Inter-organisational learning and knowledge sharing are major benefits of e-collaboration (Choi, & Ko, 2012; Levy, Loebbecke, & Powell, 2003) and it encourages e-market relationships as well as better operational performance (Howard, Vidgen, &

DOI: 10.4018/978-1-4666-9556-6.ch009

Copyright © 2016, IGI Global. Copying or distributing in print or electronic forms without written permission of IGI Global is prohibited.

Powell, 2006; Power, Hanna, Singh, & Samson, 2010). Tufekci (2008) recognised the different types of internet users and recommend a differentiation to ensure e-collaboration participants have a common objective. The essence of e-collaboration is information sharing in one way or another with a common goal. There has to be a common goal in any e-collaboration effort because without a common objective, it may not be described as e-collaboration. Part of the challenges to e-collaboration could be derived from communication barriers to knowledge sharing which emanate from internal organisational people, processes and technology (Kock, 2008; Riege, 2005). Kock (2008) believe that e-collaboration technologies could hamper communication effectiveness in complex collaborative tasks because the communication media could be distorted or inadequate by design. In this circumstance, the design distortion compels e-collaborators to seek alternative remedy as a way of compensatory adaptation to avoid the barrier.

BACKGROUND

The concept of e-collaboration is a subset of collaboration. Collaboration involves both electronic and non-electronic means of interaction between people, organisations and governments. A few of the tools of e-collaboration include e-mail, internet, wikis, online forums, chat rooms, web-conferencing, blogs, journals and crowdfunding platforms (Marks, 2011; Nosek, & McManus, 2008; Ordanini, Miceli, Pizzetti, & Parasuraman, 2011).

The level of e-collaboration has increased over a decade and the continued improvement in technology has supported its growth (Jean, Sinkovics, & Kim, 2014; Marks, 2011; Miri-Lavassani, Movahedi, & Kumar, 2010). As the development of the internet and associated tools get better and advanced, more opportunity for e-collaboration will become available (Haythornetwaite, 2005; Turban et al., 2011). Businesses that engage in e-collaboration have better competitive advantage (Nosek, & McManus, 2008). Firms use e-collaboration as an avenue for organisational coordination, learning and innovation towards competitive advantage (Fink, 2007). However, as much as many people, organisations and the governments engage in e-collaboration in one way or another, there are still challenges to the phenomenon in everyday life. Although technology has enabled the expansion of e-collaboration over a decade, Nosek, & McManus (2008) identified technology as a major challenge to the development and advancement of e-collaboration. This suggests that technology provided the necessary support for progressive e-collaboration in the past and technology also has the responsibility to resolve the challenges impacting e-collaboration today and the future.

There is no defined e-collaboration theory. E-collaboration is not confined to only computer science and it is relevant to many other areas of research including psychology, education, business and management. Different theories and arguments tend to give different focus to the subject of e-collaboration. In this research, the relevant key business and management theories for e-collaboration include social capital theory (Calabrese, & Borchert, 1996; Lin, 2002; Zheng, Li, Wu, & Xu, 2014), stakeholder theory (Ackermann, & Eden, 2011; Freeman, 1984) and computer-supported collaborative learning (CSCL) theory (Koschmann, 1996, 1999; Stahl, Koschmann, & Suthers, 2006). According to the stakeholder theory, there is need to manage the affairs of all stakeholders in a transaction in an efficient and effective manner (Ackermann, & Eden, 2011; Freeman, 1984). Therefore, e-collaboration can be classified as a business related or organisational transaction. Social capital is embedded in social network, which is made up of like-minded people (Lin, 2002; Zheng, et al., 2014). Social capital in the form of social connections and social networks can support individual and organisational goal achievement (Lin, 2002). Information technology development and network infrastructure has allowed social capital to grow (Calabrese, & Borchert, 1996). Therefore, the growth of social capital has allowed e-collaboration to grow astronomically across the internet world from individuals to organisations and to governments. CSCL was first introduced as a paradigm shift for the learning sciences in educational technology (Koschmann, 1996). Many CSCL researchers (Koschmann, 1996, 1999; Stahl, Koschmann, & Suthers, 2006) have explored the subject over a long period of time and the arguments have persisted because CSCL provides a mediating and enhancing effect for e-collaboration. For the purpose of this research, it is adequate to state that e-collaboration is one of the CSCL tools.

MAIN FOCUS OF THE CHAPTER

This study aim to provide answers to the following research questions: a) What are the barriers to electronic collaboration? b) To what extent are the barriers to electronic collaboration applicable internationally? c) To what extent are social network tools a barrier to electronic collaboration in a business context? These questions are very important in providing a knowledgebase about the challenges associated with e-collaboration in every sphere of social and human endeavours. This chapter discusses e-collaboration in terms of the challenges associated with people, process and technology. According to Haythornetwaite (2005), the communication media used for e-collaboration has an impact on the internet connectivity between e-collaborators and the quality of e-collaboration. The current e-collaboration quality derived from the available e-collaboration technologies is inadequate (Nosek, & McManus, 2008). There are weaknesses in the quality of cross organisational e-collaboration causing ineffective data exchange (Schroth, & Schmid, 2009). According to Marks (2011), student e-collaborators chose discussion board over wikis, blogs and journals. This suggests that the type of e-collaborators can determine the choice of e-collaboration tools for the task. It also shows that there are differences between e-collaboration tools in accomplishing e-collaboration tasks.

The remainder of this chapter will be divided into the following key sections: Literature review strategy; Analysis; Solutions and Recommendations; Future Research Directions and Conclusion.

LITERATURE REVIEW STRATEGY

In achieving the research aim, electronic databases (ScienceDirect, Google Scholar, EBSCO and Emerald) were explored using keyword search method. It was also necessary to search for relevant literary works published by government bodies and international organisations. In the keyword search, ‘e-collaboration barrier’, ‘electronic collaboration barrier’, ‘e-collaboration challenge’ and ‘electronic collaboration challenge’ were the keywords used. Figure 1 is an illustration model for the interaction between people, process and technology barriers in e-collaboration activities. The barriers to e-collaboration cut across the people, process and technology involved in the activity of e-collaboration. Until the barriers are identified in terms of the people, process and technology, it will be difficult to proffer any solution.

Figure 1. People, process and technology model

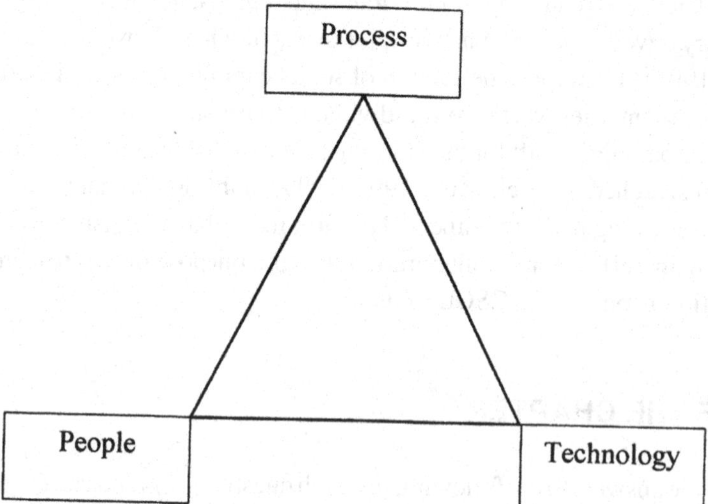

Note: E-collaboration challenge can be classified in one of people, process or technology barriers. The e-collaboration initiator or manager under stakeholder management has a responsibility to manage the three strategic classifications in any organisational setting.

ANALYSIS

People as Barriers

People as individuals, organisational people and the government constitute different barriers in e-collaboration. People are different in many ways including gender, nationality, colour, religion, educational profile and personal orientation. These people must be able to engage in an effective and efficient e-collaboration for common goal (Tufekci, 2008).

Failure of management is a major barrier to effective e-collaboration. E-collaborators and other participants in e-collaboration are called stakeholders under stakeholder theory. According to Ackermann, & Eden (2011) and Freeman (1984), the manager has the responsibility to manage all stakeholders efficiently and effectively. Unfortunately, if the manager fails to manage the people effectively and efficiently, it becomes a challenge for e-collaboration effort in the organisation.

Resistance to change is a major obstacle to e-collaboration. Although Tufekci (2008) suggest that e-collaborators should have common objective, Turban et al. (2011) believe employee resistance could destroy the e-collaboration initiative of the organisation. The introduction of e-collaboration is a major organisational change and all organisational people should be involved in making success of the change.

The security and privacy of e-collaborators is paramount to an effective e-collaboration initiative (Turban et al., 2011). They revealed the negative effect of disclosing private, sensitive information or malicious code over the organisational workspace and internet. E-collaborators must be aware and behave responsibly online to protect everyone and eliminate any negative consequences.

Internet misuse is a possibility in e-collaboration. Young (2004) discussed the possibility of internet use addiction among people with particular reference to chat rooms and online games. Therefore, the internet is a resource rich environment and if it is not used appropriately could cause undesirable outcomes for e-collaboration activities and the organisation.

Social loafing is identified as a major people barrier to group cohesion in online communities (Shiue, Chiu, & Chang, 2010). Social loafing is a human attitude of exerting less effort in group activities and more effort when working alone. Social loafing destroys group cohesion and does not support e-collaboration.

Process as Barriers

The process barriers relevant to e-collaboration are enormous. This section will discuss research based findings. The process of e-collaboration requires adequate planning (Rutkowski et al., 2002). This reflects any business activity because planning ensures adequate control, coordination and management of all e-collaboration activities.

Cai (2005) identified process management challenge associated with the management of complex and distributed e-collaboration processes. In e-collaboration, the manager has the strategic responsibility to manage and engage with all the associated stakeholders (Ackermann, & Eden, 2011; Freeman, 1984) with a view to maximising the productivity of e-collaborators. The complexity of e-collaboration projects includes the management of social aspects, context realisation and conflicts (Cai, 2005). An efficient organisational structure will be required to support electronic interactions between e-collaborators (Rutkowski et al., 2002).

New e-collaboration tools or upgrade to existing tools require huge financial resources. Supply chain management (SCM) firms are beginning to deploy modern e-business and e-marketplace tools that support e-collaboration compared to EDI (Chan et al., 2012; Howard et al., 2006). Although EDI is an obsolete technology tool for SCM, businesses may continue to use the tool to support their e-collaboration effort for lack of financial resources to upgrade the current tool. This suggests that as e-collaboration tools evolve in design to embrace modern trend, there are cost consequences in upgrading existing tools. Rutkowski, Vogel, Genuchten, Bemelmans, & Favier (2002) described this evolutionary trend as the 'reality of virtuality' (p. 219).

There are legal risks associated with the content created during e-collaboration (Turban et al., 2011). Some of the legal risks associated with e-collaboration include use of offensive language in blogs, forums and other published outlet as well as compliance issues. There are risks associated with copyright and intellectual property violations as well as publishing libellous statements (Turban et al., 2011). Researchers (Barnes, & Barnes, 2009; Turban et al., 2011) provided some risk management strategies for resolving potential risks including policy formulation, education of staffs, monitoring and filtering and legal insurance to tackle potential issues of breach.

Technology as Barriers

Every aspects of e-collaboration technology need to be managed to ensure efficient and effective system that could lead to organisational competitiveness. Therefore, technology management is a major challenge. There is need to bridge the IT support gap to advance e-collaboration effort as 'there is little support for the joint development lifecycle of planning, creating, evaluating, negotiating, and consolidating group work' (Nosek, & McManus, 2008, p. 3).

E-collaboration is associated with high cost of adoption (Chan, Chong, & Zhou, 2012). However, e-collaboration is known to be beneficial for attaining competitive advantage with specific reference to

SCM system (Chan et al., 2012). They identified an Electronic Data Interchange (EDI) to aid e-collaboration in a SCM environment. The EDI is an old system characterised by different data standards, lack of real time data and high cost of implementation. Therefore, small firms can scarcely afford to adopt the EDI for e-collaboration. However, businesses are now adopting better e-marketplace and e-business solutions to resolve their SCM need but small firms are still limited by their low financial resource base (Chan et al., 2012).

The technical nature of e-collaboration makes it complex and confusing for some organisations and individuals (Rutkowski et al., 2002). The need for modernity suggests that old obsolete e-collaboration tools should be replaced with a more modern facility that can perform a better job and improve organisational competitiveness. Better training can help to resolve technical complexity in e-collaboration and technology in general. A notable example of e-collaboration requiring training for participants is crowdfunding (Valanciene, & Jegeleviciute, 2013).

The design flaws of the e-collaboration tool can impact the application of the tools (Kock, 2008). Obsolete technology tool such as EDI is not adequate for SCM e-collaboration (Chan et al., 2012). E-collaboration tools are varied and different; they satisfy different purposes and meet perceived needs (Marks, 2011). In an attempt to adapt to a lack of an appropriate e-collaboration tool, there could be a compensatory adaptation which is an obstacle avoidance strategy (Kock, 2008). However, e-collaboration tools that mimic face-to-face communication include web-conference (Nosek, & McManus, 2008) and video-conference. Prior to the emergence of video-conference facility, there was e-collaboration using text only (e-mail) or sound only (telephone) and no video effect. Although e-collaborators were able to interact in the times of text or sound effect alone, their interaction has improved with the introduction of video-conferencing which creates a near natural view of e-collaborating groups.

The use of unlicensed software is a major barrier to e-collaboration. Software licensing for e-collaboration must be fully implemented to ensure compliance for the organisation and users across the e-collaboration environment. The use of unlicensed software and digital goods are breach of copyright and hence illegal (Tunca, & Wu, 2012). According to Trotter, & Cameron (1996), the software producers seek to protect their software before developing a finished product. Therefore, software piracy and use of unlicensed software through e-collaboration tools are copyright infringement.

There is a global limitation of e-collaboration tools and other infrastructure (Munkvold, 2005). It is stated that the implementation of infrastructure to support e-collaboration is marred by implementation difficulties caused by cultural diversity and organisational diversity in the global business terrain. According to Munkvold (2005), 'Challenges in the global implementation process were found to increase with the organizational and geographical scope of the implementation, level of autonomy in the adoption process, cultural diversity, technological heterogeneity, and level of work process support embedded in the system'(p. 78). The internet connectivity issues in developing countries have been discussed widely (InfoDev, 2013). Hence, the limitation of the global infrastructure is having detrimental effect on global e-collaboration effort.

SOLUTIONS AND RECOMMENDATIONS

The barriers to e-collaboration are people, process and technology centric. It is very important that these barriers are duly identified with a view to proffer appropriate solutions. As part of this chapter, people as barriers (e.g. failure of management, resistance to change, security and privacy issues, internet misuse and social loafing), process as barriers (e.g. inadequate planning, process management challenge, huge financial resource requirement and legal risks) and technology as barriers (e.g. technology management challenge, high cost of adoption, technically complex, unlicensed software, design flaws, obsolete e-collaboration tools and global infrastructure limitation) have been discussed. The discussion shows that the following solutions will contribute towards removing the identified barriers:

1. **Stakeholder Engagements and Management:** E-collaboration involves multi-stakeholder engagements and hence the principles of stakeholder management should apply. In e-collaboration relationships and according to Ackermann, & Eden (2011), there are multiple stakeholders who should be managed for a successful outcome. The success of e-collaboration relies on the efficiency and effectiveness of the stakeholder management of e-collaboration participants as described in Freeman (1984).
2. **Implement Change Management Policy:** E-collaboration is an online way of interacting with individuals and organisations. The introduction of e-collaboration in an organisation requires a change management policy to ensure staffs are involved in the process to avoid resistance (Turban et al., 2011). Although Fink (2007) believes that organisations use e-collaboration as a tool for organisational coordination, a good change management policy will be required to attain competitiveness. According to Cai (2005), there are complexities associated with the management of distributed e-collaboration processes. However, change management policy can support e-collaboration success.
3. **Exploit Modern and Purposeful e-Collaboration Tools:** Businesses should exploit modern e-collaboration tools (e.g. e-business and e-marketplace) to gain reduced relative cost advantage. To this end, businesses and organisations should replace or upgrade obsolete e-collaboration tools to improve organisational performance and competitiveness. According to Chan et al. (2012), small firms experienced challenges in implementing EDI systems for their e-collaboration. Although Rutkowski et al. (2002) discussed the reality of high financial cost associated with e-collaboration; other researchers (Chan et al., 2012; Howard et al., 2006; Power et al., 2010) discovered that businesses are now adopting better e-marketplace and e-business solutions to resolve their e-collaboration need. E-collaboration tools could be inadequate by design as discussed by Kock (2008) but businesses should aim to exploit modern tools that fit the purpose for improved efficiency and effectiveness.
4. **Promote e-Collaboration Policy:** Businesses and organisations should produce and promote e-collaboration policy to support relevant aspects including the use and behaviour expectations in e-collaboration activities.
5. **Provide e-Collaboration Training for Participants:** Businesses and organisations should provide e-collaboration training for staffs to improve their operational effectiveness. Although the subject of training could be simplistic in the e-collaboration environment, it is very easy to assume knowledge of e-collaboration following exposure to social networking platforms. Crowdfunding is an example of e-collaboration between project initiators and crowd investors using an internet platform (Valanciene, & Jegeleviciute, 2013). Although crowdfunding platforms are accessible to project initiators or entrepreneurs as e-collaborators, they need training to present their project ideas and to enable them operate better on the internet platform to attain their fundraising target (Valanciene, & Jegeleviciute, 2013). Fink (2007) identified learning as an organisational role in e-collaboration. The sharing of purposeful information in an organisational setting can support staff learning (Riege, 2005). Therefore, organisations should endeavour to provide adequate training for its staff e-collaborators for better performance towards competitiveness.

6. **Research Funding and Information Dissemination:** Businesses and organisations should help in funding e-collaboration research and disseminate information widely to ensure the barrier against the global e-collaboration effort is broken. The increasing popularity of crowdfunding has provided fundraising for research and information dissemination (Wheat, Wang, Byrnes, & Ranganathan, 2013). This concept must be encouraged and promoted to increase e-collaboration around the world to improve access to finance for entrepreneurs to build, innovate and expand their projects to systematically increase business opportunities and economic development.
7. **Improve e-Collaboration Infrastructure:** The improvement in technology development has supported the continuous growth of e-collaboration (Jean et al., 2014; Marks, 2011; Miri-Lavassani et al., 2010). The quality of the communication media used for e-collaboration can determine the quality of the e-collaboration effort (Haythornetwaite, 2005). To this end, the responsibility to improve e-collaboration infrastructure rests with the government, entrepreneurs and firm owners. E-collaboration is not restricted by physical geography; it is international. However, e-collaboration is a global phenomenon to a limited extent because it is driven by the availability of the internet. Thus, developing countries are facing the barrier of low availability of internet facilities with the effect of reduced interaction from those countries (InfoDev, 2013). The lack of infrastructure and other infrastructure limitations can introduce a lack of or reduced e-collaboration effort with a consequence of causing isolation in the world of e-collaboration. A notable example of e-collaboration isolation is in some developing countries as reported (InfoDev, 2013). There is need to improve IT support gap (Nosek, & McManus, 2008) to support e-collaboration infrastructure limitations and improve e-collaboration tasks.
8. **Improve Cultural and Organisational Diversity:** E-collaboration is restricted by cultural diversity and organisational diversity in the global business environment (Munkvold, 2005). They discovered that the physical environment of technology tools can impact the efficiency and effectiveness of e-collaboration in a global context noting a case study of an USA corporate project being piloted in its subsidiary in Chile but without training manual in Spanish. The project was hampered by the lack of Spanish language manual as the product was developed in USA with English language manual only.
9. **Improve Security for the e-Collaboration Environment, Participants and Tools:** Social network tools are not barriers to e-collaboration in any business or organisational context. However, the negative use of social network tools could pose barriers for e-collaboration. Turban et al. (2011) discussed the misuse and abuse of e-collaboration tools, participants and environment. They stated that the security and privacy of individual information is paramount in e-collaboration.
10. **Pursue Common Objective:** It is very important that there is a common objective in e-collaboration for effective outcome (Tufekci, 2008). E-collaboration involves online interaction between individuals and organisations but e-collaboration with a common objective eliminates social loafing (Shiue et al., 2010) which is the practice of lone performer.
11. **Engage in Risk Management:** E-collaboration activities involve the creation of copyright and intellectual property materials. E-collaboration can expose organisations to various risk factors that could pose negative impact such as publishing libellous statements (Turban et al., 2011). Therefore, risk management is a significant necessity in e-collaboration. Risk management strategies for eliminating or reducing risk as identified in Barnes, & Barnes (2009) and Turban et al. (2011) includes policy formulation, education of staffs, computer system monitoring and filtering

and legal insurance to tackle potential issues of breach. Legal insurance is one way of risk mitigation (Turban et al., 2011).

12. **Implement e-Collaboration Software Licensing and Asset Management:** Software licensing for e-collaboration is required to protect the firm against copyright infringement (Tunca, & Wu, 2012). Trotter, & Cameron (1996) show that the issue of software piracy and copyright breach has existed for more than a decade. Therefore, software piracy and use of unlicensed software through e-collaboration tools is a copyright infringement. E-collaboration tools and their associated documentation have clear instructions on use and these must be managed as part of the asset management of the organisation.

FUTURE RESEARCH DIRECTIONS

To a limited extent, e-collaboration is solely a technology phenomenon. Although there are many technology research literatures on e-collaboration, the social aspect remain largely unexplored. E-collaboration is relevant in the business and management research area but there are limited research work. It is therefore important to exploit e-collaboration with a view to investigate its relevance in the business and management research area and increase research publications accordingly. For example, stakeholder management is relevant in e-collaboration but there are very limited research work in this area. E-collaboration is also scarcely discussed in the area of psychology and it will be beneficial if human behaviour can be explained by research in identifying what behaviours that e-collaborators exhibit in their online role.

E-collaboration opportunity is not currently a global phenomenon for various reasons including infrastructure limitation, cultural diversity and organisational diversity. It is necessary to research into the global aspect of e-collaboration and disseminates research based information as far and wide as possible with a view to develop global best practice in e-collaboration.

CONCLUSION

This chapter reviews research literature on e-collaboration and the knowledgebase produced will enhance e-collaboration research and encourage collaborative engagement among people, organisations and governments wherever possible for common goal. E-collaboration is information sharing, information exchange, knowledge sharing, social networking and joint working. The challenges to e-collaboration are categorised as people, process and technology barriers because all the issues identified in e-collaboration research are rooted in one of these categories. Business owners and organisational managers are encouraged to use this knowledgebase to avoid pitfalls in the implementation and use of e-collaboration. E-collaboration is a progressive and innovative phenomenon. Although e-collaboration is often presented as a technology phenomenon, there are various multidisciplinary aspects to it. Therefore, e-collaboration cut across computer science and other multidisciplinary areas such as business management, organisational science, social psychology, training and education. Businesses, organisations and governments are encouraged to engage further in e-collaborative activities in social and human endeavours wherever possible. As e-collaboration is a source of competitiveness, businesses that fail to strategically adopt the phenomenon could lose out. Businesses that support e-collaboration strategy have the potential to have better competitive advantage with increased firm performance.

REFERENCES

Ackermann, F., & Eden, C. (2011). Strategic management of stakeholders: Theory and practice. *Long Range Planning*, *44*(3), 179–196. doi:10.1016/j.lrp.2010.08.001

Barnes, N. D., & Barnes, F. R. (2009). Equipping your organization for the social networking game. *IEEE Engineering Management Review*, *38*(3), 3–7. doi:10.1109/EMR.2010.5559137

Cai, J. (2005). A social interaction analysis methodology for improving e-collaboration over the internet. *Electronic Commerce Research and Applications*, *4*(2), 85–99. doi:10.1016/j.elerap.2004.10.007

Calabrese, A., & Borchert, M. (1996). Prospects for electronic democracy in the United States: Rethinking communications and social policy. *Media Culture & Society*, *18*(2), 249–268. doi:10.1177/016344396018002005

Chan, F. T. S., Yee-Loong Chong, A., & Zhou, L. (2012). An empirical investigation of factors affecting e-collaboration diffusion in SMEs. *International Journal of Production Economics*, *138*(2), 329–344. doi:10.1016/j.ijpe.2012.04.004

Choi, S., & Ko, I. (2012). Leveraging electronic collaboration to promote interorganizational learning. *International Journal of Information Management*, *32*(6), 550–559. doi:10.1016/j.ijinfomgt.2012.03.002

Fink, L. (2007). Coordination, learning, and innovation: The organizational roles of e-collaboration and their impacts. *International Journal of e-Collaboration*, *3*(3), 53–70. doi:10.4018/jec.2007070104

Freeman, R. E. (1984). *Strategic management: A stakeholder approach*. Boston: Pitman.

Haythornthwaite, C. (2005). Social networks and internet connectivity effects. *Information Communication and Society*, *8*(2), 125–147. doi:10.1080/13691180500146185

Howard, M., Vidgen, R., & Powell, P. (2006). Automotive e-hubs: Exploring motivations and barriers to collaboration and interaction. *The Journal of Strategic Information Systems*, *15*(1), 51–75. doi:10.1016/j.jsis.2005.06.002

InfoDev. (2013). *Crowdfunding's potential for the developing world*. Washington, DC: World Bank.

Jean, R., Sinkovics, R. R., & Kim, D. (2014). The impact of technological, organizational and environmental characteristics on electronic collaboration and relationship performance in international customer-supplier relationship. *Information & Management*, *51*(7), 854–864. doi:10.1016/j.im.2014.08.002

Kock, N. (2008). Designing e-collaboration technologies to facilitate compensatory adaptation. *Information Systems Management*, *25*(1), 14–19. doi:10.1080/10580530701777115

Kock, N., & D'Arcy, J. (2002). Resolving the e-collaboration paradox: The competing influences of media naturalness and compensatory adaptation. *Information Management and Consulting* [Special issue on Electronic Collaboration], *17*(4), 72–78.

Koschmann, T. (1996). Paradigm shifts and instructional technology: An introduction. In T. Koschmann (Ed.), *CSCL: Theory and practice of an emerging paradigm* (pp. 1–23). Mahwah, NJ: Lawrence Erlbaum Associates.

Koschmann, T. (1999). Computer support for collaboration and learning. *Journal of the Learning Sciences, 8*(3-4), 495–497. doi:10.1080/10508406.1999.9672077

Levy, M., Loebbecke, C., & Maier, R. (2003). SMEs, co-opetition and knowledge sharing: The role of information systems. *European Journal of Information Systems, 12*(1), 3–17. doi:10.1057/palgrave.ejis.3000439

Lin, N. (2002). *Social capital: A theory of social structure and action*. Cambridge, UK: Cambridge University Press.

Marks, A. (2011). Electronic group collaboration in higher education. *Proceedings of the 15th IEEE International Conference on Computer Supported Cooperative Work in Design* (pp. 742-747).

Miri-Lavassani, K., Movahedi, B., & Kumar, V. (2010). Electronic collaboration ontology: The case of readiness analysis of electronic marketplace adoption. *Journal of Management & Organization, 16*(3), 454–466. doi:10.5172/jmo.16.3.454

Munkvold, B. E. (2005). Experiences from global e-collaboration: Contextual influences on technology adoption and use. *IEEE Transactions on Professional Communication, 48*(1), 78–86. doi:10.1109/TPC.2005.843300

Nosek, J. T., & McManus, M. (2008). Collaboration challenges: Bridging the IT support gap. *Information Systems Management, 25*(1), 3–7. doi:10.1080/10580530701777081

Ordanini, A., Miceli, L., Pizzetti, M., & Parasuraman, A. (2011). Crowd-funding: Transforming customers into investors through innovative service platforms. *Journal of Service Management, 22*(4), 443–470. doi:10.1108/09564231111155079

Power, D., Hanna, V., Singh, P. J., & Samson, D. (2010). Electronic markets, data access and collaboration: Relative value to performance in firm operations. *Supply Chain Management: An International Journal, 15*(3), 238–251. doi:10.1108/13598541011039992

Riege, A. (2005). Three-dozen knowledge-sharing barriers managers must consider. *Journal of Knowledge Management, 9*(3), 18–35. doi:10.1108/13673270510602746

Rutkowski, A. F., Vogel, D. R., Van Genuchten, M., Bemelmans, T. M. A., & Favier, M. (2002). E-collaboration: The reality of virtuality. *IEEE Transactions on Professional Communication, 45*(4), 219–230. doi:10.1109/TPC.2002.805147

Schroth, C., & Schmid, B. (2009). Reference architecture for cross-company electronic collaboration. *International Journal of e-Collaboration, 5*(2), 75–91. doi:10.4018/jec.2009040105

Shiue, Y., Chiu, C., & Chang, C. (2010). Exploring and mitigating social loafing in online communities. *Computers in Human Behavior, 26*(4), 768–777. doi:10.1016/j.chb.2010.01.014

Stahl, G., Koschmann, T., & Suthers, D. (2006). Computer-supported collaborative learning: An historical perspective. In R. K. Sawyer (Ed.), *Cambridge handbook of the learning sciences* (pp. 409–426). Cambridge, UK: Cambridge University Press.

Trotter, N., & Cameron, G. (1996). Making the most of your software. *Computer Fraud & Security*, *1996*(10), 12–16. doi:10.1016/1361-3723(96)84808-1

Tufekci, Z. (2008). Grooming, gossip, Facebook and Myspace. *Information Communication and Society*, *11*(4), 544–564. doi:10.1080/13691180801999050

Tunca, T. I., & Wu, Q. (2012). Fighting fire with fire: Commercial piracy and the role of file sharing on copyright protection policy for digital goods. *Information Systems Research*, *24*(2), 436–453. doi:10.1287/isre.1120.0430

Turban, E., Bolloju, N., & Liang, T. (2011). Enterprise social networking: Opportunities, adoption, and risk mitigation. *Journal of Organizational Computing and Electronic Commerce*, *21*(3), 202–220. doi:10.1080/10919392.2011.590109

Valanciene, L., & Jegeleviciute, S. (2013). Valuation of crowdfunding: Benefits and drawbacks. *Economics and Management*, *18*(1), 39–48. doi:10.5755/j01.em.18.1.3713

Wheat, R. E., Wang, Y., Byrnes, J. E., & Ranganathan, J. (2013). Raising money for scientific research through crowdfunding. *Trends in Ecology & Evolution*, *28*(2), 71–72. doi:10.1016/j.tree.2012.11.001 PMID:23219380

Young, K. S. (2004). Internet addiction: A new clinical phenomenon and its consequences. *The American Behavioral Scientist*, *48*(4), 402–415. doi:10.1177/0002764204270278

Zheng, H., Li, D., Wu, J., & Xu, Y. (2014). The role of multidimensional social capital in crowdfunding: A comparative study in China and US. *Information & Management*, *51*(4), 488–496. doi:10.1016/j.im.2014.03.003

KEY TERMS AND DEFINITIONS

Crowdfunding: A way of raising project money in the form of small individual contributions from a large number of people using the internet.

Innovative: Applying new ideas.

Social Capital: A trusted network connection between like-minded people.

Social Loafing: A human behaviour of using less effort in group activities and more effort when working alone.

Social Network: A set of people linked by social relationships.

Stakeholder: A person or group with an interest in a business.

Chapter 10
The Impact of Social Networking Sites on the Arab Community

Mahmoud Mohamed Elkhouly
Helwan University, Egypt

ABSTRACT

Social media or social networking tools are Internet-based applications that focus on building social networks or social relations among people with shared interests and/or activities. Social media sites essentially consist of a representation of each user (often a profile), his/her social links, and a variety of additional services. Social networking sites fuss and was impressed by the community as a result of submissions from the ease and facilitated communication between people, and widened its fame and many use became their top concern, where communicating through these sites to get to know each other, and find out news each other, and receive news and themes and all that is new in the arena. However, since these sites and programs are open, there are no controls commensurate with our religion and our values and our habits of Arab and fixed principles, which impact on the lives of people in general, whether positively or negatively.

INTRODUCTION

Social media or social networking tools are Internet-based applications that focus on building social networks or social relations among people with shared interests and/or activities. Social media sites essentially consist of a representation of each user (often a profile), his/her social links, and a variety of additional services. They allow users to share ideas, activities, events, and interests within their individual networks, in addition to a wider scope of applications with increasing global impact on society and government.

Social networking sites fuss and was impressed by the community as a result of submissions from the ease and facilitated communication between people, and widened its fame and many use became their top concern, where communicating through these sites to get to know each other, and find out news each other, and receive news and themes and all that is new in the arena. However, since these sites and

DOI: 10.4018/978-1-4666-9556-6.ch010

Copyright © 2016, IGI Global. Copying or distributing in print or electronic forms without written permission of IGI Global is prohibited.

programs are open, there are no controls commensurate with religion, values and habits of Arab and fixed principles, which impact on the lives of people in general, whether positively or negatively.

This chapter aims to explore and identify the social and political implications of social networking in Arab countries and to suggest policy options and avenues for further research.

Arab Community

The Arab Region, which lies at the crossroads of Europe, Africa and Asia, is the cradle of civilization and the birthplace of the three great monotheistic religions of the world. The Region benefits from a number of similarities and opportunities, including a long, rich history spanning thousands of years, strong cultural traditions, common language and a large, educated workforce, due in part to increasing female labor force participation. Furthermore, the Region sits atop more than half of the world's oil resources. Despite these similarities, the Arab Region is characterized by enormous demographic, geographic, political and socio-economic diversity. The Region includes countries with very large populations, led by Egypt with a population of 85 million, and countries with small populations, such as Qatar at 111,000, which is the smallest. While several countries in the Region are already hovering at or near replacement level fertility (Kuwait, Lebanon, Tunisia, and United Arab Emirates), other countries and areas continue to exhibit high levels of fertility (the Occupied Palestinian Territory, Somalia, Sudan and Yemen). The Region is also characterized by extreme differences in land areas. For example, Sudan, the largest country in the Region with 2.5 million square kilometers, is the tenth largest country in the world. In contrast, the region's smallest country, Bahrain, covers just 750 square kilometers. Another distinguishing feature among the Arab countries is the sharp differences in population density. For example, Bahrain is the most densely populated with some 1,454 inhabitants per square kilometer. In comparison, Libya and Mauritania have a mere three inhabitants per square kilometer. In 2010, Arab world population reaches 359 million reside in the 22 countries and areas of the Arab Region and together account for five per cent of world population (Barry, 2010).

The number of Internet users in the Arab World is expected to rise to about 197 million users by 2017. the Internet penetration rate will jump from about 32 per cent in 2012 to over 51 per cent in 2017, which would be about 3 per cent above the world average at that time (Arab Knowledge Economy Report, 2014).

Contextual Background

One of the most remarkable and interesting aspects of the 2011 Arab revolts has been the use of social media tools - text messaging, e-mail, video and photo sharing, social networking, and the like - by small groups of activists and a large body of protesters in mobilizing, organizing, communicating and transmitting these events.

Social networking is a new driving force that has a significant global impact on political change. Few research studies have been published on the impact of social networking related to political change. During the first year of the Arab revolutions it appeared that 'Digital media provided both an awareness of shared grievances and transportable strategies for action'), which enabled the rise of the people and the fall of at least three oppressive regimes in Tunisia, Libya and Egypt.

This section discusses the impacts of social networking tools on the recent political changes in the eighteen-day Egyptian ''Revolution 2.0'' of 2011. Social network-related factors appear to have had a positive impact on Egyptians 'attitudes toward social change, which, in turn, supported their individual and aggregate behavior, leading to the revolution.

Arab Spring was perhaps the first time in Egyptian history during which events were majorly covered and reported by ordinary citizens via social networking sites rather that the mainstream media. According to the 2011 Arab Social Media Report (Arab Social Media Report Series, 2014), for example, 94 percent of Tunisians get their news from social media tools and social networking sites. This number was 88 percent in Egypt in the same year. In both countries, people relied on state-sponsored media considerably less than they do on social media (40 percent in Egypt and 36 percent in Tunisia).

In Egypt, there was considerable growth in the number of users of social media networking sites in early 2011. For example, the number of Facebook users in the country between January and February 2011 increased almost a million, reaching 5.5 million within a matter of weeks. Similarly, the number of Twitter users doubled and reached 45 thousand by the end of February 2011 (Catharine, 2013). Almost eight million Egyptians viewed videos posted on YouTube in the January revolution's first week despite the blocking of communications across the country. According to the "Internet & Revolution" study conducted by eMarketing Egypt (eMarketing Egypt Releases, 2014), an internet marketing consulting company, on the role of the Internet on the Egyptian revolution: 28% of Internet users purely relied on the Internet to stay tuned with the news and updates, among those, 63% had participated in the demonstrations.

The Internet had solely shaped the views of 17% of users regarding the recent events Facebook was the primary tool used to tie up with events and news as mentioned by 71% of users, 45% of users reported that they will increase their reliance on the Internet to tie up with coming news and events.

One of the unique features of the Egyptian Revolution was the relatively short period of time taken for the protestors to reach their goal. The protestors forced Mubarak to resign in less than three weeks after major demonstrations hit the streets in January 25th. A key aspect of this speedy transition was the effective use of social media and social networking tools as platforms through which people organized in groups, coordinated their activities and mobilized the masses. Twitter, for example, was widely used during the Egyptian revolution. Egyptian Twitter users used this service for political discourse, organization, transparency and recruitment, substantially changing the status quo. The use of Twitter continued as a revolutionary tool following the 18-days after January 25, with users sharing thoughts and opinions through this medium. Figure (1), shows the main usage of Facebook during event of 2011 in Egypt (Sean A., Henry F., Marc L., John S., & Deen F., 2012).

Figure 1. The main usage of Facebook during event of 2011 in Egypt

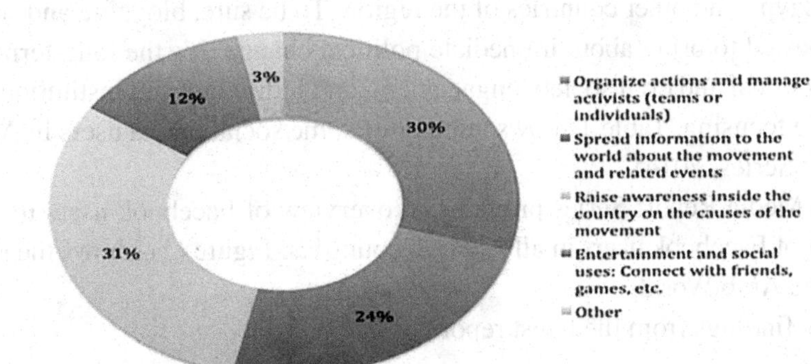

What was unique with regards to the use of social media and networking tools during the Arab Spring, however, was the effectiveness of these tools in mobilizing masses (Kamal, 2013). Although the Internet Café in the Egyptian context played a minor role during the Arab Spring, some people preferred connecting to the Internet through cafes for the purposes of anonymity and security. Not only did these platforms provide pathways to mass organized activity, but they allowed the Egyptians to talk to each other and share common grievances. Further, through informal networks—such as family members and neighbors—Egyptians who lacked access to the Internet or members of the older generations who did not use social media and networking tools received information about what was going on in the streets.

Social media and networking tools defeated the state of emergency in the country and helped disseminate knowledge about the issues such as corruption and human rights violations. They made the entire process of knowledge dissemination and sharing of ideas an easy one for the protestors. Digital activists were able to capitalize on the power of social network platforms to trigger social movements and political action. In many ways, social media and networking tools were a revelation for youth on the realities in the Egyptian streets. They created a parallel environment where people were able to organize around political ideas with social media's state of anonymity creating security that enabled people to openly discuss their ideas.

Of the four major Arab Spring protests analyzed—Tunisia, Egypt, Libya, and Bahrain—large differences were found across the four in the amount of information consumed via social media. The events in Egypt and in Libya (#jan25 and #feb17, respectively) garnered there is the simple fact that the Egyptian government shut down the Internet and short message service (SMS) on January 28. At that point, if not before, the mass of protestors was "composed primarily of people who have never updated a Facebook page or sent out a tweet in their lives"—no matter how "wired" some activists may have been (Sean A., Henry F., Marc L., John S., & Deen F., 2012).

In fact, the shutdown of the Internet may actually have spurred more people to protest—the opposite of what one might expect if Twitter, Facebook, or SMS were the primary means by which protestors were mobilized (Navid, 2011), It is also possible that new media was important for some groups involved in protests but not others.

Major Social Networking Tools That Used in the ARABIAN Countries

It's still very early in the dawn of the digital age in the Arab world. Just as Arab satellite channels helped revolutionize broadcast news, social media is arguably changing the nature of news and community engagement, which continues to evolve with increased convergence of social media and satellite broadcasts, as seen in Tunisia, Egypt, and other countries of the region. To be sure, blogging and social networking alone cannot be expected to bring about immediate political change. It's the long-term impact, the development of new political and civil society engagement, and individual and institutional competencies on which analysts are focusing. Table 1 shows number of some social media users in Arab world (Arab Social Media Report Series, 2014).

The Arab Social Media Report Series provides an overview of Facebook users in the Arab World. As such, the number of Facebook users in all 22 Arab countries. Figure (2), shows the number of active Facebook users in the Arab World.

These are the key findings from the latest report:

- The total number of Facebook users in the Arab world as of beginning of May 2014 was 81,302,064 up from 54,552,875 in May 2013.

Table 1. Number of some social media users in Arab word

Country	Estimated Twitter Users No.	Twitter %	Facebook Users No.	Facebook %	Internet Users per 100**	Mobile subscriptions per 100**
Algeria	8415	0.02%	3565180	9.50%	12.5	92.42
Bahrain	72468	5.33%	352520	25.93%	55.0	124.18
Egypt	295219	0.35%	11000000	13.1%	26.74	87.11
Iraq	11040	0.03%	1685640	5.00%	5.60	75.78
Jordan	59726	0.92%	2204500	34.14%	38.0	106.99
Kuwait	370987	12.83%	992200	34.31%	38.25	160.78
Lebanon	77722	1.81%	1403800	32.71%	31.0	68.0
Libya	4393	0.07%	545700	8.43%	14.0	171.52
Mauritania	528	0.01%	86740	2.39%	3.0	79.34
Morocco	38018	0.12%	4373660	13.42%	49.0	100.10
Oman	9832	0.34%	482680	16.62%	62.60	165.54
Palestine	33750	0.79%	906760	21.23%	37.44	
Qatar	59835	3.09%	567680	29.28%	69.0	132.43
Saudi Arabia	830291	2.89%	5506660	19.18%	41.0	187.86
Somalia	1999	0.02%	87840	0.90%		6.95
Sudan	4507	0.01%	1409634	3.08%		40.54
Syria	10839	0.05%	3228677	15.29%	20.70	57.30
Tunisia	12000	0.11%	2986700	27.90%	36.80	106.04
UAE	263070	3.25%	3293660	40.63%	78.0	145.45
Yemen	5907	0.02%	554820	2.17%	10.85	46.09

Figure 2. Facebook in the Arab Region

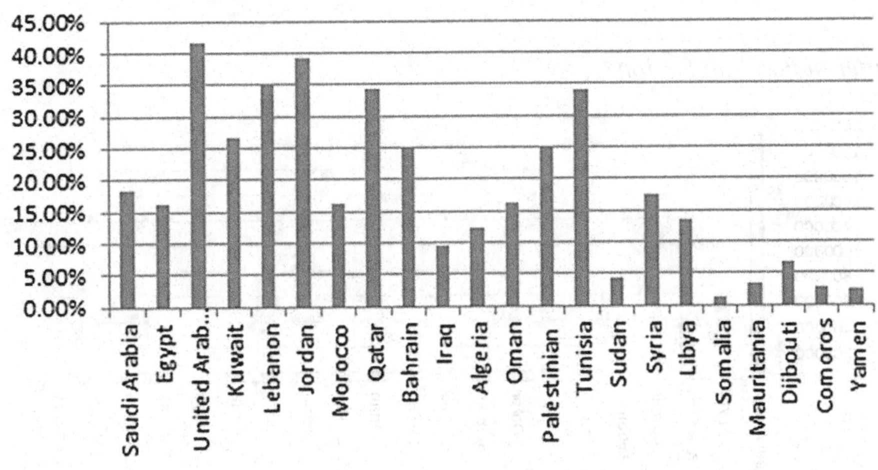

- By May 2014 the country average for Facebook penetration in the Arab region was over 21.5% up from 15% in May 2013.
- The percentage of female users has dipped slightly (from 33.4% in May 2013, to 31.75% in May 2014), after having fluctuated slightly between 33.4% and 34% in the past two years. This is still significantly lower than the global average of roughly 50%.
- The percentage of youth (those under 30) has decreased slightly due to slow and steady uptake amongst users aged 30 and above. As of May 2014 the percentage of users between 15 and 29 years old was 67%.
- In terms of Facebook penetration rate in the region, Qatar now leads in the Arab region, followed by the UAE, with Jordan, Lebanon, and Bahrain rounding out the top five countries in terms of Facebook penetration.
- Egypt continues to constitute about a quarter of all Facebook users in the region (24%) and has gained the highest number of new Facebook users since January 2014, with an increase of over 2.6 million users in that time period

While for Twitter users in the Arab World, the key findings from the latest report are:

- The total number of active Twitter users in the Arab world reached 5,797,500 users as of March 2014. Figure 3, shows the number of active Twitter users in the Arab World.
- The country with the highest number of active Twitter users in the Arab region is Saudi Arabia with 2.4 million users, accounting for over 40% of all active Twitter users in the Arab region.
- The estimated number of tweets produced by Twitter users in the Arab world in March 2014 was 533,165,900 tweets, an average of 17,198,900 tweets per day.
- Saudi Arabia, alone, produced 40% of all tweets in the Arab world, while Egypt produced 17% and Kuwait produced 10%.
- The percentage of female Twitter users in the Arab region – published for the first time in the Arab Social Media Report series - is 36.6%, slightly higher than that of female Facebook users in the region.

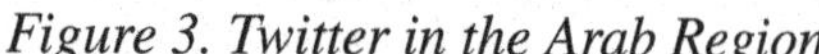

Figure 3. Twitter in the Arab Region

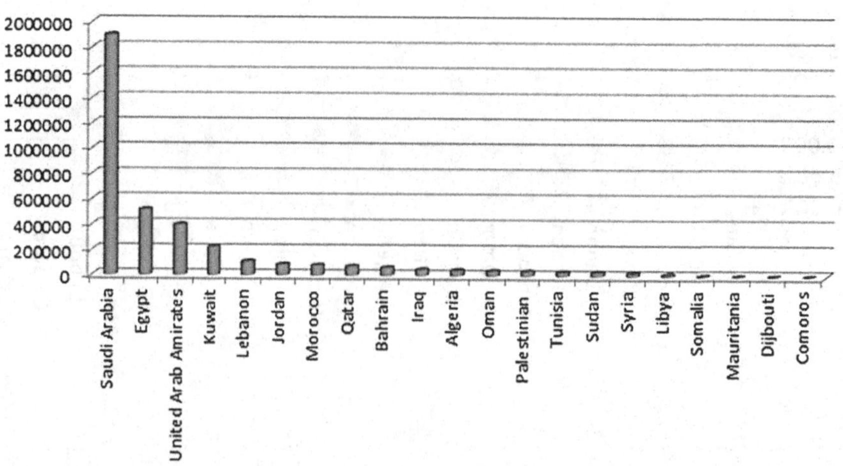

WOMEN RIGHTS IN ARAB COMMUNITY

In many societies, a woman is still regarded as a second-class citizen and deprived of various basic rights enjoyed by the male population. Deeply resenting this discrimination, they have championed a fight to obtain for themselves an equal status which unfortunately to date eludes them in the more modern Western states. Whereas the pendulum has swung to the extremes and has opened the way to licentiousness in the modern society, the West has often regarded Islamic women as being backward in a male-dominated world. On the contrary, Islam was the first religion formally to grant the

Women a status never known before. The Holy Quran, the sacred scripture of Islam, contains hundreds of teachings, which apply both to men and women alike. The moral, spiritual and economic equality of men and women as propagated by Islam is unquestionable. The specific verses of the Holy Quran, which address themselves to men or women, deal with either their physical differences or the role they each have to play in safeguarding the moral fiber of the society Islam envisages (Muhammad, 2008).

In most Arab countries, political rights of all the citizens, men and women, are severely curtailed. Even when recognized in laws, they are rarely respected in practice. Stereotypes, political party gate-keepers, the roles that societies expect women to conform to, and the lack of resources are some of the obstacles preventing women from running for high-level policy making offices in Arab world. Only two Arab countries do not recognize the right of women to vote and to stand for elections. These two, Saudi Arabia and the United Arab Emirates (UAE), do not hold elections in the first place; and Kuwait was the only country that holds regular elections but excluded women until recently in 2006. Some Middle Eastern states recognized the political rights of women relatively early—Syria in 1949, Lebanon in 1952, Egypt in 1956, and Tunisia in 1957etc. however, in a cultural and social environment inimical to women's acquisition and free exercise of their political rights; it takes more than legal edicts to make gender equality in political participation a reality (Leila, 2010).

Nowadays, Arab women are turning to media as a mean s for their empowerment, as a medium for education that overcomes barriers of distance and time, and as a tool to advance their progress and development in their communities. The new information technologies have allowed women in Arab world to be seen as equal to men in their ability to discuss, investigate, report and present various issues. They facilitated links and networks for women to interact effectively and share information and resources faster. Meanwhile, the women's movements in the region are increasingly using the electronic media to put forward their advocacy and build solidarity.

The societal and political transformations taking place across the region played an instrumental role in challenging stereotypes about Arab women as oppressed and subservient. In particular, the leading role that women have played in orchestrating and participating in social movements in Tunisia, Egypt, and Yemen has cemented their position as equal partners to men in transforming the political landscapes in their countries. The most obvious acknowledgement of this leadership role was the awarding of the Nobel Peace Prize to an Arab woman, Tawakkul Karman, a leading female Yemeni political activist. Whether Arab women's civic and political engagement will be enhanced in the aftermath of the "Arab Spring" remains to be seen. It is clear from news reports and interviews with activists that women were active in nontraditional forms of political participation–the protests, strikes, and demonstrations that characterized the Arab Spring, and till now in Egypt.

MOTIVATION AND METHODOLOGY

The Egyptian revolution carries a challenging transition phase, starting out with problems such as low foreign direct investments, a high budget deficit, a high debt rate, a high unemployment rate, a high poverty rate, and a low standard of living (Doaa & Zeinab, 2013). All these factors enforced me to close my software house company and to increase unemployment rate. However, I got a lot of contacts from old students who want to initiate many Non-Governmental Organizations (NGOs) in different areas, to help people to develop their skills and therefore, helping our new country to recover soon. I felt that this new inspire after revolution means that people started to trust and to cooperate with the new leaders.

The research conducted was analytical research and the data was collected with the help of a questionnaire in a cross sectional survey. The target population for the study was the college students, of bachelors program, of faculty of Computers and Information, Helwan university, Egypt. To explore the relationship between social networks and impact on students' academic performance, we chose a sample of 387 students (228 male, 159 female who were in the age bracket of 18 to 25 years.

After that a critical analysis was carried out of the collected facts and figures and had been compared with other 265 samples from Alhag Elkhdr University in Algeria (Naryman, 2012), 300 samples from Jordon (El-tahat & Zohier, 2013). Other samples from Saudi Arabia (Hanan, 2013), Lebanon, Syria and Tunisia (Leila, 2010), also had been included to give a wide figure about Arab community.

The Impact of Social Networking on College Students

This study is asking a question about the extent of the impact of these sites on college students on various issues? This study also sought to determine the limits of the influence of social networking sites by posing questions give clues can be read out of the many aspects of the relationship of Arab university students these sites.

The clear problem of the study is to answer the following questions:

1. What is the effect of the amount of interaction with these sites to improve political awareness among the students of Arab universities?
2. What is the effect of the amount of confidence in the information provided by these sites to improve the political awareness of the students?
3. What is the effect of the time period for the membership to improve the political awareness of the Arab Universities students?

Data Analysis

Responses to the survey were fairly similar across the three questions: a) Are you member in Facebook' group? b) Do you use your real name in Facebook?, and c) Are social networking empowered women's rights?. Figure 4 breakdowns the results on gender base.

The results can be summarized as follow:

- Social media has become an important source of news. While the credibility of some sources can clearly be contested, news channels tweet or give updates on significant happenings all over

Figure 4. Breakdowns the some results on gender base

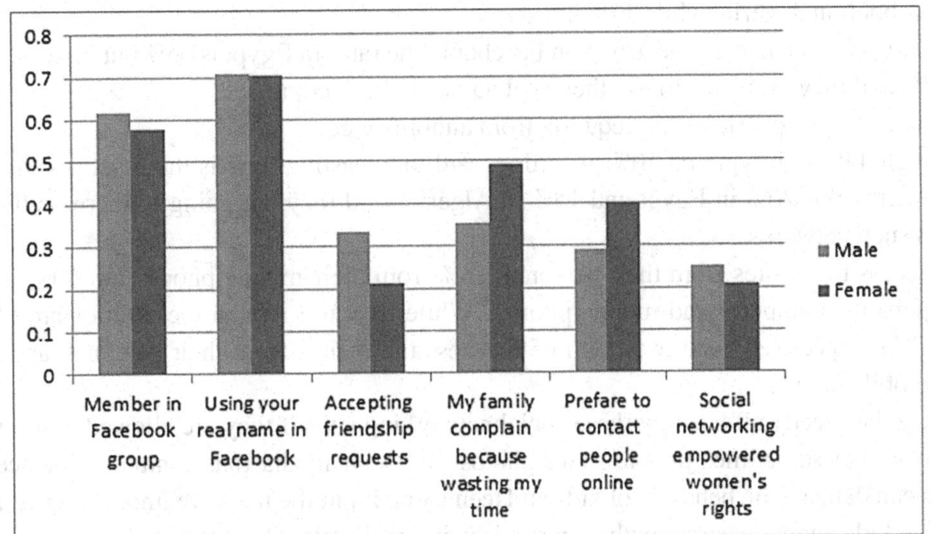

the world. Their availability on social networks makes news more accessible. Additionally, news quickly gets passed around the networks in ways never experienced before. That is why 30% showed that one of their objectives from using social media is to be aware for up-to-date news.

- Another objective with 34%, was communicate with their families, since family living abroad can be kept abreast of the latest happenings in your world as quickly as those living next door. Friends who you haven't seen since school, and who have since moved away, are able to keep in touch.
- 77% have a Facebook account in Saudi Arabiya, 45% have a Facebook account in Egypt, while 0.09% has twitter accounts, 21% have whatups accounts, and 33% have all types of accounts. This ratios increase in case of Jordon to be 83% has a Facebook account and 25% have a twitter accounts.
- One of the negative effect of social media or network is it leads to addiction. Spending countless hours on the social sites can divert the focus and attention from a particular task. It lowers the motivational level of the people, especially of students. They mainly rely on technology and the internet instead of learning the practical knowledge and expertise of the everyday life. Average time spent per day in accessing such social networking is ranging from 2 to 5 hours, while 11% spent time range from 5 to 8 hours, and 16% spent more than 8 hours per day. Among this time 39% spent time ranging from 1 to 3 hours accessing Facebook only. The majority use Facebook more than three years ago and they access it on daily basis, while in Algeria the majority use Facebook less than three years ago.
- They may access it more than 5 times per day especially at night when they access it alone.
- It's entirely possible to have hundreds of friends on Facebook. They may not be friends you know on a personal level and spend time with in the real world on a weekly basis. But they're friends nevertheless. It isn't just your inner circle of close friends and even closer family members that social networking sites allow you to communicate with easily and effectively, either. They open the world up to you, making it a smaller place than it has ever been before. In Algeria, 64%. have less than 150 friendship on Facebook, while in Egypt this ratio decreases to 34%, since 26%

have150 to 300 friendships in Egypt but 15% in Algeria, and 21% have more than 300 friendship on Facebook in Algeria, while 17% in Egypt.

- Most of users join at least one group on Facebook, the ratio in Egypt is 65% but increase in Algeria to 72%, and they preferred to use their real names in both countries.
- They used to accept friendship requests from annomnance.
- Although 44% in Egypt and 40% in Jordon, said that wasting time is the most negative affect of social networks, 20% in Egypt and 15% in Algeria, said they are going to increase their time in access such networks.
- 18% access these sites from their personal, 13% from their mobile phone, and 50% access from both personal computer and mobile phones. While in Saudi Arabia these ratios are (23%, 31%, and 47%) respectively, and in Jordon 65% access these sites from their personal, and 31% from their mobile phone.
- Kids can be greatly affected by these social networking sites if they are allowed to use them. The reason is that sometimes people share photos on social media that contains violence and sex, which can damage the behavior of kids and teenagers. It put the negative impact on overall society as these kids and teenagers involve themselves in crime related activities. 44% believe that their interaction with their families decreased after they used social networks. Therefore 11% among them are going to prevent their children in the future from using these social networks, 50% will allow them to access partially, and 20% will let them use it freely even in daily basis. This percentage change in Algeria case to be 2%, 69%, and 28% respectively.
- Social media has enabled greater political awareness and organization, which has in some cases rewritten entire political landscapes. It has particularly played a large part in inspired the political unrests in Egypt and Tunis. 66% said that social networking sites increased their awarnace about political issues both locally and internationally. 73% believe that these sites were very important tools in Arab spring during 2011.
- There is no doubting that social networking sites can lead to the breaking up of relationships. But there is another side to the tale, which is that people are moving onto other, perhaps better, relationships at the same time. Social networks can put you (back) in touch with those you have lots in common with, and that common ground is often the starting point for long-lasting relationships. As painful as break-ups can be, they can sometimes be the right thing for all concerned. What's to say that the new relationship, founded on the steps of Facebook, isn't THE one that will last? Even if it doesn't turn into a spectacular coupling, it could be the friendship that is needed at the time. Which has to be a positive? Therefore, 42% believe that Facebook is one of the factors for raising divorce rate in Egypt.

Social networking sites encourage people to be more public about their personal lives. Because intimate details of our lives can be posted so easily, users are prone to bypass the filters they might normally employ when talking about their private lives. What's more, the things they post remain available indefinitely. While at one moment a photo of friends doing shots at a party may seem harmless, the image may appear less attractive in the context of an employer doing a background check. While most sites allow their users to control who sees the things they've posted, such limitations are often forgotten, can be difficult to control or don't work as well as advertised. The analysis of negative effects of using Facebook from students point of views showed that, they truly understand the different aspects lead to these negative effects, as shown in figure (5).

Figure 5. Negatives of social networking sites

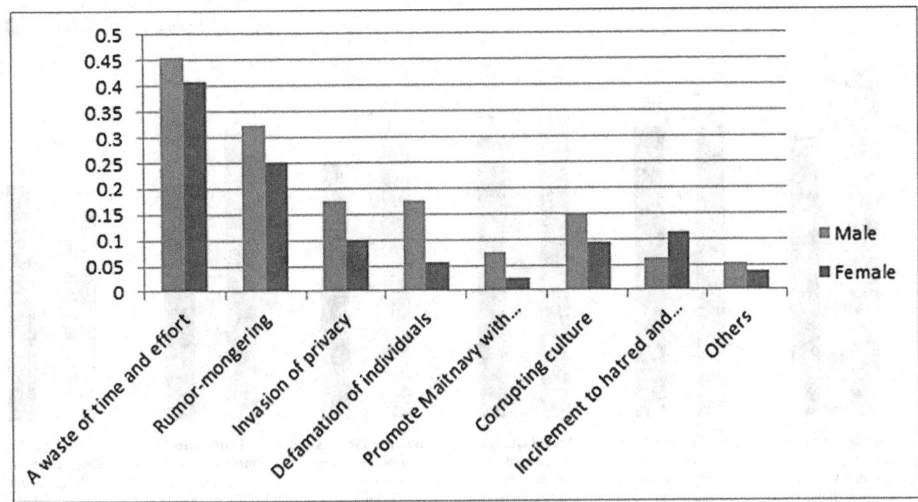

Despite the large number of benefits to use these sites, but the non-conscious use by family members toward the establishment of social relations in all its forms online, and in

The absence of effective policies for monitoring and control of these sites may pose a serious risk to the family stability, in addition to the many problems social that may arise,

Especially between spouses or between children and parents, which reflected negatively disintegration of the family? Another analysis regarding the miss use of Facebook, students gave the lack of awareness the highest ratio, as shown in figure (6).

Other results showed that the majority of men and women respondents thought that social media can be a tool for women's empowerment in their countries. Given the low ranking of most of these countries on gender equality and women's empowerment indices, the participants' optimistic responses indicate

Figure 6. Resones for misuse of social networking sites

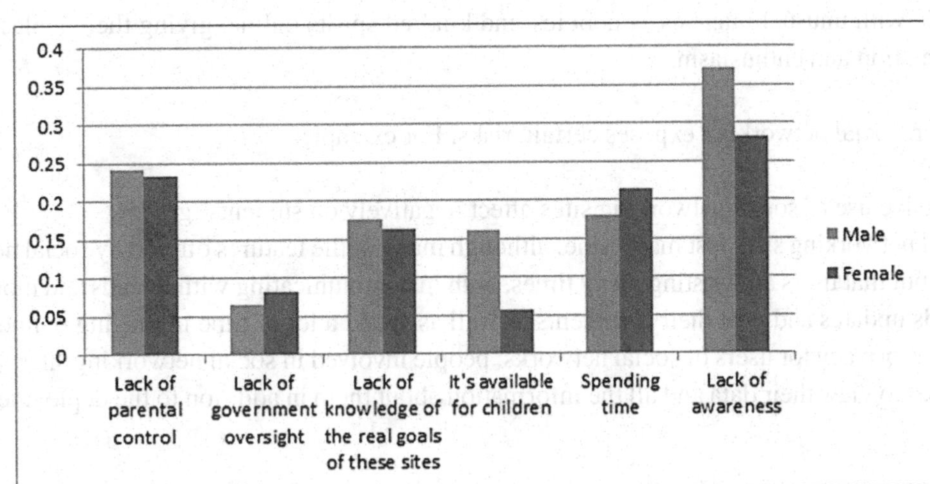

Figure 7. Changing gender inequalities

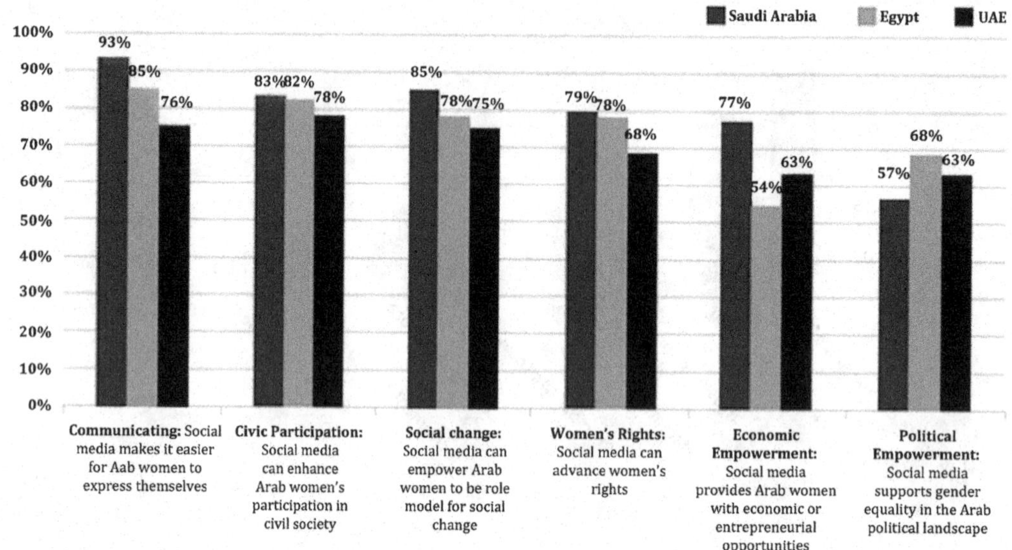

that social media users in the Arab region view this media as a potential catalyst for changing gender inequalities in the region (see Figure 7).

Pros and Cons of Social Networking Sites

No doubt that, social networking provides many benefits. For example:

- Social networking is an extension of real-world friendships. It helps us enrich and manage our social lives.
- Socializing online can give shy, socially awkward teens and women comfortable way to communicate -- one that's less intimidating than meeting face-to-face. This can boost their self-esteem and help them practice their social skills.
- People with unusual interests or hobbies find kindred spirits online, giving them a place to share information and enthusiasm.

However, social networking exposes certain risks. For example:

- Excessive use of social networking sites affect negatively on students' grades.
- Social networking sites lost many time: although many of the features offered by social networking sites, but that users are wasting many times, both in communicating with friends and monitor their friends updates and post their comments as well as spend a lot of time in playing online games.
- Lack of privacy for users of social networks: people involved in social networking sites using their profiles to view their data and all the information about them in addition to the deployment of a lot

of personal information about housing and the university it is possible to take advantage of some scammers this information to be exploited.

- Social networking sites can be used as a tool for the dissemination of false news: there are a large number of incorrect news spread through social networking sites daily, and a lot of users believe it and re-deployed again, causing a lot of rumors trading
- Use of social networking sites affect the mental state of the user: excessive use of social networking sites increases the sense of loneliness, depression and addiction to sit in front of the Internet.
- Social networking sites affect family cohesion.
- Users of social networking sites vulnerable to social isolation: social networking sites affect exacerbate feelings of unity among a lot of people, and separated from the real world, and not wanting to participate in life as well as to increase the feeling of self-confidence.

CONCLUSION

The findings of the survey show clear similarities in the views of male and female social media users in the Arab region. Arab men and women largely agree on issues related to social media and its implications for women and civic participation. They use social media in similar ways and have similar opinions on the role that social media can play in women's empowerment. Whether this is a result of using social media, or has more to do with the typical profile of a social media user, warrants further research.

A study about why accepting anonyms friendship requests on Facebook by students in Egypt and Allegra reports that most users utilize the site to keep in touch with old friends or people they knew from the past. 46% from Egypt and 62% from Algeria use the site to 'check out the Facebook profile of someone new to them', 28% from Egypt and 17% from Algeria use the site to 'waste their time', and 11% from Egypt and 21% from Algeria use the site to ' find people to date'. Other findings are:

- The students use social networks for many purposes and fulfilling different roles: for communication, entertainment, academic and professional work. They share information, build and maintain friendships, see what friends do or share, keep in touch or track them, learn more about friends, and keep connections and track of news.
- Social networks' communication and connectivity capabilities that enable to share information in various sources with many people have become an everyday habit for and students and they can be used as compensation of being away from the people with whom they usually communicate closely.
- Usually students add persons whom they know (either in person or by reference) to their network. However, adding someone they don't know in person, there should be a reason; for example, the person is the friend of friends or she/he has a relevant background.
- Students are aware that too much use or misuse of these technologies can lead to negative things, such as problems with the organizations they work in or alienation. They know they have to use social networks with caution, even restricting the time they put to them.
- Students are aware that social networks can also be a source of negative consequences. Therefore they should be careful on the kind of information shared as it can damage one's personal image or compromise privacy.

FURTHER RESEARCH

After this investigation, the same method proposed can be applied to a different sample of other professionals or more diverse user groups to see if the results are different. This study could be taken as a starting point for one more complex and ambitious with bigger and more heterogeneous samples of participants.

A future work can study if there are differences in participants' information behavior in social networks between locations, level of specialization and profession. Also, a study can analyze deeper uses of social networks, such as the information behavior in users who utilize the integration the different social networks allow.

Some of the results of this study and similar ones can be taken into account for the design of a learning management system or digital library with the features of a social network.

REFERENCES

Arab Knowledge Economy Report 2014. (2014). Retrieved from http:// www.orientplanet.com

Arab Social Media Report Series. (2014). Retrieved from [REMOVED HYPERLINK FIELD]http:// www.arabsocialmediareport.com/Facebook/LineChart.aspx?&PriMenuID=18&CatID=24&mnu=Cat #sthash.UA3EapcL.dpuf

Hanan, E. (2013). *The Effects of Using Electronic Social Networks on Social Relationships Facebook and Twitter as Example* [MSc thesis]. King Abdul Aziz University.

Kamal, S. (2013). *The role of social medial & networking in post-conflict settings – lessons learned from Egypt*, African Development Bank Conference: History and Experience of Post-conflict Reintegration and Stabilization: Reflections from DDR in Africa 5-6 June, Hotel African Tunis.

Leila R. (2010, Feb 16). *Women in Arab media: present but not heard* [Presentation]. Stanford University, California, USA.

Mirkin, B. (2010). *Population Levels, Trends and Policies in the Arab Region: Challenges and Opportunities*. United Nations Development Programme Regional Bureau for Arab States Arab Human Development Report Research Paper Series.

Muhammad, Z. K. (2008). *Woman in Islam*. Tilford, Surrey, U.K.: Islam International Publications Limited Islamabad, Sheephatch Lane.

Naryman, N. (2012). *Studying Facebook sample users from Algiera to obtain its effect on social relations* [Msc thesis]. Elhag Elkhdr University.

Navid, H. (2011). *Media Disruption Exacerbates Revolutionary Unrest: Evidence from Mubarak's Natural Experiment*. American Political Science Association Annual Meeting. Retrieved from http:// papers.ssrn.com/sol3/papers.cfm?abstract_id=1903351

Salman Abdou, D. M., & Zaazou, Z. (2013). The Egyptian revolution and post socio-economic impact. *Topics in Middle Eastern and African Economies, 15*(1). eMarketing Egypt Releases. (2014, May 23). *The First Report about the Internet and the Revolution in Egypt*. Retrieved from http://www.pr.com/press-release/336504

Sean, A., Henry, F., Marc, L., John, S., & Deen, F. (2012). *New Media and Conflict after the Arab Spring*. United States Institute of Peace.

Smith, C. (2013, May 16). Egyptian Tweeter Says Twitter was Invaluable during Protests. *Huffingtonpost.com*. Retrieved from http://www.huffingtonpost.com/2011/02/17/egypt-twitter-jan25-protests_n_824310.html

Chapter 11
e-Research, a way of Learning Together?

Paolo Diviacco
Istituto Nazionale di Oceanografia e di Geofisica Sperimentale (OGS), Italy

ABSTRACT

The aim of this chapter is to compare the two worlds of science and learning in the perspective to find commonalties that could be used to develop new methods and technologies to better support collaborative and on-line scientific research. In this perspective we claim the existence of a convergence of these two domains and highlight similarities in on-line tools that support such activities. At the same time, we bring attention to the fact that a largely overlooked aspect of existing on-line scientific collaborative research systems, which is instead well represented in learning systems, is communication among partners. To address this issue we build a collaborative on-line software tool that allows to make some interesting early observations. Further on, we report on the introduction of a discourse structuring facility that could be used, on one hand, to ease the use of communication tools and on the other as a boundary object: an artifact that allows to bridge different paradigms and backgrounds.

INTRODUCTION

This chapter will explore the possibility to extend and improve e-Research technologies applying approaches borrowed from learning. This could be possible only if a convergence is demonstrated to exist between the two domains.

In this, a starting point, could be the fact that both have undergone a severe revision in the last decades which coincided with the crackling that postmodernism was able to trigger in their, ever since, firm pillars. This irreversible process allowed switching from a scenario where science was associated with the truth and learning with its transmission, to one where both became associated with situated and socially dependent knowledge building. It was indeed the possible existence of this convergence that triggered our interest in comparing the two domains, so that we thought that new ideas can emerge comparing the different approaches taken and the different experiences done separately in the two domains. In this sense it must be said that, while, in the field of learning, there is quite a large literature on what this

DOI: 10.4018/978-1-4666-9556-6.ch011

Copyright © 2016, IGI Global. Copying or distributing in print or electronic forms without written permission of IGI Global is prohibited.

latter can borrow from scientific research, on the other side there is not so much available yet, on what science can gain from the comparison with learning.

BACKGROUND

Science

The Encyclopædia Britannica defines Science as: *any system of knowledge that is concerned with the physical world and its phenomena and that entails unbiased observations and systematic experimentation.*

In the traditional vision, science coincides with truth. This happens because scientific research is an activity that is supposed to be objective (unbiased), meaning that it is supposed to be founded on facts and logic.

This has been demonstrated to be hardly the case.

Science is not objective. Even in the perspective of the analytical tradition (Searle 2008, Diviacco 2015) the term objective is translated as "not just from someone's point of view". It essentially means that what is stated is not private, that, on the contrary, it is public, meaning that it is inevitably defined by the interactions of the members of a community. Quoting Latour and Woolgar (1979) "Science is a Social Construct".

Within the same perspective, facts and opinions themselves cannot be easily (or maybe at all) distinguished. To say that something is a fact would require the possibility to state its metaphysically objective condition. Metaphysical objectivity refers to properties of things that do not depend on experience for their existence (Diviacco 2015). This of course is something rather difficult to determine for anyone of us. What we normally try to achieve, instead, is the form of epistemological objectivity we described above, where a community finds a convergence towards a "state of affairs". This latter is not a fact, since it is epistemic, but at the same time it is not an opinion, since it is not only private. It is a merely possible situation that can be expressed by any non-contradictory true or false sentence

Paradigms, Communities and Theory-Ladenness

In the traditional view, researchers are always described as "cold" operators that, in their work, from a point A inevitably and "logically" go straightforwardly to a point B. This does not happen in reality. Researchers are much more "serendipic"[1] . Many paths can be followed during any research and often scientists can be tempted to follow a less direct one. Suchman (1987) uses the metaphor of a map where many roads can drive to the same place.

Pierce (1931) maintained that actual research drifts from the standard vision of the scientific method due to a mode of reasoning, that he called abduction.

Abductive reasoning infers the existence of a state of affairs not accessible to observations. It is a form of hypothesis that should be based on a rational analysis of other states of affairs. It is different from induction, which is predictive, as in the classic example: all ravens are black therefore the next one will also be black. In fact abduction is generally used in retrodictions, such as in the example proposed by Peirce (1931), where if I enter a room where I find a tin of white beans and a white bean on the floor I grow naturally the idea that this latter comes from the white beans tin.

This is just an hypothesis. Abduction merely suggests a state of affairs.

Although possibly at different "concentration" when not often neglected, this has always permeated almost all scientific disciplines.

Now, if the choice is not based on logic only, what is the mechanism that makes a scientist prefer one path over another? Epistemology and history of science propose that the answer lies in the fact that scientists tend to bias all their activities upon what Thomas Kuhn (1962) named paradigms. These are essentially philosophical or theoretical frameworks, traditions or schools that condition their way of thinking. Different, concurrent and incommensurable paradigms exist within any discipline. In Addition, after Lakatos (1970), it became evident that theories or paradigms can shield their core from attempts at falsification by changing a set of auxiliary and peripheral hypotheses (the protective belt) while leaving essentially unaltered the kernel of the theory.

In several domains where falsification of theories is not an easy task, where reasoning itself cannot be reduced to the inductive/deductive loop of the classic scientific method, communities of researchers tend to speciate, forming incommensurable tribes that tend to preserve their territories due to, not only ethical, but also political reasons (Diviacco 2015, 2012). In fact, following Whitley (2000), external conditions and circumstances, such as how universities, faculties and departments are organized, or the control over facilities, can and do make a difference to disciplinary status and identity. To what described so far we need to add the problem of herding and rhetorics. Being science a social construct it will strongly depend on the relationships between the partners in a research project or in the scientific community in general.

Besides, one generally overlooked issue is that paradigms condition scientists lives at every level, even at those of the observation and planning of observations. Any experiment is bound to a theory, meaning to what someone is expecting to see. Quoting Hanson (1958, p.8) "Observation of x is shaped by prior knowledge of x". The attitude to shape reality, meaning to neglect some information (or representation of information) while preferring others upon the prescriptions of a theory is named theory-ladenness (Bishop, 1992). There are evidences that theory-ladenness is relevant in perception (what is called conceptual penetrability of visual systems). For example, Hanson maintains that there is a "linguistic" element in "seeing," even thought there is nothing "linguistic" in what "meets the eyeball." (Suppe, 1977) this makes Hanson think that those who hold rival theories will make different, and logically incompatible observation statements when "looking at" the same thing.

A very interesting consequence from the point of view of what we are discussing in this work is that experience and training can alter our visual system so that experienced researchers can be able to recognize features that could be invisible to the others (Fodor, 1983), and of course the other way around. Following Fodor (1983) it should be possible to test when this is happening if a new feature is identified in a fast, mandatory and non voluntary fashion. Diviacco and Busato (2015) reports on an experiment done in the case of seismic data interpretation, where trained researchers were able to recognize geophysical features in data not originated in that domain, but represented as they were.

Learning

The Oxford Dictionary currently defines learning as: the acquisition of knowledge or skills through study, experience, or being taught. As mentioned above the traditional vision focused on the trasmission of information, recently this approach evolved moving the focus towards the learner. It can be a subject for discussion whether or not the domain of learning changed its perspective as a consequence of the ideas developed in the domain of science, as suggested by Scardamalia and Bereiter (2006). To us it seems more likely that both have responded to wider cultural changes that since the 1960s have been put forward by western culture in general. This perspective has been taken by us (Diviacco 2015) in a similar effort to what we are doing here, comparing contemporary visions of science with recent trends in understanding the Arts. Post-modernism increased the eccentricity of new visions from common sense. Personalities such as Deridda and Barthes influenced and were at the same time the gauge of a changing society. These ideas penetrated the domain of education/learning that was further moved from Piaget's constructivism and Vygotsky's socio-constructivism to Papert's Constructionism, learning by discovery and similar approaches. All these had in common the commitment to move the focus from learning intended as a process of transmission and assimilation of knowledge, to one where knowledge should emerge naturally from a knowledge building process.

Factors Conditioning Learning

Teaching was often understood as a way to impart abstracted and fixed concepts and entities. It was Piaget himself that maintained that the transmission model, or conduit methapor, of human communication won't do (Ackermann, 2001). He highlighted that any learner resists to new ideas. They have reasons to avoid changing their view in the light of external perturbation. Therefore, something is needed to overcome the resistance to embrace new knowledge. Piaget, for example, suggested that teaching should always be indirect. For him information is not something to be delivered, rather something that needs to be experienced and acquired through interaction with the world, things and people.

Context

In this sense one very important concept that has been pushed in the last decade is that Knowledge is essentially context dependent, and that reusing it in other contexts can create problems. Knowledge, following the definition of Donna Haraway (1988) becomes then situated; specific to a particular situation.

Situated knowledge is typical of learning methodologies such as trial and error, or learning from experience that are in line with the vision that moves the focus from knowledge transmission towards knowledge building. These methods acknowledge the fact that any method that tries to teach abstract concepts independently of authentic situations, overlooks the way understanding is developed through continued situation use (Brown, Collins & Duguid, 1989). In addition, concepts will continually evolve being their evolution defined by their use, which means that part of the meaning of each concept will be always inherited from the context of use.

Artifacts

For Seymour Papert Knowledge can be internalized "in a context where the learner is consciously engaged in constructing a public entity, whether it's a sand castle on the beach or a theory of the universe" (Papert, 1991). This shifts the emphasis from cognitive potentials to the actual creation of something in the real life: an artifact; and the transformation of ideas that this can trigger. Artifacts might be abstract, such as, for example, theories, or real things to experience and work with, such as in the case of Papert's software and commercial hardware derived from his work[2].

Externalization, as a mean to augment the knowing mind, allows extending widely, but of course depending on the context, the type of artifacts involved. This in our perspective is overwhelmingly important since allows to include in the discussion digital media and Information technology.

A very important point for our discussion is that, even though the importance of artifacts have been highlighted also before, for example by Vygotsky, now the expression of ideas through the creation of tangible artifacts allows sharing these latter to transmit knowledge.

The Social Dimension

If we consider the social aspects of learning, we realize that, in the early 1990s, there has been a drift from all approaches that were focusing on the individual as the knowing actor. This resembles what happened in other domains, such as Philosophy and the Arts, where, similarly, the focus was moved outside the individual. In Diviacco (2015), for example, we brought the case of artistic experiences such as Gilbert and George or The Residents, to show artists collectives that broke up with the focus on their egos.

In the perspective drawn so far, meaning is also constructed socially. It is the product of negotiation within a community. It is cultural. Learning is therefore a process of enculturation, meaning a process of adoption of the behaviour and belief system of a social group

Following the work of Lave and Wenger (1991) knowing should be rethought as a cultural practice put in action by the members of a community. Learning communities have been advocated as effective in mitigating conceptual resistance of learners and enhancing their engagement levels (Zhao & Kuh, 2004).

A learning community can be seen as a great support in the process of learning, because mimics the natural process of learning which does not pass through the use of abstract formalization but through practitioning the actual real problems

People can pick up relevant jargon, imitate behavior and start to act in accordance with the norms of that culture, which can be recondite and complex.

Tacit Knowledge

Summing up, artifacts can be thought of as epistemic tools that can be shared in a community (Sterelny, 2005). Learning the meaning of an artifact will depend on the occasions and conditions for its use (the context) but also on the norms of the specific community that employs it.

In addition to this we need to mention a very important issue, which is tacit knowledge.

In the domain of learning often two categorizations of knowledge are contrasted: on one hand what is called declarative knowledge (or knowledge “about”) and on the other hand procedural knowledge (or, even if not perfectly matching, knowledge “of”).

Declarative Knowledge enables someone to describe a rule, while procedural knowledge enables someone to apply that rule. Declarative knowledge about skiing allows you to represent what happens while your are gliding on the snow, while procedural knowledge allows you to actually ski. The former is what can be found in textbooks, while the second is generally transmitted at a different level.

Tacit knowledge is difficult to encode and transfer directly to another person. Tacit knowledge cannot be formalized because pertains to the deep maps of conceptual connections we have in our brain and that cannot be fully explored. Sharing tacit knowledge requires cooperation, understanding and trust between the person giving the knowledge and the one receiving it; such knowledge includes know-how, which is the individual’s technical skills, mind-sets, beliefs and positions, which can be obtained through observation, imitation and direct experience (Nonaka, 1994).

This can be the case of a formal relation between a mentor and an apprentice, such as in the case, for example, of doctoral or post-doctoral students (Olson & Connelly, 1995; Whitley & Oddi, 1998), but also any case of cooperation where experience accumulated is shared not only through formalized knowledge. A wide literature informs us that similar problems are common in non-academic situations as well. Organizations in general have to deal with the transmission of tacit knowledge. Duffy and Cunningham (1996) and Oliver (2001) have a different approach saying that the knowledge of an individual cannot be transferred to another person in its entirety, because this latter creates new knowledge on his/her part which can be different from the expectations. In addition, we must take into account the information asymmetries that exist between the person who possesses the knowledge and the one receiving it during the transfer of knowledge (Wilkesmann & Wilkesmann, 2011). The last two visions are not in contrast with tacit knowledge.

The Discourse

Following the ideas of Bereiter (2002) and Scardamalia and Bereiter (2006) learning by knowledge building is question-driven inquiry and explanation-driven understanding in a progressive discourse (Hakkarainen, 2003). The discourse plays a very important role, here, since records and, at the same time, stimulates the process of learning. In a community, it naturally becomes the place to exchange ideas, record experiences and activities. Scardamalia and Bereiter (2006) maintain that there are two versions of the claim that collaborative discourse plays a role in knowledge building, and namely: (i) a weak form, where findings only become contributions to community knowledge when they are brought into public discourse, and (ii) a strong version, where the discourse is itself the state of public knowledge in a community. Within this latter version the progress of knowledge coincide with the progress of the knowledge building discourse. This would mean that the state of knowledge of a community is not something in the minds of the individual members of the community, rather in the discourse itself. If the discourse takes place in an artifact, this latter will become the state of knowledge of the designated community

MAIN FOCUS OF THE CHAPTER

Linking Science and Learning

At the beginning of this paper, we claimed that, in the light of the perspective projected by postmodernism, a convergence could be found between science and learning. Can we prove this hypothesis?

The most important argument to support our thesis lies in the fact that both are concerned with knowledge building. In the case of science of course this latter is the "core-business" and main mission, while, in the case of learning it can be seen more as a mean.

A second very important feature is that both are context dependent.

Considering abductive reasoning, bias and theory-ladenness, is it easy to understand that scientific research is almost always inevitably bound to a context and to the community that lives in that context. So is learning, that, as explained above, is in fact situated.

A third important aspect is that both science and learning have strong social aspects. As we have demonstrated, the possibility to warrant an assertion in science has become rather debatable. We showed that science receives its objectivity from the condition of being public. It is a social construct, and if it would not be so, states of affairs would reduce to mere opinions. On the other hand learning is a process of enculturation and its social dimension has been demonstrated to be important for the motivation of learners.

A Fourth important point is that in scientific research, similarly to learning, there are serious problems and limits emerging while formalizing meaning. Tacit knowledge can be embedded in practices and even tools that often are available in an opaque way. Following Brown, Collins and Duguid (1989), any method that tries to teach abstract concepts independently of authentic situations overlooks the way understanding is developed through use. The meaning of a word cannot be captured by a defintion because it will be always "under construction"

In our opinion these points demonstrate the similarity between scientific research and learning, so that we can now start to address the issue of what the former can get from the experience of the latter

A Space for the Discourse

So far we pointed at several issues, and namely: knowledge building, context, social construction and tacit knowledge, that could be seen as separated entities. On the contrary, to study learning and distill what collaborative research can get from it they have to be considered within the same perspective. To address this, we need a vision based on the possibility to create tangible artifacts, such as digital media spaces, that can be shared in a community where the actual knowledge building discourse can take place.

This needs to be much more than an online versions of a "conversations". It should allow the possibility to add data, refer to them, restructure the discourse, identify progress and new ideas and create links among them. Users can think of their work in this type of Knowledge "space" as building a communal learning resource, which, contrary to online conversations that are mainly ephemeral, has lasting utility. This feature introduces the aspect of knowledge "preservation" that such spaces might have, which is very important and becomes a solid argument to support the strong version of the role of collaborative discourse in knowledge building we found in Scardamalia and Bereiter (2006).

Learning Content Management Systems (LCMS) and Virtual Research Environments (VRE)

Learning Content Management Systems (LCMS) provide tools to deliver and manage synchronous and asynchronous online learning, as well as virtual spaces for learner interaction such as discussion forums and chats.

Virtual Research Environment (VRE) are sets of online tools, systems and processes interoperating to facilitate or enhance the research process within and without institutional boundaries (Fraser, 2004). In practice, LCMS implement the functional specification we discussed above for the case of learning, while VREs are systems to support e-research.

Among the most popular open source LCMS we can recall, for example: Moodle, ATutor, .LRN, ILIAS, among commercial systems we can recall Siminars, Skillshare, Udemy and others. Of course each one has advantages and disadvantages in comparison with the others. Here, in the perspective of adopting and adapting some functionality of LCMS for e-research, we'd like to focus on what is currently offered by LCMS that is currently missing in VREs.

All LCSM offer file storage and access tools. In learning, data is mostly multimedia, while in scientific research, things are a bit more complicated because many types of observation exist that are conceptually different, and need different forms of representation (Diviacco, 2015).

Most of VREs address this aspects, such as for example, Max Plank's eSciDoc. (https://www.escidoc.org) or the Myexperiment (http://www.myexperiment.org) initiative. We personally have been involved in developing and maintaining several data access infrastructure, such as for example the EU FP7 GeoSeas project (http://www.geo-seas.eu/) or the EMODNET- Bathymetry initiative (http://www.emodnet-hydrography.eu/) and already reported on the problems related to this activity in Diviacco and Busato (2013).

Fraser's (2004) definition is rather generic, but pinpoints the fact that VREs should be online, should support interoperability and very importantly should foster collaborative attitude between researchers. We think that this last feature of VREs is a key point in the discussion here. In fact, as far as we know, all existing VREs lack integrated support for actual communication among researchers: tools to socially discuss scientific issues. Some VRE use collaborative tools such as for example MS Jammer or Alfresco, but these are not relevant here, since they focus mainly on the process of syncing partners agendas, which, is not knowledge building.

Since we showed that there is a convergence between learning and scientific research and highlighted in this perspective the importance of community driven knowledge building we find natural to emphasize the role of the discussion among partners in a scientific research.

If in the field of learning the notion of the discourse is well rooted, in scientific research, as far as we know, it seems, instead, rather overlooked. As mentioned above, in the past, this difference could have been due to the presumption of researchers to hold the truth, and the need to protect the core of their paradigms from external attacks. Nowadays this position cannot be held up any longer. Collaborative research is becoming the central tenet of science. Communication among scientists, and therefore the discourse linking their positions, theses or ideas should become the focus of our work. Practically we need to borrow from LCMS tools that are already consolidated there and that, instead, are not used in VREs, such as for example forums, chats, wikis.

COLLA

In detail we will follow the implementation and use of an asynchronous or near-synchronous messaging system within a VRE. In this analysis we will use a multipurpose collaborative framework that we developed to prototype and test our ideas and innovation. This system is called COLLA (Diviacco, 2015, 2012). Colla in italian means glue, and in fact its mission is to keep researchers together. COLLA is essentially a generic Content Management System (CMS) with a talent in handling several scientific data types. Considering that our background is geophysics, COLLA, was born with a specific focus on marine seismic and multibeam data[3]. It allows interoperability between formats, representation of georeferenced data, and, something quite peculiar for this class of software, allows representation of seismic profiles. These features correspond to data access and visualization facilities that can be sometimes found in VREs. To this COLLA adds two important items, and namely: a messaging facility and a graphic concept/entity-to-messages mapping facility

COLLA's Messaging Facility

This functionality is very similar to any forum or chat systems that can be found in most of the LCMS. Users post messages that other users can comment or reply to. All users are automatically notified of any post. There is a conversation threading, sorting and indenting function that helps readability. What is peculiar here is that messages can contain URLs that are automatically generated upon connection with the data visualization facility. Embedding data, maps or images can be of great help to corroborate partners' contributions to the discourse.

COLLA's Graphic Concept/Entity-To-Messages Mapping Facility

The graphic concept/entity-to-messages mapping facility is a rather peculiar feature of COLLA. Early in the evolution of the system, we realized that leaving threads of discussion unstructured can be confusing for users so that eventually they submit information to the wrong thread. This is a rather common experience in any forum where it is possible to read users asking to a moderator if that was the right place for their questions or comments. How to address this? The simplest solution is to provide a list of the available threads, in order that users can pick the one they are interested in. This has proven to be often insufficient. Users pick threads upon titles or labels that can be obscure or prone to tacit knowledge, and keep on making mistakes.

We adopted a different approach allowing users to define a graphical concept or entity space. This can be anything from a concept/mind map, to a diagram of a process or workflow, to data, maps or images to simple sketches that can be useful to allow partners to share a common vision. Following Diviacco and Busato(2015) and Diviacco (2012) this can be though of as a "boundary object" (Star & Griesemer, 1989). Boundary objects aim at gathering communities in the same cognitive space bridging concurrent cognitive models through abstraction from all the domains of the partners. Boundary objects are weakly structured in common use, and become strongly structured in individual use.

Within the graphical concept/entity space each node is associated with a discussion thread, so that users can click on the node and be sent to the corresponding thread.

Summing up, the tool we developed offers all the on-line data access functionalities that can be found commonly in VREs, typical LCMS features such as forums/chats, with the addition of an innovative, specifically developed, discourse structuring tool. We think that it is the interplay between the discourse and the structure provided by the boundary object that can offer the most interesting outcomes of this research.

CASE STUDY

To analyze them, we will make use of some examples where our ideas have been used, generally with good results and wide acceptance. These examples should be considered non-systematic case studies showing the possibilities and limitations of the method. We must add also a disclaimer and highlight a weak point of these case studies, which is that, of course, we were not aware of any additional discussion partners might have had outside the system we provided for example by e-mail or personal face to face conversation. Probably this could be an interesting starting point for another specific study.

Building a Shared Infrastructure

The EU FP7 project GeoSeas, aims at building an e-infrastructure of 26 marine geological and geophysical data centers, located in 17 European maritime countries. From the very beginning it was clear that all partners were bringing with them different standards, practices and vocabularies. Any imposition of one of them as a de facto standard would have induced disaffection in the other partners, so that a convergence on a new "artifact" was considered a better solution. To achieve this, it was decided to move the activities of standardization and the definition of a shared metadata model and controlled vocabulary on a project hosted by COLLA (figure 1). A mind map representing the various issues and their relations was made available as a boundary object, while to each node a specific discussion thread was linked (Diviacco, Lowry & Leadbetter, 2011).

Experts were able immediately to understand where their contribution was required so that they almost always populated the right thread. Discussions were extensive, revealing how far each partner position was from that of the others, and very importantly that they had only limited knowledge of the practices of the others. To discuss and negotiate, partners were forced to explore the other partners' cultures. As a matter of fact, and in the light of what said above, this can be thought of as a form of learning. Our experience was that after being exposed to other practices and paradigms, partners become less castled, and accept to enter proactively and collaboratively in the discussion. The discussion threads, while embedding the issues discussed above, and namely: artifact, context, community and tacit knowledge, become a reference, a form of documentation, for the Community of Practice involved in the activities,

Figure 1. Schema showing the link between the structuring facility and the data management and forum/chat facilities within the GeoSeas Project case study. In this case the structuring tool (left) was a mind map. On the right all messages can be browsed/searched. Each message can contain links to data such as images, documents or any kind of file.

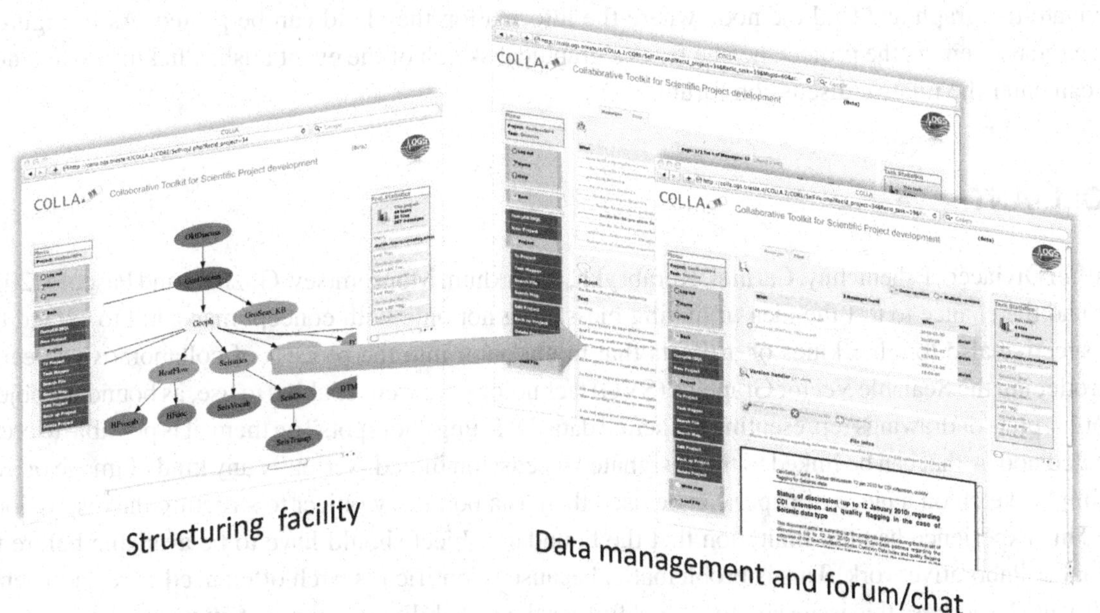

both in case they want to find something they forgot, or for novices needing to understand the reasons for the choices made by others.

Developing an Ontology

Within the EU FP7 project Eurofleets a community gathered to build an ontology for an event logger software (Diviacco, DeCawer, Leadbetter, Sorribas, Stojanov, Busato & Cova, 2015). In this case each partner was appointed as a reference for a specific scientific domain. The work then was mostly done outside the collaborative tool, which was used mainly to put "pieces" together and have versioning control. There was no big discourse running and in fact the use of the system was rather minimal.

This suggested, quite obviously, that such collaborative systems are useful when overlaps exist between partner's activities; where an actual discussion can take place. Otherwise a static knowledge base is more that sufficient.

Earthquakes Site Effects

In Diviacco, Pshenichny, Carniel, Khrabrykh, Shterkhun, Mouromtsev, Guzman and Pascolo (2014) and Diviacco and Pshenichny (2011, 2010) we tested a different approach where the graphic concept/entity-to-messages mapping facility was loaded with an interactive graph describing a physical process, in this case the site effect of earthquakes (Luzón, Palencia, Morales, Sánchez-Sesma, & García 2002) by means of the event bushes technique (Pshenichny & Kanzheleva, 2011).

This intends to give a strict and finite but extendable display/formalization of an area of reality and corresponding domain of knowledge, being at the same time sufficiently flexible to accommodate different conceptualization of the same phenomenon. For example, geophysicists and geologists have different understanding of terms like "soil", "bedrock", "sediment", etc. Geophysicists are usually mainly concerned with their mechanical characteristics, while geologists are more concerned with their genesis. Notwithstanding this, providing a common "flexible" boundary object such as the event bush they can navigate the graph and find the node where the information they hold can be posted. As in Figure 2, once the user enters the project, he/she faces a graphical sketch of the event bush. Clicking on any node he can enter the relative discussion forum.

COLL-ANT

Within Diviacco, Pshenichny, Carniel, Khrabrykh, Shterkhun, Mouromtsev, Guzman and Pascolo (2014) we had the chance to test the idea of linking messaging not only with concept maps, but to extend this perspective also to other kinds of artifacts that might enter into the process of collaborative research. Introducing the Scalable Vector Graphics (SVG) technology we were enabled to use, as boundary object: graphs, plots or drawings representing the actual data. Defining "hot spots" on them, it is possible to create labeled nodes, that can be linked to the designated discussion thread. Virtually any kind of image or even a simple sketch on a piece of paper can be used then as a boundary object to structure the discussion.

This experience had the limitation that the boundary object should have to be available before the actual collaborative work. This is problematic, because scientific research often need to re-set its environment. To address this issue and to extend further the possibilities of the system we worked on a new

Figure 2. Schema showing the link between the structuring facility and the document/messaging facility. In this case the structuring tool (left) is an Event Bush

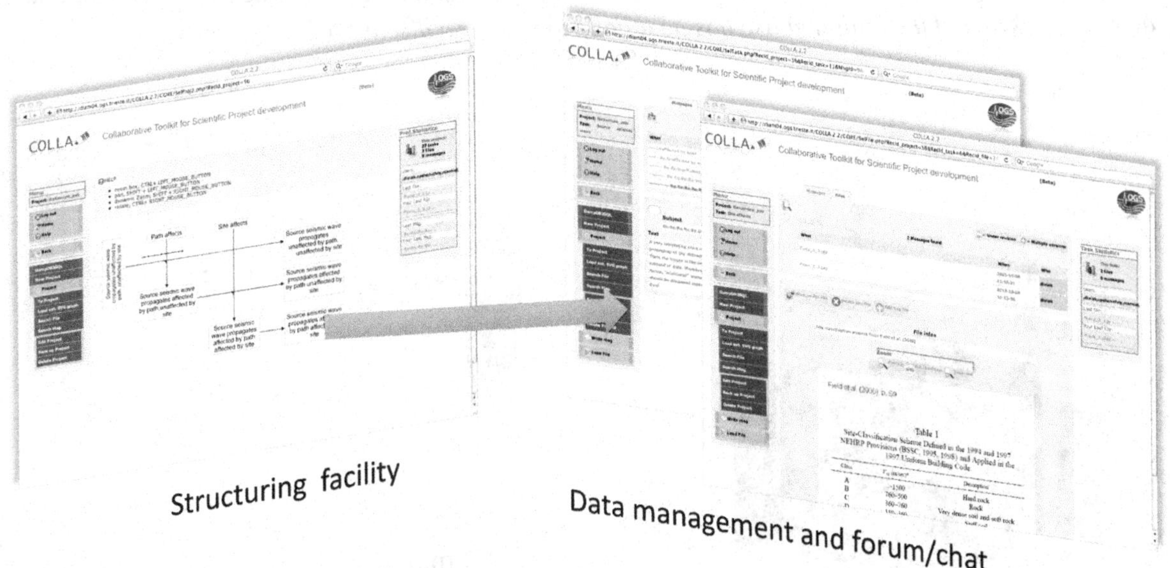

prototype that allows, not only to interactively visualize geophysical (only, for now) data as in the previous works of Diviacco and Busato (2013) and Diviacco (2005) but to create entities (nodes), drawing them directly on the data viewer, and automatically assigning them to a discussion thread (Figure 3). This prototype was named COLL-ANT being an extension of COLLA toward collaborative annotation not only of knowledge models but also of the actual data. We reported on the implementation of COLL-ANT in Diviacco and Busato (2015).

Using COLL-ANT a team of researchers can remotely identify on a dedicated viewer a feature, such as for example a geological layer or a fault, draw a sketch of it's extension and clicking on it enter a discussion thread where they can exchange their opinions. This way the interplay between annotation and data becomes the artifact that can be used as a boundary object between researchers or communities

CONCLUSION

Our previous work and publications were very much focused on web based collaborative scientific research from an insider point of view. In this work we explore a new perspective where scientific research is associated with learning. Can collaborative scientific research be considered a form of learning? If so, can practices and experiences done in on-line learning be used to improve on-line collaborative scientific research?

We demonstrated that collaborative research and learning are largely convergent human activities, therefore we claim that this should be possible.

In the quest for useful ideas in the domain of learning, we realized that the most important contribution for scientific collaboration is the discourse; meaning the communication among partners while building knowledge, which is, normally, an overlooked aspect of e-Research.

Figure 3. Schema showing the use of the COLL-ANT prototype. In this case the structuring tool is not anymore a mind map or a workflow but the actual data. A map reveals the position of a geological fault (in red, leftmost part of image). A seismic section crossing the fault reveals its extension (center). Users can draw a sketch of the fault and use this as a node to trigger a discussion.

We developed methods and software to allow users to exchange messages and there link and visualize data. After some experiences we realized that the discourse needs a framework that could on one hand structure messaging, that otherwise becomes chaotic and difficult to browse or query, and on the other hand allows to create a boundary object that could bridge different visions, practice and paradigms.

We did not test the software "in vitro", rather we preferred to use it directly in the running projects we were involved in.

Reflecting on these experiences, we realized that an important factor is the motivation of partners, that a "critical mass" is also required and that the availability of data that partners were not able to access before or otherwise, can increase the confidence in using such tools.

Most importantly, however, we saw that it is possible to make a step beyond putting in contact the structuring tool and the data themselves. In the cases we described, using the software we developed, geophysical data can be visualized on a canvas where users can identify geologic features. To each one of them a discussion thread can be associated so that the designated community can share ideas and visions, building together a knowledge base.

Interestingly enough if the forum and data base can be made available to other teams or scientists they can access and learn from what already discussed by others. A Community of Practice is created. If multiple projects are made available using the same data, multiple theories, perspectives and paradigms are then reachable and can be used to nurture the debate within and across scientific communities.

Summing up, we can eventually answer affirmatively to the question in the title of this work. E-Research can learn from e-learning, and we showed how. In addition, we proposed a new tool that, structuring the discourse and the data themselves, can support the activities of research of a small team up to large Communities of Practices.

To close the loop, back from research to learning, it could be interesting to see how the structuring tool we described could be used in e-learning environments. This, of course, is well beyond the scope of this chapter, but could be a starting point for another specific work.

FUTURE RESEARCH DIRECTIONS

The first results from the COLL-ANT project are very encouraging, but are far from being conclusive.

A lot more needs to be done.

One very important issue is the extension to other scientific domains. In fact if the geosciences are particularly representative of what we described above, similar conditions can be found in other domains, such as for example Medicine, History, Economics and many more. In this sense, one first step we are currently working on, expanding what we started in Diviacco and Busato (2015), is to develop a wider application of our ideas and techniques to the Arts, and in particular to the case of Music. Here collaborative analysis of scores, audio and ancillary information can be very important both from the point of view of research and digital curation, but also for learning as well.

Another important aspect we would like to explore is the motivation of researchers in adopting such tools. Generally researchers are quite reluctant to enter a collaborative space because they fear to be forced to change their paradigms and habits. We experienced that this anxiety is somehow relieved by the availability of information they do not have and that such systems allow them to obtain. Since this depends on the quantity of data they can access to, we are confident that with the fast growth of the availability of collaborative VREs, researchers with soon become more open. Of course this, somehow can be a dog chasing his own tail. To break this vicious circle our institution, hoping that others will do the same, decided to upload into the system all the data it was able to make available,

REFERENCES

Ackermann, E. (2001). Piaget's constructivism, Papert's constructionism: What's the difference. *Future of learning group*, 5(3).

Bereiter, C. (2002). *Education and mind in the knowledge age*. Mahwah, NJ: Lawrence Erlbaum Associates.

Bishop, M. A. (1992). Theory-Ladenness of Perception Arguments. *Proceedings of the Biennial Meeting of the Philosophy of Science Association* (Vol. 1992, pp. 287-299).

Brown, J., Collins, A., & Duguid, P. (1989). Situated cognition and the Culture of Learning. *Educational Researcher*, *18*(1), 32–42. doi:10.3102/0013189X018001032

Carey, S. (1983). Cognitive Development: The Descriptive Problem. In Gazzaniga (Ed.), Handbook for Cognitive Neurology. Hillsdale, NJ: Lawrence & Erlbaum

Dietrich, F., & List, C. (2007). Judgment aggregation under constraints. In T. Boylan & R. Gekker (Eds.), *Economics, Rational Choice and Normative Philosophy*. London: Routledge.

Diviacco, P. (2005). An open source, web based, simple solution for seismic data dissemination and collaborative research. *Computers & Geosciences*, *31*(5), 599–605. doi:10.1016/j.cageo.2004.11.008

Diviacco, P. (2012). Addressing Conflicting Cognitive Models in Collaborative e-Research: A Case Study in Exploration Geophysics. In *Collaborative and Distributed e-Research: Innovations in Technologies, Strategies and Applications*. Hershey, PA: IGI Global press; doi:10.4018/978-1-4666-0125-3.ch012

Diviacco, P. (2015). Reconciling Knowledge and Collaborative e-Research. In Diviacco, P. Fox,P., Leadbetter,A., Pshenichny, C., (Editors), Collaborative Knowledge in Scientific Research Networks. Hershey, PA: IGI Global. doi:10.4018/978-1-4666-6567-5.ch001

Diviacco, P., & Busato, A. (2013). The Geo-Seas Seismic data viewer: a tool to facilitate control of data access. *Bollettino di Geofisica Teorica ed Applicata*, 54(3), 257-270.

Diviacco, P., & Busato, A. (2015). Maps, graphs and annotations as Boundary Objects in Knowledge Networks, Distributed Cognition and Collaborative e-Research. In P. Diviacco, P. Fox, C. Pshenichny, & A. Leadbetter (Eds.), *Collaborative Knowledge in Scientific Research Networks*. Hershey, PA: IGI Global.

Diviacco, P., DeCawer, K., Leadbetter, A., Sorribas, J., Stojanov, Y., Busato, A., & Cova, A. (2014). *Bridging semantically different paradigms in the field of marine acquisition event logging, Earth Science Informatics*. Springer; doi:10.1007/s12145-014-0192-0

Diviacco, P., Lowry, R., & Leadbetter, A. (2011). Collaborative work and tools towards wide scientific community driven metadata model and vocabulary building. The case of the EU GeoSeas project. European Geosciences Union (EGU) General Assembly, Vienna (Austria), April 2010. *Geophysical Research Abstracts, 12*.

Diviacco, P., & Pshenichny, C. A. (2010). Concept-referenced spaces in computer-supported collaborative work. [). EGU, Vienna]. *Geophysical Research Abstracts, 12*.

Diviacco, P., & Pshenichny, C. A. (2011, April). A case study on the use of event bushes as a formal representation for Computer Supported Collaborative Work in the GeoSciences European Geosciences Union (EGU) General Assembly, Vienna, Austria. *Geophysical Research Abstracts* (Vol. 12).

Diviacco, P., Pshenichny, C. A., Carniel, R., Khrabrykh, Z., Shterkhun, V., Mouromtsev, D., & Pascolo, P. et al. (2014). Organization of a geophysical information space by using an event-bush-based collaborative tool. *Earth Sci Inform, 10*. doi:10.1007/s12145-014-0182-2

Duffy, T., & Cunningham, D. (1996). Constructivism: Implications for the design and delivery of instruction. Handbook of research for educational telecommunications and technology (pp. 170-198).

Fodor, J. (1983). *The Modularity of Mind*. Cambridge, MA: MIT Press.

Fraser, M. (2004). *Supporting Virtual Research Environments: how can we help?* Retrieved from http://users.ox.ac.uk/~mikef/rts/vre/img2.html

Hakkarainen, K. (2003). Emergence of progressive-inquiry culture in computer-supported collaborative learning. *Learning Environments Research*, *6*(2), 199–220. doi:10.1023/A:1024995120180

Hanson, N. R. (1958). Patterns of Discovery. Cambridge: Cambridge University Press. repr. 1975.

Haraway, D. (1988). Situated Knowledges: The Science Question in Feminism and the Privilege of Partial Perspective. *Feminist Studies*, *14*(3), 575–599.

Kuhn, T. S. (1962). *The structure of scientific revolutions*. Chicago, IL: University of Chicago Press.

Lakatos, I. (1970). (Lakatos, & Musgrave Eds.). Falsification and the Methodology of Scientific Research Programmes, in Criticism and the Growth of Knowledge. Cambridge University Press, 1970.

Latour, B., & Woolgar, S. (1979). *Laboratory life: The construction of scientific facts*. Princeton, NJ: Princeton University Press.

Lave, J., & Wenger, E. (1991). *Situated Learning: Legitimate Peripheral Participation*. Cambridge: Cambridge University Press; doi:10.1017/CBO9780511815355

Luzón, F., Palencia, V. J., Morales, J., Sánchez-Sesma, F. J., & García, J. M. (2002). Evaluation of Site effects in sedimentary basins. *Fis Tierra*, *14*, 183–214.

Nonaka, I. (1994). A Dynamic theory of Organizational Knowledge Creation. *Organization Science*, *5*(1), 14–37. doi:10.1287/orsc.5.1.14

Oliver, R. (2001). Developing e-learning environments that support knowledge construction in higher education. In Stoney, S. and Burn, J. (Eds.), Working for Excellence in the E-conomy, (pp. 407-16). Churchlands: We-B Centre.

Olson, R. K., & Connelly, L. M. (1995). Mentoring through predoctoral fellowships to enhance research productivity. [PubMed]. *Journal of Professional Nursing*, *11*(5), 270–275. doi:10.1016/S8755-7223(05)80007-9

Papert, S. (1980). *Mindstorms. Children, Computers and Powerful Ideas*. New York: Basic books.

Peirce, C. S. (1931): Collected Papers. Cambridge, Harvard University press, Scritti scelti UTET, Torino.

Pshenichny, C. A., & Kanzheleva, O. M. (2011) In K. Sinha, L. Gundersen, J. Jackson, & D. Arctur (Eds.), Theoretical foundations of the event bush method: Societal Challenges and Geoinformatics (GSA Special Paper 482) (pp. 139–165). doi:10.1130/2011.2482(12)

Ramirez, M., & Castaneda, A. (1974). *Cultural Democracy, Bicognitive Development and Education*. New York: Academic Press.

Scardamalia, M., & Bereiter, C. (2003). Knowledge Building. In *Encyclopedia of Education*. New York: MacMillan Reference.

Scardamalia, M., & Bereiter, C. (2006). Knowledge building: Theory, pedagogy, and technology. In R. K. Sawyer (Ed.), *The Cambridge handbook of the learning sciences* (pp. 97–115). New York, NY: Cambridge University Press.

Searle, J. R. (2008). Philosophy in a New Century (p. 167). New York: Cambridge.

Star, S. L., & Griesemer, J. R. (1989). Institutional Ecology, Translations and Boundary Objects: Amateurs and Professionals in Berkeley s Museum of Vertebrate Zoology. *Social Studies of Science*, *19*(4), 387–420. doi:10.1177/030631289019003001

Sterelny, K. 2005. Externalism, epistemic artefacts and the estende mind. In R. Schantz (Ed.), The Externalist Challenge: New Studies on Cognition and Intentionality. Berlin: de Gruyter.

Suchman, L. A. (1987). *Plans and situated actions: The problem of human-machine communication*. Cambridge, UK: Cambridge University Press.

Suppe, F. (1977). *The Structure of Scientific Theories* (pp. 154–156). University of Illinois Press.

Wehrwein, E. A., Lujan, H. L., & DiCarlo, S. E. (2007, June). Gender differences in learning style preferences among undergraduate physiology students. [PubMed]. *Advances in Physiology Education*, *31*(2), 153–157. doi:10.1152/advan.00060.2006

Whitley, G. G., & Oddi, L. F. (1998). Graduate student-faculty collaboration in research and publication. [PubMed]. *Western Journal of Nursing*, *20*(5), 572–583. doi:10.1177/019394599802000505

Whitley, R. (2000). *The intellectual and social organization of the sciences*. Oxford, UK: Clarendon Press.

Wilkesmann, U., Fischer, H., & Wilkesmann, M. (2009). Cultural characteristics of knowledge transfer. *Journal of Knowledge Management*, *13*(6), 464–477. doi:10.1108/13673270910997123

Zhao, C., & Kuh, G. D. (2004). Adding Value: Learning communities and student engagement. *Research in Higher Education*, *45*(2), 115–138. doi:10.1023/B:RIHE.0000015692.88534.de

ADDITIONAL READING SECTION

Sheriff, R. E. (1973). *Encyclopedic dictionary of exploration geophysics*. Tulsa: The Society of Exploration Geophysics.

KEY TERMS AND DEFINITIONS

Boundary Object: An artifact that allow two different and incommensurable communities to collaborate. They are weakly structured in common use, and become strongly structured in individual use.

Collaborative Research: Methods, tools and communities involved or supporting scientific research and knowledge building.

Discourse: the information, the tools and the network on top of which a community builds its knowledge. The state of knowledge of a community in the discourse itself. If the discourse takes place in an artifact, this latter will become the state of knowledge of the designated community.

Knowledge Building: in learning corresponds to methodologies such as trial and error, or learning from experience, that stimulates in the subject his/her capacity to understand a phenomenon or system by him/herself. Knowledge building is the very core business of Scientific Research. It is therefore claimed in this chapter that learning and scientific research are similar.

Learning: situated and socially dependent process of understanding reality that simplistically can be seen as a form of transmission of information while in wider vision could be seen as a form of knowledge building.

Virtual Research Environments: IT systems (often web based) aiming to support collaborative research, and therefore mainly devoted to orchestrate the contributions of a distributed community of researchers.

ENDNOTES

1 The ancient Persian tale of *The Three Princes of Serendip* narrates of three princes that in Horace Walpole's words *"always make discoveries, by accidents and sagacity, of things which they were not in quest of"*. The world is used often to refer to the cases in science when something has been discovered by accident, such as Alexander Fleming's discovery of penicillin in 1928.

2 In 2006 Papert had a street accident that left him with speech problems, and the need to undergo extensive rehabilitation at home. During his recovery, Papert's rehabilitation team used some of the techniques he had pioneered. In the same perspective, a well known Danish toy company, based its production of a robotic toy set on Paper's ideas. This toy set shares the name with a book Papert published in 1980.

3 Seismic data are used in reflection seismology, which is a geophysical exploration method that uses the reflection of acoustic waves below the seabottom to map the buried interfaces and rocks. Multibeam echosounder is a type of sonar that emits sound waves in a fan shape (swath) rather than a vertical sample (ping)

Chapter 12
Role Negotiation in Collaborative Projects

Jonan Donaldson
Western Oregon University, USA

ABSTRACT

The nature of the traditional approaches to collaborative group projects can often be characterized by hierarchy, clarity of roles, and assignment of tasks to participants. Digital-age collaborative projects are often characterized by impromptu and ill-defined organization, spontaneity, democratic decision-making, and continual morphing of roles. These two approaches are grounded in fundamentally different cultural frameworks. This chapter describes and analyzes an innovative collaborative process of role description, negotiation, adoption, and ongoing evolution through routine metacognitive processes which provides a structure by which to integrate positive aspects of traditional hierarchical approaches to collaborative projects and positive aspects of digital-age communication culture. This role negotiation process can clarify responsibilities and processes while nurturing the sense of personal agency and self-determination crucial to intrinsic motivation and engagement.

INTRODUCTION

Digital tools have opened an incredible range of possibilities for collaboration no longer bound by space and time. Along with these tools and possibilities comes a new ethos of communication, aspects of which produce novel challenges and opportunities for effective collaboration. In the space where traditional approaches to collaboration collide with digital-age approaches lies a bounty of innovative ideas ripe for the harvest. This chapter explores this area of collision between the way we have traditionally gone about setting up collaborative projects and the features of digital-age collaborations. This exploration will delve into these issues through the lens of a focal point on the narrowly-defined aspect of role negotiation in digitally-mediated collaborative projects.

This chapter explores academic research, theory, a case study, and the author's experience toward identifying some principles of digital-age collaborative projects, with a focus on role negotiation in technology-mediated collaborative projects in the digital age—principles which may provide insight into methods of weaving together aspects of "traditional" and "digital-age" approaches to collaboration.

DOI: 10.4018/978-1-4666-9556-6.ch012

Copyright © 2016, IGI Global. Copying or distributing in print or electronic forms without written permission of IGI Global is prohibited.

BACKGROUND

To situate ourselves intellectually, we shall begin with two mental pictures. In our first picture, we find ourselves in a pre-internet office environment in the late twentieth century where we are observing a collaborative project involving a team of twenty people. The first thing that commands our attention is that one person is going from cubicle to cubicle checking in on the progress of individuals. Our intuition that this must be the team leader is confirmed as the team gathers in a conference room for a meeting. The team leader briefly overviews the meeting agenda and then leads the team through an overview of a recent setback. The floor is opened to discussion for fifteen minutes, after which the team leader summarizes the ideas brought forward and lays out a series of next steps. One team member volunteers to take on one of the action items, but seeing no further volunteers, the team leader assigns the remaining tasks to individuals and sets completion deadlines. The meeting is dismissed and people head back to their cubicles. The team leader then heads for the airport to catch a flight to another city to meet a potential vendor and discuss their proposal.

In our second picture, we find ourselves in a current-day coffee shop looking over the shoulder of someone working on tablet computer. She replies to an email, sends a few instant messages, and then opens a collaboration app where she reads a chain of posts in a discussion thread exploring the information gathered from potential vendors who responded to a recent request for information. Several themes have emerged in the thread and the consensus seems to be that they proceed with the writing of a formal Request for Proposals (RFP). She opens another app and creates a collaborative document in which to draft the RFP, creates a rough outline, invites her team-mates, and posts a note in the collaboration app suggesting they start drafting in the collaborative document and use the comments feature to suggest edits. She then searches the internet and identifies several similar institutions which recently contracted with vendors for similar solutions. After finding the email addresses of people involved in the process, she sends five of them emails explaining her team's current situation and asking for any advice they may be able to offer. Her smartphone vibrates and she sees that a reminder from her calendar indicates it is time to start her video conference with a team-mate who recently asked her for help.

In our first scenario we see certain recognizable features. The collaboration is bound by space and time, as evidenced by the need physical meetings and face-to-face interactions. Time is also a limitation. Team members need to be at a particular place at a particular time. The team leader is physically moving from person to person to coordinate, receive updates, and set goals. Such a situation lends itself to a hierarchy in which ultimate decision-making rests with one individual who is responsible for seeing the big picture and coordinating the work done by each team member.

In the second scenario we see the limitations of time and space have been eliminated, replaced with a completely new set of issues. Less authority resides in any one individual, but each participant is expected to multitask, be involved in a wider range of decision-making, and master the use of many different digital tools for communication and collaboration. The freedom gained by being unshackled from a nine-to-five day in the cubicle has been offset by a twenty-four-hour day of rapidly shifting attention from application to application. This is exacerbated by increased uncertainty about our own responsibilities given the ever-changing nature of projects where we can never be sure who has done what, who is currently working on what, and who is planning to do what.

If we were to observe a wider range of collaborative projects we would find aspects of both scenarios. However, it could be reasonably be expected that we would tend to find collaborative projects structured like our first scenario with features of the second scenario superimposed upon it. We would not be surprised to find hierarchical structures in which decision-making power ultimately resides with one individual, and the other members of the group doing tasks assigned to them. At the structural core of the collaboration we would find more similarities with the first scenario than with the second. It would only be on the surface level where we would find aspects of the second scenario. Perhaps the project would be managed using digital tools which track progress of individual tasks on a predetermined timeline. Perhaps those involved in the project would collaborate using email and video conferencing tools. Ultimately, however, the nature of collaborative projects would bear more resemblance to the traditional model than to the digital-age collaborative projects we often see outside the realm of business or academia.

Although we are decades into the digital age, there is still a tendency to assume that projects are to be managed, and that hierarchies and roles will be well-defined. This arises from entrenched cultural forces in working environments around the world—often relatively independent of the larger cultural forces of the larger societies in which the working environments are embedded. In these environments, collaborative projects tend to have division of tasks among group members as they work toward goals formulated by superiors.

In contrast, the processes and roles produced by the wider culture of digital communications are characterized by impromptu and ill-defined organization, spontaneity, democratic decision-making, and continual morphing of roles. In this digital-age culture the individual is expected to be an innovator and creator. Collaborative projects in such an environment often have sharing of tasks and responsibilities amongst a number of group members as they work toward an ever-evolving vision for the project.

When these two paradigms meet, there is often such a degree of disconnect and incompatibility that the efficiency and effectiveness of the digitally-mediated collaborative project are severely jeopardized. Although they are not mutually exclusive, they are built on quite different cultural and theoretical foundations.

When digital natives who have grown up in the digital age—as well as digital immigrants who have become acculturated to digital-age communications—find themselves in highly formalized hierarchical working environments they often become disengaged. As of 2011, only eleven percent of workers around the world were engaged at work. The vast majority were disengaged. In fact, a significant number were so actively disengaged that their negative attitudes could spread within their workplace (Gallup Consulting, 2011, p. 2). Although there are many factors which contribute to this disengagement, some factors can clearly be traced to the differences between digital-age culture and the culture of hierarchically-structured business environments. It might be tempting to argue that we must learn to adapt to hierarchical structures in which we work, and adapt to the digital-age culture outside of the working environment. However, digital-age culture is beginning to impact even the most entrenched of hierarchical environments: "There is mounting evidence that decision-making within firms is increasingly decentralized and allocated to lower tiers of the managerial hierarchy" (Pongracic, 2009, p. 2).

One powerful aspect of digital-age culture impacting working environments can be seen in the cultural shift from the information consumer culture of the age of books, newspapers, and television to an information producer culture in which blogs, personal websites, Twitter, and Instagram put the power of information production in the hands of the average person: "The digital consumer is active, rather than passive. She programs, rather than is programmed. And in peer-to-peer manner, she spreads her creativity to the many, rather than receiving it broadcast from the few" (Lessig, 2004, pp. 2-3). This shift instils a sense of personal agency, which if not nurtured and integrated into everyday work life can lead to disengagement, frustration, and hostility.

Deci and Ryan developed the Cognitive Evaluation Theory to explain the effects of agency—or lack thereof—on academic achievement. Their theory distinguishes between intrinsic motivation and extrinsic motivation. Decades of studies have repeatedly demonstrated that situations in which intrinsic motivation is nurtured and extrinsic motivation is minimized result in increased engagement and ability (Deci, Koestner, & Ryan, 2001, p. 15). In research investigating meta-analyses of the effectiveness of computer-aided instruction, Hattie (2008) found that students performed better in situations where they were in control than in situations where teachers were in control (p. 255). Other studies have found evidence that extrinsic motivation—which often arises in situations characterized by of lack of personal agency and self-determination—has negative impacts. For example, Walker, Green and Mansell (2006) found that extrinsic motivation was correlated with "shallow cognitive engagement" (p. 9). Kohn, in summarizing research concerning a particular type of extrinsic motivation—rewards—argued that the damaging effects of rewards far outweigh any benefits (1996, p. 3). Motivation research powerfully suggests that intrinsic motivation leads to positive outcomes and extrinsic motivation leads to negative outcomes. Extrinsic motivation arises in situations characterized by lack of personal agency—often when those in positions of power believe there is a need to motivate people through systems of incentives, rewards, and punishments. Conversely, at the heart of intrinsic motivation is a personal sense of agency in which people are empowered to make decisions not only concerning how they achieve outcomes, but also decisions concerning goals and the roles they will play in the project.

In the world of educational research and theory there is a distinct movement away from the lecture-textbook-exam model towards student ownership of learning. Although the roots of this shift can be found in the work of John Dewey a century ago, educational theory has seen this shift picking up pace for over half a century in constructivist theories developed by Jean Piaget (1966; 1970; 1972; 1977), Lev Vygotsky (1978; Vygotsky & Luria, 1994), Jerome Bruner (1986; Bruner & Weinreich-Haste, 1987; Bruner, 1996), and others. Constructivist theories of learning see learning as a process by which individuals construct their own understandings. According to these theories, it is impossible to transfer knowledge from one individual to another because learners must construct their own knowledge. In other words, giving students information in the form of textbooks or lectures should be the most ineffective method of teaching, and testing students on how well they remember that information cannot truly measure learning because each individual student will have constructed a unique understanding. The influence of constructivist theories found renewed vigor since the turn of the century due to evidence from a growing body of research studies (Hattie, 2008; Mehta & Fine, 2012; Reeve, 2013; Innovation Unit, 2013; Snape & Fox-Turnbull, 2013; Hattie & Yates, 2014). Learning is a process of actively constructing a mental schema which combines existing schemas into more complex schemas (Van Merrienboer & Sweller, 2005, p. 149), and therefore no two individuals will ever have identical mental schemas. Therefore, the most effective learning situations will be those in which individuals are asked to make their own decisions concerning the processes and objectives involved.

Constructivist theory and research suggest that we must change the way we conduct teaching and learning, replacing teacher-and-textbook-centered education with student-centered collaborative project-based learning. In educational environments built around this growing body of research we find a shift away from telling students what to learn, how to learn it, and when to learn it toward empowering and guiding students to make their own decisions about what to learn, how to learn it, and when to learn it (Thomas, 2000). It should be noted that this shift can be seen primarily in educational research and theory, but is rarely found in common practice in schools:

Despite rhetoric to the contrary, the epistemological stance underlying traditional school practice is that knowledge is to be deposited in the kids' heads for an (unlikely) future use. Students are never ready, never prepared, never mature enough to put the knowledge into use, and consequently never considered capable of deciding what they should learn. (Blikstein & Cavallo, 2002, p. 16)

The most effective learning environments are constructivist environments in which learners "own" their learning at all levels, including ownership of learning objectives and ownership of methods by which they achieve those objectives. This is often at odds with the traditional structures of our educational systems which are inextricably rooted in assumptions that: 1) curriculum designers will determine the learning objectives, 2) that all students will work towards those learning objectives according to a predetermined timeline, and 3) that success will be measured by standardized tests which determine how well students mastered the learning objectives. These assumptions are incompatible with everything research tells us about the most effective practices in learning: "Paradoxically, it may be an absence of the external pressures of schooling—assessment, curriculum, lecture, and demands for note-taking that leads to the greatest achievement" (Martinez & Stager, 2013, p. 25). The fundamental reason educators find it nearly impossible to implement the findings of educational research on a large scale is that research indicates the centrality of the principles of personal agency and intrinsic motivation, while the system is premised on principles of control and extrinsic motivation. This tension in many ways mirrors the tensions which arose in the shift of the consumer-of-information culture of the previous century with the digital-age culture in which everyone can be a producer of information.

Whether in the workplace or in academia, people become deeply engaged when the situation promotes a sense of self-determinism and agency, and become deeply disengaged when rigid hierarchical situations reduce personal agency. When agency is promoted, productivity and engagement increases. This is increasingly important in light of the expectations of personal agency fostered by digital-age culture.

Another factor of digital-age culture which impacts engagement—and is inextricably related to the sense of personal agency—is the effect of digital communications technologies on collaborative processes. Personal agency is promoted in collaborative environments. Johnson and Johnson, pioneers in cooperative research and theory, found that confidence and autonomy are higher in cooperative efforts than individual work (2005, p. 311). Technologies for communication and collaboration not only increase the potential for collaboration beyond the limits of space and time, but also engender cultural features which impact our interactions with others. As Rushkoff and Purvis so eloquently stated, "The history of the internet can probably best be understood as a social medium repeatedly shaking off attempts to turn it into something else. . . . Our digital networks are biased toward social connections—toward contact" (2011, p. 99). These social connections facilitated by digital technologies shape the way we approach our interactions in digitally-mediated collaborative projects. For such collaborations to be optimally effective, the process of structuring the collaboration should be done with careful consideration given to the nature of social interactions in the digital age.

One theoretical framework which yields fruitful insights into the functioning of effective collaborations is the Community of Learners framework from the field of adult learning theory. Although this constructivist framework describes the process of collaborative learning, some features can be extrapolated to understanding of a wider range of collaborative processes. In a Community of Learners environment, each participant is responsible for both construction of individual understandings as well as facilitating individual construction of understandings by other participants. This requires metacognitive processes such as discussion and reflection on both the individual and social process levels (Garrison & Akyol,

2013, p. 85). Taking this idea beyond the original framework we could suggest that effective collaborative situations would involve three aspects: 1) individual responsibility for one's own tasks, 2) individual responsibility to help other members of the group with their tasks, and 3) metacognitive processes which facilitate self-regulation and co-regulation. Instead of group project work consisting of a simple division of tasks amongst members, we would see "ownership" of any particular task as a more complex construct involving ownership by an individual, by other group members, and by the group as a whole.

Ownership of a task involves more than responsibility. A powerful sense of ownership can best be fostered when the owner is also the creator. When we create things, the sense of "I own this" is greater than, for example, if we are given something identical. We then have a stronger sense of responsibility when the sense of ownership is stronger. In collaborative situations there is a delicate balance between collective ownership and individual ownership, which depends on effective processes of negotiation:

A main difference between collaborative interactions and an hierarchical situation is that one partner will not impose his view on the sole basis of his authority, but will - to some extent - argue for his standpoint, justify, negotiate, attempt to convince. (Dillenbourg, 1999, p. 9)

Negotiation is an ever-present feature of effective collaborative work. As such, it may be advisable to begin any collaborative project by creating an atmosphere of negotiation through a process of role negotiation. This role negotiation process not only may help create a positive atmosphere for future negotiations, but can also clarify roles and processes which in turn will facilitate future interactions between participants (Dietrich, Eskerod, Dalcher, & Sandhawalia, 2010, p. 65). The clarification of roles and processes are essential to the success of any collaborative project. Shared goals and trusting relationships are not sufficient (Maccoby, 2011, p. 60). When a goal, a process, a role, or any other aspect of a collaborative project is created through a process of negotiation there is a powerful sense of ownership and responsibility on both the collective and individual levels.

Metacognition (thinking about one's own thinking) is a crucial aspect of achievement. The most common forms of metacognition are the writing of reflection pieces, drawing of concept maps, and discussion with peers concerning processes and progress in terms of a particular objective. Through metacognitive processes we are better able improve on our strengths, adjust for our weaknesses, and self-regulate: "The role of metacognitive planning, monitoring, and control processes is central to theories of regulation, and self-regulation in particular" (Jrvel & Hadwin, 2013, p. 26). When metacognitive processes take place in a collaborative framework, they can facilitate collaborative construction.

Role negotiation is a metacognitive process in its own right. Kaplan (2014) argues that it encourages participants to engage in a process of self-reflection concerning their own needs, interests, and abilities (p. 262), an analysis which will help them negotiate and define their own roles. This metacognition in working out their own roles and helping others on the team work out their roles also helps participants to balance dependency, interdependency, and intra-dependency (p. 261).

Metacognitive processes are important at any stage of a collaborative process. A good theory, such as the Community of Learners framework, can provide useful signposts guiding us toward experiments with innovative uses of metacognitive practices. Such signposts pack a greater "punch" if research yields results which align with the predictions of the theory. There is a growing body of research indicating that metacognitive practices such as group debriefing generated through group reflection and discussion improves both individual and group effectiveness (i.e. Jarvela, Volet, & Jarvenoja, 2010; Bertucci, Johnson, Johnson, & Conte, 2012; Jrvel & Hadwin, 2013). Starting out a collaborative project with metacognition through various digital tools such as discussion boards and shared collaborative documents sets the stage for subsequent instances of metacognitive work along the way.

The digital age has given us an ever-growing selection of powerful tools by which we can collaborate, communicate, organize, gather information, and create. However, along with them come a new set of issues. We have to spend more time choosing the most appropriate tools. We face a learning curve with each new technology. We are expected to juggle multiple tools which leads to inefficiencies caused by task-switching in a futile attempt to emulate the multi-tasking capabilities of computers. In addition to dealing with these issues, we also face the frustrations of functioning in a digital-age culture of personal agency and empowerment while working in hierarchical systems in which there is little space for such personal agency and empowerment.

The problems faced by workers or students embarking on digitally-mediated collaborative projects require innovative solutions which implement principles emerging from research in motivation, engagement, collaboration, project-based learning, and constructivism. The next section brings together some of these principles.

MAIN FOCUS OF THE CHAPTER

Translating Research and Theory into Practice

There is a rich history of research and theory concerning collaboration in the field of business, and another distinct history of research and theory concerning collaboration in education. Each arena has its own unique set of assumptions. In the field of business, group collaborative projects are often assumed to be processes within hierarchical systems, while in the field of education collaborative projects are often assumed to function as self-contained non-hierarchical "democratic" structures. The latter shares some features with the "digital-age communications" paradigm, such as the assumption of equal footing amongst all participants and the expectation of democratic decision-making.

The assumptions, norms, and "best practices" surrounding collaborative projects found in the world of business often reflect the exaggerated first scenario. There are some positive aspects of the "traditional" project-management paradigm which can be adopted in our role-negotiation processes. Primary amongst these is a clarity of responsibilities. Without such clarity, a number of issues arise including redundancy when multiple members of the project group expend time and energy tackling the same aspect of the project and unrecognized gaps occurring when no member of the group realizes an aspect of the project is not being addressed by anyone else.

Another positive aspect of the "traditional" paradigm is the clarity of processes and goals. Often the processes and goals for projects in these environments are planned out in great detail by one individual or a small group of managers in conference. The result is that by the time the actual work on the project gets underway, there is a blueprint including goals, stages, timelines, roles, and so on. Such clarity is highly desirable in a world where productivity is valued above all else. It also provides a means by which managers can monitor and evaluate the progress being made by each participant.

In the second admittedly exaggerated scenario we saw the collaboration processes of an individual working in a digitally-mediated collaborative process. Just as there are positive aspects of the "traditional" approach to collaboration, there are also positive aspects of the "digital-age communications" paradigm which can be adopted in our role-negotiation process. The most obvious example is the empowerment of each member of the project group due to lack of imposition of hierarchies. When people feel that they have the authority and freedom to assume responsibilities of their own choosing, the psychological effects include a greater sense of "ownership" of the project, an increased sense that the project is personally meaningful, and an increased sense of ability to overcome difficulties.

Another aspect which we can adopt from the "digital-age communications" paradigm is the higher comfort level in turning to others for assistance. In the "traditional" paradigm, there are incentives for each individual to perform their own work well without turning to others for help, which is seen to imply lack of ability. However, in the "digital-age communications" paradigm, individuals are much more comfortable asking others for assistance and asking others to give them feedback on drafts. Furthermore, the digital age has caused a cultural shift away from individuals being consumers of information toward individuals being producers of information. Some unique features of this shift can inform our re-formulation of collaborative processes such as the phenomenon of creative modifications to works by others which has come to be known as "re-mix".

This chapter started with a discussion of two paradigms for collaborative projects. The extreme versions of these approaches are incompatible with real-world digitally-mediated collaborative projects. The purest form of the "traditional" approach leaves participants feeling controlled and disengaged. The "digital-age communications" approach leaves participants feeling overwhelmed, unfocused, and pulled in many directions.

The solution to this conundrum lies not in forcing adoption of one paradigm over the other, but rather a process which integrates positive aspects of both paradigms. The overview of research and theory suggested that the ideal locus for efforts at such an integration is in a process of role negotiation through which the effectiveness and efficiency of digitally-mediated collaborative projects, ranging from the highly formal to the highly informal, can be optimized.

As suggested earlier, the effectiveness of digitally-mediated collaboration may depend on the extent to which individuals simultaneously assume and share "ownership" and responsibilities. It was also argued that a sense of agency may be a crucial element, particularly in light of the cultural shift towards individuals being producers rather than consumers of information. Furthermore, we saw that it may be beneficial to integrate digital-age cultural attitudes and norms that inform the social interactions of group members. Finally, the power of metacognition in collaborative processes was introduced. All of these aspects could be arranged to mutually support each-other in a process by which roles are adopted by individuals within a collaborative group.

The adoption of a role is quite different than the imposition of a role. When a role is thrust upon someone, that person may end up adopting the role, but more often than not the person will "play" the role. Many teachers can attest to the fact that "group work" often fails miserably. Upon deeper analysis, we find that one of two patterns had set the situation up to fail even before it ever started. In the first pattern, the teacher outlines the goals of the project and determines group membership, but then expects the group to naturally know how to work together to achieve the stated goals—without any thought given as to who will do what. In the second pattern, the teacher tells individual students exactly what their unique roles will be. In the first pattern we may find enthusiastic students, but without clarification of any roles they either accomplish very little or one student will take over and do everything. In the second pattern we find unenthusiastic students who balk and whine, but play the roles assigned them by the person in power over them. Collaborative work without structure is ineffective, and collaborative work without participants feeling a sense of agency is often both ineffective and emotionally destructive.

A very different picture emerges when agency and structure are combined in a process of role definition, negotiation, and adoption within a collaborative project. Implicit in the adoption of any role are corresponding benefits, responsibilities, and obligations. For example, "In the role of doctor, a person must strive to avoid harming any patient. In the role of journalist, a person must attempt to report the facts of an event in an unbiased and thorough manner. In the role of citizen, a person is expected to vote, pay taxes, and participate knowledgeably in civil society." (Davis, Seider, & Gardner, 2008, p. 1104). When a role is purposefully thought out, defined, and adopted by an individual within a group in which the other members participate in the discussing, defining, negotiating, and supporting that role, a sense of "ownership" and agency empowers that individual to embrace the responsibilities and obligations thereof. This lays the groundwork for future metacognitive reflection and discussion concerning not only surface issues such as progress on tasks, but also concerning deeper issues such as how responsibilities and obligations are translating into practice and how roles may need to evolve in order to bring out the best in terms of abilities and passions of each group member.

The process of collaboratively defining, negotiating, and selecting roles in digitally-mediated collaborative group projects emphasizes equality of power amongst all members of the group, but also establishes clear expectations of responsibility. Without this process—especially when working with digital collaborative tools—it is likely that some group members will tend toward expectations arising from the traditional project-management paradigm while other members will tend toward expectations arising from the digital-age communications paradigm. This process provides clarity without resorting to the hierarchical traditions which cause resentment in people accustomed to digital-age communication cultural norms.

CASE STUDY: AN EXAMPLE OF ROLE NEGOTIATION

Methodology

The role negotiation process described in this chapter comes from research, theory, and the author's own personal experience as an educator for nearly two decades in face-to-face and online classes. As a lecturer and researcher in educational theory and educational technology, he has designed, taught, and conducted both informal and formal research studies of courses in which digitally-mediated collaboration on group projects is central. In one of these courses, in eleven weeks the students collaboratively wrote and published a book using the role negotiation process described here. The entire process was digitally mediated through a variety of tools and the participants never met in person.

Before the beginning of the project a set of collaborative documents were created, including a document in which was written a rough draft of possible roles, a document with a rough draft of possible themes/topics, and a set of blank documents for each chapter. A flexible workflow was proposed in a set of forums in an asynchronous discussion board tool inside a learning management system structured in a weekly format.

At the beginning of the project a discussion board forum and corresponding collaborative document provided the space in which participants could define, negotiate, and adopt roles. Each participant took a "lead" role in writing one of the chapters, but was assisted by several other participants who were in "support" roles. Thus, each chapter was written by three or more people collaboratively. Each participant adopted one lead writing role and two support writing roles. The term "writing" was broadly defined in this project to include topic development, research, development of perspectives, and writing.

In addition to writing roles, a set of editing roles were defined, negotiated, and adopted. Each participant adopted one lead editing role and two support editing roles. The term "editing" was broadly defined in this project to include not only the traditional meaning of the word, but also aspects such as finding a publishing platform, public relations, graphic design, and accounting.

The entire book was then collaboratively edited by everyone in the class. Each participant adopted one lead writing role, two support writing roles, one lead editing role, and two support editing roles for a total of six roles per participant. The first six weeks were devoted to production by participants in their writing roles, and the final four weeks were devoted to work in their editing roles.

In their lead writing roles, participants defined the focus for the topics and themes to be covered in their own chapters. They then conducted research, outlined, and wrote drafts of their chapters in the shared collaborative document for that chapter. Everyone was free to see what others were doing because all documents were shared with all participants. After the initial drafts of chapters were completed, the participants wrote reflection posts in a discussion board forum and engaged in discussion about their progress, difficulties they encountered, high points in the process, and thoughts about their roles.

In their support writing roles, participants went into the documents for the chapters for which they had adopted support roles and added research, writing, suggestions, and whatever else the chapter lead had asked them to do. In terms of word count, each participant contributed approximately the same amount as was initially drafted by the chapter lead, so that by the end of this stage each chapter had tripled in size.

After contributions by participants in their support roles, the participants returned to their lead writing roles and worked with the contributions of the support role participants in order to smooth out abrupt transitions, fill in gaps, and make the logic and structure of the chapter as clean as possible. Finally, they moved all content of their own chapter document to one large collaborative document, thus creating one space for the entire book.

All the work done by each participant up to this point had been limited to work in the three chapters in which they had adopted lead or support roles. After this, the work shifted to work on the project as a whole.

In their lead editing roles, participants conducted whatever research was needed to clarify the goals, processes, and tools needed to function optimally in their role. Then they spent a week engaging in the work defined by the role, after which they wrote reflection posts in the discussion board and engaged in discussion concerning the role, progress, needs, and future directions of the role.

In their support editing roles, participants did whatever the participants in the lead editing roles had indicated, as well as work they felt was appropriate.

As work on the project neared completion, all participants took a big-picture view of the whole project and identified areas which needed attention. Discussion of these needs and possible solutions was conducted in the discussion board as well as through the use of the commenting feature of the collaborative document.

Finally the manuscript was sent to the publisher, and after some back-and-forth with the publisher concerning editing and formatting the book was published and distributed through an online book marketplace.

Since the completion of this collaborative the sales of the book have been impressive and it has been translated into several languages. The participants have since reported a powerful sense of pride, ownership, and transformation of identity through this digitally-mediated collaborative process (Donaldson & Bucy, in press).

After the completion of the collaborative process described above, the Institutional Review Board (IRB) approval was obtained to conduct formal research concerning this project. All participants signed consent forms, after which they were interviewed and data was collected from the learning management system (LMS) such as discussion board posts. Because the decision to conduct a formal research study was made after the conclusion of the project, the participants and the course designer (the author) were not influenced during the project by knowing that their work would be the subject of research.

The transcriptions of the interviews (N=7) and LMS data were coded in the NVivo qualitative analysis software according to Grounded Theory procedures (Glaser, Strauss, & Strauss, 1967). Multiple rounds of coding were conducted. The first round of coding included a dozen coding categories. New coding categories emerged with each round of coding, resulting in a total of 48 coding categories according to which 49,105 words of participant data were coded.

Rounds of coding the participant data alternated with rounds of coding literature review data in the form of quotations and reading notes (N=3,294). Literature review coding was conducted in a separate instance in the NVivo qualitative analysis software where 81,000 words of literature review data were coded according to 98 coding categories.

Participant data and literature review data were analyzed for themes found in coding similarities and relationships between the coding categories which emerged from the data in this grounded research study.

Results

The qualitative analysis found that themes related to the collaborative nature of the project were related to participant views concerning their learning, engagement, motivation, and feelings of success. Participants reported that the role negotiation process was crucial to the overall success of the digitally-mediated collaborative project as well as to their individual engagement, motivation, and learning.

Participants felt that the roles they negotiated and adopted contributed to the quality of their own work. For example, they said things such as:

Every time we wrote something we'd get two different feedbacks from our peers.

The ability to read and review peer work strengthened my work.

Meshing others written work into my own was a very new experience for me and one that I found helpful and challenging. The ideas of others helped me to find different avenues and ideas to take my writing.

They also believed that the negotiation of roles and the subsequent work in those roles contributed to the overall quality of the project:

I think the roles were divided in a very fair fashion. I loved that we all had a part in each other's [work] to help edit and expand on the ideas.

When I read the book again and I see it, I cannot tell it's from different authors. It seems like one voice. I guess it's because of the discussions.

I learned how to make different voices to be one voice at the end through discussion and through editing.

The experience of digitally mediated collaboration was new for all the participants, and reported that the role negotiation and collaborative processes were effective:

The other thing would be just the collaboration. I had never experienced that before in an online class. Obviously it's different than meeting face-to-face. So that's my big takeaway, just seeing that process and how using stuff like Google Docs can be a great teaching and learning tool. Especially for people who are, you know, a great distance away, apart. Yeah, so I think that model really did work and I learned such a great deal.

My peers did an amazing job pulling this together. Who knew that working together from a distance would be this easy and possible?

SOLUTIONS AND RECOMMENDATIONS

The process of effective role negotiation for digitally-mediated collaborative projects varies from project to project. However, some principles can be formulated based on the adoption of positive aspects from the "traditional" project-management paradigm and from the "digital-age communications" paradigm.

Brainstorming Sessions

Brainstorming sessions should be arranged using digital communications tools such as discussion boards and virtual meeting tools at the beginning of the project to address questions such as:

- How can we clearly describe the intended outcomes of this project?
- What are the stages of this project?
- What is our timeline, and what milestones should we include in the timeline?
- How can we describe the various roles needed for successful completion of this project?
- Can the types of roles be categorized? For example, can we describe "planning", "creation", and "refinement/editing" role types?
- What digital tools would be most appropriate for collaboration in this project?
- What are each of our relevant strengths and weaknesses?

These brainstorming sessions are crucial in developing a collaborative atmosphere in which the sense of agency is established. The communication during such brainstorming sessions also facilitates a sense of unity as participants come to understand how their peers perceive the project and contribute their views.

Defining Vision Collaboratively

In the brainstorming session a common vision will gradually start to emerge. Although a vision is starting to take shape, there may be slight discrepancies between understandings. The creation of a project definition shared and collaboratively edited document which includes the results of the previous brainstorming sessions can help by both clarifying the vision and providing an opportunity to negotiate on differences of opinion concerning the overall vision and goals of the project.

Defining Roles Collaboratively

Once the common vision for the project has been solidified, the stage has been set for discussion, description, and negotiation of roles. This can be facilitated by creation of a role definition shared and collaboratively edited document which includes:

- A title for each role
- A clear definition of the purpose of each role
- A clear description of the responsibilities of each role

Selection of Roles

Using the collaboratively-created "roles" online document, participants can then start the process of selection of roles. There are a variety of possible logistics for role selection, a relatively simple method which aligns well with research is for each participant to take the lead on particular roles and also provide support to other group members in their lead roles.

Each member of the group will elect to take responsibility as "lead" in one or more roles, depending on the situation. If more than one "lead" role is selected, it might be good to consider the possibility of selecting roles in different categories of roles if such categories have been defined. The adoption of lead roles at this stage is essential to the development of a sense of agency and ownership, which then leads to stronger senses of responsibility and intrinsic motivation.

Each member of the group will then elect to take responsibility as "support" in two or more roles, depending on the situation. When the "support" roles are selected, it might be good to consider the possibility of selecting roles in different categories of roles if such categories have been defined. The adoption of support roles creates a stronger sense of unity in the collaboration. It makes concrete the abstract notion of ownership of the project by the entire collaborative group.

During the selection process, discussion is encouraged. Such discussions could include things such as instances in which one member sees in another member a positive quality which might make that person particularly effective in a role that person may not otherwise consider. Sometimes others are better at judging our strengths than we are at judging our own strengths.

Role Performance

Once the roles have been defined and adopted in the shared "roles" document, the foundation will have been built on which to engage in collaborative project work. The adoption of both "lead" and "support" roles is especially powerful in digitally-mediated collaborative group projects. Setting up roles in this way allows for the sharing of responsibilities, as well as the creation of an environment in which asking for and giving support is encouraged. Although the "lead" individual in each role will assume complete responsibility for that role, that individual can call upon the "support" role individuals for assistance. Furthermore, since each individual has both "lead" and "support" roles, they will not be limited to work within their own "lead" role, thus allowing for more opportunities to contribute their own skills, knowledge, and creativity.

Role Evolution: Metacognitive Practices

The process of role negotiation early in a collaborative process sets up opportunities for individual and group metacognitive processes. Regular reflection sessions should be scheduled in a predictable routine. Established routines, perhaps indicated through a shared group calendar, can help participants transition back and forth from lead role work to support role work. For example, a weekly pattern of switching from lead to support and back again can be scheduled to be conducted in a discussion board. At the end of a week, participants could summarize their progress in their lead roles, describe challenges, point out aspects they are particularly proud of, and reflect on their roles in terms of what adjustments to the role descriptions might be needed. After engaging in this reflective discussion, they could then provide pointers to the group members who have adopted roles in support of their lead roles. During the following week in our hypothetical scenario, each group member would work in their support roles, and the next week they would come back to their lead roles, and so on in an alternating pattern of lead and support.

FUTURE RESEARCH DIRECTIONS

In the literature on collaboration and digitally-mediated collaboration there has historically been an emphasis on trust and communication. Other fruitful lines of research are emerging such as metacognitive practices in collaborations, personal self-determination in collaborative environments, and the interplay between motivation, collaboration, and productivity. However, there has been very little research into the collaborative processes involved in role negotiation, description, adoption, and evolution over time. This chapter presented research, theory, and the author's experience which, taken together, provided the groundwork upon which a set of principles were extrapolated. The research study reported here was a qualitative research design. Future quantitative and mixed-methods research designs could contribute to our understanding concerning the effectiveness of various implementations of role negotiation processes. The digital tools used here were limited to a learning management system and shared Google documents. Future research could analyze the use of a variety of other digital tools such as social media and project-management tools. There is much to be done in terms of research into roles in collaborative digitally-mediated projects. The possibility of using this area as the focal point on which to ground an integration of a variety of research findings and theoretical constructs is promising.

CONCLUSION

Aspects of individual work such as productivity, motivation, agency, engagement, and development of skills are a complex network of interactions. In physically-located collaborative environments the complexity of these aspects increases dramatically. In digitally-mediated collaborative environments the complexity grows even greater. With lack of non-verbal cues such as facial expressions and body language communication takes on a completely different nature. There is an ever-growing number of digital tools which make collaboration easier, more efficient, and empowering. These tools open new possibilities for collaboration not bounded by space or time. However, these tools also bring with them new problems, including the need for rapid task-switching (often called "multitasking"), the breakdown of distinction between work life and private life, and lack of clarity of roles, goals, and processes.

A collaborative process of role description, negotiation, adoption, and ongoing evolution through routine metacognitive processes could provide a structure by which to merge positive aspects of traditional hierarchical approaches and positive aspects of digital-age communication culture. This role negotiation process can clarify responsibilities and processes while nurturing the sense of personal agency and self-determination crucial to engagement in the digital age.

Although the role negotiation process described here is grounded in principles extrapolated from research and theory in a variety of fields including motivation, engagement, agency, collaboration, and constructivism, the application thereof in real-world situations will be constrained by the unique characteristics of each digitally-mediated collaborative project. This role negotiation process is an idealized framework intended to weave together a wide range of relevant research. Whatever the unique characteristics of a real-world collaborative project, it is hoped that the principles presented here can shed valuable light by which new innovations in digitally-mediated collaborative processes may arise.

REFERENCES

Bertucci, A., Johnson, D. W., Johnson, R. T., & Conte, S. (2012). Influence of Group Processing on Achievement and Perception of Social and Academic Support in Elementary Inexperienced Cooperative Learning Groups. *The Journal of Educational Research*, *105*(5), 329–335. doi:10.1080/00220671.2011.627396

Blikstein, P., & Cavallo, D. P. (2002). *Technology as a Trojan Horse in School Environments: The Emergence of the Learning Atmosphere (II)*. Proceedings of the ICL Workshop, Austria.

Bruner, J. S. (1986). *Actual minds, possible worlds*. Cambridge, Mass: Harvard University Press.

Bruner, J. S. (1996). *The culture of education*. Cambridge, Mass: Harvard University Press.

Bruner, J. S., & Weinreich-Haste, H. (1987). *Making sense: The child's construction of the world*. London: Methuen.

Davis, K., Seider, S., & Gardner, H. (2008). When False Representations Ring True (and When They Don't). *Social Research*, *75*(4), 1085–1108.

Deci, E. L., Koestner, R., & Ryan, R. M. (2001). Extrinsic Rewards and Intrinsic Motivation in Education: Reconsidered Once Again. *Review of Educational Research*, *71*(1), 1–27. doi:10.3102/00346543071001001

Dietrich, P., Eskerod, P., Dalcher, D., & Sandhawalia, B. (2010). The dynamics of collaboration in multipartner projects. *Project Management Journal*, *41*(4), 59–78. doi:10.1002/pmj.20194

Dillenbourg, P. (1999). What do you mean by collaborative learning? In P. Dillenbourg (Ed.), *Collaborative-learning: Cognitive and Computational Approaches* (pp. 1–19). Oxford: Elsevier.

Gallup Consulting. (2011). *The state of the Global Workplace 2011: A worldwide study of employee engagement and wellbeing*. Gallup, Inc. Retrieved from http://www.gallup.com/services/177083/state-global-workplace-2011.aspx

Glaser, B. G., Strauss, A. L., & Strauss, A. L. (1967). *The discovery of grounded theory: Strategies for qualitative research*. Chicago: Aldine Pub. Co.

Hattie, J. (2008). *Visible learning: A synthesis of over 800 meta-analyses relating to achievement*. London: Routledge.

Hattie, J., & Yates, G. C. R. (2014). *Visible learning and the science of how we learn*. London: Routledge/Taylor & Francis Group.

Innovation Unit. (2013). *Redesigning Education: Shaping learning systems around the globe. Innovation Unit for the Global Education Leaders' Program*. Seattle, WA: Booktrope.

Jarvela, S., Volet, S., & Jarvenoja, H. (2010). Research on Motivation in Collaborative Learning: Moving Beyond the Cognitive-Situative Divide and Combining Individual and Social Processes. *Educational Psychologist*, *45*(1), 15–27. doi:10.1080/00461520903433539

Johnson, D. W., & Johnson, R. T. (2005). New Developments in Social Interdependence Theory. *Genetic, Social, and General Psychology Monographs*, *131*(4), 285–358. doi:10.3200/MONO.131.4.285-358 PMID:17191373

Jrvel, S., & Hadwin, A. (2013). New Frontiers: Regulating Learning in CSCL. *Educational Psychologist*, *48*(1), 25–39. doi:10.1080/00461520.2012.748006

Kaplan, S. N. (2014). Collaboration. *Gifted Child Today*, *37*(4), 261–263. doi:10.1177/1076217514545384

Kohn, A. (1996). By all available means: Cameron and Pierce's defense. *Review of Educational Research*, *66*(1), 1–4. doi:10.3102/00346543066001001

Lessig, L. (2004). The Creative Commons. *Montana Law Review*, *65*, 1–14.

Maccoby, M. (2011). Constructing collaboration. *Research Technology Management*, *54*(1), 59–60. doi:10.5437/08953608X540159

Martinez, S., & Stager, G. (2013). *Invent to Learn: Making, tinkering, and engineering in the classroom*. Torrance, Ca: Constructing Modern Knowledge Press.

Mehta, J., & Fine, S. (2012). Teaching differently...Learning deeply. *Phi Delta Kappan*, *94*(2), 31–35. doi:10.1177/003172171209400208

Piaget, J. (1966). *Psychology of Intelligence*. Totowa, NJ: Littlefield, Adams.

Piaget, J. (1970). *Science of education and the psychology of the child*. New York: Orion Press.

Piaget, J. (1972). *The principles of genetic epistemology*. New York: Basic Books.

Piaget, J. (1977). *The development of thought: Equilibration of cognitive structures*. New York: Viking Press.

Pongracic, I. (2009). *Employees and entrepreneurship: Co-ordination and spontaneity in non-hierarchical business organizations*. Cheltenham: Edward Elgar Publishing. doi:10.4337/9781848446137

Reeve, J. (2013). How Students Create Motivationally Supportive Learning Environments for Themselves: The Concept of Agentic Engagement. *Journal of Educational Psychology*, *105*(3), 579–595. doi:10.1037/a0032690

Snape, P., & Fox-Turnbull, W. (2013). Perspectives of authenticity: Implementation in technology education. *International Journal of Technology and Design Education*, *23*(1), 51–68. doi:10.1007/s10798-011-9168-2

Thomas, J. W. (2000). *A review of research on project-based learning*. San Rafael, CA: Autodesk Foundation.

Van Merrienboer, J. J., & Sweller, J. (2005). Cognitive load theory and complex learning: Recent developments and future directions. *Educational Psychology Review*, *17*(2), 147–177. doi:10.1007/s10648-005-3951-0

Vygotsky, L., & Luria, A. (1994). Tool and symbol in child development. In L. S. Vygotskiĭ, R. Veer, & J. Valsiner (Eds.), The Vygotsky reader (pp. 99-174). Oxford, UK: Blackwell.

Vygotsky, L. S. (1978). *Mind in society* (M. Cole, V. John-Steiner, S. Scribner, & E. Souberman, Eds.). Cambridge, MA: Harvard University Press.

Walker, C. O., Greene, B. A., & Mansell, R. A. (2006). Identification with academics, intrinsic/extrinsic motivation, and self-efficacy as predictors of cognitive engagement. *Learning and Individual Differences*, *16*(1), 1–12. doi:10.1016/j.lindif.2005.06.004

KEY TERMS AND DEFINITIONS

Agency: An individual's ability and authority to make and carry out decisions regarding a particular endeavor.

Collaborative Project: A clearly-defined endeavor in which a number of individuals work together to achieve a goal.

Constructivism: A theory which describes learning as a process in which knowledge and skills are constructed in the mind of the individual.

Engagement: An individual's intellectual, emotional, and participatory involvement in a project.

Metacognition: The process of observing, analyzing, and regulating one's own thinking.

Motivation: An individual's purposes or drives which lead to engagement in a project or process.

Ownership: The recognition that a process or product belongs to those involved in the creation thereof.

Role: A clearly-defined set of responsibilities, rights, and tasks adopted by an individual engaged in a project or process which involves others. Roles are often defined in relation to other roles.

Chapter 13 The Scholarship of Engagement and Generative Learning Communities: Preparing EFL Leaders for Authentic Practice at the American Spaces Philippines

Gianina O Cabanilla
University of the Philippines Diliman, Philippines

ABSTRACT

The Regional English language learning (ELL) project in the American Spaces Philippines was established at the US Department of State's Bureau of Educational and Cultural Affairs (ECA) and Bureau of International Information Programs (IIP) in the fiscal year 2013 as a response to a study which showed the modest state of English language teaching and learning in the country. The project, a cooperation between English as a Foreign Language (EFL) educators and administrators at partner schools, universities, and American spaces in the archipelago counterparts and funded by the US Department of State's Bureau of Educational and Cultural Affairs (ECA) and Bureau of International Information Programs (IIP), was aimed at assisting with the production of more and better-qualified English as a Foreign Language (EFL) educators and administrators.

INTRODUCTION

Today's students, an expression used by Marc Prensky in his paper "*Digital natives, digital immigrants*" back in 2001 represent the Net generation having grown up within digital technology. To use his own words, Prensky said for them *they have spent their entire lives surrounded by and using computers, videogames, digital music players, video cams, cell phones, and all the other toys and tools of the digital*

DOI: 10.4018/978-1-4666-9556-6.ch013

Copyright © 2016, IGI Global. Copying or distributing in print or electronic forms without written permission of IGI Global is prohibited.

age [....]. Computer games, email, the Internet, cell phones and instant messaging are integral parts of their lives.

Hence, students of the *Net Generation (Net Gen)* need a greater flexibility in their studies and studies strongly connected with current technologies. These needs of students today lead to the increasing importance of redefining educational physical & online space. On the other hand Universities are facing the experiment to make the shift from face-to-face learning in the campus to a blended environment of combining face-to-face and online activities.

The paper proposes the use of a *Learning Management System (LMS)* to support *Learning Spaces* in Universities and illustrate a guide to design and develop collaborative sequences of learning activities as a catalyst to enhance the learning process. Students implementing the sequences on their own or in *Campus* supporting by facilitators can accomplish specific educational goals in a flexible educational setting. A case study in the *Hellenic Open University* regarding the development of a learning sequence on the topic "*Implementing essays*" highlights the advantages, the requirements and the relevant constraints. The case study can be extended in all activities of supporting learning at a distance both in Open and in conventional Universities optimizing the experience in distance education, which Open Universities have conquered until now.

In particular this paper emphasizes in the development of electronic collaborative experiences at Universities based on Learning Spaces and LMS to support both students and educators in their complex work. The second unit presents the methodology and also the experience gained by Open Universities so far to support electronic collaborative experiences. The third unit defines and approaches the concept of *Learning Spaces* and how they can contribute to support e-collaboration. Next, in the fourth unit the *Learning Activity Management System (LAMS)* is proposed as an appropriate open *Learning Management System* which serves the adopted pedagogical framework. A Repository of LAMS-sequences has the potential to become an innovative Learning Space (*e-Campus-LS*) combining students' work inside and outside the Campus. The fifth unit describes an exemplar LAMS sequence aiming at supporting students who are implementing an essay as a case study in the Hellenic Open University and presents the preliminary findings from evaluating the sequence. Furthermore, the sixth unit proposes two levels of extension of the case study towards a methodology of developing collaborative sequences using *LMSs* in Open and conventional Universities too. Finally, the paper highlights discussion themes raised by working with Learning Spaces in Higher Education. Proposals for further use of Learning Spaces and conclusions are drawn and commented.

SUPPORTING ELECTRONIC COLLABORATIVE EXPERIENCES

Supporting Students at a Distance

The integration of the Information and Communication Technologies (ICT) has changed radically learning and transforms education. Advanced technologies support learning in the 21st century following all three generations of pedagogy: behaviorism, constructivism and connectivism. Universities today approach more and more distance and flexible forms of education since learning is possible to happen in areas outside the traditional campus, occurring anytime and anywhere.

The Distance Learning methodology aims at activating students guiding them towards an exploratory approach to knowledge and ensures the maximum possible flexibility in space, time and pace of learning. Most students in Distance Learning (Kokkos, 2001; Hatzilakos, Papadakis & Rossiou, 2007):

- Need human support in order to use the educational material,
- Cannot approach it critically since they have not cultivated the appropriate study skills,
- Are not familiar with the ways of approaching in depth the learning objects and using alternative learning resources,
- Are not familiar with writing essays
- Haven't cultivated appropriate self organization and learning autonomy.

These multiple levels of support are provided by educators in Distance Learning. Educators need to combine multiple roles as facilitators, coordinators of learning experiences, developers of pro learning circumstances (Athansoula-Reppa, 2006). Students on their end, expect from educators in Distance Learning (DL) coordination, encouragement, counseling, comprehension of concerns, direct response to questions, problem solving, appropriate guidance in activities and exchange of views (Fung & Carr, 2000). In addition, they expect from educators to be clear in describing the goals and the objectives of each activity, having proper administration, sensitivity in individualized needs, new ideas, proposals, DL practices, learning approaches, authentic educational material aimed at their goals, excellent knowledge of their field and the ability to enrich the educational process. The usual reasons for students' failure in e-learning courses are (Jenkins & Vissere, 2001):

- The poor instructional design of the course from not experienced educators,
- Technical issues,
- The lack of students' time,
- Students' insufficient support in general,
- The lack of supporting students' individualized learning preferences, in particular.

The development of bilateral interactions between educators and students and also among students, is most critical for achieving direct or indirect communication. Between face-to-face (f2f) meetings, communication is delivered in asynchronous mode aiming at continuing of discussion and interaction between educators and students. The emerging question is: "How to instructionally design learning experiences in which students could participate to gain high degrees of interactions and build new knowledge in a common space, in or outside the Campus?"

Teaching at a Distance

Educators in DL guide and direct students in the learning process and strategies using appropriate instructional design, providing feedback on evaluation of the essays and communicating constantly f2f or through the web. They focus on the significance of metacognitive activities for self evaluation of the learning process. Furthermore, they highlight the set of competences regarding self regulation and organization of students. Implementing the essays is the primary way for students in understanding the educational content in the framework of distance studies, whereby students regard themselves as the main responsible for their learning (Vasala, Hatziplis & Lionarakis, 2007).

Evaluating students' essays is one of the most significant features of distance teaching. Educators encourage students' engagement in activities orientated to support metacognitive issues of concern as commenting essays, structuring meta-cognitive exercises, motivating them in exchanging views and in keeping a personal diary recording thoughts regarding their attempts and ongoing progress (Fanariti & Spanaka, 2009).

According DL principles, educators use techniques which enhance the active participation and are based on experiential learning in order to achieve specific learning objectives of the course and to lead in personal goals as well. The convergence of tutor and students goals leads to eliminate the distance between them. The more effective the convergence is, the smaller the distance remains (Moore, 1973, 1980).

Collaborating in Communities of Practice

DL is highly criticized regarding the support of its methodology in collaborative learning (Avouris & Komis, 2003). Collaboration is a basic parameter in fundamental aspects of human activities as working and learning. Modern web based environments can provide students learning sequences designed particularly for the DL educators, oriented to different educational goals each time based on individualized needs. Therefore learning sequences provide personalized, interactive, just-in-time, current and user-centered services. During their implementation they can adapt in students learning needs and educators choices so as to be more effective.

Communities of practice (CoP) are groups for exchanging ideas and new practices, sharing a common interest (Lave & Wenger, 1991; Bruckman & Resnick, 1996) and provide resources and peer-support. Lave & Wenger (1998) consider as a CoP, a community of individuals which is united by common goals, interests and practices.

Communities of practice have an essential role in distance learning (Palloff & Pratt, 1999). Interactions within the community are non static and continually transforming procedures, therefore each group is characterized by its own potential.

The meta-analysis of Johnson & Johnson (1990) highlights the value of collaboration in the learning process:

- Students working in a collaborative and non competitive learning environment, have better performance,
- Students participating in groups solve easier problems,
- Students participating in groups, use more methods and metacognitive strategies,
- Collaborative learning cultivates higher level of thinking,
- New ideas and innovative solutions are being produced in working groups.

Collaboration at a distance supported from advanced learning technologies is today feasible and effective (e-collaboration) and also consists a broad field for research and experiment.

Collaborative e-learning is collaboration happening in a virtual place. Both synchronous and asynchronous communication, combined with the development of team dynamics contributes to solve many problems faced today by learners in distance education (Vasala, Hatziplis & Lionarakis, 2007). Pilot studies in the Open University (Freake & Papathanassiou, 2006, Cornelius & Macdonald, 2008) indicate that supporting student tends to be "the critical factor for successful studies" therefore educators need to use fluently all means and communication methods and adapt them depending on the case (Papadimitriou & Lionarakis, 2009).

Collaborating in a virtual place enhances interactions among members of the CoP with discussions, commenting, social networking applications and the co-creation of digital content in knowledge construction places.

Some indicative practices of collaboration according to the Toolkit of Maggie Coats (1992) are brainstorming, discussions, debates, role playing, case studies, group working, and simulations. As Rowntree, (1998) mentioned, *my recent experience taught me that all principles and practices for collaboration in face to face workshops could be applied even if everyone is in different place and time. We are able to split participants in groups, to engage them in activities related with their project, interact testing and cultivating their relevant skills.*

Discussions in forums, interactive videoconferencing, peer assessment and co-creation of digital content are three indicative dimensions of e-collaboration making deeper interactions between members of the CoP.

Discussions in Forums

Discussions in forums in learning environments regard course discussions, live seminar discussions, study groups, examinations and technical support. Students create their topics and participate in threads of comments, expressing their arguments, thoughts and questions.

Interactive Videoconference

Interactive Videoconferencing provides opportunities to students to exchange views, share data, and participate actively in a dynamic interactive environment with collaborative construction of knowledge in real time (Anastasiadis, 2007). Pedagogical, technological, administrative and financial issues should be taken into account for designing and implementing an Interactive Videoconference. The proposed pedagogical framework of using videoconferencing is based on:

- Interdisciplinary approach
- Social constructivism theories
- Project based learning
- Distance learning principles by American Distance Education Consortium (ADEC, nd) and
- Evaluation method combining qualitative and quantitative measures.

Interactive Videoconferencing is not only a tool of synchronous e-learning but it can be exploited afterwards in asynchronous format supporting CoPs. Students who haven't participated in real time are able to view the recording on demand, either in total or either partially. Segmented units of videoconferencing aiming to concrete learning objectives could be exploited asynchronously, as "social objects" to enhance interactions in CoPs (Papadimitriou et. al, 2007). Therefore, Interactive Videoconferencing consists an innovative way of building communities beyond spatial constraints.

Peer Assessment

Peer assessment is a learning process whereby students grade assignments or tests for their peers, based on benchmarks provided by the teacher. Rubrics are often used in conjunction with peer-assessment.

This practice is employed to improve students' understanding of course materials as well as their meta-cognitive skills. Students can learn from grading their peers' work, understanding the grading process and recognizing their own strengths and weaknesses. By getting involved in this process, they are moving towards a better understanding of how to construct their work and also learn better strategies for improving their test results.

Co-Creation

Co-creation is a collaborative process which takes place when many non-pre-defined problems occur . Co-Creation can be understood as a process to deal with real local or global challenges in new ways, addressing difficult and complex problems and delivering fundamental life-changing results. The *Co-creation Methodology* could be implemented following the steps below (Tsakarestou & Papadimitriou, 2014):

- Introduction
  - Exploring the concepts of collaboration and co-creation, pre-defined and non-pre-defined problems.
  - Prototyping problem insights.
  - Approaching the benefits.
- Brainstorming
  - Participants brainstorm and research in small teams on ideas by "solving" the problem-challenge and proposing subjects in their disciplines or combining them.
- Presenting and selecting the ideas. Participants:
  - present their ideas to the plenary. The educators pitch the ideas to start their project by:
  - voting for the proposed ideas and selecting a number of them.
  - shaping one group for each idea.
- Working in groups. Participants working in groups:
  - Define their needs in the synthesis of technical or conceptual materials.
  - Plan extensively experimentation in progress.
  - Explore "secrets" of successful projects and teams behind them.
  - Search and use open resources.
  - Get mentoring.
  - Develop their ideas in projects collaboration.
  - Discuss and select platforms to publish their final digital projects.
- Synthesis - Presentation
  - Groups present final versions to other teams – feedback and discussion

Co-creation at a distance can be achieved when participants are far away among them and they are able to deliver digital content or content on the cloud following the previous methodology.

E-COLLABORATION AT LEARNING SPACES

Virtual and Physical Spaces

Networks' development, web based environments and modern learning theories compose the new area of *Learning Spaces* aiming at enhancing interactivity between educators, learners and educational content, opening up new perspectives in DL and also collaboration among students.

Learning Spaces is a broader concept than "classroom" towards the convergence of the net generation (Net Gen) students, current learning theories and ICT. The Net Gen students have adopted rapidly and embraced ICT especially the web based services. "Therefore the concept of classroom has both expanded and evolved; virtual space has taken its place alongside the physical space" (Brown, 2013).

The resources used in higher education today tend to be digital and delivered via environments on the Web. In addition, internet connectivity is increasingly portable. Therefore learning is possible to happen, in areas outside the traditional classroom, occurring anytime and anywhere.

Learning Spaces towards the Net Generation Learners

The Net Gen students are social and team oriented, comfortable with multitasking, and generally positive in their outlook, and have a hands-on, "let's build it" approach—all encouraged by the IT resources at their disposal. Net Gen students have embraced IT, having a mutually influential -almost symbiotic-relationship (Brown, 2013). Universities can offer to digital natives the opportunity of a flexible model in their studies with no physical or spatial presence.

Information today is plentiful and the student's role is not to memorize or even understand everything, but being able to find and apply knowledge when and where it is needed based on connectivist learning (Anderson & Dron, 2011; Siemens, 2005; Downes, 2007). The ubiquitous networked connections between people, digital artifacts, and content, leads for seeking and defining "social objects" to enhance participation, reflections and interactions in CoP among students.

According JISC, (2013), *a Learning Space should be able to motivate learners and promote learning as an activity, support collaborative as well as formal practice, provide a personalized and inclusive environment, and be flexible in the face of changing needs*. The design of its individual LS needs to be (JISC, 2013):

- **Flexible:** To accommodate both current and evolving pedagogies.
- **Future-Proofed:** To enable space to be re-allocated and reconfigured.
- **Bold:** To look beyond tried and tested technologies and pedagogies.
- **Creative:** To energies and inspire learners and tutors.
- **Supportive:** To develop the potential of all learners.
- **Enterprising:** To make each space capable of supporting different purposes.

Table 1. Online and f2f activities in e –Campus

Online Activities in e –Campus	F2F Activities in e –Campus
Personalized Learning • Courses • Educational material • Media • Self paced e-experiments • Construction of digital artifacts • Assignments	Experiential Learning • Experiments • Problem solving based projects • Enquiry and research based projects
Active and Collaborative Learning • Active learning practices • e-Collaborative learning practices based on social objects (group work, debates, discussions, role playing, world café)	Active and Collaborative Learning • Active learning practices • Collaborative learning practices (group work, debates, discussions, role playing, world café)
Connectivist Learning • Avatars, polls • Joint activities • Study groups • e-Experiments • Webinars, e-workshops • Immersive conferencing	

Teaching and learning in Learning Spaces is integrated in a continuous blended mode combining (Table 1):

- Face-to-Face activities using methods and practices in experiential, situated, active, collaborative problem solving, project based learning.
- Online activities according personalized, adaptive and collaborative learning.

In this context, students are able to collaborate asynchronously in the Learning Space "e-Campus" (e-Campus-LS):

- Participating in forums,
- Working in groups for completing specific tasks or assignments,
- Creating collaborative projects,
- Shaping study groups, discussing and exchanging their thoughts, ideas on key points of their study or asking peer support in their assignments,
- Conducting peer evaluation of assignments.

Synchronous mode practices of collaboration in the Learning Space "e-Campus" (e-Campus-LS) include:

- Polls, real time interactions,
- Interactive videoconferences,
- Webinars (Web seminars), e-workshops,
- Serious games,
- Simulations and applications.

Students can use avatars when they log in the Learning Space, navigate e-lessons and engage in immersive conferencing. Activities in Learning Spaces should use *emotional intelligence* theory (Goleman, 2006) to create a sense of belonging in learning communities and enhance interactions in depth and large scale among students and their educators.

Flipping the Campus towards the "e-Campus-LS"

Flipping classrooms (University of Northern Colorado, 2013) is an upcoming blended method of flexible studies implemented within the following main steps; when students go to the campus they have already studied the major part of the educational material as digital resources at home available on the *e-Campus-LS*. The digital resources include lectures from their professors or eminent speakers. In the campus, the work of students is facilitated by tutors in groups or individually on their own devices aiming primarily at active learning. In this context, they try to discover knowledge through theorems, laws, software programs or experiments, collecting data, implementing statistics, creating artefacts, drawing and interpreting conclusions. Multiple learning methodologies are implemented following methods based on *the Problem Solving, Project, Enquiry or Research Based Learning methodologies.* Learning could be also *situated* in real world situations, *experiential* based on *constructivist* and *connectivist* models. Tutors facilitate and support f2f work, provide daily feedback and facilitate the necessary or optional activities on the *e-Campus-LS*. Active learning communities among students are promoted at f2f work or in study groups.

Learning Analytics

Advanced learning systems allow individualized supporting and teaching of students while they provide analytic data to educators so as to think critically the learning design and transform their views (Cameron, 2007) reforming and re-using sequences of learning activities which they have developed and proposed for supporting students. An educator can use *learning analytics* to monitor and intervene in his students' performance depending on their progress, so Learning Spaces have the potential to support differentiate teaching and *adaptive personalized learning*.

WHAT DO WE NEED FROM TECHNOLOGY TO SUPPORT LEARNING SPACES?

Learning Technologies

A learning technology is an orchestration of technologies, necessarily including pedagogies, whether implicit or explicit. Technology sets the beat and the timing while pedagogy defines the moves (Anderson, 2009). Trying to design and support such blended learning activities as mentioned in the previous units, we need learning technologies which have the potential:

- To organize sequences of collaborative activities with specific learning outcomes, which also can use the whole spectrum of the available digital resources and also the wealth of Open Educational Resources,

Figure 1. Learning space based on LAMS

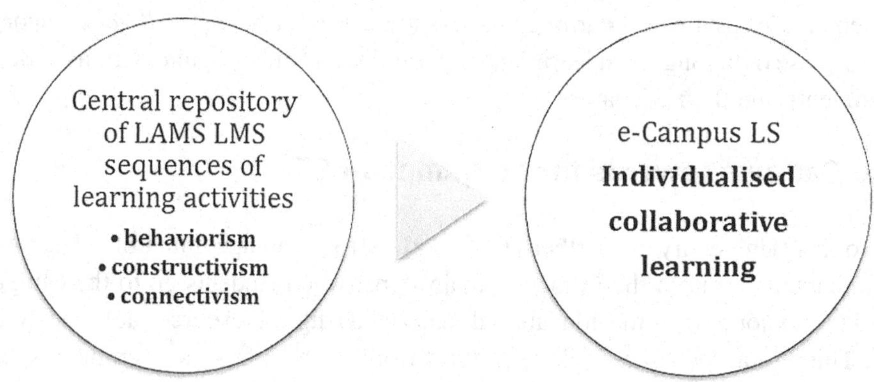

- To support designing and authoring sequences by educators on their own and
- To monitor students' progress providing relevant data aiming to support personalized learning.

Innovative *Learning Spaces* both physical and virtual can emerge then, using sequences of learning activities designed and developed from tutors in order to combine personal online use and face-to-face support.

In this paper, the use of *Learning Activity Management System (LAMS)* is proposed to approach the concept of *Learning Spaces* at Universities and illustrate a guide to design and develop sequences of collaborative learning activities as a catalyst to enhance the learning process at a distance. Educators in distance education can be supported too and that will contribute critically to their effective role in administrative, social and educational context. The *Learning Activity Management System (LAMS) is* a proposal according the *learning design standard* towards the development of learning sequences aiming to support both tutor's work and students' progress.

A *Learning Space* could be developed using LAMS sequences providing innovative and flexible learning experiences. LAMS sequences can support essentially electronic collaborative experiences among students and therefore they lead in getting higher performances and also decreasing students drop out from their studies. The goal is not to do away with the traditional campus, but rather to reinvent and to integrate it within the *Learning Spaces*, moving towards a single united learning environment (*e-Campus*). So, the proposed "e-Campus" consists of a Repository of sequences of learning activities in LAMS (Figure 1) aiming at:

- Supporting students study and collaboration outside the campus,
- Monitoring students' progress and engagement by their educators, using collaborative sequences,
- Providing an authoring environment for educators in order to design and develop sequences of learning activities.
- Supporting differentiated teaching by providing *learning analytics* to the educators for the monitoring of their students' progress.

Each student shapes his own learning profile, following specific steps in order to accomplish specific learning outcomes and create his own environment "My-Campus" including his work and outcomes in an e-portfolio.

The Learning Activities Management System (LAMS)

The LMS LAMS (LAMS, nd) is an open source freely available web based *Learning Management System* 'inspired' by the *Learning Design model* for designing and delivering online and offline collaborative learning activities. These activities can include a range of individual tasks, pair or small group work and whole class activities based on learning objects (content) and collaboration. It functions as an autonomous Learning Management System, or integrated in *Course & Content Management Systems, CMSs* as *Sakai, Blackboard, WebCT, Moodle*, etc. The user needs only one browser (*IE, Firefox, Chrome*), and the *Flash Player* while the system administrator can install it on any operating system (*Windows, Linux, Macintosh)*. Today (the end of 2014), LAMS is considered the most popular software for learning design, since more than 10,036 users (most of them are educators) from 86 countries, have used it already and has been translated in 33 languages (Dalziel, 2014).

Students implementing the LAMS sequences (Figure 2) at Learning Spaces are encouraged to interact with their peers in specifically designed reflective activities and accomplish educational goals in a flexible educational setting. The design of the sequences aims to enhance cognitive process and concept construction, and activate also critical and creative thinking.

Furthermore, each educator is able to design and develop his own learning sequences following specific steps and contribute by that in a common Repository. Building a Repository of learning sequences supports the work of educators and affects critically to their effective role in social and educational context.

Figure 2. The LessonLAMS learning space

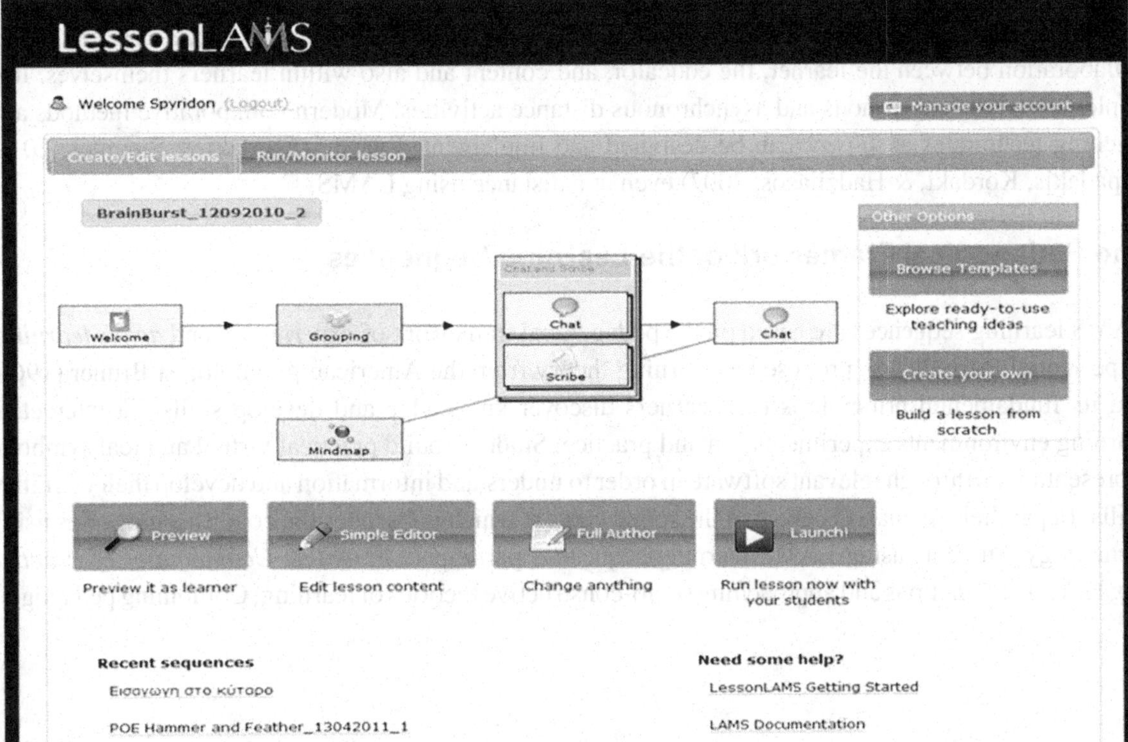

More than 2,100 sequences available in the Central LAMS Repository (LAMS Central, nd), have been downloaded more than 23,000 times and previewed more than 54,000 times!

As we approach the end of 2014, we have just passed two significant milestones, for the International (and the Greek) LAMS community (LAMS community, nd) with 10,030 members, who has already developed a Repository with more than 2,100 free lessons – good practices as LAMS sequences, 4400 discussion topics (downloaded 23,137 times /previewed 54,764 times). In the international Repository, communities of educators can upload and share their own sequences and reuse existing ones freely available with *Creative Commons* licenses or other. Furthermore an educator can *embed* LAMS lessons in his Learning Space as his personal blog and also she/he can create accounts for her/his students. Students execute the sequences and the educator supports them through *LessonLAMS* service (LessonLAMS, nd). The LessonLAMS has now over 10,000 users.

The *LessonLAMS* service disposes also a *LAMS Pedagogical Planner*, a feature which helps course's design based on prior pedagogy strategies and educational techniques by providing exemplary lessons as *templates, ready-to-use teaching ideas*.

LAMS provides a set of tools for authoring activities facilitating:

1. Information (*Notice board, Share Resources, Task list*)
2. Collaboration (*Chat and Scribe, Discussion forum, building groups*)
3. Feedback *(Questions & Answers, Survey, Poll)*
4. Evaluation (*File Submission, Evaluation, Multiple Choice Questions*).
5. Co-creation (*Chat and Scribe, Discussion forum, building groups*)

Activities tools are presented in the authoring area in a simple and comprehensive mode, so as a common user using the familiar technique *drag & drop* can place and combine them to build the modules of her/his learning sequences. The basic rationale behind the *learning design standard* is enhancing collaboration between the learner, the educator, and content and also within learners themselves. It is implemented in synchronous and asynchronous distance activities. Modern collaborative methods and teaching techniques as *Jigsaw* can be designed and implemented easily (Kordaki & Siempos, 2010; Papadakis, Kordaki, & Hadzilacos, 2007) even at a distance using LAMS.

The Pedagogical Framework of the Learning Sequences

LAMS learning sequences are based on the pedagogical framework of *experiential* and *active learning*. Experiential learning was proposed as learning theory from the American psychologist Bruner (1966) and its fundamental principle is that learners discover knowledge and develop skills via interactive learning environments experimentation and practice. Students build practical virtual and real symbolic representations through relevant software in order to understand information and develop their cognitive skills. In parallel, emphasis is given in the social context which influences the cognitive processes using technology. Students using LAMS learning sequences participate in *Online Communities of Practice* engaging in interactions and approaching socio-constructive theories of learning. Combining pedagogies of behaviorism, constructivism and connectivism is crucial for the development of *Learning Spaces* and could achieve flexibility.

Students use of LAMS sequences contributes actively in their own learning (*active learning*). Following them step by step, students participate in activities related to teaching goals and objectives, encouraging reflective and self reflective activities. Cognitive process and concept construction are enhanced, critical and creative thinking are activated and learning engages higher order thinking skills (Fragaki, Reynolds, & Vanbuel, 2009; Matsagouras, 2005: 84-95).

LAMS sequences are based on an educational framework of approaching quality and use a variety of means and tools towards *Polymorphic education* (Lionarakis, 1998). LAMS uses activity tools allowing easily the implementation of three sets of educational material which is supported by the taxonomy of West (1996, in Lionarakis 2001). In addition, it provides diverse learning opportunities for students and relevant feedback throughout their overall study and exploitation.

A CASE STUDY AT THE HELLENIC OPEN UNIVERSITY

Studying at the Hellenic Open University: An Introduction

Distance Learning is the fundamental methodology of teaching and learning at Open Universities, therefore they have already the experience from its implementation for about 50 years. Students enrolled in *Distance Learning* courses study all by themselves the educational material using various means and technologies for a long period and are asked to implement essays in order to engage in depth with the cognitive subject and to be better prepared for the final exams (Keegan, 1986; Lionarakis, 2001). The course usually includes a few face-to-face (f2f) meetings. Between two face-to-face meetings, educators can support students study and the successful implementation of their essays using web based environments. On their end, educators in *Distance Learning* can use advanced learning management systems in order to gain a more precise and clear view of the work, the difficulties faced by their students and their personal contribution in group work.

In Greece 31,000 adults benefit today of the second educational chance which the Hellenic Open University offers them by studying at a distance. Most of them work in parallel with their studies, therefore they need a high priority flexible place, time and pace of learning. Furthermore, adult learners studying at Open Universities will be more and more a part of the Net generation in forthcoming years.

The Hellenic Open University uses web based environments in a short scale and only pilot advanced learning technologies have been applied. In addition, Local Centers have been established at the Hellenic Open University in 1994 and could provide f2f facilitation using LAMS sequences for each particular activity of the distance learning methodology.

In the following units an exemplary LAMS sequence is presented, aiming to prepare and support students in the Hellenic Open University during their work on essays in (Table 2):

- A concrete topic (*Distance Learning in school education)* and
- A general format as a template for implementing essays.

Table 2. Supporting students during their work on essays

Tutor-Counselor	Student
Designing and authoring activities	**Implementing essays, projects**
Inspiring, Motivating, Guiding, Providing feedback	Having questions, Facing difficulties
Answering, Interacting, Discussing in forums	Participating and Contributing in groups, Interacting
Facilitating, Encouraging	Studying with their own pace,
Getting learning analytics, Monitoring	Self-organizing Self-regulating Self-evaluating

LAMS Sequence for Preparing and Implementing an Essay

This unit describes and discusses the design and the development of an exemplary LAMS sequence preparing and supporting students who are implementing an essay. Students are motivated by educators, to use the sequence and they are guided to think and find responses in critical issues and queries, such as:

- How do they estimate issues which should be focused?
- What can they leave out when implementing the essay?
- In which ways do they perform self evaluation?
- In which ways do they shape their criteria and questions addressed to self evaluation?
- Do they face essays' elements under multiple points of view?
- Do they recognize and adopt alternative solutions?
- Do they recognize similarities and proportions between circumstances that allow applying a broader reaction?
- How can collaboration with their peers support their progress?

Designing Activities

Designing learning and teaching activities is based on concrete principles in Distance Learning. The sequence aims at encouraging students through their interaction in a collaborative Learning Space to broaden matters related to the cognitive subject. The sequence would be a catalyst towards the implementation of the essay.

The design of the learning activities of the sequence-template includes (Figure 3):

- Goals and objectives aiming to student's evaluation on their progress (*Pre-text* or *Co-text*, according West & Lionarakis's taxonomy, 2001)
- Self evaluation activities so as students will learn by enhancing interaction with content (*Inter-text or Context,* West & Lionarakis). Plus, they allow students to control continually their progress (Matralis, 1998)

Figure 3. Authoring area in LMS LAMS

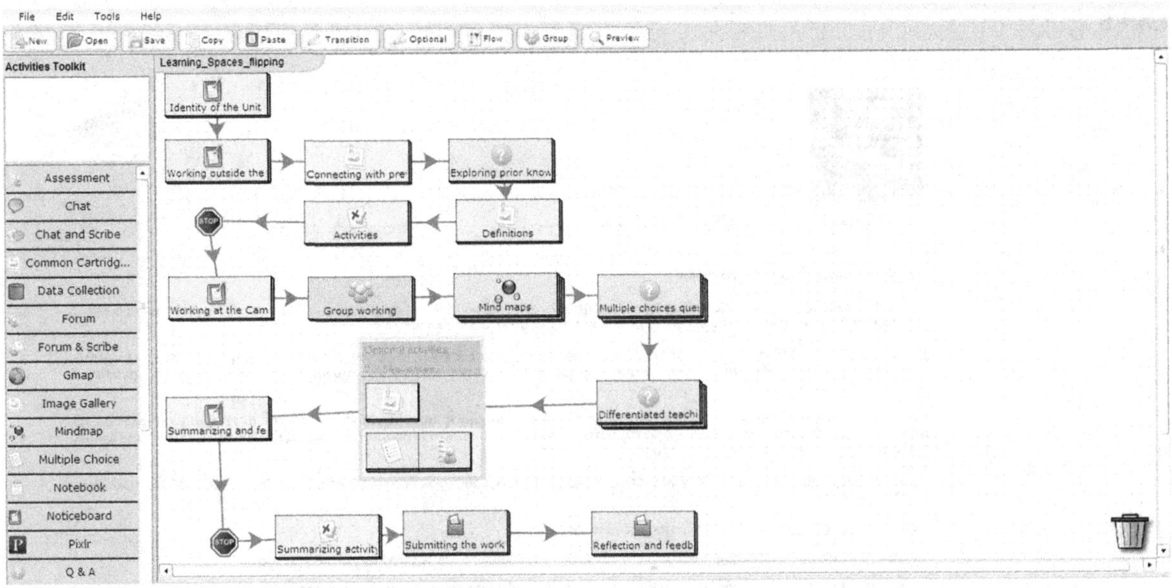

- Rewarding and encouraging comments depending on success or failure in the previous activities (Matralis, 1998)
- Activities including visualizing data which activate students
- *Open Educational Resources* aiming to broaden students' horizons regarding the topic (in the role of *Post-text* and *Multi-text as additional portfolio/material and multimedia material* according West & Lionarakis's taxonomy).
- Explanations, clarifications, hypertexts (*Over-text,* West & Lionarakis)
- Pictures, figures, diagrams (*Para-text,* West & Lionarakis)
- Case studies, examples, explanations (*Retro-text*, West & Lionarakis)
- Combining essay with the goals of the course and the personal goals of student following adult learning principles.
- Exchanging of views aiming to enhance interactions.

Authoring a Learning Sequence

The specific topic of the essay regards "*Distance learning in school education*". The first activity unfolds the title, a short description and the objectives of the sequence (Figure 4).

The second metacognitive activity regards self evaluation, spotting key-words of the essay aiming at exploring the students' prior knowledge. The next three activities are focused on the topic providing supportive material and learning resources from the web (Figure 5).

Metacognitive discussion activities follow up, aiming at motivating and exchanging views and concerns with peers. The activity poses three topics for relevant discussions in a forum and asks students to add and discuss further their own topics which they consider that they could contribute towards the implementation of the essay. Two *threads* from discussions will be exploited in their essay as an indicator of their active participation in forums.

Figure 4. Students' learning space

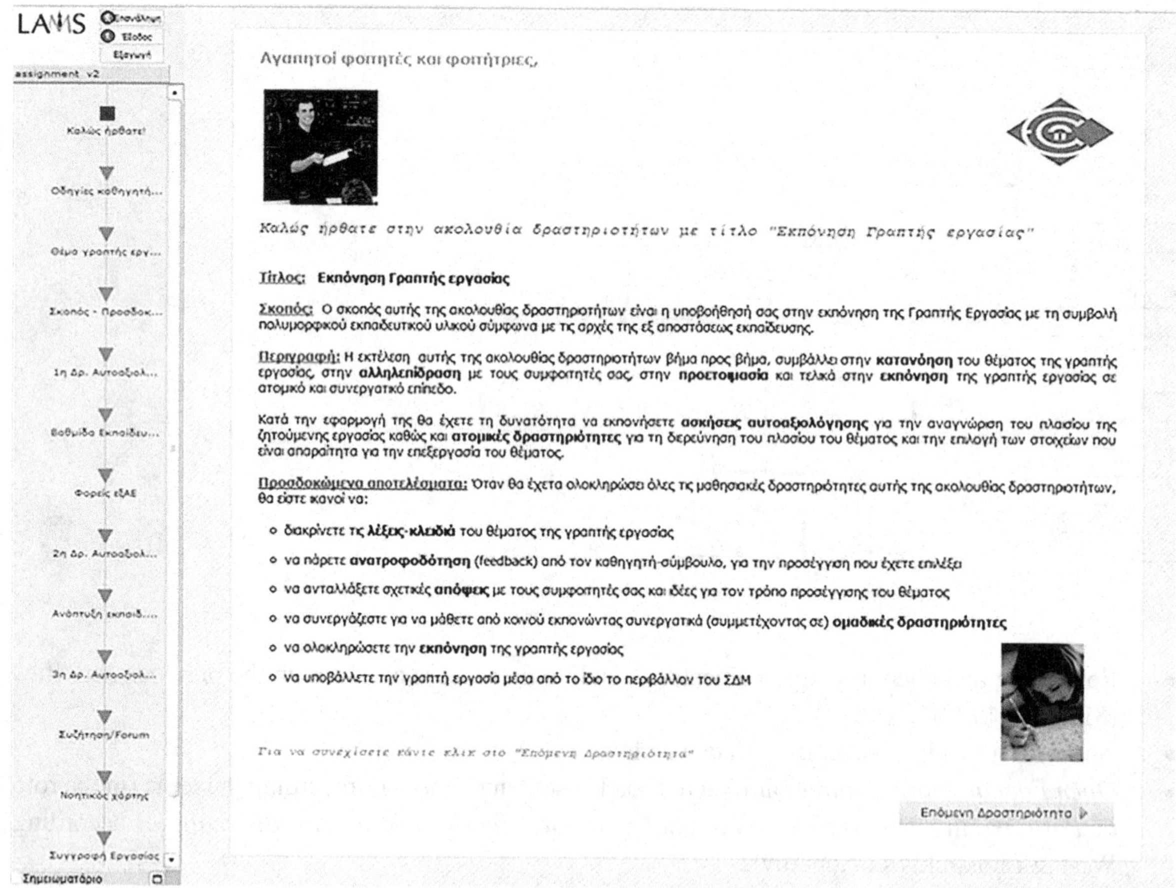

The next activity asks the expansion of a conceptual map relevant to the topic. The conceptual mapping technique is a reflective cognitive tool that enhances the construction of new knowledge and promotes interaction at the same time. This technique engages learners in active learning processes by motivating them to analyze and react critically to the content as well as to organize and represent knowledge, bearing in mind the social and civil environment (Jonassen, 2000).

All activities include guidance from tutors. They could be implemented in home individually or in Local Centers if students need the facilitation of a tutor or of their peers or just the feeling of the academic environment. In both ways, the tutor-counselor is able to view and monitor their progress through LAMS guiding them critically if it is needed. In addition, educators can get *learning analytics* from the process of implementing the activities.

The final activity of the sequence-template contains the guide "*Directions for writing an academic scientific essay*". Students can study the guide and upload the essay via the platform LAMS. All categories of LAMS tools were exploited to develop the above activities.

Figure 5. Authoring a learning activity which provides supportive material from the Web

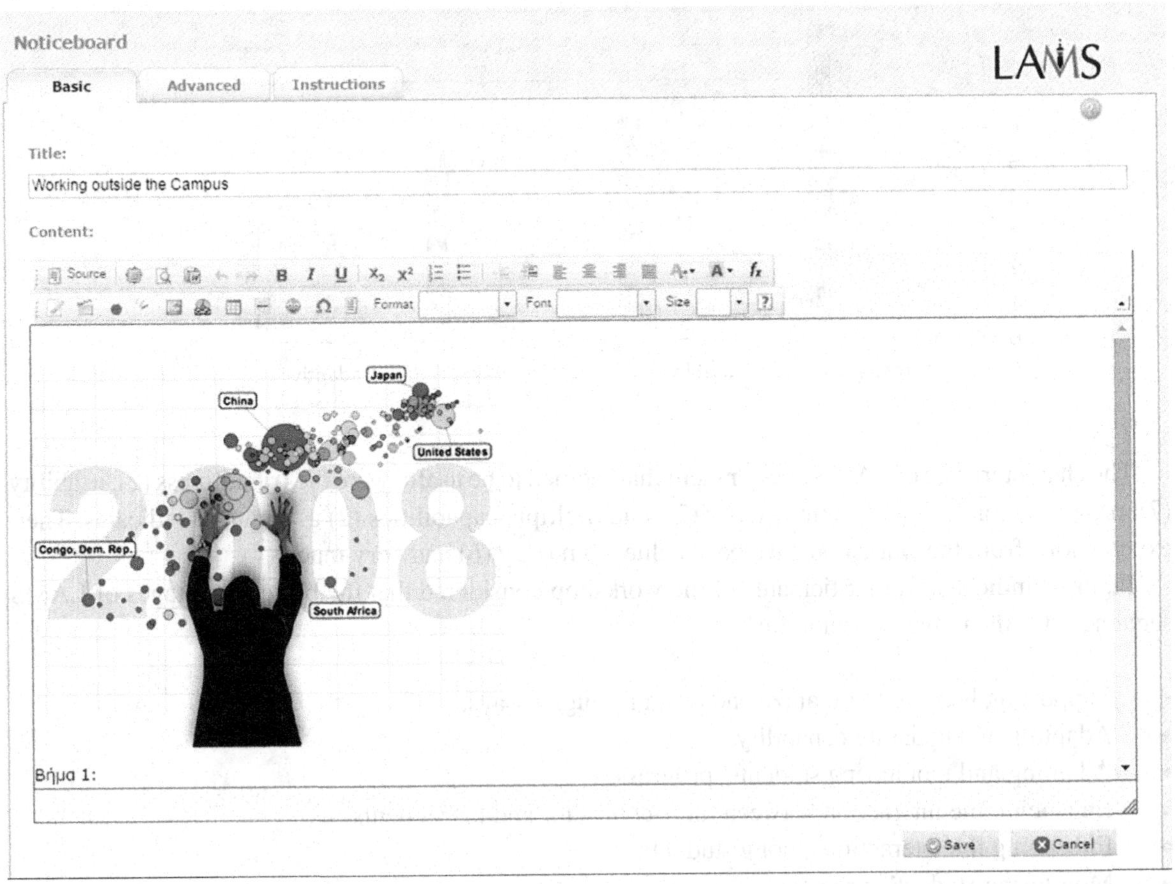

Preliminary Results from Evaluating the Sequence

During the 6th *International Conference of Open and Distance Learning* the aforementioned sequence was presented in a LAMS workshop with 14 educators coming from Higher Education and Life Long Learning in December 2011. They consist a focus group with nine men and five women. Their educational experience was the following: three of them had one to five years, four of them had six to fifteen years and seven participants had more than 15 years of experience. Participants saw interest in order to:

- Use available LAMS sequences created by other educators in their teaching at 100% (14),
- Create their own sequences or modify others for their teaching at 100% (14),
- Use exemplary sequences for the development of their own learning material, at 100% (14) and
- Contribute in enriching the sequences Repository at 78, 5% (11).

Figure 6. First impression of LAMS

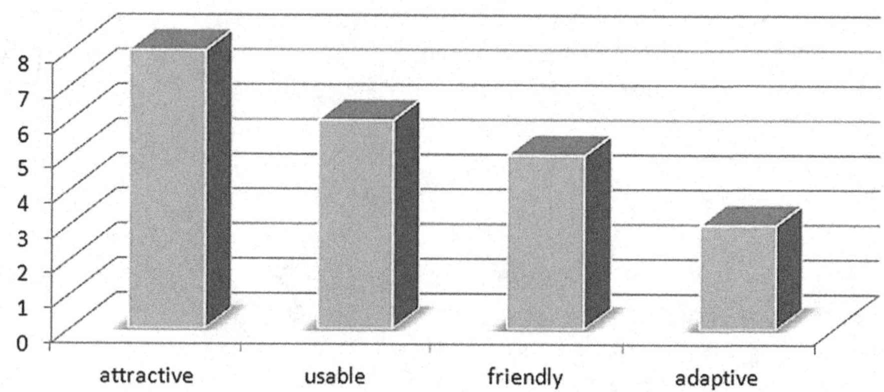

The characteristics of LAMS environment that seemed to be useful were the friendliness (2), usability (7), progress monitoring (3), interactivity (2), and multiple capabilities (2) as Figure 6 indicates. Their expectations from the workshop have been achieved mostly (6) and very much (7).

Figure 7 indicates that participants of the workshop considered that the basic advantages of LAMS sequences for the tutor-counselor are:

- Supporting her/him to organize and teach through essays.
- Adapting and updating capability.
- Adapting and monitoring students' progress.
- Enhancing the interaction between tutor-counselor and his students.
- Enhancing the interaction among students.
- Monitoring student's progress.
- Providing opportunities for reflections.

Data analysis has been conducted with descriptive statistics using percentages to display distributions and histograms to depict frequency distributions.

Figure 7. Advantages of LAMS sequences for tutor-counselors

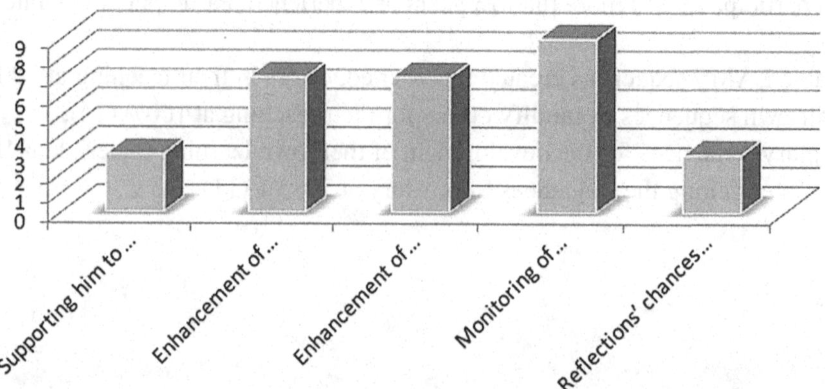

Benefits from the LAMS Sequences

Designing and developing LAMS sequences asks for educators who are familiar with web based environments. Educators can use, adapt and update sequences from repositories developed from their peers. By using them, they can direct their students to learning strategies, to focus on their feedback between f2f meetings. Key advantages from developing and using LAMS sequences on behalf of educators, are (Papadimitriou, Papadakis, Lionarakis & Kameas, 2011):

- Providing the capability to design supporting activities using a friendly environment and exploiting their own expertise.
- Providing the capability to develop integrated activities.
- Selecting tools from the environment depending on their strong characteristics.
- Providing the capability of embedding all multimedia elements.
- Providing a usable and attractive platform.
- Providing the capability of being anonymous or not.
- Uploading and delivering content from the platform.
- Providing the capability of adapting and updating sequences.
- Providing the capability of monitoring the students' progress and getting learning analytics.
- Enhancing their interaction with students.
- Supporting them to organize their teaching through essays.

In particular, the advantages for students are:

- Creative engagement (*active learning, learning by doing*).
- Discovering learning (*experiential learning*).
- Exchanging views and questions therefore enhancing interactions in virtual and physical communities of the Learning Space.

INNOVATIVE EXPERIENCES IN LEARNING SPACES FOR OPEN AND CONVENTIONAL UNIVERSITIES

This paper proposes two levels of extension of the case study (Table 3) aiming at achieving e-collaboration in Learning Spaces: the first regards face-to-face meetings in Open Universities and the second all learning activities in conventional Universities.

Extending the Case Study in f2f Meetings in Open Universities

Students using LAMS sequences could combine individualized or collaborative learning, studying alone or in Local Centers in terms of Open Universities. LAMS sequences could be developed as the general

Table 3. Extending the case study

Extending the case study	
Case study	• Essay "Distance Learning in school education" • Hellenic Open University
Case study template	• Implementing essays • Hellenic Open University
1st level of extension	• Face-to-face meetings • Open Universities
2nd level of extension	• Learning activities • Conventional Universities

Table 4. Flipped Campus sequence of learning activities for Conventional Universities

2nd Level of Extension
Session A: Students study at home the educational material from e-Campus-LS LAMS sequences include: • Hook activities aiming to engage students with the topic • Q&A activities exploring prior knowledge on the topic • Viewing recorded lectures activities • Self evaluation activities
Session B: Students work in groups of 2-3 LAMS sequences are oriented in: • Experiential learning activities • Explanatory learning activities • Situated learning activities • Problem solving/project based learning activities, • Differentiated teaching • Evaluation or Peer evaluation activities • e-Collaborative sequences in e-Campus-LS -- e-Collaborative sequences in e-Campus-LS • Real-time polling Wireless networking makes real-time or synchronous interaction among all participants in class a very real and increasingly practical possibility. • Videoconferencing Videoconferencing makes it feasible for an invited expert from a remote institution to join a class session. • Capturing and disseminating Discussions, notes, and other in-classroom events can be captured, segmented and disseminated for further study or playing the role of "social objects" to enhance collaboration in e-Campus-LS
Session C: Summarizing and feedback LAMS sequences include: • Summarizing activities • Submitting the work / essay activity • Reflection and feedback activities

Figure 8. The authoring environment in Flipped Campus

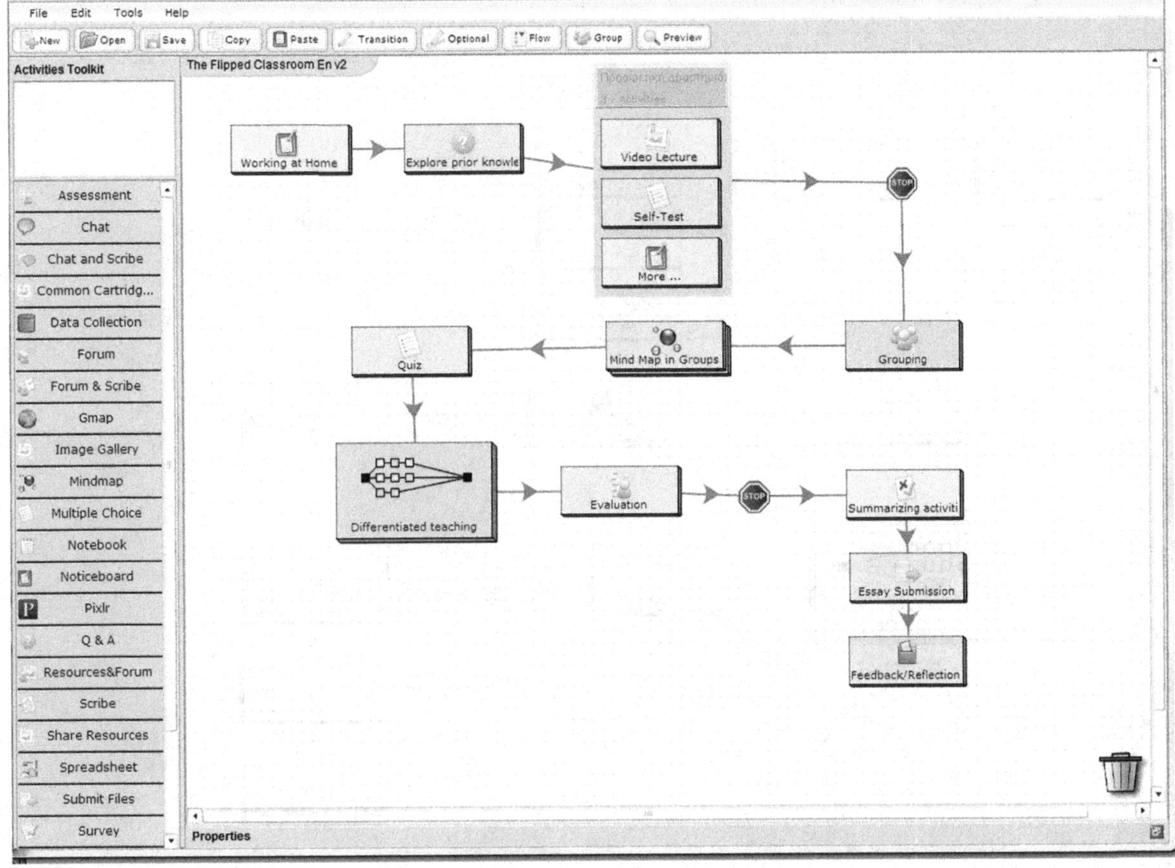

template shows in the Table 4 *(Session B)*, extending the case study towards face-to-face meetings in Open Universities. So, the first level of extension regards students' work in groups implementing activities of:

- Collaborative, experiential, explanatory, problem solving, project based learning
- Differentiated teaching
- Peer evaluation

Methodology of Developing Collaborative sequences

LAMS provides a well developed approach to the creation and sequencing of content-based, single learner, self-paced learning objects. However, there is little understanding of how to create sequences of learning activities which involve groups of learners interacting within a structured set of collaborative —environments.

Trying to enhance this understanding a methodology of developing collaborative sequences according the "Flipping model" in e-Campus is proposed. This 2nd level of extension includes three main sessions of implementing the flipped campus (Table 4).

Figure 9. The students' environment in Flipped Campus

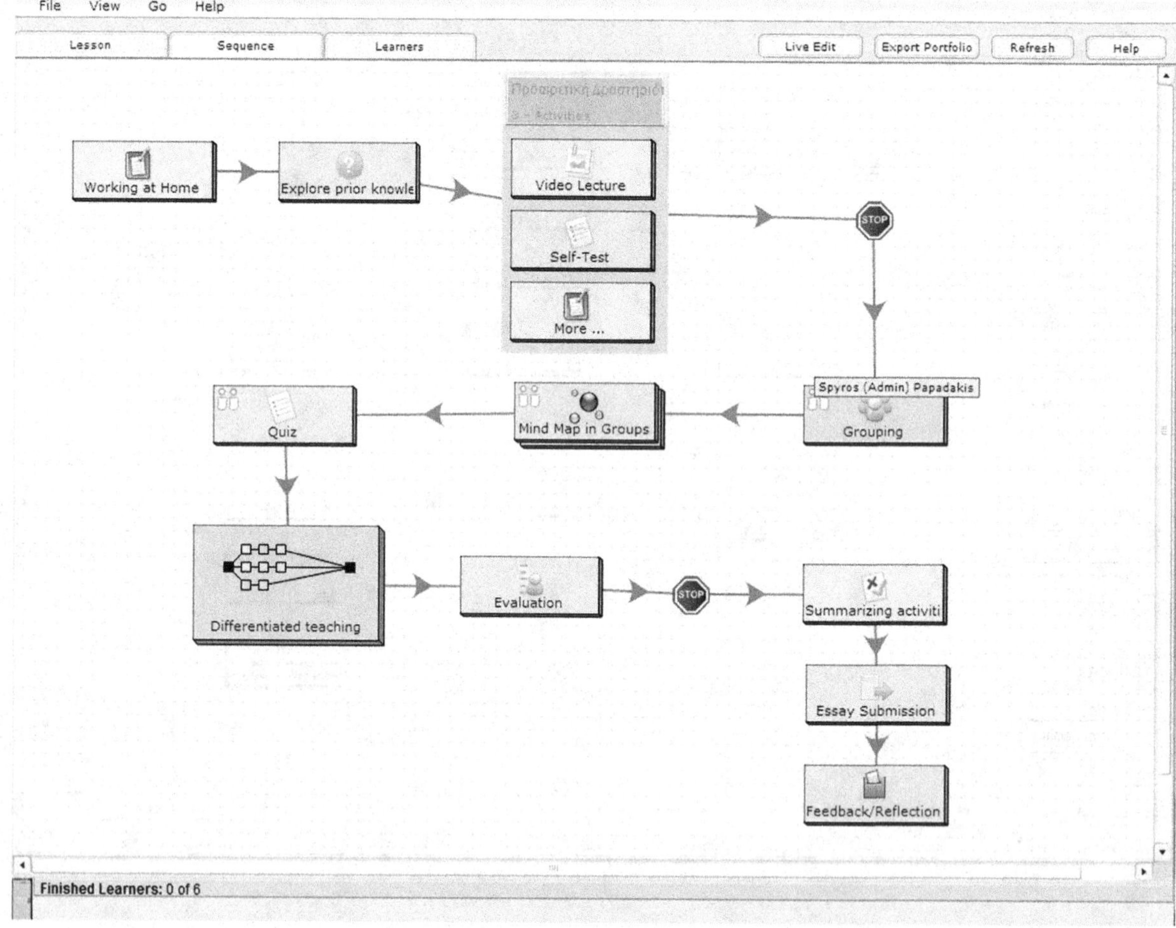

Flipped Campus sequences of learning activities for Conventional Universities can be authored by educators from scratch or based on the proposed template (Figure 8). Students run the activities step by step in home or in Campus (Figures 9 and 10). During their study they are being monitored and guided by their educators online (Figure 11). All activities of the "Flipped Campus sequence" could be implemented online. However, the B session is proposed to be implemented face-to-face.

The proposed methodology combines and elaborates best practices recorded from Open Universities' experience, the advantages from mobile technologies and wireless networking.

RESULTS AND DISCUSSION

The Learning Space of the case study aimed at achieving higher level of interactions among students and their tutor in the distance learning setting of the Hellenic Open University. It also focused on monitoring students' progress and their direct guiding between f2f meetings when they prepare an essay. Tutors participating in the case study characterize LAMS sequences as friendly, adaptive, attractive and easy

Figure 10. Working at home in Flipped Classroom

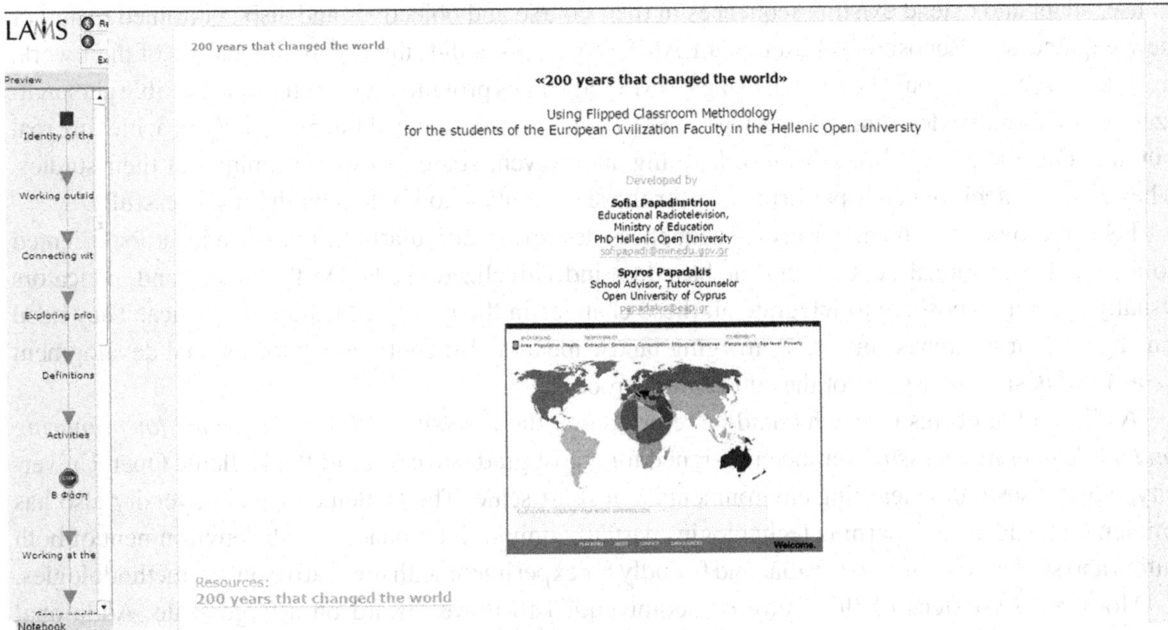

Figure 11. The monitoring student's environment in Flipped Campus

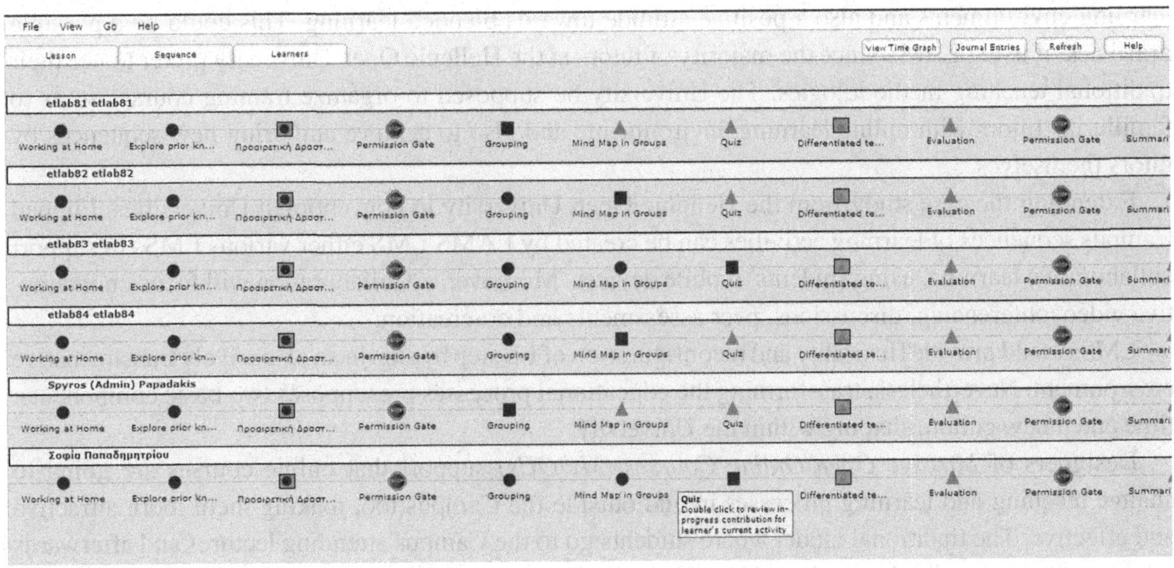

to use. Besides these advantages, they are not familiar of developing such sequences but they are keen to use, adapt and extend existing sequences in their course and objectives and also get trained to author new sequences. A Repository of exemplar LAMS sequences could support all dimensions of their work.

Learning Spaces could be created using LAMS sequences providing innovative and flexible personalized or collaborative learning experiences. LAMS sequences can contribute essentially in achieving real autonomous and personalized distance learning and prevent students from dropping out their studies. They also can achieve better performances for those students who implement them successfully.

LS can provide to students, learning sequences designed particularly from their educators, oriented to different educational goals each time based on individualized needs. On the other hand, educators usually are not so positive to integrate all these changes in their daily educational practice. They need raising of their awareness in a new emerging landscape and also continuous professional development so as to re-design all aspects of the educational process.

As limitation of this research could be referred that the case study "*LAMS sequence for preparing and implementing an essay*" has been designed for a post graduate course of the Hellenic Open University, which uses online learning environments in a short scale. The Hellenic Open University also has implemented advanced learning technologies partially only in pilot phases, so the environment of both tutors and students was not so familiar and friendly for experiment with innovative online methodologies.

However, next steps of this study is recommended to move toward on a large scale. Additional research would be needed to verify the findings from this case study so as to generalize on Open and conventional Universities.

Prerequisite of designing and developing LAMS sequences is the familiarization of tutors with online learning environments and also a positive attitude towards blended learning. This could be a possible drawback of using LAMS since the majority of tutors at the Hellenic Open University prefer to use their traditional teaching methodologies. The University be supposed to organize training courses so as to familiarize tutors with online learning environments and also to achieve authoring new sequences by tutors themselves.

Extending the case study from the Hellenic Open University to conventional Universities, Flipped Campus sequences of learning activities can be created by LAMS LMS either various LMSs to support collaborative learning, using students' mobile devices. Moreover, e-Collaboration will focus on interactive videoconferencing, discussions, peer assessments and co-creation.

LMSs could provide flexibility and reconfiguration of LS step by step in an extensively transformative environment. Nevertheless, transforming the educational processes presupposes two basic components: time and a new culture shaping within the University.

Designers of *Massive Open Online Courses (MOOCs)* support that online courses are going to change teaching and learning processes in and outside the Campus too, making them more attractive and effective. The traditional model where students go to the Campus attending lectures and afterwards implement essays individually should be "flipped". LAMS have the potential to support the implementation of new models for extending MOOCS in integrated blended Learning Spaces, where students could form study groups facilitated by tutors and also exchange knowledge and personal views in both ways online and in person.

CONCLUSION AND FUTURE PLANS

According European Union policies "There is a strong need for flexible, innovative learning approaches and delivery methods: to improve quality and relevance while expanding student numbers, to widen participation to diverse groups of learners, and to combat drop-out. One key way of achieving this, in line with the EU Digital Agenda (European Union, 2010), is to exploit the transformational benefits of ICTs and other new technologies to enrich teaching, improve learning experiences, support personalised learning, facilitate access through distance learning, and virtual mobility, streamline administration and create new opportunities for research".

The *Hellenic Quality Assurance and Accreditation Agency* according to the "Annual report 2011-12 in Higher Education" (Hellenic Quality Assurance and Accreditation Agency, 2012), considers that Universities should implement modern educational methodology, multiple bibliographies in order to enhance active participation and critical thinking in the learning process. Therefore, most universities have developed e-learning courses offering a large number of digital learning resources and some of them have begun providing Open Educational Resources and DL Courses, as well.

DL has become a scout of the new era in education and has contributed to the quality of education. Attending DL courses provides a solution to a growing majority of people who look forward to a second chance in education besides working full time. They need flexible methods beyond place and time constraints and the ICT's revolution can achieve this flexibility providing *ubiquitous learning*.

In the information age of a networked society (Castells, 1996), teaching is still the *scaffolding* (Bruner, 1976) to improve students to a new level of development each time (*zone of proximal development*, Vygotsky, 1978). The Unesco's proposed learning environments in 2002 are still active today, which means that educators use the same fundamental principles to create meaningful, collaborative and situated in real life, environments. Advanced learning technologies could support their work fostering students' e-collaboration and creativity.

All three generations of pedagogy, behaviorism, constructivism and connectivism are necessary to cover the whole spectrum of educational needs of the Net generation' students in the 21st century. Combining pedagogies is crucial for the development of Learning Spaces and could achieve the design of flexible sequences of learning activities.

Educators are always needed to ignite the fire of learning to their students. The learning context is merely common with the previous generation, however educators are able to author, use and reuse electronic collaborative experiences based on Learning Spaces in many rich and meaningful ways (Papadimitriou, 2013).

Universities have the potential to organize sequences of activities in big Repositories, authored by their educators overcoming old attitudes and perceptions. By that innovative Learning Spaces will be developed exploiting global best practices and the long experience gained from the University's educators so far. The sequences will be strongly oriented to concrete objectives of each learning unit in a course and will be available to all educators for adapting, extending and reusing them to achieve blended learning. Learning technologies today have matured to make e-collaboration feasible in diverse ways and mobile devices are evolving more and more towards *ubiquitous learning*.

REFERENCES

Anderson, T. (2009). The dance of technology and pedagogy in self-paced distance education. *Proceedings of the 17th ICDE World Congress, Maastricht*. Retrieved from http://auspace.athabascau.ca:8080/dspace/bitstream/2149/2210/1/The%20Dance%20of%20technology%20and%20Pedagogy%20in%20Self%20Paced%20Instructions.docx

Anderson, T., & Dron, J. (2011). Three Generations of Distance Education Pedagogy. *International Review of Research in Open and Distance Learning*, *12*(3), 80–97.

American Distance Education Consortium (ADEC). (n. d.). ADEC EdFuture 2014 Presentations. Retrieved rom http://www.adec.edu/conference/edfuture-2014/presentations

Avouris, N., & Komis, B. (2003). Synchronous collaboration at a distance: community and interaction issues (in Greek). In A. Lionarakis (Ed.), Proceedings of the 2nd *Hellenic Conference of Open and Distance Learning*, Patra, Hellenic Open University.

Athanasoula-Reppa, A. (2006). Tutor-counselor's role in Open and Distance Learning Lionarakis. In A. Lionarakis (Ed.), *Elements of theory and action*. Athens: Propompos. (in Greek)

Anastasiadis, P. (2007). Advanced Learning Technologies of synchronous and asynchronous transmission serving ODL (in Greek). In A. Lionarakis, (Ed.), *Proceedings of 4th International Conference of Open and Distance Learning*, Issue B Athens: Propompos.

Brown, M. (2013). Learning Spaces. In D. G. Oblinger, & J. L. Oblinger (Eds.), *Educating the net generation.* Retrieved from http://net.educause.edu/ir/library/pdf/pub71011.pdf

Bruckman, A., & Resnick, M. (1995). The MediaMOO Project: Constructionism and Professional Community. *In Convergence*, *1*(1), 94–109.

Bruner, J. (1966). *Toward a theory of instruction*. Cambridge: Belknap Press of Harvard University.

Cameron, L. (2007). Scaffolding Effective Learning Design with Pre-Service Teachers. In C. Montgomerie, & J. Seale (Eds.), *Proceedings of World Conference on Educational Multimedia, Hypermedia and Telecommunications 2007* (pp. 195-202). Chesapeake, VA: AACE.

Castells, M. (1996). *The Information Age: Economy, society and culture: The rise of the networked society* (Vol. 1). Oxford, UK: Blackwell.

Coats, M. (1992). *Open Teaching Toolkit – Effective Tutorials*. The Open University. Retrieved from http://labspace.open.ac.uk/file.php/5718/LDT_12_Intro.pdf

Cornelius, S., & Macdonald, J. (2008). Online informal professional development for distance tutors: Experiences from The Open University in Scotland. *Open Learning: The Journal of Open and Distance Learning*, *23*(1), 43–55. doi:10.1080/02680510701815319

Downes, S. (2007). An introduction to connective knowledge. *Proceedings of the International Conference on Media, knowledge & education—exploring new spaces, relations and dynamics in digital media ecologies*. Retrieved from http://www.downes.ca/post/3303

Dalziel, J. (2010). *Practical e-Teaching Strategies for Predict – Observe – Explain, Problem-Based Learning and Role Plays*. Sydney: LAMS International. Retrieved from http://www.practicaleteaching-strategies.com/

European Union, (2010). *A Digital Agenda for Europe. Digital Agenda COM 245 final*. Retrieved from http://europa.eu/legislation_summaries/information_society/strategies/si0016_en.htm

Fanariti, M., & Spanaka, Ad. (2010, November). Metacognition and learning autonomy during the implementation of essays [in Greek]. *The Open Education Journal, 6*(1), 138–151. Retrieved from http://journal.openet.gr/index.php/openjournal/article/view/105

Fragaki, M., Reynolds, S., & Vanbuel, M. (2009). A pedagogical framework for the effective use of video in class & Exemplary video- based educational scenarios. In *D6.1- A pedagogical framework for the effective use of video in class / Exemplary video-based educational scenarios, EduTubePlus -A European Curriculum Related Video Library and Hybrid e- services for the Pedagogical Exploitation of Video in Class*. Athens: Research Academic Computer Technology Institute.

Freake, St., & Papathanassiou, H. (2006). *Tutorial support for a Level 3 Electromagnetism course - using a blended approach*. Department of Physics and Astronomy, The Open University. Retrieved from http://www.open.ac.uk/picetl/activities/details/detail.php?itemId=4612257d02466&themeId=460d2aa4d3c48

Fung, Y., & Carr, R. (2000). Face-to-Face Tutorials in a Distance Learning System: Meeting student needs. *Open Learning, 15*(1), 35–46. doi:10.1080/026805100115452

Goleman, D. (2006). *Social Intelligence*. Athens: Ellinika Grammata. (in Greek)

Hadzilakos, T., Papadakis, S., & Rossiou, E. (2007). Group Counseling Conferences (in Greek). *Open Education*, 5.

Hellenic Quality Assurance and Accreditation Agency. (2012). The Annual report 2011-12 in Higher Education. Retrieved from http://www.hqaa.gr/data1/%CE%91%CE%94%CE%99%CE%A0_%CE%95%CE%A4%CE%97%CE%A3%CE%99%CE%91_%CE%95%CE%9A%CE%98%CE%95%CE%A3%CE%97_2011-12.pdf

Jekins, J., & Vissere, G. (2001). *E-learning-Everybody's Business*. Retrieved from www.imaginal.nl

JISC. (2013*). Designing Spaces for Effective Learning - A guide to 21st century learning space design*. Retrieved from http://www.jisc.ac.uk/uploaded_documents/JISClearningspaces.pdf

Johnson, D. W., & Johnson, R. T. (1996). Cooperation and the use of technology. In D. H. Jonassen (Ed.), *Handbook of research for educational communications and technology* (pp. 170–198). New York: Simon & Schuster Macmillan.

Jonassen, D. (2000). Revisiting Activity Theory as a Framework for Designing Student- Centered Learning Environments. In D. Jonassen & S. Land (Eds.), *Theoretical foundations of Learning Environments*. LEA.

Keegan, D. (1986). *The foundations of distance education* (2nd ed.). London: Routledge.

Kokkos, A. (2001). Tutor-counselor's role in Open and Distance Learning: the case of Hellenic Open University (in Greek). In A. Lionarakis (Ed.), *Proceedings of 1st International Conference of Open and Distance Learning*, Patra, Hellenic Open University.

Kordaki, M., & Siempos, H. (2010, April 7-10). The JiGSAW Collaborative Method within the online computer science classroom. *Proceedings of the 2nd International Conference on Computer Supported Education*, Valencia, Spain (pp. 65-74).

LAMS. (n. d.). *What is LAMS?* Retrieved from http://www.lamsfoundation.org/

Central, L. A. M. S. (n. d.). *Browsing LAMS sequences*. Retrieved from http://lamscommunity.org/lamscentral/

LAMS community. (n. d.). *LAMS community*. Retrieved from www.lamscommunity.org

Lesson, L. A. M. S. (n. d.). *LessonLAMS*. Retrieved from http://lessonlams.com/lams/

Lave, J., & Wenger, E. (1991). *Situated Learning: Legitimate Peripheral Participation*. New York: Cambridge University Press; doi:10.1017/CBO9780511815355

Lave, J., & Wenger, E. (1998). *Communities of Practice: Learning, Meaning, and Identity*. New York: Cambridge University Press.

Lionarakis, A. (1998). Polymorphic Education: A pedagogical framework for open and distance learning. In A. Szucs & A. Wagner (Eds.), *Transformation, Innovation and Tradition Roles and Perspectives of Open and Distance Learning* (pp. 499–504). Italy: University of Bologna, Universities in a Digital Era.

Lionarakis, A. (2001). Open and Distance polymorphic education: considerations on a qualitative approach of designing educational material. In A. Lionarakis (Ed.), *Views and considerations on ODL*. Athens: Propompos. (in Greek)

Matsagouras, E. (2002). *Critical thinking in teaching*. Athens: Gutenberg. (in Greek)

Matralis, Ch. (1998). Goal and Objectives (in Greek). In A. Kokkos, A. Lionarakis, Ch. Matralis, C. Panayotakopoulos (Eds.), The educational material and new technologies, Open and Distance Learning (vol. C). Patra: Hellenic Open University.

Moore, M. G. (1973). Toward a theory of Independent Learning and Teaching. *The Journal of Higher Education*, *44*(9), 661–679. doi:10.2307/1980599

Moore, M. G. (1980). Independent study. In R. Boyd & J. Apps (Eds.), *Redefining the Discipline of Adult Education* (pp. 16–31). San Francisco: Jossey-Bass.

Papadakis, S., Kordaki, M., & Hadzilacos, T. (2007, November 29-30). Learning Design: the views of Prospective Computer Professionals. In P. Kefalas, A., Sotiriadou, G. Davies & A. McGettrick (Eds.), *Proceedings of Informatics Education Europe II Conference*, Thessaloniki, Greece (pp. 2-11).

Papadimitriou, S., Lampropoulou, N., & Kampylis, P. (2007). The multiple use of videoconference in distance learning of Greek teachers via Greek School Network. (in Greek). In A. Lionarakis (Ed.), *Proceedings of the 4th International Conference Open and Distance Learning*. Athens: Propompos.

Papadimitriou, S., & Lionarakis, A. (2009). Tutor-counselor's role in Open and Distance Learning and the development of his support mechanism in ODL [in Greek]. *The Open Education Journal*, *6*(1), 106–122. Retrieved from http://journal.openet.gr/index.php/openjournal/article/view/103

Papadimitriou, S., Papadakis, S., Lionarakis, A., & Kameas, A. (2011, November). A proposal of using Learning Activities Management System (LAMS) to support the work of Educators in HOU. In A. Lionarakis (Ed.), *Proceedings of the 6th International Conference in Open & Distance Learning*. Retrieved from http://icodl.openet.gr/index.php/icodl/2011/paper/view/51

Papadimitriou, S. (2013). Open Educational Resources and Practices Unfold a Brand New World Towards an Open Higher Education. *Proceedings of the Open Education 2030 Contribution to the JRC-IPTS Call for Vision Papers Part III: Higher Education*. Retrieved from http://is.jrc.ec.europa.eu/pages/EAP/documents/All_OE2030_HE_v%204_author%20revised_OK.pdf

Palloff, R., & Pratt, K. (1999). *Building Learning Communities in Cyberspace: effective strategies for the online classroom*. San Franciso: Jossey-Bass.

Prensky, M. (2001). Digital natives, digital immigrants. [NCB University Press.]. *The Horizon*, *9*(5), 1–6.

Rowntree, D. (1998). Workshops role in Staff development. In C. Latsem & F. Lockwood (Eds.), *Staff development in open and flexible learning*. London: Routledge.

Siemens, G. (2005). A learning theory for the digital age. In *Instructional Technology and Distance Education*, 2(1), 3–10. Retrieved from http://www.elearnspace.org/Articles/connectivism.htm

Tsakarestou, B., & Papadimitriou, S. (2014). *Workshop Co-creation Methodology on 10 May 2014 in Athens, Greece*. Retrieved from http://www.medeanet.eu/event/workshop-%E2%80%9Cco-creation-methodology%E2%80%9D-10-may-2014-athens-greece

University of Northern Colorado. (2013). *The flipped classroom*. Retrieved from www.flippedclassroom.com

Vasala, P., Hatziplis, P., & Lionarakis, A. (2007). Views of undergraduate and postgraduate students at Hellenic Open University on essays: a comparative study of two courses (in Greek). In A. Lionarakis (Ed), *Proceedings of 4th International Conference of Open and Distance Learning*, Athens, Propompos (pp. 296-308).

UNESCO. (2002). *How students learn* (in Greek). International Bureau of Education. Retrieved from http://www.ibe.unesco.org/fileadmin/user_upload/archive/publications/EducationalPracticesSeriesPdf/prac07gr.pdf

Vygotsky, L. S., & Cole, M. (1978). *Mind in society: the development of higher psychological processes*. Cambridge, Mass.; London: Harvard University Press.

Wenger, E. (1998). *Communities of practice, Learning, meaning and identity*. New York: Cambridge University Press; doi:10.1017/CBO9780511803932

KEY TERMS AND DEFINITIONS

Adaptive Personalized Learning: A category of learning, based on the dynamic adaptation of teaching practices aiming to achieve special learning needs and personal goals for each student.

Co-Creation: A collaborative process which takes place when complex non-pre-defined problems occur and serve as challenges to implement common work in small teams proposing and optimising solutions.

Flipped Campus: An upcoming blended method of flexible studies implemented within the flipped classroom strategy. Flipped classroom is an instructional strategy and a type of blended learning that reverses the traditional educational arrangement by delivering instructional content often online, outside the classroom and by moving activities into the classroom.

Interactive Videoconference: A synchronous e-learning tool which provides opportunities to students to exchange views, share data, and participate actively in a dynamic interactive environment with collaborative construction of knowledge in real time.

LAMS LMS: An open source freely available web based *Learning Management System* 'inspired' by the *Learning Design model* for designing and delivering online and offline sequences of learning activities.

Learning Analytics: the measurement, collection, analysis and reporting of data about learners and their contexts, for purposes of understanding and optimising learning and the environments in which it occurs. Educators can use learning analytics from advanced learning systems to monitor and intervene in students' performance depending on their individual progress.

Learning Sequence: A guide of learning activities which serves as a catalyst to enhance the learning process. Students accomplish concrete educational goals in a flexible educational setting, implementing the sequences on their own or in *Campus* supporting by facilitators.

Learning Spaces: A combination of virtual and physical spaces aiming at enhancing learning experiences, interactivity and collaboration between learners of the net generation, educators and educational content, opening up new perspectives in DL.

Peer Assessment: A learning process whereby students grade assignments or tests of their peers, based on benchmarks provided by their teacher. Rubrics are often used in conjunction with peer-assessment. This practice is addressed to improve students' understanding on the learning material and also enhance meta-cognitive skills.

Chapter 14
Online Communities of Practice and Web 2.0

Amir Manzoor
Bahria University, Pakistan

ABSTRACT

In contemporary Knowledge Management, communication and collaboration play very significant role. Knowledge exists within the stakeholders of an organization. Such knowledge, when extracted and harnessed effectively, can become an extremely valuable asset to achieve organizational goals and objectives. This knowledge, embedded in the people, must be properly released through an appropriate channel to make it usable. Through dialogue and discussions, using online tools, this release and reuses of knowledge can be made possible. The Community of Practice (CoP) is a useful organizing concept for enhancing collaboration, sharing knowledge, and disseminating best practices among researchers and practitioners. This chapter explores the concept of Communities of Practice and how Web 2.0 technologies can facilitate the transformation from a conventional community of practice to online community of practice for better and effective online communities of practices.

INTRODUCTION

According to Wenger (2006), a community of practice (CoP) is a group of interested parties that come together to collaborate, and hopefully learn from one another. CoP share a concern or a passion for something they do and learn how to do it better as they interact regularly.

The impact of the Internet on our lives has been pervasive. People are increasingly turning to the social interaction available on the Internet to satisfy their needs, whether these are professional or personal. The Internet offers users fast access to social contacts such as online chat groups and discussion lists to make connections with others. Richness and vitality are important components to ensure that people continue to actively participate in such a phenomenon. Online communities have their roots firmly in the 1960's Counterculture movement (Goldberger, 2003; Matei, 2005; Sun, Rau, & Ma, 2014) which advocated authenticity, deeper social involvement, egalitarian ideals, individualism, less prejudice and

DOI: 10.4018/978-1-4666-9556-6.ch014

Copyright © 2016, IGI Global. Copying or distributing in print or electronic forms without written permission of IGI Global is prohibited.

more emotional satisfaction (Matei, 2005). From the general meeting place of people who shared ideas grew subject-specific communities and professional communities.

Online communities are being increasingly used by for professional support, guidance and inspiration (Bond, 2004; Chen & Chen, 2002; Cornu, 2004; Matei, 2005; Sun, Rau, & Ma, 2014; R. Jamali, Russell, Nicholas, & Watkinson, 2014). These have been organized around subject areas and offer participants the opportunities to develop both personally and professionally. The current popularity of online communities means that it is necessary to examine these communities and determine what characteristics are necessary for them to function effectively. The objective of this chapter is to explore how Web 2.0 technologies can facilitate developing better and effective online communities of practices. The chapter will explore the concept of Communities of Practice and the transformation from a conventional community of practice to online community of practice. . The barriers and motivations for contributing to such communities will be analyzed. The chapter will then move on to assessing how the Web 2.0 technologies facilitate Communities of Practice.

COMMUNITIES OF PRACTICE

Knowledge Management System (KMS) is also a collaborative tool. KMS can be used to create virtual Communities of Practice (CoP) (Wenger, 2006; Tsai & Bagozzi, 2014). Community is a principle feature of collaboration and sharing (Wang, Noe, & Wang, 2014). According to Rao (2002), successful knowledge management heavily relies on "groups of people who work on business-relevant topics across organizational boundaries" (p. 2). The creation of conversations among groups of interested people leads to enhancement of knowledge and business practices (Bolger, 2009). A CoP develops a "shared understanding of what it does, of how to do it, and how it is related to other communities and their practices – in all, a 'world-view' … (CoP's) are a sensible focus for Knowledge Management initiatives (sharing) some common language, purpose and ways of acting" (Walsham, 2001, p. 601). In the collaboration among like-minded people, the one idea that permeates is that multiple brains are better than one. CoPs also provide learning opportunities. As Sinclair (2006) puts it "we learn from our communities" and from our experiences "spending much of our lives learning from others and sharing our experiences and lessons learned with them in exchange" (p. 601). Such community learning promotes dialogue and development of concepts. This dialogue and concept building supports the transformation of tacit knowledge to explicit knowledge (Adams, Brock, Gordon, Grohs, & Kirk, 2014).

Most commonly, a "community of practice" (CoP) refers to a group of people united by a common goal, usually the sharing of professional knowledge or practices (Wenger, 1999; Cox, 2005). This ideal permits a community to persist over time, despite changes in the composition of the community's membership (Cox, 2005). A primary aspect of a CoP involves the cultivation of relationships between experts possessing practical knowledge of interest to the group as a whole, while a secondary concern involves the socialization of newcomers to the group. The social relationship between these two groups—established practitioners and novices—facilitates the transfer of knowledge and ensures continuity within the community (Jin, Wen, & Gough, 2010; McWilliam, 2012).

Originally for an online strategy for business, a CoP also refers to a group of individuals who share experience, comprehension, information, and resources about an area of common interest. It could be defined further as a group of individuals who share common causes, capabilities, or problems within a certain field, discipline, or context. They establish a formal community with the explicit purpose of allowing members to deepen their knowledge and expertise through ongoing interaction. This form of knowledge management and manipulation has many effects on learning in various sectors and on various scales (Saint-Onge & Wallace, 2012). There are three elements of a CoP: 1) a domain, or a defined set of issues, 2) a community, or network of relationships, and 3) practices, or standardized ways of "doing things" (Lin & Lee, 2006). These three elements—domain, community, and practices—draw upon various iterations of social and professional networking.

A CoP can be used to address any set of issues that a networked community decides to address such as collaboration on research projects, business endeavors, and technological innovations. Unlike social networking websites soliciting feedback and consumer opinion, CoPs are more than one-way channels for information dissemination or a social connection. COPs are a vehicle for knowledge management in many places at once. With differing types of knowledge, practitioners can obtain, contribute, reshape, or critique knowledge, in any manner that is consistent with a given CoP's norms and standards. This horizontal movement of communication fragments power and authority and allows more people to become producers of knowledge themselves (Wenger, 2011).

Community is not a new concept. A community is a natural part of human behavior that recognizes people need of socialization and work with others (van Winkelen, 2003). Yet CoPs are more formalized and what van Winkelen (2003) identifies as an "emergent phenomena". CoPs also contain an aspect of design and commitment and formalize their existence through the establishment of common goals and values and seek to meet predetermined needs of their participants. CoPs are also learning environments. According to Hubert, Newhouse and Vestal (2001), CoPs are groups of people who come together to share and to learn from one another. This sharing and learning occurs both face-to-face and virtually. These people are held together by a common interest in a body of knowledge. Their motivation of participation comes from their desire and need to share knowledge (Wenger, 2011).

Community members, through an ongoing daily interactions, extend their knowledge and understanding. CoPs are fundamentally social structures that foster their own learning, manage their own knowledge building and develop competencies within the group (van Winkelen, 2003). Participants become a community through interacting and experiencing common events created by the community (Tosey, 1999). CoPs differ in their effectiveness as learning communities. In some CoPs, there exist few opportunities for peripheral practice and novices find it difficult to gain entry and make a valuable contribution to the community's work. Other communities provide different ways for people to become involved at different levels of competence. Some communities religiously follow long-established traditions while others adopt their own status and practices (Wenger, 2011).

Participation in Communities of Practice

There exist many studies (Ardichvili, et al, 2003; McLure Wasko & Faraj, 2002; ;Hall & Graham, 2004; Ridings & Gefen, 2004; Zhang & Watts, 2008; Wang & Fesenmaier, 2003; Schneider, Von Krogh, & JäGer, 2013; Zhou, Wu, Zhang, & Xu, 2013; Fugelstad et al., 2012) that seek to determine what motivates/demotivates people to practice in CoPs. CoPs are not viewed as forums in which to socialize or form new relationships. According to McLure Wasko and Faraj (2000), "work units behaving as focused communities are more innovative" (p. 162). It is essential to understand what factors motivate such innovation and participation (Bolger, 2009).

Motivations for Participation

Some clear benefits for less well-informed participants to participate in any knowledge sharing activity include hope to gain more knowledge and insight of experienced people. However, there must also be some benefits for knowledge providers who are prepared to share their knowledge to these less knowledgeable members of the community. Benefits or returns for participation can be classified into two categories: tangible and intangible (McLure Wasko & Faraj, 2000; Bolger, 2009).

Tangible Returns for Participation

According to McLure Wasko and Faraj (2000), CoPs provide access to "useful information and expertise, answers to specific questions, and personal gain" (p. 163). CoPs provide quick and most up-to-date help unavailable elsewhere. CoPs are excellent source of expertise (Barab, Scott, Del Valle Martin, & Fang, 2012). Take example of online CoP that makes up DRUPAL (an interactive web-building application). While the DRUPAL technology is not revolutionary, the community that supports it is extremely proactive in knowledge collaboration (Bolger, 2009). DRUPAL is open source and members can extend DRUPAL's capabilities. Members are encouraged to develop new functionalities and make them available to the community. Members can use online forums to resolve issues they are experiencing with DRUPAL. Members can use threaded discussion forums to get help on specific problems. According to McLure Wasko and Faraj (2000), the prospect that contribution many enhance "standing in the profession, establish a reputation that will hopefully translate into a job … generate personal clients is foremost" (p. 166).

Intangible Returns for Participation

First, motivation such as satisfaction and self-actualization, exposing expertise and gaining peer recognition for such can drive participation in the community. Second, people can view community collaboration as a challenge and encouraged to refine thinking and develop new insights. Third, some people may participate in a community for fun. They gain enjoyment through learning and sharing with others. Fourth, participants can keep themselves abreast of innovations and issues in their field. With the CoP, it may be difficult and untimely to discover (Yen, Hsu, & Huang, 2011; Bolger, 2009).

Barriers to Participation

Conversely to analyzing why people participate, barriers need to be identified. First, there is no financial reward for participating in the CoP (Bolger, 2009; Hughes, Jewson, & Unwin, 2013). Such rewards could not be possibly implemented and maintained and may not align with a community spirit. However, as Walsham (2001) states, "in a context where individuals see little in the way of financial reward for knowledge-sharing activities, it is not surprising that knowledge hoarding may take place" (p. 603). Rewards exist in some form. Rewards must be viewed as individual and personal and the benefits of the intangible returns must be emphasized over tangible returns (Jeon, Kim, & Koh, 2011). Walshman studied the benefits and limitations of computer systems in the context of CoPs. According to Walsham (2001), a "strongly individual-based reward system did not encourage collaborative behavior" (p. 603). This is an area for top management need to address to promote new CoP initiatives (Bolger, 2009).

Second, McLure Wasko and Faraj (2000) states that "People must become comfortable with their own level of expertise in order to feel their participation is valuable" (p. 169). This aspect of motivation needs to be nurtured in individuals over time. However, feeling comfortable and confident certainly becomes stronger when participation increases and positive feedback is expected (Bouchamma & Michaud, 2011).

Third, Walsham (2001) noted that there is a "danger of being seen to be politically incorrect in terms of current organisational thinking" (p. 603). Users may feel hesitant to share views in a CoP that are not strictly in keeping with top management point of view. This is particularly notable for public sector organizations (Sayed and Rowland, 2004). In their discussion of Wiki technologies in public sector, Guy (2006) noted that some aspects may "go against the organisation's acceptable usage policy (and) by their very nature provide a collective view and this may not always represent an unbiased view." (p. 4). A possible solution could be restricting access to a CoP to members only. According to Walsham (2001), that means "individuals in a community of practice may share views, knowing that their organizational superiors have no access to their exchanges" (p. 603).

WEB 2.0 TECHNOLOGIES FOR COMMUNITIES OF PRACTICE

For contemporary CoPs to be most effective, Allee (1997) argues that the World Wide Web (WWW) is an ideal location for knowledge sharing. According to Alleee, knowledge requires community and Internet is the best place that illustrates this principle. Similarly, knowledge creation and transfer was described by McLure Wasko and Faraj (2000) as "social phenomena and an integral part of a community" (p. 160). When communities use a KMS as a host platform for their collaboration, knowledge is captured, organized, formalized, distributed, and accessible to other members. The system has the power to extend and transform existing knowledge and merge it with knowledgebase of other members (Hislop, 2013).

With these social and functional considerations in mind, we should keep in mind that existing CoPs are bounded by geography and, without efficient forms of communication, community members at different geographical locations cannot get optimal benefits from the dispersion of knowledge (Jin, Wen, & Gough, 2010; Wenger, 2011). The most efficient form of communicating knowledge within a CoP has been through in-person interaction (Tierney & Palmer, 2013). However, this form of communication can severely limit the scope of the conventional CoP to immediately surrounding geography (Jin, Wen, & Gough, 2010). Web 2.0 technologies offer novel ways of undertaking efficient communication despite vast geographical distances. Web 2.0 technologies confer the capability to drastically reshape the scale and scope of CoPs.

Web 2.0 facilitates communication, information sharing, interoperability, user-centric design, and collaboration on the web. Popular Web 2.0 tools include Blogs, WIKIS, RSS Feeds, Tagging, Social Networks, and Search Engines (Brown, 2012). Web 2.0 tools are fast becoming leading tools that provides more progressive use of users time spent online "contributing (to the) contents of their Knowledge Space" (Lee & Lan, 2007, p. 49). In general, people are making extended uses of the web as intranets spread within organizations. Utilizing technologies which are already existing (such as SQL databases, message boards, JavaScript etc.) and the extension of such technologies using familiar and easy-to-use tools (such as AJAX, XML, and Flash) mean the real knowledge management side of a KMS can become its true focus (Venkatesh, Croteau, & Rabah, 2014). Nissen et al. (2000) noted that some KMS's are supportive in nature. These KMS organize, formalize, and distribute knowledge in the enterprise and support people to apply, evolve, and create knowledge in the organization. Such a KMS provides sharing of knowledge with its users and has the facility and ability to create new knowledge without having an extensive technology focus (Bolger, 2009).

Note that World Wide Web has not changed to facilitate knowledge management and the development of powerful KMS. What has changed, is the increased use of interactive trends and the discovery of powerful organizational communication across the World Wide Web. Industries are replacing standalone applications with distributed enterprise applications. The focus of the World Wide Web has changed to become a space for collaboration, enhancing creativity among people/groups who share interests (Eisenstadt & Vincent, 2012).

Web 2.0 offers increased collaboration speeds in the virtual, or online, realm, thus enhancing the functionality of CoPs. Web 2.0 allows users to transmit knowledge, research, data, and practical experience more easily (Kai-Wai Chu & Kennedy, 2011). The ubiquity of the Internet allows for interaction between experts from different areas of the globe. Expert-to-expert interaction enables communities to disseminate information more quickly and effectively. Another potential benefit of virtual CoPs is their ability to foster multiculturalism, thus expanding a community's diversity and versatility. Multicultural interaction creates a higher level of understanding and fosters an increase in social skills, and these communities exist in virtual realms because of the broad access that exists through online social networking (Hossain & Aydin, 2011). Observations and practices that are common in specific parts of the globe may become accessible worldwide when the communities become part of the virtual realm.

PLANNING FOR ONLINE COMMUNITIES OF PRACTICE

Community Planning

There exist some common pitfalls of online community projects. In the process of technology evaluation, we must remember overall goals of the online community. The process of technology evaluation should be an iterative process. In this process, user scenarios and functional requirements should be determined and supporting technologies should be examined against these scenarios and functional requirements (Bolger, 2009; Kraut et al., 2012).

Community Goals

Goals of the online community should first be clearly identified before the process of technology evaluation starts. A consensus needs to be developed about the value created by the community for its members. In addition to this, how the beneficial outcomes will be achieved in near future. Potential members must be able to clearly understand the community purpose. The goals thus guide participation and growth of memberships (Meyerhoff & Strycharz, 2013).

Audience Needs

Along with goals, understanding the needs of potential members is also important. The community's purpose determines the kind of potential members to attract. A deep understanding of the requirements and online behavior of these potential members of community is needed. Functionality a technology platform should provide depends on few things needed for active engagement of all segments of community (Meyerhoff & Strycharz, 2013).

Audience Scenarios and Functional Requirements

Community initiators need to translate community's needs and objectives into a set of clear functional priorities. These functional priorities guide technology selection and configuration (Spagnoletti & Resca, 2012). User scenarios are concise statements which describe probable tasks that potential community members would perform. These scenarios may include many steps a user takes to achieve a certain goal (such as find and download a resource). These needs not be exhaustive, but they should be enough to capture all the key illustrations pertinent to the potential members of the community (Cruickshank, 2011).

Wenger, White, and Smith (2009) developed a list of common orientations that communities can have. These orientations are as follows:

- **Meeting Support:** Some communities are formed around face-to-face meetings that can result in either follow-up online meetings or a combination of online and offline meetings. Communities formed around online meetings may provide sharing of information and decision making.
- **Open-ended Conversations:** Some communities are formed around discussions and community members take part in a series of ongoing online discussions.
- **Project-Orientations:** Communities formed around projects are based on sharing key project information.
- **Content Collection and Organization:** Content-oriented communities provide collection and categorization of content useful for community members. These communities may also develop and synthesize information and dependent on file repositories to collect and categorize content.
- **Access to Expertise:** Some communities are formed around the idea that knowledge can be useful as collected content but we still we need the right person with the right expertise. These communities make experts available to community members for questions and answers.
- **Interpersonal Relationships:** Some communities form around building and maintaining interpersonal relationships. The purpose of these communities could be explicit learning or to build/ maintain a network to achieve personal/professional objectives of its members. Often closed, these communities and their members generally are very concerned about who becomes a member of the community.
- **Individual Participation:** Some communities form around user participation. In such communities, individual participate may vary from one to another. These communities offer a higher level of personalization.
- **Community Growth:** Some communities are formed around content mining. Members perform active mining of community content for valuable information. For these communities to work, active governance and accepted leadership is a must.
- **Context-Orientation:** Some communities are mission-focused and thus have a unique identity. Such communities may bring people together from different organizations or from a single organization. While some of these communities may be open or closed, the context in which they work is their key feature.

Scenarios can also be developed based on desired level of interaction, the desired kind of knowledge development, the kind of resources required for community, and community members' characteristics (Bolger, 2009; Dascalu, Bodea, Lytras, De Pablos, & Burlacu, 2014). Following is the discussion of some possible levels of interaction.

- **One-Way Dissemination of Knowledge:** In this type of interaction, producer(s) of knowledge disseminate knowledge/resources to participants who are primarily knowledge consumers. Comments might be posted and questions may be asked from participants. Participants may also post suggestions about the disseminated content /resources. However, the flow of knowledge is primarily unidirectional.
- **Shared Knowledge Development:** In this type of interaction, multiple users work in a group to achieve a common goal (e.g. managing a project) and build knowledge in multiple people at once.
- **Many-to-Many Interactions:** In this type of interaction, a small group of users is the source of knowledge for a wider group of users. However, all users are peers irrespective of whether they are knowledge provider or knowledge consumers. In these interactions, all participants act voluntarily. As such, it is the most difficult to foster. Motivating users to actually contribute knowledge can be very difficult.

However, these interactions can help in identification of relationships among users and to develop user scenarios that can guide technical requirements. Once user scenarios are identified, community initiators can prioritize them in the context of the overall community goals and members' needs. In this process, first, audience needs should be mapped to audience scenarios. Second, an importance value (on a scale of 1-5 for example) should be assigned to each audience/audience need. Third, these importance ratings should be used to prioritize the list of user scenarios. Fourth, in a parallel activity, similar importance ratings should be assigned to the community goals. Scenarios providing clear support to the most important community goals should be assigned additional priority. Some subjective analysis can also be done on top of these importance ratings to come up with the optimal set of functional priorities (Bolger, 2009).

Community designers are often tempted to create a large set of priority scenarios and technology features. However, community designers should perform a critical review of the final set of priority scenarios. The final scenarios should satisfy community goals and members' needs. The scenarios should include a few discrete, well-connected activities and provide small amount of functionality. These activities should be such that potential community members having different preferences are engaged with community without overwhelming them with technology options. Communities can be more effective when they do right a small number of activities. At their beginning, communities run into problems when they try to provide some sort of ultimate solution to many potential problems (Venkatesh et al., 2012).

Functionality and Pilot Testing

The leaders of the community need to have a set of prioritized scenarios in order determine appropriate technical functionality for the developed scenarios. Community leaders often are tempted to provide more and more functionality. However, excessive functionality can shift community focus from its core value-creating activities. Communities of professionals tend to focus on providing more functionality. This is because this audience is busy, willing to have quick technology solutions, and already overloaded with information. This audience needs quick access to information needed to do their jobs. As such, the desire of such audience is access to functionality that will help them get such information (e.g. the information needed to prepare presentation for the next meeting).

The choice of functionality plays a significant role for the community's purpose. A blog might be a better choice for a community whose key objective is knowledge sharing by a small group of knowledge providers with a large group of knowledge consumers. Using blogs, the knowledge providers can provide useful and easily consumable knowledge and get feedback from knowledge consumers. A discussion forum may be inappropriate here if knowledge consumers only want to consumer knowledge and not provide feedback to the knowledge providers. If a community's key value proposition is to connect members working on the same topics, an appropriate choice may be a discussion forum. This forum would allow its users to post and answer questions and share resources. Social networking functionality (such as user profiles and wall posts) may also help users. A blog for this community can split user's questions and conversations and might actually detract from mass of the discussion area. In both communities described above, a Wiki wouldn't work well because Wikis are often less useful for less structured communities facilitating ad-hoc, on-going knowledge sharing (Connectededucators.org, 2011).

Communities should start with a small feature set and a limited roll out w.r.t. technology and scale of community. In other words, community leaders should begin with a pilot of the community. Historically, online communities, once activated, are guided by community members who decide the community direction and purpose regardless of initial intention about the community.

This natural process pose no problems if the original community goals remain in line. Community leaders should adopt a flexible approach and be ready to accept different ways to achieve the same goals because these emerging new ways may imply modifications in technical functionality and other fine tunings to enhance the community's development. Additionally, emerging patterns of member activity may be an indication of new required functionality to improve the usability of the community. For example, an emerging pattern of members' regular access to images from discussions may suggest that providing a photo gallery functionality may be valuable feature for community. When a pilot is launched first, community designers can identify emerging activity patterns and put them into practice without risking a change in community's original direction (Valaitis, Akhtar-Danesh, Brooks, Binks, & Semogas, 2011).

Community Management

Community leaders should know that launching a community requires heavy investment of their time. Many successful communities have emerged organically due to significant effort of their members and developers. This effort included development of content for the community and norms of community interaction. Users generally do not expect very large amount of existing content from a community before becoming a member but they do expect that the available content must be seeded (Valaitis, Akhtar-Danesh, Brooks, Binks, & Semogas, 2011). Within the technological infrastructure of the community, there must exist explicit and clear directions and norms of the community. This requires skilful user experience configuration and choice of wording. User training on new technology is important but a large liability (Connected Educators, 2011).

Community users not only need static help (e.g. frequently asked questions) but also need some sort of dynamic help (such as webinars) so that they clearly understand the use of various tools and how to provide effective contribution to the community. Growing a new non-existent community requires an additional effort of recruiting participants, bringing them together, and community moderation/marketing. Community leaders must keep online discussions active and make active regular contact with the community. Community leaders must understand use of community tools by the members and the content these members consider most valuable. With this analysis, future technology use can be decided.

Web 2.0 Community Tools and their Functionality

There exist different types of valuable community tools that provide different functionalities (Bolger, 2009; Barnett, Jones, Bennett, Iverson, & Bonney, 2013; Venkatesh, Croteau, & Rabah, 2014).

Content Tools

Content Management and File Repositories: Many CoPs provide sharing and dissemination of knowledge. Community platforms should integrate traditional web content management with other forms of collaboration such as social networking. Content can be provided as either file lists with folders or as hierarchal listing of files. The amount of content a community might provide determines the choice of needed features with larger amounts of data requiring extensive browsing and organizing ability. Community size and members' familiarity with each other is also important. Smaller online communities belonging to existing offline communities often results in more useful communities.

- **Blogs:** Blogs are important tools for facilitating discussions when users want to go beyond simple questions and answers. With blogs, user can post a brief idea or opinion and invite other users for their comments. For active participation, group blogs should provide an intuitive user interface that users can use to include different forms of multimedia (such as images and videos) in blog posts. This interface should also allow highlighting the authors with their profile and pictures. With this, users can gain a clear understanding of relationships to be made and the expertise to be utilized. Examples of some blog software are WordPress, TypePad, and BlogSpot. There are other all-in-one software packages (e.g. Drupal Commons and Central Desktop) that provides blog functionality as part of their large portfolio of features.
- **Microblogs/Status Updates:** Microblogs can be called status updates. Microblogs provide anyone the ability to post short thoughts/quick observations. Twitter is one good example that users can use to send tweets (a 140-character short message). Today, microblogs provide serious community interaction. Some examples of microblog applications include Twitter and Tumblr. There are other all-in-one software packages (e.g. Jive and Drupal Commons) that provides microblog functionality as part of their large portfolio of features.
- **Wikis:** Wikis are special collaborative content development websites that users can use to add and edit pages. To develop software documentation or frequently asked questions, wikis are a good choice. Since wikis do not provide preexisting structure, they are not a good choice for novice users and often work better for more sophisticated users and for those with extensive experience of content development. Some popular examples of wiki software are MediaWiki, SocialText, PBWorks, and Confluence.

Collaborative Document Authoring Tools

One good example is Google Documents. These tools work like a familiar software (such as a word processor, spreadsheet, or a presentation tool). Simultaneous editing of a document by multiple users is possible. All edits made are tracked for reference and provide immediate feedback to principal author(s). Some more examples of collaborative document authoring tools are NoodleTools, TitanPad, Wiggio, and Writeboard. There are other all-in-one community software packages (e.g. Basecamp and ProjectSpaces) that provides collaborative document authoring functionality as part of their large portfolio of features.

- **Social Bookmarking:** Online CoPs should be able to collect links from across the web. That allows a great deal of content, already posted somewhere else, to be brought on a single page for the community so that users can easily access it. Using social bookmarking services, community leaders and members can collect and categorize external web content. Users can also provide annotation and comments that others users of social bookmarking service can see when they visit the page. Some popular examples of social bookmarking service provides include backlinksflow.com (world renowned link builder and SEO specialist), onlywire.com (a fast, secure automation tool to submit content to the top Social Media Networks like Facebook, Twitter and Google+.), Diigo.com (a social bookmarking website which allows signed-up users to bookmark and tag webpages). Additionally, it allows users to highlight any part of a webpage and attach sticky notes to specific highlights or to a whole page), Delicious.com (a social bookmarking web service owned by Yahoo and used for storing, sharing, and discovering web bookmarks), and StumbleUpon.com (a form of web search engine that finds and recommends web content to its users and allow users to discover and rate Web pages, photos and videos that are personalized to their tastes and interests using peer-sourcing and social-networking principles).
- **Media Libraries:** In many cases, communities want to share multimedia (such as videos and images) in order both capture knowledge and build comradeship. Some community tools provide a way to do this with the tool and users can also use outside services as the primary source of their content. The outside services provide an excellent user experience. Community managers are free from the worries of hosting large amounts of user content. Some examples of these outside service providers include Flickr (an image hosting and video hosting website, and web services suite that is owned by Yahoo) and YouTube (a video-sharing website that allows users to upload, view, and share videos, and it makes use of Adobe Flash Video and HTML5 technology to display a wide variety of user-generated and corporate media video). There are other all-in-one software packages (e.g. Ning and BuddyPress) that provides this functionality as part of their large portfolio of features.

Data Visualization Tools

Data visualization tools are used by communities to share information and knowledge within the data. These tools can make this data easier for members to access, use, and share across acknowledge levels in a community. Some examples of these data visualization tools are Google Spreadsheets (part of a software office suite offered by Google within its Google Drive service. The suite allows users to create and edit documents online while collaborating with other users in real-time), Many Eyes (a web community that connects visualization experts, practitioners, academics and enthusiasts, offers this technology and expertise, along with ways to share and learn from others), Swivel, Dygraphs (allows users to explore and interpret dense data sets), ZingChart (a JavaScript charting library designed to quickly render fast, beautiful charts with big data sets), InstantAtlas,Timeline, Exhibit, Modest Maps, Leaflet, WolframAlpha (an online service that answers factual queries directly by computing the answer from externally sourced curated data, rather than providing a list of documents or web pages that might contain the answer), Visual.ly (a community platform for data visualization and infographics), and Visualize Free (Connected Educators, 2011).

Member Interaction Tools

- **User Profiles:** Social networking is valuable for large communities. This is because it can help build, strengthen, and maintain participants' relationships (Cambridge, 2010). Members connect with people to involve in new types of interactions. For social networking platforms (such as Facebook) this is especially true. The Facebook profile includes both biographic information and a history of user contributions. A rich profile feature can encourage participation, help members have a more comfortable interaction, and sharing with unknown people. For tropical communities, this aspect is because in these communities users are seeking knowledge. There exist many all-in-one software packages (such as BuddyPres and Ning) that provide user profile feature.
- **Member Comments:** Many online communities provide user comments feature. Users can post comments on content posted by others. When comments are embedded in web pages, documents, and blog posts, rich discussions on content can take place and lead to an enhancement of both quality and quantity of user interaction. Communities can use advanced comments tools to provide rich discussion threads, easy access, and tracking of an individual's comments posted across different communities. Examples of some all-in-one platforms that provide this comments functionality include Disqus (a blog comment hosting service for web sites and online communities that uses a networked platform and includes various features, such as social integration, social networking, user profiles, spam and moderation tools, analytics, email notifications, and mobile commenting) and Omeka (a free, open source content management system for online digital collections that allows users to publish and exhibit cultural heritage objects, and extend its functionality with themes and plugins).
- **Discussions:** Meaningful discussions are important for knowledge sharing. In discussions, all participants have equal status. Some example of all-in-one community platforms that provide this functionality include LinkedIn, Facebook, phpBB (a free, open-source Internet forum package written in the PHP scripting language that provide support for multiple database engines (PostgreSQL, MySQL, Oracle, SQL Server), flat message structure (as opposed to threaded), hierarchical subforums, topic split/merge/lock, user groups, multiple attachments per post, full-text search, plugins and various notification options such as e-mail, Jabber instant messaging, and ATOM feeds), and ezboard (a provider of free and paid hosted Internet forums for use by webmasters and message board administrators who have little to no experience running a web site).
- **Webinars:** These tools are generally stand-alone that run alongside other community tools. Webinars provide synchronous, virtual interaction which require simultaneous presence of all members online. Users can share their screens in real time. This could provide a more powerful and efficient way to get work done. Some examples of tools used to provide webinar services include WebEx (provides on-demand collaboration, online meeting, web conferencing and video-conferencing applications), Adobe Connect (software used to create information and general presentations, online training materials, web conferencing, learning modules, and user desktop sharing), Elluminate Live (a web conferencing program that rented out virtual Spaces where virtual

schools and businesses can hold classes and meetings), and Dimdim (a web-based platform for realtime, rich-media collaboration and meetings including free web conferencing service where users could share desktops, show slides, collaborate, chat, talk and broadcast via webcam).

Member Feedback and Research

- **User-Generated Ratings:** In many communities, members can rate the utility of content. Users can comment on content, rate the content, and find the ratings and usage of content by other members. For community sites that provide less content, content ratings can be a powerful tool that users can use to quickly find the most useful content and understand its use by other members of community. Some examples of such user ratings are ratings and reviews on Amazon.com and eBay and Facebook's 'Like' feature. A Like button on Facebook is a feature where the user can express that they like, enjoy or support certain content. Facebook also display the number of users who liked each content, and show a full list of them.
- **Polls and Surveys:** These tools facilitate participation and involvement from of large group of participants. This is because not all users post to a discussion forum or a blog. These tools can reduce fear among users for posting ideas in large communities. This fear factor can result in an ecosystem of non-participation where we see only few dominant participants lead a large group of hesitant participants. Examples of tools that provide these polls and surveys include SurveyMonkey; SurveyGizmo; Wufoo. Some all-in-one community platforms (such as Jive and Drupal Commons) also provide this feature as part of a portfolio of a large feature set (Connectededucators.org, 2011).

Project Coordination

- **Event Calendars:** This tool can be used to provide a central listing of events. Using this list, members can get information about upcoming events/activities and past meetings. Some all-in-one community platforms (such as Centrla Desktop and Ning) provide this functiolaity. Meetup provides online access to commercial offline events. Eventbrite (www.eventbrite.com) is a global marketplace for live experiences that allows people to find and create events in more than 150 countries.
- **Task-management Tools:** This tool is important for a more project-oriented community that require task management and milestone tracking. Some examples of such tools include BaseCamp (a web-based project-management tool) and ProjectSpace (a total project managment solution accessed by any browser platform). Some all-in-one community platforms (such as CentralDesktop) also provide this tool as part of a portfolio of a large feature set.
- **Decision-support Tools:** Groups collaborating on projects need to have discussions and develop strategies. Decision support tools can support decision-making processes by facilitating ranking of ideas, establishing consensus, and systematically analyzing a situation. Some all-in-one project management software (such as SAS Streamworks) provide decision support tools. IdeaScale and HERMES are online idea ranking and deliberation systems. IdeaScale is a cloud-based software company that licenses an innovation management platform employing the principles and practices of crowdsourcing. HERMES is a web-based system that augments classical decision making approaches by supporting argumentative discourse among decision makers.

Incentive and Recognition Services

- **Badges:** This tool can be used to indicate levels of achievement within a community in order motivate participation and help members identify experts. Users earn, give, and receive badges that indicate their achievements. These badges become part of user profile. Edmodo is an educational website that takes the ideas of a social network and refines them and makes it appropriate for a classroom. Using Edmodo, students and teachers can reach out to one another and connect by sharing ideas, problems, and helpful tips (Connected Educators, 2011). The customized versions of all-in-one community platforms (such as BuddyPress and DrupalCommons) also provide the badge functionality.
- **Rewards Systems:** This tool is a step ahead of badges that users can use to earn physical rewards for their actions performed within community. Use of this tool could increase costs but also increases incentives. Some examples of these reward system include uBoost (an online student performance recognition and rewards platform,); Webcentiv (online incentives management system that is easy to set up, highly efficient and can be accessed at any time by any number of people in any number of locations); and Love2Reward.co.uk (one of the largest providers of reward management products and services in the UK).
- **Reputation Management Systems:** This tool can help establish whether the person making a comment is reliable or not. This tool can assess a user's behavior so that other users could establish the user's history of reputation. This tool can provide added contextual information about author's general reputation. Amazon and eBay provides "rate the seller" tool. Seller ratings function like a personal referral: before making a purchase, customer can view comments as well as star ratings submitted by previous buyers. Customer can use the link sent in reminder e-mail, or rate the seller via the "Buyer Account" link after receiving item from the seller. Slashdot (a news website that features news stories on science and technology that are submitted and evaluated by its users, and each story has a comments section attached to it) and other community news sites can also provide this functionality.

Social Media and Community Sites

- **General Social Networking Sites:** Online communities have blurred boundaries mainly due to the proliferation of social networking sites. Communities provide certain activities within site and push certain activities to third-party sites. Some communities may only focus on third-party sites though it limits community functionality. On the other hand, many communities coexist with the social networking sites. These communities provide core activities occurring onsite while some activities are extended into social networks. A number of platforms support automated linking to the Facebook or LinkedIn. Many APIs are also offered by the major social networking sites for custom integration. In some cases, community mangers use both onsite and offsite communities in parallel. The Facebook API is a platform for building applications that are available to the members of the social network of Facebook. The API allows applications to use the social connections and profile information to make applications more involving, and to publish activities to the news feed and profile pages of Facebook, subject to individual users privacy settings. With the API, users can add social context to their applications by utilizing profile, friend, Page, group, photo, and event data. The API uses RESTful protocol and responses are localized and in XML format (Facebook, 2014).

- **Topic-specific Community Sites:** These sites are platforms that serve specific contemporary sectors (e.g. education sector). Many features of these sites are shared by more general-purpose communities. These sites may also include features specific to the sector which the community is serving (in this case education). These features may include privacy and control for social networking. In some cases, these sites can provide means to recruit members because may already be participants of these types of sites but in different contexts. These sites provide high level of security and privacy and are generally tailored to meet specific audience. Some examples of such sites in education sector include edmodo.com and Edublogs.org (a web-based service that archives and supports student and teacher learning by facilitating reflection, questioning by self and others, collaboration and by providing contexts for engaging in higher-order thinking).
- **Content-type-specific Social Media Sites:** These social media sites are formed around sharing of specific content. One good example is famous Youtube.com that share videos. These sites are good choice for distributing media content around which community interaction can be encouraged. Vimeo is another famous site for sharing videos. Flickr and Picasa are popular sites for sharing photos. Slideshare is a famous site for sharing presentations and Scribd for sharing documents. Swivel and Many Eyes are two famous sites for sharing data.

Supporting Utilities

- **Notifications:** For an active community, notifications are important. Email remains the primary way communities use to notify members of community activities. Busy people can use notifications sent via email to stay informed about what's happening (such as new resources and discussions) without logging in to the community site. Content syndication standards (such as RSS and Atom) and SMS notifications are generally preferred by users. Many all-in-one community platforms (such as Basecamp and Central Desktop) provide notifications feature.
- **Public and Private Content:** Many communities place much of the community content on publically accessible pages. Password protecting the resources raises the barriers to participation and some users may be discouraged to join the community. However, password protection also provide added trust and privacy and different tools can provide different level of protection. In some cases, the whole community site can be private. Other sites may make private some sections, or some content. Many all-in-one community platforms (such as Jive and Drupal Commons) allow content protection. Facebook allows a more granular protection of the content.
- **Application Programming Interface (API):** An API provides a set of rules and specifications to be followed by web-based applications in their interactions with other applications. Use of APIs is a more recent trend. APIs can be used to develop mashup applications that combine data and functionality from multiple sources to create new information (Connected Educators, 2011).
- **Centralized User Authentication and Login:** Web-based authentications services are one of the most common techniques of user authentication and login used by today's websites. Use of this feature reduces barriers to join the community because the prospective member can use a single account to access all networked resources. There are open authentication standards available such as OpenID (an open standard and decentralized protocol by the non-profit OpenID Foundation

that allows users to be authenticated by certain co-operating sites, known as Relying Parties or RP, using a third party service) and OAuth (an open standard to authorization that provides client applications a 'secure delegated access' to server resources, on behalf of a resource owner, without sharing their credentials). Famous sites such as Facebook, Twitter, Google, and Yahoo also provide authentication/login services.

- **Web Metrics:** Increasing number of web applications offering their own set of tailored web metrics. These metrics are useful to understand tools usage i.e. who uses them and for what purposes. Google Analytics (a service offered by Google that generates detailed statistics about a website's traffic and traffic sources and measures conversions and sale) and Omniture (an online marketing and web analytics service) are examples of services that provide these metrics.

Community Architecture

To provide coherent community service, desired and available functionality must be merged together. Here 'coherent' is not necessarily a single solution. Community designers need to consider the different community orientations and map them to possible functionalities. Wenger, White and Smith (2009) provided different community orientations. Knowing the functionality requirements and functionality in hand, community designers can set up a set of tools. Available community platforms can be either a single all-in-one platform or a best-of-breed package. A best-of-breed package promises to provide in one package an extensive set of tools that cater needs of each specialty. It is a good idea to first plan for a core platform for the community that serves as a base and then add additional functionality as needed.

The Core Platform

We discussed previously that online communities should concentrate on providing a focused, simple experience doing well a small number of activities. In order to do so, a core platform for community is a logical choice. This core platform provides the major functionality used by community plus some additional supporting features. There are few significant benefits of having such a core platform.

1. **Seamless User Experience**: Users learn one system that provides them a significant portion of what they need.
2. **Simplified Management:** Community designers can develop few key channels for users to interact with the community. These channels are customized to meet the community goals and user needs. Users can then be trained and supported on using these features.
3. **Cost-Effective and Easy Pilot:** Most core platform are available either as online services or as a download. This way, community leaders can start a community with low initial investment. Core platforms provide multiple configuration options to the community managers.

Most core platforms provide many common features. These common features include document repositories, announcements, blogs, member profiles, user comments, and event calendar. Most core platforms provide some sort of control over appearance of features. Community leaders can activate a limited set of features when the community is launched and add other features as the need arise.

Example Core Collaboration Platforms

There exist various core online collaboration platforms (such as HUdle, BaseCamp, Wrike, OneHub, and Google Docs) and each platform has unique characteristics. Community designers need to carefully evaluate these characteristics before selecting a core platform. Three most important defining features of these platforms are:

1. **Feature Set**: Collaboration software vary in their approach of aggregating different features such as discussion boards, event calendars, and blogs. Community initiators need to make tradeoff between having a platform with so many complex features to understand or a platform with limited number of features but easier to understand.
2. **Open Source/Proprietary**: There exist both proprietary and open-source collaborative tools. Open source tools has the advantage of low costs and no licensing requirements. Users can have full access to the source code and there also available options for commercial implementation with an active community of developers support the product. In contrast, best proprietary software can provide very smooth functioning and supported but their licensing costs are high and users have limited choices of customizations.
3. **Hosting:** Collaborative software can also be provided under Software-as-a-service (SaS) model. In this configuration, the user hosts the collaborative software. SaaS software can be easily setup and configured. They can be updated quite easily and can be scaled when needed. SaaS-based collaborative software vary considerably and may cost fortune.

   Following are the representative selection f popular core platforms.

   - **Jive SBS:** It is a full-featured commercial software. It is a commercial Java EE-based Enterprise 2.0 collaboration and knowledge management tool. Jive integrates the functionality of online communities, microblogging, social networking, discussion forums, blogs, wikis, and IM under one unified user interface. Content placed into any of the systems (blog, wiki, documentation, etc.) can be found through a common search interface. Other features include RSS capability, email integration, a reputation and reward system for participation, personal user profiles, JAX-WS web service interoperability, and integration with the Spring Framework.
   - **Drupal Commons:** It is an open source platform that provides a significant suite of tools and allow customization to unique needs. Drupal Commons is backed by a large, global, well-organized and active developer community. Drupal Commons is a ready-to-use solution for building either internal or external communities. It provides a complete social business software solution for organizations. Drupal Commons helps organize content into topic (organic) groups with blog, discussion, document, wiki, and event content types. It also allows users to create (user) relationships with each other in order to follow each other's activities on a site. Authenticated users can view a personalized dashboard containing content from all their subscribed groups (Drupal.org, 2014).
   - **Central Desktop:** It is a proprietary, hosted collaboration application that provides collaborative workspaces. Users use these collaborative workspaces for task and docu-

ment management. It provides excellent integration with e-mail and allow users to send copies of emails to workspaces.

- Central Desktop also include an online file viewer that supports more than 200 different file types, improved wiki navigation and the ability to convert any file type into a downloadable PDF document. Central Desktop is an alternative to email, Microsoft SharePoint and lightweight file-sharing sites. It connects people, content and customers in the cloud, so everyone can get things done together from one private, secure, centralized website.
- **SharePoint:** SharePoint is a web application framework and platform developed by Microsoft. .SharePoint integrates intranet, content management, and document management. SharePoint is mostly used by midsize businesses and large departments. SharePoint comprises a multipurpose set of Web technologies backed by a common technical infrastructure. By default, SharePoint has a Microsoft Office-like interface, and it is closely integrated with the Office suite. The web tools are intended for non-technical users. SharePoint can provide intranet portals, document and file management, collaboration, social networks, extranets, websites, enterprise search, and business intelligence. It also has system integration, process integration, and workflow automation capabilities. Enterprise application software (such as enterprise resource planning (ERP) and customer relationship management (CRM) packages) often provide some SharePoint integration.
- **BuddyPress:** Built-upon WordPress, BuddyPress is an open-source social networking software. It provides many features of a typical social networking platforms plus a set of technologies for web developers. BuddyPress is supported by a large active body of developers. BuddyPress helps you run any kind of social network on your WordPress, with member profiles, activity streams, user groups, messaging, and more.
- **Edmodo:** Edmodo is a custom-built education social networking software. It is not a general collaboration platform. Main focus of Edmodo is to provide a safe, efficient way for teachers to have online collaboration in their classes. Edmodo provides a substantial teacher-to-teacher community area, social networking functionality, discussions, and document sharing. The easy-to-use Interface makes Edmodo easy to adopt.
- **PBWorks:** PBworks is a commercial real-time collaborative editing (RTCE). PBworks is a hosted application that uses its own proprietary software. Users can create free basic wiki workspaces or upgrade to a premium plan to access additional features, such as enhanced security features, customization through CSS, and more storage space. Workspaces can be public or private (only viewable by those who have been invited to join the workspace). The software is only available in English. A number of businesses and corporations use PBworks to create private wikis for employees.
- **Groupsite:** Groupsite is a platform that empowers the creation of social websites called Groupsites. Groupsites are collaboration communities that enable groups to communicate, share and network to make things happen. It is done by combining the most useful features of online groups and listservs (like Yahoo! Groups), collaboration software (like Sharepoint) and Social Networks (like Facebook and Linkedin). It is a hosted workspace software that provides an institutive, easy-to-use interface. It is easy to implement and offer various design themes and configuration options organizations can

use based on their needs. Groupsite nicely integrates with e-mail. Users can link notifications to discussions and announcements.

- **Ning:** Users and organizations can use Ning, an online software, to create custom social network based community sites having a customized look and feel. Ning-based community sites can provide multiple features such as photos, videos, forums and blogs. Similar to Facebook 'Like' feature, a 'Like' button can also be added. Users can also integrate these sites with other sites such as Facebook, Twitter, Google and Yahoo!. It is a hosted workspace software that draws large number of users and networks. It is reliable and scalable. Ning incorporates many external applications that support APIs.
- **SocialGO:** It is an integrated social networking and collaboration software. SocialGo provides online video chat feature, is simple to setup and users can send bulletins to other users. SocialGO offers premium services whereby it builds a site on behalf of a customer. The company offers two products. SocialGO Classic is a social network builder that allows users to create a custom social network using preset configuration. SocialGO Pro is a social website builder that allows users to use advanced customization to form an online community for a group, business or interest.
- **Tomoye Community Software and Social Sites:** It is a proprietary, integrated social networking and collaboration software designed for CoPs. Multiple features (such as document sharing, blogging, wikis, videos, and Q&A) are aggregated in this software. Users can interact with the site via e-mail. This software showcases community experts displaying whether they are helpful and active. Users can rate content highlight the content they think is the most valuable. Like Jive, this software can be quite expensive if the membership of community is large.
- **Alfresco Share:** It is an open-source community software. It is designed to provide collaboration on content and projects. This collaboration is done among a geographically dispersed team of people. Alfresco Share provides social networking features, such as tagging and feeds, and collaboration tools (such as document repositories, blogs, wikis, event calendar etc.). Users can use a built-in reader to view various types of documents within the software without downloading the documents. The software can be easily setup, customized, and scaled.

Supporting Services

Selected core platforms, in most cases, don't provide some features that the community needs. Some of these features may be required for particular needs (such as webinar) to support a community's offline discussions. Many other features may be required over time. As an example, successful community may be based on a document repository. Later on, the community may decide to use a social bookmarking service to gather links.

During its growth, a community explore many technologies and can integrate various incentives tools into community architecture to support community growth and activity. Using collaborative authoring tools, communities can develop and share pieces of knowledge. A community can launch a blog to highlight community activities. These are just few examples how a community can expand beyond its core platform. Available integration tools (such as APIs, feeds, and widgets) can make certain types of integration easy but others can be difficult. There is a trade-off between the benefits of more connected system and the costs of integration required. These higher costs can be justified provided that integration results in more efficient work, further community growth, and new kinds of interaction.

Third-Party Sites and Social Media

Social media sites are special support services that can play multiple roles (e.g. to provide support to community marketing strategy). A community focused on a topic (e.g. Topic "A") may post notifications on Facebook and Twitter to reach a wider audience base. Acting as an ongoing channel for information dissemination, social media sites can use their feeds to broadcast content to members of the community. The services provided by social media sites can be significant aspects of a community. Social media sites (such as LinkedIn) can provide a community formed around discussions among professionals of many types. If audience are already using a core platform in another context, making these services part of community architecture can be valuable. Community goals can be better served by using custom applications to extend such communities.

Community designers face considerable challenge to decide about activities that should take place on social media sites. Social media site communities, with broader reach, tend to be more casual. This way these sites can identify and attract active users to their community. An example can be taken from the presidential campaign of US president Barack Obama. Obama succeeded to build large Facebook communities. However, the members of these communities didn't donate for Obama's campaign. The donors were the ones who migrated from other social media sites to sites dedicated to Obama (e.g. barackobama.com). This is a clear example of ability of social media sites to act as an excellent communication channel to strengthen community efforts (Connected Educators, 2011).

PRACTICAL/MANAGERIAL IMPLICATIONS AND RECOMMENDATIONS

Efforts to encourage use of CoPs still suffer from various shortcomings. In order encourage users to use KMS tools for collaboration a stimulus is strongly needed. We need withdraw from using traditional methods of communication (such as email) in favor of new web-based applications (such as wikis). Employees need positive enforcement and encouragement to use these new applications. Employees must also be encouraged to utilize positive aspects of these applications such as feedback and enhanced user experience.

Experts also need to realize that they are not only the contributors to these new applications but also the users of the same. McLure Wasko and Faraj (2000) points out this fact by noting that "instead of experts focusing their time and attention on creating new innovations, their role shifts from that of knowledge creators to knowledge disseminators" (p. 160). The CoPs should be a valuable tool of knowledge search for both experts and newbies alike. This task is difficult and would require adequate access to, and participation in, from all levels of the community.

For CoPs, some important considerations include keeping abreast of new technologies, learning new technologies, training users, and maintaining services. Even if these considerations are taken into account, it is remain uncertain whether or not non-participants of CoP will recognize the potential provided by new technologies for CoP. There has been some exploration about web 2.0 technologies however it is insufficient. It is important that CoP participants understand and capitalize on the opportunities available through use of these emerging technologies to maintain and sustain contact by and among communities, to alleviate the challenges of distance and isolation and the lack of inconsistent information dissemination.

Educators need to focus on organizations transition from being pure teaching organization to learning organization. Teaching organizations have traditionally been run by highly skilled professionals. Today's communities have transformed to become networks of artisans who collaborate with each other but still act individually. Ultimately, a transition is needed so that these educators work together on independent learning teams. The members of a true collaborative community have different roles but perform collectively. An analogy can be taken from hockey team where each team member plays a different role but performs collectively. Developing effective independent teams is a genuine challenge. Initially the organizations should focus on building offline teams. Once these offline teams get off the ground, online collaboration should be fostered among teams.

Technology providers have traditionally considered online communities as customer or user groups. An important shift to watch for is that how these "closed boxes" (i.e. communities) evolve into an open space where open conversations will take place. Content providers can create content and share it across different groups. Content sharing and conversations among teams of educators can build huge knowledgebase. The real challenge is to find ways to leverage these knowledgebase across communities.

A fundamental goal of education is to create cross-cultural, cross-boundary collaboration. To produce true learners of 21st century, connected educators need to develop connected learners. There exist two groups of educators today. One consists of educators that are motivated, self-directed and connected. The second group consists of educators that are overwhelmed, timid, and disconnected. The growing divide between the two groups is worrisome. Current teacher evaluation programs seldom give credit for participation in online CoPs. Teachers need to be rewarded for their participation in CoPs. A 360 degree evaluation of teachers should be done where evaluation of teacher is not limited to just administration but it also includes teacher's peers and members of CoP in which the teacher participates.

Schools are constantly introducing new programs. These programs are seldom implemented fully as teacher expect another program before the last one is fully implemented. This way, provision of even something valuable can just go through the motions of implementing it. Technology is clearly here to stay. However, the same phenomenon stand in the way of technology adoption as the teachers continue to look for what benefits they can get from this technology. With each new program, teacher expects to gain something out of its use (such as salary increase or some form of appreciation). The remedy to this is to just keep putting out more content with the hope that, as the time passes, teachers will start posting their own materials.

We are still waiting for a killer app that could give online CoPs a real boost (Bolger, 2009). Current technology allows motivated persons to stay connected at their own. Surprisingly not many young teachers in their professional lives don't seem to realize the potential of technology for their benefit. The technology vendors currently sell to a market of educators that can be called a market of artisans. To this market, vendors sell technology as it is. A market of collaborative teaching practices current doesn't seem to exist probably because vendors currently lack collaborative teaching skills. The killer app mentioned earlier is expected to change this culture and increase real demand of social-networking based learning tools by educators.

Presently many communities are operational. Another important question is how new effective CoPs can built in the presence of these existing communities. The current generation of schools can be described as closed systems with conservative curriculum. The important thing is educators need to learn from their students. Free students can teach educators in a very short period of time (let's say a week or a month). Educators are not the ones to take us where educators need to go. The important question is how education can be made a profession such as medicine or law. The learning could be considered a product and teachers need to move beyond not knowing how to use technology. While a radical forward change is not possible for everyone in education community, online CoPs are great help for majority of teachers who progress gradually.

FUTURE RESEARCH DIRECTIONS

It would be interesting to analyze whether Web 2.0 technologies impact Communities of Practice and knowledge sharing the same way in both non-profit and for-profit organizations. It would be interesting because both types of the organization cover different aspects of the KM spectrum. Research is also needed to analyze in-depth situational factors that influence the impact of Web 2.0 application on KM. The outcomes would help organizations understand which levers they have to move in order to benefit from Web 2.0. Another future research area is to conduct some quantitative research in order to derive some general conclusion about the impact of Web 2.0 on KM. Innovations in mobile technology shape how mobile workers share knowledge and collaborate on the go. There exists a concept called mobile communities of practice (MCOPs) introduced as a lens for understanding how these workers self-organize. Variations in the degree of organizational alignment and individual discretion can shape these MCOPs. Further research is needed to gain a deeper understanding of MCOPs that can provide important strategic implications practical considerations for identifying, creating, and supporting MCOPs and Online COPs.

CONCLUSION

Currently we are in the early stages of using technology that supports online CoPs. We are also beginning to understand the dynamics and values of these communities. There exist great challenges regarding access, training of users, community building and engagement and integrating these online CoPs into the existing educational communities. Besides, the online communities and technology use to build these communities provide many rewards to the users.

Knowledge Management Systems (KMS) are primarily people-driven tools. Development of light, web-based tools for CoPs can encourage participation and probably barriers of adoption and implementation of CoPs. Existing communities need efficient and effective support. Web 2.0 tools can be the most effective tools for supporting online CoPs. Implementing online CoP technology is challenging but some clear roadmaps exist for successful implementation.

Developing CoPs, based on Web 2.0 tools, need careful planning. Careful mapping of goals and scenarios is required to understand the true requirements of audience in the community. We also need to think about the purpose of the community. These considerations should guide and inform the technology selection for building CoPs. Availability of resources for community management tasks (such as user training) should be ensured. Implementation should first start with a pilot program with minimum features offered. The community can grow in unexpected ways. It is need to be assured that the expansion is consistent with goals and purpose of community. Community will evolve over time and features should be added when needed. While home-based technology should be preferred, other valuable tools should also be used. In early stages, the focus should be to have few systems flow perfectly. With the passage of time, other useful systems should be fine-tuned. This chapter contributes to the existing knowledge base of knowledge management by providing insights how Web 2.0 applications can be used for developing effective Communities of Practice.

REFERENCES

Adams, A. N., Brock, R. J., Gordon, K. A., Grohs, J. R., & Kirk, G. R. (2014). Service, Dialogue, and Reflection as Foundational Elements in a Living Learning Community. *Journal of College and Character*, *15*(3), 179–188. doi:10.1515/jcc-2014-0021

Allee, V. 1997. 12 Principles of Knowledge Management. Retrieved from http://www.providersedge.com/docs/km_articles/12_principles_of_Knowledge_Management.pdf

Ardichvili, A., Page, V., & Wentling, T. (2003). Motivation and barriers to participation in virtual knowledge-sharing communities of practice. *Journal of Knowledge Management*, *7*(1), 64–77. doi:10.1108/13673270310463626

Barab, S., Scott, J., Del Valle Martin, R., & Fang, F. (2012). Coming to Terms with Communities of Practice: A definition and operational criteria.

Barnett, S., Jones, S. C., Bennett, S., Iverson, D., & Bonney, A. (2013). Usefulness of a virtual community of practice and web 2.0 tools for general practice training: Experiences and expectations of general practitioner registrars and supervisors. *Australian Journal of Primary Health*, *19*(4), 292–296. doi:10.1071/PY13024 PMID:23823006

Bolger, S. (2009). Investigating the viability of virtual communities of practice in the public sector.

Bond, P. (2004). Communities of Practice and Complexity: Conversation and Culture. *Organization and People*, *11*(4), 1–7.

Bouchamma, Y., & Michaud, C. (2011). Communities of practice with teaching supervisors: A discussion of community members' experiences. *Journal of Educational Change*, *12*(4), 403–420. doi:10.1007/s10833-010-9141-y

Brown, S. A. (2012). Seeing Web 2.0 in context: A study of academic perceptions. *The Internet and Higher Education*, *15*(1), 50–57. doi:10.1016/j.iheduc.2011.04.003

Chen, T.-L., & Chen, T.-J. (2002). A strategic analysis of the online learning community for continuing professional development of university faculty in Taiwan: A SWOT analysis. *Proceedings of the International Conference on Computers in Education 2002* (pp. 1408–1409). IEEE.

Connectededucators (2011). Technology for Online Communities of Practice. from http://connectededucators.org/wp-content/uploads/2011/03/0143_Platforms-and-Tools-march-2011.pdf

Cornu, B. (2004). Networking and collecting intelligence for teachers and learners. In A. Brown & N. Davis (Eds.), *Digital technology, communities and education* (pp. 40–45). London: Routledge Falmer.

Cox, A. (2005). What are communities of practice? A comparative review of four seminal works. *Journal of Information Science, 31*(6), 527–540. doi:10.1177/0165551505057016

Cruickshank, P. (2011). *Customer journey mapping*. Smart Cities Guide.

Dascalu, M.-I., Bodea, C.-N., Lytras, M., De Pablos, P. O., & Burlacu, A. (2014). Improving e-learning communities through optimal composition of multidisciplinary learning groups. *Computers in Human Behavior, 30*, 362–371. doi:10.1016/j.chb.2013.01.022

Drupal.org. (2014). Drupal Commons. Retrieved from https://www.drupal.org/project/commons

Eisenstadt, M., & Vincent, T. (2012). *The knowledge web: Learning and collaborating on the net*. Routledge.

Euerby, A., & Burns, C. M. (2012). Designing for Social Engagement in Online Social Networks Using Communities-of-Practice Theory and Cognitive Work Analysis A Case Study. *Journal of Cognitive Engineering and Decision Making, 6*(2), 194–213. doi:10.1177/1555343412440697

Facebook. (2014). Facebook. Retrieved from http://www.programmableweb.com/api/facebook

Fugelstad, P., Dwyer, P., Filson Moses, J., Kim, J., Mannino, C. A., Terveen, L., & Snyder, M. (2012). What makes users rate (share, tag, edit...)?: predicting patterns of participation in online communities. *Proceedings of the ACM 2012 conference on Computer Supported Cooperative Work* (pp. 969–978). ACM. doi:10.1145/2145204.2145349

Goldberg, P. (2003). Disconnected Urbanism - Metropolis Magazine. Retrieved from http://www.metropolismag.com/December-1969/Disconnected-Urbanism/

Guy, M. 2006. Wiki or Won't He? A Tale of Public Sector Wikis. Comparison of UK & US State Organisations, Changing Audiences, Participation, and Collective Intelligence. Available from: http://www.ariadne.ac.uk/issue49/guy/

Hall, H., & Graham, D. (2004). Creation and recreation: Motivating collaboration to generate knowledge capital in online communities. *International Journal of Information Management, 24*(3), 235–246. doi:10.1016/j.ijinfomgt.2004.02.004

Hislop, D. (2013). *Knowledge management in organizations: A critical introduction*. Oxford University Press.

Hossain, M., & Aydin, H. (2011). A Web 2.0-based collaborative model for multicultural education. *Multicultural Education & Technology Journal, 5*(2), 116–128. doi:10.1108/17504971111142655

Hughes, J., Jewson, N., & Unwin, L. (2013). *Communities of practice: Critical perspectives*. Routledge.

Jamali, R., H., Russell, B., Nicholas, D., & Watkinson, A. (. (2014). Do online communities support research collaboration? *Aslib Journal of Information Management, 66*(6), 603–622. doi:10.1108/AJIM-08-2013-0072

Jeon, S., Kim, Y.-G., & Koh, J. (2011). An integrative model for knowledge sharing in communities-of-practice. *Journal of Knowledge Management, 15*(2), 251–269. doi:10.1108/13673271111119682

Jin, L., Wen, Z., & Gough, N. (2010). Social virtual worlds for technology-enhanced learning on an augmented learning platform. *Learning, Media and Technology*, *35*(2), 139–153. doi:10.1080/17439884.2010.494424

Kai-Wai Chu, S., & Kennedy, D. M. (2011). Using online collaborative tools for groups to co-construct knowledge. *Online Information Review*, *35*(4), 581–597. doi:10.1108/14684521111161945

Kraut, R. E., Resnick, P., Kiesler, S., Burke, M., Chen, Y., & Kittur, N. … Riedl, J. (2012). Building successful online communities: Evidence-based social design. MIT Press.

Lee, M. R., & Lan, Y. (2007). From Web 2.0 to conversational knowledge management: Towards collaborative intelligence. *Journal of Entrepreneurship Research*, 2(2), 47–62.

Lin, M. F., & Lee, M. (2006). E-learning Localized: The case of the OOPS project. In A. Edmundson (Ed.), *Globalization in Education: Improving education quality through cross-cultural dialogue* (pp. 168–186). Hershey, PA: Idea Group.

Matei, S. A. (2005). From counterculture to cyberculture: Virtual community discourse and the dilemma of modernity. *Journal of Computer-Mediated Communication, 10*(3), 00–00.

McLure Wasko, M., & Faraj, S. (2000). It is what one does: Why people participate and help others in electronic communities of practice. *The Journal of Strategic Information Systems*, *9*(2-3), 155–173. doi:10.1016/S0963-8687(00)00045-7

McWilliam, G. (2012). Building stronger brands through online communities. *Sloan Management Review*, *41*(3).

Meyerhoff, M., & Strycharz, A. (2013). *Communities of practice*. Wiley Online Library. doi:10.1002/9781118335598.ch20

Newhouse, H. C. B., & Vestal, W. (2001). Building and Sustaining Communities of Practice. Houston: American Productivity Centre.

Nissen, M. E., Kamel, M. N., & Sengupta, K. C. (2000). Toward integrating knowledge management, processes and systems: a position paper. *Proceedings of the AAAI Symposium on Bringing Knowledge to Business Processes, Stanford, CA*.

Ridings, C. M., & Gefen, D. (2004). Virtual community attraction: Why people hang out online. *Journal of Computer-Mediated Communication, 10*(1).

Saint-Onge, H., & Wallace, D. (2012). *Leveraging communities of practice for strategic advantage*. Routledge.

Schneider, A., Von Krogh, G., & Jäger, P. (2013). "What's coming next?" Epistemic curiosity and lurking behavior in online communities. *Computers in Human Behavior*, *29*(1), 293–303. doi:10.1016/j.chb.2012.09.008

Sinclair, N. (2006). *Stealth KM, Winning Knowledge Management Strategies for the Public Sector*. Butterworth-Heinemann.

Spagnoletti, P., & Resca, A. (2012). A design theory for IT supporting online communities. *Proceedings of the 2012 45th Hawaii International Conference on System Science HICSS* (pp. 4082–4091). IEEE. doi:10.1109/HICSS.2012.54

Sun, N., Rau, P. P.-L., & Ma, L. (2014). Understanding lurkers in online communities: A literature review. *Computers in Human Behavior, 38*, 110–117. doi:10.1016/j.chb.2014.05.022

Tierney, R., & Palmer, M. (2013). Participation, interaction and learner satisfaction in a professional practice wiki for teachers. *Cyberpsychology and New Media: A Thematic Reader*, 195.

Tosey, P. (1999). The peer learning community: A contextual design for learning? *Management Decision, 37*(5), 403–010. doi:10.1108/00251749910274171

Tsai, H.-T., & Bagozzi, R. P. (2014). Contribution behavior in virtual communities: Cognitive, emotional and social influences. *Management Information Systems Quarterly, 38*(1), 143–163.

Valaitis, R. K., Akhtar-Danesh, N., Brooks, F., Binks, S., & Semogas, D. (2011). Online communities of practice as a communication resource for community health nurses working with homeless persons. *Journal of Advanced Nursing, 67*(6), 1273–1284. doi:10.1111/j.1365-2648.2010.05582.x PMID:21306424

Van Winkelen, C. 2003. Inter-organisational communities of practice. Retrieved from http://www. elearningeuropa.info/directory/index.php?page=doc&doc_id=1483&doclng=6

Venkatesh, V., Croteau, A.-M., & Rabah, J. (2014). Perceptions of effectiveness of instructional uses of technology in higher education in an era of Web 2.0. *Proceedings of the 2014 47th Hawaii International Conference on System Sciences (HICSS)* (pp. 110–119). IEEE.

Venkatesh, V., Rabah, J., Fusaro, M., Couture, A., Varela, W., & Alexander, K. (2012). Perceptions of Technology Use and Course Effectiveness in the Age of Web 2.0: A Large-Scale Survey of Québec University Students and Instructors. *Proceedings of the World Conference on E-Learning in Corporate, Government, Healthcare, and Higher Education* (Vol. 2012, pp. 1691–1699).

Walsham, G. (2001). Knowledge Management: The benefits and limitations of Computer Systems. *European Journal of Knowledge Management, 9*(6), 599–608. doi:10.1016/S0263-2373(01)00085-8

Wang, S., Noe, R. A., & Wang, Z.-M. (2014). Motivating Knowledge Sharing in Knowledge Management Systems A Quasi–Field Experiment. *Journal of Management, 40*(4), 978–1009. doi:10.1177/0149206311412192

Wang, Y., & Fesenmaier, D. R. (2003). Assessing motivation of contribution in online communities: An empirical investigation of an online travel community. *Electronic Markets, 13*(1), 33–45. doi:10.1080/1019678032000052934

Wenger, E. (1999). Communities of practice: Learning as a social system. *Systems Thinker, 9*(5), 2–3.

Wenger, E. (2006). Communities of Practice: A brief introduction. North San Juan, C.A. Available from: http://www.ewenger.com/theory/index.html

Wenger, E. (2011). *Communities of practice: A brief introduction.* Retrieved from https://scholarsbank.uoregon.edu/xmlui/bitstream/handle/1794/11736/A%20brief%20introduction%20to%20CoP.pdf?sequence=1&isAllowed=y

Wenger, E., White, N., & Smith, J. D. (2009). *Digital habitats.* Stewarding Technology for Communities.

Yen, H. R., Hsu, S. H.-Y., & Huang, C.-Y. (2011). Good soldiers on the Web: Understanding the drivers of participation in online communities of consumption. *International Journal of Electronic Commerce, 15*(4), 89–120. doi:10.2753/JEC1086-4415150403

Zhang, W., & Watts, S. (2008). Online communities as communities of practice: A case study. *Journal of Knowledge Management, 12*(4), 55–71. doi:10.1108/13673270810884255

Zhou, Z., Wu, J. P., Zhang, Q., & Xu, S. (2013). Transforming visitors into members in online brand communities: Evidence from China. *Journal of Business Research, 66*(12), 2438–2443.

ADDITIONAL READING

Bannister, F., 2007. The curse of benchmarking: an assessment of the validity and value of e-government comparisons. *International Review of Administrative Sciences,* 73, 171.

Bhatt, G. (2001). Knowledge Management in Organisations: Examining the Interactions between Technologies, Techniques and People. *Journal of Knowledge Management, 5*(1), 68–75. doi:10.1108/13673270110384419

Bixler, C. H. (2002). Applying the four pillars of Knowledge Management, *KMWorldMagazine*, 11(1)

Davenport, T. H., & Prusak, L. (2006). Working Knowledge: How organizations manage what they know (pp. 3, 11). Harvard Business School Press, Boston, MA, USA.

Gladwell, M. (2002). *The Tipping Point: How little things can make a big difference.* New York, NY: Black Ray Books.

Holland, G. A. (2006). Extended Cognition and Social Constructionism as Underpinnings for Knowledge Management Practice. *Journal of Knowledge Management Practice*, 7(1).

Nonaka, I. (1991). The knowledge-creating company. *Harvard Business Review, 69*(6), 96–104.

Orlikowski, W. J. 1992. Learning from Notes: organizational issues in groupware implementation. Proceedings of the 1992 ACM conference on Computer- supported cooperative work (pp. 362-369). ACM Press New York, NY, USA. doi:10.1145/143457.143549

Rowley, J. (1992). *Organising Knowledge* (2nd ed.). Hants, UK: Gower Publishing.

Senge, P. M. (1990). *The Fifth Discipline: The Art and Practice of the Learning Organization.* New York, NY: Doubleday.

Wiig, K. M. (1993). *Knowledge Management Foundations: Thinking About Thinking – How People and Organizations Create, Represent, and Use Knowledge.* Arlington, TX: Schema Press.

KEY TERMS AND DEFINITIONS

Collaboration: Collaboration is a joint effort of multiple individuals or work groups to accomplish a task or project.

Community: A community is a group of people living in the same place or having a particular characteristic in common.

Community of Practice: Community of practice is formed by people who engage in a process of collective learning in a shared domain of human endeavor.

Explicit Knowledge: Explicit knowledge is knowledge that has been articulated, codified, and stored in certain media.

Knowledge Management: Knowledge management is the process of capturing, developing, sharing, and effectively using organizational knowledge.

Tacit Knowledge: Tacit knowledge is the kind of knowledge that is difficult to transfer to another person by means of writing it down or verbalizing it.

Virtual Community: A virtual community is a community of people sharing common interests, ideas, and feelings over the Internet or other collaborative networks.

Chapter 15
Guidelines to Innovate Organizations by Knowledge Management via Communities of Practice

Roberta Salgado Gonçalves da Silva
University of São Paulo, Brazil

Edson Walmir Cazarini
University of São Paulo, Brazil

ABSTRACT

This study proposes to achieve an innovative environment via Communities of Practice (CoP) in companies that doesn´t know Knowledge Management (KM). The contribution of the paper is to elucidate the relevance of KM presenting a research and the literature of KM, CoP, Organizational Culture and Information and Communication Technology. A survey was performed at ten companies in the interior of São Paulo state, Brazil. Any company that doesn´t know KM and needs to be innovative may use the original twenty-two guidelines.

1. INTRODUCTION

The knowledge of a company is the result of years of organizational activity in which the knowledge of individuals is combined into a collective whole, according to Kogut & Zander (1992). Choi et al. (2008) state that knowledge is a critical source that has encouraged companies to devote attention to management, meaning that in the Knowledge-Based Economy (KBE), which has a very competitive base, companies need to settle an innovation environment. An active resource to KBE companies is knowledge; therefore, the Knowledge Management (KM) adds competitive value to assist managers.

To settle an innovation environment companies pay attention to the development of KM, which requires strategies, such as the use of Communities of Practice (CoP), to achieve employee learning. According to Skerlavaj et al. (2010), the participation perspective is derived from practice-based studies

DOI: 10.4018/978-1-4666-9556-6.ch015

Copyright © 2016, IGI Global. Copying or distributing in print or electronic forms without written permission of IGI Global is prohibited.

such as apprenticeship learning, in which no teaching was conducted; that means knowledge was not directly imparted to participants through instruction-based methods. Skerlavaj et al. (2010) explain that within this perspective, learning is understood as the function of participation in CoP, which means that learning takes place through sustaining a community where knowledge flows richly among individuals, thereby ensuring participation and interactions of individuals. While the participation perspective considers organizational learning as a relational phenomenon, it neglects the acquisition perspective. One of the KM principles cited is "assure learning".

In this context, Valenzuela et al. (2008) state that KM will stimulate companies to become more efficient and effective by using the knowledge base existence and mobilizing the available knowledge sources to create new knowledge. According to Rosini & Palmisano (2003), the development of collective knowledge and for the continuous learning, Information Technologies (IT) are strategic, so people in a company may share problems, perspectives, ideas and solutions. Harris (2001) states that the KBE is linked to technology based on computers and new IT potential. In the context, Information and Communication Technology (ICT) and IT are two inseparable concepts.

Bourhis & Dubé (2010) state that a community, whose overall objective represents an organizational priority, is embedded in an Organizational Culture (OC) submitted to organizational practices and exposed to political issues, which may all impact on its actions. Hislop (2005) highlights the potentiality of CoP in terms of knowledge processes as basis of organizational innovation by supporting and promoting the creation, development and use of knowledge, and as it facilitate and promote individual and group learning, and the sharing of knowledge.

Li et al. (2006) considers that OC and KM are correlated and critical to organizational performance. To develop KM, the use of ICT, OC and CoP should be considered. The CoP is known as a management tool for the enhancement of companies' competitiveness, according to Li et al. (2009). Organizational Culture and KM have been the target of numerous studies.

It wasn't found in the literature a known guideline to develop KM via CoP with the assistance of the OC and ICT literature. Based on this knowledge gap, the goal in this study is to propose an innovative environment to development of KM via CoP in companies that doesn´t know KM. The main question of this study is: "which are the key practices at companies that may help manage the aggregated knowledge necessary to develop an innovative environment?" The contribution of the paper is to elucidate the relevance of KM for companies presenting a research and the CoP, based on the literature of KM, CoP, OC and ICT.

2. KNOWLEDGE MANAGEMENT AND COMMUNITIES OF PRACTICE

According to Prusak (2001), KM appears as an answer to social and economic trends, as globalization, computing influence and centered view on knowledge. Although the more accepted view on scientific community about KM is presented under a methodology based on knowledge life cycle or knowledge process, according to McElroy (1999), the interest in KM has grown along with the advances in computers, networks and data management systems. Sharing and collaboration among thousands of people scattered around the globe depends on the technology of connection and the organized storage of content, and many knowledge projects have focused on building systems to connect people and capture knowledge, according to Bose (2004).

Due to KM complexity, some authors define it from the following standpoint of view: a) KM is one of the biggest strategic uses of IT, due to that many companies create KM systems to manage organizational learning and their know-how (O´BRIEN, 2004, pp.60); b) KM is the deliberate and systematic coordination of an organization's people, technology, processes, and organizational structure in order to add value through reuse and innovation (DALKIR, 2005, pp.3); c) KM appears as strengthening and a support to company's activity. Maximizing the people's potential on executing your activity in the operational system, fostering impulse to creativity and innovation, beyond the systematizing and more effective use of company's explicit and registered knowledge (HOFFMANN, 2009, pp.86).

To make the understanding easier, this study highlights five KM principles (HOFFMANN, 2009, pp.97): a) Capacitate people work in groups; b) Preserve culture and values; c) Assure learning; d) Create, discover and collect knowledge inside and outside the company; e) Share and understand models and guidelines to be used. To preserve culture values and create, discover and collect knowledge inside and outside the company are related to the CSF of KM and CoP adopted in this work.

According to Cortés et al. (2007), the horizontal structural of a company implicates communication improvement, decision making decentralization and empowerment. Cortés et al. (2007) state that the main organizational structure characteristics, which are also related to the CSF, that support KM are: a) Horizontal and flexible structure; b) Few hierarchy levels; c) Amplified communication in all the company.

Butler et al. (2008) state that CoP are one of two social and organizational groupings as being vital to the success of knowledge sharing initiative, that involves members of informal CoP which have shared knowledge interests. The knowledge sharing initiative may or may not have organizational processes as their subject. The other social and organizational grouping is a formal way of knowledge workers called a Knowledge Network (KN).

Networks and CoP are spaces and/or strategies based on which the social construction of knowledge takes place and they have become common in Knowledge Creation and Management (KCM) models, according to Gairín-Sallán et al. (2010). In this context, CoP is a good example of group in which members begin to act in a collective and coordinated manner, solving complex tasks, without explicit rules for action such as written procedures, decision rules, formal models, or even without explicit communication.

According to Erden et al. (2008) which state that organizational knowledge creation theory posits that through knowledge conversion, new tacit knowledge can become collective for the group (NONAKA, 1994).

Communities of Practice have attracted a lot of attention as a way of fostering learning among a vast array of groups, from public defenders to web specialists or textile workers, according to Bourhis & Dubé (2010), which state that CoP are seen as an innovative way to create and share knowledge in organizations and to combine working, learning and innovating.

As a work place for sharing, Wenger (1998) highlights that CoP, where members can communicate, store and share the knowledge of products and profiles. The space to be used could be at a server, in the Internet or intranet of a company. Dalkir (2005) highlights the importance of the space to be used for real time sharing and asynchronous discussion.

The concepts of CoP and Networks of Practice (NOP) are similar. According to Agterberg et al. (2010), CoP was originally defined as emergent collections of closely connected people who engaged in frequent, social, face-to-face interactions, working side by side, and shared a common situated context or practice, and NOP similarly are self-organizing groups of members who share the same practice, but are geographically dispersed.

Due to the importance of the CoP to the success of companies' innovation, some studies were developed to provide better understanding to the academic community and companies (KLEIN et. al 2005; FAHEY et al. 2007; USORO et al. 2007). Amin & Roberts (2008) state that CoP is known as "situated learning" on the learning process and on KM. That attracts the attention of academics and self-employed person due to the fact that CoP is being used to explain learning and knowledge creation across a varied environment at work, company and space.

Wenger (2014) states that create and stimulate knowledge is not pleasant to hierarchy of industrial control and command, meantime it's essential to CoP, which were till then informal inside the company, that keep up necessary needs to company, would be legalized, engaged and integrated to it.

3. MATERIAL AND METHODS

A questionnaire and an interview were presented at ten companies in the interior of São Paulo state, Brazil. They were developed and supported by the literature review on KM, CoP, CO and ICT. Both instruments were applied to the Human Resource (HR) and Information Technology (IT) managers, which were chosen for being the closest to a KM action that could have due to their access to people and technology. From a list of twenty-four companies, eleven agreed to participate in the survey, one of the responses was not considered valid.

The managers answered the questionnaire by e-mail (Appendix 1) and then answered a face-to-face interview (Appendix 2). Some questions aimed to characterize the company's economy: number of employees, annual revenues, client profile, product, processes and financing sources (Table 1).

Next it was important to identify the existence of a KM department and its time of existence, KM tools and sharing's, the ICT use by the employees (Table 2) and the time average for the use of ICT (Table 3).

The semi-structured interview intended to determine the strengths and weaknesses of the companies in the development of KM identifying the key practices. Data were collected through questionnaires, semi-structured interviews and direct observation, organized and analyzed. Data analysis was done based on content analyses. For the questionnaire's analyses, there were primarily used histograms and content analysis. Content analysis was done in three phases: recovery, in which there was transcribing the interviews, the analysis of semantic meaning and pragmatic conversation validation by the respondent.

The interview had twenty nine questions based on six CSF that were investigated with their respective units of analysis, the potentialities and deficiencies in the companies' environment to develop KM via CoP (Table 4).

Regarding the validity of the research instruments, they were submitted to experts on their knowledge field such as professors, research groups, associations and Chief Executive Officer (CEO) using the content validity. The first contacted CEOs gave permission to apply the research at the companies and contributed to the development of the questionnaire and the interview. A pretest was applied to part of the companies, which after responding the questions contributed to clarify some of them, so the people responsible for the departments and areas could respond with information that is more appropriate.

After reading the answers from the questionnaire, the specialists suggested that the CSF from KM and CoP should be identified in the literature and used in the interview guide. During the development

Table 1. Company characterization

Number of Employees	Annual Income	Productive System	Customer's Profile	Processes	Origin of Resources
2080	More than U$ 568 thousand	Industry	Brazil's legal entity	Raw material transformation to final product	Own source
328	More than U$ 568 thousand	Industry	Brazil's and exterior legal entity	Foundry, machining, forging and special materials	Own source
376	More than U$ 568 thousand	Industry	Natural person & legal entity in Brazil. Resale to Europe, Latin America, Australia and USA	Metal machining, product manufacturing and mounting	Own source
145	More than U$ 568 thousand	Industry	Brazil's legal entity	Metal machining, mounting and transformation raw material to final product	Financing agencies: FAPESP [a], FINEP [b], Public Bank BNDES[c]
720	More than U$ 568 thousand	Industry	Brazil natural person; exports to Mercosul[e] and Europe	Raw material transformation to final product	Public bank BNDES[c] and commercial banks
3000	From U$136 thousand to U$ 284 thousand	Industry	Foreigner and Brazil's legal entity	Production, administration and marketing	Public Bank BNDES[c]
550	More than U$ 568 thousand	Industry	Brazil's legal entity	Beneficiation, transformation and finishing	-
80	More than U$ 568 thousand	Industry	Natural person and legal entity in Brazil, Mercosul[e], Europe and Africa.	Manufacturing, manufacturing and quality control	Public bank CEF[d] and the program Sanitation for All and Pro Sanitation
609	From U$ 284 thousand to more than U$ 568 thousand	Services	Legal entity in São Paulo state cities: São Carlos, Mococa, Santa Rosa do Viterbo and Paraná state: Curitiba, Ponta Grossa, Araucária	Cleaning, conservation, gardening and logistics	Own source
505	More than U$ 568 thousand	Services	Natural person and legal entity (urban and country areas)	-	Own source

Note: a. Foundation supporting research in the state of São Paulo; b. Financing of studies and projects; c. National development bank; d.Federal savings bank; e.Common market of the south.

of the guidelines, they were contacted again and suggested to explain each one and to set the sequence of the facts that should be applied in the company. They also suggested a new guideline to be the last on the role, number 22: "to propose a mediator to motivate the employees to practice knowledge", as they considered it very relevant.

The interview had 29 questions related to the CSFs of KM and CoP, company structure, company members, technology and leadership.

Table 2. KM sharing tools and ICT use in the company

KM Sharing Tools and ICT	KM Department	KM Department Time of Existence	KM Sharing Tools	Open/Closed Technology Use
E-mail	Doesn't do KM	-	E-mail	E-mail, internet, forum, phone and wiki open
List of online discussions, email, intranet, instant message, phone, corporate portals	IT department does KM	-	List of online discussions, email, intranet, instant message, phone, corporate portals	Intranet, e-mail, phone, corporate portals, instant message are open; internet and online discussion list are limited
E-mail and phone	Human Resource department does KM	Ten years	E-mail e telefone	Internet, e-mail, phone are open;, instant message is limited
E-mail, intranet, phone, and repositories of knowledge	IT department does KM	About six years	E-mail, intranet, phone and knowledge repositories	Phone is open; Internet, e-mail, intranet and knowledge repositories are limited
E-mail, intranet, instant messaging and phone	Project department and the Information Center department do KM	-	E-mail, intranet, instant messaging and phone	Intranet, instant message and phone are open, Internet and e-mail are limited
E-mail, Instant Message and intranet	Human Resource department does KM	More than 30 years	E-mail, intranet and instant message	E-mail and phone are open; Internet, intranet and instant message are limited
E-mail, intranet, phone, wiki, corporate portals and repositories of knowledge	Human Resource and IT department do KM	-	E-mail, intranet, phone, wiki, corporate portals and knowledge repositories	E-mail, intranet, phone, wiki, corporate portals and knowledge repositories are open; Internet and instant message are limited
E-mail, intranet and phone	IT department does KM	8 years	E-mail, intranet and phone	Online discussion list, forum, intranet, phone; e-mail, Internet and instant message are limited
E-mail, intranet, phone, corporate portals and repositories of knowledge	Human Resource department does KM	12 years	E-mail, intranet, phone, corporate portals and knowledge repositories	Phone, corporate portals are open; e-mail, Internet, intranet and knowledge repositories are limited
E-mail and intranet	Project department does KM	18 years	E-mail and intranet	Intranet and instant message are open; e-mail, Internet, online discussion lists, phone, forum, wiki, corporate portals are limited

4. RESULT AND DISCUSSION

The companies in this study do not know that KM is a valuable strategy to become competitive and innovative on KBE society. Although they said the departments practiced KM, it was verified it didn´t happen. They didn´t act in a coordinated manner solving complex tasks without explicit rules for action or even without explicit communication, and there was not technology of connection to organize content to focus on connecting people and capturing knowledge.

Table 3. Time average for the use of ICT by employees in the company

All Day	Four Hours a Day	Two Hours a Day	Half an Hour
E-mail, Internet, phone			
Intranet, e-mail, phone, corporate portals, Internet			
	E-mail and phone		Internet
Phone, e-mail Internet, repositories of knowledge			
		Phone	E-mail, intranet, internet, instant messages
E-mail, phone, Internet, intranet and instant messages			
E-mail, phone, wiki, corporate portals, knowledge repositories and instant messaging			
E-mail, phone, wiki, corporate portals, knowledge repositories and instant messaging			
Internet, intranet and phone		Forum, e-mail and corporate portals	Online discussion list, wiki and knowledge repositories
E-mail, internet, intranet, phone, corporate portals, knowledge repositories			
	Phone	Intranet, Internet and corporate portals	Online discussion lists, forum, e-mail, repositories and instant messages

Table 4. Critical success factors of knowledge management and communities of practice

CSF	References
Organization with a little bureaucratic and a little hierarchy	Dubé et al. (2003), p. 14; Roberts (2006), p. 628; Wenger et. al (2002), p. 128
Valorisation of the culture and of the knowledge sharing	Hara et al. (2009), p. 747 ; Wenger et al. (2002), p.38
Knowledge of the information and communication technology; use to facilitate the communication and places of meeting and talks	Gongla & Rizzuto (2001), p. 849; Hara et al. (2009), p. 742; Dubé et al. (2006), p.78 and 81; Wenger et al. (2002), p.130-131
People with something in common, which the knowledge will contribute to the company	Gongla & Rizzuto (2001), p. 847; Roberts (2006), p. 625; Wenger (1998), p. 8
Issues closely related to an important issue to the company and the daily work	Dubé et al. (2003), p. 13
Include members of different backgrounds, skills, age, personality and authority	Roberts (2006), p. 627

It´s clear that there was no KM strengthening and support to company's activity. Therefore, it was found three key practices that manage the aggregated knowledge necessary to develop an innovative environment:

1. **Master-apprentice model:** Valuing the work of master-apprentice model;
2. **Mediator tool:** ICT contributes to KM and CoP as a mediator tool in changing environments and interaction, since intervening in the learning process and consolidating as means capable of connecting individuals;
3. **Socialization:** Conversion of part of the tacit to explicit knowledge from an individual to another.

In most companies the CSF found give the direction to present the twenty-two essential guidelines to the creation of CoP, such as the following nine:

1. A vertical hierarchy and departmental structure, which face is integration;
2. Information flows in print and informal place to exchange information;
3. Provide training for the dissemination and sharing of knowledge;
4. To know the competence of its employees;
5. Understand that the value of the employees occurs through courses, scholarships, training, career and promotions;
6. To have teamwork and cooperation among employees, according to the level of trust and friendship;
7. Encourage studies and provide financial assistance, training exercises, suitable environment for safety, information technology and health aid;
8. Recognize programs that appears to participate in profit sharing, career plan, contact by email from the senior management and a mural publication;
9. Financial risk is worth for better results; deny there is penalty to employees in case of mistakes.

The discourse analyses form the interview gave support for the proposed guidelines together with the CSF of CoP and KM. The result made it possible to propose the adoption of the approach based in the twenty-two sequentially guidelines, innovating management and beginning the development of KM via CoP:

1. A flat hierarchy and a structure for projects to the flow of knowledge. Therefore, employees can expose and exchange ideas and information at the same level to deepen knowledge and expertise;
2. Integration in person and via Internet to store the knowledge generated among employees with concerns and interest in a particular subject;
3. Provide physical and virtual space for information flow in dual carriageway via e-mail or a blog. The purpose is to sharing information, ideas and advices;
4. Provide informal space for exchanging experiences among employees as a recreation area designed for them. The purpose of the contact is to assist in solving problems, creating projects and developing the tacit understanding on a topic;
5. Provide training for the generation of new ideas for the development of collective knowledge, continuous learning. They help in the sharing of problems, perspectives, ideas and solutions;

6. Provide an information system for the dissemination and sharing of knowledge;
7. Valuing the company culture. By providing communication channels to make interaction and knowledge transfer easier;
8. Mapping the competence of the staff. It helps achieving their organizational goals and the company´s in order to develop innovative ideas and solutions;
9. Enhancing knowledge through courses and specializations, scholarships, internal training, career path and promotions;
10. Encourage teamwork and cooperation, if only for financial stimulus;
11. Promoting trust and friendship between people;
12. Support the development of internal activities through scholarships, training, financial incentives, appropriate environment for safety and environmental technology and implement programs;
13. Involve senior management in recognition of employee's work, and implement a career plan and profit sharing programs and results;
14. Taking financial risks innovating;
15. Don't promote the employee sanction in case of mistakes;
16. Adopt methodologies and techniques used for creating and capturing knowledge, and promote training;
17. Adopt methodologies and techniques used for the transfer and sharing of knowledge as a practice;
18. Evaluate practices of KM through a physical or electronic form or by reaction activities and career path;
19. Enable leaders to have access to different areas of the company to encourage the creation, sharing and the use of knowledge every day;
20. Development of KM practices in programs supported by the senior management;
21. Frequency or training programs to create, capture, share, use and disseminate knowledge;
22. Propose a mediator to motivate the employees to practice knowledge.

5. CONCLUSION

Any company that doesn´t know KM and needs to be innovative, now can do it using the original twenty-two guidelines. The goal was accomplished since it opened paths to an innovative environment in company and elucidates the relevance of KM and CoP at the KBE.

This study presented questionnaires and interviews answered by decision makers from HR and IT areas, in companies in the interior of São Paulo state, Brazil. The guidelines were developed based on the data from the interviews and the CSF of KM and CoP, after validated by specialists.

The KBE asks for better preparation of companies for their survival. The intention of this work was to contribute to the companies aiming to improve their management in terms of knowledge, considered a critical source for innovation. It also helps academics who study the issues presented.

There are future studies to be done such as CoP design, CoP mediation, Proximal Development Zone learning, the guidelines pilot test and learning as a function of participation in CoP.

REFERENCES

Agterberg, M., Hooff, B. V. D., Huysman, M., & Soekijad, M. (2010). Keeping The Wheels Turning: The Dynamics of Managing Networks of Practice. *Journal of Management Studies*, *47*(1), 85–108. doi:10.1111/j.1467-6486.2009.00867.x

Amin, A., & Roberts, J. (2008). Knowing in action: Beyond communities of practice. *Research Policy*, *37*(2), 353–369. doi:10.1016/j.respol.2007.11.003

Barcelo-Valenzuela, M., Sanchez-Schmitz, G., Perez-Soltero, A., Martín Rubio, F., & Marr, B. (2008). Defining the Problem: Key element for the Success of Knowledge Management. *Knowledge Management Research & Practice*, *6*(5), 322–333. doi:10.1057/kmrp.2008.22

Bose, R. (2004). Knowledge Management Metrics. *Industrial Management & Data Systems*, *104*(6), 457–468. doi:10.1108/02635570410543771

Bourhis, A., & Dubé, L. (2010). Structuring Spontaneity: Investigating the Impact of Management Practices on the Success of Virtual Communities of Practice. *Journal of Information Science*, *36*(2), 175–193. doi:10.1177/0165551509357861

Butler, T., Feller, J., Pope, A., Emerson, B., & Murphy, C. (2008). Designing a Core it Artifact for Knowledge Management Systems Using Participatory Action Research in a Government and a Non-Government Organization. *The Journal of Strategic Information Systems*, *17*(4), 249–267. doi:10.1016/j.jsis.2007.10.002

Choi, B., Poon, S. K., & Davis, J. G. (2008). Effects of Knowledge Management Strategy on Organizational Performance, a Complementarity Theory-Based Approach. *Omega-International Journal of Management Science*, *36*(2), 235–251. doi:10.1016/j.omega.2006.06.007

Cortés, C. E., Patronicio, Z. S., & Eva, P. O. (2007). Organizational Structure Features Supporting Knowledge Management Processes. *Journal of Knowledge Management*, *11*(4), 45–57. doi:10.1108/13673270710762701

Dalkir, K. (2005). *Knowledge Management in Theory and Practice*. Boston: Elsevier.

Dubé, L., Bourhis, A., & E Jacob, R. (2003). Towards a typology of virtual communities of practice. *Cahiers du GReSI*, Novembre, *3*(13).

Erden, Z., Von Krogh, G., & Nonaka, I. (2008). The Quality of Group Tacit Knowledge. *The Journal of Strategic Information Systems*, *17*(1), 4–18. doi:10.1016/j.jsis.2008.02.002

Fahey, R., Vasconcelos, A. C., & David, E. D. (2007). The Impact of Rewards within Communities of Practice: A Study of the Sap Online Global Community. *Knowledge Management Research & Practice. Hampshire*, *5*, 186–198.

Gairín-Sallán, J., Rodríguez-Gómez, D., & Armengol-Asparó, C. (2010). Who Exactly Is the Moderator? A Consideration of Online Knowledge Management Network Moderation in Educational Organizations. *Computers & Education*, *55*(1), 304–312. doi:10.1016/j.compedu.2010.01.016

Gongla, P., & Rizzuto, C. R. (2001). Evolving communities of practice: IBM Global Services experience. *IBM Systems Journal*, *40*(4), 842–862. doi:10.1147/sj.404.0842

Hara, N., Shachaf, P., & Stoerger, S. (2009). Online communities of practice typology revisited. *Journal of Information Science*, *35*(6), 740–757. doi:10.1177/0165551509342361

Harris, R. G. (2001). The Knowledge-Based Economy: Intellectual Origins and New Economic Perspectives. *International Journal of Management Reviews*, *3*(1), 21–40. doi:10.1111/1468-2370.00052

Hislop, D. (2005). *Knowledge Management in Organizations: A Critical Introduction*. Oxford: Oxford University Press.

Hoffmann, W. A. (2009). *Gestão do Conhecimento: Desafios de Aprender*. São Carlos: Compacta.

Klein, H. J., Connell, N. A., & Meyer, E. (2005). Knowledge Characteristics of Communities of Practice. *Knowledge Management Research & Practice*, *3*(2), 106–114. doi:10.1057/palgrave.kmrp.8500055

Kogut, B., & Zander, U. (1992). Knowledge of the Firm, Combinative Capabilities, and the Replication of Technology. *Organization Science*, *3*(3), 383–397.

Li, L. C., Grimshaw, J. M., Nielsen, C., Judd, M., Coyote, P. C., & Graham, I. D. (2009) Evolution of Wenger's concept of community of practice. Implementation Science, London 4(11).

Li, Z., Yezhuang, T., & Zhongying, Q. (2006) The impact of organizational culture and knowledge management on organizational performance. *Proceedings of the Information Resources Management Association International Conference*, San Diego. Hershey, PA, USA: Idea Group Co.

McElroy, M. W. (1999) The Second Generation of Knowledge Management. *Knowledge Management,* October, 86-88.

Nonaka, I. (1994). A Dynamic Theory of Organizational Knowledge Creation. *Organization Science*, *05*(01), 14–37. doi:10.1287/orsc.5.1.14

O'Brien, J. (2004). *Sistemas de informação e as decisões gerenciais na era da Internet*. São Paulo: Saraiva.

Prusak, L. (2001). Where Did Knowledge Management come from? *IBM Systems Journal*, *40*(4), 1002–1007. doi:10.1147/sj.404.01002

Roberts, J. (2006). Limits to communities of practice. *Journal of Management Studies*, *43*(3), 623–639. doi:10.1111/j.1467-6486.2006.00618.x

Rosini, A. M., & Palmisano, A. (2003). *Administração de Sistemas de Informação e a Gestão do Conhecimento*. São Paulo: Pioneira Thompson Learning.

Skerlavaj, M., Dimovski, V., & Desouza, K. C. (2010). Patterns and Structures of Intra-Organizational Learning Networks within a Knowledge-Intensive Organization. *Journal of Information Technology*, *25*(2), 189–204. doi:10.1057/jit.2010.3

Usoro, A., Sharratt, M. W., Tsui, E., & Shekhar, S. (2007). Trust as an Antecedent to Knowledge Sharing in Virtual Communities of Practice. *Knowledge Management Research & Practice*, *5*(3), 199–212. doi:10.1057/palgrave.kmrp.8500143

Wenger, E. (2014) Communities of Practice: a few frequently asked questions, www.ewenger.com on October 8th.

Wenger, E. C. (1998). *Communities of Practice, Learning Meaning and Identity*. New York: Cambridge University Press. doi:10.1017/CBO9780511803932

Wenger, E. C., McDermott, R., & Snyder, W. C. (2002). *Cultivating communities of practice: a guide to managing knowledge*. Boston: Harvard Business School Press.

APPENDIX 1

Dear,

I hereby ask for your participation on the following research about Knowledge Management as part of the master course of Roberta Salgado Gonçalves da Silva enrolled at the Production Engineering undergraduate program at Engineering School of São Carlos, University of São Paulo, under advising of the PhD Professor Edson Walmir Cazarini.

The company and employees names will be confident and the result of the research will be presented to the participants at the end of the work.

Sincerely,

Research on Knowledge Best Practices

Objective: the questionnaire will follow these goals: verify the potentialities and deficiencies on the development of KM on companies; identify the use of some tools/best practice, such as Communities of Practice.

Justification: the companies were chosen to be classified as large and for having evidences of the use of information and communication technology.

The following is the conceptualizations of some of the area terms to have uniformity and clarity regards the formulated questions.

Knowledge Management: Defined by Dalkir (2005) as a deliberate and systematic coordination of people, technology, process and structure in an organization with the objective to aggregate value by the reutilization of knowledge and innovation. Knowledge Management is the activity of management which the objective é the improvement of the process of knowledge and consequently, of the business itself and the ability to adaptation to the environment (McELROY, 1999) (see Questionnaire).

Questionnaire

1. Company characterization:

   a. Please, identify yourself. Data are confidential:

Name/ Company/Email Address/Phone Number

b. Actual number of employee.
c. Which is the size of the company in terms of annual revenue?

Until U$136 thousand/ From U$136 thousand to U$ 284 thousand/ From U$ 284 thousand to more than U$ 568 thousand/ More than U$ 568 thousand.

d. In which type of production system does the company fit: industry, trade or service?
e. What is the profile of the company's customers? Individuals or entities? Reside in which regions? What is the income? What are their preferences?
f. What are the main products?
g. In the case of industry, which are the main processes?
h. What funding is used in the company to carry out activities and projects?

2. Knowledge Management characterization:
    a. Please, identify yourself. Data are confidential:

Name/ Company/Email Address/Phone Number

b. What company department performs the tasks of knowledge management? In addition, how long does this occur?
c. Which of the following tools are used to share knowledge within the company?
    i. Mailing lists online
    ii. Virtual forums
    iii. E-mail
    iv. Intranet
    v. Instant Messaging
    vi. Telephone
    vii. Wiki
    viii. Corporate portals
    ix. Knowledge repositories
    x. None of the above

3. Employees have open or restricted access to which technologies? Open/Restrict

a. Mailing lists online
b. Virtual forums
c. E-mail
d. Intranet
e. Instant Messaging
f. Telephone
g. Wiki
h. Corporate portals
i. Knowledge repositories
j. None of the above

4. Do you use the work schedule to make use of virtual environments? If so, for how long? All day/Four hours/Two hours/Half an hour

a. Mailing lists online

b. Virtual forums
c. E-mail
d. Intranet
e. Instant Messaging
f. Telephone
g. Wiki
h. Corporate portals
i. Knowledge repositories
j. None of the above

5. Is information technology present throughout the organization? Yes/No/Other (please specify).
6. Information technology offers or competitive strategies, which favors below?

a. Cost reduction;
b. Product differentiation;
c. Service differentiation;
d. Product innovation;
e. Service innovation;
f. Developing partnerships;
g. Other (please specify)

7. Which tools of information technology are used in the company?

a. Spreadsheets
b. Database
c. Corporate portals
d. Communities of practice
e. Forum
f. Other (please specify)

8. Is information technology used outside the workplace tasks for the company?
9. Which technologies are used to improve the work practices within the company?

APPENDIX 2

Dear,

In June, a report on the results of the academic research on the practices of Knowledge Management and Communities of Practice were sent to you. The data collection was made by a questionnaire answered by the decision maker on human resource management, knowledge management or information and communication technology departments.

At this second and last phase of the research, it´s needed an interview with the same decision makers. There are 29 questions to be asked in about twenty minutes. For your knowledge, the interview guide is attached.

Your participation was fundamental until now for the success of the research and we appreciate your valuable collaboration on this final phase.

Sincerely,

Interview

1. How to classify the hierarchy of the organization, vertical, horizontal or mixed?
2. What is the organizational structure type: by departments, projects or both?
3. How is the integration between the departments?
4. Is there any way to set up the information flow within the organization?
5. Within this organizational structure, is there any informal space where employees exchange experiences?
6. Is there any training for the employees to generate new ideas and innovation? How does it occur?
7. Is there any training for the dissemination and sharing of knowledge? How does it occur?
8. Does the organization know the employee competence?
9. How is knowledge valued in the organization?
10. Is there any teamwork? How are the activities?
11. Does the success of an employee depend on the success of others?
12. What is the way of cooperation in the organization?
13. How do you evaluate the level of trust and friendship between people?
14. Does the organization support employees to develop by themselves their formal activities?
15. Does the organization demonstrate its concern for the well - being of employees?
16. What kind of recognition does the organization offer to its employees? Is there any promotion system to rise in the hierarchy?
17. Does the organization take risk to achieve better results?
18. Is there any penalty if employees make mistakes within the organization?
19. Which are the methodologies and techniques used for creating and capturing knowledge?
20. Which are the methodologies and techniques used for the transfer and sharing of knowledge?
21. Which are the methodologies and techniques used for the learning of knowledge?
22. Which are the methodologies and techniques to use the knowledge?
23. Which are the methodologies and techniques used for the evaluation of the practices of knowledge management?
24. How often do employees create and capture new knowledge for the organization?
25. How often do employees share and disseminate knowledge within the organization?
26. How often do employees use the knowledge within the organization?
27. How does the organization provide leaders in different areas to encourage the creation, sharing and use of knowledge?
28. How does the organization train leaders for knowledge management?
29. How does the top management support the management practices of knowledge?

Chapter 16
Integration of Web 2.0 Tools for Non-Formal Learning Practices:
A Study of IBM's Digital Spaces

Ayse Kok
Bogazici University, Turkey

ABSTRACT

This research tries to explore the specific benefits of online collaboration tools, and finds out how their use has been appropriated by employee volunteers for their practice of volunteering and how they influenced the process of their meaning-making. By doing so, it raised an awareness of the digital tools that provide collections of traits through which individuals can get involved in non-formal learning practices by having digital interactions with others.

1. INTRODUCTION

This study provides an insight into how online engagement enabled the continuation of non-formal workplace learning practices such as volunteering and opened up possibilities for new ways to contribute to the learning process of employees. Today's workplace settings are in constant need of recurrent learning processes interwoven with daily tasks on digital spaces. However, these digital spaces are not devoid of any issues and hence suggest the need for employees to be conscious of the emerging issues. As every knowledge-intensive entity needs to support their employees' development in non-classroom and non-instructional type of learning the crucial aspect of digital applications in terms of contributing to related processes of knowledge creation by fostering collaboration needs an emphasis. While doing this I reflect upon the strategies adopted in alignment with the umbrella term of "Web 2.0".

This research study explores how online communities are created by employee volunteers and also provides an understanding of non-formal learning practices within such fluid settings; important issues for organizations interested in non-formal learning practices of their employees are also being raised.

The study conveys a context-driven collaboration model focusing on learning through collaboration throughout a volunteering programme. This volunteering program matches communities' needs in the

DOI: 10.4018/978-1-4666-9556-6.ch016

Copyright © 2016, IGI Global. Copying or distributing in print or electronic forms without written permission of IGI Global is prohibited.

developing world to IBM employees' learning processes in a collaborative and integrated manner. This volunteering model involves a decentralized, employee-generated learning process that is driven by collaboration with colleagues, online resources and experts within the organizational setting in IBM. I identify the affordances of various digital tools from the perspective employee volunteering, and how these affordances can be leveraged to support employee choice and autonomy. The volunteers made a decision for using these online collaboration tools on their own without being under the influence of any institution, and based on their own needs and ideas they utilized these tools. In addition to being a generic space for sharing documents, the digital environment serves as a joint place populated and created by the volunteers to navigate through information, find personal routes and pathways. This set of tools provide contextual information in a seamless manner based on the learning needs of the IBM employees. My inquiry in this thesis related to different volunteering cases that deal with the changing usage patterns. I delve into the collaborative processes facilitated by the use of digital tools within their volunteering context, in other words, whether and how volunteers were supported by the content conveyed to them via means of relevant digital assets and tools. The volunteering setting embeds aspects of both virtual and physical parts of workplace learning.

2. LITERATURE REVIEW AND CONCEPTUAL FRAMEWORK

The last decade has been witness to a shift from the individual to the constructive and social aspect of knowledge in the existing epistemologies (Easterby-Smith & Lyles, 2003). Such a direct shift of focus onto the social nature of meaning and practice can result in the redefinition of the organisation itself as a community of practice (CoP), with organisational dimensions that convey meaning to these practices meaning.

The prominent scholars Lave and Wenger who firstly made a definition of CoP in their famous book with the title "*Situated Learning: Legitimate Peripheral Participation*" studied how situated learning takes place as a result of the relationships built by "master practitioners" and "newcomers". CoP's can also refer to places in which which "communicative action" occurs (Polanyi, 2002). The mutual creation of knowledge mediates these actions (Wenger, 2004). While CoP's function as a ground for knowledge creation and transfer (Lesser & Prusak, 2000; Wenger, 2004; Wenger & Snyder, 2000) they exist at the crossroads of intellectual and social capital. Within the current body of literature it is a common belief among scholars that CoP's support the basis of social capital, which is mandatory for creating knowledge and its dissemination (Lesser & Prusak, 2000, p. 124).

According to Wenger (1999), CoP framework can be implemented within both "intra" and "inter" dimensions of organizational settings due to being "an integral part of our daily lives" (Wenger, 1999, p. 6, 7). Building further upon the concept of CoP, Wenger utilized it to establish a comprehensive theory of how individuals within collective settings such as organizations work together (1999; 2000; 2004). In his book, *Communities of Practice: Learning, Meaning, and Identity*, Wenger (1999) states that organizations can be considered as assemblies of CoP which can reach even beyond their confines and be situated either within or between formal networks (1998, p. 30). In addition, some scholars utilized the concept of CoP to put cross-sector collaborations under scrutiny (Lathlean & le May, 2002; Dewhurst & Navarro, 2004). These scholars have also contributed to my motivation for approaching the CSC Program from the perspective of CoP. These studies suggest that organizational initiatives provide a fruitful ground to implement the CoP theory.

The term "joint enterprise," referred to as the shared purpose of practitioners in a particular field is used as one of the main characteristics of a CoP (Wenger & Synder, 2000). Similarly, according to O'Donnell *et* al (2003) CoP's are formed around a common interest established upon the values of their members. These shared interests are set into a negotiation on a communal basis (Wenger, 1998, p. 78) around a common purpose. Wenger (1998) describes a "practice as a process by which meaning is provided for one's engagement within the world" (p. 51). According to Wenger (1998), "mutual accountability" (p. 81), which refers to the degree of reciprocal relationship among its members, acts as a glue in terms of holding these joint enterprises together. The "shared repertoire" is another feature underpinning CoP (Wenger, 1999, p. 82) and this "shared repertoire" includes the tools and techniques in order for negotiating the meaning and making learning happen (Wenger, 1999). Possible forms for this repertoire range from an informal discussion during a coffee break to a structured meeting based on some decision-making criteria. According to Wenger & Synder (2000), as CoP's often have connotations to business units or teams; additional effort is required to integrate them into organizational settings in order for their power to be realized (Wenger & Snyder, 2000).

IBM's CSC employees can be considered as communities of voluntary practitioners and their means of communication should also be taken into account. These means of communication tange from face-to-face interactions to the use of various digital tools. In other words, it is not sufficient to focus only on the individual elements of the CSC Programme such as the volunteers or online collaboration tools, but in particular on their mutual interplay. Crossan *et* al. (1999) states that one of the main barriers against theory development with regard to any organizational practice is whether the unit of analysis should be individual, group, organizational and/or interorganizational. Furthermore, some theorists assert that an organizational practice would not be complete without the sharing of information and the development of common meaning (Daft & Weick, 1966; Huber, 1991; Stata, 1989). Consequently, as an organizational practice must be shared and integrated with the learning done by others (Brown, 1993; Daft & Huber, 1987; Daft & Weick, 1966) the unit of analysis should be the group. Other scholars assert that the unit of analysis should be the organization itself as much needs to be done by organizations themselves due to the fact that the activity is stored with organizational structures, procedures or systems (Duncan & Weiss, 1979; Hedberg, 1981; Shrivastava, 1983; Fiol & Lyles, 1985; Levitt & March, 1988; Stata, 1989; Huber, 1991; Chi-Sum *et* al., 2008). By taking into account these theoretical perspectives, the unit of analysis of this study will be the group as it focuses on the different CSC groups made up of IBM employee volunteers.

2.1. Literature about CSCL

Any academic discussion of online collaboration involves the practice and theory of CSCL (computer-supported collaborative learning). While the focus of much current CSCL work with regard to workplace learning is rooted in workplace interaction, we should keep in mind that contrary to popular belief, CSCL could especially make a difference when it comes to learning outside the boundaries of organizational settings. So, apart from the daily work practices of individuals, the social "situatedness" of learning (Winograd & Flores, 1986) should also become the focus of these discussions (Lave, 1988). Due to the adoption of such an alternative approach "outside-class" activities are considered as a crucial aspect of the social background with regard to the process of learning (Cole & Griffin, 1987).

From the theoretical perspectives of CSCL, learning should be assessed on the group level while technology can support the group processes: According to Scardamalia and Bereiter (1996), the community learns as a whole in a computer-supported learning community while the term "community" itself needs a re-conceptualization taking into account the definition provided by Lave and Wenger (1991). Engeström (1999) took a wider learning approach and studied how learning occurs during the interaction of multiple groups among each other. Stahl (2001) claims that these theoreticians (e.g: Lave, 1996; Engeström, 1999) derive their social theories based on Hegel (1967), Marx (1976) and Vygotsky (1978) and that these CSCL theories are disputative due to the increasing complexity of the history of philosophy and theory since the times of Descartes. According to Kant (1787), our conceptualization of the outer world was represented by the human mind, which involves a basic structure rather than being simply given by the material world. Hegel (1807) adopted a developmental view and grounded the process of representation in changes throughout the history. According to Marx (1867/1976), these changes are grounded within socio-economic phenomena. Later on, another famous scholar, namely Heidegger (1927), suggested another perspective in which the human being is more firmly situated in the world than Descartes' approach. Figure 1 shows a graphical representation with regard to the different social and individual theories of learning.

Figure 1. Graphic representation of individual and social theories of learning (Stahl, 2001)

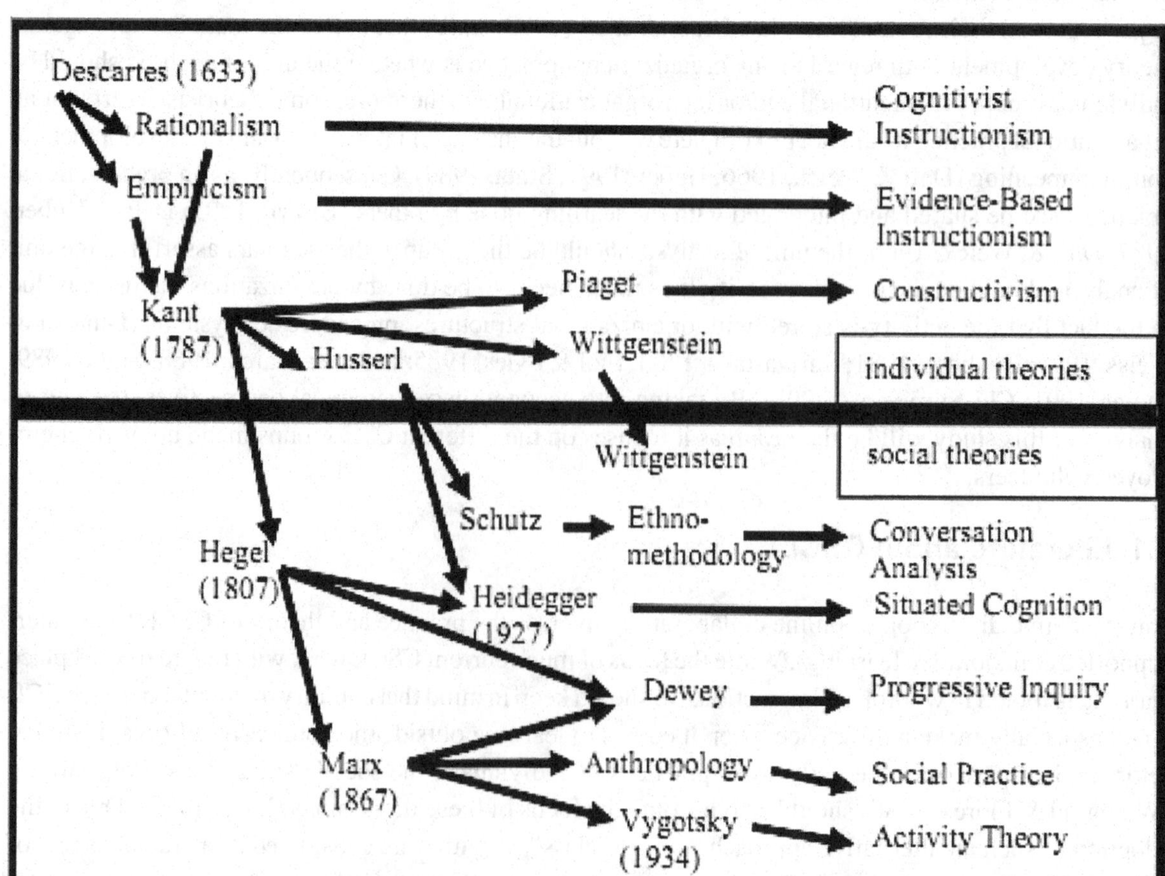

Taking into account these individual and social theories of learning there are two main approaches of defining CSCL:

- According to the first perspective, CSCL can be seen as an "umbrella term" which provides a fertile ground with regard to the development of multi-faceted perspectives on related topics. In fact, this approach provides a further ground for the creation of many new research areas such as Computer Supported Cooperative Work (CSCW) (Bannon et *al.*, 1988, Bannon & Schmidt, 1992);
- The second perspective is related to understanding the related problems and concerns in detail and establishing a shared understanding on the object of study which would further contribute to the development of the field. As there is no unified definition for CSCL, a compositional perspective might be taken in which the meaning of the term is built from its components. So, possible questions that can be asked include what do people mean by collaboration or learning and by CSCL. Rather than imposing an exclusive interpretation on the meaning of CSCL, the focus of research can shift to workplace learning, in this case to the specific initiative of employee volunteering, and how it might be supported by the online collaboration tools.

Table 1 provides the differences between traditional and collaborative learning as explained by Mandl & Krause (2001). A constructivist learning theory underpins the concept of CSCL. According to this theoretical approach, learning involves a process guided on one's own which requires a conscious knowledge creation and hence the previous experiences, skill set and mindset of the individual influence this process (Mandl & Krause, 2001). Additionally, there is a second constructivist approach with regard to knowledge-sharing: "to solve problems in a self-organized way" (Arnold & Schussler, 1998, p. 78). Within this regard it is crucial for organizational stakeholders that different types of learning are facilitated by supporting learner-oriented, social and situative learning (Mandl & Krause, 2001).

Timothy Koschmann, one of the prominent scholars in this field asserted that this shift in pedagogical models due to the use of technology represents the start of a new paradigm according to the Kuhnian perspective (Koschmann, 1996). Koschmann (1996) further stated that with CSCL the emphasis shifts from the personal development onto the group cognition and due to the incompatibility of this perspective with the conventional view which is more individualistic, it meets the requirements of a new paradigm as determined by Kuhn (1962).

Table 1. Differences between the traditional and collaborative e-learning model (Mandl & Krause, 2001)

	Traditional Approach	Collaborative Approach
The objective of learning	Being qualified for expertise	Skill
Know-how	In progress, memorized	Construed
Paradigm	Solving a problem, gaining an understanding	To enhance related experiences and practices
Technology use	Dissemination	Communication, learning in collaboration
The mode of involvement for learner	The metaphor of acquisition metaphor	The metaphor of participation
Interaction type	Delivery model	Dynamic and complex model

In my view, rather than trying to come up with a unified approach for empirical research in CSCL researchers should focus on how individuals collaborate with digital tools which might also be relevant for the CSC Programme. In my point of view, the aim should be to elaborate on the ways of using these tools in an effective way in order to obtain the commonly shared goals which is one of the underlying features of collaboration.

3. RESEARCH METHODOLOGY

This section discusses the key research questions, the overall methodological approach, the design of the study and research methods and strategies as well as ethical issues, and a short precursory description of data analysis planned including a pilot study.

3.1. Research Questions

The study aims to answer the following research questions:

- How are collaborative learning tools used for the volunteering practice of knowledge workers?
- What are their assumptions about the benefits and challenges in using these tools for such a practice?

In conceptualising the participatory nature of this research study, I have derived my approach from the framework offered by Fajerman and Treseder (2000) that specifies six different ways for involving participants ranging from no involvement at all to the involvement of the participant initiated on his own or based on decisions shared with the researcher. The methodology used in this study belongs to the group of "consulted and informed" as defined by Fajerman and Treseder (2000), in other words I as a researcher designed the study while the participants' opinions are taken seriously. Needless to say, the participants are informed of the complete research process (see Figure 2).

3.2. Data Collection

Data collection has the following main sources:

- Information based on the online survey;
- Digital artefacts such as blogs and wikis; and
- Transcripts from the interviews.

The data collection methods of this research study include an interview an online); and review of digital artefacts all of which have been utilized in both participatory design and related participatory research. A cross table in order to match the online survey and interview details was developed. Table 2 provides the data collection methods based on each stage.

Figure 2. Fajerman and Treseder (2000)'s model for levels of participant involvement

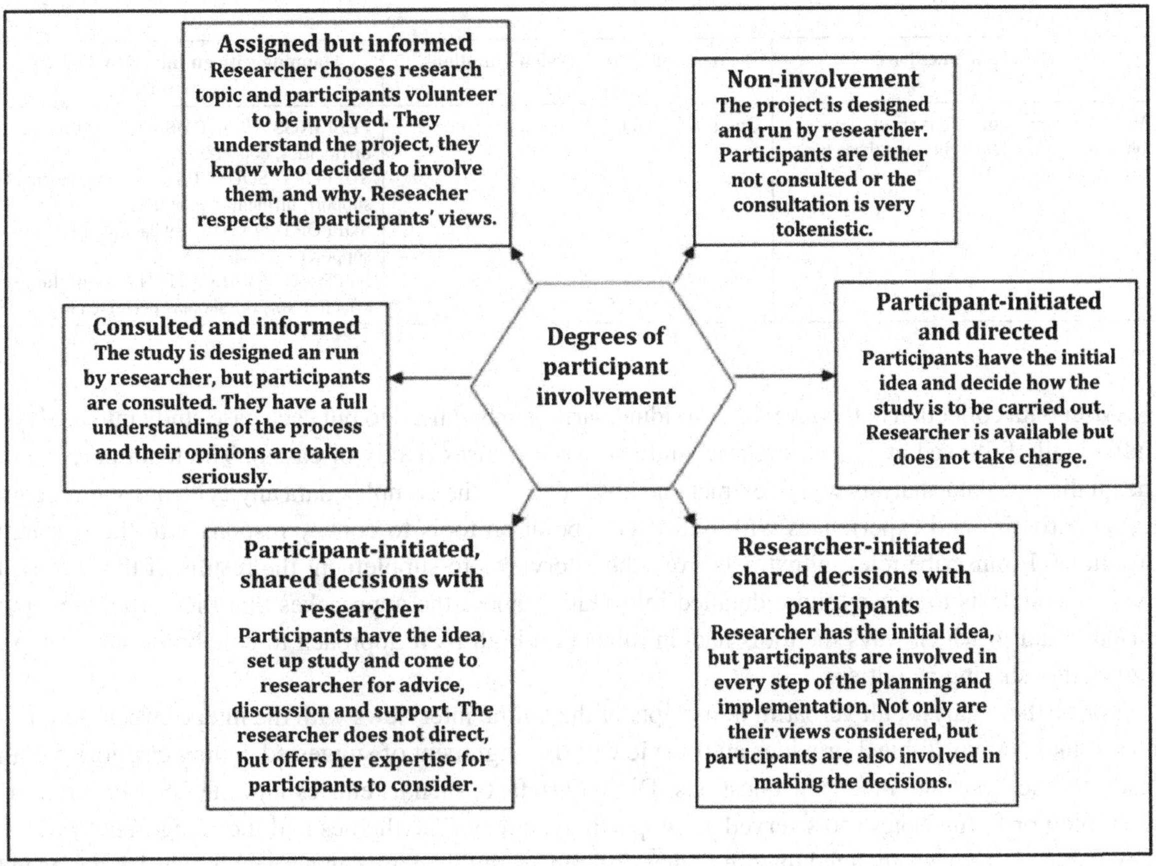

3.3. Data Analysis

To conduct the quantitative data analysis, SPSS was used while for qualitative analysis Excel was used by separating content into appropriate sections and manipulating it. Open comments provided about the answers were put into an additional column in the Excel file. In order to see whether some general patterns emerge an overall descriptive analysis was conducted based on the available dataset. A further analysis of these patterns showed whether there were differences among the volunteers. Based on the emerging patterns I coded the qualitative data and ranked the results or directly quoted to support the quantitative findings.

Table 2. Breakdown of data collected

Stage One - Context	Stage Two - Case Studies	
Survey	*Interviews*	*Digital artefacts*
12	17	30

Table 3. Overview of the alignment of the suggested interview coding categories with research questions and interview questions

Research Questions	Mapping with Interview Questions	Mapping with an Interview Coding Framework
What are their assumptions about the benefits and challenges in using these tools for such a practice?	Questions 2,4,5,6,7,9	FEELINGS ABOUT USAGE (confidence, difficulties, concerns) SUPPORT- SOURCES (who provides the support; influential people) SUPPORT- NATURE (what kind of support) SUPPORT- EVALUATION (how useful or effective was the support perceived to be)

After data collection at the level of individual participants, I tried to put each case study into analysis individually followed by an overarching study across the cases (study of cases). The main purpose of the qualitative data analysis was to extract and abstract from the complex data any evidence with regard to the activities and experiences with online collaboration tools to convey responses to the research questions. I transcribe relevant extracts from the interviews to supplement the results of the survey. I used this analysis to convey more detailed information about the approaches that the participants put into use and in which ways the tools had an impact on both their approach to collaboration and their knowledge-sharing activities.

For further analysis, all verbatim transcripts of the online interviews with the interviewees were imported into NVivo. Table 3 provides an overview of the alignment of suggested coding categories with research questions and interview questions. Digital artefacts such as entries into the CSC Programme wiki, blog or Lotus Notes tools served as supporting sources. The themes and the categories to which they belong have been changed in case of any differences until a common agreement has been reached among the participants.

4. RESULTS

In line with the approaches above the CSC participants devise and adopt a variety of approaches when using technology to support their volunteering process. The most common types of approach adopted by participants seem to be related to sharing of experiences, knowledge and best practice which can establish the ground for encouraging the use of online collaboration tools. These are outlined in Table 4.

At the heart of the CSC Programme lies the process of project-based learning that enables the individuals to gain a shared understanding and construe a common basis for knowledge creation. This does not necessarily leave aside individual contributions and perspectives, yet volunteers are not required to segregate their work into discrete tasks to be completed individually and bring them together later on. Rather, they are required to make contributions to the point of views of their team mates for the mutual negotiation of meaning and the joint construction of a project by using online collaboration tools (Roschelle & Teasely, 1995). Coordination is a necessary element only when putting together the partial results of the discrete tasks of the related project (Roschelle & Teasely, 1995). On the other hand, the construction of a joint project through genuine collaboration necessitates a coordinated effort for a joint

Table 4. Overview of the types of approaches used by CSC volunteers

Volunteers' Approaches	Examples
Having co-presence/ Sharing experience, knowledge and best practice	Using Instant messaging; participating in discussion forums; or uploading videos or photos onto the Internet
Meeting new colleagues and experience parts of the world	Having discussions through Lotus Notes communities and tracking the experience of the participants
Navigating through information, find personal routes and pathways	Using internal Lotus Notes platform
Increasing one's knowledge on CSC Programme	Using Edvisor especially before leaving for fieldwork
Reflecting on one's experiences	Blogging
Accessing, creating, sharing and continually improving ideas	Participating in exchange of ideas via blogs and wikis
Participating in networks of distributed volunteers engaging in activities	Using popular Web 2.0 tools such as Ning, FaceBook
Facilitating ongoing communication, dialogue and shared activity	Creating digital artefacts
Supporting one's learning process	Attending online trainings on culture, security and literature reading on social responsibility projects online
Receiving informal support	Using Skype or MSN to communicate with others
Aiming toward a common goal of knowledge creation	Participating in exchange of ideas via Lotus Notes communities, e-mail and wiki
Participating in a team evolution process	Observing others' online behavioural pattern on discussion forums or the wiki
Supporting online communities and relationships between people	Participating in Lotus Notes communities
Having a more authentic collaboration through the creation of digital artefacts	Posting mainly on blogs or contributing to wikis
Recombining the information shared by others to create new concepts, ideas, and services	Utilizing Web 2.0 tools (mostly blogs and wikis)
Having co-presence/ Sharing experience, knowledge and best practice	Using Instant messaging; participating in discussion forums; or uploading videos or photos onto the Internet
Meeting new colleagues and experience parts of the world	Having discussions through Lotus Notes communities and tracking the experience of the participants
Navigating through information, find personal routes and pathways	Using internal Lotus Notes platform
Increasing one's knowledge on CSC Programme	Using Edvisor especially before leaving for fieldwork
Reflecting on one's experiences	Blogging
Accessing, creating, sharing and continually improving ideas	Participating in exchange of ideas via blogs and wikis
Participating in networks of distributed volunteers engaging in activities	Using popular Web 2.0 tools such as Ning, FaceBook
Facilitating ongoing communication, dialogue and shared activity	Creating digital artefacts
Supporting one's learning process	Attending online trainings on culture, security and literature reading on social responsibility projects online
Receiving informal support	Using Skype or MSN to communicate with others
Aiming toward a common goal of knowledge creation	Participating in exchange of ideas via Lotus Notes communities, e-mail and wiki
Participating in a team evolution process	Observing others' online behavioural pattern on discussion forums or the wiki
Supporting online communities and relationships between people	Participating in Lotus Notes communities
Having a more authentic collaboration through the creation of digital artefacts	Posting mainly on blogs or contributing to wikis
Recombining the information shared by others to create new concepts, ideas, and services	Utilizing Web 2.0 tools (mostly blogs and wikis)

problem-solving (Roschelle & Teasely, 1995). It involves an interactive process that requires the participation of all group members for mutual negotiation and sharing of ideas (Roschelle & Teasely, 1995).

All these factors displayed in Table 5 lead to the emergence of a new volunteering practice that I call as 'distributed' or 'technology-enhanced' volunteering. It is the amalgamation of the social affordances of digital tools, with new informal learning goals and priorities that provide an opportunity for metamorphical shifts in employee volunteering practices.

As summarized in Figure 3 feelings and beliefs about the potential benefits of digital collaboration tools vary. Some people think that online collaboration tools offer a great potential fpr improving digital competencies of team members others think by providing connectivity and a shared belief of understanding of team members' roles and responsibilities. While connectivity is about enabling a space for activities co-presence is about requiring that everybody participate in these activities. Through participation in these forms of discussion and interaction, volunteers are provided with the ability to construct their own informal learning trajectories as well as shaping pro-actively those of others. This observed distributed cognition among CSC volunteers as supported by online collaboration tools directly leads to the temporary construction of one or more group minds. Intersubjectivity is obtained when there is a shared ownership of the activity and a common conceptualization about the objective as a result of the collaborative redefinition of that activity. So, perspectives are negotiated on an ongoing basis.

The perceived benefits of online collaboration tools can also engender epistemic fluency (Goodyear & Zenios, 2007) which allows volunteers not to underestimate the complexity of existing ideas, norms and practices. Evidence of both interdependent use (using the tools for the purpose of collaboration), independent use (e.g: independent use of tools for other purposes than collaboration) are evident throughout the study. Such practices do not often conform with the norms and practices of the conventional volunteering practice. Individual traits such as personal values act as a mediator for the methods of collaboration and learning in social contexts, such as digital environments. Volunteers' participation in digital collaboration should not be assumed as being certain in terms of improving their digital competencies. Meaning and value are important for what is afforded for them to participate in online conversations and learn and eventually improve their digital competencies.

Two individual aspects that appeared to influence participants' decisions about improving their digital competencies via use of these tools are:

- A tendency to participate in a shared endeavour;
- A feeling of co-presence.

Table 5. Mapping between research questions and the findings

Research Question	Sub-Themes
How are collaborative learning tools used for the volunteering practice of knowledge workers?	Usage & Approaches Strategies/Choices Feelings
What are their beliefs about the benefits and challenges in using these tools for such a practice?	Feelings & Assumptions Choices Skills Use & Feelings Usage & Approaches Support

Figure 3. Samples of answers to interview questions

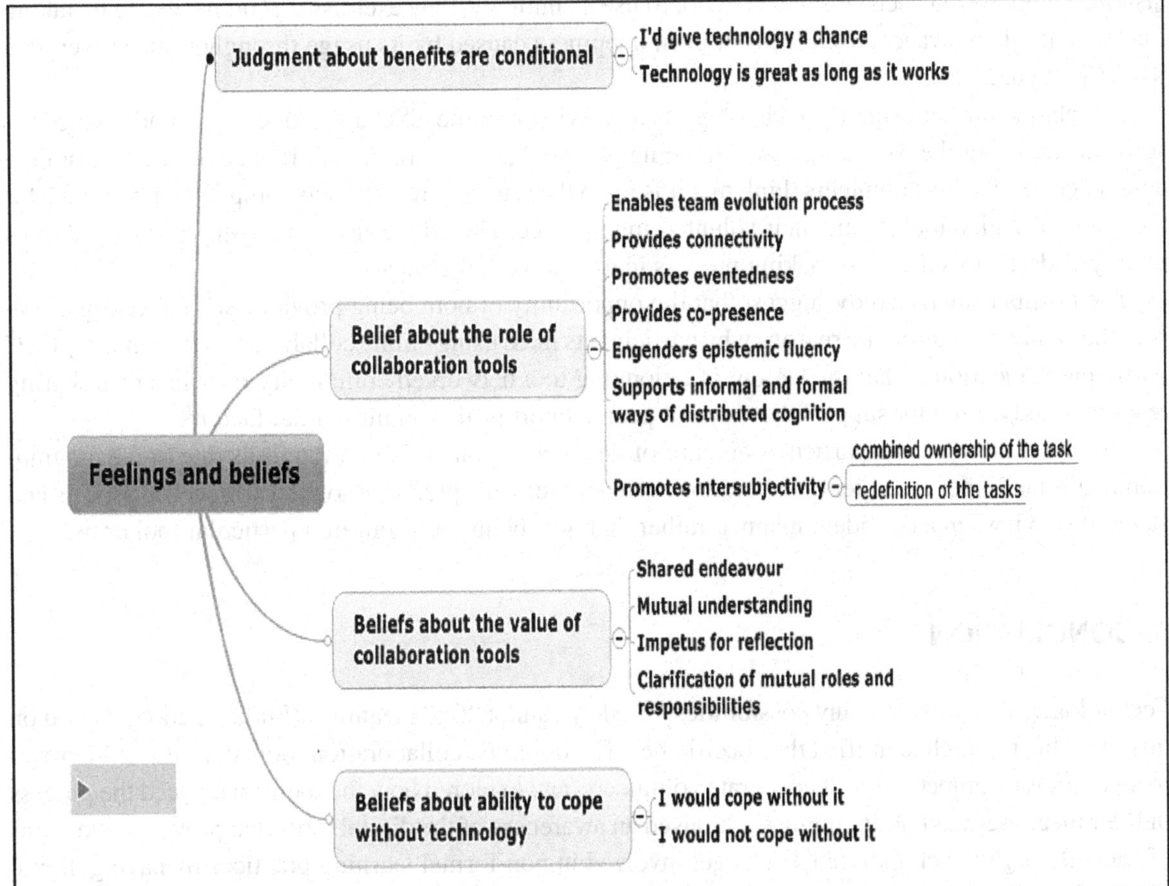

Participants equipped with various levels of expertise and areas of interests nourish the volunteering environment with ideas and knowledge that are befitted by volunteers based on their needs and digital competencies. Expertise is therefore distributed amongst all volunteers. Given the 'transformative' nature of such interactions (Pea, 1994), individuals acquire more expertise as the dialogue unfolds and they co-construct knowledge.

There is also the opportunity provided by the online collaboration tools to go through a team evolution process and recognize common patterns in communication styles of group members. Some participants expressed some issues of concern such as privacy. Still some of the participants indicated they would collaborate without technology, but they would prefer not to. The volunteers are also endowed with a flexibility that enables 'collaborative remixability' (Boyd, 2007) – a transformative process which denotes the state of the information which can be recombined to further develop new concepts, ideas, and services. The different tools enabled the volunteers to navigate through information, find personal routes and pathways. A more liberated definition of community occurred derived from the notion of social networks with an emphasis on social ties rather than geographic location. These virtual communities are place independent, liberated from geography and dependent on technology.

According to Selwyn (2006), who came up firstly with the term "digital decisions", when individuals make empowered decisions to use or not to use technology, they exercise a genuine choice by taking into account its relevance, usefulness or even happiness caused by its usage throughout their everyday lives (Selwyn, 2006).

The choice for not using the technology is also evident in the CSC data. One of the underlying reasons for not using the technology was no being able to "get on with them". It is also evident from the data that several CSC volunteers think that it is up to them to take refined and complicated decisions for the usage of digital tools to aid their volunteering practice. The affordances and features of digital tools mainly underlie this decision-making process in addition to other factors.

The results from the study suggest that the opportunity of both being provided with a feeling of co-presence and eventedness are reasons why participants liked using online collaboration tools mostly CSC participants mentioned that the feeling of belonging to a networked community of colleagues sharing resources and asking for support the value of peer support is also an influential factor

Finally, if there were a particular amount of dependence on collaboration tools due to the assumption that it facilitates an easier collaboration; CSC participants preferred to refer to specific aspects and stated their views in a confident manner, rather than just being in favour of a particular tool or using it.

5. CONCLUSION

Technologies can provide many possibilities, but they cannot "fix" meanings (Suthers, 2005). Based on this fact, this research identified the specific benefits of online collaboration tools in terms of improvement of digital competencies of corporate volunteers, and explored how the tools influenced the process of their meaning-making. By doing so, it raised an awareness of the digital tools that provide collections of traits through which individuals can get involved in non-formal learning practices by having digital interactions with others and improving their digital competencies.

It would be disingenuous and naïve of me to promise that the research study will by itself transform the online collaboration experiences of all users. I do however argue that the finding of this research study would increase an awareness amongst institutional stakeholders interested in the practice of improvement of digital competencies via employee volunteering to take further action and to provide direct responses to what the participants have said and done.

Furthermore, this research study elaborates that participants have created a variety of refined and customized strategies for putting the digital tools into practice to aid their digital competencies. Volunteers' participation in digital collaboration should not be assumed as being certain in terms of improving their digital competencies. Meaning and value are important for what is afforded for them to participate in online conversations and learn and eventually improve their digital competencies. Two individual aspects that appeared to influence participants' decisions about improving their digital competencies via use of these tools are:

- A tendency to participate in a shared endeavour;
- A feeling of co-presence.

I assert that the most pragmatic way to view online collaboration tools with respect to supporting digital competencies is to consider it an enabling medium through which the individuals can structure and complete their activities. The possibility of making use of the tools to reach beyond the individual volunteering activity and facilitate improvement of digital competencies which can be reciprocally supportive breaks down some of the employee volunteering stereotypes that have been moved back and forth for such a long time.

One of the main challenges faced during technology-enhanced volunteering programs will be the composition of the available digital tools and activities so that each tool can be utilized for its affordance. Despite the fact that this study has taken a step in that direction, there is certainly a need for more studies about what works and what does not in a project-based learning environment. The alignment all the affordances in such a way that volunteers gain an understanding of them and make use of the many affordances can be difficult. So, online collaboration tools should better be distributed within the network of volunteers and embodies within their practice of volunteering so that volunteers have more opportunities to realize and take benefit from the affordances of the digital tools. For this purpose, a thorough structuration of the complete environment and the various actors within that context are required: volunteers, digital competencies, digital tools, digital resources and other project stakeholders such as managers.

In the final analysis, the incorporation of online collaboration tools into the CSC Programme is about change in the way the volunteers collaborate with each other, not about technology. This collaborative phenomenon raises the point about socio-technical systems thinking, which stipulates that technology in itself has little meaning. Within the context of employee volunteering, technology gains its value with regard to the collaborative interactions of the volunteers. It's about people and their behavior, not computers. It is about inventing new visions of employee volunteering in the context of a digital world. While the lack of online collaboration tools is a barrier to improve the digital competencies within the context of non-formal learning practices such as employee volunteering, the presence of these tools does not guarantee further improvement of these digital competencies.

REFERENCES

Anderson, K., Dittlau, A., & Funkel, K. (2004, June 29-July 1). Probing students. In M. Agger Eriksen, L. Malmborg, & J. Nielsen (Eds.), *Web Proceedings of Computers in Art and Design Education Conference CADE2004*. Copenhagen Business School, Denmark and Malmö University, Sweden. Copenhagen: CADE.

Anderson, P. (2007). *What is Web 2.0? Ideas, technologies and implications for education* [Online]. JISC. Retrieved from www.jisc.ac.uk/media/documents/techwatch/tsw0701b.pdf

Clark, H. H. (1996). *Using Language*. Cambridge: Cambridge University Press. doi:10.1017/CBO9780511620539

Cogburn, D. L. (2002). HCI in the so-called developing world: What's in it for everyone. *Interactions (New York, N.Y.)*, *10*(2), 80–87. doi:10.1145/637848.637866

Cohen, W. M., & Levinthal, D. A. (1990). Absorptive capacity: A new perspective on learning and innovation. *Administrative Science Quarterly*, *35*(1), 128–152. doi:10.2307/2393553

Cole, M., & Griffin, P. (Eds.). (1987). *Contextual Factors in Education*. Madison: Wisconsin Center for Educational Research.

Conole, G. (2007). Describing learning activities -Tools and resources to guide practice. In H. Beetham & R. Sharpe (Eds.), *Rethinking Pedagogy for a Digital Age: Designing and Delivering E-learning* (pp. 81–91). London: Routledge.

Conole, G., & Fill, K. (2005). *The learning taxonomy in DialogusPlus Toolkit*. University of South Hampton. Retrieved from http://joker.ecs.soton.ac.uk/dialogplustoolkit/userarea/

Cook, S. D. N., & Brown, J. S. (1999). Bridging epistemologies: The generative dance between organizational knowledge and organizational knowing. *Organization Science*, *10*(4), 381–400. doi:10.1287/orsc.10.4.381

Cornwall, A., & Jewkes, R. (1995). What is participatory research? *Social Science & Medicine*, *41*(12), 1667–1676. doi:10.1016/0277-9536(95)00127-S PMID:8746866

Creanor, L., & Trinder, K. et al.. (2006). *LEX: The learner experience of e-learning – final project report, August 2006*. JISC.

Crossan, M. M., Lane, H. W., & White, R. E. (1999). An organizational learning framework: From Intuition to Institution. *Academy of Management Review*, *24*(3), 522–537.

Daft, R., & Huber, G. P. (1987). How organizations learn: A communications framework. *Research in the Sociology of Organizations*, *5*, 1–36.

Dewey, J. (1938). *Logic: The Theory of Inquiry*. New York: Holt.

Dewhurst, F. W., & Cegarra Navarro, J. G. (2004). External communities of practice and relational capital. *The Learning Organization*, *11*(4/5), 322–331. doi:10.1108/09696470410538224

Dewsbury, G., Rouncefield, M., Clarke, K., & Sommerville, I. (2004). Depending on digital design: Extending inclusivity. *Housing Studies*, *19*(5), 811–825. doi:10.1080/0267303042000249224

Dillenbourg, P. (1999). What do you mean by "collaborative learning"? In P. Dillenbourg (Ed.), *Collaborative Learning: Cognitive and Computational Approaches* (pp. 1–16). Amsterdam: Pergamon.

Dirckinck-Holmfeld, L. (2002). Designing virtual learning environments based on problem oriented project pedagogy. In L. Dirckinck-Holmfeld, & B. Fibiger (Eds.), Learning in virtual environments (pp. 31-54). Fredriksberg Denmark: Samfundslitteratur.

Dohn, N. (2010). Web 2.0: Inherent tensions and evident challenges for education. *International Journal of Computer-Supported Collaborative Learning*, *4*(3), 343–363. doi:10.1007/s11412-009-9066-8

Downes, S. (2010). *E-learning 2.0*. National Research Council of Canada. Retrieved from <http://www.elearnmag.org/subpage.cfm?section=articles&article=29-1

Druin, A. (2007). *Connecting Generations: Developing Co-Design Methods for Older Adults and Children*. Retrieved from http://hcil.cs.umd.edu/trs/2007-15/2007-15.pdf

Duckett, P. S., & Fryer, D. (1998). Developing empowering research practices with people who have learning disabilities. *Journal of Community & Applied Social Psychology*, *8*(1), 57–65. doi:10.1002/(SICI)1099-1298(199801/02)8:1<57::AID-CASP438>3.0.CO;2-8

Easterby-Smith, M., & Lyles, M. A. (2003). *The Blackwell Handbook of Organizational Learning and Knowledge Management*. Oxford: Blackwell.

Edwards, R., & Usher, R. (2008). *Globalisation and pedagogy: Space, place and identity* (2nd ed.). Milton Park, England: Routledge.

Engeström, Y. (1999). Activity theory and individual and social transformation. In Y. Engeström, R. Miettinen, & R. L. Punamäki (Eds.), *Perspectives on activity theory* (pp. 19–38). Cambridge: Cambridge University Press. doi:10.1017/CBO9780511812774.003

Engeström, Y. (2001). Expansive learning at work: Toward an activity theoretical reconceptualization. *Journal of Education and Work, 14*(1), 133–156. doi:10.1080/13639080020028747

Engeström, Y., & Middleton, D. (1996). Introduction: Studying work as mindful practice. In Y. Engestrom & D. Middleton (Eds.), *Cognition and Communication at Work* (pp. 1–14). Cambridge: Cambridge University Press. doi:10.1017/CBO9781139174077.001

Etzioni, A. (1975). An Engineer-Social Science Team at Work. *Technology Review, 1975*, 26–31.

Everitt, A., Hardiker, P., Littlewood, J., & Mullender, A. (1992). *Applied Research for Better Practice*. London: Macmillan.

Facebook. (2014). Statistics. Retrieved from http://www.facebook.com/press/info.php?statistics

Fajerman, L., & Treseder, P. (2000). *Children are Service Users too: A Guide to Consulting Children and Young People*. London: Save The Children.

Finholt, T., & Sproull, L. S. (1990). Electronic groups at work. *Organization Science, 1*(1), 41–64. doi:10.1287/orsc.1.1.41

Fiol, C. M., & Lyles, M. A. (1985). Organizational learning. *Academy of Management Review, 10*(4), 803–813.

Fischer, G., & Ostwald, J. (2002). Seeding, Evolutionary Growth, and Reseeding: Enriching Participatory Design with Informed Participation. *Proceedings of the Participatory Design Conference (PDC'02)*, Malmo, Sweden (pp. 135-143).

Foth, M. (2004). Animating personalised networking in a student apartment complex through participatory design. *Proceedings of the Participatory Design Conference*, Toronto. Retrieved from http://eprints.qut.edu.au/archive/00001904/01/foth_id172_shortpaper.pdf

French, S., & Swain, J. (2004). Researching together: a participatory approach. In S. French & J. Sim (Eds.), *Physiotherapy: A Psychosocial Approach* (3rd ed., pp. 50–64). Oxford: Butterworth-Heinemann.

Gee, J. P. (2004). *Situated Language and Learning: A Critique of Traditional Schooling*. New York: Palmgrave-McMillan.

Gibb, T., & Fenwick, T. (2008) 'Older' professionals' learning in an ageist culture: Beneath and between the borders. In J. Groen & S. Guo (Eds.), *Online Proceedings of the Canadian Association for the Study of Adult Education.* Vancouver, British Columbia. Retrieved from http://www.oise.utoronto.ca/CASAE/cnf2008/OnlineProceedings-2008/CAS2008-Gibb.pdf

Giddens, A. (1984). *The constitution of society*. Berkeley: University of California Press.

Johansen, R. (1988). *Groupware: Computer Support for Business Teams*. New York: The Free Press.

Jones, N. B., & Laffey, J. (2002). How to facilitate e-collaboration and e-learning in organizations. In A. Rosset (Ed.), *The ASTD E-Learning Handbook* (pp. 80–101). New York, USA: McGraw-Hill.

Myers, M. (1991) Cooperative learning in heterogeneous classes. *Cooperative Learning, 11*(4).

Naylor, P., Wharf-Higgins, J., Blair, L., Green, L., & O'Connor, B. (2002). Evaluating the participatory process in a community based heart health project. *Social Science & Medicine*, *55*(7), 1173–1187. doi:10.1016/S0277-9536(01)00247-7 PMID:12365529

Neilson, R. (1997). *Collaborative Technologies & Organizational Learning*. Hershey, PA: Idea Group Publishing.

Nelson, G., Ochocka, J., Griffin, K., & Lord, J. (1998). Nothing about me, without me: Participatory Action Research with self-help/mutual aid organizations for psychiatric consumer/survivors. *American Journal of Community Psychology*, *26*(6), 881–912. doi:10.1023/A:1022298129812 PMID:10085536

Newell, A., Carmichael, J., & Morgan, M. (2007). Methodologies for involving older adults in the design process. *Proceedings of the 4th International Conference on Universal Access in HCI*. Retrieved from http://www.springerlink.com/content/53t5026735v65721/fulltext.pdf

Newman, D., Griffin, P., & Cole, M. (1989). *The Construction Zone: Working for Cognitive Change in School*. New York: Cambridge University Press.

Nightingale, C. (2006). *Nothing About Me, Without Me. Involving Learners with Learning Difficulties or Disabilities*. London: Learning Skills Development Agency.

O'Reilly, T. (2005). *What is Web 2.0: design patterns and business models for the next generation of software* [Online]. Available from: <http://www.oreillynet.com/pub/a/oreilly/tim/news/2005/09/30/what-is-web-20.html> (Accessed January 30, 2010).

O'Reilly, T. (2007). *Web 2.0 Compact Definition: Trying Again*. Retrieved from http://www.oreillynet.com/pub/a/oreilly/tim/news/2005/09/30/what-is-web-20.html

Orlikowski, W. (1992). The duality of technology: Rethinking the concept of technology in organizations. *Organization Science*, *3*(3), 398–427. doi:10.1287/orsc.3.3.398

Pain, R., & Francis, P. (2003). Reflections on participatory research. *Area*, *35*(1), 46–54. doi:10.1111/1475-4762.00109

Patton, M. Q. (1980). *Qualitative Evaluation Methods*. Beverly Hills, CA, USA: Sage Publications.

Patton, M. Q. (1990). *Qualitative Evaluation and Research Methods*. Newbury Park; London, UK: Sage.

Pea, R. D. (1994). Seeing what we build together: Distributed multimedia learning environments for transformative communications. *Journal of the Learning Sciences*, *3*(3), 285–299. doi:10.1207/s15327809jls0303_4

Putnam, R. D. (2000). *Bowling alone: The collapse and revival of American community*. New York: Simon & Schuster. doi:10.1145/358916.361990

Radermacher, H. (2006). *Participatory Action Research With People With Disabilities: Exploring Experiences Of Participation*. Melbourne: Victoria University.

Reason, P., & Heron, J. (1986). Research with people: The paradigm of co-operation experiential enquiry. *Person-Centred Review*, *1*(4), 456–476.

Schrage, M. (1990). *Shared Minds: The New Technologies of Collaboration*. New York: Random House.

Selwyn, N. (2006). Digital division or digital decision? A study of non-users and low-users of computers, poetics. *Journal of Empirical Research in Culture. Medical Art*, *34*(4-5), 273–292.

Sfard, A. (1998). On two metaphors for learning and the dangers of choosing just one. *Educational Researcher*, *27*(2), 4–13. doi:10.3102/0013189X027002004

Sharpe, R., Benfield, G., Lessner, E., & De Cicco, E. (2005) *Learner Scoping Study: Final Report*. JISC. Retrieved from http://www.jisc.ac.uk/uploaded_documents/scoping%20study%20final%20report%20v4.1.doc

Shrivastava, P. (1983). A typology of organizational learning systems. *Journal of Management Studies*, *20*(1), 7–28. doi:10.1111/j.1467-6486.1983.tb00195.x

Silva & Breuleux. (1994) The Use of Participatory Design in the Implementation of Internet-based Collaborative Learning Activities in K-12 Classrooms. Retrieved from http://www.helsinki.fi/science/optek/1994/n3/silva.txt

Sim, J. (1998). Collecting and analysing qualitative data: Issues raised by the focus group. *Journal of Advanced Nursing*, *28*(2), 345–352. doi:10.1046/j.1365-2648.1998.00692.x PMID:9725732

Simon, H. A. (1991). Bounded rationality and organizational learning. *Organization Science*, *2*(1), 125–134. doi:10.1287/orsc.2.1.125

Sleeman, D., & Brown, J. S. (Eds.), (1982). *Intelligent Tutoring Systems*. New York: Academic Press.

Smith, J. A., & Osborn, M. (2003). Interpretative Phenomenological Analysis. In A. Smith (Ed.), *Qualitative Psychology* (pp. 40–52). London: Sage.

Sproull, L., & Kiesler, S. (1995). *Connections: New Ways of Working In the Networked Organization*. Cambridge, MA: The MIT Press.

Stahl, G. (Ed.), (2001). Computer Support for Collaborative Learning: Foundations for a CSCL Community. Hillsdale, NJ: Lawrence Erlbaum.

Weick, K. E. (1990). Technology as equivoque: Sense-making in new technologies. In P. S. Goodman & L. S. Sproull (Eds.), *Technology and Organizations* (pp. 78–93). San Francisco: Jossey-Bass.

Wenger, E. (1999). *Communities of Practice: Learning, Meaning and Identity*. Cambridge: Cambridge University Press.

Wenger, E. (2000). Communities of practice: The key to knowledge strategy. In E. L. Lesser, M. A. Fontaine, & J. A. Slusher (Eds.), *Knowledge and Communities* (pp. 3–20). Boston: Butterworth Heinemann. doi:10.1016/B978-0-7506-7293-1.50004-4

Wenger, E. (2004). Communities of practice and social learning systems. In K. Starkey, S. Tempest, & A. McKinlay (Eds.), *How Organizations Learn: Managing the Search for Knowledge* (pp. 238–258). London: Thomson.

Wenger, E., & Snyder, W. M. (2000). Communities of practice: The organizational frontier. *Harvard Business Review*, *78*(6), 139. PMID:11184968

Zack, M. H., & McKenney, J. L. (1995). Social context and interaction in ongoing computer-supported management groups. *Organization Science*, *6*(4), 394–422. doi:10.1287/orsc.6.4.394

Zarb, G. (1992). On the Road to Damascus: First steps towards changing the relations of research production. *Disability, Handicap & Society*, *7*(2), 125–138. doi:10.1080/02674649266780161

Zhao, S. (2001). The increasing presence of telecopresence in the Internet era. Paper presented at the annual conference of the American Sociological Association, Anaheim, CA.

Compilation of References

Ackermann, E. (2001). Piaget's constructivism, Papert's constructionism: What's the difference. *Future of learning group*, 5(3).

Ackermann, F., & Eden, C. (2011). Strategic management of stakeholders: Theory and practice. *Long Range Planning*, *44*(3), 179–196. doi:10.1016/j.lrp.2010.08.001

Adam, A. (1998). *Artificial Knowing, Gender and the Thinking Machine*. London, New York: First Routledge.

Adams, A. N., Brock, R. J., Gordon, K. A., Grohs, J. R., & Kirk, G. R. (2014). Service, Dialogue, and Reflection as Foundational Elements in a Living Learning Community. *Journal of College and Character*, *15*(3), 179–188. doi:10.1515/jcc-2014-0021

Agterberg, M., Hooff, B. V. D., Huysman, M., & Soekijad, M. (2010). Keeping The Wheels Turning: The Dynamics of Managing Networks of Practice. *Journal of Management Studies*, *47*(1), 85–108. doi:10.1111/j.1467-6486.2009.00867.x

Aitchison, C. (n. d.). WebQuests from the National Museums Online Learning Project. Retrieved from http://www.aitchisonmedia.net/NMOLP/

Akyol, Z., Garrison, D. R., & Ozden, M. Y. (2009). Online and Blended Communities of Inquiry: Exploring the Developmental and Perceptional Differences. *International Review of Research in Open and Distance Learning*, *10*(6), 65–83.

Ali, I. M., Pascoe, C., & Warne, L. (2002). Interactions of organizational culture and collaboration in working and learning. *Journal of Educational Technology & Society*, *5*(2), 60–68.

Allee, V. 1997. 12 Principles of Knowledge Management. Retrieved from http://www.providersedge.com/docs/km_articles/12_principles_of_Knowledge_Management.pdf

American Distance Education Consortium (ADEC). (n. d.). ADEC EdFuture 2014 Presentations. Retrieved rom http://www.adec.edu/conference/edfuture-2014/presentations

Amin, A., & Roberts, J. (2008). Knowing in action: Beyond communities of practice. *Research Policy*, *37*(2), 353–369. doi:10.1016/j.respol.2007.11.003

Anastasiadis, P. (2007). Advanced Learning Technologies of synchronous and asynchronous transmission serving ODL (in Greek). In A. Lionarakis, (Ed.), *Proceedings of 4th International Conference of Open and Distance Learning*, Issue B Athens: Propompos.

Anderson, K., Dittlau, A., & Funkel, K. (2004, June 29-July 1). Probing students. In M. Agger Eriksen, L. Malmborg, & J. Nielsen (Eds.), *Web Proceedings of Computers in Art and Design Education Conference CADE2004*. Copenhagen Business School, Denmark and Malmö University, Sweden. Copenhagen: CADE.

Anderson, P. (2007). *What is Web 2.0? Ideas, technologies and implications for education* [Online]. JISC. Retrieved from www.jisc.ac.uk/media/documents/techwatch/tsw0701b.pdf

Anderson, T. (2009). The dance of technology and pedagogy in self-paced distance education. *Proceedings of the 17th ICDE World Congress, Maastricht.* Retrieved from http://auspace.athabascau.ca:8080/dspace/bitstream/2149/2210/1/The%20Dance%20of%20technology%20and%20Pedagogy%20in%20Self%20Paced%20Instructions.docx

Anderson, S. E., & Harris, J. B. (1997). Factors associated with amount of use and benefits obtained by users of a statewide educational telecomputing network. *Educational Technology Research and Development, 45*(1), 19–50. doi:10.1007/BF02299611

Anderson, T., & Dron, J. (2011). Three Generations of Distance Education Pedagogy. *International Review of Research in Open and Distance Learning, 12*(3), 80–97.

Antonopoulou, A. & Dare, E. (2008). 'The Phi Books,' Single edition artist's books.

Antonopoulou, A. & Dare, E. (2012). Phi territories: Neighbourhoods of collaboration and participation. *Journal of Writing in Creative Practice*, 5(1), 85–105.

Antonopoulou, A., & Dare, E. (2009, November 16-18). Berlin Freie Universität, Graduiertenkolleg "InterArt" International Research Training Group "Interart Studies." Berlin.

Antonopoulou, A., & Dare, E. (2013). The digital dreamhacker: Crowdsourcing the dream imaginary. In K. Cleland, L. Fisher, & R. Harley (Eds.), *Proceedings of the19th International Symposium of Electronic Art*, ISEA '13, Sydney.

Antonopoulou, A., & Dare, E. (2010, March). *Inter-art Symposium, Goldsmiths-University of London*, London.

Arab Knowledge Economy Report 2014. (2014). Retrieved from http:// www.orientplanet.com

Arab Social Media Report Series. (2014). Retrieved from [REMOVED HYPERLINK FIELD]http://www.arabsocialmediareport.com/Facebook/LineChart.aspx?&PriMenuID=18&CatID=24&mnu=Cat#sthash.UA3EapcL.dpuf

Ardichvili, A., Page, V., & Wentling, T. (2003). Motivation and barriers to participation in virtual knowledge-sharing communities of practice. *Journal of Knowledge Management, 7*(1), 64–77. doi:10.1108/13673270310463626

Arvaja, M., Häkkinen, P., & Kankaanranta, M. (2008). Collaborative Learning and Computer-Supported Collaborative Learning Environments. In J. Voogt & G. Knezek (Eds.), *International Handbook of Information Technology in Primary and Secondary Education* (Vol. 20, pp. 267–279). Springer, US. doi:10.1007/978-0-387-73315-9_16

Asquith, A. (1998). Non-elite Employees' Perceptions of Organizational Change in English Local Government. *International Journal of Public Sector Management, 11*(4), 262–280. doi:10.1108/09513559810225825

Athanasoula-Reppa, A. (2006). Tutor-counselor's role in Open and Distance Learning Lionarakis. In A. Lionarakis (Ed.), *Elements of theory and action.* Athens: Propompos. (in Greek)

Attwell, G. (2007). The personal learning environments: The future of eLearning? *eLearning Papers, 2*(1), 1-8.

Avgerou, C., & Walsham, G. (2000). Introduction: IT in Developing Countries. In C. Avgerou & G. Walsham (Eds.), *Information Technology in Context: Studies from the Perspective of Developing Countries* (pp. 1–8). Ashgate: Aldershot Press.

Avouris, N., & Komis, B. (2003). Synchronous collaboration at a distance: community and interaction issues (in Greek). In A. Lionarakis (Ed.), Proceedings of the 2nd *Hellenic Conference of Open and Distance Learning*, Patra, Hellenic Open University.

Azevedo, R. (2002). Beyond Intelligent Tutoring Systems: Using Computers as META Cognitive Tools to Enhance Learning? *Instructional Science*, *30*, 31–45.

Bahl, R. W., & Linn, J. F. (1992). *Urban Public Finance in Developing Countries*. New York, N.Y.: Oxford University Press.

Baker, R., & Siemens, G. (2014). Educational Data Mining and Learning Analytics. In R. K. Sawyer (Ed.), *Cambridge Handbook of the Learning Sciences* (2nd ed., pp. 253–274). New York, NY: Cambridge University Press.

Baldwin, C. Y., & Clark, K. B. (1999). *Design Rules: The Power of Modularity* (Vol. 1). MIT Press.

Baldwin, T. T., Magjuka, R. J., & Loher, B. T. (1991). The perils of participation: Effects of choice of trainee motivation and learning. *Personnel Psychology*, *44*(1), 51–65. doi:10.1111/j.1744-6570.1991.tb00690.x

Bandura, A. (1977). *Social learning theory*. NY: General Learning Press.

Bandura, A. (1986). *Social foundations of thought and action: A social cognitive theory*. Englewood Cliffs, NJ: Prentice-Hall.

Bang, J., & Dalsgaard, C. (2006). Rethinking e-learning: Shifting the focus to learning activities. In E. K. Sorensen & D. Murchú (Eds.), *Enhancing learning through technology* (pp. 184–202). Information Science Publishing. doi:10.4018/978-1-59140-971-7.ch008

Bannock, G., Baxter, R. E., & Davis, E. (1987). *The Penguin Dictionary of Economics* (4th ed.). London: Penguin Books.

Bannon, L. J. (1991). From Human Factors to Human Actors: The Role of Psychology and Human Computer Interaction Studies in System Design. In J. Greenbaum & M. Kyng (Eds.), *Design At Work: Cooperative Design of Computer Systems* (pp. 25–44). New Jersey, N.J.: Lawerence Erlbaum Associates Inc., Publishers.

Barab, S., Scott, J., Del Valle Martin, R., & Fang, F. (2012). Coming to Terms with Communities of Practice: A definition and operational criteria.

Barab, S. (2006). Design-Based Research: A Methodological Toolkit for the Learning Scientist. In R. K. Sawyer (Ed.), *The Cambridge Handbook of the Learning Sciences* (pp. 153–169). Cambridge, UK: Cambridge University Press.

Barcelo-Valenzuela, M., Sanchez-Schmitz, G., Perez-Soltero, A., Martín Rubio, F., & Marr, B. (2008). Defining the Problem: Key element for the Success of Knowledge Management. *Knowledge Management Research & Practice*, *6*(5), 322–333. doi:10.1057/kmrp.2008.22

Barkley, E. F., Cross, K. P., & Major, C. H. (2014). *Collaborative Learning Techniques: A Handbook for College Faculty* (2nd ed.). San Francisco, CA: John Wiley & Sons.

Barnes, N. D., & Barnes, F. R. (2009). Equipping your organization for the social networking game. *IEEE Engineering Management Review*, *38*(3), 3–7. doi:10.1109/EMR.2010.5559137

Barnett, S., Jones, S. C., Bennett, S., Iverson, D., & Bonney, A. (2013). Usefulness of a virtual community of practice and web 2.0 tools for general practice training: Experiences and expectations of general practitioner registrars and supervisors. *Australian Journal of Primary Health*, *19*(4), 292–296. doi:10.1071/PY13024 PMID:23823006

Basu, S. (2004). E-Government and Developing Countries: An Overview. *International Review of Law Computers & Technology*, *18*(1), 109–132. doi:10.1080/13600860410001674779

Battrawi, B., & Muhtaseb, R. (2013). Assessing the Role of Social Networks in Increasing Interest in Science and Science Literacy among a Sample of Facebook Users.*Proceedings of the 10th International Conference on Hands-on Science*; Košice, Slovakia.

Battrawi, B., & Muhtaseb, R. (2013). The Use of Social Networks as a Tool to Increase Interest in Science and Science Literacy: A Case Study of 'Creative Minds' Facebook Page.*Proceedings of the Second Edition of the International Conference New Perspectives in Science Education*; Florence, Italy.

Battrawi, B., & Muhtaseb, R. (2014). Real-Time Monitoring and Facebook Events: New Social Media Tools for Promoting Online Interaction and Public Engagement in Science.*Proceedings of the 8th International Technology, Education and Development Conference*; Valencia, Spain.

Beinhocker, E. D. 2006. The Origin of Wealth: Evolution, Complexity and the Radical Remaking of Economics. Boston, M.A.: Harvard Business School Press.

Bellamy, C. (2000). The Politics of Public Information Systems. In G. David Garson (Ed.), *Handbook of Public Information Systems* (pp. 85–98). New York, N.Y.: Marcel Dekker Inc.

Bellamy, C., & Taylor, J. A. (1994). Introduction: Exploiting IT in Public Administration. *Public Administration, 72*(1), 1–12. doi:10.1111/j.1467-9299.1994.tb00996.x

Ben Ammar, M., Neji, M., Alimi, A. M., & Gouardères, G. (2010). The Affective Tutoring System. *Expert Systems with Applications, 37*(4), 3013–3023. doi:10.1016/j.eswa.2009.09.031

Bennett, W. L. (2004a). Communicating Global Activism: Strengths and Vulnerabilities of Networked Politics. In W. Van Der Donk, B. D. Loader, & P. G. Nixon et al. (Eds.), *Cyberprotest: New Media, Citizens and Social Movements* (pp. 123–146). London: Routledge.

Benton, L. (2013). *Participatory Design and Autism: Supporting the participation, contribution and collaboration of children with ASD during the technology design process* [Doctor of Philosophy]. University of Bath. Retrieved from http://opus.bath.ac.uk/40576/

Bereiter, C. (2002). *Education and mind in the knowledge age.* Mahwah, NJ: Lawrence Erlbaum Associates.

Bertucci, A., Johnson, D. W., Johnson, R. T., & Conte, S. (2012). Influence of Group Processing on Achievement and Perception of Social and Academic Support in Elementary Inexperienced Cooperative Learning Groups. *The Journal of Educational Research, 105*(5), 329–335. doi:10.1080/00220671.2011.627396

Bettoni, M. (2005). Wissenskooperation – Die Zukunft des Wissensmanagements. *Lernende Organisation – Zeitschrift für Systemisches Management und Organisation, 25*(3), 6-24.

Bettoni, M., Andenmatten, S., & Mathieu, R. (2007). Knowledge Cooperation in Online Communities: A Duality of Participation and Cultivation. *Electronic Journal of Knowledge Management, 5*(1), 1–6.

Bettoni, M., & Eggs, C. (2010). User-centred Knowledge Management: A Constructivist and Socialized View. *Constructivist Foundations, 5*(3), 130–143.

Bettoni, M., Schiller, G., & Bernhard, W. (2011). A CoP for Research Activities in Universities. In O. R. Hernáez & E. Bueno Campos (Eds.), *Handbook of Research on Communities of Practice for Organizational Management and Networking: Methodologies for Competitive Advantage* (pp. 396–420). Hershey, PA: IGI Global.

Beun, R.-J., De Vos, E., & Witteman, C. (2003). *Embodied Conversational Agents: Effects on Memory Performance and Anthropomorphisation.* Paper presented at the Intelligent Virtual Agents IVA 2003. doi:10.1007/978-3-540-39396-2_52

Bezemer, J., & Kress, G. (2008). Writing in Multimodal Texts: A Social Semiotic Account of Designs for Learning. *Written Communication, 25*(2), 166–195. doi:10.1177/0741088307313177

Bhatnagar, S. (2004). *E-Government: From Vision to Implementation.* New Delhi: SAGE Publications.

Biggs, J., & Tang, C. (2011). *Teaching for Quality Learning at University* (4th ed.). Maidenhead, UK: The Society for Research into Higher Education and Open University Press.

Bingham, T., & Conner, M. (2010). *The new social learning: A guide to transforming organizations through social media*. San Francisco, CA: Berrett-Koehler Publishers, Inc.

Bishop, M. A. (1992). Theory-Ladenness of Perception Arguments.*Proceedings of the Biennial Meeting of the Philosophy of Science Association* (Vol. 1992, pp. 287-299).

Blikstein, P., & Cavallo, D. P. (2002). *Technology as a Trojan Horse in School Environments: The Emergence of the Learning Atmosphere (II)*. Proceedings of the ICL Workshop, Austria.

Bolger, S. (2009). Investigating the viability of virtual communities of practice in the public sector.

Bond, P. (2004). Communities of Practice and Complexity: Conversation and Culture. *Organization and People*, *11*(4), 1–7.

Borgatti, S. P., Mehra, A., Brass, D. J., & Labianca, G. (2009, February13). Network Analysis in the Social Sciences. *Science*, *323*(5916), 892–895. doi:10.1126/science.1165821 PMID:19213908

Bose, R. (2004). Knowledge Management Metrics. *Industrial Management & Data Systems*, *104*(6), 457–468. doi:10.1108/02635570410543771

Bossen, C., Dindler, C., & Iversen, O. S. (2010). *User gains and PD aims: Assessment from a participatory design project*. Paper presented at the Proceedings of the Participatory Design Conference PDC 2010, Sydney, Australia. doi:10.1145/1900441.1900461

Bouchamma, Y., & Michaud, C. (2011). Communities of practice with teaching supervisors: A discussion of community members' experiences. *Journal of Educational Change*, *12*(4), 403–420. doi:10.1007/s10833-010-9141-y

Bourdieu, P. (2004). *Science of Science and Reflexivity*. Chicago: University of Chicago Press.

Bourhis, A., & Dubé, L. (2010). Structuring Spontaneity: Investigating the Impact of Management Practices on the Success of Virtual Communities of Practice. *Journal of Information Science*, *36*(2), 175–193. doi:10.1177/0165551509357861

Branch, R. M. (2009). *Instructional Design: The ADDIE Approach*. New York, NY: Springer.

Branch, R. M., & Merrill, M. D. (2012). Characteristics of Instructional Design Models. In R. A. Reiser & J. V. Dempsey (Eds.), *Trends and Issues in Instructional Design and Technology* (3rd ed., pp. 8–16). Boston, MA: Pearson Education.

Bray, E., Aoki, K., & Dlugosh, L. (2008). Predictors of learning satisfaction in Japanese online distance learners. *International Review of Research in Open and Distance Learning*, *9*(3), 1–24.

Bremmer, J., & Roodenburg, H. (Eds.). (1993). *A Cultural History of Gesture from Antiquity to the Present Day*. Oxford: Polity Press.

Breslin, J. G., Passant, A., & Decker, S. (2009). *The Social Semantic Web*. Berlin: Springer. doi:10.1007/978-3-642-01172-6

Brew, A., & Boud, D. (1995). Research and Learning in Higher Education. In B. Smith & S. Brown (Eds.), *Research, Teaching, and Learning in Higher Education: 192*. London; Washington, D.C.: Kogan Page.

Brown, M. (2013). Learning Spaces. In D. G. Oblinger, & J. L. Oblinger (Eds.), *Educating the net generation*. Retrieved from http://net.educause.edu/ir/library/pdf/pub7101l.pdf

Brown, J. S., Collins, A., & Duguid, P. (1989). Situated cognition and the culture of learning. *Educational Researcher*, *18*(1), 32–42. doi:10.3102/0013189X018001032

Brown, S. A. (2012). Seeing Web 2.0 in context: A study of academic perceptions. *The Internet and Higher Education, 15*(1), 50–57. doi:10.1016/j.iheduc.2011.04.003

Brown, T. (2008). Design thinking. *Harvard Business Review, 2008*(June). Retrieved from http://hbr.org/2008/06/design-thinking/ar/1 PMID:18605031

Bruckman, A., & Resnick, M. (1995). The MediaMOO Project: Constructionism and Professional Community. *In Convergence, 1*(1), 94–109.

Bruner, J. (1966). *Toward a theory of instruction.* Cambridge: Belknap Press of Harvard University.

Bruner, J. S. (1986). *Actual minds, possible worlds.* Cambridge, Mass: Harvard University Press.

Bruner, J. S. (1996). *The culture of education.* Cambridge, Mass: Harvard University Press.

Bruner, J. S., & Weinreich-Haste, H. (1987). *Making sense: The child's construction of the world.* London: Methuen.

Burton, B., & Willis, D. A. (2014). Gartner's Hype Cycle Special Report for 2014. *Gartner Research Report.* Retrieved from https://www.gartner.com/doc/2816917/gartners-hype-cycle-special-report?docdisp=share

Burt, R. S. (1992). *Structural Holes: The Social Structure of Competition.* Cambridge, MA: Harvard University Press.

Butler, T., Feller, J., Pope, A., Emerson, B., & Murphy, C. (2008). Designing a Core it Artifact for Knowledge Management Systems Using Participatory Action Research in a Government and a Non-Government Organization. *The Journal of Strategic Information Systems, 17*(4), 249–267. doi:10.1016/j.jsis.2007.10.002

Cai, J. (2005). A social interaction analysis methodology for improving e-collaboration over the internet. *Electronic Commerce Research and Applications, 4*(2), 85–99. doi:10.1016/j.elerap.2004.10.007

Calabrese, A., & Borchert, M. (1996). Prospects for electronic democracy in the United States: Rethinking communications and social policy. *Media Culture & Society, 18*(2), 249–268. doi:10.1177/016344396018002005

Calongne, C., Stricker, A., Truman, B., Murray, J., Lavieri, E., Jr., & Martini, D. (2014, April 22-24). Slippery rocks and ALGAE: A multiplayer educational roleplaying game and a model for adaptive learning game design. *Proceedings of the 19th Annual TCC Worldwide Online Conference.* Retrieved from http://etec.hawaii.edu/proceedings/2014/Calongne.pdf

Calongne, C. (2008). Educational frontiers: Learning in a virtual world. *EDUCAUSE Review, 43*(5), 36–48. Retrieved from http://net.educause.edu/ir/library/pdf/ERM0852.pdf

Cameron, L. (2007). Scaffolding Effective Learning Design with Pre-Service Teachers. In C. Montgomerie, & J. Seale (Eds.), *Proceedings of World Conference on Educational Multimedia, Hypermedia and Telecommunications 2007* (pp. 195-202). Chesapeake, VA: AACE.

Cameron, R., & Harrison, J. L. (2012). The interrelatedness of formal, non-formal and informal learning: Evidence from labour market program participants. *Australian Journal of Adult Learning, 52*(2), 277–309.

Carayon, P., Hoonakker, P., & Smith, M. J. (2012). Human Factors in Organizational Design and Management. In G. Salvendy (Ed.), *Handbook of Human Factors and Ergonomics* – (4th ed., pp. 534–552). New Jersey, N.J.: John Wiley and Sons. doi:10.1002/9781118131350.ch18

Carey, S. (1983). Cognitive Development: The Descriptive Problem. In Gazzaniga (Ed.), Handbook for Cognitive Neurology. Hillsdale, NJ: Lawrence & Erlbaum

Carter, P. (2004). *Material Thinking: the Theory and Practice of Creative Research.* Melbourne, Vic: Melbourne University Press.

Carter, R. (1999). *Mapping the mind.* Los Angeles, CA: University of California Press.

Casely, J. (2004, March13th). Public Sector Reform and Corruption: CARD Facade in Andhra Pradesh. *Economic and Political Weekly*, 1151–1156.

Castells, M. (1996). *The Information Age: Economy, society and culture: The rise of the networked society* (Vol. 1). Oxford, UK: Blackwell.

Central, L. A. M. S. (n. d.). *Browsing LAMS sequences.* Retrieved from http://lamscommunity.org/lamscentral/

Cerezo, E., Baldassarri, S., Hupont, I., & Seron, F. J. (2008). Affective embodied conversational agents for natural interaction. In O. Jimmy (Ed.), *Affective Computing* (pp. 329–354). Vienna, Austria: I-Tech Education and Publishing. doi:10.5772/6173

Chan, F. T. S., Yee-Loong Chong, A., & Zhou, L. (2012). An empirical investigation of factors affecting e-collaboration diffusion in SMEs. *International Journal of Production Economics, 138*(2), 329–344. doi:10.1016/j.ijpe.2012.04.004

Charbonneau-Gowdy, P., & Cechova, I. (2009). Moving from analogue to high definition e-tools to support empowering social learning approaches. *Electronic Journal of e-Learning, 7*(3), 225-238.

Chen, T.-L., & Chen, T.-J. (2002). A strategic analysis of the online learning community for continuing professional development of university faculty in Taiwan: A SWOT analysis. *Proceedings of the International Conference on Computers in Education 2002* (pp. 1408–1409). IEEE.

Chen, B., & Bryer, T. (2012). Investigating instructional strategies for using social media in formal and informal learning. *International Review of Research in Open and Distance Learning, 13*(1), 87–104.

Choi, B., Poon, S. K., & Davis, J. G. (2008). Effects of Knowledge Management Strategy on Organizational Performance, a Complementarity Theory-Based Approach. *Omega-International Journal of Management Science, 36*(2), 235–251. doi:10.1016/j.omega.2006.06.007

Choi, S., & Ko, I. (2012). Leveraging electronic collaboration to promote interorganizational learning. *International Journal of Information Management, 32*(6), 550–559. doi:10.1016/j.ijinfomgt.2012.03.002

Ciborra, C. (2005). Interpreting e-government and development: Efficiency, transparency or governance at a distance? *Information Technology & People, 18*(3), 260–279. doi:10.1108/09593840510615879

Clara Moskowitz. (2013, May 29). Asteroid Miners to Launch World's 1st Crowdfunded Space Telescope. Retrieved from http://www.space.com/21345-asteroid-mining-crowdfunding-space-telescope.html

Clark, H. H. (1996). *Using Language.* Cambridge: Cambridge University Press. doi:10.1017/CBO9780511620539

Coats, M. (1992). *Open Teaching Toolkit – Effective Tutorials.* The Open University. Retrieved from http://labspace.open.ac.uk/file.php/5718/LDT_12_Intro.pdf

Cogburn, D. L. (2002). HCI in the so-called developing world: What's in it for everyone. *Interactions (New York, N.Y.), 10*(2), 80–87. doi:10.1145/637848.637866

Cohen, W. M., & Levinthal, D. A. (1990). Absorptive capacity: A new perspective on learning and innovation. *Administrative Science Quarterly, 35*(1), 128–152. doi:10.2307/2393553

Cole, M. (1996). *Cultural psychology: A once and future discipline.* Cambridge, MA: Harvard University Press.

Cole, M., & Engeström, Y. (1993). A cultural-historical approach to distributed cognition. In G. Salomon (Ed.), *Distributed cognitions: Psychological and educational considerations* (pp. 1–46). New York, NY: Cambridge University Press.

Cole, M., & Griffin, P. (Eds.). (1987). *Contextual Factors in Education*. Madison: Wisconsin Center for Educational Research.

Collins, A., Brown, J. S., & Newman, S. E. (1989). Cognitive apprenticeship: Teaching the craft of reading, writing, and mathematics. In L. B. Resnick (Ed.), *Knowing, learning, and instruction: Essays in honor of Robert Glaser* (pp. 453–494). Hillsdale, NJ: Lawrence Erlbaum Associates.

Colquitt, J. A., LePine, J. A., & Noe, R. A. (2000). Toward an integrative theory of training motivation: A meta-analytic path analysis of 20 years of research. *The Journal of Applied Psychology*, *85*(5), 678–707. doi:10.1037/0021-9010.85.5.678 PMID:11055143

Connectededucators (2011). Technology for Online Communities of Practice. from http://connectededucators.org/wp-content/uploads/2011/03/0143_Platforms-and-Tools-march-2011.pdf

Conole, G., & Fill, K. (2005). *The learning taxonomy in DialogusPlus Toolkit*. University of South Hampton. Retrieved from http://joker.ecs.soton.ac.uk/dialogplustoolkit/userarea/

Conole, G. (2007). Describing learning activities -Tools and resources to guide practice. In H. Beetham & R. Sharpe (Eds.), *Rethinking Pedagogy for a Digital Age: Designing and Delivering E-learning* (pp. 81–91). London: Routledge.

Conole, G. (2013). Tools and Resources to Guide Practice. In H. Beetham & R. Sharpe (Eds.), *Rethinking Pedagogy for a Digital Age: Designing for 21st Century Learning* (pp. 78–100). London, UK: Routledge.

Conte, R., & Paolucci, M. (2001). Intelligent social learning. *Journal of Artificial Societies and Social Simulation*, *4*(1). Retrieved from http://jasss.soc.surrey.ac.uk/4/1/3.html

Contreras-Castillo, J., Favela, J., Perez-Fragoso, C., & Santamaria-del-Angel, E. (2004). Informal interactions and their implications for online courses. *Computers & Education*, *42*(2), 149–168. doi:10.1016/S0360-1315(03)00069-1

Cook, S. D. N., & Brown, J. S. (1999). Bridging epistemologies: The generative dance between organizational knowledge and organizational knowing. *Organization Science*, *10*(4), 381–400. doi:10.1287/orsc.10.4.381

Cornelius, S., & Macdonald, J. (2008). Online informal professional development for distance tutors: Experiences from The Open University in Scotland. *Open Learning: The Journal of Open and Distance Learning*, *23*(1), 43–55. doi:10.1080/02680510701815319

Cornu, B. (2004). Networking and collecting intelligence for teachers and learners. In A. Brown & N. Davis (Eds.), *Digital technology, communities and education* (pp. 40–45). London: Routledge Falmer.

Cornwall, A., & Jewkes, R. (1995). What is participatory research? *Social Science & Medicine*, *41*(12), 1667–1676. doi:10.1016/0277-9536(95)00127-S PMID:8746866

Cornwell, B., Curry, T. J., & Schwirian, K. P. (2003). Revisiting Norton Long's Ecology of Games: A Network Approach. *City & Community*, *2*(2), 121–142. doi:10.1111/1540-6040.00044

Cortés, C. E., Patronicio, Z. S., & Eva, P. O. (2007). Organizational Structure Features Supporting Knowledge Management Processes. *Journal of Knowledge Management*, *11*(4), 45–57. doi:10.1108/13673270710762701

Coverdale, A. (2008). Critique of Connectivism [blog post]. Retrieved fromhttps://sites.google.com/site/andycoverdale/texts/critique-of-connectivism

Cox, A. (2005). What are communities of practice? A comparative review of four seminal works. *Journal of Information Science*, *31*(6), 527–540. doi:10.1177/0165551505057016

Creanor, L., & Trinder, K. et al.. (2006). *LEX: The learner experience of e-learning – final project report, August 2006*. JISC.

Crossan, M. M., Lane, H. W., & White, R. E. (1999). An organizational learning framework: From Intuition to Institution. *Academy of Management Review*, *24*(3), 522–537.

Cross, J. (2007). *Informal learning: Rediscovering the natural pathways that inspire innovation and performance*. San Francisco, CA: John Wiley & Sons, Inc.

Crozier, M., & Friedberg, E. (1980). [University of Chicago Press.]. *Actors and Systems. Chicago*, *I*, L.

Cruickshank, P., Edelmann, N., & Smith, C. F. (2010). Signing an e-Petition as a Transition from Lurking to Participation. *Electronic Government and Electronic Participation*.

Cruickshank, P. (2011). *Customer journey mapping*. Smart Cities Guide.

Czaja, S. J., & Nair, S. N. (2012). Human Factors Engineering and Systems Design. In G. Salvendy (Ed.), *Handbook of Human Factors and Ergonomics* (4th ed., pp. 38–56). New Jersey, N.J.: John Wiley and Sons. doi:10.1002/9781118131350.ch2

Dada, D. (2006). The Failure of E-Government in Developing Countries: A Literature Review. *The Electronic Journal on Information Systems in Developing Countries*, *26*(7), 1–10.

Daft, R., & Huber, G. P. (1987). How organizations learn: A communications framework. *Research in the Sociology of Organizations*, *5*, 1–36.

Dalkir, K. (2005). *Knowledge Management in Theory and Practice*. Boston: Elsevier.

Dalziel, J. (2010). *Practical e-Teaching Strategies for Predict – Observe – Explain, Problem-Based Learning and Role Plays*. Sydney: LAMS International. Retrieved from http://www.practicaleteachingstrategies.com/

Dalziel, J. (2007). Building communities of designers. In H. Beetham & R. Sharpe (Eds.), *Rethinking pedagogy for a digital age: Designing and delivering e-learning* (pp. 193–206). London, UK: Routledge.

Dascalu, M.-I., Bodea, C.-N., Lytras, M., De Pablos, P. O., & Burlacu, A. (2014). Improving e-learning communities through optimal composition of multidisciplinary learning groups. *Computers in Human Behavior*, *30*, 362–371. doi:10.1016/j.chb.2013.01.022

Davis, K., Seider, S., & Gardner, H. (2008). When False Representations Ring True (and When They Don't). *Social Research*, *75*(4), 1085–1108.

Deci, E. L., Koestner, R., & Ryan, R. M. (2001). Extrinsic Rewards and Intrinsic Motivation in Education: Reconsidered Once Again. *Review of Educational Research*, *71*(1), 1–27. doi:10.3102/00346543071001001

Dennen, V. P. (2004). Cognitive apprenticeship in educational practice: Research on scaffolding, modeling, mentoring, and coaching as instructional strategies. In D. H. Jonassen (Ed.), *Handbook of research on educational communications and technology* (2nd ed., pp. 813–828). NJ: Lawrence Erlbaum Associates.

Dennett, D. (1988). Quining Qualia. In A. Marcel, & E. Bisiach (Eds.), Consciousness in Contemporary Society (pp. 43-77). Oxford University Press.

Dewey, J. (1938). *Logic: The Theory of Inquiry*. New York: Holt.

Dewhurst, F. W., & Cegarra Navarro, J. G. (2004). External communities of practice and relational capital. *The Learning Organization*, *11*(4/5), 322–331. doi:10.1108/09696470410538224

Dewsbury, G., Rouncefield, M., Clarke, K., & Sommerville, I. (2004). Depending on digital design: Extending inclusivity. *Housing Studies*, *19*(5), 811–825. doi:10.1080/0267303042000249224

Dietrich, F., & List, C. (2007). Judgment aggregation under constraints. In T. Boylan & R. Gekker (Eds.), *Economics, Rational Choice and Normative Philosophy*. London: Routledge.

Dietrich, P., Eskerod, P., Dalcher, D., & Sandhawalia, B. (2010). The dynamics of collaboration in multipartner projects. *Project Management Journal*, *41*(4), 59–78. doi:10.1002/pmj.20194

Dillenbourg, P. & Fischer, F. (2007). Basics of Computer-Supported Collaborative Learning. *Zeitschrift für Berufs- und Wirtschaftspädagogik*. *21*, 111-130.

Dillenbourg, P. (1999). What do you mean by "collaborative learning"? In P. Dillenbourg (Ed.), *Collaborative Learning: Cognitive and Computational Approaches* (pp. 1–16). Amsterdam: Pergamon.

Dillenbourg, P. (1999). What do you mean by collaborative learning? In P. Dillenbourg (Ed.), *Collaborative-learning: Cognitive and Computational Approaches* (pp. 1–19). Oxford: Elsevier.

Dillenbourg, P., & Hong, F. (2008). The mechanics of CSCL macro scripts. *International Journal of Computer-Supported Collaborative Learning*, *3*(1), 5–23. doi:10.1007/s11412-007-9033-1

Dillenbourg, P., & Jermann, P. (2010). Technology for Classroom Orchestration. In M. S. Khine & I. M. Saleh (Eds.), *New Science of Learning* (pp. 525–552). New York, NY: Springer. doi:10.1007/978-1-4419-5716-0_26

Dillinger, W. (1988). Urban Property Taxation in Developing Countries. *World Bank Policy Research Working Paper Series*, no. 41. Retrieved from http://ideas.repec.org/p/wbk/wbrwps/41.html

DiMaggio, P., Hargittai, E., Neuman, W. R., & Robinson, J. P. (2001). Social Implications of the Internet. In H. Nissenbaum & M. E. Price (Eds.), *Academy & the Internet*., doi:10.1146/annurev.soc.27.1.307

DiMicco, J., Millen, D. R., Geyer, W., Dugan, C., Brownholtz, B., & Muller, M. (2008). Motivations for social networking at work. *Proceedings of the 2008 ACM conference on Computer supported cooperative work CSCW '08* (pp. 711-720).

Dirckinck-Holmfeld, L. (2002). Designing virtual learning environments based on problem oriented project pedagogy. In L. Dirckinck-Holmfeld, & B. Fibiger (Eds.), Learning in virtual environments (pp. 31-54). Fredriksberg Denmark: Samfundslitteratur.

Dirckinck-Holmfeld, L. (2002). Designing Virtual Learning Environments based on Problem Oriented Project Pedagogy. In L. Dirckinck-Holmfeld & B. Fibiger (Eds.), *Learning in Virtual Environments: Forlaget.*

Diviacco, P. (2015). Reconciling Knowledge and Collaborative e-Research. In Diviacco, P. Fox,P., Leadbetter,A., Pshenichny, C., (Editors), Collaborative Knowledge in Scientific Research Networks. Hershey, PA: IGI Global. doi:10.4018/978-1-4666-6567-5.ch001

Diviacco, P., & Busato, A. (2013). The Geo-Seas Seismic data viewer: a tool to facilitate control of data access. *Bollettino di Geofisica Teorica ed Applicata*, 54(3), 257-270.

Diviacco, P., & Pshenichny, C. A. (2011, April). A case study on the use of event bushes as a formal representation for Computer Supported Collaborative Work in the GeoSciences European Geosciences Union (EGU) General Assembly, Vienna, Austria. *Geophysical Research Abstracts* (Vol. 12).

Diviacco, P. (2005). An open source, web based, simple solution for seismic data dissemination and collaborative research. *Computers & Geosciences*, *31*(5), 599–605. doi:10.1016/j.cageo.2004.11.008

Diviacco, P. (2012). Addressing Conflicting Cognitive Models in Collaborative e-Research: A Case Study in Exploration Geophysics. In *Collaborative and Distributed e-Research: Innovations in Technologies, Strategies and Applications.* Hershey, PA: IGI Global press; doi:10.4018/978-1-4666-0125-3.ch012

Diviacco, P., & Busato, A. (2015). Maps, graphs and annotations as Boundary Objects in Knowledge Networks, Distributed Cognition and Collaborative e-Research. In P. Diviacco, P. Fox, C. Pshenichny, & A. Leadbetter (Eds.), *Collaborative Knowledge in Scientific Research Networks*. Hershey, PA: IGI Global.

Diviacco, P., DeCawer, K., Leadbetter, A., Sorribas, J., Stojanov, Y., Busato, A., & Cova, A. (2014). *Bridging semantically different paradigms in the field of marine acquisition event logging, Earth Science Informatics*. Springer; doi:10.1007/s12145-014-0192-0

Diviacco, P., Lowry, R., & Leadbetter, A. (2011). Collaborative work and tools towards wide scientific community driven metadata model and vocabulary building. The case of the EU GeoSeas project. European Geosciences Union (EGU) General Assembly, Vienna (Austria), April 2010. *Geophysical Research Abstracts, 12*, •••.

Diviacco, P., & Pshenichny, C. A. (2010). Concept-referenced spaces in computer-supported collaborative work.[]. EGU, Vienna]. *Geophysical Research Abstracts, 12*, •••.

Diviacco, P., Pshenichny, C. A., Carniel, R., Khrabrykh, Z., Shterkhun, V., Mouromtsev, D., & Pascolo, P. et al. (2014). Organization of a geophysical information space by using an event-bush-based collaborative tool. *Earth Sci Inform, 10*. doi:10.1007/s12145-014-0182-2

Dohn, N. (2010). Web 2.0: Inherent tensions and evident challenges for education. *International Journal of Computer-Supported Collaborative Learning*, *4*(3), 343–363. doi:10.1007/s11412-009-9066-8

Dong, B., Zheng, Q., Yang, J., Li, H., & Qiao, M. (2009). *An E-learning Ecosystem Based on Cloud Computing Infrastructure.* Paper presented at the International Conference on Advanced Learning Technologies ICALT 2009, Riga, Latvia. doi:10.1109/ICALT.2009.21

Dossick, C., Anderson, A., Iorio, J., Neff, G., & Taylor, J. (2012). Messy talk and mutual discovery: exploring the necessary conditions for synthesis in virtual teams. In A. Javernick-Will & A. Mahalingam (Eds.), *Proceedings of the Engineering Project Organizations Conference.* Retrieved from http://www.epossociety.org/EPOC2012/Papers/Dossick_Anderson_Iorio_Neff_Taylor.pdf

Dourish, P. (2000). A Foundational Framework for Situated Computing. Position paper for the CHI 2000 *Workshop on Situated Computing: A Research Agenda.*

Downes, S. (2007). An introduction to connective knowledge. *Proceedings of the International Conference on Media, knowledge & education—exploring new spaces, relations and dynamics in digital media ecologies.* Retrieved from http://www.downes.ca/post/3303

Downes, S. (2010). *E-learning 2.0.* National Research Council of Canada. Retrieved from <http://www.elearnmag.org/subpage.cfm?section=articles&article=29-1

Downs, A. (1964). Inside Bureaucracy. Boston, M.A.: Little Brown.

Drakos, N. (2013). Agenda Overview for Social Software and Collaboration. *Gartner Research Report* ID G00245492. Retrieved from https://www.gartner.com/doc/2291615/agenda-overview-social-software-collaboration

Druin, A. (2007). *Connecting Generations: Developing Co-Design Methods for Older Adults and Children.* Retrieved from http://hcil.cs.umd.edu/trs/2007-15/2007-15.pdf

Drupal.org. (2014). Drupal Commons. Retrieved from https://www.drupal.org/project/commons

Dubé, L., Bourhis, A., & E Jacob, R. (2003). Towards a typology of virtual communities of practice. *Cahiers du GReSI*, Novembre, *3*(13).

Duckett, P. S., & Fryer, D. (1998). Developing empowering research practices with people who have learning disabilities. *Journal of Community & Applied Social Psychology*, *8*(1), 57–65. doi:10.1002/(SICI)1099-1298(199801/02)8:1<57::AID-CASP438>3.0.CO;2-8

Duffy, T., & Cunningham, D. (1996). Constructivism: Implications for the design and delivery of instruction. Handbook of research for educational telecommunications and technology (pp. 170-198).

Duke, B., Harper, G., & Johnston, M. (2013). Connectivism as a Digital Age Learning Theory. *The HETL Review* (Special Issue), 2013. Retrieved from https://www.hetl.org/ihr-special-issues/

Dutton, W. H. (1992). The Ecology of Games Shaping Telecommunications Policy. *Communication Theory*, *2*(4), 303–324. doi:10.1111/j.1468-2885.1992.tb00046.x

Dutton, W. H., Schneider, V., & Vedel, T. (2012). Large Technical Systems as Ecologies of Games: Cases from Telecommunications to the Internet. In J. Bauer, A. Lang, & V. Schneider (Eds.), *Innovation Policy and Governance in High-Tech Industries: The Complexity of Coordination*. Berlin: Springer Link. doi:10.1007/978-3-642-12563-8_3

Easterby-Smith, M., & Lyles, M. A. (2003). *The Blackwell Handbook of Organizational Learning and Knowledge Management*. Oxford: Blackwell.

Edwards, J. (2011). A Process View of Knowledge Management: It Ain't What you do, it's the way That you do it. *Electronic Journal of Knowledge Management*, *9*(4), 297–306.

Edwards, J. S. (2009). Business processes and knowledge management. In M. Khosrow-Pour (Ed.), *Encyclopedia of Information Science and Technology* (Vol. I, pp. 471–476). Hershey, PA: IGI Global. doi:10.4018/978-1-60566-026-4.ch078

Edwards, R., & Usher, R. (2008). *Globalisation and pedagogy: Space, place and identity* (2nd ed.). Milton Park, England: Routledge.

Eisenhardt, K. M. (1989). Building Theories from Case Study Research. *Academy of Management Review*, *14*(4), 532–550.

Eisenstadt, M., & Vincent, T. (2012). *The knowledge web: Learning and collaborating on the net*. Routledge.

Endress, E., & Wehner, T. (Eds.). (1996). *Zwischenbetriebliche Kooperation. Die Gestaltung von lieferbedingungen*. Weinheim: Psychologie Verlags Union.

Engeström, Y. (1999). Activity theory and individual and social transformation. In Y. Engeström, R. Miettinen, & R. L. Punamäki (Eds.), *Perspectives on activity theory* (pp. 19–38). Cambridge: Cambridge University Press. doi:10.1017/CBO9780511812774.003

Engeström, Y. (2001). Expansive learning at work: Toward an activity theoretical reconceptualization. *Journal of Education and Work*, *14*(1), 133–156. doi:10.1080/13639080020028747

Engeström, Y., & Middleton, D. (1996). Introduction: Studying work as mindful practice. In Y. Engestrom & D. Middleton (Eds.), *Cognition and Communication at Work* (pp. 1–14). Cambridge: Cambridge University Press. doi:10.1017/CBO9781139174077.001

Erden, Z., Von Krogh, G., & Nonaka, I. (2008). The Quality of Group Tacit Knowledge. *The Journal of Strategic Information Systems*, *17*(1), 4–18. doi:10.1016/j.jsis.2008.02.002

Ertl, B. (2008). E-Collaborative Knowledge Construction. In N. Kock (Ed.), *Encyclopedia of E-Collaboration* (pp. 233–239). Hershey, PA: Information Science Reference. doi:10.4018/978-1-59904-000-4.ch036

Etzioni, A. (1975). An Engineer-Social Science Team at Work. *Technology Review, 1975*, 26–31.

Euerby, A., & Burns, C. M. (2012). Designing for Social Engagement in Online Social Networks Using Communities-of-Practice Theory and Cognitive Work Analysis A Case Study. *Journal of Cognitive Engineering and Decision Making, 6*(2), 194–213. doi:10.1177/1555343412440697

European Union, (2010). *A Digital Agenda for Europe. Digital Agenda COM 245 final*. Retrieved from http://europa.eu/legislation_summaries/information_society/strategies/si0016_en.htm

Everett, M., & Borgatti, S. P. (2005). Ego network betweenness. *Social Networks, 27*(1), 31–38. doi:10.1016/j.socnet.2004.11.007

Everitt, A., Hardiker, P., Littlewood, J., & Mullender, A. (1992). *Applied Research for Better Practice*. London: Macmillan.

Ewing, J., & Miller, D. (2002). A framework for evaluating computer supported collaborative learning. *Journal of Educational Technology & Society, 5*(1), 112–118.

Facebook. (2014). Facebook. Retrieved from http://www.programmableweb.com/api/facebook

Facebook. (2014). Statistics. Retrieved from http://www.facebook.com/press/info.php?statistics

Fahey, R., Vasconcelos, A. C., & David, E. D. (2007). The Impact of Rewards within Communities of Practice: A Study of the Sap Online Global Community. *Knowledge Management Research & Practice. Hampshire, 5*, 186–198.

Fajerman, L., & Treseder, P. (2000). *Children are Service Users too: A Guide to Consulting Children and Young People*. London: Save The Children.

Fanariti, M., & Spanaka, Ad. (2010, November). Metacognition and learning autonomy during the implementation of essays [in Greek]. *The Open Education Journal, 6*(1), 138–151. Retrieved from http://journal.openet.gr/index.php/openjournal/article/view/105

Fehr, E., & Gachter, S. (1998). Reciprocity and Economics: The Economic Implications of *Homo Reciprocans. European Economic Review, 42*(3), 845–859. doi:10.1016/S0014-2921(97)00131-1

Fehr, E., & Gachter, S. (2002). Altruistic Punishment in Humans. *Nature, 415*(6868), 137–145. doi:10.1038/415137a PMID:11805825

Feng, X. (2008). *Ship Collaborative Design Based on Multi-agent and Ontology Cooperative Design, Visualization, and Engineering* (pp. 249–252). Berlin: Springer. doi:10.1007/978-3-540-88011-0_35

Ferguson, R., & Shum, S. B. (2012). *Social Learning Analytics: Five Approaches*. Paper presented at the Proceedings of the International Conference on Learning Analytics and Knowledge LAK '12.

Ferriter, B. (n. d.). Using videoconferencing to connect your class to the world. Retrieved from http://www.learnnc.org/lp/pages/6559

Finholt, T., & Sproull, L. S. (1990). Electronic groups at work. *Organization Science, 1*(1), 41–64. doi:10.1287/orsc.1.1.41

Fink, L. (2007). Coordination, learning, and innovation: The organizational roles of e-collaboration and their impacts. *International Journal of e-Collaboration, 3*(3), 53–70. doi:10.4018/jec.2007070104

Fiol, C. M., & Lyles, M. A. (1985). Organizational learning. *Academy of Management Review, 10*(4), 803–813.

Firestone, W. A. (1989). Educational Policy as an Ecology of Games. *Educational Researcher, 18*(7), 18–24. doi:10.2307/1177165

Fischer, G., & Ostwald, J. (2002). Seeding, Evolutionary Growth, and Reseeding: Enriching Participatory Design with Informed Participation.*Proceedings of the Participatory Design Conference (PDC'02)*, Malmo, Sweden (pp. 135-143).

Fodor, J. (1983). *The Modularity of Mind*. Cambridge, MA: MIT Press.

Foth, M. (2004). Animating personalised networking in a student apartment complex through participatory design. *Proceedings of the Participatory Design Conference*, Toronto. Retrieved from http://eprints.qut.edu.au/archive/00001904/01/foth_id172_shortpaper.pdf

Fox, Z. (2011, August 11). 5 Ways Museums Are Reaching Digital Audiences. *Mashable.com*. Retrieved from http://mashable.com/2011/08/11/museums-digital/

Fragaki, M., Reynolds, S., & Vanbuel, M. (2009). A pedagogical framework for the effective use of video in class & Exemplary video- based educational scenarios. In *D6.1- A pedagogical framework for the effective use of video in class / Exemplary video-based educational scenarios, EduTubePlus -A European Curriculum Related Video Library and Hybrid e- services for the Pedagogical Exploitation of Video in Class*. Athens: Research Academic Computer Technology Institute.

Fraser, M. (2004). *Supporting Virtual Research Environments: how can we help?* Retrieved from http://users.ox.ac.uk/~mikef/rts/vre/img2.html

Freake, St., & Papathanassiou, H. (2006). *Tutorial support for a Level 3 Electromagnetism course - using a blended approach*. Department of Physics and Astronomy, The Open University. Retrieved from http://www.open.ac.uk/picetl/activities/details/detail.php?itemId=4612257d02466&themeId=460d2aa4d3c48

Freeman, R. E. (1984). *Strategic management: A stakeholder approach*. Boston: Pitman.

French, S., & Swain, J. (2004). Researching together: a participatory approach. In S. French & J. Sim (Eds.), *Physiotherapy: A Psychosocial Approach* (3rd ed., pp. 50–64). Oxford: Butterworth-Heinemann.

Fryer, M. (2012). Facilitative leadership: Drawing on Jürgen Habermas' model of ideal speech to propose a less impositional way to lead. *Organization*, *19*(1), 25–43. doi:10.1177/1350508411401462

Fugelstad, P., Dwyer, P., Filson Moses, J., Kim, J., Mannino, C. A., Terveen, L., & Snyder, M. (2012). What makes users rate (share, tag, edit...)?: predicting patterns of participation in online communities.*Proceedings of the ACM 2012 conference on Computer Supported Cooperative Work* (pp. 969–978). ACM. doi:10.1145/2145204.2145349

Fullan, M. (2013). The New Pedagogy: Students and Teachers as Learning Partners. *LEARNing Landscapes*, *6*(2).

Fung, Y., & Carr, R. (2000). Face-to-Face Tutorials in a Distance Learning System: Meeting student needs. *Open Learning*, *15*(1), 35–46. doi:10.1080/026805100115452

Gagné, R. M., Wager, W. W., Golas, K. C., & Keller, J. M. (2005). *Principles of Instructional Design* (5th ed.). Belmont, CA: Wadsworth.

Gairín-Sallán, J., Rodríguez-Gómez, D., & Armengol-Asparó, C. (2010). Who Exactly Is the Moderator? A Consideration of Online Knowledge Management Network Moderation in Educational Organizations. *Computers & Education*, *55*(1), 304–312. doi:10.1016/j.compedu.2010.01.016

Gallup Consulting. (2011). *The state of the Global Workplace 2011: A worldwide study of employee engagement and wellbeing*. Gallup, Inc. Retrieved from http://www.gallup.com/services/177083/state-global-workplace-2011.aspx

Garrett, N. (2011). An e-portfolio design supporting ownership, social learning, and ease of use. *Journal of Educational Technology & Society*, *14*(1), 187–202.

Garrison, D. R., Anderson, T., & Archer, W. (1999). Critical Inquiry in a Text-Based Environment: Computer Conferencing in Higher Education. *The Internet and Higher Education, 2*(2), 87–105. doi:10.1016/S1096-7516(00)00016-6

Gaskill, M. (2014, December 30). Astronaut Photographs Inspire Next Generation of Scientists. Retrieved from http://www.nasa.gov/mission_pages/station/research/news/EEAB

Gaver, B., Boucher, A., Pennington, S., & Walker, B. (2004). Cultural Probes and The value of Uncertainty. *Interaction, 11*(5), 53–56. doi:10.1145/1015530.1015555

Gee, J. P. (2004). *Situated Language and Learning: A Critique of Traditional Schooling*. New York: Palmgrave-McMillan.

Gibb, T., & Fenwick, T. (2008) 'Older' professionals' learning in an ageist culture: Beneath and between the borders. In J. Groen & S. Guo (Eds.), *Online Proceedings of the Canadian Association for the Study of Adult Education.* Vancouver, British Columbia. Retrieved from http://www.oise.utoronto.ca/CASAE/cnf2008/OnlineProceedings-2008/CAS2008-Gibb.pdf

Gibbs, M. R., Wadley, G., & Ng, S. (2012, October 27-29). Using "simple" technology to support geographically distributed communities of practice. Proceedings of the 2012 IEEE Conference on Technology and Society in Asia (T&SA) (pp. 1, 6).

Gibson, S. K. (2004). Social learning (cognitive) theory and implications for human resource development. *Advances in Developing Human Resources, 6*(2), 193–210. doi:10.1177/1523422304263429

Giddens, A. (1984). *The constitution of society*. Berkeley: University of California Press.

Gintis, H. (2006). *The Economy as a Complex Adaptive System - A Review of Eric D. Beinhocker.* MacArthur Research Foundation Paper Series. Retrieved from http://www.umass.edu/preferen/Class%20Material/Readings%20in%20Market%20Dynamics/Complexity%20Economics.pdf

Gintis, H. (2000). *Game Theory Evolving*. Princeton, N.J.: Princeton University Press.

Glaser, B. G., Strauss, A. L., & Strauss, A. L. (1967). *The discovery of grounded theory: Strategies for qualitative research.* Chicago: Aldine Pub. Co.

Glick, J. (1997). Discourse and development: Notes from the field. In *Discourse, Tools, and Reasoning: Essays on Situated Cognition, edited by Resnick, Saljo, Pontecorvo, and Burge*. Berlin: Springer. doi:10.1007/978-3-662-03362-3_11

Gloor, P. (2006). *Swarm Creativity, Competitive Advantage Through Collaborative Innovation Networks*. Oxford: Oxford University Press. doi:10.1093/acprof:oso/9780195304121.001.0001

Goffman, E. (1963). *Behavior in public places: notes on the social organization of gatherings*. New York: Free Press of Glencoe.

Goldberg, P. (2003). Disconnected Urbanism - Metropolis Magazine. Retrieved from http://www.metropolismag.com/December-1969/Disconnected-Urbanism/

Goleman, D. (2006). *Social Intelligence*. Athens: Ellinika Grammata. (in Greek)

Gongla, P., & Rizzuto, C. R. (2001). Evolving communities of practice: IBM Global Services experience. *IBM Systems Journal, 40*(4), 842–862. doi:10.1147/sj.404.0842

Good, J., & Robertson, J. (2006). CARSS: A framework for learner-centred design with children. *International Journal of Artificial Intelligence in Education, 16*(4), 381–413.

Goodson, I., & Cole, A. (1994). Exploring the Teacher's Professional Knowledge: Constructing Identity and Community. *Teacher Education Quarterly, 21*(1), 85–105.

Granovetter, M. (1973). The Strength of Weak Ties. *American Journal of Sociology*, *78*(6), 1360–1380. doi:10.1086/225469

Grimpe, B., Hartswood, M., & Jirotka, M. (2014). *Towards a Closer Dialogue between Policy and Practice: Responsible design in HCI.* Paper presented at the Proceedings of the Conference on Human Factors in Computing Systems CHI '14, Toronto. doi:10.1145/2556288.2557364

Grosser, M. (2004). *Gossamer Odyssey. The Triumph of Human-Powered Flight.* St. Paul, MN: Zenith Press.

Guy, M. 2006. Wiki or Won't He? A Tale of Public Sector Wikis. Comparison of UK & US State Organisations, Changing Audiences, Participation, and Collective Intelligence. Available from: http://www.ariadne.ac.uk/issue49/guy/

Hadzilakos, T., Papadakis, S., & Rossiou, E. (2007). Group Counseling Conferences (in Greek). *Open Education*, 5.

Hakkarainen, K. (2003). Emergence of progressive-inquiry culture in computer-supported collaborative learning. *Learning Environments Research*, *6*(2), 199–220. doi:10.1023/A:1024995120180

Hall, P. A., & Taylor, R. C. R. (1996). Political Science and the Three New Institutionalisms. *MPIFG Discussion Paper 96/9*.

Hall, S. (2014, February 17). Zooniverse Reaches One Million Volunteers. *Universe Today.* Retrieved from http://www.universetoday.com/109413/zooniverse-reaches-one-million-volunteers/

Hall, H., & Graham, D. (2004). Creation and recreation: Motivating collaboration to generate knowledge capital in online communities. *International Journal of Information Management*, *24*(3), 235–246. doi:10.1016/j.ijinfomgt.2004.02.004

Hampton, J. A. (1997). Emergent attributes in combined concepts. In T.B. Ward, S.M. Smith, & J. Vaid (Eds.), Creative thought: An investigation of conceptual structures and processes (pp. 83-110). Washington, DC: American Psychological Association. doi:10.1037/10227-004

Hanan, E. (2013). *The Effects of Using Electronic Social Networks on Social Relationships Facebook and Twitter as Example* [MSc thesis]. King Abdul Aziz University.

Hanneman, R. A. (2001). Introduction to Social Network Methods. Retrieved from http://www.researchmethods.org/NETTEXT.pdf

Hanson, N. R. (1958). Patterns of Discovery. Cambridge: Cambridge University Press. repr. 1975.

Hara, N., Shachaf, P., & Stoerger, S. (2009). Online communities of practice typology revisited. *Journal of Information Science*, *35*(6), 740–757. doi:10.1177/0165551509342361

Haraway, D. (1988). Situated Knowledges: The Science Question in Feminism and the Privilege of Partial Perspective. *Feminist Studies*, *14*(3), 575–599.

Harris, R. G. (2001). The Knowledge-Based Economy: Intellectual Origins and New Economic Perspectives. *International Journal of Management Reviews*, *3*(1), 21–40. doi:10.1111/1468-2370.00052

Hartley, J. (2005). Case Study Research. In C. Cassell & G. Symon (Eds.), *Essential Guide to Qualitative Methods in Organisational Research* (pp. 323–333). London: SAGE Publications.

Hasan, H., & Pfaff, C. C. (2006). The wiki: an environment to revolutionize employees' interaction with corporate knowledge.*Proceedings of the Australasian Computer-Human Interaction Conference*, Sydney (pp. 377-380). doi:10.1145/1228175.1228250

Hattie, J. (2008). *Visible learning: A synthesis of over 800 meta-analyses relating to achievement.* London: Routledge.

Hattie, J., & Yates, G. C. R. (2014). *Visible learning and the science of how we learn.* London: Routledge/Taylor & Francis Group.

Hayles, K. N. (2002). *Writing Machines*. Cambridge: MIT Press.

Haythornthwaite, C. (2005). Social networks and internet connectivity effects. *Information Communication and Society, 8*(2), 125–147. doi:10.1080/13691180500146185

Hechter, M., & Kanazawa, S. (1997). Sociological Rational Choice Theory. *Annual Review of Sociology, 23*(1), 191–214. doi:10.1146/annurev.soc.23.1.191

Heeks, R. 2003. Most eGovernment-for-Development Projects Fail: How Can the Risks be Reduced? *i-Government Working Paper Series - Paper No. 14*, IDPM, 2003.

Hellenic Quality Assurance and Accreditation Agency. (2012). The Annual report 2011-12 in Higher Education. Retrieved from http://www.hqaa.gr/data1/%CE%91%CE%94%CE%99%CE%A0_%CE%95%CE%A4%CE%97%CE%A3%CE%99%CE%91_%CE%95%CE%9A%CE%98%CE%95%CE%A3%CE%97_2011-12.pdf

Helms, R., Ignacio, R., Brinkkemper, S., & Zonneveld, A. (2010). Limitations of Network Analysis for Studying Efficiency and Effectiveness of Knowledge Sharing. *Electronic Journal of Knowledge Management, 8*(1), 53–68. Retrieved from www.ejkm.com

Hernández-Leo, D., Romeo, L., Carralero, M. A., Chacón, J., Carrió, M., Moreno, P., & Blat, J. (2011). LdShake: Learning design solutions sharing and co-edition. *Computers & Education, 57*(4), 2249–2260. doi:10.1016/j.compedu.2011.06.016

Heston, J. (2013, February 6). Collaborative Learning: Leveraging Social Learning Sites. Retrieved fromhttp://blog.cengage.com/collaborative-learning-leveraging-social-learning-sites-part-1-of-2/

Hill, J. R., Song, L., & West, R. E. (2009). Social learning theory and web-based learning environments: A review of research and discussion of implications. *American Journal of Distance Education, 23*(2), 88–103. doi:10.1080/08923640902857713

Hislop, D. (2005). *Knowledge Management in Organizations: A Critical Introduction*. Oxford: Oxford University Press.

Hislop, D. (2013). *Knowledge management in organizations: A critical introduction*. Oxford University Press.

Hoffmann, W. A. (2009). *Gestão do Conhecimento: Desafios de Aprender*. São Carlos: Compacta.

Holmes, B., & Gardner, J. (2006). *E-learning: Concepts and Practice*. London, UK: Sage.

Holstein, J. A., & Gubrium, F. J. (2000). *The self we live by: narrative identity in a postmodern world*. New York: Oxford University Press, Inc.

Hossain, M., & Aydin, H. (2011). A Web 2.0-based collaborative model for multicultural education. *Multicultural Education & Technology Journal, 5*(2), 116–128. doi:10.1108/17504971111142655

Howard, M., Vidgen, R., & Powell, P. (2006). Automotive e-hubs: Exploring motivations and barriers to collaboration and interaction. *The Journal of Strategic Information Systems, 15*(1), 51–75. doi:10.1016/j.jsis.2005.06.002

Hughes, J., Jewson, N., & Unwin, L. (2013). *Communities of practice: Critical perspectives*. Routledge.

Illeris, K. (2009). *Contemporary Theories of Learning: Learning Theorists -- in Their Own Words*. London, New York: Taylor & Francis Routledge.

InfoDev. (2013). *Crowdfunding's potential for the developing world*. Washington, DC: World Bank.

Innovation Unit. (2013). *Redesigning Education: Shaping learning systems around the globe. Innovation Unit for the Global Education Leaders' Program*. Seattle, WA: Booktrope.

Isaac-Henry, K. (1997). Development and Change in the Public Sector. In K. Isaac-Henry, C. Painter, & C. Barnes (Eds.), *Management in the Public Sector: Challenge and Change* (pp. 1–25). London: International Thomson Business Press.

Jacko, J. A., Yi, J. S., Sainfort, F., & McClellan, M. (2012). Human Factors and Ergonomic Methods. In G. Salvendy (Ed.), *Handbook of Human Factors and Ergonomics* (4th ed., pp. 289–329). New Jersey, N.J.: John Wiley and Sons. doi:10.1002/9781118131350.ch10

Jackson, A., Yates, J., & Orlikowski, W. (2007). Corporate blogging: Building community through persistent digital talk. *Proceedings of the 40th Hawaii International Conference on System Sciences* (pp. 1530-1605). doi:10.1109/HICSS.2007.155

Jamali, R., H., Russell, B., Nicholas, D., & Watkinson, A. (. (2014). Do online communities support research collaboration? *Aslib Journal of Information Management, 66*(6), 603–622. doi:10.1108/AJIM-08-2013-0072

Jankowski, N. W. (2006). Creating Community with Media: History, Theories and Scientific Investigations. In L. A. Lievrouw & S. Livingstone (Eds.), The Handbook of New Media (Updated Student ed., pp. 55-74). London, UK: Sage.

Jarvela, S., Volet, S., & Jarvenoja, H. (2010). Research on Motivation in Collaborative Learning: Moving Beyond the Cognitive-Situative Divide and Combining Individual and Social Processes. *Educational Psychologist, 45*(1), 15–27. doi:10.1080/00461520903433539

Jean, R., Sinkovics, R. R., & Kim, D. (2014). The impact of technological, organizational and environmental characteristics on electronic collaboration and relationship performance in international customer-supplier relationship. *Information & Management, 51*(7), 854–864. doi:10.1016/j.im.2014.08.002

Jekins, J., & Vissere, G. (2001). *E-learning-Everybody's Business.* Retrieved from www.imaginal.nl

Jeon, S., Kim, Y.-G., & Koh, J. (2011). An integrative model for knowledge sharing in communities-of-practice. *Journal of Knowledge Management, 15*(2), 251–269. doi:10.1108/13673271111119682

Jin, L., Wen, Z., & Gough, N. (2010). Social virtual worlds for technology-enhanced learning on an augmented learning platform. *Learning, Media and Technology, 35*(2), 139–153. doi:10.1080/17439884.2010.494424

JISC. (2013*). Designing Spaces for Effective Learning - A guide to 21st century learning space design.* Retrieved from http://www.jisc.ac.uk/uploaded_documents/JISClearningspaces.pdf

Johansen, R. (1988). *Groupware: Computer Support for Business Teams.* New York: The Free Press.

Johnson, D. W., & Johnson, R. T. (1996). Cooperation and the use of technology. In D. H. Jonassen (Ed.), *Handbook of research for educational communications and technology* (pp. 170–198). New York: Simon & Schuster Macmillan.

Johnson, D. W., & Johnson, R. T. (2005). New Developments in Social Interdependence Theory. *Genetic, Social, and General Psychology Monographs, 131*(4), 285–358. doi:10.3200/MONO.131.4.285-358 PMID:17191373

Jonassen, D. (2000). Revisiting Activity Theory as a Framework for Designing Student- Centered Learning Environments. In D. Jonassen & S. Land (Eds.), *Theoretical foundations of Learning Environments.* LEA.

Jonassen, D. H., & Land, S. M. (2000). *Theoretical Foundations of Learning Environments.* Mahwah, NJ: Lawrence Erlbaum Associates.

Jones, N. B., & Laffey, J. (2002). How to facilitate e-collaboration and e-learning in organizations. In A. Rosset (Ed.), *The ASTD E-Learning Handbook* (pp. 80–101). New York, USA: McGraw-Hill.

Joosten, T. (2012). *Social media for educators: Strategies and best practices.* John Wiley & Sons.

Jrvel, S., & Hadwin, A. (2013). New Frontiers: Regulating Learning in CSCL. *Educational Psychologist, 48*(1), 25–39. doi:10.1080/00461520.2012.748006

Kahn, P. H. Jr, Ishiguro, H., Friedman, B., Kanda, T., Freier, N. G., Severson, R. L., & Miller, J. (2007). What is a Human?: Toward psychological benchmarks in the field of human–robot interaction. *Interaction Studies: Social Behaviour and Communication in Biological and Artificial Systems*, *8*(3), 363–390. doi:10.1075/is.8.3.04kah

Kai-Wai Chu, S., & Kennedy, D. M. (2011). Using online collaborative tools for groups to co-construct knowledge. *Online Information Review*, *35*(4), 581–597. doi:10.1108/14684521111161945

Kamal, S. (2013). *The role of social medial & networking in post-conflict settings – lessons learned from Egypt*, African Development Bank Conference: History and Experience of Post-conflict Reintegration and Stabilization: Reflections from DDR in Africa 5-6 June, Hotel African Tunis.

Kaplan, S. N. (2014). Collaboration. *Gifted Child Today*, *37*(4), 261–263. doi:10.1177/1076217514545384

Kapp, K. M., & O'Driscoll, T. (2010). *Learning in 3D: Adding a new dimension to enterprise learning and collaboration*. San Francisco, CA: Pfeiffer and John Wiley, Inc.

Kateman, B. (2012, February 29). Social Media and the Love of Science. Retrieved from http://blogs.ei.columbia.edu/2012/02/29/social-media-and-the-love-of-science/

Keegan, D. (1986). *The foundations of distance education* (2nd ed.). London: Routledge.

Keeler, L. C. (2006). Student satisfaction and types of interaction in distance education courses. *Dissertation Abstracts International*, *67*, 9.

Keitt, T. J., & Schadler, T. (2012). The Road To Social Business Transformation Starts With A Burning Platform. *Forrester Research Report Abstract*. Retrieved from http://www.forrester.com/The+Road+To+Social+Business+Transformation+Starts+With+A+Burning+Platform

Keitt, T. J., Brown, M., Koplowitz, R., Schadler, T., Karcher, P., Fenwick, N., & Smit, A. (2012). The Social CIO. *Forrester Research Report Abstract*. Retrieved from http://www.forrester.com/The+Social+CIO/fulltext/-/E-RES72881

Kelly, L., & Russo, A. (2008). From ladders of participation to networks of participation: Social media and museum audiences. *Proceedings of Museums and the Web 2008*.

Kelly, K. (2010). *What technology wants*. New York, NY: Viking.

Kelty, C. (2005). Geeks, Social Imaginaries, and Recursive Publics. *Cultural Anthropology*, *20*(2), 185–214. doi:10.1525/can.2005.20.2.185

Kenman, H. (1996). Konkordanzdemokratie und Korporatismus aus der Perspektive eines rationalen Institutionalismus. *Politische Vierteljahresschrift*, *37*, 494–515.

Kietzmann, J. H., Hermkens, K., McCarthy, I. P., & Silvestre, B. S. (2011). Social media? Get serious! Understanding the functional building blocks of social media. *Business Horizons*, *54*(3), 241–251. doi:10.1016/j.bushor.2011.01.005

Kimble, C., & Hildreth, P. (2004). Communities of Practice: Going One Step Too Far? Proceedings of 9e colloque de l'AIM, (May 2004). p. 304.

Kim, S. T., Lee, C. K., & Hwang, T. (2008). Investigating the influence of employee blogging on IT workers' organizational citizenship behavior. *International Journal of Information Technology and Management*, *7*(2), 178–189. doi:10.1504/IJITM.2008.016604

Klein, H. J., Connell, N. A., & Meyer, E. (2005). Knowledge Characteristics of Communities of Practice. *Knowledge Management Research & Practice*, *3*(2), 106–114. doi:10.1057/palgrave.kmrp.8500055

Kluge, S., & Riley, L. (2008). Teaching in Virtual Worlds: Opportunities and Challenges. *Issues in Informing Science and Information Technology*, *5*, 127–135.

Kobbe, L., Weinberger, A., Dillenbourg, P., Harrer, A., Hämäläinen, R., Häkkinen, P., & Fischer, F. (2007). Specifying Computer-Supported Collaboration Scripts. *International Journal of Computer-Supported Collaborative Learning*, *2*(2-3), 211–224. doi:10.1007/s11412-007-9014-4

Kock, N. (2005). What is E-Collaboration? *International Journal of e-Collaboration*, *1*(1), i–vii.

Kock, N. (2008). A Basic Definition of E-Collaboration and its Underlying Concepts. In N. Kock (Ed.), *Encyclopedia of E-Collaboration* (pp. 48–53). Hershey, PA: Information Science Reference. doi:10.4018/978-1-59904-000-4.ch008

Kock, N. (2008). Designing e-collaboration technologies to facilitate compensatory adaptation. *Information Systems Management*, *25*(1), 14–19. doi:10.1080/10580530701777115

Kock, N., & D'Arcy, J. (2002). Resolving the e-collaboration paradox: The competing influences of media naturalness and compensatory adaptation. *Information Management and Consulting* [Special issue on Electronic Collaboration], *17*(4), 72–78.

Kogut, B., & Zander, U. (1992). Knowledge of the Firm, Combinative Capabilities, and the Replication of Technology. *Organization Science*, *3*(3), 383–397.

Kohn, A. (1996). By all available means: Cameron and Pierce's defense. *Review of Educational Research*, *66*(1), 1–4. doi:10.3102/00346543066001001

Kok, A. (2011). In Defence of Mobile Technologies: Exploring the Socio-Technological Dimensions of M-Learning. In A.G. Abdel-Wahab, & A.A. El-Masry (Eds.), Mobile Information Communication Technologies Adoption in Developing Countries: Effects and Implications (pp. 67-78). Hershey, PA: Information Science Reference.

Kokkos, A. (2001). Tutor-counselor's role in Open and Distance Learning: the case of Hellenic Open University (in Greek). In A. Lionarakis (Ed.), *Proceedings of 1st International Conference of Open and Distance Learning*, Patra, Hellenic Open University.

Kolaczyk, E. D., & Krivitsky, P. N. (2012). On the Question of Effective Sample Size in Network Modeling, Cornell University Library. Retrieved from http://arxiv.org/abs/1112.0840

Koplowitz, R., Schooley, C., Karcherwith Khalid Kark, P., & Murphy, K. (2013.) Social Business And Collaboration Success Hinges On Effective Change Management. *Forrester Research Report Abstract*. Retrieved from https://www.forrester.com/Social+Business+And+Collaboration+Success+Hinges+On+Effective+Change+Management/fulltext/-/E-res81003 [REMOVED HYPERLINK FIELD]

Kordaki, M., & Siempos, H. (2010, April 7-10). The JiGSAW Collaborative Method within the online computer science classroom.*Proceedings of the 2nd International Conference on Computer Supported Education*, Valencia, Spain (pp. 65-74).

Koschmann, T. (1996). Paradigm shifts and instructional technology: An introduction. In T. Koschmann (Ed.), *CSCL: Theory and practice of an emerging paradigm* (pp. 1–23). Mahwah, NJ: Lawrence Erlbaum Associates.

Koschmann, T. (1999). Computer support for collaboration and learning. *Journal of the Learning Sciences*, *8*(3-4), 495–497. doi:10.1080/10508406.1999.9672077

Kozulin, A. (2003). Psychological Tools and Mediated Learning. In A. Kozulin, B. Gindis, V. S. Ageyev, & S. M. Miller (Eds.), *Vygotsky's educational theory in cultural context* (pp. 15–38). Cambridge, UK: Cambridge University Press. doi:10.1017/CBO9780511840975.003

Krathwohl, D. R. (2002). A Revision of Bloom's Taxonomy: An Overview. *Theory into Practice*, *41*(4), 212–218. doi:10.1207/s15430421tip4104_2

Kraut, R. E., Resnick, P., Kiesler, S., Burke, M., Chen, Y., & Kittur, N. … Riedl, J. (2012). Building successful online communities: Evidence-based social design. MIT Press.

Kreijns, K., Kirschner, P. A., & Jochems, W. (2003). Identifying the pitfalls for social interaction in computer-supported collaborative learning environments: A review of the research. *Computers in Human Behavior*, *19*(3), 335–353. doi:10.1016/S0747-5632(02)00057-2

Kreijns, K., Kirschner, P. A., Jochems, W., & van Buuren, H. (2007). Measuring perceived sociability of computer-supported collaborative learning environments. *Computers & Education*, *49*(2), 176–192. doi:10.1016/j.compedu.2005.05.004

Kuhn, T. S. (1962). *The structure of scientific revolutions*. Chicago, IL: University of Chicago Press.

Kukulska-Hulme, A., & Traxler, J. (2007). Designing for mobile and wireless learning. In H. Beetham & R. Sharpe (Eds.), *Rethinking pedagogy for a digital age: Designing and delivering e-learning* (pp. 180–192). London, UK: Routledge.

Kulczycki, E. (2013). *Transformation of Science Communication in the Age of Social Media*. Adam Mickiewicz University. Department of Philosophy.

Kuutti, K. 1996. Activity Theory as a Potential Framework for Human Computer Interaction Research. In B. A. Nardi (Ed.), Context and Consciousness: Activity Theory and Human Computer Interaction (pp. 17 – 44). Boston, M.A.: M.I.T. Press.

Lai, K. W. (1993). Teachers as Facilitators in a Computer-supported Learning Environment. *Journal of Information Technology for Teacher Education*, *2*(2), 127–137. doi:10.1080/0962029930020202

Lakatos, I. (1970). (Lakatos, & Musgrave Eds.). Falsification and the Methodology of Scientific Research Programmes, in Criticism and the Growth of Knowledge. Cambridge University Press, 1970.

LAMS community. (n. d.). *LAMS community*. Retrieved from www.lamscommunity.org

LAMS. (n. d.). *What is LAMS?* Retrieved from http://www.lamsfoundation.org/

Laningham, S. (Interviewer), & Berners-Lee, T. (Interviewee). (2006). developerWorks Interviews: Tim Berners-Lee. Retrieved from http://www.ibm.com/developerworks/podcast/dwi/cm-int082206txt.html

Latour, B., & Woolgar, S. (1979). *Laboratory life: The construction of scientific facts*. Princeton, NJ: Princeton University Press.

Laurillard, D. (2008). Technology Enhanced Learning as a Tool for Pedagogical Innovation. *Journal of Philosophy of Education*, *42*(3-4), 521–533. doi:10.1111/j.1467-9752.2008.00658.x

Laurillard, D. (2009). The pedagogical challenges to collaborative technologies. *International Journal of Computer-Supported Collaborative Learning*, *4*(1), 5–20. doi:10.1007/s11412-008-9056-2

Laurillard, D. (2012). *Teaching as a design science: Building Pedagogical Patterns for Learning and Technology*. New York, NY: Routledge.

Laurillard, D., Charlton, P., Craft, B., Dimakopoulos, D., Ljubojevic, D., Magoulas, G., & Whittlestone, K. et al. (2013). A constructionist learning environment for teachers to model learning designs. *Journal of Computer Assisted Learning*, *29*(1), 15–30. doi:10.1111/j.1365-2729.2011.00458.x

Lave, J., & Wenger, E. (1991). *Situated learning: Legitimate peripheral participation*. Cambridge, UK: Cambridge University Press. doi:10.1017/CBO9780511815355

Lave, J., & Wenger, E. (1998). *Communities of Practice: Learning, Meaning, and Identity*. New York: Cambridge University Press.

Laver, M., & Schofield, N. (1990). *Multiparty Government: The Politics of Coalition in Europe*. Oxford: Oxford University Press.

Lavoy, D. (2013, February 13). Collaboration Isn't Working: What We Have Here is a Chasm. *CMSWire.com*. Retrieved from http://www.cmswire.com/cms/social-business/collaboration-isnt-working-what-we-have-here-is-a-chasm-019597.php

Lawson, B. (2005). *How Designers Think: The Design Process Demystified* (4th ed.). Oxford, UK: Architectural Press.

Lee, A., Danis, C., Miller, T., & Jung, Y. (2001). Fostering Social Interaction in Online Spaces.*Proceedings of the Conference on Human-Computer Interaction* (pp. 59-66).

Lee, H., & Bonk, C. (2010). Implementation, challenges, and future plans of social learning in the workplace. In J. Sanchez, & K. Zhang (Eds.), *Proceedings of World Conference on E-Learning in Corporate, Government, Healthcare, and Higher Education 2010* (pp. 2581-2587). Chesapeake, VA: AACE.

Lee, M. R., & Lan, Y. (2007). From Web 2.0 to conversational knowledge management: Towards collaborative intelligence. *Journal of Entrepreneurship Research*, *2*(2), 47–62.

Leila R. (2010, Feb 16). *Women in Arab media: present but not heard* [Presentation]. Stanford University, California, USA.

LeNoue, M., Hall, T., & Eighmy, M. A. (2011). Adult education and social media revolution. *Adult Learning*, *22*(2), 4–12. doi:10.1177/104515951102200201

Lessig, L. (2004). The Creative Commons. *Montana Law Review*, *65*, 1–14.

Lesson, L. A. M. S. (n. d.). *LessonLAMS*. Retrieved from http://lessonlams.com/lams/

Levy, S., & Yupangco, J. (2008, August 11). Overcoming the challenges of social learning in the workplace. *Learning Solutions e-Magazine*.

Levy, M., Loebbecke, C., & Maier, R. (2003). SMEs, co-opetition and knowledge sharing: The role of information systems. *European Journal of Information Systems*, *12*(1), 3–17. doi:10.1057/palgrave.ejis.3000439

Lewark, S. (2010). Learning, knowledge transfer and competence development in forestry operations small and medium sized enterprises (SMEs). Institute for Forest Utilization and Work Science. Albert-Ludwigs-University Freiburg, Breisgau, Germany.

Lewin, K. (1943). Defining the Field at a given time. *Psychological Review*, *50*(3), 292–310. doi:10.1037/h0062738

Lewis, A. (1982). *The Psychology of Taxation*. Oxford: Martin Robertson & Company.

Li, L. C., Grimshaw, J. M., Nielsen, C., Judd, M., Coyote, P. C., & Graham, I. D. (2009) Evolution of Wenger's concept of community of practice. Implementation Science, London 4(11).

Li, Z., Yezhuang, T., & Zhongying, Q. (2006) The impact of organizational culture and knowledge management on organizational performance. *Proceedings of the Information Resources Management Association International Conference*, San Diego. Hershey, PA, USA: Idea Group Co.

Lin, M. F., & Lee, M. (2006). E-learning Localized: The case of the OOPS project. In A. Edmundson (Ed.), *Globalization in Education: Improving education quality through cross-cultural dialogue* (pp. 168–186). Hershey, PA: Idea Group.

Lin, N. (2002). *Social capital: A theory of social structure and action*. Cambridge, UK: Cambridge University Press.

Lionarakis, A. (1998). Polymorphic Education: A pedagogical framework for open and distance learning. In A. Szucs & A. Wagner (Eds.), *Transformation, Innovation and Tradition Roles and Perspectives of Open and Distance Learning* (pp. 499–504). Italy: University of Bologna, Universities in a Digital Era.

Lionarakis, A. (2001). Open and Distance polymorphic education: considerations on a qualitative approach of designing educational material. In A. Lionarakis (Ed.), *Views and considerations on ODL*. Athens: Propompos. (in Greek)

Lippincott, J., Hemmasi, H., & Lewis, V. (2014, June 16). Trends in Digital Scholarship Centers. Retrieved from http://www.educause.edu/ero/article/trends-digital-scholarship-centers/

Long, N. E. (1958). The Local Community as an Ecology of Games. *American Journal of Sociology*, *64*(3), 251–261. doi:10.1086/222468

Luckin, R., Koedinger, K. R., & Greer, J. (2007). *Artificial Intelligence in Education: Building Technology Rich Learning Contexts That Work* (Vol. 158). Amsterdam: IOS Press.

Luzón, F., Palencia, V. J., Morales, J., Sánchez-Sesma, F. J., & García, J. M. (2002). Evaluation of Site effects in sedimentary basins. *Fis Tierra*, *14*, 183–214.

Maccoby, M. (2011). Constructing collaboration. *Research Technology Management*, *54*(1), 59–60. doi:10.5437/08953608X540159

Macy, M. W., & Willer, R. (2002). From Factors to Actors: Computational Sociology and Agent-Based Modeling. *Annual Review of Sociology*, *28*(1), 143–166. doi:10.1146/annurev.soc.28.110601.141117

Maddux, C. D., Johnson, D. L., & Willis, J. W. (1997). *Educational computing: Learning with tomorrow's technologies*. Boston: Allyn & Bacon.

Madon, S. (1997). Information-based Global Economy and Socio-Economic Development: The Case of Bangalore. *The Information Society*, *13*(3), 227–243. doi:10.1080/019722497129115

Madon, S. (2004). Evaluating the Developmental Impact of E-Governance Initiatives: An Exploratory Framework. *Electronic Journal of Information Systems in Developing Countries*, *20*(5), 1–13.

Madon, S., Sahay, S., & Sahay, J. (2004). Implementing Property Tax Reforms in Bangalore: An Actor-Network Perspective. *Information and Organization*, *14*(4), 269–295. doi:10.1016/j.infoandorg.2004.07.002

Magagnino, F. (2008). The Web 2.0 Approach and its Repercussions on E-learning Applications: The Development of a Prototype for Informal Learning. *Journal of e-Learning and Knowledge Society*, *4*(3), 223-232.

Magnisalis, I., Demetriadis, S., & Karakostas, A. (2011). Adaptive and Intelligent Systems for Collaborative Learning Support: A Review of the Field. *IEEE Transactions on Learning Technologies*, *4*(1), 5–20. doi:10.1109/TLT.2011.2

March, J. G., & Olsen, J. P. (1984). The New Institutionalism: Organisational Factors in Political Life. *The American Political Science Review*, *78*(3), 734–749. doi:10.2307/1961840

March, J. G., & Olsen, J. P. (1989). *Rediscovering Institutions: The Organisational Basis of Politics*. New York, N.Y.: The Free Press.

Margetts, H. Z. (2006). Transparency and Digital Government. In C. Hood & D. Heald (Eds.), *Transparency: the Key to Better Governance?* (pp. 197–210). London: The British Academy. doi:10.5871/bacad/9780197263839.003.0012

Margetts, H. Z., John, P., Escher, T., & Reissfelder, S. (2011). Social Information and Political Participation on the Internet: An Experiment. *European Political Science Review*, *3*(3), 321–344. doi:10.1017/S1755773911000129

Marin, A., & Wellman, B. (2011). Social network analysis: An introduction. In J. Scott & P. J. Carrington (Eds.), *The SAGE Handbook of Social Network Analysis* (pp. 11–25). London: SAGE.

Marks, A. (2011). Electronic group collaboration in higher education. *Proceedings of the15th IEEE International Conference on Computer Supported Cooperative Work in Design* (pp. 742-747).

Martinez, S., & Stager, G. (2013). *Invent to Learn: Making, tinkering, and engineering in the classroom*. Torrance, Ca: Constructing Modern Knowledge Press.

Masterman, L., & Vogel, M. (2007). Practices and processes of design for learning. In H. Beetham & R. Sharpe (Eds.), *Rethinking Pedagogy for a Digital Age: Designing and delivering elearning* (pp. 52–63). London, UK: Routledge.

Mateas, M., & Sengers, P. (Eds.), (2003). *Narrative Intelligence*. Amsterdam: John Benjamins Publishing. doi:10.1075/aicr.46

Matei, S. A. (2005). From counterculture to cyberculture: Virtual community discourse and the dilemma of modernity. *Journal of Computer-Mediated Communication, 10*(3), 00–00.

Mathieu, J. E., Tannenbaum, S. I., & Salas, E. (1992). Influences of individual and situational characteristics on measures of training effectiveness. *Academy of Management Journal, 35*(4), 828–847. doi:10.2307/256317

Matralis, Ch. (1998). Goal and Objectives (in Greek). In A. Kokkos, A. Lionarakis, Ch. Matralis, C. Panayotakopoulos (Eds.), The educational material and new technologies, Open and Distance Learning (vol. C). Patra: Hellenic Open University.

Matsagouras, E. (2002). *Critical thinking in teaching*. Athens: Gutenberg. (in Greek)

McCubbins, M. D., & Sullivan, T. (1987). *Congress: Structure and Policy*. Cambridge: Cambridge University Press.

McDonald, J., & Gibson, C. C. (1998). Interpersonal dynamics and group development in computer conferencing. *American Journal of Distance Education, 12*(1), 7–25. doi:10.1080/08923649809526980

McElroy, M. W. (1999) The Second Generation of Knowledge Management. *Knowledge Management,* October, 86-88.

McLure Wasko, M., & Faraj, S. (2000). It is what one does: Why people participate and help others in electronic communities of practice. *The Journal of Strategic Information Systems, 9*(2-3), 155–173. doi:10.1016/S0963-8687(00)00045-7

McMahon, M. (1997, December). *Social constructivism and the world wide web: A paradigm for learning*. Paper presented at the ASCILITE conference. Perth, Australia.

McNeill, D. (2005). *Gesture and Thought.* Chicago: University of Chicago Press. doi:10.7208/chicago/9780226514642.001.0001

McWilliam, G. (2012). Building stronger brands through online communities. *Sloan Management Review, 41*(3).

Mehta, J. (2010). Ideas and Politics: Towards a Second Generation. *Perspectives on Politic*. Retrieved from http://www.allacademic.com//meta/p_mla_apa_research_citation/0/2/2/1/1/pages22111/p22111-1.php

Mehta, J., & Fine, S. (2012). Teaching differently...Learning deeply. *Phi Delta Kappan, 94*(2), 31–35. doi:10.1177/003172171209400208

Mejias, U. A. (2006). *The tyranny of nodes: Towards a critique of social network theories.* Retrieved from http://blog.ulisesmejias.com/2006/10/09/the-tyranny-of-nodes-towards-a-critique-of-social-network-theories/

Merriam, S., Caffarella, R., & Baumgartner, L. (2007). *Learning in adulthood: A comprehensive guide* (3rd ed.). NY: Willey.

Meyerhoff, M., & Strycharz, A. (2013). *Communities of practice*. Wiley Online Library. doi:10.1002/9781118335598.ch20

Miller, M. D., Linn, R. L., & Gronlund, N. E. (2009). *Measurement and Assessment in Teaching* (10th ed.). Upper Saddle River, NJ: Merrill.

Miller, N. E., & Dollard, J. C. (1941). *Social learning and imitation*. New Haven, CT: Yale University Press.

Mintzberg, H. (1985). The Organisation as Political Arena. *Journal of Management Studies*, *22*(2), 133–154. doi:10.1111/j.1467-6486.1985.tb00069.x

Miri-Lavassani, K., Movahedi, B., & Kumar, V. (2010). Electronic collaboration ontology: The case of readiness analysis of electronic marketplace adoption. *Journal of Management & Organization*, *16*(3), 454–466. doi:10.5172/jmo.16.3.454

Mirkin, B. (2010). *Population Levels, Trends and Policies in the Arab Region: Challenges and Opportunities*. United Nations Development Programme Regional Bureau for Arab States Arab Human Development Report Research Paper Series.

Mishra, P., & Koehler, M. (2006). Technological Pedagogical Content Knowledge: A Framework for Teacher Knowledge. *Teachers College Record*, *108*(6), 1017–1054. doi:10.1111/j.1467-9620.2006.00684.x

Misra, S. (2005). eGovernance: Responsive and Transparent Service Delivery Mechanism. In A. Singh (Ed.), Administrative Reforms: Towards Sustainable Practices (pp. 283-302). New Delhi: SAGE Publications.

Molina, A. (2003). The Digital Divide: The Need for a Global e-Inclusion Movement. *Technology Analysis and Strategic Management*, *15*(1), 137–152. doi:10.1080/0953732032000046105

Moll, L. C. (1990). Introduction. In L. C. Moll (Ed.), *Vygotsky and education: Instructional implications and applications of sociohistorical psychology* (pp. 1–27). NY: Cambridge University Press. doi:10.1017/CBO9781139173674.002

Monclar, R. S., Oliveira, J., de Faria, F. F., Ventura, L., de Souza, J. M., & Campos, M. L. M. (2011, June 8-10). Using social networks analysis for collaboration and team formation identification. Proceedings of the *2011 15th International Conference on Computer Supported Cooperative Work in Design CSCWD* (pp. 562-569). doi:10.1109/CSCWD.2011.5960128

Moon, M. J. (2002). The Evolution of E-Government among Municipalities: Rhetoric or Reality? *Public Administration Review*, *62*(4), 424–433. doi:10.1111/0033-3352.00196

Moon, S. B. (2010). *Basic concepts and applications of structural equation modeling*. Seoul: Haksisa.

Moon, S., & Lee, Y. (2009). The impacts of social network activities on company employees' organizational commitment and job satisfaction. *Journal of Korea Human Resource Management*, *6*(2), 55–67.

Moore, M. G. (1973). Toward a theory of Independent Learning and Teaching. *The Journal of Higher Education*, *44*(9), 661–679. doi:10.2307/1980599

Moore, M. G. (1980). Independent study. In R. Boyd & J. Apps (Eds.), *Redefining the Discipline of Adult Education* (pp. 16–31). San Francisco: Jossey-Bass.

Moore, M. G. (1989). Three types of interaction. *American Journal of Distance Education*, *3*(2), 1–6. doi:10.1080/08923648909526659

Morozov, E. (2012). *The Net Delusion: How Not to Liberate The World*. London: Penguin Books.

Muhammad, Z. K. (2008). *Woman in Islam*. Tilford, Surrey, U.K.: Islam International Publications Limited Islamabad, Sheephatch Lane.

Munkvold, B. E. (2005). Experiences from global e-collaboration: Contextual influences on technology adoption and use. *IEEE Transactions on Professional Communication*, *48*(1), 78–86. doi:10.1109/TPC.2005.843300

Myers, M. (1991) Cooperative learning in heterogeneous classes. *Cooperative Learning,* 11(4).

Naryman, N. (2012). *Studying Facebook sample users from Algiera to obtain its effect on social relations* [Msc thesis]. Elhag Elkhdr University.

NASA. (2015). Social Media at NASA. Retrieved from http://www.nasa.gov/socialmedia/

National Institute of Urban Affairs (NIUA). (2004). *Reforming the Property Tax System. Research Study Series no. 94.* New Delhi: NIUA Press.

Navid, H. (2011). *Media Disruption Exacerbates Revolutionary Unrest: Evidence from Mubarak's Natural Experiment.* American Political Science Association Annual Meeting. Retrieved from http://papers.ssrn.com/sol3/papers.cfm?abstract_id=1903351

Naylor, P., Wharf-Higgins, J., Blair, L., Green, L., & O'Connor, B. (2002). Evaluating the participatory process in a community based heart health project. *Social Science & Medicine, 55*(7), 1173–1187. doi:10.1016/S0277-9536(01)00247-7 PMID:12365529

Neilson, R. (1997). *Collaborative Technologies & Organizational Learning*. Hershey, PA: Idea Group Publishing.

Nelson, G., Ochocka, J., Griffin, K., & Lord, J. (1998). Nothing about me, without me: Participatory Action Research with self-help/mutual aid organizations for psychiatric consumer/survivors. *American Journal of Community Psychology, 26*(6), 881–912. doi:10.1023/A:1022298129812 PMID:10085536

Newell, A., Carmichael, J., & Morgan, M. (2007). Methodologies for involving older adults in the design process. *Proceedings of the 4th International Conference on Universal Access in HCI.* Retrieved from http://www.springerlink.com/content/53t5026735v65721/fulltext.pdf

Newhouse, H. C. B., & Vestal, W. (2001). Building and Sustaining Communities of Practice. Houston: American Productivity Centre.

Newman, D., Griffin, P., & Cole, M. (1989). *The Construction Zone: Working for Cognitive Change in School.* New York: Cambridge University Press.

Newman, M., Barabási, A. L., & Watts, D. J. (2006). *The Structure and Dynamics of Networks.* Oxford: Princeton University Press.

Nielsen, M. (2010, May 1). Introduction to the Polymath Project and Density Hales-Jewett and Moser Numbers. Retrieved from http://michaelnielsen.org/blog/introduction-to-the-polymath-project-and-density-hales-jewett-and-moser-numbers/

Nightingale, C. (2006). *Nothing About Me, Without Me. Involving Learners with Learning Difficulties or Disabilities.* London: Learning Skills Development Agency.

Nissen, M. E., Kamel, M. N., & Sengupta, K. C. (2000). Toward integrating knowledge management, processes and systems: a position paper.*Proceedings of the AAAI Symposium on Bringing Knowledge to Business Processes, Stanford, CA.*

Noble, J., Davy, S., & Franks, D. W. (2004). Effects of the topology of social networks on information transmission. In S. Schaal, A. J. Ijspeert, A. Billard, & S. Vijayakumar (Eds.), *From Animals to Animats 8: Proceedings of the Eighth International Conference on Simulation of Adaptive Behavior* (pp. 395-404). MIT Press. Retrieved from http://eprints.soton.ac.uk/265249/1/sabNetTopology.pdf

Noe, R. A. (1986). Trainee attributes and attitudes: Neglected influences on training effectiveness. *Academy of Management Review, 11*, 736–749.

Nonaka, I. (1994). A Dynamic theory of Organizational Knowledge Creation. *Organization Science*, *5*(1), 14–37. doi:10.1287/orsc.5.1.14

Nonaka, I., & Konno, N. (1998). The concept of "ba": Building a foundation for knowledge creation. *California Management Review*, *40*(3), 40–54. doi:10.2307/41165942

Noorden, R. (2014, August 15). Online collaboration: Scientists and the social network. Retrieved from http://www.nature.com/news/online-collaboration-scientists-and-the-social-network-1.15711

Northern Illinois University. (2005). Stages of Collaboration. Retrieved from http://www.niu.edu/rcrportal/collabresearch/stages/stages.html

Nosek, J. T., & McManus, M. (2008). Collaboration challenges: Bridging the IT support gap. *Information Systems Management*, *25*(1), 3–7. doi:10.1080/10580530701777081

O'Brien, J. (2004). *Sistemas de informação e as decisões gerenciais na era da Internet*. São Paulo: Saraiva.

Oliver, R. (2001). Developing e-learning environments that support knowledge construction in higher education. In Stoney, S. and Burn, J. (Eds.), Working for Excellence in the E-conomy, (pp. 407-16). Churchlands: We-B Centre.

Olsen, J. K., Belenky, D. M., Aleven, V., & Rummel, N. (2014, June 5-9,). Using an Intelligent Tutoring System to Support Collaborative as well as Individual Learning. In S. Trausan-Matu, K. E. Boyer, M. Crosby & K. Panourgia (Eds.), *Intelligent Tutoring Systems: Proceedings* of the *12th International Conference, ITS 2014, Honolulu, HI, USA* (pp. 134-143). Cham, Switzerland: Springer International Publishing. doi:10.1007/978-3-319-07221-0_16

Olson, R. K., & Connelly, L. M. (1995). Mentoring through predoctoral fellowships to enhance research productivity. [PubMed]. *Journal of Professional Nursing*, *11*(5), 270–275. doi:10.1016/S8755-7223(05)80007-9

Ordanini, A., Miceli, L., Pizzetti, M., & Parasuraman, A. (2011). Crowd-funding: Transforming customers into investors through innovative service platforms. *Journal of Service Management*, *22*(4), 443–470. doi:10.1108/09564231111155079

O'Reilly, T. (2005). *What is Web 2.0: design patterns and business models for the next generation of software* [Online]. Available from: <http://www.oreillynet.com/pub/a/oreilly/tim/news/2005/09/30/what-is-web-20.html> (Accessed January 30, 2010).

O'Reilly, T. (2007). *Web 2.0 Compact Definition: Trying Again*. Retrieved from http://www.oreillynet.com/pub/a/oreilly/tim/news/2005/09/30/what-is-web-20.html

Orlikowski, W. (1992). The duality of technology: Rethinking the concept of technology in organizations. *Organization Science*, *3*(3), 398–427. doi:10.1287/orsc.3.3.398

Ostrom, E., Gardner, R., & Walker, J. (1994). Rules, Games and Common-Pool Resources. Ann Arbor, M.I.: University of Michigan Press.

Pain, R., & Francis, P. (2003). Reflections on participatory research. *Area*, *35*(1), 46–54. doi:10.1111/1475-4762.00109

Palloff, R., & Pratt, K. (1999). *Building Learning Communities in Cyberspace: effective strategies for the online classroom*. San Franciso: Jossey-Bass.

Papadakis, S., Kordaki, M., & Hadzilacos, T. (2007, November 29-30). Learning Design: the views of Prospective Computer Professionals. In P. Kefalas, A., Sotiriadou, G. Davies & A. McGettrick (Eds.), *Proceedings of Informatics Education Europe II Conference*, Thessaloniki, Greece (pp. 2-11).

Papadimitriou, S. (2013). Open Educational Resources and Practices Unfold a Brand New World Towards an Open Higher Education. *Proceedings of the Open Education 2030 Contribution to the JRC-IPTS Call for Vision Papers Part III: Higher Education.* Retrieved from http://is.jrc.ec.europa.eu/pages/EAP/documents/All_OE2030_HE_v%204_author%20revised_OK.pdf

Papadimitriou, S., Lampropoulou, N., & Kampylis, P. (2007). The multiple use of videoconference in distance learning of Greek teachers via Greek School Network. (in Greek). In A. Lionarakis (Ed.), *Proceedings of the 4th International Conference Open and Distance Learning.* Athens: Propompos.

Papadimitriou, S., Papadakis, S., Lionarakis, A., & Kameas, A. (2011, November). A proposal of using Learning Activities Management System (LAMS) to support the work of Educators in HOU. In A. Lionarakis (Ed.), *Proceedings of the 6th International Conference in Open & Distance Learning.* Retrieved from http://icodl.openet.gr/index.php/icodl/2011/paper/view/51

Papadimitriou, S., & Lionarakis, A. (2009). Tutor-counselor's role in Open and Distance Learning and the development of his support mechanism in ODL[in Greek]. *The Open Education Journal, 6*(1), 106–122. Retrieved from http://journal.openet.gr/index.php/openjournal/article/view/103

Papert, S. (1980). *Mindstorms. Children, Computers and Powerful Ideas.* New York: Basic books.

Park, S., Lim, C., Lee, J., & Choi, J. (2010). *Understanding of educational methods in educational technology.* Seoul: Educational Science Inc.

Parsons, S., & Cobb, S. (2014). Reflections on the role of the 'users': Challenges in a multi-disciplinary context of learner-centred design for children on the autism spectrum. *International Journal of Research & Method in Education, 37*(4), 421–441. doi:10.1080/1743727X.2014.890584

Patton, M. Q. (1980). *Qualitative Evaluation Methods.* Beverly Hills, CA, USA: Sage Publications.

Patton, M. Q. (1990). *Qualitative Evaluation and Research Methods.* Newbury Park; London, UK: Sage.

Pea, R. D. (1994). Seeing what we build together: Distributed multimedia learning environments for transformative communications. *Journal of the Learning Sciences, 3*(3), 285–299. doi:10.1207/s15327809jls0303_4

Peirce, C. S. (1931): Collected Papers. Cambridge, Harvard University press, Scritti scelti UTET, Torino.

Peters, B. G. (2000). *Institutional Theory in Political Science: The New Institutionalism.* London: Continuum Press.

Peterson, C., & Seligman, M. E. P. (2004). *Character strengths and virtues: A handbook and classification. New York: Oxford University Press and Washington.* DC: American Psychological Association.

Piaget, J. (1966). *Psychology of Intelligence.* Totowa, NJ: Littlefield, Adams.

Piaget, J. (1970). *Science of education and the psychology of the child.* New York: Orion Press.

Piaget, J. (1972). *The principles of genetic epistemology.* New York: Basic Books.

Piaget, J. (1977). *The development of thought: Equilibration of cognitive structures.* New York: Viking Press.

Pileggi, S. F., Fernandez-Llatas, C., & Traver, V. (2012). When the Social Meets the Semantic: Social Semantic Web or Web 2.5. *Future Internet, 4*(3), 852–864. doi:10.3390/fi4030852

Planetary Resources. (2013, May 29). Planetary Resources Announces World's First Crowdfunded Space Telescope Campaign. Retrieved from http://www.planetaryresources.com/2013/05/planetary-resources-announces-worlds-first-crowdfunded-space-telescope-campaign/

Polanyi, M. (1967) (reissue edition 2009). The Tacit Dimension. Chicago: Chicago University Press.

Pólya, G. (1945). *How to Solve It*. New York: Princeton University Press.

Pongracic, I. (2009). *Employees and entrepreneurship: Co-ordination and spontaneity in non-hierarchical business organizations*. Cheltenham: Edward Elgar Publishing. doi:10.4337/9781848446137

Power, D., Hanna, V., Singh, P. J., & Samson, D. (2010). Electronic markets, data access and collaboration: Relative value to performance in firm operations. *Supply Chain Management: An International Journal*, *15*(3), 238–251. doi:10.1108/13598541011039992

Prensky, M. (2001). Digital natives, digital immigrants.[NCB University Press.]. *The Horizon*, *9*(5), 1–6.

Price, V., & Archbold, J. (1995). Development and application of social learning theory. *British Journal of Nursing (Mark Allen Publishing)*, *4*(21), 1263–1268. doi:10.12968/bjon.1995.4.21.1263 PMID:8574105

Procter, W. (2014, June 11). Social Media and Language Learning. *Education First Blog*. Retrieved from http://www.ef.com/blog/corporate/social-media-and-language-learning/

Proctor, R. W., & Vu, K.-P. L. (2012). Selection and Control of Action. In G. Salvendy (Ed.), *Handbook of Human Factors and Ergonomics* (4th ed., pp. 95–116). New Jersey, N.J.: John Wiley and Sons. doi:10.1002/9781118131350.ch4

Prusak, L. (2001). Where Did Knowledge Management come from? *IBM Systems Journal*, *40*(4), 1002–1007. doi:10.1147/sj.404.01002

Pshenichny, C. A., & Kanzheleva, O. M. (2011) In K. Sinha, L. Gundersen, J. Jackson, & D. Arctur (Eds.), Theoretical foundations of the event bush method: Societal Challenges and Geoinformatics (GSA Special Paper 482) (pp. 139–165). doi:10.1130/2011.2482(12)

Putnam, R. D. (2000). *Bowling alone: The collapse and revival of American community*. New York: Simon & Schuster. doi:10.1145/358916.361990

Radermacher, H. (2006). *Participatory Action Research With People With Disabilities: Exploring Experiences Of Participation*. Melbourne: Victoria University.

Raike, A., Keune, A., Lindholm, B., & Muttilainen, J. (2013). Concept design for a collaborative digital learning tool for film post-production. *Journal of Media Practice*, *14*(4), 307–329. doi:10.1386/jmpr.14.4.307_1

Ramirez, M., & Castaneda, A. (1974). *Cultural Democracy, Bicognitive Development and Education*. New York: Academic Press.

Reason, P., & Heron, J. (1986). Research with people: The paradigm of co-operation experiential enquiry. *Person-Centred Review*, *1*(4), 456–476.

Reeve, J. (2013). How Students Create Motivationally Supportive Learning Environments for Themselves: The Concept of Agentic Engagement. *Journal of Educational Psychology*, *105*(3), 579–595. doi:10.1037/a0032690

Reigeluth, C. M., & Keller, J. B. (2009). Understanding instruction. In C. M. Reigeluth & A. A. Carr-Chellman (Eds.), *Instructional-design theories and models: Building a common knowledge base* (Vol. III, pp. 27–39). NY: Routlege.

Reimann, P. (2013). Design-Based Research—Designing as Research. In R. Luckin, S. Puntambekar, P. Goodyear, B. Grabowski, J. Underwood, & N. Winters (Eds.), *Handbook of Design in Educational Technology* (pp. 44–52). New York, NY: Routledge.

Resnick, M. (July, 1996). Distributed constructionism. In *Proceedings of the International Conference on the Learning Sciences Association for the Advancement of Computing in Education*, Northwestern University.

Rheingold, H. (2000). *The Virtual Community: Homesteading on the Electronic Frontier* (Revised ed.). Cambridge, MA: MIT press.

Ridings, C. M., & Gefen, D. (2004). Virtual community attraction: Why people hang out online. *Journal of Computer-Mediated Communication, 10*(1).

Riege, A. (2005). Three-dozen knowledge-sharing barriers managers must consider. *Journal of Knowledge Management, 9*(3), 18–35. doi:10.1108/13673270510602746

Roberts, J. (2006). Limits to communities of practice. *Journal of Management Studies, 43*(3), 623–639. doi:10.1111/j.1467-6486.2006.00618.x

Rodriguez Robles, F. M. (2006). Learner characteristic, interaction and support service variables as predictors of satisfaction in web-based distance education. *Dissertation Abstracts International, 67*, 7.

Rogoff, B. (1990). *Apprenticeship in thinking: Cognitive development in social context.* NY: Oxford University Press.

Roschelle, J. M., Pea, R. D., Hoadley, C. M., Gordin, D. N., & Means, B. M. (2000). Changing How and What Children Learn in School with Computer-Based Technologies. *The Future of Children, 10*(2), 76–101. doi:10.2307/1602690 PMID:11255710

Roschelle, J., & Teasley, S. D. (1995). The construction of shared knowledge in collaborative problem solving. In C. E. O'Malley (Ed.), *Computer-Supported Collaborative Learning* (pp. 69–197). Berlin: Springer-Verlag. doi:10.1007/978-3-642-85098-1_5

Rosedale, P. (2014, November 8). Philip Rosedale keynote: What is the metaverse? *Proceedings of the Open Simulator Community Conference.* [YouTube Video]. Retrieved from https://www.youtube.com/watch?v=iR3uUVPyjhU

Rosengard, J. K. (1998). Property Tax Reform in Developing Countries. Boston, M.A.: Kluwer Academic Publications. doi:10.1007/978-1-4615-5667-1

Rosini, A. M., & Palmisano, A. (2003). *Administração de Sistemas de Informação e a Gestão do Conhecimento.* São Paulo: Pioneira Thompson Learning.

Rotter, J. B. (1954). *Social learning and clinical psychology.* NY: Prentice-Hall. doi:10.1037/10788-000

Rotter, J. B. (1982). *The development and application of social learning theory: Selected papers.* NY: Praeger.

Rowntree, D. (1998). Workshops role in Staff development. In C. Latsem & F. Lockwood (Eds.), *Staff development in open and flexible learning.* London: Routledge.

Royston, C. (2009, April 18). WebQuests - National Museums Online Learning Project. Retrieved from http://www.museumsandtheweb.com/mw2009/abstracts/prg_335002093.html

Russo, A., Watkins, J. J., Kelly, L., & Chan, S. (2006, December 7- 9). How will social media affect museum communication? Proceedings of the Nordic Digital Excellence in Museums NODEM, Oslo, Norway.

Russo, A., Watkins, J., & Chan, S. (2007). Look who's talking.[Museum and Gallery Services New South Wales.]. *The MAG, 2*, 14–15.

Russo, A., Watkins, J., Kelly, L., & Chan, S. (2007). Social media and cultural interactive experiences in museums. *Nordic Journal of Digital Literacy, 1*, 19–29.

Rutkowski, A. F., Vogel, D. R., Van Genuchten, M., Bemelmans, T. M. A., & Favier, M. (2002). E-collaboration: The reality of virtuality. *IEEE Transactions on Professional Communication, 45*(4), 219–230. doi:10.1109/TPC.2002.805147

Saint-Onge, H., & Wallace, D. (2012). *Leveraging communities of practice for strategic advantage*. Routledge.

Salman Abdou, D. M., & Zaazou, Z. (2013). The Egyptian revolution and post socio-economic impact. *Topics in Middle Eastern and African Economies, 15*(1). eMarketing Egypt Releases. (2014, May 23). *The First Report about the Internet and the Revolution in Egypt*. Retrieved from http://www.pr.com/press-release/336504

Salmon, G. (2003). e-moderating: the Key to Teaching and Learning Online (2nd ed.). London: Routledge.

Savin-Baden, M. (2008). *Learning Spaces: Creating Opportunities for Knowledge Creation in Academic Life*. Maidenhead: Open University Press.

Sawyer, R. K. (2006). Introduction: The New Science of Learning. In R. K. Sawyer (Ed.), *The Cambridge Handbook of the Learning Sciences* (pp. 1–16). Cambridge, UK: Cambridge University Press.

Scaife, M., Rogers, Y., Aldrich, F., & Davies, M. (1997). *Designing For or Designing With? Informant Design For Interactive Learning Environments*. Paper presented at the Proceedings of the Conference on Human Factors in Computing Systems CHI '97, Atlanta, GA. doi:10.1145/258549.258789

Scardamalia, M., & Bereiter, C. (2003). Knowledge Building. In *Encyclopedia of Education*. New York: MacMillan Reference.

Scardamalia, M., & Bereiter, C. (2006). Knowledge Building: Theory, Pedagogy, and Technology. In R. K. Sawyer (Ed.), *The Cambridge Handbook of the Learning Sciences* (pp. 97–115). Cambridge, UK: Cambridge University Press.

Scardamalia, M., & Bereiter, C. (2006). Knowledge building: Theory, pedagogy, and technology. In R. K. Sawyer (Ed.), *The Cambridge handbook of the learning sciences* (pp. 97–115). New York, NY: Cambridge University Press.

Scariot, C. A., Heemann, A., & Padovani, S. (2012). Understanding the collaborative-participatory design. *Work (Reading, Mass.), 41*, 2701–2705. PMID:22317129

Scharmer, C. O. (2000). Presencing: Learning from the future as it emerges [PDF document]. Presentation at the *Conference on Knowledge and Innovation, Helsinki School of Economics, Finland.* Retrieved from http://www.ottoscharmer.com/docs/articles/2000_Presencing.pdf

Scharpf, F. W. (1997). *Games Real Actors Play: Actor-Centered Institutionalism in Policy Research*. Oxford: Westview Press.

Schneider, A., Von Krogh, G., & Jäger, P. (2013). "What's coming next?" Epistemic curiosity and lurking behavior in online communities. *Computers in Human Behavior, 29*(1), 293–303. doi:10.1016/j.chb.2012.09.008

Schrage, M. (1990). *Shared Minds: The New Technologies of Collaboration*. New York: Random House.

Schroth, C., & Schmid, B. (2009). Reference architecture for cross-company electronic collaboration. *International Journal of e-Collaboration, 5*(2), 75–91. doi:10.4018/jec.2009040105

Schwarz, R. (2005). The Skilled Facilitator Approach. In R. Schwarz, A. Davidson, P. Carlson, & S. McKinney (Eds.), *The Skilled Facilitator Fieldbook* (pp. 3–13). San Francisco: Jossey-Bass.

Sean, A., Henry, F., Marc, L., John, S., & Deen, F. (2012). *New Media and Conflict after the Arab Spring*. United States Institute of Peace.

Searle, J. R. (2008). Philosophy in a New Century (p. 167). New York: Cambridge.

Selwyn, N. (2006). Digital division or digital decision? A study of non-users and low-users of computers, poetics. *Journal of Empirical Research in Culture. Medical Art, 34*(4-5), 273–292.

Selwyn, N. (2011). *Education and Technology: Key Issues and Debates*. London, UK: Continuum.

Sfard, A. (1998). On two metaphors for learning and the dangers of choosing just one. *Educational Researcher*, *27*(2), 4–13. doi:10.3102/0013189X027002004

Sharpe, R., Benfield, G., Lessner, E., & De Cicco, E. (2005) *Learner Scoping Study: Final Report*. JISC. Retrieved from http://www.jisc.ac.uk/uploaded_documents/scoping%20study%20final%20report%20v4.1.doc

Shiue, Y., Chiu, C., & Chang, C. (2010). Exploring and mitigating social loafing in online communities. *Computers in Human Behavior*, *26*(4), 768–777. doi:10.1016/j.chb.2010.01.014

Shrivastava, P. (1983). A typology of organizational learning systems. *Journal of Management Studies*, *20*(1), 7–28. doi:10.1111/j.1467-6486.1983.tb00195.x

Shultz, T. R. (2011). Connectionism and Learning. In V. G. Aukrust (Ed.), *Learning and Cognition in Education* (pp. 25–33). Oxford, UK: Elsevier.

Siemens, G. (2005). A learning theory for the digital age. In *Instructional Technology and Distance Education*, 2(1), 3–10. Retrieved from http://www.elearnspace.org/Articles/connectivism.htm

Siemens, G. (2005). Connectivism: A Learning Theory for the Digital Age. *International journal of instructional technology and distance learning*, *2*(1), 3-10.

Siemens, G. (2014). Connectivism: A Learning Theory for the Digital Age. *Elearnspace*. Retrieved from http://www.elearnspace.org/Articles/connectivism.htm

Silva & Breuleux. (1994) The Use of Participatory Design in the Implementation of Internet-based Collaborative Learning Activities in K-12 Classrooms. Retrieved from http://www.helsinki.fi/science/optek/1994/n3/silva.txt

Sim, J. (1998). Collecting and analysing qualitative data: Issues raised by the focus group. *Journal of Advanced Nursing*, *28*(2), 345–352. doi:10.1046/j.1365-2648.1998.00692.x PMID:9725732

Simon, H. A. (1955). A Behavioural Model of Rational Choice. *The Quarterly Journal of Economics*, *69*(1), 99–118. doi:10.2307/1884852

Simon, H. A. (1991). Bounded rationality and organizational learning. *Organization Science*, *2*(1), 125–134. doi:10.1287/orsc.2.1.125

Sinclair, N. (2006). *Stealth KM, Winning Knowledge Management Strategies for the Public Sector*. Butterworth-Heinemann.

Skerlavaj, M., Dimovski, V., & Desouza, K. C. (2010). Patterns and Structures of Intra-Organizational Learning Networks within a Knowledge-Intensive Organization. *Journal of Information Technology*, *25*(2), 189–204. doi:10.1057/jit.2010.3

Slavin, R. E. (1995). *Cooperative learning: Theory, research, and practice* (2nd ed.). Englewood Cliffs, NJ: Prentice Hall.

Sleeman, D., & Brown, J. S. (Eds.), (1982). *Intelligent Tutoring Systems*. New York: Academic Press.

Sloep, P., Hummel, H., & Manderveld, J. (2005). Basic Design Procedures for E-learning Courses. In R. Koper & C. Tattersall (Eds.), *Learning Design: A Handbook on Modelling and Delivering Networked Education and Training* (pp. 139–160). Berlin: Springer. doi:10.1007/3-540-27360-3_8

Smith, C. (2013, May 16). Egyptian Tweeter Says Twitter was Invaluable during Protests. *Huffingtonpost.com*. Retrieved from http://www.huffingtonpost.com/2011/02/17/egypt-twitter-jan25-protests_n_824310.html

Smith, S. M. (1995). Fixation, incubation, and insight in memory and creative thinking. In S. M. Smith, T. B. Ward, & R. A. Finke (Eds.), The creative cognition approach (pp. 135-156). Cambridge, MA: MIT Press.

Smith, J. A., & Osborn, M. (2003). Interpretative Phenomenological Analysis. In A. Smith (Ed.), *Qualitative Psychology* (pp. 40–52). London: Sage.

Smith, P. J., & Sadler-Smith, E. (2006). *Learning in Organizations: Complexities and diversities*. Oxon, UK: Routledge.

Snape, P., & Fox-Turnbull, W. (2013). Perspectives of authenticity: Implementation in technology education. *International Journal of Technology and Design Education, 23*(1), 51–68. doi:10.1007/s10798-011-9168-2

Spagnoletti, P., & Resca, A. (2012). A design theory for IT supporting online communities. *Proceedings of the 2012 45th Hawaii International Conference on System Science HICSS* (pp. 4082–4091). IEEE. doi:10.1109/HICSS.2012.54

Sproull, L., & Kiesler, S. (1995). *Connections: New Ways of Working In the Networked Organization*. Cambridge, MA: The MIT Press.

Stahl, G. (Ed.), (2001). Computer Support for Collaborative Learning: Foundations for a CSCL Community. Hillsdale, NJ: Lawrence Erlbaum.

Stahl, G., Koschmann, T., & Suthers, D. (2006). Computer-supported collaborative learning: An historical perspective. In R. K. Sawyer (Ed.), *Cambridge handbook of the learning sciences* (pp. 409–426). Cambridge, UK: Cambridge University Press.

Stanforth, C. (2006). Analysing eGovernment in Developing Countries Using Actor-Network Theory. *iGovernment Working Paper Series Paper no. 17*.

Stankov, S., Glavinić, V., & Rosić, M. (2011). *Intelligent Tutoring Systems in E-learning Environments: Design, Implementation and Evaluation*. Hershey, PA: Information Science Reference. doi:10.4018/978-1-61692-008-1

Star, S. L., & Griesemer, J. R. (1989). Institutional Ecology, Translations and Boundary Objects: Amateurs and Professionals in Berkeley s Museum of Vertebrate Zoology. *Social Studies of Science, 19*(4), 387–420. doi:10.1177/030631289019003001

Sterelny, K. 2005. Externalism, epistemic artefacts and the estende mind. In R. Schantz (Ed.), The Externalist Challenge: New Studies on Cognition and Intentionality. Berlin: de Gruyter.

Sthapornnanon, N., Sakulbumrungsil, R., Theeraroungchaisri, A., & Watcharadamrongkun, S. (2009). Instructional design and assessment: Social constructivist learning environment in an online professional practice course. *American Journal of Pharmaceutical Education, 73*(1), 1–8. doi:10.5688/aj730110 PMID:19513138

Stricker, A., Holm, J., Calongne, C., & McCrocklin, M. (2011). Collaborative prototyping of learning innovations across loosely coupled educational communities. *International Journal of Learning and Media*, Winter 2011, 3(1).

Suchman, L. A. (1987). *Plans and situated actions: The problem of human-machine communication*. Cambridge, UK: Cambridge University Press.

Sullivan, G. (2005). *Art Practice as Research*. Thousand Oaks, CA: Sage.

Sun, N., Rau, P. P.-L., & Ma, L. (2014). Understanding lurkers in online communities: A literature review. *Computers in Human Behavior, 38*, 110–117. doi:10.1016/j.chb.2014.05.022

Suppe, F. (1977). *The Structure of Scientific Theories* (pp. 154–156). University of Illinois Press.

Tchounikine, P., Rummel, N., & McLaren, B. M. (2010). Computer Supported Collaborative Learning and Intelligent Tutoring Systems. In R. Nkambou, J. Bourdeau, & R. Mizoguchi (Eds.), *Advances in Intelligent Tutoring Systems* (pp. 447–463). Berlin: Springer. doi:10.1007/978-3-642-14363-2_22

Thomas, J. W. (2000). *A review of research on project-based learning*. San Rafael, CA: Autodesk Foundation.

Tierney, R., & Palmer, M. (2013). Participation, interaction and learner satisfaction in a professional practice wiki for teachers. *Cyberpsychology and New Media: A Thematic Reader*, 195.

Tosey, P. (1999). The peer learning community: A contextual design for learning? *Management Decision*, *37*(5), 403–010. doi:10.1108/00251749910274171

Trotter, N., & Cameron, G. (1996). Making the most of your software. *Computer Fraud & Security*, *1996*(10), 12–16. doi:10.1016/1361-3723(96)84808-1

Truman, B. (2013). *Transformative interactions using embodied avatars in collaborative virtual environments: Towards transdisciplinarity* [Doctoral dissertation]. ProQuest Dissertations & Theses Global. (1560886039).

Tsai, H.-T., & Bagozzi, R. P. (2014). Contribution behavior in virtual communities: Cognitive, emotional and social influences. *Management Information Systems Quarterly*, *38*(1), 143–163.

Tsakarestou, B., & Papadimitriou, S. (2014). *Workshop Co-creation Methodology on 10 May 2014 in Athens, Greece*. Retrieved from http://www.medeanet.eu/event/workshop-%E2%80%9Cco-creation-methodology%E2%80%9D-10-may-2014-athens-greece

Tsebelis, G. (1990). Nested Games: Rational Choice in Comparative Politics. Berkley, C.A.: University of California Press.

Tufekci, Z. (2008). Grooming, gossip, Facebook and Myspace. *Information Communication and Society*, *11*(4), 544–564. doi:10.1080/13691180801999050

Tunca, T. I., & Wu, Q. (2012). Fighting fire with fire: Commercial piracy and the role of file sharing on copyright protection policy for digital goods. *Information Systems Research*, *24*(2), 436–453. doi:10.1287/isre.1120.0430

Turban, E., Bolloju, N., & Liang, T. (2011). Enterprise social networking: Opportunities, adoption, and risk mitigation. *Journal of Organizational Computing and Electronic Commerce*, *21*(3), 202–220. doi:10.1080/10919392.2011.590109

UNESCO. (2002). *How students learn* (in Greek). International Bureau of Education. Retrieved from http://www.ibe.unesco.org/fileadmin/user_upload/archive/publications/EducationalPracticesSeriesPdf/prac07gr.pdf

University of Northern Colorado. (2013). *The flipped classroom*. Retrieved from www.flippedclassroom.com

Usoro, A., Sharratt, M. W., Tsui, E., & Shekhar, S. (2007). Trust as an Antecedent to Knowledge Sharing in Virtual Communities of Practice. *Knowledge Management Research & Practice*, *5*(3), 199–212. doi:10.1057/palgrave.kmrp.8500143

Valaitis, R. K., Akhtar-Danesh, N., Brooks, F., Binks, S., & Semogas, D. (2011). Online communities of practice as a communication resource for community health nurses working with homeless persons. *Journal of Advanced Nursing*, *67*(6), 1273–1284. doi:10.1111/j.1365-2648.2010.05582.x PMID:21306424

Valanciene, L., & Jegeleviciute, S. (2013). Valuation of crowdfunding: Benefits and drawbacks. *Economics and Management*, *18*(1), 39–48. doi:10.5755/j01.em.18.1.3713

Van Dijk, J. A. G. M. (1997). The reality of virtual communities. *Trends in communication, 1*(1), 39-63.

Van Dijk, J. A. G. M. (2005). *The Deepening Divide: Inequality in the Information Society*. Thousand Oaks, CA: Sage Publications.

Van Merrienboer, J. J., & Sweller, J. (2005). Cognitive load theory and complex learning: Recent developments and future directions. *Educational Psychology Review*, *17*(2), 147–177. doi:10.1007/s10648-005-3951-0

Van Winkelen, C. 2003. Inter-organisational communities of practice. Retrieved from http://www. elearningeuropa.info/directory/index.php?page=doc&doc_id=1483&doclng=6

Vasala, P., Hatziplis, P., & Lionarakis, A. (2007). Views of undergraduate and postgraduate students at Hellenic Open University on essays: a comparative study of two courses (in Greek). In A. Lionarakis (Ed), *Proceedings of 4th International Conference of Open and Distance Learning*, Athens, Propompos (pp. 296-308).

Vedel, T. (1989). Télématique et Configurations d'Acteurs: Une Perspective Européenne. *Reseaux*, *7*(37), 9–28.

Venkatesh, V., Croteau, A.-M., & Rabah, J. (2014). Perceptions of effectiveness of instructional uses of technology in higher education in an era of Web 2.0. *Proceedings of the 2014 47th Hawaii International Conference on System Sciences (HICSS)* (pp. 110–119). IEEE.

Venkatesh, V., Rabah, J., Fusaro, M., Couture, A., Varela, W., & Alexander, K. (2012). Perceptions of Technology Use and Course Effectiveness in the Age of Web 2.0: A Large-Scale Survey of Québec University Students and Instructors. *Proceedings of theWorld Conference on E-Learning in Corporate, Government, Healthcare, and Higher Education* (Vol. 2012, pp. 1691–1699).

Virkar, S. (2011). *The Politics of Implementing e-Government for Development: The Ecology of Games Shaping Property Tax Administration in Bangalore City, India* [Unpublished Doctoral Thesis]. University of Oxford, Oxford.

Vollmer, A., & Wehner, T. (2007). Innovation und wissensorientierte Kooperation. *Profile*, *13*, 31–36.

Voss, A., Mascord, M., Casteleiro, M. A., Asgari-Targhi, M., Procter, R., Fraser, M., . . . Anderson, S. (2007). e-Infrastructure Development and Community Engagement. Paper presented at the e-Social Science Conference, Ann Arbor, Michigan, US.

Vygotsky, L. S. (1962). In E. Hanfmann & G. Vakar (Eds., Trans., Original work published 1934). Thought and language. Cambridge, MA: MIT Press. doi:10.1037/11193-000

Vygotsky, L., & Luria, A. (1994). Tool and symbol in child development. In L. S. Vygotskiĭ, R. Veer, & J. Valsiner (Eds.), The Vygotsky reader (pp. 99-174). Oxford, UK: Blackwell.

Vygotsky, L. S. (1978). *Mind and society*. Cambridge, MA: Harvard University Press.

Vygotsky, L. S. (1978). *Mind in society* (M. Cole, V. John-Steiner, S. Scribner, & E. Souberman, Eds.). Cambridge, MA: Harvard University Press.

Vygotsky, L. S. (1978). *Mind in Society: The Development of Higher Psychological Processes* (M. Cole, V. John-Steiner, S. Scribner, & E. Souberman, Eds.). Cambridge, MA: Harvard University Press.

Vygotsky, L. S. (1978). *Mind in society: The development of higher psychological processes*. Cambridge, MA: Harvard University.

Vygotsky, L. S. (1979). The development of higher forms of attention in childhood. *Social Psychology*, *18*, 67–115.

Vygotsky, L. S., & Cole, M. (1978). *Mind in society: the development of higher psychological processes*. Cambridge, Mass.; London: Harvard University Press.

Walker, C. O., Greene, B. A., & Mansell, R. A. (2006). Identification with academics, intrinsic/extrinsic motivation, and self-efficacy as predictors of cognitive engagement. *Learning and Individual Differences*, *16*(1), 1–12. doi:10.1016/j.lindif.2005.06.004

Walker, E., Rummel, N., & Koedinger, K. R. (2009). CTRL: A research framework for providing adaptive collaborative learning support. *User Modeling and User-Adapted Interaction*, *19*(5), 387–431. doi:10.1007/s11257-009-9069-1

Walsham, G. (2001). Knowledge Management: The benefits and limitations of Computer Systems. *European Journal of Knowledge Management*, *9*(6), 599–608. doi:10.1016/S0263-2373(01)00085-8

Wang, S., Noe, R. A., & Wang, Z.-M. (2014). Motivating Knowledge Sharing in Knowledge Management Systems A Quasi–Field Experiment. *Journal of Management*, *40*(4), 978–1009. doi:10.1177/0149206311412192

Wang, Y., & Fesenmaier, D. R. (2003). Assessing motivation of contribution in online communities: An empirical investigation of an online travel community. *Electronic Markets*, *13*(1), 33–45. doi:10.1080/1019678032000052934

Ward, T. B., Smith, S. M., & Finke, R. A. (1999). Creative cognition. In R.J. Sternberg (Ed.), The handbook of creativity (pp. 189-212). Cambridge, MA: MIT Press.

Ward, T. B., Finke, R. A., & Smith, S. M. (1995). *Creativity and the mind: Discovering the genius within.* New York, NY: Plenum Press. doi:10.1007/978-1-4899-3330-0

Warschauer, M. (1997). Computer-Mediated Collaborative Learning: Theory and Practice. *The Modern Language Journal* (Special Issue), *81*(4), 470-481.

Warschauer, M. (2007). The paradoxical future of digital learning. *Learning Inquiry*, *1*(1), 41–49. doi:10.1007/s11519-007-0001-5

Wasserman, S., & Faust, K. (1994). *Social Network Analysis.* Cambridge: Cambridge University Press. doi:10.1017/CBO9780511815478

Watkins, K., & Marsick, V. (1990). *Informal and incidental learning in the workplace.* London.

Wehrwein, E. A., Lujan, H. L., & DiCarlo, S. E. (2007, June). Gender differences in learning style preferences among undergraduate physiology students.[PubMed]. *Advances in Physiology Education*, *31*(2), 153–157. doi:10.1152/advan.00060.2006

Weick, K. E. (1990). Technology as equivoque: Sense-making in new technologies. In P. S. Goodman & L. S. Sproull (Eds.), *Technology and Organizations* (pp. 78–93). San Francisco: Jossey-Bass.

Weidner, D. (Director) (2007, April 23). KM Essentials. *Certified Knowledge Manager Training Program (CKM).* Lecture conducted from KM Institute, Basel.

Wellman, B. (2002). Little boxes, glocalization, and networked individualism. In M. Tanabe, P. van den Besselaar, & T. Ishida (Eds.), Digital cities II: Computational and sociological approaches (pp. 10–25). Berlin: Springer; Retrieved from http://www.chass.utoronto.ca/~wellman/publications/littleboxes/littlebox.PDF doi:10.1007/3-540-45636-8_2

Wellman, B. (1997). An electronic group is virtually a social network. In S. Kiesler (Ed.), *Culture of the Internet* (pp. 179–205). Mahwah, NJ: Lawrence Erlbaum Associates.

Wellman, B., Salaff, J., Dimitrova, D., Garton, L., Gulia, M., & Haythornthwaite, C. (1996). Computer networks as social networks: Collaborative work, telework, and virtual community. *Annual Review of Sociology*, *22*(1), 213–238. doi:10.1146/annurev.soc.22.1.213

Wenger, E. (2006). Communities of Practice: A brief introduction. North San Juan, C.A. Available from: http://www.ewenger.com/theory/index.html

Wenger, E. (2006). *Communities of practice: a brief introduction.* Retrieved from http://wenger-trayner.com/wp-content/uploads/2013/10/06-Brief-introduction-to-communities-of-practice.pdf

Wenger, E. (2011). *Communities of practice: A brief introduction.* Retrieved from https://scholarsbank.uoregon.edu/xmlui/bitstream/handle/1794/11736/A%20brief%20introduction%20to%20CoP.pdf?sequence=1&isAllowed=y

Wenger, E. (2014) Communities of Practice: a few frequently asked questions, www.ewenger.com on October 8th.

Wenger, E., White, N., & Smith, J. D. (2009) Digital Habitats: stewarding technology for communities. Portland, OR: CPsquare.

Wenger, E. (1998). *Communities of practice: Learning, meaning, and identity*. New York, NY: Cambridge University Press. doi:10.1017/CBO9780511803932

Wenger, E. (1999). Communities of practice: Learning as a social system. *Systems Thinker*, *9*(5), 2–3.

Wenger, E. (1999). *Communities of Practice: Learning, Meaning and Identity*. Cambridge: Cambridge University Press.

Wenger, E. (2000). Communities of practice: The key to knowledge strategy. In E. L. Lesser, M. A. Fontaine, & J. A. Slusher (Eds.), *Knowledge and Communities* (pp. 3–20). Boston: Butterworth Heinemann. doi:10.1016/B978-0-7506-7293-1.50004-4

Wenger, E. (2004). Communities of practice and social learning systems. In K. Starkey, S. Tempest, & A. McKinlay (Eds.), *How Organizations Learn: Managing the Search for Knowledge* (pp. 238–258). London: Thomson.

Wenger, E. C., McDermott, R., & Snyder, W. C. (2002). *Cultivating communities of practice: a guide to managing knowledge*. Boston: Harvard Business School Press.

Wenger, E., McDermott, R., & Snyder, W. M. (2002). *Cultivating communities of practice: A guide to managing knowledge*. Boston: Harvard Business School Press.

Wenger, E., & Snyder, W. M. (2000). Communities of practice: The organizational frontier. *Harvard Business Review*, *78*(6), 139. PMID:11184968

Wenger, E., White, N., & Smith, J. D. (2009). *Digital habitats*. Stewarding Technology for Communities.

Wertsch, J. V. (1984). The Zone of Proximal Development: Some Conceptual Issues. *New Directions for Child and Adolescent Development*, *1984*(23), 7–18. doi:10.1002/cd.23219842303

Wertsch, J. V. (1985). *Vygotsky and the social formation of mind*. Cambridge, MA: Harvard University Press.

Wertsch, J. V., & Tulviste, P. (1992). L. S. Vygotsky and contemporary developmental psychology. *Developmental Psychology*, *28*(4), 548–557. doi:10.1037/0012-1649.28.4.548

Wheat, R. E., Wang, Y., Byrnes, J. E., & Ranganathan, J. (2013). Raising money for scientific research through crowdfunding. *Trends in Ecology & Evolution*, *28*(2), 71–72. doi:10.1016/j.tree.2012.11.001 PMID:23219380

Whitley, G. G., & Oddi, L. F. (1998). Graduate student-faculty collaboration in research and publication.[PubMed]. *Western Journal of Nursing*, *20*(5), 572–583. doi:10.1177/019394599802000505

Whitley, R. (2000). *The intellectual and social organization of the sciences*. Oxford, UK: Clarendon Press.

Wiley, D. A., & Edwards, E. K. (2002). Online self-organizing social systems: The decentralized future of online learning. Retrieved from http://wiley.ed.usu.edu/docs/ososs.pdf

Wilkesmann, U., Fischer, H., & Wilkesmann, M. (2009). Cultural characteristics of knowledge transfer. *Journal of Knowledge Management*, *13*(6), 464–477. doi:10.1108/13673270910997123

Wilson, S. (1996). Art as Research. Retrieved from http://userwww.sfsu.edu/~swilson/

Wink, J., & Putney, L. G. (2002). *A vision of Vygotsky*. Boston: Allyn & Bacon.

Wisniewski, E. J. (1997). Conceptual combination: Possibilities and aesthetics. In T. B. Ward, S. M. Smith, & J. Vaid (Eds.), Creative thought: An investigation of conceptual structures and processes (pp. 83-110). Washington, DC: American Psychological Association.

Woo, Y., & Reeves, T. C. (2007). Meaningful interaction in web-based learning: A social constructivist interpretation. *The Internet and Higher Education, 10*(1), 15–25. doi:10.1016/j.iheduc.2006.10.005

Yakhlef, A. (2010). The three facets of knowledge: A critique of the practice-based learning theory. *Research Policy, 39*(1), 39–46. doi:10.1016/j.respol.2009.11.005

Yap, R., & Robben, J. (2010). A model for leveraging social learning technologies in corporate environments.*Proceedings of the 7th International Conference on Networked Learning 2010.*

Yen, H. R., Hsu, S. H.-Y., & Huang, C.-Y. (2011). Good soldiers on the Web: Understanding the drivers of participation in online communities of consumption. *International Journal of Electronic Commerce, 15*(4), 89–120. doi:10.2753/JEC1086-4415150403

Yin, R. K. (2003). Applied Social Research Methods Series: Vol. 5. *Case Study Research: Design and Methods.* London: SAGE Publications.

Young, K. S. (2004). Internet addiction: A new clinical phenomenon and its consequences. *The American Behavioral Scientist, 48*(4), 402–415. doi:10.1177/0002764204270278

Zack, M. H., & McKenney, J. L. (1995). Social context and interaction in ongoing computer-supported management groups. *Organization Science, 6*(4), 394–422. doi:10.1287/orsc.6.4.394

Zarb, G. (1992). On the Road to Damascus: First steps towards changing the relations of research production. *Disability, Handicap & Society, 7*(2), 125–138. doi:10.1080/02674649266780161

Zemke, R., & Zemke, S. (1984, March). 30 things we know for sure about adult learning. *Innovation Abstracts, 6*(8).

Zhang, W., & Watts, S. (2008). Online communities as communities of practice: A case study. *Journal of Knowledge Management, 12*(4), 55–71. doi:10.1108/13673270810884255

Zhang, X., Olfman, L., & Firpo, D. (2010). Supporting social constructivist learning through the KEEP SLS e-portfolio system. *International Journal on E-Learning, 9*(3), 411–426.

Zhao, S. (2001). The increasing presence of telecopresence in the Internet era. Paper presented at the annual conference of the American Sociological Association, Anaheim, CA.

Zhao, C., & Kuh, G. D. (2004). Adding Value: Learning communities and student engagement. *Research in Higher Education, 45*(2), 115–138. doi:10.1023/B:RIHE.0000015692.88534.de

Zheng, H., Li, D., Wu, J., & Xu, Y. (2014). The role of multidimensional social capital in crowdfunding: A comparative study in China and US. *Information & Management, 51*(4), 488–496. doi:10.1016/j.im.2014.03.003

Zhou, Z., Wu, J. P., Zhang, Q., & Xu, S. (2013). Transforming visitors into members in online brand communities: Evidence from China. *Journal of Business Research, 66*(12), 2438–2443.

Zywica, J., Richards, K. A., & Gomez, K. (2011). Affordances of a scaffolded-social learning network. *On The Horizon, 19*(1), 33–42. doi:10.1108/10748121111107690

About the Contributors

Ayse Kok has over 8 years of experience in the field of social, mobile and digital technologies both from a practitioner and from a researcher perspective. She participated in various projects in partnership with international organizations such as UN, NATO and the EU. Previously, she was working for an international bank in Turkey where she established the Digital Learning Unit and has been awarded by Brandon Hall- a leading global institute in L & D practices- in two different categories for her projects. Ayse also acted as an adjunct faculty member in her home town Turkey. Ayse attended various international conferences as a speaker and published several articles in both peer-reviewed journals and academic books. She is the first female graduate student for both MSc and MLitt degrees in her academic field in Oxford University where she also became a member of Oxford Educational Technology Research Group. She is also passionate about philanthropy and is the co-founder of the first non-for-profit Turkish MooC (http://www.UniversitePlus.com) which aims to revolutionize higher education in Turkey.

Hyunkyung Lee has been in the Human Resource Development field for the past 10 years. In her career of 10 years, she has worked with four companies, namely The MASIE Center, HYUNDAI Research Institute & Learning Center, Manager Society Inc., and MAEKYUNG Human Resource Institute. Her professional experiences in the workplace have focused on (1) analyzing the needs of organizations and designing, developing, implementing, and evaluating online and offline training programs; and (2) creating and managing competency development programs for staffs, managers, and executives. She also holds a Ph.D. in Educational Technology and her area of interests are instructional design, educational technology in learning and teaching, collaborative learning, and learning performance in organizations. As an educational technology expert and HRD professional, she is currently teaching undergraduate and graduate students at Yonsei University and conducting various research projects, such as instructional design and development of ICT training programs for K-12 teachers from developing countries and effects analysis on collaborative learning for improving pre-service teachers' competencies.

* * *

Alexandra Antonopoulou is currently a Senior Lecturer and Course Leader in the UK, teaching a broad range of Art and Design courses in several institutions. Her research explores the uses of storymaking, fiction and play in learning, designing and research, as well as ideas of shared authorship and collaboration.

Willi Bernhard Dipl. El. Ing. HTL/FH. Since 1984, he has been engineer, lecturer and researcher in industrial and academic organisations in the domains of Telecommunication, eLearning, Modelling & Simulation, Business-Creativity & Innovationmanagement, eCollaboration, Technology Enhanced Learning as well as Simulation- & Game Based Training and Complexity Management. In 1992 he was leading a Swiss National Competence-Center for the Simulation of Enterprises at the CIM-Centre of the Nordwestern University of Applied Sciences in Muttenz. In 1998 he was also leading the cantonal impulse-project for improving Creativity & Innovation at SME in the region of Basel. Since 2002, he is also founder and CEO of the Basle Institute of Technology and the Swiss Simulation Engineering GmbH. Since 2006, he is Professor and Head of Consulting Services in the e-Collaboration team of the IFeL-Institute at the Swiss Distance University of Applied Sciences in Brig, where he is doing consultancy, research and lecturing. He is also in the steering committee of the Swiss Engineering Association SE-STV in the section of Basel. His research interests are in the fields of Knowledge-Sharing through Collaborative-Creativity, Serious Games and Communities of Practice in conjunction with new technologies and digital worlds. He is also interested in unconventional methods to solve existing problems or to create new practical applications which will help to challenge the future in business & education, mainly by using todays digital & e-technologies.

Marco C. Bettoni since September 2005 Bettoni has worked for Fernfachhochschule Schweiz (Swiss Distance University of Applied Sciences) as member of the directory board; until 2008 he was also Director R&D, then 2008-2014 Head of the Research Management Unit and since June 2014 Co-Director of IFeL (Institute for Research in Open-, Distance- and eLearning). After receiving his master's degree in 1977 (ETH Zürich) he have been active until 1987 with various functions for industrial (Rieter, Siemens), banking (UBS), non profit (SPE) and academic (ETH) organizations in the domains of machine design, engineering education, vocational education, IT management and IT development. From 1987 to 1991 he has been project leader and knowledge engineer in the development of knowledge-based systems and since 1981 he has been involved in cognitive science research. Between July 1991 and March 2004 at the Basel University of Applied Sciences (FHBB) he has been involved in teaching post-graduate courses, consulting with enterprises and government and doing applied research. His main domain of competence is that of Knowledge Technologies which includes Artificial Intelligence (especially Knowledge Engineering) and Knowledge Management (focusing on human aspects). In June 2003 ETH Zürich appointed him as a 'guest researcher' as special recognition for his research in the human aspects of Knowledge Management.

Nicole Bittel graduated with a Master of Arts from the University of Zurich. Her research focuses on the topics of organizational and educational storytelling, e-collaboration, knowledge management and e-learning as well as on methodological skills in (applied) research and management. Since 2011 she is working as research associate in the e-Collaboration team of the IFeL-Institute at the Swiss Distance University of Applied Sciences in Brig. Her experience includes working within a geographically diverse team, implementing research and service projects in the fields of e-collaboration and new working spaces for knowledge work, writing and publishing activities, organising research events and performing research services as well as participating in various (inter)national research communities. In 2014 Nicole was appointed as leader of the research field "storytelling for working and learning".

Cynthia Calongne, also known as Lyr Lobo, joined CTU's Computer Science department in 1996, and prior to it, was a software engineer for 13 years, supporting Air Force Space Command and an environmental organization in Washington, DC. She has hosted 150+ research presentations and workshops. Her team won the $25,000 Grand Prize in the 2010 Federal Virtual World Challenge for the Mars Expedition Strategy Challenge, a space simulation, and in 2005, she completed an artificial intelligence grant for the National Science Foundation. In 1995, she evaluated the creation of a user interface paradigm to support virtual environments on a PC.

Edson Walmir Cazarini graduated in Mechanical Engineering (1971), Master in Computer Science (1976) and PhD in Mechanical Engineering (1992), all from University of São Paulo, Brazil. He is researcher and mentor at masters and doctoral program in the Graduate Program in Production Engineering from Engineering School of São Carlos, University of São Paulo, in the following areas: Decision Support Systems, Modeling and Organizational Distance Education. Belongs to the editorial board of two journals and is reviewer of two other journals. The more frequent key words on his resume are in the context of scientific, technological and artistic-cultural production terms: Decision Support Systems, Information Systems, Organizational Intelligence, Knowledge Management, Organizational Modeling, Educational Technology, Distance Education, Environment learning and Collaborative Learning.

Eleanor Dare holds a PHD in Arts and Computational Technology from Goldsmiths, Department of Computing, University of London. She is currently an Associate Lecturer in the Departments of Maths and Computing at the University of Derby and the Open University.

Paolo Diviacco is a geophysicist at Istituto Nazionale di Oceanografia e di Geofisica Sperimentale (OGS). He holds a PhD in exploration geophysics, and has 20 years of experience in seismic data processing. He always maintained an interest in computer science and programming, developing software in the field of geophysics and web based data management. At the same time, he has always been interested in the philosophical and sociological aspects of scientific production in general and in the geo-sciences in particular. In this perspective he has been active in developing ideas and web based systems that could support scientists while collaborating and foster the collaborative attitude among research institutions. In this context he worked within several international projects, such as, for example, FP7 ODIP, FP7 Geo-Seas, FP7 Emodnet, FP7 Eurofleets, the Antarctic Seismic Data Library.

Jonan Donaldson is an educational professional. His specialties include open educational resources, digital portfolios, and best practices in online course design. He primarily teaches graduate-level courses on technology in education including courses such as Big Thinkers in Educational Technology, Digital Portfolios in Education, Instructional Design, Designing Information, and Web 2.0 Tools for Teaching and Learning. He is currently experimenting with designing courses in which students create open educational resources in a paradigm he calls "authorship learning".

Mahmoud Mohamed El-Khouly is an assistant professor at Helwan University, Egypt. He received his BSc degree from Helwan University in (1983), his first Master Degree from the same University, Egypt (1994), his second Master Degree from Cairo University in computer sciences Egypt (1995), and his Doctorate of Philosophy from Saitama University in computer sciences, Japan (2000). Dr. El-Khouly held different academic positions at Temple University Japan (TUJ) (2001), Visiting Professor at Qatar

University (2003-2004), culture attache' at Egyptian embassy in London/UK (2005-2008). He acted as a Head of E-learning Project funded from HEEPF, Egypt (2005), and a Head of Management Information System Project, Helwan University, Egypt (2009). Dr. El-Khouly has participated with more than 50 research papers in conferences and published many journal articles. He is acting now as vice dean for education and students affairs, faculty of Computers & Information, Helwan university. His research interests are Software Agent, e-learning, Information Retrieval.

Roberta Salgado Gonçalves da Silva is a PhD student (qualified) and Master for Production Engineering from University of São Paulo (USP), Brazil, in 2011. At the Master worked on issues such as communities of practice, knowledge management and information and communication technologies. The PhD studies are on competences for teamwork. Has a degree in Social Communication/Journalism by PUC Campinas (1998) and used to be a journalist at print media and corporate communication (1995-2008). The most frequent keywords in the context of scientific and technological production are agribusiness, organizational learning, competences, communities of practice, distance education, knowledge management, innovation, information technology and communication and teamwork. Has additional training in: virtual mentoring, collaborative learning and at tutoring training. Used to be a communication advisor and made technological foresight in the Project of Innovation and Technological Prospection for Agribusiness Network (2007-2009) at USP. She is a co-author of 'Professional Profile in Rural Areas: Subsidies for Diagnostics and Strategies Definition - Productive Chain of Beekeeping, Dairy Cattle and Sheep', published by Embrapa (ISSN 1518-7179), in 2008. Was head of division relationship with productive sector and head of relationship combined technology and innovation institutions at São Carlos (Brazil) city hall, from 2007 to 2009. Has worked as assistant in political development of science, technology and innovation programs and sustainable economic development activities incentive to quality program implementation and productivity in industry and services, receiving foreign entrepreneur for being bilingual (English) and disseminating science through annual exhibitions promoted by the Brazilian Ministry of Science, Technology and Innovation. She volunteered at MD Anderson Cancer Center Medical Center (Houston, USA) and others.

Bernard Owens Imarhiagbe is a lecturer at Kingston University and a Member of the British Computer Society. Prior to academia, he worked as an IT Consultant with a major global IT consulting organisation in the UK. His academic research area includes small firm finance, entrepreneurship, research methods and technology innovation.

Antonis Emm Lionarakis is Greek national, currently Associate Professor of Open and Distance Education at the Hellenic Open University, School of Humanities and has been a tutor – counselor at the Open University / United Kingdom. He was a member of the Governing Board of the Institute of Continuing Adult Education and founder, as well as president of the Hellenic Network of Open and Distance Education. He was member of the planning Committee for the development of the Hellenic Open University and member of the Implementation Unit for the development of the institution. Since 2003, he is the editor-in-chief of the international Journal 'Open Education – the journal for ODL and Educational Technology'. Every two year he is organizing an international conference for open and distance learning in Greece (ICODL) with hundreds of participants from all over the world. He has contributed to writing chapters in 25 books about distance learning. He is in charge of several research projects and member of the Global Advisory Council (GAC) of The Observatory on Borderless Higher Education. He was invited to present his work in several countries, such as France, Iceland, Bulgaria, Turkey and Japan.

Amir Manzoor holds a bachelor's degree in engineering from NED University, Karachi, an MBA from Lahore University of Management Sciences (LUMS), and an MBA from Bangor University, United Kingdom. He has many years of diverse professional and teaching experience working at many renowned national and internal organizations and higher education institutions. His research interests include electronic commerce and technology applications in business.

Victoria Mirata has a degree in Work Psychology, English and German and works since 2014 as a research associate at FFHS where her research is focusing on the topic of "New Working Spaces for Knowledge Work". Her main research interests are in the domain of work & organizational psychology and include e.g. motivation, creativity at work, recruitment & selection process of employees, human resource management and team development.

Rami Wael Muhtaseb is the information technician at the Walid & Helen Kattan Science Education Project of the A.M. Qattan Foundation. Rami received his bachelor's degree in Computer Science from Mutah University, Jordan. He received his master's degree in Business Economics and Management from MAICH institute in Greece. Rami is the moderator of the EnglishPAL community website, and he is the co-admin of the Creative Minds bilingual Facebook Page which aims to popularize science culture and literacy in Palestine and the Arab world. He has participated in many conferences and workshops related to science education, his research contributions focused on employing social media as a virtual informal learning environment, and on highlighting the role of social media in promoting online interaction and public engagement in science. His research and work topics of interest include; ICT in Science Education, Social Media for Science Outreach and Science Communication, the Impact of Social media on Informal Learning in Museums, and Employing Social Media in Crowdsourcing for Science.

Spyros Papadakis is School Advisor at Ministry of Education and Religious Affairs. He lectures Educational Technology as Adjunct Faculty in Information and Communications Systems Master Program at the Open University of Cyprus. He holds a Ph.D in Computer Science and Information Systems from the School of Science and Technology (HOU), a Master (M.Ed) in Adult Education (HOU), a Postgraduate Certificate (PGCE) in Open and Distance Education (HOU) and a Bachelor (B.Sc.) in Mathematics from the University of Patras, Greece. He has extensive teaching experience as teacher and lecturer in the schools sector teaching Computer Science and Adult Education from secondary to professional development. Spyros is member of editorial board of one international jurnal and he serves as a reviewer for journals and conferences. He is passionate in teaching and enjoys sharing learning resources and collaborating with others. Spyros is the coordinator of the Greek Educator LAMS Community.

Sofia Papadimitriou has studied Mathematics and Computer Science (M.Sc) in the Athens National University. Her PhD entitled "The role of tutor-counsellor and the development of his supporting mechanism in a collaborative learning environment in distance education" regards in the field of Open and Distance Learning in Higher Education and has been developed in the School of Humanities at the Hellenic Open University. She has been an ICT Secondary teacher since 1990 and also an educator in

ICT training courses for primary and secondary teachers. She has been working in the Educational Radio-Television of the Ministry of Education, since September 2007 and she coordinates its Social and Digital Media. Furthermore, she has coordinated 5 working groups on behalf of the Educational RadioTelevision for the European projects: EduTubePlus:, MEDEAnet, March (MAke science Real in sCHools). Sofia has also participated in the "Energy-bits", a cross media European project distributed in Television and the Web. Plus, she has participated at the development of the "Photodentro/Educational Video" which is the Greek Educational Video Repository for primary and secondary education, designed and developed by CTI Diophantus in the framework of the "Digital School". Sofia has co-authored three book chapters and published 26 papers in scientific conferences and journals on the topics of Open and Distance Learning, using Media in Education, Open Educational Resources, Academic staff development and STEM.

Andrew Stricker serves Air University by helping to design, develop, and implement advanced and emerging learning technologies into Air Force educational and professional military education programs. Prior to his arrival to Air University Andrew served Vanderbilt University as Associate Provost for Innovation through Technology. He was responsible for working with academic, technology and administrative leaders to prioritize, plan and execute the infusion of educational technologies and enabling innovations for improving learning, teaching and research. Andrew also served 27 years as an Air Force officer and scientist specializing in technology systems integration and human-factors engineering. His graduate work was conducted at Texas A&M University, College Station, Texas and Yale University, New Haven, Connecticut.

Shefali Virkar is a research student at the University of Oxford, UK, currently reading for a D.Phil. in Politics. Her doctoral research seeks to explore the growing use of Information and Communication Technologies (ICTs) to promote better governance in the developing world, with special focus on the political and institutional impacts of ICTs on local public administration reform in India.Shefali holds an M.A. in Globalisation, Governance and Development from the University of Warwick, UK. Her Master's dissertation analysed the concept of the Digital Divide in a globalising world, its impact on developing countries, and the ensuing policy implications. At Oxford, Shefali is a member of Keble College.

Alexandros Xafopoulos (A'leksanðros Ksa'fopulos) was raised in Greece. He is currently an MA student in Education & Technology at the University College London (UCL) Institute of Education (IOE), and private tutor in Mathematics and Computer Programming. He is also an excellent Computer Science and Theology graduate of the Aristotle University of Thessaloniki (AUTh). He was a Phd student in Informatics at AUTh. During his studies in Informatics he was an undergraduate scholar of the (Greek) State Scholarship Foundation (IKY) and the Hellenic Telecommunications Organization (OTE) and a postgraduate scholar of the Research Committee of AUTh. He worked as a researcher-programmer in 2 EU funded R&D projects at the Artificial Intelligence and Information Analysis (AIIA) laboratory of AUTh. He was an academic assistant at the School of Informatics of AUTh and a visiting researcher at the Tampere International Center for Signal Processing (TICSP) in Tampere, Finland. His portfolio includes 6 publications, 2 journal and 4 conference peer-reviewed co-authored papers, as well as 3 conference presentations and 2 academic seminar talks with about 80 citations. His research interests lie in the areas of Educational Technology, Learning Design, Computer Supported Collaborative Learning, and Mathematics Education.

Jingjing Zhang received her BSc in Computer Science from BNU, an MRes from University College London (UCL), an MSc and a DPhil from the University of Oxford. As an undergraduate, she was awarded 2003 AIEJ Scholarship for a one-year exchange study at Tokyo Gakugei University. At Oxford (MSc, DPhil), she was a Clarendon scholar and a member of Brasenose College (funded by ORS scholarship). She is now an Associate Professor at the Faculty of Education of BNU, specialising in learning and technology. Before joining BNU, she was first trained in Directorate for Education, OECD Paris, and then interned at the Department of Management, the UN headquarters New York.

Index

H

I

J

K

L

M

N

O

P

Q

R

S

T

V

W

Become an IRMA Member

Members of the **Information Resources Management Association (IRMA)** understand the importance of community within their field of study. The Information Resources Management Association is an ideal venue through which professionals, students, and academicians can convene and share the latest industry innovations and scholarly research that is changing the field of information science and technology. Become a member today and enjoy the benefits of membership as well as the opportunity to collaborate and network with fellow experts in the field.

IRMA Membership Benefits:

- **One FREE Journal Subscription**
- **30% Off Additional Journal Subscriptions**
- **20% Off Book Purchases**
- Updates on the latest events and research on Information Resources Management through the IRMA-L listserv.
- Updates on new open access and downloadable content added to Research IRM.
- A copy of the Information Technology Management Newsletter twice a year.
- A certificate of membership.

IRMA Membership $195

Scan code to visit irma-international.org and begin by selecting your free journal subscription.

Membership is good for one full year.

www.irma-international.org

Printed in the United States
By Bookmasters

Printed in the United States
By Bookmasters